Music and the Aging Brain

Music and the Aging Brain

Edited by

Lola L. Cuddy
Department of Psychology, Queen's University, Kingston,
ON, Canada

Sylvie Belleville
Department of Psychology, University of Montreal, Montreal, QC,
Canada; Research Centre, Institut Universitaire de Gériatrie de Montréal,
Montreal, QC, Canada

Aline Moussard
Research Centre, Institut Universitaire de Gériatrie de Montréal,
Montreal, QC, Canada

ACADEMIC PRESS

An imprint of Elsevier

ELSEVIER

Academic Press is an imprint of Elsevier
125 London Wall, London EC2Y 5AS, United Kingdom
525 B Street, Suite 1650, San Diego, CA 92101, United States
50 Hampshire Street, 5th Floor, Cambridge, MA 02139, United States
The Boulevard, Langford Lane, Kidlington, Oxford OX5 1GB, United Kingdom

British Library Cataloguing-in-Publication Data
A catalogue record for this book is available from the British Library

Library of Congress Cataloging-in-Publication Data
A catalog record for this book is available from the Library of Congress

ISBN: 978-0-12-817422-7

For Information on all Academic Press publications
visit our website at https://www.elsevier.com/books-and-journals

Publisher: Nikki Levy
Acquisitions Editor: Melanie Tucker
Editorial Project Manager: Barbara Makinster
Production Project Manager: Punithavathy Govindaradjane
Cover Designer: Matthew Limbert

Typeset by MPS Limited, Chennai, India

Working together
to grow libraries in
developing countries

www.elsevier.com • www.bookaid.org

Contents

5.   Stroke and acquired amusia   151

Aleksi J. Sihvonen and Teppo Särkämö

6.   "Curious" cases of preservation of music
compositional ability in the presence of organic brain
disease: historical examples   173

Lola L. Cuddy and Jacalyn M. Duffin

Part 3
The Power of Music as Neuroprotection in Normal Aging

**11. Toward music-based auditory rehabilitation for older
      adults**   293

Benjamin Rich Zendel and Sarah Sauvé

Part 4
The Power of Music in Rehabilitation and Care in Disordered Aging

**12. Benefits and limits of musical interventions in
      pathological aging**   317

Hervé Platel and Mathilde Groussard

List of Contributors

Claude Alain Department of Psychology, University of Toronto, Toronto, ON, Canada; Rotman Research Institute, Baycrest, Toronto, ON, Canada; Institute of Medical Sciences, University of Toronto, Toronto, ON, Canada; Faculty of Music, University of Toronto, Toronto, ON, Canada

Eckart Altenmüller Institute of Music Physiology and Musicians' Medicine (IMMM), University of Music, Drama and Media, Hanover, Germany

Elia Benhamou Dementia Research Centre, UCL Queen Square Institute of Neurology, University College London, London, United Kingdom

Louis Bherer Centre de Recherche, Institut Universitaire de Gériatrie de Montréal, Montréal, QC, Canada; Centre de Recherche, Institut de Cardiologie de Montréal, Montréal, QC, Canada; Département de Médecine, Université de Montréal, Montréal, QC, Canada

T.M. Vanessa Chan Department of Psychology, University of Toronto, Toronto, ON, Canada; Rotman Research Institute, Baycrest, Toronto, ON, Canada

Annabel J. Cohen Department of Psychology, University of Prince Edward Island, Charlottetown, PE, Canada

Lola L. Cuddy Department of Psychology, Queen's University, Kingston, ON, Canada

Simone Dalla Bella International Laboratory for Brain, Music, and Sound Research (BRAMS), Montreal, QC, Canada; Department of Psychology, University of Montreal, Montreal, QC, Canada; Centre for Research on Brain, Language and Music (CRBLM), Montreal, QC, Canada

Jacalyn M. Duffin Professor Emerita, Hannah Chair of the History of Medicine, Queen's University, Kingston, ON, Canada

Mathilde Groussard Normandy Univ, UNICAEN, PSL Research University, EPHE, INSERM, U1077, CHU de Caen, Cyceron, Caen, France

Andrea R. Halpern Psychology Department, Bucknell University, Lewisburg, PA, United States

Brenda Hanna-Pladdy Center for Advanced Imaging Research, Department of Diagnostic Radiology & Nuclear Medicine, University of Maryland School of Medicine, Baltimore, MD, United States

Lise Hobeika Université de Lille, EA 4072 – PSITEC – Psychologie: Interactions, Temps, Emotions, Cognition, Equipe Neuropsychologie et Audition, Lille, France; Sciences et Technologies de la Musique et du Son, IRCAM, CNRS, Sorbonne Université, Paris, France

Clara E. James University of Applied Sciences and Arts Western Switzerland HES-SO, School of Health Sciences, Geneva, Switzerland; Faculty of Psychology and Educational Sciences, University of Geneva, Geneva, Switzerland

Stefan Koelsch Department for Biological and Medical Psychology, University of Bergen, Bergen, Norway

Yuko Koshimori Music and Health Research Collaboratory, University of Toronto, Toronto, ON, Canada

Miriam Menken Center for Advanced Imaging Research, Department of Diagnostic Radiology & Nuclear Medicine, University of Maryland School of Medicine, Baltimore, MD, United States

Margaret Kathleen Pichora-Fuller Department of Psychology, University of Toronto, Toronto, ON, Canada; Department of Gerontology, Simon Fraser University, Vancouver, BC, Canada; Rotman Research Institute, Baycrest, Toronto, ON, Canada

Hervé Platel Normandy Univ, UNICAEN, PSL Research University, EPHE, INSERM, U1077, CHU de Caen, Cyceron, Caen, France

David Predovan Centre de Recherche, Institut Universitaire de Gériatrie de Montréal, Montréal, QC, Canada; Département de Psychologie, Université du Québec à Montréal, Montréal, QC, Canada

Séverine Samson Université de Lille, EA 4072 – PSITEC – Psychologie: Interactions, Temps, Emotions, Cognition, Equipe Neuropsychologie et Audition, Lille, France; AP-HP, GHU Pitié-Salpêtrière-Charles Foix, Unité d'épilepsie, Paris, France

Teppo Särkämö Department of Psychology and Logopedics, University of Helsinki, Helsinki, Finland

Sarah Sauvé Faculty of Medicine, Memorial University of Newfoundland, St. John's, NL, Canada

Aleksi J. Sihvonen Department of Psychology and Logopedics, University of Helsinki, Helsinki, Finland

Geir Olve Skeie The Grieg Academy – Department of Music, University of Bergen, Bergen, Norway; Department of Neurology, Haukeland University Hospital, Bergen, Norway

Michael Thaut Music and Health Research Collaboratory, University of Toronto, Toronto, ON, Canada

Jason D. Warren Dementia Research Centre, UCL Queen Square Institute of Neurology, University College London, London, United Kingdom

Benjamin Rich Zendel Faculty of Medicine, Memorial University of Newfoundland, St. John's, NL, Canada; Aging Research Centre - Newfoundland and Labrador, Grenfell Campus, Memorial University, Corner Brook, NL, Canada

About the editors

Lola L. Cuddy is Professor Emerita in the Department of Psychology, Queen's University, Canada, where she founded and directed the Music Cognition Laboratory. Research interests include the perceptual, cognitive, and emotional processes involved in music appreciation and understanding. Recent work has focused on individual differences in musical and prosodic skills and sensitivities, and such topics as absolute pitch, tone deafness, effects of music lessons on nonmusical cognitive skills, musical dyslexia, aging and music, amusia following stroke, and sparing of musical memories in Alzheimer's disease. She was editor of the flagship journal *Music Perception* (2002–17) and is a current associate editor of *Cognitive Processing*.

Sylvie Belleville is a full professor at the Psychology Department of University of Montreal, Canada, and Director of the Research Center of the Institut Universitaire de Gériatrie de Montréal, Canada. She is recognized for her work on the use of cognitive training to prevent age-related cognitive decline. She identified processes of compensation and plasticity in mild cognitive impairment using brain imaging techniques and also contributed to a better understanding of the neuropsychological deficits found in persons with very early signs of Alzheimer's disease or mild cognitive impairment. She has published more than 200 peer-reviewed articles and holds a Tier 1 Canada Research Chair on the Cognitive Neuroscience of Aging and Brain Plasticity.

Aline Moussard is a neuropsychologist specializing in applied research related to the use of music as a tool for cognitive stimulation in healthy and clinical populations. She is also a project manager at the Research Center of the Institut Universitaire de Gériatrie de Montréal, Canada, and is currently coordinating a multisite research project on dementia prevention that uses cognitive training and stimulating leisure activities (including music practice) to build and strengthen cognitive reserve in healthy older adults.

Foreword

As a "mature" neuroscientist, I wish to believe that by returning to my active musical life, after 35 years of abstinence, I am slowing the aging of my brain. Is this only wishful thinking? Or is there a real possibility that music engagement protects us from cognitive losses? Here, you will find the science behind this hope.

Cuddy, Belleville, and Moussard have succeeded in assembling a remarkable panel of scientists to address from a scholarly perspective the potential of music to aid older adults and to alleviate age-related disorders. The aging population has led to increased interest in the effects of various lifestyle choices that can mitigate or prevent the cognitive decline that accompanies aging. Although the therapeutic use of music, for example, healing songs, exists in all human societies (Mehr et al., 2019), it is only recently that healthcare professionals and politicians have taken a formal interest and are asking experts for their recommendations regarding music and health.

Music is widely accessible, easy to use, and enjoyed by the majority of people, making it a potentially useful tool for improving well-being and thereby health. Furthermore, learning music may feed a "cognitive reserve." The concept of cognitive reserve is often associated with the efficacy of music in slowing cognitive aging. The "more trained" brain would have the ability to optimize cognitive functioning despite neurobiological aging. Like intellectual activity, often associated with a high level of education, music engagement may compensate for the negative effects of aging. However, music is not magic. Music is shaped and constrained by the functioning of our brain. How our brain responds to music may reflect large individual differences.

Let's be optimistic. Music brings people together and makes them feel better. As this book testifies, there is an explosion of fundamental research on music in the aging brain. Thus there are "grounds for optimism that the ancient hope of using music as medicine may finally be realized" (Benhamou & Warren, this volume, p. 107).

Isabelle Peretz

University of Montreal, Montreal, QC, Canada

2019

Reference

Mehr, S. A., Singh, M., Knox, D., Ketter, D. M., Pickens-Jones, D., Atwood, S., ... Howard, R. M. (2019). Universality and diversity in human song. *Science*, *366*(6468).

Preface

This book develops our understanding of the deep and mysterious power of music. It explores the effect of music on the aging brain and age-related neurological disorders, such as stroke or dementia. Music may offer protection against some of the sensory and cognitive declines that accompany aging and may even alleviate the symptoms of aging-related brain diseases. Here our approach is twofold—first, to present the current state of knowledge about music and brain processes, and second to apply this evidence to normal aging (for prevention) and pathological aging (for rehabilitation or quality of life). We consider the role of music training but also that of *musicality*, a term which applies to the universal capacity to perceive and enjoy music (see Honing, 2018).

Why is this important? To address this question, reflect that, worldwide, we are an aging population. According to the National Institute of Health (United States), 8.5% of people worldwide (617 million) are aged 65 or older—a percentage projected to jump to nearly 17% by 2050. In the United States alone, the 65-and-older population is expected to double from 48 to 88 million by 2050. Such increases will be accompanied by increases in the incidence and prevalence of age-related neurological disorders. They present heavy economic and social challenges to provide resources directed to the physical, mental, and social welfare of older generations. How can we allay the physical and cognitive effects of aging, so that older individuals maintain good mental health and independence? Aging can become an opportunity at many levels. Older adults, if they keep their health and cognitive capacities, can contribute their experience and expertise to other generations and to society.

What can music contribute? Through music, we may alleviate the pain, distress, and social isolation of incapacitated individuals as well as help sustain cognitive and physical health. Thus music can offer directions for meeting the social and economic challenges of aging.

The chapters are written for clinicians and researchers, both established and aspiring, in the cross-disciplinary fields of music psychology, psychology, neuroscience, neuropsychology, neurology, and rehabilitation. They are also intended for those in other fields who have an interest in the neurological substrates for music. In many places, authors point out that conclusions to date regarding the power of music are flawed due to imperfect research designs and conceptualization. Valuable improved techniques and directions are suggested for future research to undertake exciting new projects and discoveries.

Preparation of this volume was facilitated by the dedicated support of Barbara Makinster at Academic Press; Ritu Sikka, editorial assistant; and Anja Cui, research assistant. We also warmly thank the chapter authors for their contributions and thoughtful reviews of the contributions of others, as well as Isabelle Peretz for supportive encouragement and for contributing the foreword.

Lola L. Cuddy, Sylvie Belleville, and Aline Moussard

Reference

Honing, H. (2018). *The origins of musicality*. Cambridge, MA: The MIT Press.

Introduction

Music is a powerful, universally available, force in our lives. We sing to our infants, use music to direct energy and to teach language and behavior patterns to preschoolers, introduce music to children on TV and audio devices, engage them in choirs and music lessons, and as adults, whether or not the music lessons ended productively, encounter music regularly in social and cultural contexts such as group singing, concerts, rituals, and dances. In some settings, music is available to aging adults for pleasure, relaxation, anxiety reduction, and reminiscence.

Yet much remains to be understood about music and its effects on us. What parts and interconnections within the brain are responsible for the appreciation of and the response to music? How does music affect us across the life span, and, the focus of this book, interact with aging processes and difficulties? First, it requires a synergy of musical, medical, therapeutic, and neuroscientific knowledge, and second, as Levitin (2019) points out, the rigorous application of the scientific principles of experimental design and observation. The chapters of this volume illustrate exciting progress in meeting these challenges.

The book comprises three sections; all three coeditors collaborated in reviewing and editing each of the three sections. Chapters in the first section deal with the musical brain and the effects of normal and pathological aging on music perception and cognition. Chapters in the second section cover music and neuroprotection and evaluate the proposal that music may help preserve the brain from the effects of normal aging. Chapters in the third section cover music therapy and intervention and evaluate the proposal that music may alleviate the symptoms of disease.

Chapter 1, *The musical brain*, by Koelsch and Skeie, presents an overview of the brain regions and networks activated by the musical brain. It includes diagrams (brain maps) of the multiple brain regions involved. These illustrations were created with subsequent chapters in mind so that they might be consulted along with the text of the chapters. The authors offer a description, based on neuroscientific evidence, of the neuroarchitecture of brain organization for music. This organization comprises complex interconnected processes and structures, from simple visceral reaction to sound and basic feature detection at subcortical levels to memory and pattern formation at cortical levels. Koelsch and Skeie then cover the processing of musical expectancy and prediction by hierarchically organized structures, and discuss musical meaning and music-evoked emotions. Throughout, the chapter emphasizes the sensory, cognitive, emotional, and social aspects of musical responding, and music's relations with language.

Chapter 2, *Processing of musical pitch, time, and emotion in older adults*, and Chapter 3, *Age-related hearing loss*, by Halpern and by Pichora-Fuller, respectively, are concerned with normal aging processes and the accompanying effects of normal sensory and cognitive declines on music processing. In Chapter 2, Halpern reviews pitch processing from single intervals to melody and time processing from single intervals to overall tempo, and, in a final section, examines the role of emotion. Pitch and time processing are integral to the overall structure of music, and declines in these domains will necessarily affect music processing. Overall, while age-related declines are found in tasks involving pitch and time processing, as well as emotion detection and memory, there is encouraging evidence that some of these declines may be offset by top-down knowledge based on experience. In Chapter 3, Pichora-Fuller describes various forms of age-related hearing loss (ARHL) and considers the consequences for speech and music perception. It foreshadows Chapter 11 by Zendel and Sauvé, in proposing that music training may prevent or ameliorate the adverse effects of ARHL.

Chapter 4, *Disorders of music processing in dementia*, and Chapter 5, *Stroke and acquired amusia*, continue the story by considering disorders of musical perception and memory resulting from age-related neuropathology—dementia and stroke. In Chapter 4, Benhamou and Warren outline the various manifestations of dementia (of which Alzheimer's disease is the most common) and the distinctive musical phenotypes accompanying each. The authors build on the descriptions of the musical brain presented in Chapter 1, here they show how neurodegenerative disease may selectively target the hierarchically organized, distributed networks of the musical brain. They propose that such evidence contributes to our understanding of brain processes for music, and also that it may inform the development of musical therapies. In Chapter 5, Sihvonen and Särkämö deal with the (sometimes devastating) consequences of stroke for the musical brain. Stroke can cause multiple impairments in perception, cognition, and motor skills, impairments that include *amusia* or the loss of perception and abilities specifically in the musical domain. However, with stroke, unlike dementia, there may be recovery of function with time and appropriate intervention. Although modern imaging techniques tracking loss and recovery following stroke have yielded insight into the brain regions subserving music, more research into the potential of rehabilitation of amusia is needed.

Chapter 6, *"Curious" cases of preservation of music compositional ability in the presence of organic brain disease: historical examples*, by Cuddy and Duffin, is an interlude intended to provide a historical context for the chapters that follow. Biographical sketches of seven composers (16–20th century) are presented; all seven were afflicted with a form of neurodegenerative brain disease, but all seven continued to compose successfully in the eyes of their contemporaries and their physicians. While acknowledging the many limitations of drawing conclusions from historical documents, the authors cautiously propose that these historical records stand, in their words, "as an inspiration to research that musical ability resides, resilient and irrepressible, in many damaged brains." If it does, then before damage occurs, might music not offer neuroprotection?

In Chapter 7, *Theories of cognitive aging: a look at potential benefits of music training on the aging brain*, T.M. Vanessa Chan and Alain present how musical training and active musicianship can contribute to mitigating the effect of aging on cognition. They assess this important question in the context of modern theories of cognitive aging by reviewing evidence emerging from behavioral as well as neuroimaging studies. Hanna-Pladdy and Menken also address this key question in Chapter 8, *Training-induced cognitive and neural changes in musicians: implications for healthy aging*, with a focus on neuroplastic processes and how musical practice can result in a form of neural or cognitive reserve that would delay the expression of brain pathology. In Chapter 9, *Singing and choirs*, Cohen examines the impact of vocal training and choir participation on the brain and cognition of older adults. Cohen argues that singing activities engage neuroplastic processes similar to those involved in learning to play an instrument and thus has potential as a way to promote brain health in older age. Capitalizing on the impact of physical activity on neuroplastic processes, Predovan and Bherer examine in Chapter 10, *Effects on cognition of physical activity with or without music and of dance*, the effect of physical activity with or without music and the impact of dance on the brain of older adults. Although there are still a limited number of well-designed empirical studies, results are encouraging and suggest that music used in combination with physical activity might provide added benefit. In Chapter 11, *Toward music-based auditory rehabilitation for older adults*, Zendel and Sauvé show that musical training can be used to improve hearing abilities in older adults. They argue that the benefit might be due to an enhancement of the speech—motor system that allows individuals to better process the acoustic features of incoming speech.

The following chapters examine how music-based interventions can alleviate symptoms and increase quality of life in age-related neurological disorders. Chapter 12, *Benefits and limits of musical interventions in pathological aging*, and Chapter 13, *Why do music-based interventions benefit persons with neurodegenerative disease?*, focus on music interventions in dementia. In Chapter 12, Platel and Groussard present different approaches targeting behavioral and cognitive outcomes throughout the spectrum of dementia severity. They explain how music can be used to decrease depression and anxiety symptoms that are commonly associated with the early stages of Alzheimer's disease, or to reduce apathy and provide some form of cognitive stimulation in the moderate and severe stages of the disease. In Chapter 13, Hobeika and Samson are interested in the effect of musical interventions on the social functioning of persons with dementia. They propose that the interpersonal coordination promoted by active music-based interventions can improve patients' nonverbal communication and their social interactions.

In Chapter 14, *Neurorehabilitation in aging through neurologic music therapy*, Thaut and Koshimori introduce the concept of neurologic music therapy and present several science-informed rehabilitation techniques applied to cognitive, language, and motor rehabilitation that can be used in age-related neurological disorders. They also explore the potential neural mechanisms underlying the therapeutic effects of music and rhythm on the aging brain. Chapter 15, *The use of rhythm in rehabilitation for patients with movement disorders*, by Dalla Bella, focuses on the rehabilitation of motor functions through synchronization to music rhythm. Dalla Bella illustrates the principle and underlying mechanisms of rhythmic auditory cueing using gait rehabilitation in Parkinson's disease as an example. He also presents how new technologies such as smartphone apps or tablet serious games can be used to better implement and disseminate rhythm-based music interventions. Finally, in Chapter 16, *The impact of music interventions on motor rehabilitation following stroke in elderly*, Altenmüller and James present music-supported therapy methods to improve poststroke recovery, with a focus on upper limb and gait rehabilitation, as well as on studies targeting cognitive and psychological outcomes. In line with the previous chapters of this section, they conclude that music listening and active musical training can be a strong stimulant for neuroplastic adaptations and behavioral improvements in neurological rehabilitation, mediated by sensory, motor, cognitive, emotional, and neurophysiological processes. Nonetheless, all these authors emphasize methodological limitations to current music-based intervention studies. They provide very important recommendations to consider when designing and assessing the next studies so that music-based interventions in neurorehabilitation can be grounded within a neurobiological understanding of how and why particular brain systems are affected. These considerations should help to improve the relevance of clinical interventions and the scientific demonstration of their efficacy, ultimately increasing patients' functioning, autonomy, and well-being.

Lola L. Cuddy, Sylvie Belleville, and Aline Moussard

Reference

Levitin, D. J. (2019). Medicine's melodies: Music, health and well-being. *Music and Medicine*, *11*(4), 236−244.

Chapter 1

The musical brain

Stefan Koelsch[1] and Geir Olve Skeie[2,3]

[1]*Department for Biological and Medical Psychology, University of Bergen, Bergen, Norway,*
[2]*The Grieg Academy — Department of Music, University of Bergen, Bergen, Norway,*
[3]*Department of Neurology, Haukeland University Hospital, Bergen, Norway*

Introduction

"Music" is a special case of sound: as opposed to a noise, or noise-textures (e.g., wind, fire crackling, rain, water bubbling, etc.), musical sounds have a particular structural organization in both the time and in the frequency domain. In the time domain, the most fundamental principle of musical structure is the temporal organization of sounds based on an isochronous pulse (the tactus, or "beat"), although there are notable exceptions (such as some kinds of meditation music, or some pieces of modern art music). In the frequency (pitch) domain, the most fundamental principle of musical structure is an organization of pitches according to the overtone series, resulting in simple (e.g., pentatonic) scales. Note that the production of overtone-based scales is, in turn, rooted in the perceptual properties of the auditory system, especially in "octave equivalence" and "fifth equivalence" (Terhardt, 1991). Inharmonic spectra (e.g., of inharmonic metallophones) give rise to different scales, such as the pelog and slendro scales (Sethares, 2005). Thus for a vast amount of musical traditions around the globe, and presumably throughout human history, these two principles (pulse and scale) build the nucleus of a *universal musical grammar*. Out of this nucleus, a seemingly infinite number of musical systems, styles, and compositions evolved. This evolvement appears to have followed computational principles described, for example, in the Chomsky hierarchy[1]

---

1. The Chomsky hierarchy is a hierarchy of formal grammatical systems for describing various classes of languages; the hierarchy can apply to both human and computer languages. This hierarchy was first published in 1956 by the linguist Chomsky. These grammatical systems were referred to by Chomsky as transformational grammars. Other linguists have since developed a variety of similar grammars; together these are known as generative grammars. The basic idea of a generative grammar is to provide a set of rules which are capable of generating all possible grammatical sentences in some language; the rules must constrain the generation so that only grammatical sentences are generated. The rules can also be used in reverse to parse a sentence and check if it is grammatical. (*Source*: https://www.conservapedia.com/Chomsky_hierarchy.)

Music and the Aging Brain. DOI: https://doi.org/10.1016/B978-0-12-817422-7.00001-8

and their extensions (Rohrmeier, Zuidema, Wiggins, & Scharff, 2015)—that is, local relationships between sounds based on a finite state grammar, and nonlocal relationships between sounds based on a context-free grammar (possibly even a context-sensitive grammar; Rohrmeier et al., 2015).

By virtue of its fundamental structural principles (pulse and scale), music immediately allows several individuals to produce sounds together. Notably, only humans can synchronize their movements (including vocalizations) flexibly in a group to an external pulse (see also Merchant & Honing, 2014; Merker, Morley, & Zuidema, 2015). This ability is possibly the simplest cognitive function that just separates us from animals (Koelsch, 2018), which would make music the decisive evolutionary step of the *Homo sapiens*, maybe even of the genus homo. Animals have "song" and "drumming" (e.g., bird song, ape drumming etc.), but gorillas do not drum in synchrony, and whales do not sing unison in choirs. Making music together in a group, that is, joint synchronized action, is a potent elicitor of social bonding, associated with the activation of pleasure-, and sometimes even "happiness-"circuits in the brain. Analogous to Robin Dunbar's *vocal grooming hypothesis* (Dunbar, 1993), music might have replaced manual grooming as the main mechanism for social bonding during human evolution. Dunbar's hypothesis (according to which vocal grooming has paved the way for the evolution of language) is based on the observation that, similar to manual grooming, human language plays a key role in building and maintaining affiliative bonds and group cohesion. This process is putatively driven by increased group size, which increases the number of social relationships an individual needs to maintain and monitor. Once the number of relationships becomes too large, an individual can no longer maintain its social networks with tactile interactions alone, and selection will favor alternative mechanisms such as talking to several individuals at the same time. However, many more individuals can make music in a group (compared to the group size typical for conversations), and thus establish and foster social relationships. This makes music the more obvious candidate to maintain social networks, and increase social cohesion in large groups. Thus a *musical grooming hypothesis* seems at least as likely to explain the emergence of music as a vocal grooming hypothesis for the emergence of language.

Like music, the term "language" refers to structured sounds that are produced by humans, and similar to music, spoken language also has melody, rhythm, accents, and timbre. However, language is a special case of music because it does not *need* a pulse nor a scale, and because it has very rich and specific meaning (it can, e.g., be used very effectively to express who did what to whom). Ulrich Reich (personal communication) once noted that "language is music distorted by (propositional) semantics." Thus the terms "music" and "language" both refer to "structured sounds that are produced by humans as a means of social interaction, expression, diversion or evocation of emotion" (Koelsch, 2014), with language, in addition, affording the property of propositional semantics. However, in language normally only one individual speaks at a time (otherwise the language cannot be understood, and the sound is unpleasant). By contrast, music provides the possibility that several individuals may produce sounds *at the same time*. In this sense, language is the music of the individual, and music is the language of the group.

These introductory thoughts illustrate that, at its core, music is not a cultural epiphenomenon of modern human societies, but at the heart of what makes us human, and thus deeply rooted in our brain. Engaging in music elicits a large array of cognitive and affective processes, including perception, multimodal integration, attention, social cognition, memory, communicative functions (including syntactic processing and processing of meaning information), bodily responses, and—when making music—action. By virtue of this richness, we presume that there is no structure of the brain in which activity cannot be modulated by music, which would make music the ideal tool to investigate the workings of the human brain. The following sections will review neuroscientific research findings about some of these processes.

We do not only hear with our cochlea

The auditory system evolved phylogenetically from the vestibular system. Interestingly, the vestibular nerve contains a substantial number of acoustically responsive fibers. The otolith organs (saccule and utricle) are sensitive to sounds and vibrations (Todd, Paillard, Kluk, Whittle, & Colebatch, 2014), and the vestibular nuclear complex in the brainstem exerts a major influence on spinal (and ocular) motoneurons in response to loud sounds with low frequencies, or with sudden onsets (Todd & Cody, 2000; Todd et al., 2014). Moreover, both the vestibular nuclei and the auditory cochlear nuclei in the brainstem project to the reticular formation (also in the brainstem), and the vestibular nucleus also projects to the parabrachial nucleus, a convergence site for vestibular, visceral, and autonomic processing in the brainstem (Balaban & Thayer, 2001; Kandler & Herbert, 1991). Such projections initiate and support movements, and contribute to the arousing (or calming) effects of music. Moreover, the inferior colliculus encodes consonance/dissonance (as well as auditory signals evoking fear or feelings of security), and this encoding is associated with preference for more consonant over more dissonant music. Notably, in addition to its projections to the auditory thalamus, the inferior colliculus hosts numerous other projections, for example, into both the somatomotor and the visceromotor (autonomic) system, thus initiating and supporting activity of skeletal muscles, smooth muscles, and cardiac muscles. These brainstem connections are the basis of our visceral reactions to music, and represent the first stages of the *auditory-limbic pathway*, which also includes the medial geniculate body of the thalamus, the auditory cortex (AC), and the amygdala (see Fig. 1.1). Thus subcortical

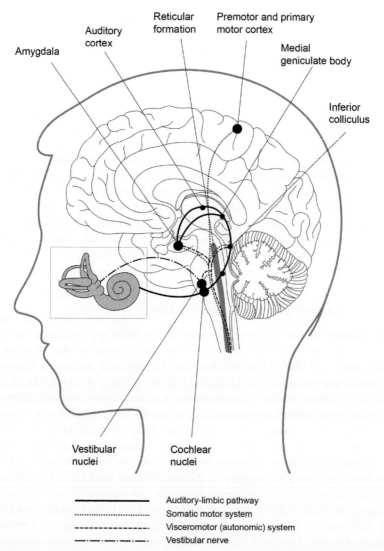

FIGURE 1.1   Illustration of the auditory-limbic pathway. Several nuclei of the auditory pathway in the brainstem, as well as the central nuclei group of the amygdala, give rise to somatomotor and autonomic responses to sounds. Note that, in addition to the auditory nerve, the vestibular nerve also contains acoustically responsive fibers. Also note that nuclei of the medial geniculate body of the thalamus project to both the auditory cortex and the amygdala. The auditory cortex also projects to the orbitofrontal cortex and the cingulate cortex (projections not shown). Moreover, amygdala, orbitofrontal cortex, and cingulate cortex have numerous projections to the hypothalamus (not shown) and thus also exert influence on the endocrine system, including the neuroendocrine motor system.

processing of sounds does not only give rise to auditory sensations, but also to somatomotor and autonomic responses, and the stimulation of motoneurons and autonomic neurons by low-frequency beats might contribute to the human impetus to "move to the beat" (Grahn & Rowe, 2009; Todd & Cody, 2000).

In addition to vibrations of the vestibular apparatus and cochlea, sounds also evoke resonances in vibration receptors, that is, in the Pacinian corpuscles (which are sensitive from 10 Hz to a few kHz, and located mainly in the skin, the retroperitoneal space in the belly, the periosteum of the bones, and the sex organs), and maybe even responses in mechanoreceptors of the skin that detect pressure. The international concert percussionist Dame Evelyn Glennie is profoundly deaf, and hears mainly through vibrations felt in the skin (personal communication with Dame Glennie), probably with contributions of the vestibular organ. Thus we do not only hear with our cochlea, but also with the vestibular apparatus and mechanoreceptors distributed throughout our body.

Auditory feature extraction in brainstem and thalamus

Neural activity originating in the auditory nerve is progressively transformed in the auditory brainstem, as indicated by different neural response properties for the periodicity of sounds, timbre (including roughness, or consonance/dissonance), sound intensity and interaural disparities in the superior olivary complex and the inferior colliculus (Pickles, 2008; Schnupp, Nelken, & King, 2011). The inferior colliculi can initiate flight and defensive behavior in response to threatening stimuli (even before the acoustic information reaches the AC; Cardoso, Coimbra, & Brandão, 1994; Lamprea et al., 2002), providing evidence of relatively elaborated auditory processing already in the brainstem. This stands in contrast to the visual system: Bard (1934) observed that decortication, that is, removing the neocortex, led to blindness in cats and dogs, but not to deafness (the hearing thresholds appeared to be elevated, but the animals were capable of differentiating sounds). From the thalamus, particularly via the medial geniculate body, neural impulses are mainly projected into different divisions of the AC (but note that the thalamus also projects auditory impulses into the amygdala and the medial orbitofrontal cortex (Kaas, Hackett, & Tramo, 1999; LeDoux, 2000; Öngür & Price, 2000).

The exact mechanisms underlying pitch perception are not known (and will not be discussed here), but it is clear that both information originating from the tonotopic organization of the cochlea (space information), and information originating from the integer time intervals of neural spiking in the auditory nerve (time information) contribute to pitch perception (Moore, 2008; Plack, 2005). Importantly, the auditory pathway does not only consist of bottom-up, but also of top-down projections, and nuclei such as the dorsal nucleus of the inferior colliculus presumably receive even more descending than ascending projections from diverse auditory cortical fields (Huffman & Henson, 1990). Given the massive top-down projections within the auditory pathway, it also becomes increasingly obvious that top-down *predictions* play an important role in pitch perception (Koelsch, Skouras, & Lohmann, 2018; Koelsch, Vuust, & Friston, 2018; Malmierca, Anderson, & Antunes, 2015, in addition to space and time information). Within the *predictive coding framework* (currently one of the dominant theories on sensory perception), such top-down projections are thought to afford passing on top-down predictions, while sensory information is passed bottom-up, signaling prediction errors, that is, sensory information that does not match a prediction (Koelsch, Skouras, et al., 2018; Koelsch, Vuust, et al., 2018).

Numerous studies investigated decoding of frequency information in the auditory brainstem using the *frequency-following response* (FFR; Kraus & Chandrasekaran, 2010). The FFR can be elicited preattentively, and is thought to originate mainly from the inferior colliculus (but note also that it is likely that the AC is at least partly involved in shaping the FFRs, e.g., by virtue of top-down projections to the inferior colliculus, see also above). Using FFRs, Wong, Skoe, Russo, Dees, and Kraus (2007) measured brainstem responses to three Mandarin tones that differed only in their (F0) pitch contours. Participants were amateur musicians and nonmusicians, and results revealed that musicians had more accurate encoding of the pitch contour of the phonemes (as reflected in the FFRs) than nonmusicians. This finding indicates that the auditory brainstem is involved in the encoding of pitch contours of speech information (vowels), and that the correlation between the FFRs and the properties of the acoustic information may be modulated by musical training. Similar training effects on FFRs elicited by syllables with a dipping pitch contour were observed in native English speakers (nonmusicians) after a training period of 14 days (with eight 30-min sessions of training on lexical pitch patterns, Song, Skoe, Wong, & Kraus, 2008). The latter results show the contribution of the brainstem in language learning, and its neural plasticity in adulthood.

A study by Strait, Kraus, Skoe, and Ashley (2009) also reported musical training effects on the decoding of the acoustic features of an affective vocalization (an infant's unhappy cry), as reflected in auditory brainstem potentials. This suggests (1) that the auditory brainstem is involved in the auditory processing of communicated states of emotion (which substantially contributes to the decoding and understanding of *affective prosody*), and (2) that musical training can lead to a finer tuning of such (subcortical) processing.

Acoustical equivalency of "timbre" and "phoneme." With regard to a comparison between music and speech, it is worth mentioning that, in terms of acoustics, there is *no* difference between a phoneme and the timbre of a musical sound (and it is only a matter of convention that some phoneticians rather use terms such as "vowel quality" or "vowel color," instead of "timbre"). Both are characterized by the two physical correlates of timbre: *spectrum envelope* (i.e., differences in the relative amplitudes of the individual "harmonics," or "overtones") and *amplitude envelope* (also sometimes called the amplitude contour or energy contour of the sound wave, i.e., the way that the loudness of a sound changes over time, particularly with regard to the on- and offset of a sound). Aperiodic sounds can also differ in spectrum envelope (see, e.g., the difference between /S/ as in "ship" and /s/ as in "sip"), and timbre differences related to amplitude envelope play a role in speech, for example, in the shape of the attack for /b/ versus /w/ and /S/ versus /Ù/ (as in "chip").

Auditory feature extraction in the AC. As mentioned above, auditory information is projected mainly via the subdivisions of the medial geniculate body into the primary AC [PAC, corresponding to Brodmann's area (BA) 41] and adjacent secondary auditory fields (corresponding to BAs 42 and 52). For a detailed description of primary auditory "core," and secondary auditory "belt" fields, as well as their connectivity, see Kaas and Hackett (2000). Large parts of the AC are buried in brain fissures, while other parts are located on the lateral surface of the superior and middle temporal gyri (see Fig. 1.2). For example, the lateral sulcus (also referred to as "Sylvian fissure," not indicated in Fig. 1.2) is a deep fissure, part of which separates the superior temporal gyrus (STG) from the frontal and the parietal lobe. Within this fissure (and thus not visible from the outside), on top of the STG, lies the "superior temporal plane" which hosts the PAC (see also Fig. 1.5), and numerous auditory belt and parabelt regions (the region of the superior temporal plane anterior of the PAC is also referred to as "planum polare," and the region posterior of the PAC as "planum temporale").

With regard to the functional properties of primary and secondary auditory fields, a study by Petkov, Kayser, Augath, and Logothetis (2006) showed that, in the macaque monkey, all of the PAC core areas, and most of the surrounding belt areas, show a tonotopic organization. (*Tonotopic* refers to the spatial arrangement of sounds in the brain. Tones close to each other in terms of frequency are mapped in spatially neighboring regions in the brain.) Tonotopic organization is clearest in the field A1, and some belt areas seem to show only weak, or no, tonotopic organization. These auditory areas perform a more fine-grained, and more specific, analysis of acoustic features compared to the auditory brainstem.

Tramo, Shah, and Braida (2002) reported that a patient with bilateral lesion of the PAC (1) had normal detection thresholds for sounds (i.e., the patient could say whether there was a tone or not); but (2) had elevated thresholds for determining whether two tones had the same pitch or not (i.e., the patient had difficulties to detect fine-grained frequency differences between two subsequent tones); and (3) had markedly increased thresholds for determining the pitch direction [i.e., the patient had great difficulties in saying whether the second tone was higher or lower in pitch than the first

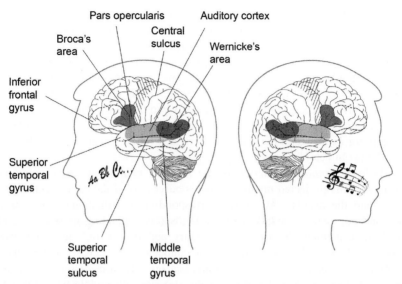

FIGURE 1.2   Lateral views on the left and right hemispheres of the brain. The auditory cortex (gray area) corresponds to large parts of the superior temporal gyrus, the superior temporal sulcus, and parts of the middle temporal gyrus (the approximate borders of the gyri are indicated by dashed lines). In the left hemisphere, the superior posterior part of the temporal gyrus is referred to as "Wernicke's area," and the posterior part of the inferior frontal gyrus (indicated by a dotted line) is referred to as "Broca's area" (see dotted area). While these areas in the left hemisphere appear to be more strongly engaged during the processing of language than of music, the homotope areas in the right hemisphere appear to be more strongly engaged during the processing of music than of language. The hashed area indicates the (lateral) premotor cortex.

tone, *even though* he could tell that both tones differed; for similar results obtained from patients with (right) PAC lesions, see Johnsrude, Penhune, & Zatorre, 2000; Zatorre, 2001].

The (primary) AC is involved in the transformation of acoustic features (such as frequency information) into percepts (such as pitch height and pitch chroma). For example, a sound with the *frequencies* 200, 300, and 400 Hz is transformed into the *pitch percept* of 100 Hz (thus the "missing fundamental" of 100 Hz is actually perceived as the pitch of the sound, a phenomenon also referred to as "residue pitch" or "virtual pitch"). Lesions of the (right) PAC result in a loss of the ability to perceive residue pitch in both animals (Whitfield, 1980) and humans (Zatorre, 1988), and neurons in the anterolateral region of the PAC show responses to a missing fundamental frequency (Bendor & Wang, 2005). Moreover, magnetoencephalographic data indicate that response properties in the PAC depend on whether or not a missing fundamental of a complex tone is perceived (Patel & Balaban, 2001). Note, however, that "combination tones" emerge already in the cochlea, and that the periodicity of complex tones is coded in the spike pattern of auditory brainstem neurons; therefore different mechanisms contribute to the perception of residue pitch on at least three different levels (basilar membrane, brainstem, and AC). However, the studies mentioned above suggest that, compared to the brainstem or the basilar membrane, the AC plays a more prominent role for the transformation of acoustic features into auditory percepts (such as the transformation of information about the frequencies of a complex sound, as well as about the periodicity of a sound, into a pitch percept).

Beyond pitch perception, the AC is also involved in a number of other functions, including auditory sensory memory (ASM), extraction of inter-sound relationships, discrimination and organization of sounds, as well as sound patterns, stream segregation, automatic change detection, and multi-sensory integration (for reviews see Hackett & Kaas, 2004; Winkler, 2007). With regard to functional differences between the left and the right PAC, as well as neighboring auditory association cortex, several studies suggest that the left AC has a higher resolution of temporal information than the right AC, and that the right AC has a higher spectral resolution than the left AC (Hyde, Peretz, & Zatorre, 2008; Perani et al., 2010; Zatorre, Belin, & Penhune, 2002). This might explain why the left AC reacts more strongly to language (in which phonemes usually occur more rapidly than tones of melodies), while the right AC reacts more strongly to music (in which sound sequences usually have higher pitch variation than in language). Finally, the AC also prepares acoustic information for further conceptual and conscious processing. For example, with regard to the meaning of sounds, just a short single tone can sound, for example, "bright," "rough," or "dull." That is, the timbre of a single sound is already capable of conveying meaningful information.

Operations within the (primary and adjacent) AC related to auditory feature analysis are reflected in electrophysiological recordings in brain-electric responses that have latencies of about 10−100 ms, particularly middle-latency responses, including the auditory P1 (a response with positive polarity and a latency of around 50 ms), and the later auditory N1, or N100, component (the N1 is a response with negative polarity and a latency of around 100 ms). Such brain-electric responses are also referred to as "event-related potentials" (ERPs) or "evoked potentials."

Echoic memory and Gestalt formation in the auditory cortex

While auditory features are extracted, the acoustic information enters the ASM (or "echoic memory"), and representations of auditory Gestalten (or "auditory objects" Griffiths & Warren, 2004) are formed. The ASM retains information only for a few seconds, and information stored in the ASM fades quickly. The ASM is thought to store physical features of sounds (such as pitch, intensity, duration, location, timbre, etc.), sound patterns, and even abstract features of sound patterns (e.g., Paavilainen, Simola, Jaramillo, Naatanen, & Winkler, 2001). Operations of the ASM are at least partly reflected electrically in the *mismatch negativity* (MMN, e.g., Näätänen, Tervaniemi, Sussman, Paavilainen, & Winkler, 2001). The MMN is typically elicited in so-called "auditory oddball paradigms": when individuals are presented with a sequence of repeating "standard" sounds or sound sequences (such as a repeating pitch, or a repeating sequence of a few pitches), the occurrence of a "deviant" sound (such as a sound with a different pitch) elicits an MMN. The MMN is an ERP with negative polarity and a peak latency of about 100−200 ms, and appears to receive its main contributions from neural sources located in the PAC and adjacent auditory (belt) fields, with additional (but smaller) contributions from frontal cortical areas (for reviews, see Deouell, 2007; Schönwiesner et al., 2007).

Numerous MMN studies have contributed to the understanding of the neural correlates of music processing by investigating different response properties of the ASM to musical and speech stimuli, by using melodic and rhythmic patterns to investigate auditory Gestalt formation, or by studying effects of long- and short-term musical training on processes underlying ASM operations. Especially the latter studies have contributed substantially to our understanding of neuroplasticity (i.e., to changes in neuronal structure and function due to experience), and thus to our understanding of the neural basis of learning (for a review see Tervaniemi, 2009). Here, suffice it to say that MMN studies showed differences between musicians and nonmusicians on the processing of sound localization, pitch, melody, rhythm, musical key, timbre, tuning, and timing (e.g., Koelsch, Schröger, & Tervaniemi, 1999; Putkinen, Tervaniemi, Saarikivi, de Vent, & Huotilainen, 2014; Rammsayer & Altenmüller, 2006; Tervaniemi, Castaneda, Knoll, & Uther, 2006; Tervaniemi, Janhunen, Kruck, Putkinen, & Huotilainen, 2016).

Auditory oddball paradigms were also used to investigate processes of melodic and rhythmic grouping of tones occurring in tone patterns (such grouping is essential for auditory Gestalt formation, see also Sussman, 2007), as well as effects related to musical long-term training on these processes. These studies showed musician/nonmusician differences (1) on the processing of 4- or 5-tone melodic patterns (Fujioka, Trainor, Ross, Kakigi, & Pantev, 2004; Tervaniemi, Ilvonen, Karma, Alho, & Näätänen, 1997; Tervaniemi, Rytkönen, Schröger, Ilmoniemi, & Näätänen, 2001; Zuijen, von Sussman, Winkler, Näätänen, & Tervaniemi, 2004); (2) on the encoding of the number of elements in a tone pattern (Zuijen, von Sussman, Winkler, Näätänen, & Tervaniemi, 2005); and (3) on the processing of patterns consisting of two voices (Fujioka, Trainor, Ross, Kakigi, & Pantev, 2005).

The formation of auditory Gestalten entails processes of perceptual separation, as well as processes of melodic, rhythmic, timbral, and spatial grouping. Such processes have been summarized under the concepts of *auditory scene analysis* and *auditory stream segregation* (Bregman, 1994). Grouping of acoustic events follows Gestalt principles such as similarity, proximity, and continuity (for acoustic cues used for perceptual separation and auditory grouping see Darwin, 1997, 2008). In everyday life, such operations are not only important for music processing, but also, for instance, for separating a speaker's voice during a conversation from other sound sources in the environment. That is, these operations are important because their function is to recognize and to follow acoustic objects, and to establish a cognitive representation of the acoustic environment. It appears that the planum temporale (located posterior of the PAC) is a crucial structure for auditory scene analysis and stream segregation, particularly due to its role for the processing of pitch intervals and sound sequences (Griffiths & Warren, 2002; Patterson, Uppenkamp, Johnsrude, & Griffiths, 2002; Snyder & Elhilali, 2017).

Musical expectancy formation: processing of local dependencies

The processing of regularities inherent in sound sequences can be performed based on two different principles. The first is based on the regularities inherent in the acoustical properties of the sounds. For example, after a sequence of several sounds with the same pitch, a sound with a different pitch sounds irregular. This type of processing is assumed to be performed by the ASM, and processing of irregular sounds is reflected in the MMN (see above). Note that the extraction of the regularity underlying such sequences does *not* require memory capabilities beyond the ASM (i.e., the regularity is extracted in real time, on a moment-to-moment basis). I have referred previously to such syntactic processes as "knowledge-free structuring" (Koelsch, 2012).

The second principle is that, the local arrangement of elements in language and music includes numerous regularities that cannot simply be extracted on a moment-to-moment basis, but have to be learned over an extended period of time ("local" refers here to the arrangement of adjacent, or directly succeeding, elements). For example, it usually takes months, or even years, to learn the syntax of a language, and it takes a considerable amount of exposure and learning to establish (implicit) knowledge of the statistical regularities of a certain type of music. I have referred previously to such syntactic processes as "musical expectancy formation" (Koelsch, 2012).

An example of local dependencies in music captured by "musical expectancy formation" is the bigram table of chord transition probabilities extracted from a corpus of Bach chorales in a study by Rohrmeier and Cross (2008). That table, for example, showed that after a dominant seventh chord, the most likely chord to follow is the tonic. It also showed that a supertonic is nine times more likely to follow a tonic than a tonic following a supertonic. This is important, because the acoustic similarity of tonic and supertonic is the same in both cases, and therefore it is very difficult to explain this statistical regularity simply based on acoustic similarity. Rather, this regularity is specific for this kind of major—minor tonal music, and thus has to be learned (over an extended period of time) to be represented accurately in the brain of a listener.

Notably, even nonmusicians are sensitive to such statistical regularities and pick up statistical structures without explicit intent. This ability is explored within the framework of *statistical learning* and *implicit learning*, both of which, it has been argued, investigate the same underlying learning phenomenon (for reviews see Dienes, 2012; Rohrmeier & Rebuschat, 2012). Although statistical learning appears to be domain-general (Conway & Christiansen, 2005), it has most prominently been investigated in the context of language acquisition, especially word learning and music (for reviews see Ettlinger, Margulis, & Wong, 2011; François & Schön, 2014; Rohrmeier & Rebuschat, 2012). With regard to statistical learning paradigms, word learning has been argued to be grounded, at least in part, in sequence prediction: in a continuous stream of syllables, sequences of events linked with high statistical conditional probability likely correspond to words, whereas syllable transitions with low predictability may likely be indicative of word-boundaries. Thus tracking conditional probability relations between syllables has been regarded as relevant for the extraction of candidate word forms. In music, representations of musical regularities guiding local dependencies serve the formation of a *musical* expectancy ("musical" is italic here to clearly differentiate this type of expectancy formation from the formation of expectancies based simply on acoustical regularities).

In addition, integrating information across the extracted units eventually reveals distributional properties (Hunt & Aslin, 2010; Thiessen, Kronstein, & Hufnagle, 2013). Extracted statistical properties provide an important basis for predictions which guide the processing of sensory information (Friston, 2010; Friston & Kiebel, 2009; Thiessen et al., 2013). Stimuli that are hard to predict (e.g., the syllable after a word boundary) have been hypothesized to increase processing load (Friston, 2010; Friston & Kiebel, 2009). Such an increase in processing load has been found to be reflected neurophysiologically in ERP components such as the N100 mentioned above and the N400a negative deflection that peaks around 400 ms poststimulus onset. During successful stream segmentation, word-onsets evoke larger N100 and N400 ERPs compared to more predictable positions within the word in adults (e.g., Abla, Katahira, & Okanoya, 2008; Francois & Schön, 2011; François & Schön, 2014; François, Chobert, Besson, & Schön, 2013; Schön & François, 2011; Teinonen & Huotilainen, 2012), and similar ERP responses have been observed even in newborns (Teinonen, Fellman, Näätänen, Alku, & Huotilainen, 2009). The N400 will be explained in more detail below.

When participants learn local dependencies (i.e., statistical regularities underlying the succession of sounds), irregular sounds elicit a *statistical MMN* (or sMMN; Koelsch, Busch, Jentschke, & Rohrmeier, 2016; Tsogli, Jentschke, Daikoku, & Koelsch, 2019), which is maximal between around

130–220 ms, and has a frontal distribution (see also studies by Daikoku, Yatomi, & Yumoto, 2014, 2015; Furl et al., 2011; Koelsch et al., 2016; Paraskevopoulos, Kuchenbuch, Herholz, & Pantev, 2012). So far, the sMMN has been investigated in statistical learning paradigms in which participants are presented over a period of several dozens of minutes with streams of "triplets" (i.e., sounds arranged in threes), with the triplets being designed such that the succession of tones within and between triplets follows exactly specified statistical regularities.

It is important to understand that, within the Chomsky hierarchy, a finite state automaton is required to process both the regularities underlying the generation the "classical" MMN on the one hand (i.e., "knowledge-free structuring"), and the sMMN on the other (i.e., *musical* expectancy formation"). In other words, a finite state grammar is sufficient to describe these two types of regularities. However, they are represented psychologically and neurophysiologically in fundamentally different ways (because the processing of regularities that do not require long-term memory, i.e., "knowledge-free structuring," differs neurocognitively from the processing of regularities stored in long-term memory, i.e., "musical expectancy formation"). The local transition probabilities underlying the generation of the "classical" MMN (e.g., the MMN elicited by a deviant pitch) are stored in the ASM (and if the probabilities change, the sensory representations of the new transition probabilities are dynamically updated). By contrast, deviants in statistical learning paradigms, like those employed in the sMMN studies described above, require an extended period of learning, and the mismatch response associated with statistical learning reflects the processing of local dependencies based on (implicit) knowledge about statistical regularities. That is, the mismatch response associated with statistical learning is based on memory representations beyond the capabilities of sensory memory. With regard to music, this also means that fundamentally different neurocognitive systems process different types of local syntactic dependencies in music, even though they can both be mastered by a finite state automaton.

Musical structure building: processing of nonlocal dependencies

As described in the previous section, tonal music involves representations of single events and local relationships on short timescales. However, many composers designed nested hierarchical syntactic structures spanning longer timescales, potentially up to entire movements of symphonies and sonatas (for academic approaches see Schenker, 1956; Salzer, 1962). Hierarchical syntactic structure (involving the potential for nested nonlocal dependencies) is a key component of the human language capacity (Chomsky, 1995; Fitch & Hauser, 2004; Friederici, Bahlmann, Heim, Schubotz, & Anwander, 2006; Hauser, Chomsky, & Fitch, 2002; Nevins, Pesetsky, & Rodrigues, 2009), and frequently produced and perceived in everyday life. For example, in the sentence "the boy who helped Peter kissed Mary," the subject relative clause "who helped Peter" is nested into the main clause "the boy kissed Mary," creating a nonlocal hierarchical dependency between "the boy" and "kissed Mary" (note that a finite state automaton will only (mis)understand that "Peter kissed Mary"!). Music theorists have described analogous hierarchical structures for music. Schenker (1956) was the first to describe musical structures as organized hierarchically, in a way that musical events are elaborated (or prolonged) by other events in a recursive fashion. According to this principle, for example, a phrase (or set of phrases) can be conceived of as an elaboration of a basic underlying tonic–dominant–tonic progression. Schenker further argued that this principle can be expanded to even larger musical sequences, up to entire musical movements. In addition, Hofstadter (1979) was one of the first to argue that a change of key embedded in a superordinate key (such as a tonal modulation away from, and returning to an initial key) constitutes a prime example of recursion in music. Based on similar ideas, several theorists have developed formal descriptions of the analysis of hierarchical structures in music (Lerdahl & Jackendoff, 1983; Rohrmeier, 2011; Steedman, 1984), including the generative theory of tonal music by Lerdahl and Jackendoff (1983), and the generative syntax model by Rohrmeier (2011).

Humans are capable of processing hierarchically organized structures including nonlocal dependencies in music (Dibben, 1994; Koelsch, Rohrmeier, Torrecuso, & Jentschke, 2013; Koelsch, Skouras, et al., 2013; Lerdahl & Krumhansl, 2007; Serafine, Glassman, & Overbeeke, 1989), driven by the human capacity to perceive and produce hierarchical, potentially recursive structures (Chomsky, 1995; Hauser et al., 2002; Jackendoff & Lerdahl, 2006). Using chorales by J.S. Bach (see Fig. 1.3) a study (Koelsch, Rohrmeier, et al., 2013; Koelsch, Skouras, et al., 2013) showed that hierarchically incorrect final chords of a musical period (violating the nonlocal prolongation of the beginning of the period) elicit a negative brain-electric potential which is maximal between 150 and 300 ms and has frontal preponderance, the *early right-anterior negativity* (ERAN). These results were replicated in studies by Zhou, Liu, Jiang, Jiang, and Jiang (2019), who also reported that the ERAN was not evoked in individuals with amusia; by Ma, Ding, Tao, and Yang (2018), who reported that the ERAN was only evoked in individuals proficient in Western music; and by Zhang, Zhou, Chang, and Yang (2018).

Note that the term "hierarchical" is used here to refer to a syntactic organizational principle of musical sequences by which elements are organized in terms of subordination and dominance relationships (Lerdahl & Jackendoff, 1983; Rohrmeier, 2011; Steedman, 1984). Such hierarchical structures can be established through the recursive application of rules, analogous to the establishment of hierarchical structures in language (Chomsky,

BWV 373 (*Liebster Jesu, wir sind hier*)

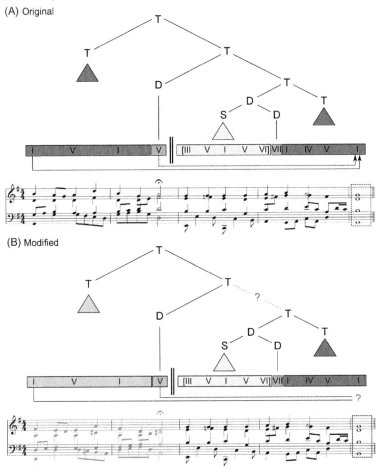

FIGURE 1.3 Nonlocal dependencies in music. (A) Original version of J.S. Bach's chorale "Liebster Jesu, wir sind hier." The first phrase ends on an open dominant (see chord with fermata) and the second phrase ends on a tonic (*dotted rectangle*). The tree structure above the scores represents a schematic diagram of the harmonic dependencies. The two thick vertical lines (separating the first and the second phrase) visualize that the local dominant (V, *rectangle* above the fermata) is not immediately followed by a resolving tonic chord, but implies its resolution with the final tonic (indicated by the *dotted arrow*). The same dependency exists between initial and final tonic (indicated by the *solid arrow*). This illustrates the nonlocal (long-distance) dependency between the initial and final tonic regions and tonic chords, respectively (also illustrated by the *solid arrow*). The chords belonging to a key other than the initial key (see function symbols in *square brackets*) represent one level of embedding. (B) Modified version (the first phrase, i.e., notes up to the fermata, was transposed downward by the pitch interval of one fourth, see light gray scores). The tree structure above the scores illustrates that the second phrase is not compatible with an expected tonic region (indicated by the *dotted line*), and that the last chord (a tonic of a local cadence, *dotted rectangle*) neither prolongs the initial tonic, nor closes the open dominant (see *solid and dotted lines* followed by question mark). In both (A) and (B), roman numerals indicate scale degrees. T, S, and D indicate the main tonal functions (tonic, subdominant, dominant) of the respective part of the sequence. Squared brackets indicate scale degrees relative to the local key (in the original version, the function symbols in square brackets indicate that the local key of C major is a subdominant region of the initial key of G major).

1995). In both linguistics and music theory, such hierarchical dependency structures are commonly represented using tree graphs. The term "hierarchical" is sometimes also used in a different sense, namely to indicate that certain pitches, chords, or keys within pieces occur more frequently than others and thus establish a frequency-based ranking of structural importance (Krumhansl & Cuddy, 2010). That is not the sense intended here.

The ERAN is usually followed by a frontal negativity that is maximal at around 500−600 ms and referred to as N5, or N500. The N5 possibly reflects processes of harmonic integration (for more information on the functional significance of the N5 see also the section on musical meaning below). ERAN and N5 can be elicited even in nonmusicians (as long as they are well familiar with the regularities of the musical style used in an experiment). Moreover, both ERAN and N5 are reduced by strong attentional demands, but can be elicited even if participants ignore the musical stimulus (for a review see Koelsch, 2012).

Most studies reporting an ERAN used harmonies as stimuli, but the ERAN can also be elicited by melodies (e.g., Carrus, Pearce, & Bhattacharya, 2013; Fiveash, Thompson, Badcock, & McArthur, 2018; Miranda & Ullman, 2007; Zendel, Lagrois, Robitaille, & Peretz, 2015). Moreover, a study by Sun et al. (2018) reported that the ERAN can also be elicited by rhythmic syntactic processing. Interestingly, a study by Przysinda, Zeng, Maves, Arkin, and Loui (2017) showed differential ERAN responses in classical and jazz musicians depending on their preferences for irregular, or unusual harmonies. The ERAN is relatively immune to predictions: the ERAN peak latency, but not amplitude, is decreased by veridical expectations, for example, when participants know the irregular chord that is about to occur (Guo & Koelsch, 2016). However, Vuvan, Zendel, and Peretz (2018) reported that random feedback (including false feedback) on participants' detection of out-of-key tones in melodies modulated the ERAN amplitude, possibly suggesting that attention-driven changes in the confidence in predictions (i.e., changes in the precision of predictions) might alter the ERAN amplitude. Moreover, recent studies reported that the ERAN is absent in individuals with "amusia" (Sun, Liu, Zhou, & Jiang, 2018), and that pitch-judgment tasks can eliminate the ERAN in such individuals (Zendel et al., 2015). Functional neuroimaging studies using chord sequences (Koelsch et al., 2002; Koelsch, Fritz, Schulze, Alsop, & Schlaug, 2005; Koelsch, Gunter, Wittfoth, & Sammler, 2005; Maess, Koelsch, Gunter, & Friederici, 2001; Tillmann, Janata, & Bharucha, 2003; Villarreal, Brattico, Leino, Østergaard, & Vuust, 2011) or melodies (Janata, Birk, et al., 2002; Janata, Tillmann, & Bharucha, 2002) suggest that music-syntactic processing involves the pars opercularis of the inferior frontal gyrus bilaterally, but with right-hemispheric weighting (see Fig. 1.2 for anatomical illustration). The pars opercularis corresponds to two cytoarchitectonic regions (BA 44v and BA 44d; Amunts et al., 2010), and in the left hemisphere, the pars opercularis is part of Broca's area (the term "Broca's area" usually refers to both the pars opercularis and the pars triangularis of the inferior frontal gyrus in the left hemisphere; see also Fig. 1.2). It seems likely that the involvement of BA 44v in music-syntactic processing is mainly due to nested (usually hierarchical) processing: this part of Broca's area is involved in the hierarchical processing of syntax in language (e.g., Makuuchi, Bahlmann, Anwander, & Friederici, 2009), the hierarchical processing of action sequences (e.g., Fazio et al., 2009), and possibly also in the processing of hierarchically organized mathematical formulas and termini (Friedrich & Friederici, 2009). Supporting this notion, a recent study by Cheung, Meyer, Friederici, and Koelsch (2018) using an artificial musical grammar reported activation of BA 44v associated with the processing of nonlocal (nested) dependencies (dependencies in that study were not hierarchically organized). Finally, a study with sung sentences by Kunert, Willems, Casasanto, Patel, and Hagoort (2015) showed interactions between processing demands of musical syntax (harmony) and language syntax in Broca's area, indicating that music- and language-syntactic processing relies on shared neural resources, at least in this brain structure. This finding is consistent with other studies showing interactions between music-syntactic and language-syntactic processing (Carrus et al., 2013; Fedorenko, Patel, Casasanto, Winawer, & Gibson, 2009; Koelsch, Fritz, et al., 2005; Koelsch, Gunter, et al., 2005; Patel, Iversen, Wassenaar, & Hagoort, 2008; Slevc, Rosenberg, & Patel, 2009; Steinbeis & Koelsch, 2008b). In these studies, chord sequences or melodies were played simultaneously with (visually presented) sentences, and it was shown, for example, that the ERAN elicited by irregular chords interacted with the left anterior negativity (LAN) elicited by linguistic (morphosyntactic) violations (Koelsch, Fritz, et al., 2005; Koelsch, Gunter, et al., 2005; Steinbeis & Koelsch, 2008b). Thus music-syntactic processes can interfere with language-syntactic processes. This is important because even if neural populations for processing syntax in music and language are located in the same brain area, entirely different (nonoverlapping) neural populations could serve the syntactic processing of music and language *within the same area*. Therefore the strongest evidence for shared neural populations mediating language- and music-syntactic processing stems from studies showing interactions between the two domains. The assumption of shared neural resources for the syntactic processing of music and language is also supported by studies showing impaired processing of musical syntactic relations in individuals with Broca's aphasia (Patel et al., 2008), and a reduced ERAN in patients with a lesion in Broca's area (Sammler, Koelsch, & Friederici, 2011).

It appears that BA 44v is not the only structure involved in music-syntactic processing: additional structures include BA 44d (i.e., the superior part of the pars opercularis), premotor cortex (PMC; see also Fig. 1.2), the anterior portion of the STG, and the posterior region of the temporal lobe, including part of Wernicke's area (e.g., Janata, Birk, et al., 2002; Janata, Tillmann, et al., 2002; Koelsch et al., 2002; Minati et al., 2008; Sammler et al., 2013; Villarreal et al., 2011; for anatomical illustration see also Fig. 1.2). The PMC (especially the inferior, or "ventral" PMC, vPMC) possibly contributes to the processing of local music-syntactic dependencies (i.e., information based on a finite state grammar): activations of vPMC have been reported in a variety of functional imaging studies on auditory processing using musical stimuli, linguistic stimuli, auditory oddball paradigms, pitch discrimination tasks, and serial prediction tasks, underlining the importance of these structures for the sequencing of structural information, the recognition of structure, and the prediction of sequential information (Janata & Grafton, 2003). With regard to language, Friederici (2004) reported that activation foci of functional neuroimaging studies on the processing of hierarchically organized long-distance dependencies and transformations are located in the posterior inferior frontal gyrus (with the mean of the coordinates reported in that article being located in the inferior pars opercularis), whereas activation foci of functional neuroimaging studies on the processing of local dependency violations are located in the vPMC (see also Friederici et al., 2006; Makuuchi et al., 2009; Opitz & Kotz, 2011). Moreover, patients with a lesion in the vPMC show disruption of the processing of finite state, but not phrase-structure grammar (Opitz & Kotz, 2011).

Note that the ability to process phrase-structure (or "context-free") grammar is available to humans, whereas nonhuman primates are apparently not able to master such grammar (Fitch & Hauser, 2004). Thus it is highly likely that only humans can adequately process music-syntactic information at the phrase-structure level. It is also worth noting that numerous studies showed that even "nonmusicians" (i.e., individuals who have not received formal musical training) have a highly sophisticated (implicit) knowledge about musical syntax (e.g., Rohrmeier & Rebuschat, 2012). Such knowledge is presumably acquired during listening experiences in everyday life.

Finally, it is important to note that violations of musical expectancies also have emotional effects, such as surprise, or tension (Huron, 2006; Koelsch, 2014; Lehne & Koelsch, 2015; Meyer, 1956). Consequently, musical irregularity confounds emotion-eliciting effects, and it is difficult to disentangle cognitive and emotional effects of music-syntactic irregularities in neuroscientific experiments. For example, a study by Koelsch, Fritz, et al. (2005), Koelsch, Gunter, et al. (2005) reported activation foci in both BA 44 and BA 47 (among other structures) in response to musical expectancy violations. BA 47 corresponds to lateral orbitofrontal cortex (located inferiorly of BA 44 and 45). This cortex is a paralimbic, five-layered palaeocortex (not neocortex), and activation of this region with musical irregularities is most likely due to emotional effects (this is also consistent with an fMRI study reporting that musical tension correlates with neural activity in BA 47; Lehne, Rohrmeier, & Koelsch, 2014). Note that, because BA 47 is not neocortex, it is highly problematic to consider this region as a "language area." Moreover, BA 47 is adjacent to BA 44/45/46, thus activation foci originating in Broca's area can easily be misplaced in BA 47. Based on receptorarchitectonic (and cytoarchitectonic) data, a study by Amunts et al. (2010) showed that BA 47 does not cluster together with BA 44/45/46 (Broca's area in the wider sense), nor with BA 6 (PMC).

In summary, very strong evidence has amassed indicating that music- and language-syntactic processes share specific neuronal resources located in the inferior frontolateral cortex including Broca's area and its right-hemispheric homologue. This evidence stems from experiments showing interactions between ERP components reflecting music- and language-syntactic processing (in particular LAN and ERAN), and fMRI measurements showing interactions between processing demands of musical syntax and language syntax in Broca's area. Shared neural resources of music and language specifically engaged for syntactic processing have been proposed in the "syntactic equivalence hypothesis" (Koelsch, 2012), and more specifically with regard to syntactic integration in the "shared syntactic integration resource hypothesis" (Patel, 2003).

Processing meaning in music

Music is a means of communication. During music-making in a group, social meaning emerges due to the participatory engagement in music. During music-listening meaning emerges through the interpretation of (musical) information. A musical composition can intentionally convey meaningful information. There is consensus that no type of music has propositional semantics (unless music imitates language): music does not have semantic content in the narrow, classical sense (as, e.g., formulated in the philosophy of mind), that is, musical statements do not have semantic content in the sense that they express "who did what to whom," and they are not "true" or "false," but rather express community, social cohesion, feelings, etc. However, music can refer to the external world such that a set of things or states can be attributed to a musical sound or a musical sequence; such a set would be the extension of the musical sound or sequence, and in this sense, music can have extensional meaning, and we can thus even speak of an *extensional musical semantics*.

The meaning of music referring to the external world has also been referred to as *extramusical meaning* (for a review see Koelsch, 2012). I (Koelsch, 2012) have suggested to distinguish three dimensions within this class of meaning: iconic, indexical, and symbolic musical meaning.

Iconic musical meaning emerges from common patterns or forms, such as musical sound patterns that resemble sounds of objects, or qualities of objects. For example, acoustic events may sound "warm," "round," "sharp," or "colorful," and a musical passage may sound, for example, "like a bird," or "like a thunderstorm." Thus for example, the extensional meaning of music that sounds "bright" would be the set of all bright things (thereby attributing an extensional content to bright musical sounds). Interestingly, both chimpanzees and humans associate high pitch with high luminance, and low pitch with low luminance (Ludwig, Adachi, & Matsuzawa, 2011), suggesting that processing of iconic extramusical meaning is not unique to humans (for a study on music−color associations see Palmer, Schloss, Xu, & Prado-León, 2013).

Indexical musical meaning emerges from associations to motor-related patterns (such as movements and prosody) that index the presence of a psychological state, for example, an emotion, or an intention. Juslin and Laukka (2003) compared in a metaanalysis the acoustical signs of emotional expression in music and speech, finding that the acoustic properties that code emotional expression in speech are highly similar to those coding these expressions in music. Similar to the recognition of affective prosody, which is to a large degree universal, perception of indexical musical meaning is, at least in part, universal (e.g., even individuals who have never heard Western music can recognize expressions of joy, fear, and sadness in Western music, or associate affective movement patterns with basic musical features of emotion expression; Sievers, Polansky, Casey, & Wheatley, 2013; Fritz et al., 2009). Cross (2009) referred to this dimension of musical meaning as "motivational−structural" due to the relationship between affective−motivational states of individuals on the one side, and the structural−acoustical characteristics of (species-specific) vocalizations on the other.

Symbolic musical meaning emerges from explicit (or conventional) extramusical associations (e.g., any national anthem). It is important to understand the difference between the different extramusical sign qualities of music, because they are implemented by different brain systems: patients with the behavioral variant of frontotemporal dementia (bvFTD) can recognize iconic musical sign quality (e.g., if music sounds like a birdcall, sunrise, raindrops, snow, etc.), but they are impaired in recognizing the indexical sign quality of music (e.g., they are impaired in recognizing whether music sounds stressed, comforting, heroic, melancholic etc.; Downey et al., 2012). On the other hand, a case study by Omar, Hailstone, Warren, Crutch, and Warren (2010) reports that recognition of indexical musical meaning was not impaired in a patient with Alzheimer's disease, whereas this patient was impaired in recognizing the symbolic sign quality of music (e.g., the patient could not tell titles or composers of songs), in contrast to bvFTD patients. For further discussion of disorders of music processing in dementia, see Benjamou and Warren, Chapter 4, Disorders of music processing in dementia, this volume.

Musical meaning also emerges from the reference of one musical element to another musical element, for example, a chord that concludes a harmonic sequence or an unexpected chord as part of a "deceptive cadence." Such meaning has also been referred to as *intramusical meaning*. Again, we can apply the framework of extensional semantics and claim that, for example, the extensional meaning of music that sounds "surprising" would be the set of all surprising events, thereby attributing an "intramusical" extensional content to musical sounds that sound surprising due to their syntactic relation to a previous context. The same logic can be applied to "certainty" (of a prediction), "tension," and "relaxation." Of course, because "intramusical" meaning is directly related to musical structure, it is a legitimate question if a separate "semantic" framework is necessary to explain a phenomenon that can also be described within the framework of musical syntax.

To understand intramusical meaning, an individual has to be familiar with the *musical* regularities of a certain musical idiom, for example, with the probabilities of occurrence of tones or harmonies given a preceding context of tones or harmonies (a deceptive cadence can only elicit surprise in individuals familiar with Western tonal music). The differentiation between extra- and intramusical meaning is not a clear-cut one, because any musical sound or sequence has intramusical properties (and in this sense all extramusical meaning is conveyed by intramusical features), and intramusical meaning can always have extensional extramusical meaning (such that an unexpected chord refers to the set of events that are unexpected). However, an important differentiating feature is that understanding extramusical meaning does not require knowledge of intramusical principles: even individuals unfamiliar with Western music can recognize emotions expressed in that music (Fritz et al., 2009), and understanding intramusical meaning does not require knowledge of the extramusical world.

The processing of extramusical meaning has been investigated in semantic priming paradigms using the N400 component (e.g., Daltrozzo & Schön, 2009a; Grieser-Painter & Koelsch, 2011; Koelsch et al., 2004; Steinbeis & Koelsch, 2008a, 2011). In an initial study (Koelsch et al., 2004), sentences and musical excerpts were presented as prime stimuli. The prime stimuli were semantically either related or unrelated to a target word that followed the prime stimulus (see top of Fig. 1.4 for an example).

In the language condition (i.e., when target words followed the presentation of sentences), the classical semantic priming effect was observed: unrelated words elicited an N400 potential which was clearly larger compared with the N400 evoked by related words (the N400 is an ERP component taken to reflect lexicosemantic processing; Friederici & Wartenburger, 2010). Importantly, this semantic priming effect was also observed when target words followed musical excerpts. That is, target words that were semantically unrelated to a preceding musical excerpt also elicited a clear N400. The N400 effects did not differ between the language condition (in which the target words followed sentences) and the music condition (in which the target words followed musical excerpts), neither with respect to amplitude nor with respect to latency or scalp distribution.

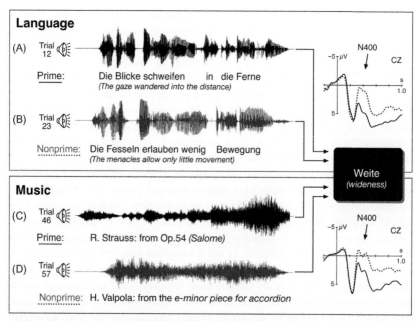

FIGURE 1.4 Processing of musical meaning. Left: Examples of the four experimental conditions preceding a visually presented target word. Top panel: Prime sentence semantically related to (A), and unrelated to (B) the target word wideness. The diagram on the right shows grand-averaged ERPs elicited by target words after the presentation of semantically related (*solid line*) and unrelated prime sentences (*dotted line*), recorded from a central electrode. Unprimed target words elicited a clear N400 component in the ERP (compared to the primed target words). Bottom panel: musical semantically related to (C), and unrelated to (D) the same target word. The diagram on the right shows grand-averaged ERPs elicited by target words after the presentation of semantically related (*solid line*) and unrelated prime sentence (*dotted line*). As after the presentation of sentences, unprimed target words elicited a clear N400 component (compared to primed target words). Each trial was presented once, conditions were distributed in random order, but counterbalanced across the experiment. Note that the same target word was used for the four different conditions. Thus condition-dependent ERP effects elicited by the target words can only be due to the different preceding contexts. *ERP*, Event-related potential. *Reprinted from Koelsch, S., Kasper, E., Sammler, D., Schulze, K., Gunter, T. C., & Friederici, A. D. (2004). Music, language, and meaning: Brain signatures of semantic processing. Nature Neuroscience, 7(3), 302−307.*

The N400 effect in the music condition revealed that music can activate representations of meaningful concepts, and thus that musical information can have a systematic influence on the semantic processing of words. The N400 effect was observed for both concrete (e.g., "river") and abstract (e.g., "illusion") words, showing that music can convey both abstract and concrete meaning information.

Due to the length of musical excerpts (~ 10 seconds), musical information could not be used as target stimulus, thus only words were used as target

stimuli (and the N400 was only elicited by words, not by musical information). However, subsequent studies using music stimuli with a duration of
only ~ 1 second showed that music stimuli that are semantically unrelated to
a preceding word prime also elicit an N400 effect (Daltrozzo & Schön,
2009a, 2009b). Other studies investigated the processing of musical meaning
using only single chords (Steinbeis & Koelsch, 2008a, 2008b) or single tones
(Grieser-Painter & Koelsch, 2011). The studies using single chords
(Steinbeis & Koelsch, 2008a, 2008b) employed an affective priming paradigm in which (1) consonant/dissonant chords, (2) chords with pleasant/
unpleasant timbre, and (3) major or minor chords primed either more positive words (e.g., "love," "grace," "charm") or more negative words (e.g.,
"hatred," "disgust," "violence"). The study using single tones (Grieser-
Painter & Koelsch, 2011) used sounds with different timbres, and observed
N400 priming effects when the sounds did not match a target word (e.g.,
"tense," "open," "strong"). These studies showed that even single chords and
tones can prime the meaning of words (in both musicians and nonmusicians),
and that even chords (in musicians) and tones (in nonmusicians and therefore
presumably also in musicians) can elicit N400 effects. Interestingly, recent
studies showed that both iconic and indexical musical meaning are associated with N400 effects. A study by Zhou, Jiang, Delogu, and Yang (2014)
used musical primes associated with the concepts of "open" or "closed"
space, and photographs of an "open space" (e.g., a beach) or a "close space"
(e.g., a cave) as targets. Meaningfully unrelated photos elicited an N400
effect, suggesting that iconic musical sign quality alone can initiate semantic
priming effects as reflected in the N400. The findings were substantiated by
another study from this group of authors (Zhou, Jiang, Wu, & Yang, 2015)
using the (iconic) musical meaning quality of "in motion" and "at rest."
Photographs of objects "in motion" (such as a flying bird) or "at rest" (such
as a sitting bird) followed musical primes associated with movement or rest.
Again, meaningfully unrelated photos elicited an N400 effect (during both a
recognition or an object decision task).

With regard to indexical extramusical meaning, Goerlich et al. (2012)
used musical excerpts sounding "happy" or "sad" as primes in one condition,
and as targets in another condition, in association with words that had a positive (e.g., "satin") or negative emotional valence (e.g., "grave"). In additional
conditions, "happy" or "sad" prosody was used instead of music. N400
effects were observed both when musical excerpts were used as primes or as
targets (but only when participants judged the un/pleasantness of the target).
The same results were observed for the conditions in which prosody stimuli
were used instead of music stimuli. Results were replicated in another study
by the same group of authors (Goerlich, Witteman, Aleman, & Martens,
2011). In addition, that study (Goerlich et al., 2011) also reported that alexithymia (lack of emotional awareness in the self or others) was correlated
negatively with the N400 amplitudes. Similarly, using photographs of

"happy" or "sad" faces as primes, and "happy" or "sad" musical excerpts as targets, a study by Kamiyama, Abla, Iwanaga, and Okanoya (2013) reported that incongruent musical targets elicit an N400 effect (compared to congruent targets). The combined results show that processing of both iconic and indexical musical sign quality (i.e., both iconic and indexical extramusical meaning) is reflected electrophysiologically in the N400.

We (Steinbeis & Koelsch, 2008a) also obtained fMRI data using an affective priming paradigm, and found that the semantic processing of words was related primarily to temporal lobe structures, namely the posterior portion of the middle temporal gyrus extending into the superior temporal sulcus, corresponding to BAs 21/37 (Lau, Phillips, & Poeppel, 2008; for anatomical illustration see also Fig. 1.2). These temporal regions play a role for the storage and activation of lexical representations (Lau et al., 2008), and are part of *Wernicke's area* (see Fig. 1.2). Damage of Wernicke's area leads to Wernicke's aphasia, which is characterized by an impairment in the understanding of language (i.e., a semantic impairment).

As described above, the N400 indexes processing of extramusical meaning. In addition, it has been suggested that processing of "intramusical meaning" is reflected in the N5 (for details see Koelsch, 2012). Support for this hypothesis stems from an experiment investigating the simultaneous processing of chords and words (Steinbeis & Koelsch, 2008b). When an unexpected chord occurred together with a word that was semantically less probable, the N5 (elicited due to the unexpectedness of the chord) was smaller compared to when an unexpected chord was presented together with a word that was semantically highly probable. By contrast, syntactically incorrect words did not influence the N5. Thus the semantic properties of words influenced the N5, perhaps indicating that the N5 reflects, at least in part, processing of meaning. However, these findings need to be substantiated and specified further by future experiments.

Finally, in addition to extra- and intramusical meaning, a third class of musical meaning has been suggested: *musicogenic meaning* (Koelsch, 2012). Musicogenic meaning emerges from the participatory nature of music, and is the most important form of musical meaning in many non-Western cultures (in Western cultures, this type of meaning is particularly important in non-classical social contexts such as in clubs or at parties). This form of musical meaning can emerge from joint, coordinated activity (e.g., dancing, singing, clapping), that is, from individuals synchronizing their movements to the musical pulse. In effect, this leads in a group of individuals to coordinated physical activity. Humans may be unique in that they can understand other individuals as intentional agents, share their intentionality, and act jointly to achieve a shared goal. Musicogenic meaning emerges immediately, and naturally, from engaging in these social functions while singing, playing instruments, or dancing together (for a review of the social functions of music see also Koelsch, 2013).

Brain correlates of music-evoked emotions

A metaanalysis of functional neuroimaging studies on music and emotion (Koelsch, 2014) reported activity changes in numerous brain structures known to be crucially involved in emotion (Fig. 1.5). The studies included in that analysis used various experimental approaches, such as investigating music-evoked experiences of intense pleasure (Blood & Zatorre, 2001; Salimpoor, Benovoy, Larcher, Dagher, & Zatorre, 2011), emotional responses to more consonant or permanently dissonant music (Blood, Zatorre, Bermudez, & Evans, 1999; Koelsch, Fritz, Cramon, Müller, & Friederici, 2006; Mueller et al., 2011, e.g.), happy- or sad-sounding music (Brattico et al., 2011; Caria, Venuti, & de Falco, 2011; Mitterschiffthaler, Fu, Dalton, Andrew, & Williams, 2007, e.g.), joy- or fear-evoking music (Eldar, Ganor, Admon, Bleich, & Hendler, 2007; Koelsch, Rohrmeier, et al., 2013; Koelsch, Skouras, et al., 2013), musical expectancy violations (Koelsch, Fritz, & Schlaug, 2008), and music-evoked tension (Lehne et al., 2014). Two aspects were striking in the results of this metaanalysis: first, all structures of the reward-system (or pleasure-system) were indicated. This system comprises the nucleus accumbens (located in the ventral striatum), the dorsal striatum (caudate nucleus), the amygdala, anterior cingulate cortex, the anterior insula, orbitofrontal cortex, secondary somatosensory cortex, and the mediodorsal thalamus (for a metaanalysis of functional neuroimaging studies on reward processing see Sescousse, Caldú, Segura, & Dreher, 2013). This underlines the pleasurable properties of music, and is consistent with the pain-reducing effects of music (e.g., Linnemann et al., 2015), due to the considerable overlap of the pleasure- and the pain-system in the brain. Second, in addition to the entire reward network, the (anterior) hippocampal formation (bilaterally) was indicated in that metaanalysis. This stays in striking contrast to (monetary, food-related, and erotic) rewards, which do not activate the hippocampus (Sescousse et al., 2013), indicating that music-evoked emotions are not related to reward alone.

It has been suggested that the (anterior) hippocampus is the neural substrate of attachment-related emotions, which give rise to subjective feelings such as joy, happiness, and being moved when social attachments are experienced, or to feelings such as sadness when social attachments are severed (Koelsch, 2014; Koelsch et al., 2015). The activation of hippocampal activity with music might be due to the extraordinary capacity of music to engage social functions associated with social attachment and social bonding (Koelsch, 2013). However, future research needs to specify the emotions associated with activity changes in the hippocampus (beyond negative emotions such as anxiety reported in animal studies). Note that music studies on emotion revealed that the (anterior) hippocampus also plays a crucial role in human emotions. This significantly expands the traditional view on the hippocampus, which focused only, unfortunately, on its cognitive functions, particularly learning, memory, and spatial navigation.

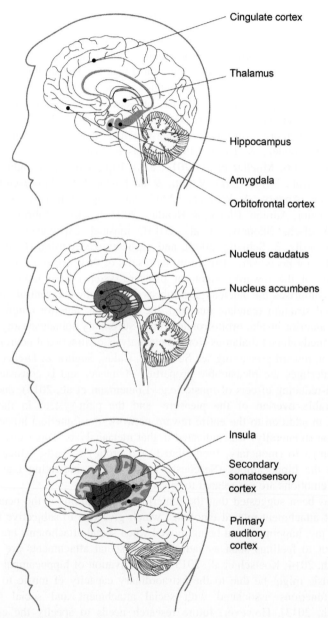

Cingulate cortex

Thalamus

Hippocampus

Amygdala

Orbitofrontal cortex

Nucleus caudatus

Nucleus accumbens

Insula

Secondary
somatosensory
cortex

Primary
auditory
cortex

FIGURE 1.5 Brain correlates of music-evoked emotions.

Importantly, the results of that metaanalysis (Koelsch, 2014), together with evidence of the influence of music on affective processes in the brainstem (reported above), show that music can change activity throughout all major emotion systems in the brain. Fig. 1.6 illustrates four "affect systems,"

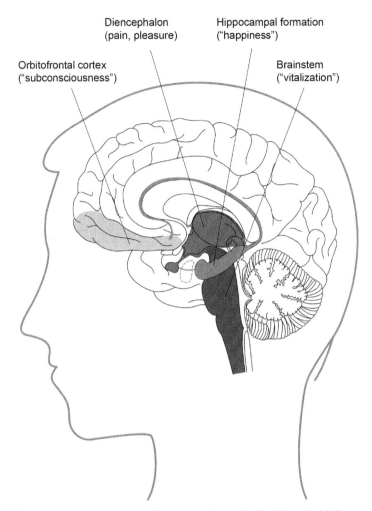

Diencephalon
(pain, pleasure)

Hippocampal formation
("happiness")

Orbitofrontal cortex
("subconsciousness")

Brainstem
("vitalization")

FIGURE 1.6 The four "affect systems," as proposed recently (Koelsch et al., 2015).

as proposed recently in the "Quartet Theory of Human Emotions" (Koelsch et al., 2015). These four systems are (1) a brainstem-centered system, which generates, for example, activation/deactivation (via the autonomic system), and thus contributes to the vitalizing or calming effects of music; (2) a diencephalon-centered system generating, for example, pain/pleasure, with the thalamus being a center for pain and the hypothalamus being a center for pleasure (the hypothalamus is also involved in homeostatic emotions, i.e., the generation of "bodily need states," and the pleasure when bodily needs are satisfied); (3) a hippocampus-centered system which generates, for example, attachment-related emotions—thus this system is the major source of "happiness," as opposed to the merely hedonic experiences generated by the diencephalon-centered system; and (4) an orbitofrontal-centered system generating, for example, moral emotions (because the orbitofrontal cortex also stores moral norms and societal rules for behavior, it can be understood as the neural correlate of the "subconsciousness"). The activity of these systems is coordinated by limbic/paralimbic coordination structures such as the amygdala, basal ganglia, striatum, insula, and cingulate cortex. The details about the affect- and coordination-systems and are provided in the original article (Koelsch et al., 2015) and will not be elaborated further here.

Importantly, as reported in this chapter, music can change activity in all of these affect- and coordination-systems. This renders music on the one hand a valuable tool for the investigation of the neural correlates of emotions, and on the other opens exciting new perspectives to use music in the therapy of psychiatric and neurological disorders and diseases associated with dysfunction in these systems. For example, the finding that music can change activity in the anterior hippocampus gives rise to the investigation of the effects of music interventions on functional and plastic changes in this brain structure in patients with Alzheimer's disease, depression, posttraumatic stress disorder, and chronic diseases of the immune system.

The role of the auditory cortex in emotions

Importantly, activity differences in the auditory cortex (AC) associated with different emotions are not simply due to acoustical differences between, for example, happy- and sad-sounding music: several recent music studies show that the AC plays a much more important role in emotions than previously believed, beyond the traditional view that sensory cortices have merely perceptual functions. For example, a recent studies (Koelsch, Skouras, et al., 2018; Koelsch, Vuust, et al., 2018) suggest that the AC hosts regions that are influential within emotion networks associated with the processing of music evoking feelings of joy or fear. That study identified computational hubs with high eigenvector centrality in different regions of the AC, and found that the functional connectivity between such processing hubs in the auditory association cortex and a number of limbic/paralimbic regions (ventral striatum, as well as orbitofrontal, cingulate, parahippocampal and insular cortex) interacted with the emotions elicited by the musical stimulus (joy or fear). Thus it appears that neurons in the AC directly incite and modulate emotional processes, consistent, for example, with work from Joseph LeDoux and colleagues showing that inputs from the AC to the (lateral) amygdala mediate fear conditioning (LeDoux, 2000). This sheds new light on the role of sensory cortices in emotion and suggests that the auditory association cortex does not only process perceptual information, but also influences emotional processes as a function of perceptual input. Consistent with these results, a study by Liu et al. (2017) reported auditory-limbic functional connectivity during listening to pop/rock songs, and a study by Salimpoor et al. (2013) reported increased functional connectivity between the (right) AC and the ventral striatum/nucleus accumbens with increasing reward value of music (as measured by the amount of money participants were willing to spend on the music they heard in the fMRI scanner), thus predicting reward value. Correspondingly, functional connectivity between the AC and the nucleus accumbens is reduced in individuals with "specific musical anhedonia," whereas individuals with average or greater-than-average reward sensitivity to music show enhanced connectivity between these structures (Martinez-Molina, Mas-Herrero, Rodriguez-Fornells, Zatorre, & Marco-Pallarés, 2016).

The effects of music-evoked emotions on brain aging

Emotions are associated with neurochemical effects, such as dopamine release. For example, a study by Salimpoor et al. (2011) showed increased striatal dopamine availability associated with listening to highly pleasurable music. Moreover, a wealth of literature has shown that music can induce strong stress-reducing effects (Koelsch & Jäncke, 2015). Both increased dopamine availability and reduced negative stress have important effects on the aging of the brain, and thus make the brain more resistant to dementia. Degeneration of dopaminergic systems contributes particularly to the declines of age-related gross and fine motor skills, and even to higher cognitive deficits. On the other hand, activities associated with dopamine release (especially motor activity, but also other activities such as experience of pleasure) therefore probably ameliorate motor deficits in older adults, and help to prevent cognitive decline (for a review see Seidler et al., 2010).

Interestingly, a study comparing brain age, as assessed by structural MRI between professional musicians, amateur musicians, and nonmusicians, reported that musicians had younger brains than their actual chronological age (Rogenmoser, Kernbach, Schlaug, & Gaser, 2018). Participants in that study were in their mid-20s, and the brains of amateur musicians were on average 3 years and 8 months younger than their actual age. It is highly likely that similar effects can also be measured in older musicians, since such effects have also been reported in a sample of long-term meditation practitioners including individuals in their 70s (Luders, Cherbuin, & Gaser, 2016, the brain age of this sample was on average even about 7.5 years younger than that of a control sample). Correspondingly, in a population-based study of twins where only one of the twins played music, the musically active twins were reported to have a lower risk of developing dementia (Balbag, Pedersen, & Gatz, 2014).

With regard to stress-reducing effects of music and their effects on aging, it is well-documented that increased life-stress (both in childhood and later in life), depression, and/or anxiety can lead to increased telomere shortening

(Shalev et al., 2013). Telomeres are nucleoprotein structures that define the ends of linear chromosomes. The length of the telomere is variable and telomeres tend to shorten with every cell division, thus telomeres shorten throughout life, and telomere dynamics has been found to be a better predictor of survival and mortality than chronological age. Therefore telomere length has been used as a marker for life expectancy and health. Due to the stress- and anxiety-reducing effects of music-making and music-listening, it has been hypothesized that music reduces telomere shortening, and thus slows down aging (Spivak et al., 2018). This assumption is supported by studies suggesting that meditation might be able to reduce telomere shortening (Schutte & Malouff, 2014). However, research on possible effects of music on telomerase activity, and possibly even on telomere shortening, is in its infancy, and future large-scale trials are necessary to establish and substantiate such effects.

Concluding remark

As a concluding remark we would like to emphasize that even individuals without formal musical training show sophisticated abilities with regard to the decoding of musical information, the acquisition of knowledge about musical syntax, the processing of musical information according to that knowledge, the understanding of music, and emotional responses to music. This finding supports the notion that musicality is a natural ability of the human brain—an observation that is also founded on the observation that all known human cultures do not only have language, but also music. Such musical abilities are important for making music together in groups, and thus for the beneficial social and emotional effects promoted by musical group activities. Because musicality is a natural human ability, everybody can benefit from the positive effects of music on the aging brain.

References

Abla, D., Katahira, K., & Okanoya, K. (2008). On-line assessment of statistical learning by event-related potentials. *Journal of Cognitive Neuroscience*, *20*(6), 952–964.

Amunts, K., Lenzen, M., Friederici, A. D., Schleicher, A., Morosan, P., Palomero-Gallagher, N., & Zilles, K. (2010). Broca's region: Novel organizational principles and multiple receptor mapping. *PLoS Biology*, *8*(9), e1000489.

Balaban, C. D., & Thayer, J. F. (2001). Neurological bases for balance—anxiety links. *Journal of Anxiety Disorders*, *15*(1), 53–79.

Balbag, M. A., Pedersen, N. L., & Gatz, M. (2014). Playing a musical instrument as a protective factor against dementia and cognitive impairment: A population-based twin study. *International Journal of Alzheimer's Disease*, *2014*.

Bard, P. (1934). On emotional expression after decortication with some remarks on certain theoretical views: Part II. *Psychological Review*, *41*(5), 424.

Bendor, D., & Wang, X. (2005). The neuronal representation of pitch in primate auditory cortex. *Nature, 436*(7054), 1161−1165.

Blood, A. J., Zatorre, R., Bermudez, P., & Evans, A. C. (1999). Emotional responses to pleasant and unpleasant music correlate with activity in paralimbic brain regions. *Nature Neuroscience, 2*(4), 382−387.

Blood, A. J., & Zatorre, R. J. (2001). Intensely pleasurable responses to music correlate with activity in brain regions implicated in reward and emotion. *Proceedings of the National Academy of Sciences, 98*(20), 11818.

Brattico, E., Alluri, V., Bogert, B., Jacobsen, T., Vartiainen, N., Nieminen, S., & Tervaniemi, M. (2011). A functional MRI study of happy and sad emotions in music with and without lyrics. *Frontiers in Psychology, 2*, 1−16.

Bregman, A. S. (1994). *Auditory scene analysis: The perceptual organization of sound.* The MIT Press.

Cardoso, S. H., Coimbra, N. C., & Brandão, M. L. (1994). Defensive reactions evoked by activation of NMDA receptors in distinct sites of the inferior colliculus. *Behavioural Brain Research, 63*(1), 17−24.

Caria, A., Venuti, P., & de Falco, S. (2011). Functional and dysfunctional brain circuits underlying emotional processing of music in autism spectrum disorders. *Cerebral Cortex, 21*(12), 2838−2849.

Carrus, E., Pearce, M. T., & Bhattacharya, J. (2013). Melodic pitch expectation interacts with neural responses to syntactic but not semantic violations. *Cortex, 49*(8), 2186−2200.

Cheung, V., Meyer, L., Friederici, A. D., & Koelsch, S. (2018). The right inferior frontal gyrus processes hierarchical non-local dependencies in music. *Scientific Reports, 8*(2018), 1−12.

Chomsky, N. (1995). *The minimalist program* (Vol. 28). Cambridge University Press.

Conway, C. M., & Christiansen, M. H. (2005). Modality-constrained statistical learning of tactile, visual, and auditory sequences. *Journal of Experimental Psychology: Learning, Memory, and Cognition, 31*(1), 24.

Cross, I. (2009). The evolutionary nature of musical meaning. *Musicae Scientiae, 13*(2), 179−200.

Daikoku, T., Yatomi, Y., & Yumoto, M. (2014). Implicit and explicit statistical learning of tone sequences across spectral shifts. *Neuropsychologia, 63*, 194−204.

Daikoku, T., Yatomi, Y., & Yumoto, M. (2015). Statistical learning of music-and language-like sequences and tolerance for spectral shifts. *Neurobiology of Learning and Memory, 118*, 8−19.

Daltrozzo, J., & Schön, D. (2009a). Conceptual processing in music as revealed by N400 effects on words and musical targets. *Journal of Cognitive Neuroscience, 21*(10), 1882−1892.

Daltrozzo, J., & Schön, D. (2009b). Is conceptual processing in music automatic? An electrophysiological approach. *Brain Research, 1270*, 88−94.

Darwin, C. (2008). Listening to speech in the presence of other sounds. *Philosophical Transactions of the Royal Society B: Biological Sciences, 363*(1493), 1011−1021.

Darwin, C. J. (1997). Auditory grouping. *Trends in Cognitive Sciences, 1*(9), 327−333.

Deouell, L. Y. (2007). The frontal generator of the mismatch negativity revisited. *Journal of Psychophysiology, 21*(3/4), 188−203.

Dibben, N. (1994). The cognitive reality of hierarchic structure in tonal and atonal music. *Music Perception, 12*(1), 1−25.

Dienes, Z. (2012). Conscious versus unconscious learning of structure. In P. Rebuschat, & J. Williams (Eds.), *Statistical learning and language acquisition* (pp. 337−364). Boston/Berlin: Walter de Gruyter, Inc.

Downey, L. E., Blezat, A., Nicholas, J., Omar, R., Golden, H. L., Mahoney, C. J., . . . Warren, J. D. (2012). Mentalising music in frontotemporal dementia. *Cortex, 49*(7), 1844–1855.

Dunbar, R. I. (1993). Coevolution of neocortical size, group size and language in humans. *Behavioral and Brain Sciences, 16*(4), 681–694.

Eldar, E., Ganor, O., Admon, R., Bleich, A., & Hendler, T. (2007). Feeling the real world: Limbic response to music depends on related content. *Cerebral Cortex, 17*(12), 2828–2840.

Ettlinger, M., Margulis, E. H., & Wong, P. C. (2011). Implicit memory in music and language. *Frontiers in Psychology, 2*.

Fazio, P., Cantagallo, A., Craighero, L., D'Ausilio, A., Roy, A. C., Pozzo, T., . . . Fadiga, L. (2009). Encoding of human action in Broca's area. *Brain, 132*(7), 1980–1988.

Fedorenko, E., Patel, A., Casasanto, D., Winawer, J., & Gibson, E. (2009). Structural integration in language and music: Evidence for a shared system. *Memory & Cognition, 37*(1), 1–19.

Fitch, W. T., & Hauser, M. D. (2004). Computational constraints on syntactic processing in a nonhuman primate. *Science, 303*(5656), 377–380.

Fiveash, A., Thompson, W. F., Badcock, N. A., & McArthur, G. (2018). Syntactic processing in music and language: Effects of interrupting auditory streams with alternating timbres. *International Journal of Psychophysiology, 129*, 31–40.

François, C., Chobert, J., Besson, M., & Schön, D. (2013). Music training for the development of speech segmentation. *Cerebral Cortex, 23*(9), 2038–2043.

Francois, C., & Schön, D. (2011). Musical expertise boosts implicit learning of both musical and linguistic structures. *Cerebral Cortex, 21*(10), 2357–2365.

François, C., & Schön, D. (2014). Neural sensitivity to statistical regularities as a fundamental biological process that underlies auditory learning: The role of musical practice. *Hearing Research, 308*, 122–128.

Friederici, A. D. (2004). Processing local transitions versus long-distance syntactic hierarchies. *Trends in Cognitive Sciences, 8*(6), 245–247.

Friederici, A. D., Bahlmann, J., Heim, S., Schubotz, R. I., & Anwander, A. (2006). The brain differentiates human and non-human grammars: Functional localization and structural connectivity. *Proceedings of the National Academy of Sciences, 103*(7), 2458–2463.

Friederici, A. D., & Wartenburger, I. (2010). Language and brain. *Wiley Interdisciplinary Reviews: Cognitive Science, 1*(2), 150–159.

Friedrich, R., & Friederici, A. D. (2009). Mathematical logic in the human brain: Syntax. *PLoS One, 4*(5), e5599.

Friston, K. (2010). The free-energy principle: A unified brain theory? *Nature Reviews Neuroscience, 11*(2), 127–138.

Friston, K., & Kiebel, S. (2009). Predictive coding under the free-energy principle. *Philosophical Transactions of the Royal Society B: Biological Sciences, 364*(1521), 1211–1221.

Fritz, T., Jentschke, S., Gosselin, N., Sammler, D., Peretz, I., Turner, R., . . . Koelsch, S. (2009). Universal recognition of three basic emotions in music. *Current Biology, 19*(7), 573–576.

Fujioka, T., Trainor, L. J., Ross, B., Kakigi, R., & Pantev, C. (2004). Musical training enhances automatic encoding of melodic contour and interval structure. *Journal of Cognitive Neuroscience, 16*(6), 1010–1021.

Fujioka, T., Trainor, L. J., Ross, B., Kakigi, R., & Pantev, C. (2005). Automatic encoding of polyphonic melodies in musicians and nonmusicians. *Journal of Cognitive Neuroscience, 17*(10), 1578–1592.

Furl, N., Kumar, S., Alter, K., Durrant, S., Shawe-Taylor, J., & Griffiths, T. D. (2011). Neural prediction of higher-order auditory sequence statistics. *NeuroImage, 54*(3), 2267–2277.

Goerlich, K. S., Witteman, J., Aleman, A., & Martens, S. (2011). Hearing feelings: Affective categorization of music and speech in alexithymia, an ERP study. *PLoS One*, *6*(5), e19501.

Goerlich, K. S., Witteman, J., Schiller, N. O., Van Heuven, V. J., Aleman, A., & Martens, S. (2012). The nature of affective priming in music and speech. *Journal of Cognitive Neuroscience*, *24*(8), 1725−1741.

Grahn, J. A., & Rowe, J. B. (2009). Feeling the beat: Premotor and striatal interactions in musicians and nonmusicians during beat perception. *The Journal of Neuroscience*, *29*(23), 7540−7548.

Grieser-Painter, J., & Koelsch, S. (2011). Can out-of-context musical sounds convey meaning? An ERP study on the processing of meaning in music. *Psychophysiology*, *48*(5), 645−655.

Griffiths, T. D., & Warren, J. D. (2002). The planum temporale as a computational hub. *Trends in Neurosciences*, *25*(7), 348−353.

Griffiths, T. D., & Warren, J. D. (2004). What is an auditory object? *Nature Reviews Neuroscience*, *5*(11), 887−892.

Guo, S., & Koelsch, S. (2016). Effects of veridical expectations on syntax processing in music: Event-related potential evidence. *Scientific Reports*, *6*.

Hackett, T. A., & Kaas, J. (2004). Auditory cortex in primates: Functional subdivisions and processing streams. In M. S. Gazzaniga (Ed.), *The cognitive neurosciences* (pp. 215−232). Cambridge, MA: MIT Press.

Hauser, M. D., Chomsky, N., & Fitch, W. T. (2002). The faculty of language: What is it, who has it, and how did it evolve. *Science*, *298*, 1569−1579.

Hofstadter, D. R. (1979). *Gödel, escher, bach*. Basic Books.

Huffman, R. F., & Henson, O. W. (1990). The descending auditory pathway and acousticomotor systems: Connections with the inferior colliculus. *Brain Research Reviews*, *15*(3), 295−323.

Hunt, R. H., & Aslin, R. N. (2010). Category induction via distributional analysis: Evidence from a serial reaction time task. *Journal of Memory and Language*, *62*(2), 98−112.

Huron, D. B. (2006). *Sweet anticipation: Music and the psychology of expectation*. The MIT Press.

Hyde, K. L., Peretz, I., & Zatorre, R. J. (2008). Evidence for the role of the right auditory cortex in fine pitch resolution. *Neuropsychologia*, *46*(2), 632−639.

Jackendoff, R., & Lerdahl, F. (2006). The capacity for music: What is it, and what's special about it? *Cognition*, *100*(1), 33−72.

Janata, P., Birk, J. L., Van Horn, J. D., Leman, M., Tillmann, B., & Bharucha, J. J. (2002). The cortical topography of tonal structures underlying Western music. *Science*, *298*(5601), 2167−2170.

Janata, P., & Grafton, S. T. (2003). Swinging in the brain: Shared neural substrates for behaviors related to sequencing and music. *Nature Neuroscience*, *6*(7), 682−687.

Janata, P., Tillmann, B., & Bharucha, J. J. (2002). Listening to polyphonic music recruits domain-general attention and working memory circuits. *Cognitive, Affective, & Behavioral Neuroscience*, *2*(2), 121−140.

Johnsrude, I. S., Penhune, V. B., & Zatorre, R. J. (2000). Functional specificity in the right human auditory cortex for perceiving pitch direction. *Brain*, *123*(1), 155−163.

Juslin, P. N., & Laukka, P. (2003). Communication of emotions in vocal expression and music performance: Different channels, same code? *Psychological Bulletin*, *129*(5), 770−814.

Kaas, J. H., & Hackett, T. A. (2000). Subdivisions of auditory cortex and processing streams in primates. *Proceedings of the National Academy of Sciences of the United States of America*, *97*(22), 11793.

Kaas, J. H., Hackett, T. A., & Tramo, M. J. (1999). Auditory processing in primate cerebral cortex. *Current Opinion in Neurobiology, 9*(2), 164–170.

Kamiyama, K. S., Abla, D., Iwanaga, K., & Okanoya, K. (2013). Interaction between musical emotion and facial expression as measured by event-related potentials. *Neuropsychologia, 51*(3), 500–505.

Kandler, K., & Herbert, H. (1991). Auditory projections from the cochlear nucleus to pontine and mesencephalic reticular nuclei in the rat. *Brain Research, 562*(2), 230–242.

Koelsch, S. (2012). *Brain and music*. Wiley.

Koelsch, S. (2013). From social contact to social cohesion – the 7 cs. *Music and Medicine, 5* (4), 204–209.

Koelsch, S. (2014). Brain correlates of music-evoked emotions. *Nature Reviews Neuroscience, 15*(3), 170–180.

Koelsch, S. (2018). Investigating the neural encoding of emotion with music. *Neuron, 98*(6), 1075–1079.

Koelsch, S., Busch, T., Jentschke, S., & Rohrmeier, M. (2016). Under the hood of statistical learning: A statistical MMN reflects the magnitude of transitional probabilities in auditory sequences. *Scientific Reports, 6.*

Koelsch, S., Fritz, T., Cramon, D. Y., Müller, K., & Friederici, A. D. (2006). Investigating emotion with music: An fMRI study. *Human Brain Mapping, 27*(3), 239–250.

Koelsch, S., Fritz, T., & Schlaug, G. (2008). Amygdala activity can be modulated by unexpected chord functions during music listening. *Neuroreport, 19*(18), 1815–1819.

Koelsch, S., Fritz, T., Schulze, K., Alsop, D., & Schlaug, G. (2005). Adults and children processing music: An fMRI study. *NeuroImage, 25*(4), 1068–1076.

Koelsch, S., Gunter, T. C., Cramon, D. Y., von, Zysset, S., Lohmann, G., & Friederici, A. D. (2002). Bach speaks: A cortical "language-network" serves the processing of music. *NeuroImage, 17*, 956–966.

Koelsch, S., Gunter, T. C., Wittfoth, M., & Sammler, D. (2005). Interaction between syntax processing in language and in music: An ERP study. *Journal of Cognitive Neuroscience, 17*(10), 1565–1577.

Koelsch, S., Jacobs, A., Liebal, K., Klann-Delius, G., Scheve, C., von, Menninghaus, W., & Gebauer, G. (2015). The quartet theory of human emotions: An integrative and neurofunctional model. *Physics of Life Reviews, 13*, 1–27.

Koelsch, S., & Jäncke, L. (2015). Music and the heart. *European Heart Journal, 36*(44), 3043–3049.

Koelsch, S., Kasper, E., Sammler, D., Schulze, K., Gunter, T. C., & Friederici, A. D. (2004). Music, language, and meaning: Brain signatures of semantic processing. *Nature Neuroscience, 7*(3), 302–307.

Koelsch, S., Rohrmeier, M., Torrecuso, R., & Jentschke, S. (2013). Processing of hierarchical syntactic structure in music. *Proceedings of the National Academy of Sciences, 110*(38), 15443–15448.

Koelsch, S., Schröger, E., & Tervaniemi, M. (1999). Superior pre-attentive auditory processing in musicians. *Neuroreport, 10*(6), 1309–1313.

Koelsch, S., Skouras, S., Fritz, T., Herrera, P., Bonhage, C., Küssner, M. B., & Jacobs, A. M. (2013). The roles of superficial amygdala and auditory cortex in music-evoked fear and joy. *NeuroImage, 81*, 49–60.

Koelsch, S., Skouras, S., & Lohmann, G. (2018). The auditory cortex hosts network nodes influential for emotion processing: An fMRI study on music-evoked fear and joy. *PLoS One, 13*(1), e0190057.

Koelsch, S., Vuust, P., & Friston, K. (2018). Predictive processes and the peculiar case of music. *Trends in Cognitive Sciences*, *23*(1), 63−77.

Kraus, N., & Chandrasekaran, B. (2010). Music training for the development of auditory skills. *Nature Reviews Neuroscience*, *11*(8), 599−605.

Krumhansl, C. L., & Cuddy, L. L. (2010). A theory of tonal hierarchies in music. *Music Perception*, *36*, 51−87.

Kunert, R., Willems, R. M., Casasanto, D., Patel, A. D., & Hagoort, P. (2015). Music and language syntax interact in Broca's area: An fMRI study. *PLoS One*, *10*(11), e0141069.

Lamprea, M. R., Cardenas, F. P., Vianna, D. M., Castilho, V. M., Cruz-Morales, S. E., & Brandão, M. L. (2002). The distribution of fos immunoreactivity in rat brain following freezing and escape responses elicited by electrical stimulation of the inferior colliculus. *Brain Research*, *950*(1−2), 186−194.

Lau, E. F., Phillips, C., & Poeppel, D. (2008). A cortical network for semantics: (De)constructing the N400. *Nature Reviews Neuroscience*, *9*(12), 920−933.

LeDoux, J. E. (2000). Emotion circuits in the brain. *Annual Review of Neuroscience*, *23*, 155−184.

Lehne, M., & Koelsch, S. (2015). Toward a general psychological model of tension and suspense. *Frontiers in Psychology*, *6*.

Lehne, M., Rohrmeier, M., & Koelsch, S. (2014). Tension-related activity in the orbitofrontal cortex and amygdala: An fMRI study with music. *Social Cognitive and Affective Neuroscience*, *9*(10), 1515−1523.

Lerdahl, F., & Jackendoff, R. (1983). *A generative theory of tonal music*. Cambridge, MA: MIT Press.

Lerdahl, F., & Krumhansl, C. L. (2007). Modeling tonal tension. *Music Perception*, *24*(4), 329−366.

Linnemann, A., Kappert, M. B., Fischer, S., Doerr, J. M., Strahler, J., & Nater, U. M. (2015). The effects of music listening on pain and stress in the daily life of patients with fibromyalgia syndrome. *Frontiers in Human Neuroscience*, *9*, 434.

Liu, C., Brattico, E., Abu-Jamous, B., Pereira, C., Jacobsen, T., & Nandi, A. K. (2017). Effect of explicit evaluation on neural connectivity related to listening to unfamiliar music. *Frontiers in Human Neuroscience*, *11*, 611.

Luders, E., Cherbuin, N., & Gaser, C. (2016). Estimating brain age using high-resolution pattern recognition: Younger brains in long-term meditation practitioners. *NeuroImage*, *134*, 508−513.

Ludwig, V. U., Adachi, I., & Matsuzawa, T. (2011). Visuoauditory mappings between high luminance and high pitch are shared by chimpanzees (pan troglodytes) and humans. *Proceedings of the National Academy of Sciences*, *108*(51), 20661−20665.

Ma, X., Ding, N., Tao, Y., & Yang, Y. F. (2018). Syntactic complexity and musical proficiency modulate neural processing of non-native music. *Neuropsychologia*, *121*, 164−174.

Maess, B., Koelsch, S., Gunter, T. C., & Friederici, A. D. (2001). Musical syntax is processed in the area of Broca: An MEG-study. *Nature Neuroscience*, *4*(5), 540−545.

Makuuchi, M., Bahlmann, J., Anwander, A., & Friederici, A. D. (2009). Segregating the core computational faculty of human language from working memory. *Proceedings of the National Academy of Sciences*, *106*(20), 8362.

Malmierca, M. S., Anderson, L. A., & Antunes, F. M. (2015). The cortical modulation of stimulus-specific adaptation in the auditory midbrain and thalamus: A potential neuronal correlate for predictive coding. *Frontiers in Systems Neuroscience*, *9*, 19.

Martinez-Molina, N., Mas-Herrero, E., Rodriguez-Fornells, A., Zatorre, R. J., & Marco-Pallarés, J. (2016). Neural correlates of specific musical anhedonia. *Proceedings of the National Academy of Sciences*, *113*(46), E7337–E7345.

Merchant, H., & Honing, H. (2014). Are non-human primates capable of rhythmic entrainment? Evidence for the gradual audiomotor evolution hypothesis. *Frontiers in Neuroscience*, *7*, 274.

Merker, B., Morley, I., & Zuidema, W. (2015). Five fundamental constraints on theories of the origins of music. *Philosophical Transactions of the Royal Society B*, *370*(1664), 20140095.

Meyer, L. B. (1956). *Emotion and meaning in music*. Chicago, IL: University of Chicago Press.

Minati, L., Rosazza, C., D'Incerti, L., Pietrocini, E., Valentini, L., Scaioli, V., ... Bruzzone, M. G. (2008). FMRI/ERP of musical syntax: Comparison of melodies and unstructured note sequences. *Neuroreport*, *19*(14), 1381–1385.

Miranda, R. A., & Ullman, M. T. (2007). Double dissociation between rules and memory in music: An event-related potential study. *NeuroImage*, *38*(2), 331–345.

Mitterschiffthaler, M. T., Fu, C. H., Dalton, J. A., Andrew, C. M., & Williams, S. C. (2007). A functional MRI study of happy and sad affective states evoked by classical music. *Human Brain Mapping*, *28*, 1150–1162.

Moore, B. C. J. (2008). *An introduction to the psychology of hearing* (5th ed.). Bingley, UK: Emerald.

Mueller, K., Mildner, T., Fritz, T., Lepsien, J., Schwarzbauer, C., Schroeter, M. L., & Möller, H. E. (2011). Investigating brain response to music: A comparison of different fMRI acquisition schemes. *NeuroImage*, *54*(1), 337–343.

Näätänen, R., Tervaniemi, M., Sussman, E., Paavilainen, P., & Winkler, I. (2001). Primitive intelligence' in the auditory cortex. *Trends in Neurosciences*, *24*(5), 283–288.

Nevins, A., Pesetsky, D., & Rodrigues, C. (2009). Pirahã exceptionality: A reassessment. *Language*, *85*(2), 355–404.

Omar, R., Hailstone, J. C., Warren, J. E., Crutch, S. J., & Warren, J. D. (2010). The cognitive organization of music knowledge: A clinical analysis. *Brain*, *133*(4), 1200–1213.

Öngür, D., & Price, J. L. (2000). The organization of networks within the orbital and medial prefrontal cortex of rats, monkeys and humans. *Cerebral Cortex*, *10*(3), 206–219.

Opitz, B., & Kotz, S. A. (2011). Ventral premotor cortex lesions disrupt learning of sequential grammatical structures. *Cortex*, *48*(6), 664–673.

Paavilainen, P., Simola, J., Jaramillo, M., Naatanen, R., & Winkler, I. (2001). Preattentive extraction of abstract feature conjunctions from auditory stimulation as reflected by the mismatch negativity (MMN). *Psychophysiology*, *38*(02), 359–365.

Palmer, S. E., Schloss, K. B., Xu, Z., & Prado-León, L. R. (2013). Music–color associations are mediated by emotion. *Proceedings of the National Academy of Sciences*, *110*(22), 8836–8841.

Paraskevopoulos, E., Kuchenbuch, A., Herholz, S. C., & Pantev, C. (2012). Statistical learning effects in musicians and non-musicians: An MEG study. *Neuropsychologia*, *50*(2), 341–349.

Patel, A. D. (2003). Language, music, syntax and the brain. *Nature Neuroscience*, *6*(7), 674–681.

Patel, A. D., & Balaban, E. (2001). Human pitch perception is reflected in the timing of stimulus-related cortical activity. *Nature Neuroscience*, *4*(8), 839–844.

Patel, A. D., Iversen, J. R., Wassenaar, M., & Hagoort, P. (2008). Musical syntactic processing in agrammatic Broca's aphasia. *Aphasiology*, *22*(7), 776–789.

Patterson, R. D., Uppenkamp, S., Johnsrude, I. S., & Griffiths, T. D. (2002). The processing of temporal pitch and melody information in auditory cortex. *Neuron, 36*(4), 767–776.

Perani, D., Saccuman, M. C., Scifo, P., Spada, D., Andreolli, G., Rovelli, R., ... Koelsch, S. (2010). Functional specializations for music processing in the human newborn brain. *Proceedings of the National Academy of Sciences, 107*(10), 4758–4763.

Petkov, C. I., Kayser, C., Augath, M., & Logothetis, N. K. (2006). Functional imaging reveals numerous fields in the monkey auditory cortex. *PLoS Biology, 4*(7), e215.

Pickles, J. O. (2008). *An introduction to the physiology of hearing* (3rd ed.). Bingley, UK: Emerald.

Plack, C. J. (2005). *The sense of hearing*. New York: Lawrence Erlbaum.

Przysinda, E., Zeng, T., Maves, K., Arkin, C., & Loui, P. (2017). Jazz musicians reveal role of expectancy in human creativity. *Brain and Cognition, 119*, 45–53.

Putkinen, V., Tervaniemi, M., Saarikivi, K., de Vent, N., & Huotilainen, M. (2014). Investigating the effects of musical training on functional brain development with a novel melodic MMN paradigm. *Neurobiology of Learning and Memory, 110*, 8–15.

Rammsayer, T., & Altenmüller, E. (2006). Temporal information processing in musicians and nonmusicians. *Music Perception, 24*(1), 37–48.

Rogenmoser, L., Kernbach, J., Schlaug, G., & Gaser, C. (2018). Keeping brains young with making music. *Brain Structure and Function, 223*(1), 297–305.

Rohrmeier, M. (2011). Towards a generative syntax of tonal harmony. *Journal of Mathematics and Music, 5*(1), 35–53.

Rohrmeier, M., & Cross, I. (2008). Statistical properties of tonal harmony in Bach's chorales. In: *Proceedings of the 10th international conference on music perception and cognition*.

Rohrmeier, M., & Rebuschat, P. (2012). Implicit learning and acquisition of music. *Topics in Cognitive Science, 4*(4), 525–553.

Rohrmeier, M., Zuidema, W., Wiggins, G. A., & Scharff, C. (2015). Principles of structure building in music, language and animal song. *Philosophical Transactions of the Royal Society B, 370*(1664), 20140097.

Salimpoor, V. N., Benovoy, M., Larcher, K., Dagher, A., & Zatorre, R. J. (2011). Anatomically distinct dopamine release during anticipation and experience of peak emotion to music. *Nature Neuroscience, 14*, 257–262.

Salimpoor, V. N., Bosch, I., van den, Kovacevic, N., McIntosh, A. R., Dagher, A., & Zatorre, R. J. (2013). Interactions between the nucleus accumbens and auditory cortices predict music reward value. *Science, 340*, 216–219.

Salzer, F. (1962). *Structural hearing: Tonal coherence in music* (Vol. 1). Dover Publications.

Sammler, D., Koelsch, S., Ball, T., Brandt, A., Grigutsch, M., Huppertz, H.-J., ... Elger, C. E. (2013). Co-localizing linguistic and musical syntax with intracranial EEG. *NeuroImage, 64*, 134–146.

Sammler, D., Koelsch, S., & Friederici, A. D. (2011). Are left fronto-temporal brain areas a prerequisite for normal music-syntactic processing? *Cortex, 47*, 659–673.

Schenker, H. (1956). *Neue musikalische Theorien und Phantasien: Der freie satz* (2nd ed.). Wien.

Schnupp, J., Nelken, I., & King, A. (2011). *Auditory neuroscience: Making sense of sound*. MIT Press.

Schön, D., & François, C. (2011). Musical expertise and statistical learning of musical and linguistic structures. *Frontiers in Psychology, 2*.

Schönwiesner, M., Novitski, N., Pakarinen, S., Carlson, S., Tervaniemi, M., & Näätänen, R. (2007). Heschl's gyrus, posterior superior temporal gyrus, and mid-ventrolateral prefrontal cortex have different roles in the detection of acoustic changes. *Journal of Neurophysiology*, *97*(3), 2075−2082.

Schutte, N. S., & Malouff, J. M. (2014). A meta-analytic review of the effects of mindfulness meditation on telomerase activity. *Psychoneuroendocrinology*, *42*, 45−48.

Seidler, R. D., Bernard, J. A., Burutolu, T. B., Fling, B. W., Gordon, M. T., Gwin, J. T., ... Lipps, D. B. (2010). Motor control and aging: Links to age-related brain structural, functional, and biochemical effects. *Neuroscience & Biobehavioral Reviews*, *34*(5), 721−733.

Serafine, M. L., Glassman, N., & Overbeeke, C. (1989). The cognitive reality of hierarchic structure in music. *Music Perception*, *6*(4), 397−430.

Sescousse, G., Caldú, X., Segura, B., & Dreher, J.-C. (2013). Processing of primary and secondary rewards: A quantitative meta-analysis and review of human functional neuroimaging studies. *Neuroscience & Biobehavioral Reviews*, *37*(4), 681−696.

Sethares, W. A. (2005). *The gamelan. Tuning, timbre*, spectrum, scale (pp. 165−187). Springer.

Shalev, I., Entringer, S., Wadhwa, P. D., Wolkowitz, O. M., Puterman, E., Lin, J., & Epel, E. S. (2013). Stress and telomere biology: A lifespan perspective. *Psychoneuroendocrinology*, *38*(9), 1835−1842.

Sievers, B., Polansky, L., Casey, M., & Wheatley, T. (2013). Music and movement share a dynamic structure that supports universal expressions of emotion. *Proceedings of the National Academy of Sciences*, *110*(1), 70−75.

Slevc, L. R., Rosenberg, J. C., & Patel, A. D. (2009). Making psycholinguistics musical: Self-paced reading time evidence for shared processing of linguistic and musical syntax. *Psychonomic Bulletin & Review*, *16*(2), 374−381.

Snyder, J. S., & Elhilali, M. (2017). Recent advances in exploring the neural underpinnings of auditory scene perception. *Annals of the New York Academy of Sciences*, *1396*(1), 39−55.

Song, J. H., Skoe, E., Wong, P. C. M., & Kraus, N. (2008). Plasticity in the adult human auditory brainstem following short-term linguistic training. *Journal of Cognitive Neuroscience*, *20*(10), 1892−1902.

Spivak, I. M., Smirnova, T. Y., Urazova, A. S., Runov, A. L., Vasilishina, A. A., Kropotov, A. V., & Spivak, D. L. (2018). Influence of music therapy on the telomere length: A brief review and a pilot study. *Biologija*, *64*(4).

Steedman, M. J. (1984). A generative grammar for jazz chord sequences. *Music Perception*, *2*(1), 52−77.

Steinbeis, N., & Koelsch, S. (2008a). Comparing the processing of music and language meaning using EEG and fMRI provides evidence for similar and distinct neural representations. *PLoS One*, *3*(5), e2226.

Steinbeis, N., & Koelsch, S. (2008b). Shared neural resources between music and language indicate semantic processing of musical tension-resolution patterns. *Cerebral Cortex*, *18*(5), 1169−1178.

Steinbeis, N., & Koelsch, S. (2011). Affective priming effects of musical sounds on the processing of word meaning. *Journal of Cognitive Neuroscience*, *23*, 604−621.

Strait, D. L., Kraus, N., Skoe, E., & Ashley, R. (2009). Musical experience and neural efficiency − effects of training on subcortical processing of vocal expressions of emotion. *European Journal of Neuroscience*, *29*(3), 661−668.

Sun, L., Liu, F., Zhou, L., & Jiang, C. (2018). Musical training modulates the early but not the late stage of rhythmic syntactic processing. *Psychophysiology*, *55*(2), e12983.

Sun, Y., Lu, X., Ho, H. T., Johnson, B. W., Sammler, D., & Thompson, W. F. (2018). Syntactic processing in music and language: Parallel abnormalities observed in congenital amusia. *NeuroImage: Clinical*, *19*, 640−651.

Sussman, E. S. (2007). A new view on the MMN and attention debate: The role of context in processing auditory events. *Journal of Psychophysiology*, *21*(3), 164−175.

Teinonen, T., Fellman, V., Näätänen, R., Alku, P., & Huotilainen, M. (2009). Statistical language learning in neonates revealed by event-related brain potentials. *BMC Neuroscience*, *10*(1), 21.

Teinonen, T., & Huotilainen, M. (2012). Implicit segmentation of a stream of syllables based on transitional probabilities: An MEG study. *Journal of Psycholinguistic Research*, *41*(1), 71−82.

Terhardt, E. (1991). Music perception and sensory information acquisition: Relationships and low-level analogies. *Music Perception: An Interdisciplinary Journal*, *8*(3), 217−239.

Tervaniemi, M. (2009). Musicians − same or different? *Annals of the New York Academy of Sciences*, *1169*, 151−156. (The neurosciences and music III disorders and plasticity).

Tervaniemi, M., Castaneda, A., Knoll, M., & Uther, M. (2006). Sound processing in amateur musicians and nonmusicians: Event-related potential and behavioral indices. *Neuroreport*, *17*(11), 1225−1228.

Tervaniemi, M., Ilvonen, T., Karma, K., Alho, K., & Näätänen, R. (1997). The musical brain: Brain waves reveal the neurophysiological basis of musicality in human subjects. *Neuroscience Letters*, *226*(1), 1−4.

Tervaniemi, M., Janhunen, L., Kruck, S., Putkinen, V., & Huotilainen, M. (2016). Auditory profiles of classical, jazz, and rock musicians: Genre-specific sensitivity to musical sound features. *Frontiers in Psychology*, *6*, 1900.

Tervaniemi, M., Rytkönen, M., Schröger, E., Ilmoniemi, R. J., & Näätänen, R. (2001). Superior formation of cortical memory traces for melodic patterns in musicians. *Learning & Memory*, *8*(5), 295−300.

Thiessen, E. D., Kronstein, A. T., & Hufnagle, D. G. (2013). The extraction and integration framework: A two-process account of statistical learning. *Psychological Bulletin*, *139*(4), 792.

Tillmann, B., Janata, P., & Bharucha, J. J. (2003). Activation of the inferior frontal cortex in musical priming. *Cognitive Brain Research*, *16*(2), 145−161.

Todd, N., Paillard, A., Kluk, K., Whittle, E., & Colebatch, J. (2014). Vestibular receptors contribute to cortical auditory evoked potentials. *Hearing Research*, in press.

Todd, N. P. M., & Cody, F. W. (2000). Vestibular responses to loud dance music: A physiological basis of the "rock and roll threshold"? *The Journal of the Acoustical Society of America*, *107*, 496.

Tramo, M. J., Shah, G. D., & Braida, L. D. (2002). Functional role of auditory cortex in frequency processing and pitch perception. *Journal of Neurophysiology*, *87*(1), 122−139.

Tsogli, V., Jentschke, S., Daikoku, T., & Koelsch, S. (2019). When the statistical MMN meets the physical MMN. *Scientific Reports*, *9*(1), 5563.

Villarreal, E. A. G., Brattico, E., Leino, S., Østergaard, L., & Vuust, P. (2011). Distinct neural responses to chord violations: A multiple source analysis study. *Brain Research*, *1389*, 103−114.

Vuvan, D. T., Zendel, B. R., & Peretz, I. (2018). Random feedback makes listeners tone-deaf. *Scientific Reports*, *8*(1), 7283.

Whitfield, I. (1980). Auditory cortex and the pitch of complex tones. *The Journal of the Acoustical Society of America*, *67*(2), 644−647.

Winkler, I. (2007). Interpreting the mismatch negativity. *Journal of Psychophysiology*, *21*(3−4), 147−163.

Wong, P. C. M., Skoe, E., Russo, N. M., Dees, T., & Kraus, N. (2007). Musical experience shapes human brainstem encoding of linguistic pitch patterns. *Nature Neuroscience, 10*(4), 420−422.

Zatorre, R. J. (1988). Pitch perception of complex tones and human temporal-lobe function. *Journal of the Acoustic Society of America, 84,* 566−572.

Zatorre, R. J. (2001). Neural specializations for tonal processing. *Annals of the New York Academy of Sciences, 930,* 193−210. (The biological foundations of music).

Zatorre, R. J., Belin, P., & Penhune, V. B. (2002). Structure and function of auditory cortex: Music and speech. *Trends in Cognitive Sciences, 6*(1), 37−46.

Zendel, B. R., Lagrois, M.-É., Robitaille, N., & Peretz, I. (2015). Attending to pitch information inhibits processing of pitch information: The curious case of amusia. *Journal of Neuroscience, 35*(9), 3815−3824.

Zhang, J., Zhou, X., Chang, R., & Yang, Y. (2018). Effects of global and local contexts on chord processing: An ERP study. *Neuropsychologia, 109,* 149−154.

Zhou, L., Jiang, C., Delogu, F., & Yang, Y. (2014). Spatial conceptual associations between music and pictures as revealed by N400 effect. *Psychophysiology, 51*(6), 520−528.

Zhou, L., Jiang, C., Wu, Y., & Yang, Y. (2015). Conveying the concept of movement in music: An event-related brain potential study. *Neuropsychologia, 77,* 128−136.

Zhou, L., Liu, F., Jiang, J., Jiang, H., & Jiang, C. (2019). Abnormal neural responses to harmonic syntactic structures in congenital amusia. *Psychophysiology, 56*(6), e13394.

Zuijen, T. L., von, Sussman, E., Winkler, I., Näätänen, R., & Tervaniemi, M. (2004). Grouping of sequential sounds—an event-related potential study comparing musicians and nonmusicians. *Journal of Cognitive Neuroscience, 16*(2), 331−338.

Zuijen, T. L., von, Sussman, E., Winkler, I., Näätänen, R., & Tervaniemi, M. (2005). Auditory organization of sound sequences by a temporal or numerical regularity—a mismatch negativity study comparing musicians and non-musicians. *Cognitive Brain Research, 23*(2−3), 270−276.

Part 1

Effects of Aging on Music Processing

Chapter 2

Processing of musical pitch, time, and emotion in older adults

Andrea R. Halpern

Psychology Department, Bucknell University, Lewisburg, PA, United States

The examination of musical processing in healthy older adults (OAs) is a comparatively recent endeavor, compared to a longer history of tracking musical development in infants and children. Although it is sometimes tempting to assume most perceptual and cognitive skills decline with age, the application of this pattern to musical processing is not straightforward. On the one hand, music exists in time, which requires moment-to-moment processing and other fluid abilities like a reasonable working memory span in order to appreciate musical structures. On the other hand, most people listen to styles of music that they have been familiar with since childhood, which should enable effective operation of top-down schematic knowledge even for unfamiliar pieces—of course favorite pieces will likely be represented accurately in semantic memory, thus providing more top-down processing support.

An additional factor is that music by its nature is an aesthetic and sometimes emotional stimulus (both in the sense of conveying and inducing emotion). This information may assist processing by the extra cues conveyed by the emotional message, but also possibly may trigger associated memories consistent with the emotion. Considering pieces inducing a positive mood, we know that all else being equal, positive affect enhances processing. A final interesting factor is that compared to many other kinds of information studied in cognitive aging, people vary in their specific musical training. This opens up the possibility that older experts might show less decline than nonexperts in age-related musically relevant cognitive skills (age $\times$ experience interaction), although that pattern is by no means guaranteed (Halpern & Bartlett, 2010).

Music and the Aging Brain. DOI: https://doi.org/10.1016/B978-0-12-817422-7.00002-X

The following sections consider three domains of musical processing in their relationship to typical aging. I begin with two fundamental aspects of music: pitch and time. Pitch relationships are perhaps the most commonly thought-of hallmark of music compared to other types of auditory input, so are considered first. I then consider a musical dimension that is arguably at least as important as pitch, namely, the detection and production of temporal relationships. Finally, I consider a more multidimensional aspect of music: the emotional message (which no doubt depends on pitch and temporal elements), including detection of emotion, induction of a felt emotion, and the relationship of musical emotion to memory for music. Although I document some expected age-related declines, I also describe situations showing remarkable stability (and in some cases enhancement) of musical processing in senior adults.

Aging and pitch relationships

Music is constructed from a tonal system, which specifies the small set of notes that a melody draws from in a given musical culture, and with what probabilities. For instance, in the tune *Twinkle Twinkle Little Star*, the first two phrases end on stable notes of the scale (fifth and tonic respectively). But the next two phrases ("so *high*" and "in the *sky*") end on the second degree of the scale, which is unstable and conveys momentum to get to the final phrase, which ends comfortably on the tonic again. Exposure to examples of melodies leads to implicit learning of a tonal framework, which is a type of musical schema. The schema captures relationships among all the pitches of the scale. A listener must detect and process pitches before fitting them into these learned schemas, illustrating the bottom-up/top-down components operative in most cognitive processes. One does not need musical training to detect and respond to these relationships, just as passive exposure to language can engender implicit knowledge of schemas for syntax. On the other hand, we would not be surprised if musicians had superior skills in both the top-down and bottom-up components of pitch processing, whether due to predisposition, training, or both.

While substantial research has traced the development of tonal sensitivity in children (Lamont, 2016), the literature on tonal processing in healthy OAs is much sparser. But interesting questions do emerge from the fact that OAs have had decades more exposure to music in general than young adults, and particularly to culturally familiar music. It might therefore be the case that behavioral, as well as neural, sensitivity to different aspects of tonal processing might increase over the life span, or at least not decrease after some age. On the other hand, musical processing takes place in real time; this requires working memory resources, which on average are less available to older compared to younger adults (YAs). The studies reviewed in this section look at some basic tonal processing mechanisms (in most cases, after accounting for age differences in peripheral skills like hearing acuity), using behavioral and neural approaches, and in some cases, comparing musicians to nonmusician listeners.

Single notes

Some researchers, while not claiming to study actual musical patterns, have examined age-related differences in processing the building blocks of music. For instance, Zendel and Alain (2012) examined thresholds for pure tone-detection and detection of mistunings in harmonic complexes. In this latter task, the complexes comprised 12 pure tones with a fundamental frequency of 200 Hz. In the tuned complex, the upper harmonics were whole number multiples of the fundamental frequency; in the mistuned complex, the second harmonic was slightly above that value. Musicians and nonmusicians over a large age range (18–91) were asked, in a forced-choice procedure, to find the smallest detectable mistuning. Pure-tone detection thresholds rose with age, not surprisingly, and the loss profile did not vary by musical training. Detection of mistuning also was worse with age, but musicians had lower (i.e., better) detection thresholds than nonmusicians; this superiority was correlated with time per week practicing her or his instrument. Thus it appears that over and above some basic loss of frequency detection, older musicians (OMs) retain their advantage in recognizing when an instrument or ensemble is well or poorly tuned.

Using similar stimuli, O'Brien, Nikjeh, and Lister (2015) examined electroencephalographic (EEG) responses in a preattentive oddball paradigm. In this paradigm a frequent stimulus is sometimes replaced with a different (oddball) stimulus, and brain response is measured when the person is paying attention to another, primary task. In this case, OMs and older nonmusicians (ONs) passively listened to sequences of harmonic complexes while watching a movie. Mistunings of the fundamental frequency occurred 25% of the time (both a small 1% and larger 6% deviation were presented; the latter is about a semitone or musical half-step in the Western scale). Data were compared with a set of younger musicians (YMs) and younger nonmusicians (YNs) from a prior study, and both early (P1, N1, and P2) as well as later [mismatch negativity (MMN) and P3a] EEG responses were compared among the four groups. (The EEG picks up synchronized electrical activity from detectors on the scalp. The temporal precision is very fine in this technique; spatial (anatomical) origin of the signals is much less precise.) Pure-tone thresholds up to 3 kHz were normal in the older listeners.

A few early EEG responses (i.e., reflecting basic detection of the acoustic signal) were responsive to age (P1 latency was shorter for older listeners and P2 shorter for younger) and none reflected musicianship differences. However, later responses more linked to complex processing showed both the main effects of musicianship and an age × musicianship interaction: YM and

OM showed similarly short MMN latencies whereas the ONs had significantly longer latency than the other three groups. OM and ON had similar MMN amplitude, which meant that the OM's short latencies did not require larger neural responses; this was also largely true of the P3a signal. The authors concluded that age affects responsivity to the simple onset of an acoustic signal, but the later components, reflecting operation of sensory memory and "distraction" by the oddball stimulus, were more sensitive to musical background. Of course as the authors rightly point out, we cannot with this typical cross-sectional method separate out the influence of musical training from inborn neural differences. But, regardless of the influence of each, we see evidence that the OM maintains musical sensitivity to this important aspect of musical pitch, being in or out of tune. Untrained OAs had less sensitive responses compared to the other groups, having apparently the advantages neither of youth nor training/predisposition.

Turning now to somewhat more musical, but still basic stimuli of note intervals (the relationship of two notes to one another), Bones and Plack (2015) presented ON and YN with intervals comprising two simultaneously sounded notes that were either consonant in the Western scale system (such as a perfect fifth) or dissonant (such as a tritone). Listeners had to rate each stimulus for pleasantness, thus this was a conscious task in contrast to the paradigm presented earlier. EEG signal was recorded and the component of interest was the frequency following response (FFR), which originates in the precortical region of the brainstem and is responsive to the periodicity (regularity) in auditory stimuli (consonant intervals having a more periodic waveform than dissonant intervals). Given that consonance and dissonance are basic distinctions in most musical cultures, we might expect either similar response patterns to consonance and dissonance in the age groups, or perhaps more differentiation between consonance and dissonance among the older group given their longer experience with music listening. However, consistent with some of the patterns seen in emotional response to music (later in this chapter), OAs actually differentiated the intervals less on pleasantness than did the younger listeners, who rated the intervals as would be predicted in the Western tonal system. In particular, the older listeners rated dissonant chords as more pleasing than did the younger; that is, their "consonance preference" was less pronounced. In a verbal condition, younger listeners also rated happy voices as happier than did older people, but this was a smaller effect than for the musical stimuli. Considering the neural response, the FFR to consonant compared to dissonant chords was also less differentiated in the OA compared to YA.

Taken together, these few studies suggest that the average OA is not as responsive to some of the fundamental dimensions comprising tonality in music, compared to young adults. This is true despite the longer exposure to music accrued over the lifetime and is over and above peripheral hearing loss. This might suggest some age-related decline in sensitivity to psychophysical relationships associated with basic perceptual mechanisms. However, so far we have considered reaction to tonal "primitives" that do not have much if any musical context. Does this age pattern still obtain with somewhat richer musical material?

Pitches in a musical context

In real music pitches are heard in the context of a melody. A study from one of my research programs looked at ratings of how well different pitches fit into a tonal context (Halpern, Kwak, Bartlett, & Dowling, 1996). Using the probe-tone technique developed by Krumhansl (Krumhansl & Kessler, 1982), we presented on each trial a four-note context consisting of the major chord triad (do-mi-sol-do) to establish a strong tonal sense. Listeners (OM and ON and YM and YN) then heard a probe note, which sometimes did but sometimes did not belong to the scale established by the context. Listeners rated how well the probe tone fit the tonal context. Good implicit knowledge of the tonal hierarchy is reflected in a profile where the notes of the major triad are rated most highly, followed by other scale notes, followed by non-scale notes. We found that whereas musicians showed a somewhat more strongly hierarchical profile than nonmusicians, OAs had as differentiated (and in one analysis, a more differentiated) a profile as young adults. This pattern was shown when the tones were constructed so as to minimize pitch proximity effects (Shepard tones, which have a clear frequency class such as "C sharp" but ambiguous pitch height, or the actual frequency range). However, when sine waves were used, which have a definite pitch height, the OAs had a small tendency to be "captured" by pitch height (i.e., to rate tones closer in frequency to the tonic as being a better fit, rather than closer in the musical scale space), which could be considered an irrelevant dimension in this task. We did not find an interaction of musical training with age; both OMs and ONs had a good sense of the musical hierarchy.

Another study reflecting well-learned tonal relations used actual melodies, drawn from either the familiar Western tonal scale, a less often used Western scale (augmented: alternating semitones and minor thirds), or a Javanese scale that uses pitch relationships different than those in Western music (Lynch & Steffens, 1994). ON and YN judged two melodies as same or different on each trial. For the "different" trials, a randomly selected note was increased in pitch by 5%. The same procedure was done with single tones. The YA and OA performed equivalently with the single tones and the familiar Western melodies. However, the young adults were superior to the older in the two less familiar tonal contexts. The authors interpreted this pattern as reflecting the equivalent knowledge of the Western tonal schema in the two groups. But when processing what seems to be a sequence of notes rather than a melody, that is, without a schema to guide the processing, the task draws more heavily on working memory, which is typically less robust in senior adults. This dissociation reflects particularly well the top-down/bottom-up reciprocal interaction in music processing alluded to at the beginning of this section: the crystallized knowledge of the tonal hierarchy is an advantage for seniors; lacking access to that, working memory limitations, or a decline in fluid abilities, show up in musical tasks as they do in other tasks.

Melodic processing

The examples discussed so far have examined processing of single pitches or pitch complexes, even if embedded in a melodic context. I next turn to studies that queried melodic processing in a more holistic manner. One of the most basic aspects of melody is its contour, or pattern of ups and downs in the pitches. Since the foundational work of Dowling (1978), many researchers have shown that listeners can extract the contour of a melody relatively easily, and use it to identify a melody, at least over short temporal intervals (reviewed by Schmuckler, 2016). Jeong and Ryu (2016) used pairs of melodic five-note sequences, synthesized with instrument sounds, and asked ON and YN listeners to indicate the contours using diagrams of arrows. In successively harder conditions, simultaneous distraction was provided by environmental sounds or by another note pattern in a different instrument. In the latter case, listeners had to follow only one of the patterns (selective attention) or alternate between them. The young adults showed modest decline in accuracy and increase in reaction time as conditions became harder; the OAs were at a disadvantage in both tasks, and particularly declined between the easiest and intermediate difficulty levels. Findings from simultaneous functional near-infrared spectroscopy (a technique that can monitor blood oxygen levels) showed younger, but not OAs, had increased levels of oxygenated hemoglobin during the task in the right dorsolateral prefrontal cortex (DLPFC). DLPFC apparently plays an important role in extraction of contours, and other neuroimaging work also points to this area as being important in working memory tasks and as being vulnerable in aging (Keller et al., 2015). The question of whether this pattern would be obtained in OMs remains open.

Other examples of tonality processing come from studies that used fully melodic material. Lagrois, Peretz, and Zendel (2018) composed melodies consistent with the Western tonal system, on average about 10 notes long. The critical note was in the same position in all stimuli and was either a note consistent with the scale, or a semitone different from that note so was not in the key of the melody, or was a quartertone away from the note, and thus sounded out of tune (flat or sharp). Participants had none to a small amount of training in older and younger age ranges. Two different behavioral tasks were presented while EEG data were collected. In the click detection task, after hearing each melody, participants had to indicate if a soft click occurred just after the critical note, so was an indirect measure of whether the wrong note was processed and had distracted them. In the direct test, the task was to indicate if a wrong note had been played and is the task of more interest for the current point. The two age groups were equally adept at identifying out of tune notes, while at the same time, the late EEG components (ERAN and P600) were smaller in the OAs. The OAs were actually superior to the younger at identifying the out of key notes, and in this case the EEG amplitudes were similar in both groups. In both groups the P600 amplitude correlated with accuracy on this task. The authors interpreted this pattern as reflecting the robust representation of tonality in the context of a melody: the seniors were performing well in both tasks, while using *fewer* (but qualitatively similar) neural resources.

Another example of tonality processing in a fully melodic context comes from one of my projects (Halpern et al., 2017). We commissioned a composer to construct melodies that were well-formed up until the last note. The composer was asked to provide two possible final notes to each melody: one with a note highly expected according to the tonal system, and one unexpected. Importantly, the unexpected note was neither mistuned nor out of the key, but rather violated the composer's intuitions about appropriate phrasal endings. Those intuitions were confirmed both by judge ratings of the piano-synthesized melodies, and an analysis of information content using the IDyOM model (Pearce, 2005): unexpected final notes had a higher IC than expected notes.

The ON and YN listened to each melody and were asked to rate the goodness of fit of the last note, while undergoing EEG recording. Behavioral ratings were identical across the groups: the expected endings were judged as significantly better fits than the unexpected endings. The early EEG component (N1), tracking the onset response to the final note, was also identical in amplitude and latency. But beginning with the P2 and extending to P600, amplitude for both types of endings were larger for the OAs and also more widespread in locus (signal emanating from a wider span of electrodes or what is called a dedifferentiation pattern). All participants had to generate expectations as the melody unfolded, and then evaluate the degree of match to that prediction. As P200 enhancement for musicians compared to nonmusicians has been observed in other auditory tasks (Marie, Magne, & Besson, 2011) and as nonmusicians become more expert on an auditory task (Tremblay & Kraus, 2002), an interpretation of the higher amplitude found here is that the OAs were paying more conscious attention to structure than young adults in this complex task. The dedifferentiation pattern, compared to the more localized processing seen in YAs, is consistent with other aging studies (Park & Reuter-Lorenz, 2009) and suggests more marshaling of resources to accomplish tasks.

In summary, these studies on tonality and aging suggest that age-related declines are more apparent when tonal components are considered in isolation, either as single stimuli, or with sparse context. To the extent the task draws on more holistic implicit knowledge of the tonal system, we see either parity among the age groups, or sometimes better or more efficient performance in the older listeners. However, with a few exceptions, comparisons between musically trained and untrained groups are yet to be done; as we saw, different task components may be differentially sensitive to age versus musical background. It is also the case that studies even with the most musically rich stimuli considered here use simple melodies, so that the combined influence of melody, harmony, instrumentation, and style are yet to be investigated. Particularly useful would be cross-cultural studies, to see if people brought up with differing tonal systems nevertheless showed the same age-related patterns to culturally familiar music, as those reviewed here.

Aging and temporal processing

The average person, when asked to define "music" might give priority to the tonal aspects of music: the contour, height, timbre, and scale of a series of notes all make music different than speech and other auditory objects. However, a reasonable argument can be made that temporal aspects of music are even more essential to labeling a series of sounds as music rather than sounds. For instance, most people would agree that a solo on a nonpitched instrument like a drum set has timing but no pitches, and constitutes music, whereas it is hard to imagine music that only has notes but no temporal structure. Even a flowing musical style like Gregorian chant has a temporal contour deriving from the Latin words. Temporal structures of music have several dimensions. The overall speed, or *tempo*, is easily differentiated when comparing songs like the slower *Silent Night* with the faster *Jingle Bells*. Music also has a *meter*, or the periodicity of strong and weak beats; this is the pulse that people clap along or dance to. Waltzes have a three-beat pattern (strong-weak-weak) compared to marches that have a two- or four-beat pattern. Finally, music typically has *rhythm* or a coherent series of shorter and longer duration of notes (and silences), such as the timings of the long and short notes in *Happy Birthday*.

Timing is of course critical to many skilled behaviors, language, and social interactions. It is not completely obvious to what extent typical aging would be expected to modify these timing skills. On the one hand, many aspects of timing seem to have neural origins in lower brain structures (Tzounopoulos & Kraus, 2009) and may operate automatically, and thus be less vulnerable to the usual age-related diminutions in functions like reductions in working memory span. On the other hand, psychologists have posited that as a general rule, cognition slows with age at least partly due to decline in frontal lobe function and less efficient white matter conduction throughout the brain (Bucur et al., 2008; Bugg, Zook, DeLosh, Davalos, & Davis, 2006). So it is interesting to consider to what extent music, depending as it does on real-time temporal processing, sometimes on very short timescales, would reflect changes with age. One speculation has been that if the internal timekeeper is slowed with age, then OAs might report that a familiar recorded piece might sound "too fast" compared with listening to that piece earlier in life (Ragot, Ferrandez, & Pouthas, 2002).

The literature on timing and aging is large, but much of the research considers processing of temporal patterns outside of a musical context, such as psychophysical studies of gap detection between clicks or duration discrimination of pure tones. Other studies consider temporal aspects of production, usually in paradigms such as synchronizing tapping with a paced signal, or continuing the pattern after the pacing signal ends. In both perception and production studies, researchers typically try to separate out peripheral processes, such as hearing thresholds or motor speed, from more central aspects of temporal processing and coordination. I consider some psychophysical studies but emphasize studies that do have at least somewhat of a musical context, and make a case for needing more such studies.

Temporal perception

Considering temporal perception first, I begin with some very basic tasks of detection of a gap within one noise burst. Harris, Eckert, Ahlstrom, and Dubno (2010) related performance on this task to particular aspects of cognitive aging. They gave a battery of cognitive tests in addition to hearing tests and found that an age-related disadvantage in tests of processing speed and self-report of mental workload predicted gap detection threshold, but only in the more demanding condition where the location of the gap varied randomly within the noise burst. The age-related increase in threshold of gap detection within one noise burst age was confirmed in a recent study by Ozmeral, Eddins, Frisina, and Eddins (2016) with a particularly large sample (1071) and a particularly large age range (18–98 years).

The more important temporal gap important in music listening is the time between the offset of one note and the onset of the next, which may convey inaccuracy (if quite obvious for instance in an ensemble performance) or expressivity (if the variability is perceived as being deliberate). For discrimination of very short time intervals (a 50 ms standard, in this case), Rammsayer, Lima, and Vogel (1993) found no difference in duration thresholds in younger, middle-aged, and OAs. However, Gordon-Salant and Fitzgibbons (1999) found that OAs showed less sensitive thresholds for duration discrimination of longer (250 ms) durations as well as gaps, both when the durations were just presented in isolation or whether presented as part of a short tone sequence. This pattern obtained even among OAs without hearing loss. A review of 36 studies using nonspeech stimuli by Humes et al. (2012) showed a consistent OA disadvantage in temporal gap detection, temporal discrimination, and temporal order discrimination, with hearing loss seldom accounting for the effects. This same conclusion was reached in a more recent literature review that was part of a study on audiovisual temporal perception by Brooks, Chan, Anderson, and Mckendrick (2018). Given that perception of rhythm and perception and production of synchronized ensemble playing likely depends on sensitivity to time intervals in about this range, this suggests some basic age-related disadvantages for OAs in detection of small expressive timing deviations.

Fitzgibbons and Gordon-Salant (2010) created sequences that were a little more musical by virtue of having an accented note, created by lengthening the duration of one note (all pitches were identical otherwise). Discrimination threshold for intertone temporal interval was tested among younger listeners, and older listeners with and without significant hearing loss. Again, an age-related increase in threshold was noted [approximately 5% relative difference limen (DL) vs approximately 10%], with no difference between the older hearing status groups, and without much influence of the position of the target interval or whether the sequence had an accent (although the accent increased the DL for all groups, not surprisingly). The evidence is therefore quite robust that a basic musically related task, perception of time between temporal events, is less acute in older listeners. We cannot be certain that these threshold differences would result in lowered music appreciation, given that many styles of music (outside of electronic or techno styles) have a certain elasticity in timing patterns; thus less sensitivity to small timing deviations might not result in a perception of oddness or inaccuracy. However, as above, implications for detection (and production) of intentional temporal deviation in music production will be addressed later.

Another aspect of temporal processing considered by several researchers is arguably even closer to a truly musical task: that of discriminating the order of sounds in a sequence. Understanding a melody requires perception and memory not just of the sounded notes, but their ordering. Composers of course can deliberately alter the ordering of notes, for instance, when using an inversion or retrograde of a theme in a fugue, or a more free variation of a kernel idea. Several studies have examined ability to distinguish sequence ordering. In a foundational study, Trainor and Trehub (1989) asked listeners to distinguish two repeating patterns that differed in the ordering of a higher and lower note. Using different response modes (categorization of same/different tasks) and variants of the sequences over four experiments, the researchers found less adept performance among older than younger in sensitivity to tone order. This occurred even with more practice at the task or more distinctive sequences.

A similar age-related deficit in distinguishing temporal order in short sequences was found by Fitzgibbons, Gordon-Salant, and Friedman (2006), which did not depend on the speed of the sequence. This suggested to them an age-related process independent of generalized slowing, in agreement with Trainor and Trehub (1989). Finally, as part of a larger test battery, Murphy et al. (2018) included a "frequency pattern test" requiring actual naming of the order of three notes (using labels of low or high) in adults aged 50–70. Performance was not related to basic hearing thresholds, but was related to working memory span, more so than age. Together these studies suggest that temporal order processing declines with age, but due to declines in central cognitive processing like working memory rather than peripheral issues like pure-tone thresholds or an overall pattern of generalized slowing.

Temporal production

Producing a signal at the "correct" musical time can involve anything from a simple tap, to a dance move, to the complex fingering of a note on wind instrument. Numerous studies have investigated whether the typical age-related slowing of many motor and cognitive processes slows overall production behavior like spontaneous tempo or also has downstream consequences in diminished ability to monitor temporal performance or increasing different types of variability (error).

Just looking at the simple speed of spontaneous tempo, Turgeon and Wing (2012) showed age-related slowing in a sample ranging from 19 to 98 years of age, with a small increase in variability of tapping with age. They also found more overestimation in OAs when asked to tap at a specified interval (e.g., 1 or 2 taps tap per second) and increased variability with evidence for a "preferred period": people of all ages produced intervals more accurately that were closer to their spontaneous tempo. There was no age difference in relative performance: that is the ratio of the 1–2 taps per second did not differ according to age.

Ability to produce a regular beat is typically studied by asking people either to tap along with a pacing signal (synchronization) or requiring continuation of the tapping pattern after the pacing beat is no longer audible, to capture the internalization of the signal and coordinated motor response. Turgeon, Wing, and Taylor (2011) found that synchronization to a signal at interonset intervals (IOIs) of 300–900 ms did not vary by age even when the IOI was changed during the sequence (i.e., the time to compensate to the new period). Similar results were found by Drewing, Aschersleben, and Li (2006) in their large sample that also included children from age 6 (stability improved from childhood until young adulthood). However, when asked to continue tapping, accuracy at least for some IOIs was lower in the OAs, and variability generally increased with age (Turgeon & Wing, 2012). In other words, it was not the case that OAs tapped more slowly than YAs but rather they had less consistency in tapping pattern. In fact, OAs were the most consistent at the fastest IOI of 300 ms.

Other researchers have tried to identify conditions under which age differences would be most apparent. Krampe, Mayr, and Kliegl (2005) asked younger and older people to continue tapping to an isochronous sequence, a simple rhythm, and a complex rhythm. Age differences in variability of the tapping were only apparent for the complex rhythms or when participants were asked to switch tapping patterns at unpredictable times. The authors contend that low-level timing mechanisms are relatively stable with aging but aspects that require higher level executive control are more prone to age-related declines. In an even more challenging situation, Krampe, Doumas, Lavrysen, and Rapp (2010) asked people to perform continuation timing either as the sole task, or concurrently with working memory tasks of varying difficulty. In the easier continuation task (with a moderate rather than very long interstimulus interval), concurrent task increased tapping variability for everyone. In the harder, slower-paced tapping, although there were no age differences in single-task variability, the dual-task condition caused OAs to have a large disadvantage in variability compared to younger.

So far, then, it seems like OAs can maintain lower level timing performance in favorable conditions, such as without a concurrent task, with a simple rhythm or when tapping at a period close to their preferred tempo. What about studies that present a somewhat more musically realistic paradigm? Kim, Cho, and Yoo (2017) asked YAs, healthy OAs, and OAs with mild dementia to use drumsticks to beat along with a pacing signal on an electronic drum pad. They beat with both hands simultaneously and also in the arguably more natural rhythm of alternating the hands; tempos were the participant's own preferred tempo and then speeds faster and slower than that. Synchronization errors were equivalent in the two healthy groups in both tapping conditions (and larger in the dementia group) but variability was lowest in the young group for both conditions. Performance on cognitive measures of memory span and executive function (trail-making) predicted variability in the group as a whole, but only for tempos faster and slower than preferred tempo. These authors agreed with other researchers that the simpler aspects of time-keeping seem to be age-invariant in healthy people, with more risk of instability in more complex tasks; in this case the complexity of beating to nonpreferred tempos.

Musical training

The studies reviewed so far in this section comprised participants without specific musical training. Given likely predispositions in timing accuracy to enter the profession, plus years of training, we might not be surprised to see mitigation in OMs of the older-age-typical slower and more variable tapping. As one indirect indication this might be so, Wöllner and Halpern (2016) gave a suite of cognitive tasks to older (professional) and younger (conservatory student) pianists and conductors, both of whom need to maintain consistent timing in their performance situations. One of the overall findings was that the professionals showed *enhanced* performance compared to students in tests of working memory for notes and words, and selective and divided attention for melodies. This pattern is thus contrary to the usual age-related declines seen in such fluid abilities.

Two studies relevant to this question took different approaches to the training variable. Iannarilli, Pesce, Persichini, and Capranica (2013) recruited ON and YN, and a sample of trained musicians (details of training were not reported), aged 60−79. The participants were presented with three different rhythms of varying complexity, and the task was to reproduce the rhythms by tapping on an electronic pad. Reproduction errors and instability were higher for the older compared to younger general groups (except for the simplest rhythm, which was at ceiling). However, in a comparison of the 12 OMs and 12 age-matched ONs, the OMs were significantly more accurate and stable than their counterparts, and equivalent to the YAs.

Given that musical training in a natural situation is a correlational variable, and, as above, likely to encompass influences both of predisposition and training, it is useful to also examine short-term training studies. Although limited in scope, any training/no training differences must ipso facto be ascribed to the training. Fujioka and Ross (2017) compared a group of OAs who engaged in piano training for 4−6 weeks, to a no-training control group, in tests of tapping synchronization and continuation to isochronous sequences at three different tempos. Although the groups were not assigned randomly (participants knew there was a more intense commitment in the training group), their background musical training was modest and equivalent, and there was no difference in pretest tapping performance. Posttest, only the trained group showed improved tapping stability, although only in the continuation, not synchronization task, and primarily for a sequence quite a bit faster than the typical range of preferred tempo. The major focus of the study was reactivity to listening to a metronome beat, as indicated by magnetoencephalography; this measure showed more brain entrainment to the beat in the trained compared to untrained participants. It would be useful to repeat this approach with true random assignment, and also an active control condition.

In summary then, it seems that timing performance can be characterized as having lower level components that are manifest in synchronization to a steady beat, and reflect overall slowing in the production of spontaneous beats. Higher level components are required to maintain an internal tempo or react to temporal changes. Those latter components are sensitive to age-related changes in cognitive resources. However, even short-term training may benefit this more advanced temporal processing, consistent with the precise timing abilities shown by trained musicians in many domains.

Music and emotion

Much of the experimental literature in cognition explores perception and memory for items like words, pictures, and faces. And although some items simply are simply "things" in everyday life, and often the experimental literature asks people to remember items without any particular emotional context, we also encounter information that conveys affect. Basic to our evolutionary past, we may be scared by wild animals charging toward us, and feel happy when we see a smiling baby. We may also have similar reactions to *depictions* of objects and events, which we could consider a second-order representation. But humans are also capable of recognizing and feeling emotion to more abstract representations such as an abstract painting or a piece of music. We could therefore call this a third-order representation: a symbol of a depiction.

In music, a composer deliberately creates these third-order representations. To quote Bernstein (1976): "And it is thus that poetry and music, but especially music, through its specific and far reaching metaphorical powers, can and does name the unnameable. And communicate the unknowable" (p. 140). An important goal of music composition is certainly conveyance of emotion (for current purposes, we are considering music that does not contain words; songs would have a more direct pathway to meaning). This can perhaps be seen most obviously in "program music" such as the dissonant chords in the famous shower scene of *Psycho*. But many other kinds of music can convey emotion. Although we can also appreciate music for its aesthetic qualities, it is very likely that the voluntary self-exposure to music (e.g., the ubiquity of personal music listening devices in the 21st century) has much to do with people's engagement with the emotional tone of music. The question here is whether processing of music's emotional message is affected by normal aging processes.

I will consider three kinds of cognition/emotion links: the first is a consideration of how age may affect ability to *detect* (or decode) the emotion conveyed in a piece of music. A second question, dependent to some extent on the first, but different from it, is to what extent people of different ages actually *feel* an emotion from a piece of music, or what is called induced emotion. A third question is whether, with age, memory is better for more versus less emotional music, and if the former, whether the particular emotion matters.

Why might emotion/music relationships even vary with age? If we consider that emotion conveys extra information in any situation, then we might expect that typical age-related losses, such as sensory impairment, or loss of efficiency in creation of new long-term memories (Old & Naveh-Benjamin, 2008) might be mitigated with that richer kind of material. Processing emotion might be particularly robust to aging given reliance on limbic system structures and not just cortical pathways (Hsieh, Hornberger, Piguet, & Hodges, 2012). On the other hand, if emotional processing is somewhat impaired in older age, then we might find even larger age differences for that kind of material (because YAs would have an extra advantage). A final point of interest is that some researchers have proposed that OAs have a processing bias in perception, liking, and memory toward positively valenced materials (positivity effect; Reed, Chan, & Mikels, 2014) more so than YAs (who sometimes show a negativity effect). Is this equally true in music, where emotion is often intrinsic to the object?

Emotion decoding

We turn first to the question of whether age is related to ability to decode emotion in music. One challenge in all this research is to select or create materials that people within a musical culture would agree is conveying an emotion. This is typically done in one of two ways. Laukka and Juslin (2007) took one theme (from Mozart Piano Sonata in A Major, K. 331) and asked four musicians to play that one theme on an electric guitar to convey the emotions of fear, anger, happiness, and sadness (and neutral), respectively. The performances that best conveyed the emotion in a pretest were presented to OA and YA, along with speech stimuli, for categorization into emotions. YA were superior to OA only for categorizing fear and sadness; in fact OA were at chance in categorizing fear. This pattern is therefore somewhat consistent with the positivity effect (there was no difference for anger, although this emotion was also by far the most accurately categorized by both groups). The advantage of this approach was that the same tune was used, so rhythm, pitches, etc., were controlled. However, it is possible that this particular theme has unique aspects that would not generalize to other music.

Vieillard et al. (2008) published a set of short piano melodies especially composed (and validated) to convey four emotions of happiness, sadness, threat, and peacefulness, hereafter referred to as the Vieillard melodies. For instance, the happy melodies were in a major mode and at a high-pitch range, and the threatening pieces had irregular rhythms and minor, sometimes dissonant, chords. Many researchers have used those melodies in OA/YA comparisons. Lima and Castro (2011) included a middle-aged group, and asked everyone to rate the excerpts on each of the four emotions. Again consistent with a positivity pattern, accuracy for putative peaceful and happy melodies was the same across ages, whereas accuracy for threatening and sad music was lower in older compared to middle-aged, compared to younger listeners. In a later study using only OA and YA (Castro & Lima, 2014) they included musicians and nonmusicians. The prior effect was replicated in the nonmusicians. The musicians were on average more accurate, with years of training predicting accuracy; furthermore, musicians used structural cues such as temporal irregularities more consistently than nonmusicians to make judgments, which could account for that accuracy. Strikingly, among musicians, age was not correlated with accuracy. Whether due to training, propensity, or both, it seems that the musicians' more effective use of cues mitigated against the reduced capacity to decode, using perhaps more holistic strategies, seen in the nonmusicians with age (although we should note that Sutcliffe, Rendell, Henry, Bailey, and Ruffman (2017) did not find a correlation of years of training, here a continuous variable, with superiority on recognition of emotion in melodies selected from this same corpus).

Two other studies suggest potential mechanisms for the lesser decoding ability in OAs, particularly for negatively valenced music. Vieillard, Didierjean, and Maquestiaux (2012) again used the 2008 melodies and asked OA and YA participants to rate the melodies on what they called valence (pleasant to unpleasant), arousal (relaxing vs stimulating), liking (not at all to very much), and hedonic value (positive to negative). They also asked the listeners to do a free grouping of the melodies by dragging icons representing each melody into proximal areas of the screen. After covarying out educational level, and measures of fluid IQ (Raven's progressive matrices, and working memory span), the authors reported that the groups did not differ in liking or hedonic values, but the OA failed to discriminate peaceful from threatening emotional music on the arousal dimension (which the YA did), and the multidimensional scaling solution of the clustering data showed less differentiation of emotions in the OA compared to YA. Sutcliffe et al. (2017) added angry excerpts and also tested for emotion recognition from faces. The OA were worse at emotion detection in all melodies except the peaceful, after controlling for fluid IQ. The researchers also found that OAs were worse than YAs in detection of negative but not positive emotion in faces, but emotion detection in faces and music was unrelated on a per person basis.

Although there are some differences among these studies, overall it seems that emotion detection is never superior and sometimes worse in OAs, particularly nonmusicians. This might be due partly to their more global representation of emotions, rather than the valence/arousal dimensional model apparently used by YAs. This global approach seems to be particularly deleterious in classifying the negative emotions in music. The possibility that OAs have in addition a bias to classify melodies as pleasant should also be considered.

Emotion induction

If older listeners are on average less successful in classifying emotionality of melodies, we would not be surprised if they also felt the intended emotion less reliably or less intensely. Of course, asking people to feel emotions in a lab setting, and to respond to different melodies in rapid succession, is inevitably somewhat artificial, but we need to take at face value reports of felt emotions. Schubert (2007) used orchestral excerpts selected to convey/induce four "quadrants" of high/low arousal and positive/negative valence. He asked for judgments both of detected and felt emotions in OA and YA. The OA rated negative pieces as less negative and also detected lower arousal on average, similar to other studies. The felt emotions were also rated as less intense by the OAs. Vieillard and Bigand (2014) similarly showed that OA reported lower activation in felt emotion, but only to threatening excerpts; overall OA reported more positive emotions. Interestingly, OA took longer to detect a note target in threatening than happy excerpts, suggesting that vigilance may be particularly enhanced when older participants are hearing happy music/feeling the induced emotion (these are hard to separate in that paradigm). Pearce and Halpern (2015) presented 1-minute excerpts of film scores previously validated by Vuoskoski and Eerola (2011) as conveying different emotions. Using the nine-item GEMS scale (Zentner, Grandjean, & Scherer, 2008) to capture felt emotion, the results showed reduced reactivity among OA to all four kinds of music (happy, sad, peaceful, threatening) although the smallest age difference was in happy music, again somewhat consistent with a positivity effect.

The age difference in felt emotion was measured physiologically by Vieillard and Gilet (2013). Facial movements were recorded while OA and YA listened to the Vielliard melodies and rated their felt emotion. Again, OAs reported more intense reaction to happy compared to other music, and they showed larger facial movements in the muscles normally used for smiling (zygomatic muscles) than younger listeners, especially to threatening music. The authors speculated that the facial movements might serve to help diminish the negative affect of high-arousing, negatively valenced music. A different method used by Juslin, Liljeström, Laukka, Västfjäll, and Lundqvist (2011) employed retrospective reports from a sample of 762 adults who were asked to rate how often (never to always) they felt each of 44 emotions in music. OA reported more positive and fewer negative emotions in their memories of induced emotion. The YA reported that they more often use music to enhance negative emotions, such as sadness.

In summary, we do have evidence for overall reduction in emotional intensity felt in response to music, particularly for negative emotions. This seems to fit to a first approximation, the socioemotional selectivity theory suggested by Carstensen and colleagues (Carstensen, Fung, & Charles, 2003). They propose that over time, adults have an increasing tendency to derive emotional satisfaction from current life circumstances, and are less interested in "expanding their horizons." The idea is that OAs can use emotional regulation strategies effectively as a coping strategy to be more content with their life, by emphasizing and giving processing priority to triggers of positive emotion. However, without longitudinal investigations, we cannot exclude the possibility of cohort and generational effects: it is possible that having lived life in a different way and at a different time compared to YAs may also play a role in this approach.

Emotion and memory

The final issue we consider here is how emotional processing of music might affect memory of the music. Generally speaking, people better remember information that has emotional tone compared to neutral information. This could result from emotion being an additional attentional, encoding, and retrieval cue (Pool, Brosch, Delplanque, & Sander, 2016; Talmi, Schimmack, Paterson, & Moscovitch, 2007), and/or because emotional information conveys extra information that would have been useful for survival in our evolutionary past (Nairne, Pandeirada, & Thompson, 2008). Evidence is mixed on whether positively versus, negatively valenced material is typically more memorable; higher arousal material is typically better remembered than less arousing material (Lee, Greening, & Mather, 2015).

The prediction for age-related differences in the emotion—memory connection is intriguing: on the one hand, if the emotion—memory connection is a basic mechanism and linked to our evolutionary past, then we might predict no age-related changes. This first possibility was illustrated by Alonso, Dellacherie, and Samson (2015), who presented symphonic excerpts to OA and YA, and tested explicit recognition immediately and after 24 hours. Although there were some interesting patterns with retention interval (positive > negative for low-arousal pieces at immediate testing; high-arousal, negative pieces were the winners for longer retention) and the expected overall lower memory scores of the seniors, they found no age-related interactions. Consistent with prior work, the OA rated the emotions detected less specifically than did the YA.

A second possibility is that to the extent emotion serves as an extra cue, seniors would show a larger memory advantage for emotional versus neutral information, than do young adults. This was the pattern found by Deffler and Halpern (2011) who presented affectively neutral melodies for later recognition. They paired each melody with a category label (patriotic), a label plus a neutral fact ("this tune is played at military events"), or an emotional fact ("this tune is played at military funerals") in an attempt to imbue context (emotional or not) to the melody. Learning the neutral fact reduced tune recognition performance for OAs relative to no fact, but if the fact were emotional, that erased the disadvantage to bring memory back to baseline (but did not enhance memory above baseline). Young adults' tune memory was not affected by the type of fact. However, in this study, emotional facts were not separated by valence or arousal categories.

A third possibility is that to the extent that OA feel and recognize emotions in a less differentiated way than YA, they might show a smaller memory advantage for these materials than YA in tunes intended to convey emotion. Narme, Peretz, Strub, and Ergis (2016) used both an explicit and an implicit recognition task for the Vieillard excerpts the reader is now familiar with. Participants rated their liking for each excerpt on each of several presentations, and the researchers interpreted an increase in liking (some pieces were presented twice, and others six times) as a measure of implicit memory. The OAs were less proficient on both memory tasks, and the implicit task was not responsive to the emotional message for either group. However, in the explicit task, OA had enhanced recognition of positive and high-arousal pieces (which was not so for YA) so that age effects were minimized for the happy excerpts, which they also liked more strongly than did the YA (performance on implicit and explicit tasks was not correlated on a per person basis).

Thus we have some evidence that for emotions to which the OA are sensitive (high valence and arousal, typically), the emotion can serve as an encoding and retrieval cue to mitigate the usual age-related memory loss. In this context, it is interesting that fearful/threatening music, which one might consider to be quite salient from an evolutionary perspective, was not privileged by older listeners. It is also notable that, in a linkage of all three of the topics in this section, there appears to be a relationship between the lower overall precision of detection and induction of emotion in seniors. This can be interpreted as emotion overall conveying less information (in the sense of uncertainty reduction) to older compared to younger listeners, which in turn reduces the overall value of emotion as a memory cue. This pattern though is not as apparent when the emotion is positive, so that senior adults both decode positive emotions and can use them as a cue for memory encoding or retrieval.

Conclusion

This chapter began with consideration of the two main domains of music: pitch and time. In some ways, the pattern of age-related change in each domain was the inverse of the other. In the pitch domain, we saw age-related disadvantage in processing isolated pitches or in unfamiliar tonal systems. However, consistent with both the accrual of tonal knowledge over a lifetime, and the processing benefits conferred by relying on schema-driven top-down processes (when appropriate), OAs showed maintenance or even gains (considered as efficiency) in processing some aspects of tonal relationships. In the domain of time, production of timing patterns was relatively robust in OAs, perhaps because of the use of neural entrainment not dependent on cortical resources. Perception of fine temporal distinctions and production of complex patterns, particularly under divided attention conditions, showed declines consistent with overall less efficiency of neural transmission. Note that OAs are not necessarily "slower" in these tasks, but often show more instability from trial to trial, consistent with less effective management of executive resources.

In the area of emotion, the evidence suggests some reduction in both detection of emotion conveyed in music and the emotional and memory response to the music. These are both more apparent in negatively valenced music. These could be causally related: it would be logical that reduced reaction could result from reduced decoding. However, it is also possible that there are separable mechanisms in perceptual analysis and emotional response systems. It is notable that the relevant studies used materials both sparse (piano melodies) and rich (film scores) so that it is unlikely the reduced responsivity is due to declines in detection of basic musical cues, like mode or timbre. And given the lesser, and sometimes nonexistent, age differences in response to positive compared to negative valence in music (and in other domains), this response pattern is likely due to changes not particularly tied to musical response per se, but a more general processing bias. One thing to keep in mind in this area of research is that emotion is of course a self-reported entity. There may be some age-related biases in the reportage of emotion that would be interesting to pursue in future research.

Finally, we saw that in some (but not all) cases, musically trained older individuals showed less age-related disadvantage than their untrained age-mates. As noted several times, it would be imprudent, and inconsistent with increasingly well-documented evidence about genetic contributions to musical (and other) skills (Mosing & Ullén, 2018) to attribute this difference solely to an effect of training. As with many choices humans make, musicians choose to begin and continue training, which very likely reflects predisposition for fine pitch or temporal discrimination and well-controlled production. However, it is obvious that training is also an important variable, which can be demonstrated in experimental training studies, even when short-term in duration (Fujioka & Ross, 2017).

Taken together, we may conclude that OAs, even with somewhat less precise response/production patterns, are fully capable of understanding, performing, enjoying, and reacting to music, particularly from a familiar tone system. Future research would benefit from more cross-cultural comparisons, training studies (including longitudinal approaches), and, in studies involving OMs, more consideration of the type of training and performing genre. A study of temporal skills in older and younger percussionists, for instance, would be very illuminating for understanding of temporal skills, and the same goes for comparing older and younger singers (who serve as their own instruments!) in the area of pitch.

Acknowledgment

I would like to dedicate this chapter to a long-time friend and colleague, James Bartlett, who was to have been my coauthor but who became ill during the planning stages, and passed away after its completion. His many contributions to psychology and his university will be appreciated for many years to come.

References

Alonso, I., Dellacherie, D., & Samson, S. (2015). Emotional memory for musical excerpts in young and older adults. *Frontiers in Aging Neuroscience, 7.* Available from https://doi.org/10.3389/fnagi.2015.00023.

Bernstein, L. (1976). *The unanswered question: Six talks at Harvard* (Vol. 33). Cambridge MA: Harvard University Press.

Bones, O., & Plack, C. J. (2015). Losing the music: Aging affects the perception and subcortical neural representation of musical harmony. *Journal of Neuroscience, 35,* 4071−4080.

Brooks, C. J., Chan, Y. M., Anderson, A. J., & Mckendrick, A. M. (2018). Audiovisual temporal perception in aging: The role of multisensory integration and age-related sensory loss. *Frontiers in Human Neuroscience, 12.* Available from https://doi.org/10.3389/fnhum.2018.00192.

Bucur, B., Madden, D. J., Spaniol, J., Provenzale, J. M., Cabeza, R., White, L. E., & Huettel, S. A. (2008). Age-related slowing of memory retrieval: Contributions of perceptual speed and cerebral white matter integrity. *Neurobiology of Aging, 29,* 1070−1079.

Bugg, J. M., Zook, N. A., DeLosh, E. L., Davalos, D. B., & Davis, H. P. (2006). Age differences in fluid intelligence: Contributions of general slowing and frontal decline. *Brain and Cognition, 62,* 9−16. Available from https://doi.org/10.1016/j.bandc.2006.02.006.

Carstensen, L. L., Fung, H. H., & Charles, S. T. (2003). Socioemotional selectivity theory and the regulation of emotion in the second half of life. *Motivation and Emotion, 27,* 103−123.

Castro, S. L., & Lima, C. F. (2014). Age and musical expertise influence emotion recognition in music. *Music Perception: An Interdisciplinary Journal, 32,* 125−142. Available from https://doi.org/10.1525/mp.2014.32.2.125.

Deffler, S. A., & Halpern, A. R. (2011). Contextual information and memory for unfamiliar tunes in older and younger adults. *Psychology and Aging, 26,* 900−904. Available from https://doi.org/10.1037/a0023372.

Dowling, W. J. (1978). Scale and contour: Two components of a theory of memory for melodies. *Psychological Review, 85,* 341−354. Available from https://doi.org/10.1037/0033-295x.85.4.341.

Drewing, K., Aschersleben, G., & Li, S. (2006). Sensorimotor synchronization across the life span. *International Journal of Behavioral Development, 30,* 280−287. Available from https://doi.org/10.1177/0165025406066764.

Fitzgibbons, P. J., & Gordon-Salant, S. (2010). Age-related differences in discrimination of temporal intervals in accented tone sequences. *Hearing Research, 264,* 41−47. Available from https://doi.org/10.1016/j.heares.2009.11.008.

Fitzgibbons, P. J., Gordon-Salant, S., & Friedman, S. A. (2006). Effects of age and sequence presentation rate on temporal order recognition. *The Journal of the Acoustical Society of America, 120,* 991−999. Available from https://doi.org/10.1121/1.2214463.

Fujioka, T., & Ross, B. (2017). Beta-band oscillations during passive listening to metronome sounds reflect improved timing representation after short-term musical training in healthy older adults. *European Journal of Neuroscience, 46,* 2339−2354. Available from https://doi.org/10.1111/ejn.13693.

Gordon-Salant, S., & Fitzgibbons, P. J. (1999). Profile of auditory temporal processing in older listeners. *Journal of Speech, Language, and Hearing Research, 42,* 300−311. Available from https://doi.org/10.1044/jslhr.4202.300.

Halpern, A. R., & Bartlett, J. C. (2010). Memory for melodies. In M. R. Jones, A. N. Popper, & R. R. Fay (Eds.), *Music perception.* New York: Springer-Verlag.

Halpern, A. R., Kwak, S. Y., Bartlett, J. C., & Dowling, W. J. (1996). The effects of aging and musical experience on the representation of tonal hierarchies. *Psychology and Aging, 11,* 235–246. Available from https://doi.org/10.1037/0882-7974.11.2.235.

Halpern, A. R., Zioga, I., Shankleman, M., Lindsen, J., Pearce, M. T., & Bhattacharya, J. (2017). That note sounds wrong! Age-related effects in processing of musical expectation. *Brain & Cognition, 113,* 1–9. Available from https://doi.org/10.1016/j.bandc.2016.12.006.

Harris, K. C., Eckert, M. A., Ahlstrom, J. B., & Dubno, J. R. (2010). Age-related differences in gap detection: Effects of task difficulty and cognitive ability. *Hearing Research, 264,* 21–29. Available from https://doi.org/10.1016/j.heares.2009.09.017.

Hsieh, S., Hornberger, M., Piguet, O., & Hodges, J. (2012). Brain correlates of musical and facial emotion recognition: Evidence from the dementias. *Neuropsychologia, 50,* 1814–1822. Available from https://doi.org/10.1016/j.neuropsychologia.2012.04.006.

Humes, L. E., Dubno, J. R., Gordon-Salant, S., Lister, J. J., Cacace, A. T., Cruickshanks, K. J., ... Wingfield, A. (2012). Central presbycusis: A review and evaluation of the evidence. *Journal of the American Academy of Audiology, 23,* 635–666. Available from https://doi.org/10.3766/jaaa.23.8.5.

Iannarilli, F., Pesce, C., Persichini, C., & Capranica, L. (2013). Age-related changes of rhythmic ability in musically trained and untrained individuals. *Sport Sciences for Health, 9,* 43–50. Available from https://doi.org/10.1007/s11332-013-0144-y.

Jeong, E., & Ryu, H. (2016). Nonverbal auditory working memory: Can music indicate the capacity? *Brain and Cognition, 105,* 9–21. Available from https://doi.org/10.1016/j.bandc.2016.03.003.

Juslin, P. N., Liljeström, S., Laukka, P., Västfjäll, D., & Lundqvist, L. (2011). Emotional reactions to music in a nationally representative sample of Swedish adults: Prevalence and causal influences. *Musicae Scientiae, 15,* 174–207. Available from https://doi.org/10.1177/102986491101500204.

Keller, J. B., Hedden, T., Thompson, T. W., Anteraper, S. A., Gabrieli, J. D., & Whitfield-Gabrieli, S. (2015). Resting-state anticorrelations between medial and lateral prefrontal cortex: Association with working memory, aging, and individual differences. *Cortex, 64,* 271–280. Available from https://doi.org/10.1016/j.cortex.2014.12.001.

Kim, S. J., Cho, S., & Yoo, G. E. (2017). Age-related changes in bimanual instrument playing with rhythmic cueing. *Frontiers in Psychology, 8.* Available from https://doi.org/10.3389/fpsyg.2017.01569.

Krampe, R. T., Doumas, M., Lavrysen, A., & Rapp, M. (2010). The costs of taking it slowly: Fast and slow movement timing in older age. *Psychology and Aging, 25,* 980–990. Available from https://doi.org/10.1037/a0020090.

Krampe, R. T., Mayr, U., & Kliegl, R. (2005). Timing, sequencing, and executive control in repetitive movement production. *Journal of Experimental Psychology: Human Perception and Performance, 31,* 379–397. Available from https://doi.org/10.1037/0096-1523.31.3.379.

Krumhansl, C. L., & Kessler, E. J. (1982). Tracing the dynamic changes in perceived tonal organization in a spatial representation of musical keys. *Psychological Review, 89,* 334–368. Available from https://doi.org/10.1037/0033-295X.89.4.334.

Lagrois, M. É., Peretz, I., & Zendel, B. R. (2018). Neurophysiological and behavioral differences between older and younger adults when processing violations of tonal structure in music. *Frontiers in Neuroscience, 12,* 54. Available from https://doi.org/10.3389/fnins.2018.00054.

Lamont, A. (2016). Musical development from the early years onwards. In S. Hallam, I. Cross, & M. Thaut (Eds.), *The Oxford handbook of music psychology* (2nd ed., pp. 399–414). New York: Oxford University Press.

Laukka, P., & Juslin, P. N. (2007). Similar patterns of age-related differences in emotion recognition from speech and music. *Motivation and Emotion, 31*, 182–191. Available from https://doi.org/10.1007/s11031-007-9063-z.

Lee, T., Greening, S. G., & Mather, M. (2015). Encoding of goal-relevant stimuli is strengthened by emotional arousal in memory. *Frontiers in Psychology, 6*. Available from https://doi.org/10.3389/fpsyg.2015.01173.

Lima, C. F., & Castro, S. L. (2011). Emotion recognition in music changes across the adult life span. *Cognition & Emotion, 25*, 585–598. Available from https://doi.org/10.1080/02699931.2010.502449.

Lynch, M. P., & Steffens, M. L. (1994). Effects of aging on processing of novel musical structure. *Journal of Gerontology, 49*, P165–P172.

Marie, C., Magne, C., & Besson, M. (2011). Musicians and the metric structure of words. *Journal of Cognitive Neuroscience, 23*, 294–305.

Mosing, M. A., & Ullén, F. (2018). Genetic influences on musical specialization: A twin study on choice of instrument and music genre. *Annals of the New York Academy of Sciences, 1423*, 427–434.

Murphy, C. F., Rabelo, C. M., Silagi, M. L., Mansur, L. L., Bamiou, D. E., & Schochat, E. (2018). Auditory processing performance of the middle-aged and elderly: Auditory or cognitive decline? *Journal of the American Academy of Audiology, 29*, 5–14. Available from https://doi.org/10.3766/jaaa.15098.

Nairne, J. S., Pandeirada, J. N., & Thompson, S. R. (2008). Adaptive memory. *Psychological Science, 19*, 176–180. Available from https://doi.org/10.1111/j.1467-9280.2008.02064.x.

Narme, P., Peretz, I., Strub, M., & Ergis, A. (2016). Emotion effects on implicit and explicit musical memory in normal aging. *Psychology and Aging, 31*, 902–913. Available from https://doi.org/10.1037/pag0000116.

O'Brien, J. L., Nikjeh, D. A., & Lister, J. J. (2015). Interaction of musicianship and aging: A comparison of cortical auditory evoked potentials. *Behavioural Neurology, 12*. Available from https://doi.org/10.1155/2015/545917.

Old, S. R., & Naveh-Benjamin, M. (2008). Differential effects of age on item and associative measures of memory: A meta-analysis. *Psychology and Aging, 23*, 104–118. Available from https://doi.org/10.1037/0882-7974.23.1.104.

Ozmeral, E. J., Eddins, A. C., Frisina, D. R., & Eddins, D. A. (2016). Large cross-sectional study of presbycusis reveals rapid progressive decline in auditory temporal acuity. *Neurobiology of Aging, 43*, 72–78. Available from https://doi.org/10.1016/j.neurobiolaging.2015.12.024.

Park, D. C., & Reuter-Lorenz, P. (2009). The adaptive brain: Aging and neurocognitive scaffolding. *Annual Review of Psychology, 60*, 173–196.

Pearce, M. T. (2005). *The construction and evaluation of statistical models of melodic structure in music perception and composition* (Doctoral dissertation). London, UK: Department of Computing, City University.

Pearce, M. T., & Halpern, A. R. (2015). Age-related patterns in emotions evoked by music. *Psychology of Aesthetics and Creative Arts, 9*, 248–253. Available from https://doi.org/10.1037/a0039279.

Pool, E., Brosch, T., Delplanque, S., & Sander, D. (2016). Attentional bias for positive emotional stimuli: A meta-analytic investigation. *Psychological Bulletin, 142*, 79–106. Available from https://doi.org/10.1037/bul0000026.

Ragot, R., Ferrandez, A.-M., & Pouthas, V. (2002). Time, music, and aging. *Psychomusicology: A Journal of Research in Music Cognition, 18*, 28–45. Available from https://doi.org/10.1037/h0094053.

Rammsayer, T. H., Lima, S. D., & Vogel, W. H. (1993). Aging and temporal discrimination of brief auditory intervals. *Psychological Research, 55*, 15−19. Available from https://doi.org/10.1007/bf00419889.

Reed, A. E., Chan, L., & Mikels, J. A. (2014). Meta-analysis of the age-related positivity effect: Age differences in preferences for positive over negative information. *Psychology and Aging, 29*, 1−15. Available from https://doi.org/10.1037/a0035194.

Schmuckler, M. A. (2016). Tonality and contour in melodic processing. In S. Hallam, I. Cross, & M. Thaut (Eds.), *The Oxford handbook of music psychology* (2nd ed., pp. 143−166). New York: Oxford University Press.

Schubert, E. (2007). Locus of emotion: The effect of task order and age on emotion perceived and emotion felt in response to music. *Journal of Music Therapy, 44*, 344−368. Available from https://doi.org/10.1093/jmt/44.4.344.

Sutcliffe, R., Rendell, P. G., Henry, J. D., Bailey, P. E., & Ruffman, T. (2017). Music to my ears: Age-related decline in musical and facial emotion recognition. *Psychology and Aging, 32*, 698−709. Available from https://doi.org/10.1037/pag0000203.

Talmi, D., Schimmack, U., Paterson, T., & Moscovitch, M. (2007). The role of attention and relatedness in emotionally enhanced memory. *Emotion, 7*, 89−102. Available from https://doi.org/10.1037/1528-3542.7.1.89.

Trainor, L. J., & Trehub, S. E. (1989). Aging and auditory temporal sequencing: Ordering the elements of repeating tone patterns. *Perception & Psychophysics, 45*, 417−426. Available from https://doi.org/10.3758/bf03210715.

Tremblay, K. L., & Kraus, N. (2002). Auditory training induces asymmetrical changes in cortical neural activity. *Journal of Speech, Language, and Hearing Research, 45*, 564−572.

Turgeon, M., & Wing, A. M. (2012). Late onset of age-related difference in unpaced tapping with no age-related difference in phase-shift error detection and correction. *Psychology and Aging, 27*, 1152−1163. Available from https://doi.org/10.1037/a0029925.

Turgeon, M., Wing, A. M., & Taylor, L. W. (2011). Timing and aging: Slowing of fastest regular tapping rate with preserved timing error detection and correction. *Psychology and Aging, 26*, 150−161. Available from https://doi.org/10.1037/a0020606.

Tzounopoulos, T., & Kraus, N. (2009). Learning to encode timing: Mechanisms of plasticity in the auditory brainstem. *Neuron, 62*, 463−469.

Vieillard, S., & Bigand, E. (2014). Distinct effects of positive and negative music on older adults' auditory target identification performances. *Quarterly Journal of Experimental Psychology, 67*, 2225−2238. Available from https://doi.org/10.1080/17470218.2014.914548.

Vieillard, S., Didierjean, A., & Maquestiaux, F. (2012). Changes in the perception and the psychological structure of musical emotions with advancing age. *Experimental Aging Research, 38*, 422−441. Available from https://doi.org/10.1080/0361073X.2012.699371.

Vieillard, S., & Gilet, A. (2013). Age-related differences in affective responses to and memory for emotions conveyed by music: A cross-sectional study. *Frontiers in Psychology, 4*. Available from https://doi.org/10.3389/fpsyg.2013.00711.

Vieillard, S., Peretz, I., Gosselin, N., Khalfa, S., Gagnon, L., & Bouchard, B. (2008). Happy, sad, scary and peaceful musical excerpts for research on emotions. *Cognition & Emotion, 22*, 720−752. Available from https://doi.org/10.1080/02699930701503567.

Vuoskoski, J. K., & Eerola, T. (2011). Measuring music-induced emotion: A comparison of emotion models, personality biases, and intensity of experiences. *Musicae Scientiae, 15*, 159−173. Available from https://doi.org/10.1177/102986491101500203.

Wöllner, C., & Halpern, A. R. (2016). Attentional flexibility and memory capacity in conductors and pianists. *Attention, Perception, & Psychophysics, 78*, 198−208. Available from https://doi.org/10.3758/s13414-015-0989-z.

Zendel, B. R., & Alain, C. (2012). Musicians experience less age-related decline in central auditory processing. *Psychology and Aging, 27,* 410–417.

Zentner, M., Grandjean, D., & Scherer, K. R. (2008). Emotions evoked by the sound of music: Characterization, classification, and measurement. *Emotion, 8,* 494–521. Available from https://doi.org/10.1037/1528-3542.8.4.494.

Chapter 3

Age-related hearing loss

Margaret Kathleen Pichora-Fuller[1,2,3]

[1]*Department of Psychology, University of Toronto, Toronto, ON, Canada,* [2]*Department of Gerontology, Simon Fraser University, Vancouver, BC, Canada,* [3]*Rotman Research Institute, Baycrest, Toronto, ON, Canada*

Overview

The prevalence of hearing impairment is high in older adults. Starting in middle age, hearing impairment increases markedly with increasing age. By 70 years of age, about half of the population have clinically significant hearing impairment. Age-related hearing loss (ARHL) is heterogeneous and may result from damage to one or more structures in the auditory system. Importantly, listening in everyday life may be compromised even without clinically significant impairment defined by audiometric thresholds.

Some types of damage result in clinically significant elevations in audiometric pure-tone detection thresholds. The audiogram summarizes the results of the basic clinical test used to measure hearing thresholds. Sound pressure or intensity, measured in decibels (dB), is the physical dimension of sound that corresponds primarily to the perceptual dimension of loudness. Audiometric thresholds, measured in dB hearing level (HL), quantify the lowest sound pressure level (SPL) at which a person can detect pure tones of specific frequencies. Frequency, measured as the number of cycles per second or Hertz (Hz), is the physical dimension of sound that corresponds primarily to the perceptual dimension of pitch. A hallmark of auditory aging is increased difficulty detecting high-frequency sounds at low dB levels. These threshold changes render the high-frequency components of complex sounds such as speech or music inaudible. Such reduced access to complex sound signals can hamper perception.

Other types of damage can reduce older adults' efficiency or accuracy in processing suprathreshold sounds (i.e., sounds that remain audible). Declines in processing the temporal properties of sounds may explain the ubiquitous complaints of older adults that it is difficult for them to understand speech in noise and that sounds are loud enough but seem unclear or jumbled. Thus age-related changes in auditory thresholds and/or suprathreshold processing

Music and the Aging Brain. DOI: https://doi.org/10.1016/B978-0-12-817422-7.00003-1
69

may undermine listening to speech and music. Importantly, individuals with similar audiometric pure-tone thresholds may vary in how they experience the everyday consequences of ARHL due to differences in their abilities to process complex suprathreshold sounds such as speech or music. Even older adults with relatively good audiograms can experience difficulties because of declines in suprathreshold auditory processing, especially in challenging listening conditions.

ARHL may differ from other types of hearing impairment and it should not be considered merely in terms of changes in the ear or which sounds older adults can or cannot detect or discriminate. Self-reported hearing problems and associated difficulties functioning in everyday life are not always accurately predicted by audiometric thresholds alone. It is important to consider ARHL in terms of not just how much older adults can hear but also how well they are able to use what they hear to function as listeners in real-world situations. ARHL can affect how well a person functions when participating in just about any activity that involves auditory communication and social interaction. Both speech and music serve communication and social interaction, but we know relatively little about the effects of ARHL on music communication compared to what we know about its effects on speech communication.

Everyday functioning and participation in many activities, including listening to and producing sounds such as speech or music, depend on brain networks that link bottom-up processing of incoming acoustic signals and top-down cognitive processing involving attention, memory, and speed of processing. In the short term, ARHL may impede cognitive processing during listening. In the long term, ARHL may accelerate cognitive declines. However, age-related declines in sensory and cognitive processing can be compensated by lifelong gains in expertise and knowledge. Accordingly, there are both age-related losses and gains in sensory—cognitive interactions during listening. Everyday functioning will depend on how well an older listener's sensory and cognitive abilities can be used to meet the demands of listening and on the extent to which situations either support or challenge functioning. Functioning will also depend on social and psychological factors that influence a person's motivation and goals for communication (Pichora-Fuller et al., 2016). Ultimately, quality of life may be influenced by older listeners' self-perceptions of their ability to function as much as by their clinically measured hearing thresholds. Thus interventions to foster the optimal functioning of aging listeners in everyday life will likely need to extend beyond treatments focused on hearing for speech communication by incorporating a more comprehensive combination of sensory, cognitive, and social approaches within a broad ecological view that includes music communication in the context of healthy aging.

In addition to the short-term effects of ARHL on everyday functioning in healthy older adults, ARHL can have widespread long-term consequences for the health of older adults. ARHL is associated with incident dementia and with increased risk for other physical, psychological, and social health issues such as falls, depression, and loneliness. The mechanisms underlying these increased health risks in people with ARHL have not yet been determined, but various hypotheses have been proposed. There may be causal links or common biological or neurological causes. Other hypotheses propose that the links are mediated by lifestyle or psychosocial factors. A better understanding of these possible mechanisms could be used to promote aging well and to optimize prevention and rehabilitation for various age-related health problems.

Language and music have been considered to be distinct systems; however, there is also evidence that they share some common stages of auditory processing (Jentschke, 2016). The perception of both speech and music is served not only by the initial encoding of sound inputs in the auditory periphery, but also by subcortical and higher levels of bottom-up central auditory processing combined with top-down cognitive processing and the use of knowledge concerning multiple levels of structure (see Chan and Alain, Chapter 7: Theories of cognitive aging: a look at potential benefits of music training on the aging brain). Nevertheless, compared to its effects on speech communication, the effects of hearing loss and hearing aids on music communication have been relatively unexplored (Kirchberger & Russo, 2015). Also, relatively unexplored are the converse effects of music on ARHL and healthy aging. Interestingly, emerging research suggests that training and engagement in music communication may protect older adults from some aspects of both auditory and cognitive aging (e.g., Dubinsky, Wood, Nespoli, & Russo, 2019; see also Zendel, Chapter 12).

The present chapter describes the causes, perceptual consequences, and prevalence of ARHL. Interactions between auditory and cognitive aging in healthy aging and links between ARHL and dementia are outlined. Then health, the functional importance of hearing in everyday life, and the potential use of music to promote healthy aging in older adults with ARHL are explored.

Normal versus impaired hearing in older adults

Distinguishing the effects of age and hearing impairment

Research investigating the listening abilities of older adults has often confounded the effects of aging and the effects of hearing impairment (Pichora-Fuller & Souza, 2003). It is difficult to disentangle the effects of hearing impairment from the effects of aging because many people with impaired hearing are older and many older people have impaired hearing. Some researchers have attempted to control for the effects of hearing impairment by setting strict eligibility criteria when recruiting participants for experimental groups that differ in age. Extensive screening is required to find samples of older adults with normal hearing thresholds, but even those who may be deemed to have clinically normal hearing seldom have hearing thresholds that match those of younger adults. Furthermore, it is problematic to compare younger adults with hearing impairment to older adults with hearing impairment because controls based on matching hearing thresholds across age groups do not necessarily control for differences in the etiologies or the perceptual consequences of the hearing impairments typical in different age groups. Two other approaches to address the confounds of age and hearing impairment have been to use simulations of auditory aging to test younger adults in within-subject experimental designs or to use correlational studies with large samples spanning a range of ages and degrees of hearing loss. Some studies of the effect of hearing loss on music perception have tested for multicollinearity between age and audiometric hearing loss and controlled for age (e.g., Kirchberger & Russo, 2015). Other studies have attempted to isolate the effects of age from the effects of hearing loss on music perception by testing only older adults with normal audiograms (e.g., Russo, Ives, Goy, Pichora-Fuller, & Patterson, 2012). Importantly, there seem to be independent effects of audiometric hearing loss and age on music perception that warrant further investigation. Future research may benefit from considering hearing thresholds and advances in diagnostic methods to differentiate hearing impairments based on etiology, including tests to differentiate subtypes of ARHL.

Heterogeneity and subtypes of age-related hearing loss

ARHL can result from changes in one or more structures of the auditory system (Yamasoba et al., 2013). Damage to the outer hair cells (OHCs) of the cochlea (inner ear) in the peripheral auditory system is typical in adult-onset hearing impairment. OHC damage often results from exposure to noise or ototoxic substances (e.g., drugs or hazardous chemicals). The OHCs are under efferent neural control and serve as a kind of amplifier to enable listeners to hear quiet sounds. Clinically, the status of the OHCs can be evaluated by testing the otoacoustic emissions that they generate in response to sounds. OHC damage can have permanent effects on the ability of people of any age to hear quiet sounds (Hoben, Easow, Pevzner, & Parker, 2017). There is no cure for OHC damage and it accumulates as people age. More specific to adult aging is another type of hearing impairment that has been likened to reduced voltage in a battery; it results from a decrease in the endocochlear potential of the cochlear fluids associated with changes to the cochlear blood supply in the stria vascularis (Mills, Schmiedt, Schulte, & Dubno, 2006).

The frequency of a sound is coded in part by place of activation along the length of the cochlea, with high frequencies coded at the base and low frequencies at the apex. This tonotopic coding of frequencies is preserved as the mechanical activation at specific places in the cochlea results in corresponding tonotopic neural transmission in the afferent neural pathways from the right and left cochleas to the cortex. Damage to the base of the cochlea can manifest as reduced audibility of high-frequency sounds. Both OHC damage and decreases in endocochlear potentials typically affect the audibility of high-frequency sounds sooner and to a greater degree than they affect the audibility low-frequency sounds, but the progression and pattern of loss across different frequencies can vary depending on the type as well as the degree of damage. Differences in the patterns of audiometric thresholds have been used to define different phenotypes of ARHL, including a sensory phenotype associated primarily with OHC loss and a metabolic phenotype associated primarily with changes in endocochlear potentials (Dubno, Eckert, Lee, Matthews, & Schmiedt, 2013).

Another subtype of ARHL is thought to involve age-related neural changes that disrupt suprathreshold auditory processing, especially the processing of temporal cues in complex sounds. Based on the observation of long-term neural degeneration after recovery from temporary shifts in the detection thresholds of animals exposed to noise, it has been suggested that age-related declines in suprathreshold auditory processing could be caused by synaptopathy that results in a disruption of neural transmissions from the sensory inner hair cells (IHCs) in the cochlea to the auditory nerve (Liberman & Kujawa, 2017). There is also considerable psychoacoustic evidence in humans that points to age-related disruptions in auditory temporal processing. Importantly, age-related changes in the temporal processing of suprathreshold sounds may occur even in older adults who have audiometric pure-tone detection thresholds that are considered to be within normal clinical limits.

Audiometric thresholds and definitions of hearing impairment

Usually, normal hearing and degrees of hearing impairment are defined using criteria based on pure-tone detection thresholds measured by audiometry. Audiometry is a standardized behavioral procedure for testing hearing thresholds using unnaturally simple pure-tone signals presented in highly controlled and artificial test conditions. In standard clinical audiometry (ANSI, 1997a), detection thresholds are measured in dB HL for pure tones (single frequency tones with a sinusoidal waveform) presented at octave test frequencies from 250 to 8000 Hz. A qualified tester, usually an audiologist, measures air-conducted thresholds for each ear by presenting pure tones produced by an audiometer over headphones to a person seated in a sound-attenuating booth. This equipment is calibrated to meet strict standards for clinical audiometry (ANSI, 1996, 2003). The person being tested is asked to respond whenever a pure tone is heard. A bracketing procedure is used to determine the audiometric thresholds in each ear. For each frequency, threshold is the lowest level in dB HL at which pure tones can be detected on 50% of the trials. A threshold of 0 dB HL occurs when the individual being tested can detect quiet sounds that have the same sound pressure level as the level used as the reference for the dB HL scale at a given frequency; the reference levels are based on the limits of audibility for each frequency in a population deemed to have normal hearing (i.e., the dB HL scale is calibrated to measure human hearing and differs from the dB SPL scale which is referenced to the same physical level for all frequencies). Pure-tone audiometric thresholds are used clinically to differentiate normal from impaired hearing when individuals are tested and they are used by epidemiologists to characterize the prevalence of hearing loss in a population for purposes such as recommending or setting public health policies.

The International Organization for Standardization has documented the median audiometric thresholds for a screened population of men and women in decades from 20 to 80 years of age [International Organization for Standardization (ISO), 2079, 2017]. Sometimes these audiometric profiles are used to describe hearing thresholds that are "normal for age." Based on these median thresholds for individuals with no history of hearing loss due to known causes other than aging, ARHL can be characterized clinically as a progressive, bilaterally symmetrical, high-frequency pure-tone hearing impairment. This description is similar for males and females, but hearing loss progresses faster in males (results for males are shown in Fig. 3.1). Males more often have a history of noise exposure resulting in the sensory audiometric phenotype compared to females who more often have the metabolic audiometric phenotype (Dubno et al., 2013). Differences in audiometric phenotypes of ARHL are shown in Fig. 3.2.

Currently, the audiometric criterion used by the World Health Organization (WHO) (2018) to define normal hearing is a pure-tone average (PTA) of thresholds at 500, 1000, 2000, and 4000 Hz in the better ear less than or equal to 25 dB HL. As illustrated in the panel A of Fig. 3.1, hearing impairment defined based on audiometric thresholds is classified as mild (26−40 dB HL), moderate (41−60 dB HL), severe (61−80 dB HL), or profound (>80 dB HL). The Global Burden of Disease Expert Hearing Loss Group (Stevens et al., 2013) has proposed shifting the criterion for normal hearing to a PTA in the better ear of less than 20 dB HL, adding a new category (moderately severe), and adjusting the boundaries between different categories of impairment to be lower than the current boundaries (see panel B of Fig. 3.1). The WHO is considering this proposal (Humes, 2019) and if it is accepted then the number of older adults who are categorized as have impaired hearing would increase. For example, a PTA of 20 dB HL for 70-year-old men based on the median thresholds shown in Fig. 3.1 could be recategorized from normal hearing to mild hearing impairment such that about half of the men who are 70 years of age would be deemed to have mild or worse hearing impairment if the proposed criteria are adopted.

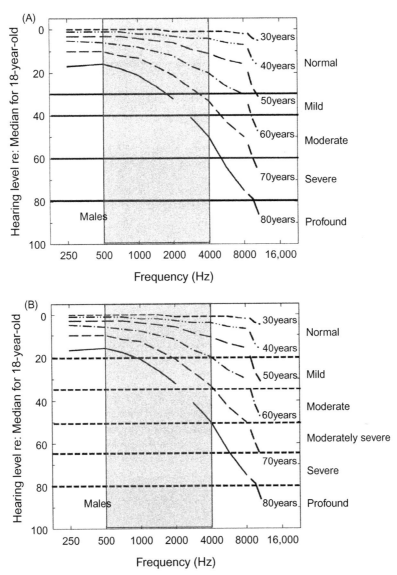

FIGURE 3.1 Progression of age-related high-frequency audiometric pure-tone hearing impairment (in dB HL) by decade of age for males based on median values from ISO (2017). Boundaries between normal hearing and categories of hearing loss are defined based on the PTA threshold at 500, 1000, 2000, and 4000 Hz in the better ear (frequency range shown in the gray area). In panel (A), the current boundaries between normal hearing and categories of impaired hearing are indicated by solid horizontal lines (WHO, 2018). In panel (B), the boundaries for proposed categories are indicated by dotted horizontal lines (Stevens et al., 2013). *PTA*, Pure-tone average.

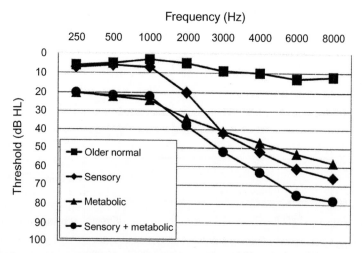

FIGURE 3.2 Mean audiometric thresholds for four audiometric phenotypes: older normal (squares), sensory (diamonds), metabolic (triangles), and sensory + metabolic (circles). *Based on Figure 2 (pg 693) of Dubno, J. R., Eckert, M. A., Lee, F. S., Matthews, L. J., & Schmiedt, R. A. (2013). Classifying human audiometric phenotypes of age-related hearing loss from animal models.* Journal of the Association for Research in Otolaryngology, *14(5), 687–701. <https://doi.org/10.1007/s10162-013-0396-x>; <https://www.ncbi.nlm.nih.gov/pmc/articles/PMC3767874/>.*

Relating audiometric thresholds to speech intelligibility

One reason that audiometric thresholds are used for categorizing degrees of hearing impairment is because speech perception becomes increasingly difficult as audiometric thresholds increase and more of the speech signal becomes inaudible. The four frequencies used by the WHO to calculate the PTA span the frequencies (500–4000 Hz) where most of the energy in the speech signal is concentrated, with vowels having energy predominantly in the lower frequencies and consonants having energy predominantly in the higher frequencies. As high-frequency thresholds worsen, vowel perception remains relatively preserved while consonant perception, which is crucial for speech understanding, becomes increasingly difficult (Humes & Dubno, 2010). The intelligibility of speech is predicted well by the Speech Intelligibility Index (SII; ANSI, 1997b), a measure of how much speech information is audible based on calculations using audiometric thresholds and the long-term average spectrum of the speech signal (and the spectrum of background noise if the intelligibility of speech in noise is calculated). This general calculation is possible because the long-term average speech spectrum has been found to be similar across many languages (Byrne et al., 1994). The SII has been very useful in designing and evaluating hearing aids insofar as a key goal of amplification is to restore the audibility of speech for people who have hearing impairment. Importantly, it is assumed that functioning in everyday life depends on speech communication and relies on speech sounds being sufficiently audible for speech to be intelligible.

Relating audiometric thresholds to music

A calculation like the SII is not available to quantify the expected effects of pure-tone hearing impairment on music perception. As shown in Fig. 3.3, the typical ranges of sound pressure levels (dB) and frequency (Hz) for speech and music differ, with music having a greater range than speech in both the dimensions (Fastl & Zwicker, 2007). Whereas the peak level of speech rarely exceeds 100 dB sound pressure level (SPL), levels for classical music may peak at 125 dB SPL and at higher dB levels for rock music (Chasin, 2006). Furthermore, variation in the acoustics of music due to differences between musical instruments and types of music is greater than the variation in the acoustics of speech due to differences between talkers and languages (Zakis, 2016). For example, music can have significant harmonic energy at frequencies up to 10,000 Hz where there is usually very little speech energy, and

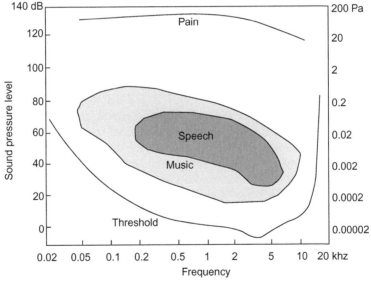

FIGURE 3.3 Region of human audibility (from detection threshold to threshold of pain) shown scaled in dB SPL and in Pascals over the frequency range of human hearing (20−20,000 Hz). *From figure (pg 6) of Gebeshuber, I. C., & Rattay, F. (2001). Coding efficiency of inner hair cells at the threshold of hearing. In S. Greenberg & M. Slaney (Eds.), Computational models of auditory function [Proceedings of the NATO Advanced Study Institute on Computational Hearing] (p. 5−16). NATO Science Series. Series A: Life Sciences 1387-6686, v. 312. Amsterdam: IOS Press. Figure is adapted based on Zwicker, E. (1982). Psychoakustik (p. 34). Berlin: Springer-Verlag; also reproduced in Fastl, H., & Zwicker, E. (2007). Psychoacoustics: Facts and models (3rd ed.). Berlin: Springer.*

instruments such as cymbals can produce sound up to 16,000 Hz (Revit, 2009) and the harmonics of piano tones can go as high as 20,000 Hz such that the highest note with a fundamental frequency of 4186 Hz has few overtones, whereas the lowest note at 27.5 Hz can have upwards of 100 overtones (Galembo, Askenfelt, Cuddy, & Russo, 2004; Russo, Cuddy, Galembo, & Thompson, 2007). The sound pressure and frequency ranges of sung speech also exceed the ranges of spoken speech; for example, the fundamental frequency of the voice for singing can be two or three octaves higher than for speech.

In everyday life, listening to live speech, either in-person or using transmitting technologies (e.g., phone), happens more frequently than listening to recorded natural speech or synthesized speech, whereas listening to recorded or synthesized music is more common than listening to live music. Recorded or synthesized speech and music both differ from live productions, but the effects may have more varied consequences for music than for speech. Fig. 3.4 illustrates differences in the spectra for different types of recorded music. Another difference between speech and music listening is that almost all people monitor their speech production during social interaction, but fewer people are musicians who regularly listen when producing music alone or with others.

Furthermore, whether for speech or music, characterizing sound signals in terms of the long-term average spectrum does not account for differences in the temporal or timing properties of the signal that are important for pitch and rhythm perception. Different sources of vibration (e.g., strings, reeds) in acoustical musical instruments can result in a wider range of fundamental frequencies, harmonics, and temporal structures than are produced when humans produce speech. Instruments also differ from speech in the temporal properties related to attack or onset times and the durations of notes or phonemes. These temporal characteristics range even more for electric and computer-generated music. In everyday life, recordings of speech and music may be listened to in a range of environments (over the radio, in the car, in theaters, places of worship, or shopping malls) such that the source signal is altered during transmission or by room acoustics. These effects further increase variation and differences in the spectrotemporal properties of speech and music that may be heard by a listener. Thus for a variety of reasons, compared to speech, although music perception will likely be altered as audibility is reduced for older adults with ARHL, it is more difficult to make generalized predictions about the correspondence between audiometric threshold elevations and consequences to music communication.

Self-report measures of hearing

Self-report measures can be used to assess functioning in everyday life. One of the most common questionnaires used to assess the psychosocial effects

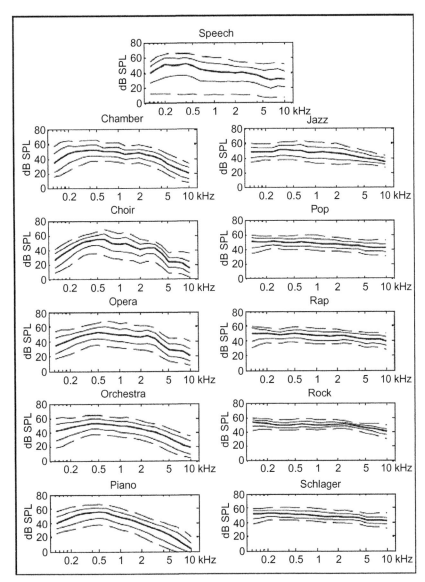

FIGURE 3.4 Dynamic range of speech and 10 different music genres. The lines represent percentiles in dB SPL across frequency in kHz (99th: upper *dashed line*, 90th: upper *solid line*, 30th: lower *solid line*, and 10th: lower *dashed line*). *Figure 1 from Kirchberger, M., & Russo, F. A. (2016). Dynamic range across music genres and the perception of dynamic compression in hearing-impaired listeners.* Trends in Hearing, 20, 2331216516630549. *<https://doi.org/ 10.1177/2331216516630549>.*

of hearing impairment on older adults is the 10-item Hearing Handicap Inventory for the Elderly–Screening (HHIE-S) (Ventry & Weinstein, 1983). An analysis of factors contributing to scores on the HHIE-S found that the PTA explained between half to two-thirds of the systematic variance (Humes, Pichora-Fuller, & Hickson, in press). One of the most widely used questionnaires designed to assess speech understanding is the Speech, Spatial, and Qualities of Hearing Scale (SSQ) and it includes four questions about music (Gatehouse & Noble, 2004). Significant age-related differences have been found on the SSQ even when the older adults had normal audiometric thresholds below 4000 Hz, including significant age-related differences on three of the four items about music (Banh, Singh, & Pichora-Fuller, 2012). Questionnaires to assess music listening in older adults with hearing impairment have been used in a few studies examining benefit from using hearing aids. One study reported that 30% of a sample of older adults who used hearing aids had diminished enjoyment of music, with about half complaining that music was too loud or too soft (Leek, Molis, Kubli, & Tufts, 2008). Similar results were reported in another study, with 76% of hearing aid users reporting benefit for listening to recorded music and 62% reporting benefit for live music (Madsen & Moore, 2014). Overall, self-report measures provide insights into the effects of auditory aging on psychosocial functioning, speech understanding, and music listening that are not fully accounted for by the PTA and that are not fully addressed by amplification.

Prevalence of age-related hearing loss

The prevalence of hearing loss based on the WHO criteria of a PTA for 500, 1000, 2000, and 4000 Hz in the better ear ≤ 25 dB HL is shown in Fig. 3.5 for men and women based on two population studies conducted in the United States. Also shown is the prevalence of self-reported hearing loss. Prevalence increases whether the criteria for defining normal hearing are based on audiometry or self-report measures, but the increase is more marked when audiometric criteria are used. In general, middle-aged adults self-report their hearing to be worse than would be expected based on their audiograms, whereas, beginning in their 60s, older adults self-report their hearing to be better than would be expected based on their audiograms and the discrepancy between self-report and clinical measures of hearing becomes more marked with increasing age (e.g., Bainbridge & Wallhagen, 2014). The discrepancy between audiometric and self-report measures has been attributed to age (e.g., Nondahl et al., 1998), as well as social (e.g., Chang, Ho, & Chou, 2009), health (Wiley, Cruickshanks, Nondahl, & Tweed, 2000), personality (e.g., Jang et al., 2002), and cognitive factors (e.g., Gatehouse, 1990). Similar disparities between speech-in-noise thresholds and self-report measures have also been attributed to these various

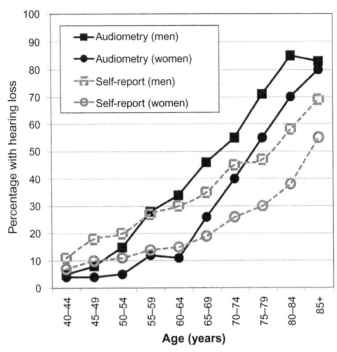

FIGURE 3.5 Percentage of the population of men and women in the United States at each age who have hearing loss defined by bilateral audiometric thresholds of mild or worse (pure-tone average of 500, 1000, 2000, and 4000 Hz in both ears >25 dB HL) based on data from the National Health and Nutrition Examination Survey or by self-report of at least a little trouble hearing based on the National Health Interview Survey. *Based on Figure 1 (pg 143) of Bainbridge, K. E., & Wallhagen, M. I. (2014). Hearing loss in an aging American population: Extent, impact, and management.* The Annual Review of Public Health, *35, 139–52. <https:// doi.org/10.1146/annurev-publhealth-032013-182510>.*

factors (e.g., Pronk, Deeg, & Kramer, 2018). Thus although audiometric thresholds are clearly associated with self-report measures, other factors besides the audibility of sound also contribute to the everyday functioning of many older adults.

Suprathreshold auditory temporal processing

Speech understanding in ideal quiet situations may pose relatively little problem for most older adults, especially for those who have normal or near-normal audiograms. However, speech understanding becomes disproportionately difficult for older compared to younger listeners in nonideal situations where competing background noise or distracting sounds (e.g., the speech of other talkers) interfere with listening. Over the last three decades, research has been undertaken to investigate age-related changes in suprathreshold auditory processing because age-related changes in audiometric thresholds could not adequately explain the disproportionate difficulties of older compared to younger adults in understanding speech in noise (Committee on Hearing, Bioacoustics and Biomechanics, 1988). Much progress has been made in understanding how auditory aging affects speech understanding in challenging listening conditions such as those encountered in everyday life, but little research has investigated music listening or made comparisons between speech and music communication. Nevertheless, music is part of the everyday lives of older adults and speech and music often cooccur in social situations. In some situations, such as when having a conversation in a restaurant, speech may be the target and music is the competing signal. In other situations, such as when attending a concert, music is the target and speech could be a competing signal. In typical singing activities, music and speech are combined. Audiometric thresholds or spectrum-based derivatives of the audiogram such as the SII are highly predictive of speech understanding when a single voice is heard in quiet, but they are less predictive of speech understanding when speech is distorted or when there is temporally fluctuating masking noise. If speech is sufficiently audible, using amplification if needed, age-related declines in suprathreshold auditory temporal and pitch processing are of little consequence to speech understanding in ideal conditions; however, suprathreshold auditory and cognitive processing provide the most likely explanation for older adults' difficulties understanding speech in noise (Humes, 2007; Humes, Kidd, & Lentz, 2013). Age-related differences in speech understanding in noise vary depending on the type of masking and implicate age-related declines in auditory temporal processing that have been observed in psychoacoustic experiments. For music, age-related declines in auditory temporal processing may be more relevant insofar as music (and also emotion perception) depends to a greater extent than speech on the temporal or pitch properties of sound. Furthermore, the issue of masking may differ given the ecology of speech compared to music listening, although this has received little or no consideration in hearing assessment or rehabilitation (Coffey, Arseneau-Bruneau, Zhang, & Zatorre, 2019).

Energetic and informational masking

Masking by competing sounds can make it difficult to listen to a target sound. For complex maskers like those encountered in everyday life, it is useful to consider energetic masking and informational masking. Energetic acoustical masking occurs when the background sound overlaps the target sound spectrally and temporally (i.e., both have a common frequency range and occur at the same time). To the extent that music and speech overlap spectrally and temporally, one could be an energetic masker of the other. In addition, there can be both energetic and informational masking when the background and target sounds are both speech because potential confusions arise from similarities in the acoustical and linguistic properties of the background and target signals. Insofar as the spectral and temporal patterns of music and speech are similar, there could be informational masking of one by the other. However, since the similarities between two speech signals are greater than the similarities between music and speech, there should be more informational masking when speech masks speech compared to when music masks speech or speech masks music. In relatively rare circumstances music from one source could compete with and mask music from another source (e.g., two radios playing at the same time).

In general, older listeners are disadvantaged compared to younger listeners when there is masking. For maskers with a speech-shaped spectrum, age-related differences are greater when the masker is fluctuating than when it is steady (Helfer & Freyman, 2014). For fluctuating maskers composed of the voices of one or more competing talkers, there are variations depending on the number of talkers. A single competing voice is a less effective energetic masker compared to multitalker babble because the degree of overlap varies more when there is only one competing talker than when there are more talkers in the background. Older adults benefit less than younger adults from listening in the dips in overlap when critical information in the target speech signal happens to occur when there is a drop or a silent gap in the competing speech signal. However, a single voice may be a more effective informational masker than multitalker babble because the listener is more likely to understand and be distracted when there is a single competing voice. Importantly, age-related differences increase as the number of competing voices decreases, implicating both auditory and cognitive factors (Tun, O'Kane, & Wingfield, 2002). Notably, however, even when the competing voice is not intelligible (e.g., when the talker is speaking a foreign language or speech is played in reverse time or distorted by removing temporal fine-structure cues such as those used to differentiate voices), there are still age-related differences when the masker is competing speech. Age-related differences when the contribution of linguistic similarity to informational masking is minimized suggest that older adults have more difficulty and are slower segregating competing voices, likely due to age-related differences in auditory temporal processing (e.g., Ezzatian, Li, Pichora-Fuller, & Schneider, 2015).

Few studies have examined the effects of music maskers on speech and no studies were found that examined the effects of speech masking on music listening. One study found that speech understanding in younger adults was better when familiar music was the masker than when the masker was unfamiliar music or multitalker speech babble, but that the familiar music and unfamiliar music and speech maskers had similar deleterious effects on speech understanding in older adults; the pattern of findings suggests that, compared to older listeners, younger listeners were less susceptible to informational masking by music and more able to segregate the speech target from the competing music and divide attention between the speech and music streams (Russo & Pichora-Fuller, 2008). Another study of younger and middle-aged adults compared the effectiveness of a single talker masker and various musical maskers varying in the complexity of their hierarchical and temporal structures (e.g., classical music vs. jazz) and found that masking effects for intact and distorted maskers were more similar between speech and classical music than between speech and jazz, suggesting the importance of structural expectancies in both speech and music, consistent with the auditory stream segregation theory (Shi & Law, 2010). Age-related differences in suprathreshold auditory processing may help to explain why older adults would be more susceptible than younger adults to informational masking by music during speech understanding because of declines in their ability to use structurally relevant temporal cues. A new test, the Music-In-Noise Task (Coffey et al., 2019), was developed to evaluate the effects of various multimusic maskers on music recognition and may provide new ways to measure the contributions of visual, spatial, and predictive cues on stream segregation, but age-related differences have not yet been investigated using the test. In older adults, top-down deployment of knowledge of speech and music structures may offset declines in bottom-up auditory processing so long as access to the predictive cues is not reduced.

Auditory temporal processing and speech understanding

In psychoacoustical studies of suprathreshold auditory processing in which degree of audiometric hearing loss has been controlled, age-related differences persist in monaural (Füllgrabe, Moore, & Stone, 2014) and binaural (Eddins & Eddins, 2018) measures of auditory temporal processing, while intensity and spectral coding are relatively unaffected by age (Fitzgibbons & Gordon-Salant, 2010). Auditory temporal processing relies on the neural coding of the various time structures of acoustic signals underlying multiple temporal phenomena. These phenomena include pitch based on periodicity coding, temporal segmentation of sound representations based on the coding of temporal properties such as amplitude envelope cues, including the onsets and offsets defining gaps and signal durations, and spatial perception of sound based on interaural timing cues that serve localization and binaural unmasking (Phillips, 1995). Declines in auditory temporal processing could impede access to important structural cues in speech and possibly also in music.

The relevance of these time structures for speech communication are well established (Greenberg, 1996; Rosen, 1992) and they have been investigated extensively in studies of older adults in which the degree of audiometric hearing loss has been controlled (e.g., Pichora-Fuller & Souza, 2003). Importantly, age-related deficits in auditory temporal processing can affect all levels of speech processing by diminishing the cues used to extract voice, phonemic, and/or syntactic information, especially at faster rates of speech when phonemes and words are shorter (Pichora-Fuller, Alain, & Schneider, 2017). Fine-structure periodicity cues conveyed by the voice contribute to the perception of a talker's age, sex, health, emotional state, and the identity of familiar individuals. Fast temporal fluctuations with periods of 10−20 ms correspond to the fundamental frequency at which a talker's vocal folds vibrate (roughly 100 Hz for males and double for females; Goy, Fernandes, Pichora-Fuller, & Van Lieshout, 2013). Temporal properties of the speech envelope such as silent gaps and differences in the durations of speech sounds can serve phoneme and word recognition. Critical durations for phonemic contrasts span several voice periods (about 50 ms; Gordon-Salant, Yeni-Komshian, Fitzgibbons, & Barett, 2006; Pichora-Fuller, Schneider, Hamstra, Benson, & Storzer, 2006). Prosodic cues conveyed by the pattern of syllabic fluctuations and rhythmic patterns in the speech envelope impart syntactic information serving sentence comprehension (Hoyte, Brownell, & Wingfield, 2009). The durations of syllables could range from 50 to 500 ms (median about 150 ms) in spontaneous speech, depending on the talker's speech rate and whether the syllables are unstressed or stressed (Greenberg & Arai, 2004) and vocal music tends to be slower than spoken speech (Kilgour, Jakobson, & Cuddy, 2000). Age-related changes in auditory temporal processing across the various levels of speech processing likely interact with cognitive slowing or declines in speed of processing (Pichora-Fuller, 2003; Wingfield, Poon, Lombardi, & Lowe, 1985). Insights into age-related declines in auditory temporal processing and their connections to cognitive aging have been gained from behavioral and physiological experiments.

Periodicity and voice

The frequency of sound is coded tonotopically by place and also by the timing of activation in the auditory system, beginning at the cochlea and continuing to higher levels. In general, place coding is dominant at higher frequencies (above 1500 Hz), whereas temporal coding is dominant at lower frequencies. For periodic sounds (e.g., pure tones) or quasiperiodic sounds (e.g., vowels), the temporal coding of low frequencies is possible because the firing of primary auditory neurons is phase-locked to the signal. Firing in the auditory nerve can occur once for each period, or cycle, of a sound wave (e.g., for a 1000-Hz pure-tone signal, there are 1000 cycles per second and the period of one cycle is 1 ms in duration). This phase-locked or synchronized timing of neural firing in response to signals is robust for low-frequency sounds, but the speed of firing would exceed the limits of the neural response for high-frequency sounds.

At lower frequencies, where older adults typically have normal audiometric thresholds, age-related differences have been found in psychoacoustic measures of temporal processing that involve the use of periodicity cues.

Such measures include monaural frequency difference limens (the just noticeable differences) between sounds of different frequencies (e.g., Abel, Krever, & Alberti, 1990) and binaural masking-level differences or the advantage of detecting dichotic compared to diotic or monotic presentations of sounds in noise (e.g., Grose & Mamo, 2010; Pichora-Fuller & Schneider, 1992). These age-related differences are not explained by audiometric thresholds and suggest that increased neural noise or temporal jitter (i.e., reduced synchrony or less precise periodicity coding) is a characteristic of at least some types of auditory aging (Anderson, Parbery-Clark, White-Schwoch, & Kraus, 2012; Hopkins & Moore, 2011; Pichora-Fuller, Schneider, MacDonald, Brown, & Pass, 2007).

Physiological studies provide further evidence of age-related differences in the neural coding of frequency based on temporal cues. In a study of monaural frequency difference limens using the frequency following response, a type of electroencephalogram measure which is sensitive to phase-locked neural activity, there were no significant age-related differences to lower frequency 500-Hz tone bursts, but the responses of older adults had reduced phase coherence and amplitudes compared to those of younger adults when 1000-Hz tone bursts were presented (Clinard, Tremblay, & Krishnan, 2010). In a study of binaural temporal processing using magnetoencephalography, the frequency range of cortical responses to interaural phase differences became more restricted with increasing age, even when audiometric thresholds were normal; respectively, younger, middle-aged, and older adults had responses up to 1225, 940, and 760 Hz (Ross, Fujioka, Tremblay, & Picton, 2007). Overall, as adults age, their ability to code periodicity becomes limited to an increasingly smaller range of lower frequencies where firing rates are slower and they gradually lose the ability to code frequencies that would require faster firing rates. In everyday listening by older adults, reduced ability to code the faster periodicity cues corresponding to higher frequencies of sound can undermine the use of pitch based on the fundamental frequency and harmonic structure of the voice to segregate one talker from another speaking concurrently (Snyder & Alain, 2005; Vongpaisal & Pichora-Fuller, 2007). Similarly, age-related differences have been found in melodic perception of low-frequency tones that can be accounted for by manipulating the upper limit of phase locking in a time-domain model of auditory perception (Russo et al., 2012).

Gaps, durations and phonemes

Many experiments have documented age-related differences in abilities to detect silent gaps between sequential sounds or discriminate differences in the durations of silent gaps or sounds, even in older adults with normal or near-normal audiograms. Age-related differences are more pronounced when the gaps or sound durations are short (Schneider & Hamstra, 1999) or when speech is fast (Haubert & Pichora-Fuller, 1999). This aspect of auditory aging can be deleterious to phonemic or word discrimination when it relies on the detection of a short silent gap [e.g., the stop consonant gap of (p) can be used to differentiate *spoon* from *soon*; Pichora-Fuller et al., 2006] or consonant–vowel transition duration cues (e.g., the contrast between *beat* and *wheat*; Gordon-Salant et al., 2006). In a physiological study using auditory evoked responses to silent gaps between 250 and 350 ms (about the duration of a syllable), the neural activation patterns of older adults differed qualitatively and were more frontally oriented in the brain compared to findings for younger adults, with these differences suggesting slower neural travel time and altered auditory inhibition or arousal by irrelevant stimuli in older adults (Lister, Maxfield, Pitt, & Gonzalez, 2011). In another ERP study that measured gap detection, attention, and cortical speed of processing, the pattern of results suggested that some older adults may be less able to compensate for declines in early or automatic auditory temporal processing by attending to the stimulus (Harris, Wilson, Eckert, & Dubno, 2012).

Envelopes and syllables

Age-related differences in following syllable fluctuations in the temporal envelope of sound sequences can also affect speech understanding, especially for artificially time-compressed speech or fast rates of natural speech (Gordon-Salant & Fitzgibbons, 1993), or when speech is heard in a background of fluctuating masking noise or speech from competing talkers (Ezzatian et al., 2015). Declines in auditory temporal processing compromise the use of the prosodic cues such as syllable rate and speech rhythm that support the processing of syntactic information (Wingfield et al., 1985; Wingfield, Tun, Koh, & Rosen, 1999). Physiological studies using the auditory steady state response (ASSR; Grose, Mamo, & Hall, 2009) have confirmed age-related deficits in temporal envelope processing for higher envelope frequencies. However, in another study, despite age-related declines in the ASSR to tones, there were age-related enhancements in envelope tracking for running speech associated with the difficulty of listening (Decruy, Vanthornhout, & Francart, 2019). The authors suggested that the differential effect of age on envelope tracking compared to ASSR may depend on the repetition rate of the stimuli, with older adults being less able to follow faster modulations. They further suggested that age-related enhancements in envelope tracking may reflect increases in brain activity as greater listening effort is expended to compensate for the degradation of peripheral auditory inputs.

In summary, age-related changes in hearing thresholds and suprathreshold auditory temporal processing can disrupt access to and efficient analysis of complex sound inputs, with deleterious consequences to speech understanding in noise. Declines in temporal processing affect periodicity coding of voice cues, coding of local envelope gap and duration cues serving phonemic contrasts and patterns of envelope cues serving syntax. Impoverished access to sound inputs during speech communication can hamper the segregation of target speech from competing maskers, especially competing speech, and impede or slow cognitive processing, but top-down cognitive processing using knowledge of linguistic structures may compensate for diminished efficiencies in bottom-up auditory processing (Henry, Herrmann, Kunke, & Obleser, 2017). There may be some similar consequences for music listening in older adults.

Auditory temporal processing and music

The imperative to discover why older adults have difficulties understanding speech in noise has motivated researchers to examine how age-related changes on psychoacoustic measures of auditory temporal processing might correspond to diminished speech and language processing. There has not been a similar imperative to examine the correspondence between psychoacoustic measures of auditory aging and music listening. A recent increase in research to investigate the effects of hearing impairment on music listening has been motivated largely to improve the design of hearing aids to meet the needs of musicians and to increase listeners' enjoyment of music. Clearly, this research on hearing loss and music listening applies to older adults who have audiometric threshold elevations. By describing the perceptual domains relevant to music listening in adults with hearing impairment, this research provides a starting point for considering how age-related changes in suprathreshold auditory temporal processing might also affect music listening in older adults with normal or near-normal audiograms. Declines in thresholds and/or auditory temporal processing in ARHL may disrupt the use of fine temporal structure cues for pitch or frequency-based, as well as gross temporal structure or time-based aspects of music listening such as beat perception (Henry, Herrmann, & Grahn, 2017).

The musical percepts of rhythm, pitch, melody, and timbre may be affected by hearing impairment and/or signal processing by hearing aids (Zakis, 2016). The Adaptive Music Perception (AMP) test was developed to assess auditory abilities relevant for music perception in people who have hearing impairment (Kirchberger & Russo, 2015). The AMP test measures discrimination thresholds for low-level acoustical dimensions in the context of four broad domains of music: meter, harmony, melody, and timbre (Kirchberger & Russo, 2015). Meter is the division of a rhythmic pattern according to equal periods or measures with strong and weak beats being organized into larger units in the pattern. In the meter test, level, pitch, and duration cues are manipulated in different subtests in which the listener judges whether a tone sequence is duple or triple in meter. Harmony corresponds to the organization of pitch cues in chords of simultaneous notes or sequences or chords in harmonic progressions. In the harmony test, the listener judges the stability of the chord sequences in subtests assessing dissonance and intonation (tonality). Melodies are sequences of tones that are perceived as an entity, with a pattern based on melodic contour (direction of pitch change) and interval size (magnitude of pitch change). In the melody test, the listener judges whether a comparison melody is the same as a standard melody when presented in transposition and in the context of a chordal accompaniment that serves as a mask, yielding two melody-to-chord ratios as measures of when the target melody is masked by the chords. Timbre enables sounds (e.g., different instruments) to be discriminated using criteria other than simply duration, loudness, or pitch, with attack time and brightness being likely attributes of timbre (e.g., Grey, 1977). In the timbre test, the listener judges which of two comparison tones is different in timbre from a standard tone for each of three timbral dimensions: rapidity of attack, brightness, or spectral fine structure.

Results on the AMP test were obtained for 19 participants with normal hearing who ranged from 27 to 67 years of age and 21 participants with hearing impairment who ranged from 38 to 83 years of age, with both groups having equivalent ranges of musical experience. The group with impaired hearing had significantly higher discrimination thresholds than the group with normal hearing on seven of the 10 low-level physical dimensions: frequency discrimination in the meter test, dissonance and intonation perception in the harmony test, melody-to-chord ratio for both melody types in the melody test, and the perception of brightness and spectral irregularity in the timbre test. After taking age into account using a multiple regression approach to analyses, hearing loss remained a significant factor in the pitch discrimination meter subtest, the intonation harmony subtest, and the melody detection subtests. In follow-up linear regression analyses, age significantly predicted results on the timbre brightness test ($P < .006$) when all 40 participants were included and age predicted the results on the meter duration test ($P < .034$) when only participants with a PTA < 25.5 dB HL were included. For older adults with audiometric hearing impairment, reduced performance on the frequency discrimination meter test, the intonation harmony test and the melody subtests would be consistent with declines in periodicity coding. Notably, in those with normal or near-normal audiograms, age predicted poorer performance on the brightness timbre test, possibly due to declines in periodicity coding, and age predicted poorer performance on the duration meter test, possibly due to declines in gap and duration coding of envelope cues. In general, these findings suggest that threshold elevations and suprathreshold auditory temporal processing declines in ARHL seem to have consequences for the perception of music that may be akin to the consequences for speech understanding.

Apart from acoustical differences between voices and instruments, speech and music can differ in many aspects of their structure, the functions they serve in the everyday lives of listeners, and the ecologies in which people listen to them. The demands of auditory processing are minimal during listening to a monologue or to a solo musician playing a flute. In group conversations, polite turn-taking would increase the demands on cognitive processing because the listener would need to switch attention from one talker to the next, and demands could be increased further if the listener also took turns as one of the talkers. For sequential rather than simultaneous talk in conversation, little masking would originate from the speech of simultaneous talkers and most masking would originate from the conversations of other nearby groups that a listener would more likely be trying to ignore unless divided attention were required for eavesdropping. Music, however, is often performed with multiple instruments playing both simultaneously and sequentially such that the demands on the listener involve integrating the productions of multiple instruments or singing voices, possibly including the listener's own productions if they are engaged in a group performance. ARHL may have somewhat similar effects on genres of music (e.g., jazz) that can be more similar to conversations in terms of turn-taking. However, the effects of ARHL on speech understanding in noise that involve susceptibility to masking and reduced ability to segregate the voice of a target talker from interfering maskers may differ from the effects of ARHL on music listening depending on the genre of music and familiarity with genres and specific works. Unlike speech at a cocktail party, ignoring competing maskers may not be relevant for some genres of music performed by ensembles of simultaneous instruments (e.g., classical music played by an orchestra) or voices (e.g., choirs). Although listeners are familiar with linguistic structures and have world knowledge that can be deployed during speech communication, with some exceptions (e.g., prayers, poems, play or movie scripts), listeners would not have prior verbatim knowledge of the incoming speech signal. In contrast, a listener may be familiar with specific pieces of music or even specific performances that they have listened to repeatedly over many years. Furthermore, hearing impairment, with or without hearing aids, clearly compromises the transactional purpose of communication which relies on receiving linguistic information, but the interactional purpose serving relationships that may rely more on emotion has been largely unstudied. Older adults are less able to identify vocal emotion compared to younger adults and these age-related differences are not explained by audiometric loss (e.g., Dupuis & Pichora-Fuller, 2015). Vocal emotion affects speech understanding in noise, but the patterns of these effects is similar for younger and older adults, even though overall performance is poorer for the older listeners (Dupuis & Pichora-Fuller, 2014). Furthermore, compared to younger adults, the communication priorities of older adults may emphasize interaction over information transactions (e.g., Carstensen et al., 2011; Mikels et al., 2010) and ARHL may impede their goals for interaction less than their goals for transaction (Villaume, Brown, & Darling, 1994). Thus there may be similarities as well as differences between speech and music in terms of how the bottom-up auditory declines in ARHL interact with top-down deployment of knowledge and familiarity to affect functioning.

Hearing aids for speech and music

Hearing aids would be a perfect solution if the everyday difficulties of older listeners with ARHL were caused solely by sounds not being audible or sufficiently loud. Hearing aids can restore the audibility of sounds insofar as they amplify to provide a frequency response that is customized according to an individual's audiometric thresholds. Hearing aids are the most common treatment for ARHL. The average first-time hearing aid user is 63 years old (Abrams & Kihm, 2015), the majority of hearing aid users are over 60 years of age (Strom, 2018), and the prevalence of hearing aid use increases as the degree and prevalence of ARHL increases with age, rising from less than 5% of those who are 50−59 years old to about 22% of those who are 80 years of age or older (Chien & Lin, 2012). A systematic review of evidence from randomized control trials concluded that adults with mild or moderate degrees of hearing impairment benefited from hearing aids in terms of improved listening ability and increases in both hearing-specific health-related and general health-related quality of life (Ferguson et al., 2017). Nevertheless, of those who would be categorized as having impaired hearing based on their audiometric thresholds, many often delay getting a hearing aid by a decade or more (Davis, Smith, Ferguson, Stephens, & Gianopoulos, 2007), only a minority (about one fifth) use a hearing aid (e.g., Bisgaard & Ruf, 2017), almost a third of those who own hearing aids are not satisfied with them (Wong, Hickson, & McPherson, 2003). Therefore amplification to address the inaudibility or loudness of sound can be an effective solution for some, but it does not provide a complete solution for all older adults (Humes et al., 2019).

Notably, beyond simply making sounds audible, signal processing by hearing aids has been designed primarily to enhance speech perception with relatively little consideration of how best to enhance music (or emotion) perception. While amplifying sound may be advantageous for both music and speech perception, some aspects of signal processing by hearing aids may not improve music or emotion perception (e.g., Goy, Pichora-Fuller, Singh, & Russo, 2018) and they may even have deleterious effects. Compression ratio and knee-points or the number of channels that are designed to improve speech perception may be disadvantageous for music perception (Zakis, 2016). For example, amplitude compression to ensure that sounds are not amplified so much that they become uncomfortably loud could optimize the availability of speech cues but reduce music cues, especially when electronic music has already been compressed (Chasin & Russo, 2004; Croghan, Arehart, & Kates, 2014; Kirchberger & Russo, 2016a). For some people with high-frequency hearing loss, frequency lowering may be an alternative to amplification in order to provide access to the high-frequency components of speech; however, depending on how the frequency lowering is implemented there may be unwanted consequences for music listening (Kirchberger & Russo, 2016b). Innovations in the design of technologies for older adults will be guided by knowledge of how suprathreshold auditory processing is altered in ARHL and how these age-related changes have similar or different effects on speech and music perception once audibility has been restored.

Links between age-related hearing loss, cognition, and health

There are age-related changes in cognition, including aspects of memory, attention, and speed of processing (see Halpern, Chapter 2: Processing of musical pitch, time, and emotion in older adults). Age-related changes in auditory processing, even in older adults with normal or near-normal audiograms, can exacerbate age-related difficulties when older adults perform cognitive tasks involving spoken language, including auditory tasks measuring discourse comprehension (e.g., Schneider, Daneman, Murphy, & Kwong See, 2000), working memory (Baldwin & Ash, 2011), and lexical decision speed (Goy, Pelletier, Coletta, & Pichora-Fuller, 2013). With increasing age, the separate effects of auditory, visual, motor, and cognitive declines on functioning become compounded. These compounding effects are seen when older adults multitask in everyday activities such as walking while listening (Campos, Ramkhalawansingh, & Pichora-Fuller, 2018; Carr, Pichora-Fuller, Li, Phillips, & Campos, 2019). The combined effects of sensory, motor, and cognitive declines challenge an increasing number of people, including those without major cognitive impairment who live in the community (Heyl & Wahl, 2012), and those with cognitive impairment who are receiving home care or residential institutional care (Guthrie et al., 2018). Ultimately, age-related sensory declines may accelerate cognitive decline (Humes, Busey, Craig, & Kewley-Port, 2013) or even increase the risk of dementia (Albers et al., 2015).

These links between hearing impairment and cognitive function have become a public health concern because, with the aging of the population, hearing loss and dementia are both expected to increase as causes of burden of disease in high-income countries (Mathers & Loncar, 2006). ARHL is a significant risk factor for cognitive decline and dementia (for reviews see Loughrey, Kelly, Kelley, Brennan, & Lawlor, 2018; Panza et al., 2019; Yuan, Sin, Sang, Pham, & Long, 2018). A recent meta-analysis calculated that the overall combined relative risk of people with hearing impairment to develop Alzheimer's disease was almost five times greater compared to controls with normal hearing (Zheng et al., 2017). The cognitive reduction associated with a 25-dB loss in hearing was calculated to be equivalent to the reduction associated with an increase of 7 years in age (Lin, 2011).

Importantly, hearing loss has been identified as the most potentially modifiable mid-life risk factor for dementia based on a systematic review of factors contributing to dementia prevention, intervention, and care (Livingston et al., 2017). There is a pressing need to understand sensory—cognitive links in aging and to investigate possible approaches to reducing the risk of dementia. At present, a randomized control trial in the United States is being conducted to investigate whether or not hearing rehabilitation can reduce the risk of dementia in older adults who have impaired hearing (Deal et al., 2017).

In addition to the important links between ARHL and cognitive health and dementia, many older adults with ARHL experience a variety of comorbid health issues (Besser, Stropahl, Urry, & Launer, 2018; Stam et al., 2014). For example, ARHL also seems to increase risk for a range of other age-related mental and physical health issues besides dementia, including depression (e.g., Huang, Dong, Lu, Yue, & Liu, 2010), difficulties walking (e.g., Viljanen et al., 2009), falls (e.g., Lin & Ferrucci, 2012), poorer physical functioning and increased risk in women of incident nursing care requirements (e.g., Chen et al., 2015), frailty (e.g., Kamil, Li, & Lin, 2014), and even mortality (e.g., Genther et al., 2015).

It is not yet known if these links between ARHL and cognition, dementia, or other age-related health issues have a causal explanation or if there is a common cause that might account for the associations found in epidemiological research. Nevertheless, it seems clear that ARHL plays an important role not only in how older adults access sound or understand speech, but also in their overall health and prospects for aging well and participating fully in everyday life.

Conclusion and implications for music

There has been a general shift in health from a predominantly biomedical physical view that has a fairly narrow focus on diagnoses and treatments for acute diseases to a more holistic bio-psycho-social-environmental view that is better suited to addressing the prevention and management of chronic disorders to promote healthy aging (Stineman & Streim, 2010). Hearing loss is more than an ear problem. Hearing is an important aspect of the capacity for people to age well and live their lives optimally. By providing access to sound, hearing enables people to interact with the auditory world, to monitor their own productions of sound, to understand the sounds produced by others, and to communicate with them. Sound provides us with critical information about our surroundings; for example, a melody from the washing machine alerts us that the clothes are clean. Sound provides us with feedback about our own actions; for example, we hear our steps as we dance, our voices as we sing, and music as we play the piano. Beyond passive hearing, active listening serves the intentional goals of the listener and requires the allocation of attention. Whether the signal is speech or music, comprehension involves interpreting the meaning of what was just heard in relation to a listener's recall of prior knowledge and emotions. Communication entails an exchange between a sender and a receiver of a message, either speech or music, as they coconstruct meaning for a shared purpose in a given situational context.

Communication relies on hearing, but also on other sensory, motor, and cognitive abilities to coordinate the understanding and expression of messages in the contexts of everyday life. The interactions of sensory and cognitive aging play out in everyday life as people with ARHL communicate, participate in social activities, and maintain social roles and relationships. Limited or atypical opportunities to communicate can have psychological and social consequences that compromise health and well-being. The mismatch between the abilities or capacities of older adults and the demands they encounter in their social and physical environmental contexts makes it difficult for them to achieve a wide range of goals. Associated reactions (e.g., feelings of loss of control, exclusion or withdrawal from social interactions, frustration, and/or reduced enjoyment of activities) may increase stress and decrease ability to cope with a variety of life issues.

Music is a relatively unexplored aspect of auditory aging. ARHL can affect audiometric threshold and/or suprathreshold auditory processing. In particular, age-related declines in temporal processing include reductions in periodicity coding, the use of envelope cues to segment sound representations, and binaural processing of spatial cues for localization and unmasking. In comparisons with the effects of ARHL on speech understanding, there may be some similar effects on music listening; however, there may also be important differences. On the one hand, ARHL could have more negative effects on music compared to speech because of the greater importance of pitch and timing cues for music perception. On the other hand, ARHL may have less negative effects on music insofar as music has more emotional and interactional significance, whereas speech is more important for transacting information. Much remains to be learned about how ARHL affects music listening and, conversely, how music training and practice may help to preserve listening abilities. Such new knowledge about how ARHL affects music listening and how music could contribute to aging well promises to open valuable new approaches to hearing rehabilitation. These new approaches could be applied in designing technologies for people that restore cues that are important for music perception, implementing new types of auditory training involving music listening and production, and enriching social interactions using music to promote positive emotions and improve the quality of life.

References

Abel, S. M., Krever, E. M., & Alberti, P. W. (1990). Auditory detection, discrimination and speech processing in ageing, noise-sensitive and hearing-impaired listeners. *Scandinavian Audiology*, *19*, 49−54. Available from https://doi.org/10.3109/01050399009070751.

Abrams, H. B., & Kihm, J. (2015). An introduction to MarkeTrak IX: A new baseline for the hearing aid market. *Hearing Review, 22,* 16.

Albers, M. W., Gilmore, G. C., Kaye, J., Murphy, C., Wingfield, A., Bennett, D. A., ... Zhang, L. I. (2015). At the interface of sensory and motor dysfunctions and Alzheimer's disease. *Alzheimer's and Dementia, 11*(1), 70−98. Available from https://doi.org/10.1016/j. jalz.2014.04.514.

Anderson, S., Parbery-Clark, A., White-Schwoch, T., & Kraus, N. (2012). Aging affects neural precision of speech encoding. *Journal of Neuroscience, 32*(41), 14156−14164. Available from https://doi.org/10.1523/JNEUROSCI.2176-12.2012.

ANSI. (1996). *American National Standard specification for audiometers. ANSI S3.6-1996.* New York: American National Standards Institute.

ANSI. (1997a). *American National Standard method for manual pure-tone threshold audiometry. ANSI S3.21-1978 (R 1997).* New York: American National Standards Institute.

ANSI. (1997b). *American National Standard methods for the calculation of the Speech Intelligibility Index. ANSI S3.21-1978 (R 1997).* New York: American National Standards Institute.

ANSI. (2003). *American National Standard maximum permissible ambient noise levels for audiometric test rooms. ANSI S3.1-1999 (R 2003).* New York: American National Standards Institute.

Bainbridge, K. E., & Wallhagen, M. I. (2014). Hearing loss in an aging American population: Extent, impact, and management. *The Annual Review of Public Health, 35,* 139−152. Available from https://doi.org/10.1146/annurev-publhealth-032013-182510.

Baldwin, C. L., & Ash, I. K. (2011). Impact of sensory acuity on auditory working memory span in young and older adults. *Psychology and Aging, 26*(1), 85−91. Available from https://doi. org/10.1037/a0020360.

Banh, J., Singh, G., & Pichora-Fuller, M. K. (2012). Age affects responses on the Speech, Spatial, and Qualities of Hearing Scale (SSQ) for adults with minimal audiometric loss. *Journal of the American Academy of Audiology, 23,* 81−91. Available from https://doi.org/ 10.3766/jaaa.23.2.2.

Besser, J., Stropahl, M., Urry, E., & Launer, S. (2018). Comorbidities of hearing loss and the implications of multimorbidity for audiologic care. *Hearing Research, 369,* 3−14. Available from https://doi.org/10.1016/j.heares.2018.06.008.

Bisgaard, N., & Ruf, S. (2017). Findings from the EuroTrak surveys from 2009 to 2015: Hearing loss prevalence, hearing aid adoption, and benefits from hearing aid use. *American Journal of Audiology, 26,* 451−461. Available from https://doi.org/10.1044/2017_AJA-16-0135.

Byrne, D., Dillon, H., Tran, K., Arlinger, S., Wilbraham, K., Cox, R., ... Ludvigsen, C. (1994). An international comparison of long-term average speech spectra. *Journal of the Acoustical Society of America, 96,* 2108−2120. Available from https://doi.org/10.1121/1.410152.

Campos, J., Ramkhalawansingh, R., & Pichora-Fuller, M. K. (2018). Hearing, self-motion perception, mobility, and aging. *Hearing Research, 369,* 42−55. Available from https://doi.org/ 10.1016/j.heares.2018.03.025.

Carr, S., Pichora-Fuller, M. K., Li, K. Z. H., Phillips, N., & Campos, J. L. (2019). Multisensory, multi-tasking performance of older adults with and without subjective cognitive decline. *Multisensory Research.* Available from https://doi.org/10.1163/22134808-20191426.

Carstensen, L. L., Turan, B., Scheibe, S., Ram, N., Ersner-Hershfield, H., Samanez-Larkin, G. R., ... Nesselroade, J. R. (2011). Emotional experience improves with age: Evidence based on over 10 years of experience sampling. *Psychology and Aging, 26,* 21−33. Available from https://doi.org/10.1037/a0021285.

Committee on Hearing, Bioacoustics and Biomechanics. (1988). Speech understanding and aging. *Journal of the Acoustical Society of America, 83*, 859–895. Available from https://doi.org/10.1121/1.395965.

Chang, H.-P., Ho, C.-Y., & Chou, P. (2009). The factors associated with a self-perceived hearing handicap in elderly people with hearing impairment—Results from a community-based study. *Ear Hear, 30*(5), 576–583. Available from https://doi.org/10.1097/AUD.0b013e3181ac127a.

Chasin, M. (2006). Hearing aids for musicians. *Hearing Review, 13*, 11–16.

Chasin, M., & Russo, F. A. (2004). Hearing aids and music. *Trends in Amplification, 8*(2), 35–47. Available from https://doi.org/10.1177/108471380400800202.

Chen, D. S., Betz, J., Yaffe, K., Ayonayon, H. N., Kritchevsky, S., Martin, K. R., . . . For Health ABC Study. (2015). Association of hearing impairment with declines in physical functioning and the risk of disability in older adults. *Journals of Gerontology Series A: Biological Sciences & Medical Sciences, 70*, 654–661. Available from https://doi.org/10.1093/gerona/glu207.

Chien, W., & Lin, F. R. (2012). Prevalence of hearing aid use among older adults in the United States. *Archives of Internal Medicine, 172*(3), 292–293. Available from https://doi.org/10.1001/archinternmed.2011.1408.

Clinard, C. G., Tremblay, K. L., & Krishnan, A. (2010). Aging alters the perception and physiological representation of frequency: Evidence from human FFR recordings. *Hearing Research, 264*(1-2), 48–55. Available from https://doi.org/10.1016/j.heares.2009.11.010.

Coffey, E. B. J., Arseneau-Bruneau, I., Zhang, X., & Zatorre, R. J. (2019). The Music-In-Noise Task (MINT): A tool for dissecting complex auditory perception. *Frontiers in Neuroscience, 13*, 199. Available from https://doi.org/10.3389/fnins.2019.00199.

Croghan, N. B. H., Arehart, K. H., & Kates, J. M. (2014). Music preferences with hearing aids: Effects of signal properties, compression settings, and listener characteristics. *Ear and Hearing, 35*, e170–e184. Available from https://doi.org/10.1097/AUD.0000000000000056.

Davis, A., Smith, P., Ferguson, M., Stephens, D., & Gianopoulos, I. (2007). Acceptability, benefit and costs of early screening for hearing disability: A study of potential screening tests and models. *Health Technology Assessment, 11*(42), 1–294. Available from https://doi.org/10.3310/hta11420.

Deal, J. A., Albert, M. S., Arnold, M., Bangdiwala, S. I., Chisolm, T., Davis, S., . . . Lin, F. R. (2017). A randomized feasibility pilot trial of hearing treatment for reducing cognitive decline: Results from the Aging and Cognitive Health Evaluation in Elders (ACHIEVE) pilot study. *Alzheimer's & Dementia, 3*(3), 410–415. Available from https://doi.org/10.1016/j.trci.2017.06.003.

Decruy, L., Vanthornhout, J., & Francart, T. (2019). Evidence for enhanced neural tracking of the speech envelope underlying age-related speech-in-noise difficulties. *Journal of Neurophysiology, 122*, 601–615. Available from https://doi.org/10.1152/jn.00687.2018.

Dubinsky, E., Wood, E. A., Nespoli, G., & Russo, F. A. (2019). Short-term choir singing supports speech-in-noise perception and neural pitch strength in older adults with age-related hearing loss. *Frontiers in Neuroscience, 13*, 1153. Available from https://doi.org/10.3389/fnins.2019.01153.

Dubno, J. R., Eckert, M. A., Lee, F. S., Matthews, L. J., & Schmiedt, R. A. (2013). Classifying human audiometric phenotypes of age-related hearing loss from animal models. *Journal of the Association for Research in Otolaryngology, 14*(5), 687–701. Available from https://doi.org/10.1007/s10162-013-0396-x.

Dupuis, K., & Pichora-Fuller, M. K. (2014). Intelligibility of emotional speech in younger and older adults. *Ear and Hearing, 35*, 695−707. Available from https://doi.org/10.1097/AUD.0000000000000082.

Dupuis, K., & Pichora-Fuller, M. K. (2015). Aging affects identification of vocal emotions in semantically neutral sentences. *Journal of Speech, Language and Hearing Research, 58*(3), 1061−1076. Available from https://doi.org/10.1044/2015_JSLHR-H-14-0256.

Eddins, A. C., & Eddins, D. A. (2018). Cortical correlates of binaural temporal processing deficits in older adults. *Ear & Hearing, 39*, 594−604. Available from https://doi.org/10.1097/AUD.0000000000000518.

Ezzatian, P., Li, L., Pichora-Fuller, M. K., & Schneider, B. A. (2015). Delayed stream segregation in older adults: More than just informational masking. *Ear and Hearing, 36*(4), 482−484. Available from https://doi.org/10.1097/AUD.0000000000000139.

Fastl, H., & Zwicker, E. (2007). *Psychoacoustics: Facts and models* (3rd ed.). Berlin: Springer.

Ferguson, M. A., Kitterick, P. T., Chong, L. Y., Edmondson-Jones, M., Barker, F., & Hoare, D. J. (2017). Hearing aids for mild to moderate hearing loss in adults. *The Cochrane Database of Systematic Reviews, 9*(9), CD012023. Available from https://doi.org/10.1002/14651858.CD012023.pub2.

Fitzgibbons, P. J., & Gordon-Salant, S. (2010). Behavioral studies with aging humans: Hearing sensitivity and psychoacoustics. In S. Gordon-Salant, R. D. Frisina, A. Popper, & R. R. Fay (Eds.), *The aging auditory system: Perceptual characterization and neural bases of presbycusis*. Berlin: Springer Handbook of Auditory Research. Springer. Available from https://doi.org/10.1007/978-1-4419-0993-0.

Füllgrabe, C., Moore, B. C. J., & Stone, M. A. (2014). Age-group differences in speech identification despite matched audiometrically normal hearing: Contributions from auditory temporal processing and cognition. *Frontiers in Aging Neuroscience, 6*, 347. Available from https://doi.org/10.3389/fnagi.2014.00347.

Galembo, A., Askenfelt, A., Cuddy, L., & Russo, F. (2004). Perceptual relevance of inharmonicity and spectral envelope in the piano bass range. *Acta Acustica United with Acustica, 90*, 528−536.

Gatehouse, S. (1990). Determinants of self-reported disability in older subjects. *Ear and Hearing, 11*, 57S−65S.

Gatehouse, S., & Noble, W. (2004). The Speech, Spatial and Qualities of Hearing Scale (SSQ). *International Journal of Audiology, 43*(2), 85−99. Available from https://doi.org/10.1080/14992020400050014.

Genther, D., Betz, J., Pratt, S., Kritchevsky, S., Martin, K., Harris, T., . . . For the Health ABC Study. (2015). Association of hearing impairment and mortality in older adults. *Journals of Gerontology Series A: Biological Sciences & Medical Sciences, 70*, 85−90. Available from https://doi.org/10.1093/gerona/glu094.

Gordon-Salant, S., & Fitzgibbons, P. J. (1993). Temporal factors and speech recognition performance in young and elderly listeners. *Journal of Speech and Hearing Research, 36*, 1276−1285. Available from https://doi.org/10.1044/jshr.3606.1276.

Gordon-Salant, S., Yeni-Komshian, G. H., Fitzgibbons, P. J., & Barett, J. (2006). Age-related differences in identification and discrimination of temporal cues in speech segments. *Journal of the Acoustical Society of America, 119*, 2455−2466. Available from https://doi.org/10.1121/1.2171527.

Goy, H., Fernandes, D. N., Pichora-Fuller, M. K., & Van Lieshout, P. (2013). Normative voice data for younger and older adults. *Journal of Voice, 27*, 545−555. Available from https://doi.org/10.1016/j.jvoice.2013.03.002.

Goy, H., Pelletier, M., Coletta, M., & Pichora-Fuller, M. K. (2013). The effects of semantic context and the type and amount of acoustical distortion on lexical decision by younger and older adults. *Journal of Speech, Language and Hearing Research, 56*, 1715−1732. Available from https://doi.org/10.1044/1092-4388(2013/12-0053).

Goy, H., Pichora-Fuller, M. K., Singh, G., & Russo, F. A. (2018). Hearing aids benefit recognition of words in emotional speech but not emotion identification. *Trends in Hearing, 22*. Available from https://doi.org/10.1177/2331216518801736, 2331216518801736.

Greenberg, S. (1996). Auditory processing of speech. In N. J. Lass (Ed.), *Principles of experimental phonetics* (pp. 362−467). St. Louis, MO: Mosby.

Greenberg, S., & Arai, T. (2004). What are the essential cues for understanding spoken language?. *IEICE Transactions on Information and Systems, E87-D*(5), 1059−1070. <http://www.splab.net/papers/2004/2004_01.pdf> Retrieved 06.08.18.

Grey, J. M. (1977). Multidimensional perceptual scaling of musical timbres. *Journal of the Acoustical Society of America, 61*, 1270−1277. Available from https://doi.org/10.1121/1.381428.

Grose, J. H., & Mamo, S. K. (2010). Processing of temporal fine structure as a function of age. *Ear and Hearing, 31*(6), 755−760. Available from https://doi.org/10.1097/AUD.0b013e3181e627e7.

Grose, J. H., Mamo, S. K., & Hall, J. W., III (2009). Age effects in temporal envelope processing: Speech unmasking and auditory steady state responses. *Ear and Hearing, 30*(5), 568−575. Available from https://doi.org/10.1097/AUD.0b013e3181ac128f.

Guthrie, D. M., Davidson, J. G. S., Williams, N., Campos, J., Hunter, K., Mick, P., ... Wittich, W. (2018). Combined impairments in vision, hearing and cognition are associated with greater levels of functional and communication difficulties than cognitive impairment alone: Analysis of interRAI data for home care and long-term care recipients in Ontario. *PLoS One, 13*(2), e0192971. Available from https://doi.org/10.1371/journal.pone.0192971.

Harris, K. C., Wilson, S., Eckert, M. A., & Dubno, J. R. (2012). Human evoked cortical activity to silent gaps in noise: Effects of age, attention, and cortical processing speed. *Ear and Hearing, 33*(3), 330−339. Available from https://doi.org/10.1097/AUD.0b013e31823fb585.

Haubert, N., & Pichora-Fuller, M. K. (1999). The perception of spoken language by elderly listeners: Contributions of auditory temporal processes. *Canadian Acoustics, 27*, 96−97.

Helfer, K. S., & Freyman, R. L. (2014). Stimulus and listener factors affecting age-related changes in competing speech perception. *Journal of the Acoustical Society of America, 136*(2), 748−759. Available from https://doi.org/10.1121/1.4887463.

Henry, M. J., Herrmann, B., & Grahn, J. A. (2017). What can we learn about beat perception by comparing brain signals and stimulus envelopes? *PLoS One, 12*(2), e0172454. Available from https://doi.org/10.1371/journal.pone.0172454.

Henry, M. J., Herrmann, B., Kunke, D., & Obleser, J. (2017). Aging affects the balance of neural entrainment and top-down neural modulation in the listening brain. *Nature Communications, 8*, 15801. Available from https://doi.org/10.1038/ncomms15801.

Heyl, V., & Wahl, H.-W. (2012). Managing daily life with age-related sensory loss: Cognitive resources gain in importance. *Psychology and Aging, 27*, 510−521. Available from https://doi.org/10.1037/a0025471.

Hoben, R., Easow, G., Pevzner, S., & Parker, M. A. (2017). Outer hair cell and auditory nerve function in speech recognition in quiet and in background noise. *Frontiers in Neuroscience, 11*, 157. Available from https://doi.org/10.3389/fnins.2017.00157.

Hopkins, K., & Moore, B. C. J. (2011). The effects of age and cochlear hearing loss on temporal fine structure sensitivity, frequency selectivity, and speech reception in noise. *Journal of the*

Acoustical Society of America, *130*, 334−339. Available from https://doi.org/10.1121/1.3585848.

Hoyte, K. J., Brownell, H., & Wingfield, A. (2009). Components of speech prosody and their use in detection of syntactic structure by older adults. *Experimental Aging Research*, *35*(1), 129−151. Available from https://doi.org/10.1080/03610730802565091.

Huang, C. Q., Dong, B. R., Lu, Z. C., Yue, J. R., & Liu, Q. X. (2010). Chronic diseases and risk for depression in old age: A meta-analysis of published literature. *Ageing Research Reviews*, *9*, 131−141. Available from https://doi.org/10.1016/j.arr.2009.05.005.

Humes, L. E. (2007). The contributions of audibility and cognitive factors to the benefit provided by amplified speech to older adults. *Journal of the American Academy of Audiology*, *18*, 590−603. Available from https://doi.org/10.3766/jaaa.18.7.6.

Humes, L. E. (2019). The World Health Organization's hearing-impairment grading system: An evaluation for unaided communication in age-related hearing loss. *International Journal of Audiology*, *58*(1), 12−20. Available from https://doi.org/10.1080/14992027.2018.1518598.

Humes, L. E., Busey, T. A., Craig, J., & Kewley-Port, D. (2013). Are age-related changes in cognitive function driven by age-related changes in sensory processing? *Attention, Perception & Psychophysics*, *75*(3), 508−524. Available from https://doi.org/10.3758/s13414-012-0406-9.

Humes, L. E., & Dubno, J. R. (2010). Factors affecting speech understanding in older adults. In S. Gordon-Salant, R. D. Frisina, A. Popper, & R. R. Fay (Eds.), *The aging auditory system: Perceptual characterization and neural bases of presbycusis* (pp. 211−258). Berlin: Springer Handbook of Auditory Research. Springer. Available from https://doi.org/10.1007/978-1-4419-0993-0_8.

Humes, L. E., Kidd, G. R., & Lentz, J. J. (2013). Auditory and cognitive factors underlying individual differences in aided speech-understanding among older adults. *Frontiers in Systems Neuroscience*, *7*, 55. Available from https://doi.org/10.3389/fnsys.2013.00055.

Humes, L. E., Pichora-Fuller, M. K., & Hickson, L. (2020). Functional consequences of impaired hearing in older adults and implications for intervention. In K. Helfer, E. Bartlett, A. Popper, & R. R. Fay (Eds.), *The aging auditory system* (2nd ed.). Berlin: Springer Handbook of Auditory Research. Springer, in press.

International Organization for Standardization (ISO). (2017). *ISO 7029:2017 acoustics— Statistical distribution of hearing thresholds related to age and gender*. Geneva: International Organization of Standards. Available from https://www.iso.org/standard/42916.html.

Jang, Y., Mortimer, J. A., Haley, W. E., Chisolm, T. E., & Graves, A. B. (2002). Nonauditory determinants of self-perceived hearing problems among older adults: The role of stressful life conditions, neuroticism, and social resources. *J Gerontol: Med Sci*, *57A*(7), M466−M469. Available from https://doi.org/10.1093/gerona/57.7.M46.

Jentschke, S. (2016). The relationship between music and language. In S. Hallam, I. Cross, & M. Thaut (Eds.), *The Oxford handbook of music psychology* (2nd ed.). https://doi.org/10.1093/oxfordhb/9780198722946.013.24. Downloaded from Oxford Handbooks Online (www.oxfordhandbooks.com). January 16, 2019.

Kamil, R., Li, L., & Lin, F. R. (2014). Association between hearing impairment and frailty in older adults. *Journal of the American Geriatrics Society*, *62*, 1186−1188. Available from https://doi.org/10.1111/jgs.12860.

Kilgour, A. R., Jakobson, L. S., & Cuddy, L. L. (2000). Music training and rate of presentation as mediators of text and song recall. *Memory and Cognition*, *28*(5), 700−710. Available from https://doi.org/10.3758/bf03198404.

Kirchberger, M. J., & Russo, F. A. (2015). Development of the Adaptive Music Perception test. *Ear and Hearing, 36*(2), 217−228. Available from https://doi.org/10.1097/AUD.0000000000000112.

Kirchberger, M., & Russo, F. A. (2016a). Dynamic range across music genres and the perception of dynamic compression in hearing-impaired listeners. *Trends in Hearing, 20.* Available from https://doi.org/10.1177/2331216516630549, 2331216516630549.

Kirchberger, M., & Russo, F. A. (2016b). Harmonic frequency lowering: Effects on the perception of music detail and sound quality. *Trends in Hearing.* Available from https://doi.org/10.1177/2331216515626131.

Leek, M. R., Molis, M. R., Kubli, L. R., & Tufts, J. B. (2008). Enjoyment of music by elderly hearing-impaired listeners. *Journal of the American Academy of Audiology, 19*(6), 519−526. Available from https://doi.org/10.3766/jaaa.19.6.7.

Liberman, M. C., & Kujawa, S. G. (2017). Cochlear synaptopathy in acquired sensorineural hearing loss: Manifestations and mechanisms. *Hearing Research, 349,* 138−147. Available from https://doi.org/10.1016/j.heares.2017.01.003.

Lin, F. R. (2011). Hearing loss and cognition among older adults in the United States. *The Journals of Gerontology, Series A: Biological Sciences and Medical Sciences, 66A*(10), 1131−1136. Available from https://doi.org/10.1093/gerona/glr115.

Lin, F., & Ferrucci, L. (2012). Hearing loss and falls among older adults in the United States. *Archives of Internal Medicine, 172,* 369−371. Available from https://doi.org/10.1001/archinternmed.2011.728.

Lister, J. J., Maxfield, N. D., Pitt, G. J., & Gonzalez, V. B. (2011). Auditory evoked responses to gaps in noise: Older adults. *International Journal of Audiology, 50*(4), 211−225. Available from https://doi.org/10.3109/14992027.2010.526967.

Livingston, G., Sommerlad, A., Orgeta, V., Costafreda, S. G., Huntley, J., Ames, D., ... Mukadam, N. (2017). Dementia prevention, intervention, and care. *The Lancet, 390*(10113), 2673−2734. Available from https://doi.org/10.1016/S0140-6736(17)31363-6.

Loughrey, D. G., Kelly, M. E., Kelley, G. A., Brennan, S., & Lawlor, B. A. (2018). Association of age-related hearing loss with cognitive function, cognitive impairment, and dementia: A systematic review and meta-analysis. *JAMA Otolaryngology—Head & Neck Surgery, 144*(2), 115−126. Available from https://doi.org/10.1001/jamaoto.2017.2513.

Madsen, S. M. K., & Moore, B. C. J. (2014). Music and hearing aids. *Trends in Hearing.* Available from https://doi.org/10.1177/2331216514558271.

Mathers, C. D., & Loncar, D. (2006). Projections of global mortality and burden of disease from 2002 to 2030. *PLoS Medicine, 3,* e442. Available from https://doi.org/10.1371/journal.pmed.0030442.

Mikels, J., Löckenhoff, C., Maglio, S., Goldstein, M., Garber, A., & Carstensen, L. L. (2010). Following your heart or your head: Focusing on emotions versus information differentially influences the decisions of younger and older adults. *Journal of Experimental Psychology: Applied, 16,* 87−95. Available from https://doi.org/10.1037/a0018500.

Mills, J. H., Schmiedt, R. A., Schulte, B. A., & Dubno, J. R. (2006). Age-related hearing loss: A loss of voltage, not hair cells. *Seminars in Hearing, 27*(4), 228−236. Available from https://doi.org/10.1055/s-2006-954849.

Nondahl, D. M., Cruickshanks, K. J., Wiley, T. L., Tweed, T. S., Klein, R., & Klein, B. E. K. (1998). Accuracy of self-reported hearing loss. *Audiology, 37,* 295−301. Available from https://doi.org/10.3109/00206099809072983.

Panza, F., Lozupone, M., Sardone, R., Battista, P., Piccininni, M., Dibello, V., ... Logroscino, G. (2019). Sensorial frailty: Age-related hearing loss and the risk of cognitive impairment and dementia in later life. *Therapeutic Advances in Chronic Disease*. Available from https://doi.org/10.1177/2040622318811000.

Phillips, D. (1995). Central auditory processing: A view from auditory neuroscience. *American Journal of Otology, 16*(3), 338–352.

Pichora-Fuller, M. K. (2003). Processing speed and timing in aging adults: Psychoacoustics, speech perception, and comprehension. *International Journal of Audiology, 42*(Supp 1), S59–S67. Available from https://doi.org/10.3109/14992020309074625.

Pichora-Fuller, M. K., Alain, C., & Schneider, B. (2017). Older adults at the cocktail party. In J. Middlebrooks, J. Simon, A. Popper, & R. R. Fay (Eds.), *The auditory system at the cocktail party* (pp. 227–259). Berlin: Springer Handbook of Auditory Research. Springer. Available from https://doi.org/10.1007/978-3-319-51662-2_9.

Pichora-Fuller, M. K., Kramer, S. E., Eckert, M., Edwards, B., Hornsby, B., Humes, L., ... Wingfield, A. (2016). Hearing impairment and cognitive energy: The Framework for Understanding Effortful Listening (FUEL). *Ear and Hearing, 37*(Supp.), 5S–S27. Available from https://doi.org/10.1097/AUD.0000000000000312.

Pichora-Fuller, M. K., & Schneider, B. A. (1992). The effect of interaural delay of the masker on masking-level differences in young and old adults. *Journal of the Acoustical Society of America, 91*, 2129–2135. Available from https://doi.org/10.1121/1.403673.

Pichora-Fuller, M. K., Schneider, B., Hamstra, S., Benson, N., & Storzer, E. (2006). Effect of age on gap detection in speech and non-speech stimuli varying in marker duration and spectral symmetry. *Journal of the Acoustical Society of America, 119*, 1143–1155. Available from https://doi.org/10.1121/1.2149837.

Pichora-Fuller, M. K., Schneider, B., MacDonald, E., Brown, S., & Pass, H. (2007). Temporal jitter disrupts speech intelligibility: A simulation of auditory aging. *Hearing Research, 223*, 114–121. Available from https://doi.org/10.1016/j.heares.2006.10.009.

Pichora-Fuller, M. K., & Souza, P. (2003). Effects of aging on auditory processing of speech. *International Journal of Audiology, 42*(Supp 2), S11–S16. Available from https://doi.org/10.3109/14992020309074638.

Pronk, M., Deeg, D. J. H., & Kramer, S. (2018). Explaining discrepancies between the Digit Triplet Speech-in-Noise Test score and self-reported hearing problems in older adults. *Journal of Speech, Language, and Hearing Research, 61*, 986–999. Available from https://doi.org/10.1044/2018_JSLHR-H-17-0124.

Revit, L. J. (2009). What's so special about music? *Hearing Review, 16*, 12–19.

Rosen, S. (1992). Temporal information in speech: Acoustic, auditory and linguistic aspects. *Philosophical Transactions of the Royal Society London B Biological Sciences, 336*, 367–373. Available from https://doi.org/10.1098/rstb.1992.0070.

Ross, B., Fujioka, T., Tremblay, K. L., & Picton, T. W. (2007). Aging in binaural hearing begins in mid-life: Evidence from cortical auditory-evoked responses to changes in interaural phase. *Journal of Neuroscience, 27*(42), 11172–11178. Available from https://doi.org/10.1523/JNEUROSCI.1813-07.2007.

Russo, F. A., Cuddy, L. L., Galembo, A., & Thompson, W. F. (2007). Sensitivity to tonality across the pitch range. *Perception, 36*(5), 781–790. Available from https://doi.org/10.1068/p5435.

Russo, F., Ives, T., Goy, H., Pichora-Fuller, M. K., & Patterson, R. (2012). Age-related differences in melodic perception are probably mediated by temporal processing: Empirical and computational evidence. *Ear and Hearing, 33*, 177–186. Available from https://doi.org/10.1097/AUD.0b013e318233acee.

Russo, F., & Pichora-Fuller, M. K. (2008). Tune in or tune out: Age-related differences in listening when speech is in the foreground and music is in the background. *Ear and Hearing, 29*, 746–760. Available from https://doi.org/10.1097/AUD.0b013e31817bdd1f.

Schneider, B. A., Daneman, M., Murphy, D. R., & Kwong See, S. (2000). Listening to discourse in distracting settings: The effects of aging. *Psychology and Aging, 15,* 110—125. Available from https://doi.org/10.1037/0882-7974.15.1.110.

Schneider, B. A., & Hamstra, S. J. (1999). Gap detection thresholds as a function of tonal duration for younger and older listeners. *Journal of the Acoustical Society of America, 106*(1), 371—380. Available from https://doi.org/10.1121/1.427062.

Shi, L.-F., & Law, Y. (2010). Masking effects of speech and music: Does the masker's hierarchical structure matter? *International Journal of Audiology, 49*(4), 296—308. Available from https://doi.org/10.3109/14992020903350188.

Snyder, J. S., & Alain, C. (2005). Age-related changes in neural activity associated with concurrent vowel segregation. *Brain Research. Cognitive Brain Research, 24*(3), 492—499. Available from https://doi.org/10.1016/j.cogbrainres.2005.03.002.

Stam, M., Kostense, P. J., Lemke, U., Merkus, P., Smit, J. H., Festen, J. M., & Kramer, S. E. (2014). Comorbidity in adults with hearing difficulties: Which chronic medical conditions are related to hearing impairment? *International Journal of Audiology, 53*(6), 392—401. Available from https://doi.org/10.3109/14992027.2013.879340.

Stevens, G., Flaxman, S., Brunskill, E., Mascarenhas, M., Mathers, C. D., Finucane, M., & for the Global Burden of Disease Hearing Loss Expert Group. (2013). Global and regional hearing impairment prevalence: An analysis of 42 studies in 29 countries. *European Journal of Public Health, 23,* 146—152. Available from https://doi.org/10.1093/eurpub/ckr176.

Stineman, M. G., & Streim, J. E. (2010). The biopsycho-ecological paradigm: A foundational theory for medicine. *PM & R: The Journal of Injury, Function, and Rehabilitation, 2*(11), 1035—1045. Available from https://doi.org/10.1016/j.pmrj.2010.06.013.

Strom, K. E. (2018). Hearing aid sales increase by 3.4% in 2017. *Hearing Review, 25*(2), 6.

Tun, P. A., O'Kane, G., & Wingfield, A. (2002). Distraction by competing speech in young and older adult listeners. *Psychology and Aging, 17*(3), 453—467. Available from https://doi.org/10.1037/0882-7974.17.3.453.

Ventry, I. M., & Weinstein, B. E. (1983). Identification of elderly people with hearing problems. *ASHA, 25,* 37—42.

Viljanen, A., Kaprio, J., Pyykkö, I., Sorri, M., Koskenvuo, M., & Rantanen, T. (2009). Hearing acuity as a predictor of walking difficulties in older women. *Journal of the American Geriatrics Society, 57,* 2282—2286. Available from https://doi.org/10.1111/j.1532-5415.2009.02553.x.

Villaume, W. A., Brown, M. H., & Darling, R. (1994). Presbycusis, communication and older adults. In M. L. Hummert, J. M. Wiemann, & J. F. Nussbaum (Eds.), *Interpersonal communication in older adulthood: Interdisciplinary theory and research* (pp. 83—106). Thousand Oaks, California: Sage. Available from https://doi.org/10.4135/9781483326832.n5.

Vongpaisal, T., & Pichora-Fuller, M. K. (2007). Effect of age on F_0 difference limen and concurrent vowel identification. *Journal of Speech, Language and Hearing Research, 50,* 1139—1156. Available from https://doi.org/10.1044/1092-4388(2007/079).

Wiley, T. L., Cruickshanks, K. J., Nondahl, D. M., & Tweed, T. S. (2000). Self-reported hearing handicap and audiometric measures in older adults. *The Journal of the American Academy of Audiology, 11,* 67—75.

Wingfield, A., Poon, L. W., Lombardi, L., & Lowe, E. (1985). Speed of processing in normal aging: Effects of speech rate, linguistic structure, and processing time. *Journal of Gerontology, 40*(5), 579—585. Available from https://doi.org/10.1093/geronj/40.5.579.

Wingfield, A., Tun, P. A., Koh, C. K., & Rosen, M. J. (1999). Regaining lost time: Adult aging and the effect of time restoration on recall of time-compressed speech. *Psychology and Aging, 14*(3), 380—389. Available from https://doi.org/10.1037/0882-7974.14.3.380.

Wong, L. L. N., Hickson, L., & McPherson, B. (2003). Hearing aid satisfaction: What does research from the past 20 years say? *Trends in Amplification, 7*(4), 117–161. Available from https://doi.org/10.1177/108471380300700402.

World Health Organization (WHO). (2018). *Grades of hearing impairment.* Geneva: World Health Organization. Available from: <https://www.who.int/pbd/deafness/hearing_impairment_grades/en/>.

Yamasoba, T., Lin, F. R., Someya, S., Kashio, A., Sakamoto, T., & Kondo, K. (2013). Current concepts in age-related hearing loss: Epidemiology and mechanistic pathways. *Hearing Research, 303*, 30–38. Available from https://doi.org/10.1016/j.heares.2013.01.021.

Yuan, J., Sin, Y., Sang, S., Pham, J. H., & Long, W.-J. (2018). The risk of cognitive impairment associated with hearing function in older adults: A pooled analysis of data from eleven studies. *Scientific Reports, 8*, 2137. Available from https://doi.org/10.1038/s41598-018-20496-w.

Zakis, J. A. (2016). Music perception and hearing aids. In G. R. Popelka, B. C. J. Moore, R. R. Fay, & A. N. Popper (Eds.), *Springer handbook of auditory research: Hearing aids* (56, pp. 217–252). Switzerland: Springer International Publishing AG. <https://doi.org/10.1007/978-3-319-33036-5>.

Zheng, Y., Fan, S., Liao, W., Fang, W., Xiao, S., & Lui, J. (2017). Hearing impairment and risk of Alzheimer's disease: A meta-analysis of prospective cohort studies. *Neurological Science, 38*(2), 233–239. Available from https://doi.org/10.1007/s10072-016-2779-3.

Further reading

Eckert, M. A., Vaden, K. I., Jr, & Dubno, J. R. (2019). Age-related hearing loss associations with changes in brain morphology. *Trends in Hearing, 23*. Available from https://doi.org/10.1177/2331216519857267, 2331216519857267.

Part 2

Disorders of Musical Perception and Memory

Chapter 4

Disorders of music processing in dementia

Elia Benhamou and Jason D. Warren
Dementia Research Centre, UCL Queen Square Institute of Neurology, University College London, London, United Kingdom

Introduction

Music and dementia have had a long journey together. The taming of Saul's "evil spirit" by David's lyre in the Book of Samuel and the Fool's singing to Lear in Shakespeare attest to an ancient belief that music is a balm for the ailing brain. The apparent power of music to unlock memories and other cognitive capacities in people with dementia, to soothe the agitated, and to comfort the bereft have always captured the popular imagination. For neurologists as well as the lay public, the chief motivation for studying music in dementia has traditionally been the prospect of musical therapies. Only recently has it come to be appreciated that music might also serve as a tool to understand the neurobiology of neurodegenerative diseases and in particular, the pathways and mechanisms by which molecular pathologies give rise to complex cognitive and behavioral effects. This has led to a growing body of studies exploiting techniques derived from neuropsychology, structural and functional neuroimaging [in particular, magnetic resonance imaging (MRI)] to delineate the cognitive and neuroanatomical landscape of the musical brain in dementia.

"Dementia" refers to a syndrome of acquired progressive decline in cognitive function or behavior, often due to a primary neurodegenerative pathology. Most neurodegenerative diseases become markedly more common with age, and dementia accordingly imposes a huge and increasing socioeconomic and human burden on societies with aging populations. The most common causes of dementia in later life are Alzheimer's disease (AD) and diseases associated with Lewy body deposition: dementia with Lewy bodies and Parkinson's disease (PD), which have largely convergent cognitive and motor phenotypes (Halpern, Golden, Magdalinou, Witoonpanich, & Warren, 2015; Weil et al., 2016). However, there are a number of other

Music and the Aging Brain. DOI: https://doi.org/10.1016/B978-0-12-817422-7.00004-3

neurodegenerative dementias and these have distinctive clinical, neurobiological, and musical features. The frontotemporal dementias (FTDs) collectively constitute a major cause of dementia beginning in mid-life (Sivasathiaseelan et al., 2019; Warren, Rohrer, & Rossor, 2013); this is a diverse spectrum of diseases, spanning syndromes led by relatively selective impairment of speech and language, production [progressive nonfluent aphasia (PNFA)], erosion of semantic memory [vocabulary, object, and conceptual knowledge: semantic dementia (SD)] or loss of socioemotional awareness and executive dysfunction [behavioral variant FTD (bvFTD)]. Better understanding of musical disorders in these diseases promises to inform the design of rational music-based therapies that build on residual capacities in people with a range of dementia syndromes. Equally, through the lens of neurodegenerative disease we have gained a fresh perspective on the musical brain, in particular, its critical neural network architecture and its role in directing complex social and emotional behaviors.

In this chapter, we firstly consider a neurobiological rationale for studying music processing in dementia and the particular challenges this poses. We then outline a taxonomy of music processing disorders in some important neurodegenerative diseases causing dementia and their major musical phenotypes. We review the available evidence concerning the neuroanatomical substrates for disorders of music processing in these diseases, in terms of the selective disintegration of distributed brain networks. Finally, we conclude with a prospect of future progress and suggest ways in which improved understanding and measurement of music processing disorders in people with dementia may help direct the development and evaluation of musical interventions.

A neurobiological rationale for studying music processing in dementia

Listening to music (like other complex cognitive functions) presents the brain with a challenging computational problem of information processing, comprising a number of component operations (see Koelsch, this volume). Contemporary cognitive models of music processing have characterized these operations and their interactions in some detail (Clark, Golden, & Warren, 2015; Koelsch, 2011; Patel, 2008; Peretz, 1990; Peretz & Coltheart, 2003; Peretz et al., 2006), while studies of patients with amusia secondary to focal brain damage and functional neuroimaging studies of the healthy brain have partly defined their neural substrates (Clark et al., 2015; Salimpoor et al., 2013; Stewart, Von Kriegstein, Warren, & Griffiths, 2006; Zatorre & Salimpoor, 2013). For our purposes in this chapter, it is useful to consider a general formulation of musical brain function that aligns with the changes wrought by neurodegenerative diseases: we present such a formulation in Fig. 4.1.

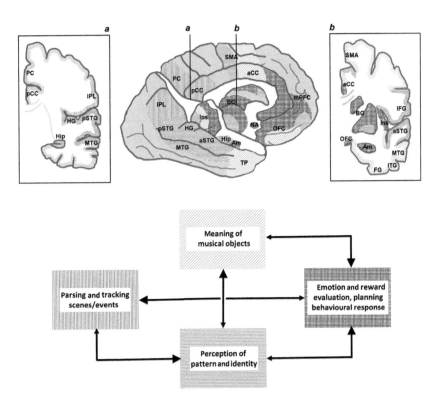

FIGURE 4.1 Cognitive and neuroanatomical organization of the musical brain.

The brain cartoon (top center) shows a right lateral cutaway view of the crerebral hemispheres with the right hemisphere projected forward (right frontal lobe and right anterior superior temporal cortex removed) to reveal the major corticosubcortical networks implicated in music processing, based on studies of focal brain damage and functional imaging of the healthy brain (see also Table 4.2). Coronal hemisections through the intact (rear) left hemsphere at levels **a** (posterior) and **b** (anterior) are also provided, to orient the projected neural networks three-dimensionally. These brain networks mediate key cognitive operations or processing stages that extract different kinds of information from musical stimuli: the major operations and their interactions are diagramed below. The shading code indicates the corresponding neural network substrate for each cognitive operation (see text for details); arrows indicate major pathways of information transfer between musical processing stages (as indicated by the relative size and direction of the arrow heads, information exhange at each stage is generally reciprocal, allowing for predictive updating according to musical context but with a predominant flow of information from earlier perceptual stages (left of diagram) to subsequent semantic and evaluative stages (right of diagram) that ultimately mediate behavioral responses). Auditory working memory is not diagramed here but is likely to interact importantly with each of the processings stages shown. Where not indicated explicitly, the diagram corresponds to the following main text sections: "tracking of musical events," musical episodic memory; "pattern," pitch and temporal patterns, and musical halucinations (excessive pattern perception); "identity" timbre perception; "meaning," musical semantic memory (see also Table 4.2). *aCC*, Anterior cingulate cortex; *Am*, amygdala; *aSTG*, anterior superior temporal gyrus; *BG*, basal ganglia; *FG*, fusiform gyrus; *HG*, Heschl's gyrus; *Hip*, hippocampus; *IFG*, inferior frontal gyrus; *Ins*, insula; *IPL*, inferior parietal lobe; *ITG*, inferior temporal gyrus; *mPFC*, medial prefrontal cortex; *MTG*, middle temporal gyrus; *NA*, nucleus accumbens; *OFC*, orbitofrontal cortex; *PC*, precuneus; *pCC*, posterior cingulate cortex; *pSTG*, posterior superior temporal gyrus; *SMA*, supplementary motor area; *TP*, temporal pole.

According to this formulation, music cognition has a modular organization: decoding the information content of a musical stimulus or memory engages four core component cognitive operations or stages of processing, underpinned by four large-scale, distributed neural networks. These processing stages and networks are linked in a broadly hierarchical organization that mediates a flow of musical information from the initial representation of acoustic features to the output of musically oriented behavior. To begin this transformation, musical sources must first be parsed from the background auditory environment and/or musical events retrieved from personal memory: this tracking of the musical sensory stream engages a posterior temporoparietal and medial temporal lobe network (Golden & Josephs, 2015; Goll et al., 2012; Slattery et al., 2019). Perceptual characterization of musical patterns and identities (e.g., melodies, rhythms, instrumental timbres) extracted from the musical stream engages a peri-Sylvian cortical network centered on superior temporal gyrus (Golden et al., 2016; Overath et al., 2010; Patterson, Uppenkamp, Johnsrude, & Griffiths, 2002; Stewart, Overath, Warren, Foxton, & Griffiths, 2008; Wiener, Turkeltaub, & Coslett, 2010); within this network, pitch, temporal and timbral attributes and relationships are analyzed by overlapping but separable neural mechanisms. Attribution of meaning to spectrotemporal patterns (e.g., recognition of a familiar tune) depends on a semantic appraisal network grounded in anterior temporal and dorsal medial prefrontal cortices (Groussard, La Joie, et al., 2010; Sikka, Cuddy, Johnsrude, & Vanstone, 2015; Slattery et al., 2019). Processing of the emotional and behavioral relevance of music and generation of an appropriate behavioral response recruit an extensive corticosubcortical network, including areas that code emotional value and salience (amygdala, insula, orbitofrontal and ventral medial prefrontal cortices) and structures that evaluate reward potential (in particular, the striatal dopaminergic system) (Koelsch, 2014; Lehne, Rohrmeier, & Koelsch, 2014; Salimpoor et al., 2013; Salimpoor, Zald, Zatorre, Dagher, & McIntosh, 2015; Zatorre & Salimpoor, 2013). These processing stages and neural mechanisms that together comprise the musical brain are dissociable and can be separately targeted by brain lesions and diseases, motivating information-processing accounts of amusia that foreground the involvement of particular cognitive modules in the development of musical deficits (Clark et al., 2015).

A common theme in the pathophysiology of neurodegenerative diseases is the spread of pathogenic proteins through large-scale, distributed brain networks: though not absolutely specific for particular diseases, the pattern of protein deposition and spread is relatively selective for particular networks, giving rise to the predictable clinicoanatomical phenotypes that characterize major dementia syndromes at presentation (Rohrer et al., 2011; Warren, Rohrer, Schott, et al., 2013; Zhou et al., 2010). Essential clinical, neuroanatomical and histopathological features of the dementia syndromes considered in this chapter are summarized in Table 4.1. Aside from their clinical

TABLE 4.1 Cardinal (extramusical) characteristics of some major dementia syndromes associated with impaired music processing.

Syndrome	Leading cognitive deficits	Neuroimaging findings[a]	Major histopathological association
Alzheimer's disease	Episodic memory followed by visual and auditory spatial, working memory, word retrieval, praxis[b]	Bilateral hippocampal and temporoparietal atrophy/hypometabolism	Extracellular plaques containing beta-amyloid, intracellular neurofibrillary tangles containing hyperphosphorylated tau
Behavioral variant frontotemporal dementia	Emotional awareness and reactivity, social conduct, executive functions	Variable, generally asymmetric frontotemporal lobar atrophy/hypometabolism, may have relatively focal atrophy of right temporal lobe	Variable, cellular inclusions containing proteins TDP-43, hyperphosphorylated tau or FUS; substantial proportion of cases genetic in origin (mainly GRN, MAPT, C9orf72)
Semantic dementia	Semantic memory: knowledge of words, visual objects, sounds, concepts; later behavioral changes similar to bvFTD	Focal anteromedial and inferior, predominantly left-sided temporal lobe atrophy/hypometabolism	Cellular inclusions containing TDP-43 (type C morphology)
Progressive nonfluent aphasia	Production of speech sounds and connected speech (grammar), later executive and speech input processing	Relatively focal, predominantly left-sided anterior peri-Sylvian atrophy/hypometabolism, variable posterior extension	Variable, most have cellular inclusions containing hyperphosphorylated tau
Lewy body diseases (Parkinson's disease, dementia with Lewy bodies)	Visual (less often auditory) hallucinations, cognitive fluctuations, attention, executive, episodic and working memory, visuoperceptual	Diffuse cortical atrophy, reduced dopamine uptake in basal ganglia on DAT brain scanning	Cellular inclusions containing alpha-synuclein and deficiency of dopamine-secreting neurons

bvFTD, Behavioral variant frontotemporal dementia; C9orf72, mutation in chromosome 9 open reading frame 72; DAT, dopamine active transporter; FDG-PET, fluorodeoxyglucose positron emission tomography; FUS, fused-in-sarcoma protein; GRN, progranulin gene; MAPT, microtubule-associated protein tau gene; MRI, magnetic resonance imaging; TDP-43, transactive response DNA-binding protein 43.

[a]Chiefly brain MRI or FDG-PET.

[b]This refers to typical (memory-led) Alzheimer's disease, major variant syndromes with underlying Alzheimer's pathology are led by visuospatial deficits (posterior cortical atrophy) and language decline (logopenic aphasia; reviewed in Warren et al., 2012).

importance, these diseases target the same neural networks that together comprise the musical brain. It therefore follows that major dementias should produce distinctive musical phenotypes: these phenotypes are predicted to reflect the relative extent of involvement of the music processing stages instantiated in particular brain regions and the connections between regions (outlined in Fig. 4.1). Indeed, our emerging picture of music processing disorders in the dementias has largely corroborated this neuroanatomical prediction. Although amusia is rarely the presenting symptom of dementia, music contributes substantially to the quality of life of people with dementia and those who care for them. Alterations of music processing may therefore assume disproportionate clinical significance; patients may be less able or willing to participate in musical activities, or may exhibit intrusive "craving" for music (musicophilia) that constitutes a management issue in its own right (Fletcher et al., 2015; Fletcher, Downey, Witoonpanich, & Warren, 2013).

Issues in studying music processing in dementia

There are a number of caveats around the study of music processing in dementia that should be acknowledged when interpreting the extant literature. Despite longstanding interest in the musical capacities of patients with dementia, most information to date has been gleaned from studies of single patients or small case series. General conclusions about musical disorders in neurodegenerative disease populations based on the existing literature should therefore be drawn with caution and, for the present, be regarded as tentative. Issues of ascertainment bias similar to those confronted by studies of amusia after focal brain damage (notably, stroke) also apply in dementia: musical functions are more likely to be studied (and are certainly easier to assess and interpret) in individuals who possess premorbid musical training and in the absence of aphasia. Relatively few studies have attempted to take direct account of the wide variation in musical expertise in the population at large. A related limitation is the general lack of widely accepted or standardized tools to assess musical functions, particularly in musically untrained listeners; this tends to further confound comparisons between studies.

In addition, the study of music processing in patients with dementia encounters issues more particularly relevant to neurodegenerative disease. In contrast to stroke (following which at least some functional recovery is anticipated, with an ensuing, essentially stable chronic deficit), neurodegenerative disorders are inherently progressive: this means that musical phenotypes (like other aspects of cognition and behavior) are likely to evolve over time. Any cross-sectional study can therefore only provide a "snapshot" of musical competence and comparisons between patients should take account of disease stage. This is one (though not the sole) important source of the wide individual variation frequently observed between patients carrying a particular diagnosis, which tends to be obscured in the reporting of group performance profiles but may hold important clues to the factors that influence musical function in the setting of neurodegenerative pathologies. Moreover, many dementias (though initially selective in the profile of cognitive impairment they produce) affect executive, attentional, and other general intellectual functions as they progress: correct interpretation of musical deficits demands that such "background" cognitive impairments are taken into account. Particularly important is working memory capacity, the dimension of executive function that allows short-term sensory traces to be monitored, mentally manipulated, and compared: as music (like all sounds) necessarily evolves in time, auditory working memory is likely to be integral to tracking and perceiving musical patterns as they evolve (Golden et al., 2017; White & Murphy, 1998), but it is not clear to what extent musical working memory and perceptual mechanisms can be dissociated. As neurodegenerative diseases tend to develop in later life, comorbidities (such cerebrovascular disease or second neurodegenerative pathologies) are common, underlining the importance of detailed phenotyping rather than adopting the undifferentiated label of "dementia" when reporting musical deficits in patients with neurodegenerative pathologies. A further practical requirement is an adequate assessment of peripheral hearing function for comparison with age norms.

Several further factors bear on the interpretation of published studies of music processing in dementia. In practice, assessment of musical capacities in patients with dementia has often relied on examiners' interpretation of their emotional reactions or musical skills (e.g., when playing an instrument): ideally, the assessment of musical functions should be objective and quantitative, following the widely accepted standards and procedures used in other domains of cognitive neuropsychology. Furthermore, work to date has focused chiefly on musical memory in dementia; much less information is available concerning more elementary perceptual musical processes or complex musical behaviors that reflect social and emotional cognition. Within the broad province of "musical memory," it is important to distinguish which memory system (typically, episodic, semantic, or procedural) is principally being assessed; this distinction is not always clearly drawn in the literature. Testing musical cognition entails challenges that are not encountered in other areas of neuropsychology. For example, within the domain of musical semantic memory, certain response procedures (such as familiarity decisions on melodies) are widely used but problematic to compare with extramusical semantic tests that probe quite specific knowledge about object properties. Tests have been devised that assess specific knowledge about melodies without relying on verbal identification (e.g., match/mismatch decisions on musical motifs derived from the same or different pieces: Golden, Downey, et al., 2015) but these have not been widely employed.

A taxonomy of music processing disorders in dementia

We now outline a taxonomy of disorders of music processing for some major dementias in which musical functions have been studied in some detail. Disorders affecting each of the key stages in processing musical information are considered in turn. Neural substrates for these disorders are inferred from neuroimaging studies in the healthy brain and with brain disease. The taxonomy is hierarchical, tracing the flow of musical information through the brain networks outlined in Fig. 4.1 and the effects of neural network damage at each processing stage. The main features of the disorders, neuropsychological tests that can be used to elicit them and their neuroanatomical associations, are summarized in Table 4.2.

Parsing musical scenes

As is the case for any sound, perception of music begins with parsing of the auditory environment into its constituent sound "objects," the process of "auditory scene analysis" (Bregman, 1990), or here, more particularly, "musical scene analysis." An "auditory object" might be defined operationally as a conjunction of acoustic features bound in a common perceptual representation and disambiguated from the auditory scene (Goll, Crutch, & Warren, 2010; Griffiths & Warren, 2004): "musical objects" could include particular melodies or instruments, while the "scene" could refer to extramusical background sounds or other patterns within the music itself (e.g., in polyphonic music), depending on current behavioral goals.

Parsing the musical scene into its constituent sounds, tracking and disambiguating musical sources and patterns are computationally highly demanding processes that are likely to be particularly reliant on neural mechanisms involved in integrating sensory information in space and time. It might therefore be anticipated that deficient musical scene analysis should sensitively signal the onset of neurodegenerative pathologies that tax the computational resources of damaged neural circuits. While little information is presently available concerning the effects of dementias on musical scene analysis per se, auditory scene analysis more generally has indeed been shown to be impaired early in the course of AD. Patients with AD have difficulty identifying target sounds (such as a spoken name) in background noise, in localizing sounds in space, in segregating overlapping sound sources with different timbres or in grouping sound sequences (e.g., tone series with different rhythms) into streams (Golden, Agustus, et al., 2015; Golden, Nicholas, et al., 2015; Goll et al., 2012; Kurylo, Corkin, Allard, Zatorre, & Growdon, 1993). These generic processes are directly relevant to music perception and AD is therefore likely a priori to be associated with deficits of musical scene analysis. On the other hand, it has been shown that at least some patients with earlier stage AD are able to identify highly familiar melodies embedded

TABLE 4.2 Summary of music processing disorders and neuroanatomical associations in some major dementia syndromes.

Musical function	Neuropsychological test paradigm[a]	AD	bvFTD	SD	PNFA	PD	Major neuroanatomical associations										Selected references
							HG	pTL	PMC	IPL	aTL	mTL	Ins	IFC	mPFC	Other	
Parsing and tracking of musical scenes/events																	
Parsing musical scenes	Dual sound stream grouping and segregation	D	NA	NA	NA	NA		+	+	+		+					Goll et al. (2012) and Golden et al. (2015)
Perceiving polyphony	Detecting familiar tunes embedded in polyphony	N	NA	NA	N	NA		+		+							Ragert et al. (2014)[b] and Golden et al. (2017)
Episodic memory	Detection of melodies presented earlier in session (discrimination from de novo)	D	NA	NA	NA	NA			+			+					Groussard et al. (2019) and Slattery et al. (2019)[c]
Perception of pattern and identity																	
Pitch interval: local	Change detection/direction, interval discrimination, deviant detection	N	NA	NA	D	D	+	+									Patterson et al. (2002), Stewart et al. (2008)[b], Troche et al. (2012), Grube et al. (2016), and Golden et al. (2017)
Pitch contour (melody): global	Contour discrimination, detection of contour deviants	D	D	D	D	NA		+		+	+						Patterson et al. (2002)[b], Stewart et al. (2008)[b], Grube et al. (2016), and Golden et al. (2017)
Key/scale	Detection of deviants, harmonically resolved versus unresolved melodies	D	D	N	N	NA		+	+	+	+			+	+		Janata et al. (2002)[b], Clark et al. (2018), and Tsai et al. (2019)[b]

(Continued)

TABLE 4.2 (Continued)

Musical function	Neuropsychological test paradigm[a]	AD	bvFTD	SD	PNFA	PD	Major neuroanatomical associations							Selected references
Rhythm: local	Discrimination of timing intervals, regularity judgment, detection of rhythm deviants	N	NA	NA	D[d]	D[d]	+	+	+	+	+	+	Basal ganglia, cerebellum	Hellström et al. (1997), Wiener et al. (2010)[b], Troche et al. (2012), Grube et al. (2016), Golden et al. (2017), and Vikene et al. (2019)[c]
Meter: global	Discrimination of meters, detection of metrical deviants	N	NA	NA	D[d]	NA	+	+	+	+	+			Wiener et al. (2010)[b], Grube et al. (2016), and Golden et al. (2017)
Timbre[e]	Spectral/temporal shape discrimination, modulation detection/discrimination, instrument discrimination	N[f]	NA	D	D	NA	+	+	+					Warren, Wise, and Warren (2005)[b], Goll et al. (2010, 2011), Omar et al. (2010), and Overath et al. (2010)[b]
Excessive perception: musical hallucinations	Patient or caregiver reports/ratings, notation of own hallucinations	D	N[g]	N	N	D	+	+	+	+			Motor cortex basal ganglia, cerebellum	Griffiths (2000), Kumar et al. (2014), and Golden and Josephs (2015)
Meaning of musical objects														
Familiar melody recognition	Familiarity/distortion decisions, within/cross-modal identity matching, naming of melodies	N	N	D[h]	N	NA	+	+						Groussard et al. (2010)[b] 2019), Sikka et al. (2015)[b], Jacobsen et al. (2015)[b], Omar et al. (2010), Hsieh et al. (2011), Johnson et al. (2011), Golden et al. (2017), and Slattery et al. (2019)[c]
Instrument recognition	Within/cross-modal identity matching, instrument naming	NA	D[h]	D	NA	NA								Omar et al. (2010) and Hailstone et al. (2010)

Emotion and reward evaluation

												Neuroanatomical correlate	References
Emotion recognition	Matching of melodies to emotion names/facial pictures, naming emotions	N	D	N	D	D[h]		+	+	+	+	+	Subcortical mesolimbic circuits	Drapeau et al. (2009), Gagnon et al. (2009), Van Tricht et al. (2010), Omar et al. (2010, 2011), Hsieh et al. (2012), and Saenz et al. (2013)
Mentalizing	Matching of melodies to mental states	NA	D	NA	NA	NA	+					+		Steinbeis and Koelsch (2009)[b] and Downey et al. (2013)
Reward valuation	Rate pleasantness of melodies (harmonically resolved/unresolved)	N	D	N	D	NA	+	+	+	+	+	+		Salimpoor et al. (2013, 2015[b]), Lehne et al. (2014)[b], Agustus et al. (2015)[c], and Clark et al. (2018)

Musical behaviors

													Neuroanatomical correlate	References
Procedural memory: playing an instrument	Objective/blinded rating of performance quality	N	N	NA	N	NA		+					Basal ganglia, cerebellum, sensorimotor cortices	Kleber et al. (2010)[b], Omar et al. (2010), Weinstein et al. (2011), and Groussard et al. (2019)
Musicophilia/aversion, creativity	Patient or caregiver reports/ratings	N	D	N	D	NA	+	+	+	+		+	Subcortical mesolimbic circuits	Miller et al. (2000) and Fletcher et al. (2013, 2015)

[a] Largely experimental and not widely validated.

[b] Neuroanatomical associations based on functional neuroimaging work in healthy brain (see also Fig. 4.1); AD, Alzheimer's disease; aTL, anterior temporal lobe (superior temporal gyrus/temporal pole).

[c] fMRI study in patients; bvFTD, behavioral variant frontotemporal dementia; D, deficit/abnormality (referenced to healthy age-matched controls); HG, Heschl's gyrus (lateral/nonprimary); IFC, inferior frontal cortex (inferior frontal gyrus/orbitofrontal cortex); Ins, insula; IPL, inferior parietal lobe; mPFC, medial prefrontal cortex (anterior cingulate/supplementary motor area); mTL, medial temporal lobe (amygdala/hippocampus/entorhinal cortex); N, normal or none (referenced to healthy age-matched controls); NA, insufficient or no data available; PD, Parkinson's disease; PMC, posteromedial cortex (posterior cingulate/precuneus); PNFA, progressive nonfluent aphasia; pTL, posterior temporal lobe (superior temporal gyrus/planum temporale); SD, semantic dementia.

[d] Evidence not consistent across studies, possibly influenced by executive and working memory factors.

[e] Multidimensional, spectral shape and dynamic spectrotemporal modulation may be mainly affected.

[f] Impaired in logopenic aphasia.

[g] Reported in some patients; +, neuroanatomical correlate identified (most patient studies based on voxel-based morphometry, unless otherwise indicated).

[h] Patients may have relatively preserved competence.

in polyphonic harmony as accurately as healthy age-matched individuals (Golden et al., 2017), perhaps signifying the importance of "top-down" predictive processing in disambiguating musical objects (see Fig. 4.1). Clearly, the analysis of musical scenes is likely to engage executive attentional and working memory resources; these cognitive capacities have been shown to affect (though do not entirely account for) performance on tasks that probe auditory scene analysis in AD (Goll et al., 2012). Since executive processing depends on widely distributed brain networks, impairments of musical scene analysis might also be anticipated in other neurodegenerative diseases such as FTD and Lewy body disease, though this remains to be substantiated.

In structural and functional MRI studies, deficits of auditory scene analysis in AD have been linked to regional atrophy and altered activity of a posterior temporoparietal network including precuneus, posterior cingulate, posterior superior temporal, and inferior parietal cortices (Golden et al., 2016; Golden, Agustus, et al., 2015; Golden, Nicholas, et al., 2015; Goll et al., 2012). This clinical evidence is in line with the picture emerging from functional neuroimaging studies in the healthy brain showing that temporoparietal mechanisms are integral to auditory scene analysis (Griffiths & Warren, 2002; Gutschalk & Dykstra, 2014; Isenberg, Vaden, & Saberi, 2012; Ragert, Fairhurst, & Keller, 2014; Teki et al., 2012; Zündorf, Lewald, & Karnath, 2013; see Fig. 4.1). Furthermore, the posterior temporoparietal and posteromedial cortices linked to deficits of auditory scene analysis in AD are components of the core brain network that is primarily targeted by the pathological process in AD (Warren, Fletcher, & Golden, 2012). This network is designated the "default-mode" network because it acts as a monitoring interface between bodily states, memories, and the external environment that instantiates a fundamental mode of normal brain operation.

From a clinical perspective, difficulty parsing musical scenes is anticipated in diseases—notably, AD—that involve attentional brain networks and, more specifically, posterior temporoparietal areas engaged in deconstructing auditory scenes of all kinds. While limited neuropsychological evidence suggests that musical scene analysis may in fact be relatively spared at least earlier in the course of AD, it is possible that difficulty hearing out separate voices in complex orchestral or polyphonic music contributes to the reduced enjoyment of music reported by some patients (Fletcher et al., 2015).

Musical events: episodic memory for music

Musical (like all auditory) scenes necessarily evolve in time, and musical events may become part of the brain's record of personal experience, with an associated spatial and temporal context (where and when the music was heard). This autobiographical record constitutes episodic memory for music: the memory system responsible for retrieving musical (and other) events over time frames ranging from around 30 seconds to a lifetime. Tracking musical scenes as they evolve and tracking musical events in the episodic memory record may present the brain with somewhat analogous problems, albeit usually instantiated over very different temporal scales; this interpretation is supported by available neuroimaging evidence suggesting that a common neural network is engaged in both processes (see Table 4.2).

In contrast to the paucity of studies of musical scene analysis, musical episodic memory has been widely studied in AD (recently reviewed by Groussard, Chan, Coppalle, & Platel, 2019). Taken together, these studies share the limitations of the wider literature on music processing in dementia, including small case numbers and widely varying test procedures and response criteria. The body of evidence suggests that episodic memory for music (like other kinds of material) is impaired from an early stage of AD and deteriorates over the course of the illness (Bartlett, Halpern, & Dowling, 1995; Campanelli et al., 2016; Ménard & Belleville, 2009; Quoniam et al., 2003; Samson, Baird, Moussard, & Clément, 2012; Vanstone & Cuddy, 2010; Vanstone, Cuddy, Duffin, & Alexander, 2009), however this has not been an invariable finding (Moussard, Bigand, Clément, & Samson, 2008). Although not strictly germane to music processing per se, a related issue which is of considerable interest to potential therapeutic applications concerns the evocation of (extramusical) autobiographical memories by music. Music appears to be more potent in evoking personal memories than certain other kinds of stimuli (e.g., photographs) and music-evoked memories tend to be emotionally salient, specific and "involuntary" (Baird, Brancatisano, Gelding, & Thompson, 2018; Cuddy, Sikka, & Vanstone, 2015; El Haj, Antoine, Nandrino, Gély-Nargeot, & Raffard, 2015; El Haj, Fasotti, & Allain, 2012): these characteristics are consistent with a rapid "template-matching" process that reactivates a previous strong association between a (musical) perceptual cue and the relevant autobiographical event (El Haj et al., 2012).

Neuroanatomical evidence concerning the neural mechanisms that support musical episodic memory in AD remains scarce. However, using activation fMRI it has recently been shown that, relative to healthy age-matched individuals, patients with AD pathology have abnormal engagement of default network hub regions in precuneus and posterior cingulate cortex during incidental episodic encoding and recall of melodies (Slattery et al., 2019). This neuroanatomical profile in AD accords with functional neuroimaging evidence in the healthy brain showing that musical episodic memory is subserved by the same core network, including precuneus, posterior cingulate cortex, and connected medial temporal lobe structures (also cardinal targets of AD pathology: Ford, Addis, & Giovanello, 2011; Platel, Baron, Desgranges, Bernard, & Eustache, 2003; Watanabe, Yagishita, & Kikyo, 2008). In the study of musical episodic memory by Slattery et al. and in other work addressing the "cocktail party effect" (Golden, Agustus, et al., 2015), patients with AD showed abnormally enhanced cortical activation, suggesting that functional network alterations are not simply the result of gray matter loss but rather reflect aberrant or potentially compensatory, heightened engagement of musical processing mechanisms. Involvement of the temporoparietal default-mode network in both auditory scene analysis and musical episodic memory further suggests that these processes may call on neural resources that are at least partly shared; both musical scene analysis and musical episodic memory are likely to entail maintenance of a detailed mental timeline and a stable sense of self continuity over time, while calibrating for dynamic internal (in particular, emotional) states. This formulation is supported by neuropsychological evidence for the "self-defining" nature of musical memories (El Haj et al., 2015), as well as neuroanatomical evidence that the default-mode network normally codes events in memory with precise short-term temporal duration information (Burunat, Alluri, Toiviainen, Numminen, & Brattico, 2014; Thavabalasingam, O'Neil, Tay, Nestor, & Lee, 2019).

From a clinical perspective, episodic memory for music, the recall of musical events (like other kinds of memoranda), is vulnerable in AD, due to degeneration of core temporoparietal circuitry that supports this memory system. However, it is important to distinguish episodic memory from other memory systems that may be relatively resilient to AD pathology—notably musical semantic memory, which we consider below.

Pitch pattern perception

Following the initial parsing of the musical scene, the auditory sources and patterns in the scene are subject to detailed perceptual analysis and decoding. Pitch is one fundamental building block of musical patterns. The relationships between the pitch values of individual notes convey musical structure as intervals (pitch change between successive notes), melody (the contour of "up" and "down" pitch shifts in a note sequence), and key (the harmonic rules that determine how notes are grouped into chords and scales). Borrowing concepts from visual gestalt psychology, pitch intervals can be considered "local" characteristics while pitch contours are "global" characteristics of melodic objects; these characteristics correspond to different levels of neuropsychological analysis and (more controversially) may have separate neural substrates (Liegeois-Chauvel, Peretz, & Babai, 1998; Peretz, 1990; Schuppert, Münte, Wieringa, & Altenmüller, 2000; Stewart et al., 2008).

Pitch is a percept that is actively "constructed" by auditory cortex from incoming sensory data. This is illustrated by the phenomenon of the "missing fundamental," whereby the pitch of a harmonic series is perceived by normal listeners even though the corresponding fundamental frequency is physically absent. Patients with AD may have difficulty forming early pitch percepts and fail to detect the missing fundamental (Abe et al., 2018). At the level of pitch pattern decoding, patients with AD syndromes (typical amnestic and language-led or "logopenic" presentations) have been shown to detect deviant notes in a tone sequence that disrupt pitch interval but not pitch contour, while patients with PNFA have difficulty detecting both interval and contour deviants (Golden et al., 2017). In line with this, patients with AD have been shown to have difficulty detecting pitch variation in tone sequences (Golden et al., 2017), while patients with PNFA have more severe difficulty processing pitch changes across tone sequences than between tone pairs (Grube et al., 2016). These deficits were not attributable to working memory effects; however, auditory working memory contributes importantly to the processing of sequential pitch changes, perhaps accounting for the less consistent deficits of pitch change detection documented in AD, FTD syndromes, and PD in other studies (Campanelli et al., 2016; Clark et al., 2018; Goll et al., 2011, 2012; Hsieh, Hornberger, Piguet, & Hodges, 2011; Johnson et al., 2011; Omar, Hailstone, Warren, Crutch, & Warren, 2010; Troche, Troche, Berkowitz, Grossman, & Reilly, 2012). Deficits of musical pitch sequence contour (melody) processing in AD and PNFA resonate with other cognitive features of these syndromes. In AD, there is evidence for impaired processing of global stimulus characteristics in cognitive domains beyond music (Delis et al., 1992; Massman et al., 1993; Matsumoto, Ohigashi, Fujimori, & Mori, 2000; Slavin, Mattingley, Bradshaw, & Storey, 2002), perhaps signifying a more general impairment of sensory feature integration. In PNFA, impaired processing of musical melody suggests an analogy with the processing of speech prosody, which is likely to present similar neural computational challenges and is likewise impaired in this syndrome (Rohrer, Sauter, Scott, Rossor, & Warren, 2012).

Data on the processing of harmonic tonal relationships (keys and scales) in the dementias remain limited. In one study, after adjusting for auditory working memory and elementary pitch discrimination performance patients with AD and bvFTD had impaired ability to determine whether novel melodies were harmonically resolved or unresolved, whereas patients with PNFA and SD performed comparably to healthy age-matched individuals (Clark et al., 2018).

The functional neuroanatomy of pitch processing has been extensively studied in the healthy brain (Janata et al., 2002; Koelsch, Fritz, Schulze, Alsop, & Schlaug, 2005; Patterson et al., 2002; Golden et al., 2016; Tsai & Li, 2019; Fig. 4.1), delineating a peri-Sylvian network in which elementary pitch percepts are achieved in lateral Heschl's gyrus and pitch patterns of increasing complexity are analyzed hierarchically in posterior and anterior superior temporal and inferior frontal cortices. A central role for this network would predict impairments of pitch pattern analysis in AD, PNFA, and bvFTD, since these syndromes target posterior and anterior peri-Sylvian cortices (Grossman, 2012; Herholz, 1995; Rohrer et al., 2010; Warren et al., 2012). However, direct evidence for the neuroanatomical substrates of pitch pattern processing in these diseases remain limited. Patients with AD have been shown to activate posterior superior temporal cortex less strongly than healthy older individuals during the processing of pitch sequences (Golden et al., 2016). Using voxel-based morphometry of patients' brain MR images, impaired detection of harmonic structure has been shown to correlate with atrophy of entorhinal, anterior superior temporal, and inferior frontal cortices targeted by AD and FTD pathologies (Clark et al., 2018).

From a clinical perspective, deficits of various aspects of pitch (interval, melody, and key) perception occur in diverse neurodegenerative syndromes linked to the distributed peri-Sylvian brain networks mediating pitch pattern analysis, notably AD, PNFA, and bvFTD. Executive and working memory deficits may contribute to altered perception of pitch in these syndromes, particularly at the level of more extended patterns (melodies).

Temporal pattern perception

Structure in time is also integral to the creation of musical patterns. Analogous with processing of pitch patterns, musical sequences can be characterized as having "local" and "global" temporal properties: rhythm is conveyed by short-range "local" relationships between successive time intervals, while meter reflects longer-range "global" interval structure. Neuropsychological studies of patients with focal brain damage suggest that the neural mechanisms that process pitch and temporal patterns are at least partly dissociable (Mendez & Geehan, 1988; Samson, Ehrlé, & Baulac, 2001).

Temporal pattern processing has been found to be relatively spared in AD, after taking working memory capacity into account (Beatty, 1999; Golden et al., 2017; Hellström & Almkvist, 1997; Strouse, Hall, & Burger, 1995). In PNFA, the evidence is inconsistent across studies, perhaps reflecting an intimate dependence on working memory for temporal analysis in this syndrome (Golden et al., 2017; Grube et al., 2016). It has been proposed (Grube et al., 2016) that impaired processing of longer-duration metrical patterns in PNFA may relate to the speech output deficits that characterize this syndrome (Ballard et al., 2014; Josephs et al., 2012), perhaps via loss of the "temporal scaffolding" that normally supports the mapping of auditory input (including feedback about own vocalizations) to speech output (Grube et al., 2013; Warren, Wise, & Warren, 2005). Patients with bvFTD (but not AD, PNFA, or SD) were found to have a defect of externally and self-paced timekeeping in a tapping task cued by a tone sequence (Henley et al., 2014).

In PD, deficits of interval and rhythm perception have also been reported (Geiser & Kaelin-Lang, 2011; Grahn & Brett, 2009; Hellström, Lang, Portin, & Rinne, 1997; Troche et al., 2012; Vikene, Skeie, & Specht, 2019), though (as in PNFA) not consistently across studies, suggesting that executive working memory and attentional factors may play an important role

(Guehl et al., 2008). Deficits may also be sensitive to dopaminergic tone and therefore, the phase of therapeutic replacement of levodopa (a precursor of dopamine, the neurotransmitter principally deficient in PD) (Cameron, Pickett, Earhart, & Grahn, 2016; Geiser & Kaelin-Lang, 2011). Patients with Lewy body disease have been shown to have particular difficulty on timed tasks requiring inhibition of responses to particular dimensions of a musical stimulus (Halpern et al., 2015), a musical Garner interference task which taxes executive function. On the other hand, patients with PD can use rhythmic and especially "groovy" music to improve walking speed, stride length or even to dance (Dalla Bella, Benoit, Farrugia, Schwartze, & Kotz, 2015; Hove & Keller, 2015; Lim et al., 2005; Volpe, Signorini, Marchetto, Lynch, & Morris, 2013), probably by engaging a sensorimotor timing interface in which an external cue (musical beat induction) overrides failing endogenous motor scheduling mechanisms (Grahn & Brett, 2007; Honing, 2012; Large & Snyder, 2009).

In the healthy brain, temporal structure is processed in distributed cortico-subcortical networks that overlap those implicated in pitch pattern processing (Wiener et al., 2010); engagement of particular structures within these networks is modulated by the temporal analysis window and by the behavioral task, basal ganglia and cerebellum being particularly engaged during precise timekeeping over short intervals, superior temporal cortex in the processing of longer-duration temporal patterns, and prefrontal and supplementary motor cortices governing attention control, working memory, and monitoring, particularly when there is a requirement to reproduce intervals or rhythms (Abrams, Bhatara, & Ryali, 2011; Agustus et al., 2018; Cadena-Valencia, García-Garibay, Merchant, Jazayeri, & de Lafuente, 2018; Chen, Penhune, & Zatorre, 2008; Chen, Zatorre, & Penhune, 2006; Grahn & Brett, 2007; Grahn, 2012; Griffiths, Johnsrude, & Dean, 1999; Herdener, Humbel, & Esposito, 2014; Konoike, Kotozaki, & Miyachi, 2012; Mathiak, Hertrich, & Grodd, 2004; Stevens, Kiehl, Pearlson, & Calhoun, 2007). The neuroanatomy of musical temporal pattern processing has not been defined in AD. However, using voxel-based morphometry in a combined cohort of patients with progressive aphasia, reduced performance on a temporal regularity judgment task was found to correlate with gray matter loss in supplementary motor area and basal ganglia (caudate nucleus) (Hardy et al., 2017a) while fMRI in patients with PNFA revealed reduced activation of anterior cingulate cortex in response to temporal irregularity relative to healthy older individuals (Hardy et al., 2017b). Though the findings accord with previous neuroimaging work, these studies employed spoken syllable sequences to convey temporal duration changes, so it is not clear to what extent the findings apply more specifically to musical stimuli. Degradation of self-paced tempo reproduction in bvFTD has been found to correlate with gray matter atrophy in cerebellum and posterior temporal cortex, and with increased axial diffusivity in superior longitudinal fasciculus (a key dorsal white matter pathway linking frontal and parietal cortices) on MRI tractography (Henley et al., 2014). A more pertinent and detailed analysis of musical rhythm processing using fMRI in PD revealed increased engagement of posterior superior temporal and inferior parietal cortices and an abnormal sequence of activation changes across anterior cingulate, bilateral anterior insula, and supplementary motor cortices in patients relative to healthy controls (Vikene et al., 2019). This hyperactivity of cortical network elements in PD may reflect primary dysfunction of subcortical basal ganglia circuitry.

From a clinical perspective, impaired processing of rhythmic and metrical information in music is likely to be particularly salient in diseases—such as PD and bvFTD—that affect corticosubcortical (including basal ganglia) circuits governing the analysis of temporal patterns. However, at least in PD, timing deficits may be to some extent redressed by external cueing or dopaminergic replacement.

Timbre perception

Timbre, which can be defined negatively as the acoustic property that distinguishes two sounds with the same pitch, duration, and loudness (Bregman, 1990), is integral to the identification of musical sources (instruments and voices). It is a multidimensional property, comprising a set of spectral and temporal features and their dynamic interaction that together characterize a particular musical (or other auditory) object (Hailstone, Omar, & Henley, 2009; McAdams & Cunible, 1992; Samson, Zatorre, & Ramsay, 2002). In addition to conveying identity, timbre contributes importantly to the emotional resonance of particular instruments (Hailstone, Omar, Henly, et al., 2009; Juslin & Laukka, 2003).

Deficits of timbre processing ("dystimbria") are uncommonly reported and timbre processing has not been widely studied in the dementias. Impaired discrimination of musical instrument timbres has been described in expert musicians with SD and AD (Omar et al., 2010). These cases with predominant temporal lobe degeneration recall descriptions of dystimbria following anterior temporal lobectomy, particularly on the right side (Milner, 1962; Samson & Zatorre, 1994; Samson et al., 2002). In group studies probing key components of timbre perception in dementia syndromes, patients with PNFA were impaired on discrimination of spectral "shapes" (the frequency profiles defining complex sounds) and spectrotemporal "ripples" (dynamic modulation patterns) (Goll et al., 2010), though not more elementary frequency modulation detection, relative to healthy age-matched controls (Goll et al., 2011; Grube et al., 2016). Patients with typical amnestic AD and SD performed normally on such tests of timbre discrimination, while timbral deficits in patients with the logopenic aphasic variant of AD have been variable (Goll et al., 2010, 2011; Grube et al., 2016). These studies underline the multidimensional nature of timbre and associated deficits of timbre processing. Moreover, neuropsychological evidence in dementia syndromes has chiefly been amassed for generic spectrotemporal properties that could underpin the timbre of any sound; more work is needed to address the processing of specifically musical timbral stimuli.

In the healthy brain, processing of timbral properties such as spectral shape and acoustic texture engages superior and lateral temporal cortices (Overath, Kumar, von Kriegstein, & Griffiths, 2008; Overath et al., 2010; Warren, Jennings, & Griffiths, 2005). Involvement of these mechanisms could potentially account for the timbral deficits observed in PNFA, however this awaits substantiation.

From a clinical perspective, impaired perception of timbre by people with temporal lobe degenerations may degrade appreciation of musical textures and instrument colors, though more generic effects of "dystimbria" on human voice and environmental sound identification may be more noticeable.

Musical hallucinations

A further dimension to abnormal perception of musical patterns is excessive perception, manifesting as musical hallucinations. These occur more frequently in Lewy body disease but may also accompany AD and (less often) FTD (Golden & Josephs, 2015); in Lewy body disease, musical hallucinations are part of a wider spectrum of auditory hallucinations and appear overall to be rather uncommon (Eversfield & Orton, 2018). Peripheral hearing loss promotes the emergence of musical hallucinations but is neither necessary nor sufficient to account for the phenomenon. Patients often report hearing banal tunes without particular personal significance that have a "choral" or "hymn-like" character; insight into the nature of the hallucination is frequently lacking. Although the hallucinated music is often described as a familiar tune, it tends to degrade and fragment over time; when musical hallucinations were notated by a patient with premorbid musical training, they were found to comprise novel, simple melodic motifs (Warren & Schott, 2006). These features are in line with a current neurobiological model according to which musical hallucinations reflect abnormal spontaneous activity in auditory cortical areas beyond primary cortex and motor and subcortical areas previously implicated in auditory imagery, which may be facilitated by peripheral sensory deafferentation (analogous to the development of visual hallucinations following peripheral visual loss in Charles Bonnet syndrome) (Griffiths, 2000; Kumar et al., 2014). Musical hallucinations could therefore be considered a further manifestation of aberrant musical pattern processing. On this view, reduced acoustic input and eroded cortical regulatory controls interact to release abnormal patterns of auditory cortical activity, which tend to conform to the "predictable" template patterns accumulated through a lifetime's exposure to musical rules and structures.

From a clinical perspective, musical hallucinations are more likely to emerge in the setting of peripheral deafness and, while hallucinatory music does not carry the sinister psychiatric overtones of auditory verbal hallucinations, it may be a harbinger of a neurodegenerative process (in particular, dementia with Lewy bodies) and may be very troublesome and intrusive in its own right. Correction of peripheral hearing loss (where possible) is the most rational approach to management, although some patients benefit from masking strategies, as well as reassurance that their complaint does not signify a more sinister psychiatric illness.

Meaning of musical objects: semantic memory for music

The initial stages of musical pattern and musical source analysis generate musical object representations: attribution of meaning to these object representations requires semantic processing, in which percepts become associated with stored knowledge about the objects of experience. Music is one of the sensory categories processed by the semantic memory system, which mediates the storage and mobilization of an encyclopedic lexicon of verbal and nonverbal concepts, derived from the individual's accumulated experience of the world. As a classical tenet of neuropsychology, semantic memory dissociates both from perceptual mechanisms and from other memory systems (in particular, episodic memory). This tenet has been found to apply to music, with well attested cases of selective sparing or impairment of musical semantic memory (musical "associative agnosia") following focal brain damage (Eustache, Lechevalier, & Viader, 1990; Finke, Esfahani, & Ploner, 2012; Peretz, 1996; Schuppert et al., 2000; Wilson, Baddeley, & Kapur, 1995). Musical semantic memory is engaged during recognition of familiar melodies, musical instruments, and (in those with musical training) musical symbols and notation systems, as well as explicit knowledge of the "rules" that govern musical compositions. An important issue in assessing musical semantic memory in patients with dementia is the frequent presence of word retrieval or verbal semantic deficits, so that naming tasks in general do not reliably index music recognition.

The balance of evidence suggests that melody recognition is relatively preserved in AD, at least in the earlier stages of the illness (Bartlett et al., 1995; Beatty et al., 1994; Cuddy & Duffin, 2005; Cuddy et al., 2012; Golden et al., 2017; Hsieh et al., 2011; Johnson et al., 2011; Kerer et al., 2013; Platel & Groussard, 2010; Polk & Kertesz, 1993; Samson et al., 2012; Vanstone & Cuddy, 2010; Vanstone et al., 2009). Most of these studies have assessed recognition of melodies based on decisions about their familiarity or fidelity (presence of false notes). Tests that probe more detailed associative knowledge about musical pieces (e.g., decisions about the composer or solo instrument from the orchestral introduction to a concerto) may expose musical semantic deficits in patients with AD (Omar et al., 2010), however experience with such tests is limited and (because they tend to rely on premorbid musical expertise) the generalizability of the findings is not clear. Whereas patients with bvFTD and PNFA may recognize melodies normally, SD is usually associated with impaired melody recognition as part of a pervasive disintegration of semantic memory across cognitive domains and modalities (Golden et al., 2017; Golden, Downey et al., 2015; Hsieh et al., 2011; Johnson et al., 2011); this deficit is not attributable to conjoint verbal or cross-modal impairments, since it is elicited by within-modality matching tasks (deciding whether two serially presented melodic fragments belong to the same or different pieces) (Golden, Downey, et al., 2015). It is noteworthy, however, that a substantial minority of patients with SD show relatively well preserved knowledge of melodies which may dissociate from other aspects of semantic function and is not contingent on prior musical expertise (Hailstone, Omar, & Warren, 2009; Hsieh et al., 2011; Omar et al., 2010; Weinstein, Koenig, & Gunawardena, 2011). A similar isolation of musical semantic competence has been reported after focal brain damage (Finke et al., 2012). However, associative agnosia for melodies has been described in association with a rather wide cerebral distribution of culprit lesions (Clark et al., 2015): neuroanatomical inferences from neurodegenerative syndromes (notably, SD) with selective temporal lobe degeneration should therefore be qualified.

There has been little work to date on other aspects of musical semantic memory in dementia. In single case studies, recognition of musical instruments was found to be impaired in SD and bvFTD but relatively intact in association with right anteromedial temporal lobe atrophy (Hailstone, Crutch, & Vestergaard, 2010; Omar et al., 2010); in these cases, there was evidence for a dissociation of musical instrument knowledge from knowledge of other auditory objects (voices and environmental sounds) as well as melody recognition. Expert musicians with SD have been found to have retained competence recognizing notated musical symbols and even intact absolute pitch (Omar et al., 2010; Weinstein et al., 2011). Taken together, this evidence suggests that musical knowledge is a highly fractionated semantic domain, mediated by neural mechanisms that are at least partly independent from those subserving other knowledge categories. The organization of the semantic memory system for music may reflect a fundamental distinction between musical objects that arise from physical sound sources in the world at large (instruments) and musical objects constituted from abstract patterns (melodies) (Hailstone Omar, & Warren, 2009; Omar et al., 2010; Weinstein et al., 2011). A distinction of this kind might also account for cases of selective sparing of melody recognition in SD despite widespread semantic disintegration affecting the recognition of other object categories.

Functional neuroimaging studies of musical semantic memory in the healthy brain have delineated an extensive cerebral network including anterior temporal, insular, inferior, and dorsomedial prefrontal cortices (Agustus et al., 2018; Freitas et al., 2018; Groussard, La Joie et al., 2010; Groussard, Rauchs et al., 2010; Herholz, Halpern, & Zatorre, 2012; Jacobsen et al., 2015; Platel et al., 2003; Sikka et al., 2015; Slattery et al., 2019; Fig. 4.1). Using voxel-based morphometry, melody recognition across FTD and AD syndromes has been correlated with regional gray matter volume in anterior superior temporal and temporal polar cortex, extending into medial temporal lobe, insula, and orbitofrontal cortex (Hsieh et al., 2011; Johnson et al., 2011). Within the musical semantic memory network, the supplementary motor area is likely to mediate affective salience and preparedness to move on listening to familiar music and may play a pivotal role in modulating the effects of neurodegenerative pathologies. It has been proposed that sparing of this region may account for the relative preservation of musical semantic memory in AD (Jacobsen et al., 2015) and it is noteworthy that this area is also relatively spared in SD. Functional MRI evidence suggests that patients with AD activate supplementary motor cortex comparably to healthy age-matched individuals in response to familiar melodies (Slattery et al., 2019) and show enhanced activity and connectivity of this region following exposure to favorite music (King et al., 2019). Conversely, reduced activation of inferior frontal cortex in AD during processing of musical familiarity (Slattery et al., 2019) suggests at least partial loss of the functional integrity of the network that may account for musical semantic deficits documented in some previous studies (Groussard et al., 2019).

From a clinical perspective, retained ability to recognize familiar music in AD suggests that individualized playlists of favorite songs and other musical pieces might be beneficial—as a bridge to patients' personal pasts, to help maintain quality of life, and perhaps (more controversially) to access autobiographical events and related extramusical cognitive functions (Garrido, Stevens, Chang, Dunne, & Perz, 2018; Garrido, Stevens, Chang, Dunne, & Perz, 2019; Groussard et al., 2019). On the other hand, many people with impaired recognition of tunes (e.g., in SD) nevertheless also continue to enjoy listening to music.

Musical emotion and reward

The capacity of music to generate emotional responses is the key to its appeal for most listeners: considering that abstract tone patterns have no intrinsic biological value, this capacity is indeed remarkable, as illustrated by the intense autonomic arousal that accompanies musical "chills" or "shiver" (Blood & Zatorre, 2001). Largely as a result of its emotional charge, music carries substantial reward potential for many people and this motivates behaviors such as music seeking and repeated exposures to particular music. Musical emotion and reward processing has emerged as a major theme in contemporary music neuroscience; the recognition that music engages the neural machinery of biological reward processing has in turn prompted a reappraisal of the evolutionary "purpose" of music and its possible role in human social cognition, in particular the signaling of affective mental states (Clark et al., 2015; Clark, Downey, & Warren, 2014; Lima et al., 2016; Zatorre & Salimpoor, 2013). Although the nature of musical emotion and its similarity to "animate" emotions remains controversial (Juslin & Laukka, 2003), musical emotion processing has been most widely studied neuropsychologically by labeling or matching of emotions expressed in music to "universal emotions" of human facial and vocal expressions (usually happiness, sadness, anger, and fear).

Using such procedures, patients with AD have been shown to have retained ability to identify different musical emotions (Drapeau, Gosselin, Gagnon, Peretz, & Lorrain, 2009; Omar et al., 2010) and can use mode and tempo cues to classify "happy" and "sad" music (Gagnon, Peretz, & Fülöp, 2009). This ability may dissociate from recognition of facial expressions (Drapeau et al., 2009). In contrast, recognition of basic emotions from music is impaired in bvFTD and SD, usually (though not invariably) as part of a pervasive difficulty interpreting emotional and other social signals in these syndromes (Hailstone et al., 2010; Hsieh, Hornberger, Piguet, & Hodges, 2012; Omar et al., 2011; Sivasathiaseelan et al., 2019; Warren, Rohrer, Rossor, 2013). The rare phenomenon of selective musical anhedonia has been described following focal lesions of amygdala and insula (Griffiths, Warren, Dean, & Howard, 2004), prime sites of involvement in FTD syndromes. Compared with healthy older controls, patients with bvFTD also have difficulty inferring more complex affective mental states (though not nonmental representations) from music (Downey et al., 2013); again, music here is signaling a core deficit of bvFTD affecting mentalizing or "theory of mind" (Bora, Walterfang, & Velakoulis, 2015). On the other hand, patients with bvFTD can reliably detect dissonance and change in musical (major/ minor) mode (Agustus et al., 2015), arguing that their deficit lies predominantly with higher order "symbolic" processing of emotions rather than the perception of more elementary affective cues in music. In PD, recognition of musical emotions appears to be more variable (Lima, Garrett, & Castro, 2013; Saenz et al., 2013). One relevant factor may be the degree of stimulus ambiguity, as these patients seem to be more susceptible to response bias (Laskowska, Gawryś, Łęski, & Koziorowski, 2015).

Assignment of reward value to music has been little addressed in people with dementia. Building on evidence that normal listeners find melodies with a harmonic structure that fulfils expectations subjectively pleasurable or rewarding but unresolved melodies unpleasant (Koelsch, Kilches, Steinbeis, & Schelinski, 2008; Salimpoor et al., 2015), one study found that patients with bvFTD and SD rated the pleasantness of "unfinished" melodies differently from healthy age-matched individuals, whereas patients with AD and PNFA performed comparably to controls (Clark et al., 2018). A further consideration here is that impaired explicit understanding of musical emotions does not preclude a patient continuing to derive pleasure from music (Matthews, Chang, De May, Engstrom, & Miller, 2009).

The functional neuroanatomy of musical emotion and reward processing has been quite widely studied in the healthy brain (Blood & Zatorre, 2001; Blood, Zatorre, Bermudez, & Evans, 1999; Koelsch, 2014; Lehne et al., 2014; Menon & Levitin, 2005; Salimpoor et al., 2013, 2015; Steinbeis & Koelsch, 2009; Zatorre & Salimpoor, 2013; Fig. 4.1). This work has demonstrated that the neural substrates of musical emotion are very extensive. These substrates encompass structures that analyze relatively elementary affective attributes (such as roughness and dissonance) or mediate autonomic responses, in medial temporal lobe and insula; higher order areas that evaluate salience and behavioral relevance and the representation of mental states, in medial prefrontal and orbitofrontal cortices; and subcortical (mesolimbic) dopaminergic circuits involved in coding reward value, including nucleus accumbens and ventral striatum. There is an important overlap with the musical semantic memory network, underscoring the role of familiarity in musical preference (Brown, Martinez, & Parsons, 2004; Lehne et al., 2014; Pereira et al., 2011). The neuroanatomical evidence in dementia syndromes aligns with this picture in the normal brain. Music emotion recognition across dementia syndromes has been correlated with gray matter loss in a similar distributed cerebral network including insula, orbitofrontal cortex, anterior cingulate and medial prefrontal and anterior temporal cortices, amygdala, and the subcortical mesolimbic system (Hsieh et al., 2012; Omar et al., 2011). More specifically, musical mental state attribution in bvFTD correlated with atrophy of anterior temporal and ventromedial prefrontal cortices (Downey et al., 2013), while processing of musical affective reward value correlated with atrophy of orbitofrontal cortex (Clark et al., 2018), all areas that have been implicated in theory of mind and musical reward processing in the healthy brain (Lehne et al., 2014; Salimpoor et al., 2015; Steinbeis & Koelsch, 2009; Zahn et al., 2007, 2009). In a functional MRI study (Agustus et al., 2015), the processing of musical mode variation was associated with reduced activation of brainstem raphe nuclei in bvFTD compared with healthy older controls: these brainstem nuclei are hubs of serotonergic and noradrenergic transmission and regulate emotional arousal.

Musical behaviors

Ultimately, the meaning and emotional resonance of musical objects must be integrated into an appropriate behavioral response. This might be attentive listening, dancing, or singing along. However, more specific behavioral outputs—both functional and dysfunctional—are possible, and progress has been made toward characterizing these in people with dementia.

Playing a musical instrument is a specialized skill that depends on musical procedural memory: the implicit memory system that governs the performance of learned motor skills and routines. A number of case studies of patients with AD have reported retained proficiency on a previously learned instrument and ability to learn new pieces, even in more severe disease stage (Baird & Samson, 2009; Beatty, 1999; Beatty et al., 1994; Cowles et al., 2003; Fornazzari et al., 2006; Polk & Kertesz, 1993). These studies also demonstrate that competence playing an instrument may be maintained despite ideomotor apraxia (Beatty et al., 1994, 1999). Although studies are scarce, preserved and even acquired competence playing an instrument are also well documented in SD and bvFTD (Cho et al., 2015; Miller, Boone, Cummings, Read, & Mishkin, 2000; Omar et al., 2010; Weinstein et al., 2011). On the other hand, inability to regulate tempo when playing the piano has been described as an early feature of PD (Rossi, Cerquetti, & Merello, 2015). While direct neuroanatomical correlation is lacking, musical procedural memory is likely to be mediated by subcortical structures (basal ganglia and cerebellum) and primary sensorimotor cortices that are relatively resistant to the pathological process in many dementias, though relatively more susceptible in PD (Groussard et al., 2019; Kleber, Veit, Birbaumer, Gruzelier, & Lotze, 2010).

Alterations in musical behavior resulting from neurodegenerative disease are less often addressed by psychologists and music therapists but may be a striking feature of some dementia syndromes, particularly SD and bvFTD. A number of these patients develop intense, intrusive craving for music (musicophilia) or aversion to music, usually as part of a more widespread alteration of hedonic reactivity to sounds and diverse other stimuli (including food and sex) with biological reward potential (Boeve & Geda, 2001; Fletcher et al., 2013; Fletcher, Clark, & Warren, 2014, 2015; Geroldi et al., 2000; Mendez & Shapira, 2013; Perry et al., 2014; Woolley et al., 2007). There may be quite striking alteration of musical tastes (Boeve & Geda, 2001; Geroldi et al., 2000). Other patients with FTD exhibit a drive to create music that was not evident prior to onset of the illness, sometimes very competently (Miller et al., 2000); this appears to be part of a spectrum of liberated artistic creativity reported in FTD and has been particularly linked to the presence of atrophy involving the left anterior temporal lobe and its connections. It has been proposed that this phenomenon reflects paradoxical facilitation of relatively intact right cerebral mechanisms that mediate creativity in the context of damaged left-sided inhibitory controls (Miller et al., 2000; Seeley et al., 2008). Marked behavioral shifts in music-seeking behavior appear to be substantially less common in AD and other dementia syndromes.

While the brain basis for these behaviors remains poorly understood, available structural neuroanatomical evidence implicates a network of brain regions previously linked to reward valuation and appetitive behaviors. Using voxel-based morphometry, music aversion has been associated with atrophy of hippocampus and amygdala, entorhinal cortex, and insula, while development of musicophilia may correlate with relative preservation of hippocampus and concurrent atrophy of orbitofrontal cortex (Fletcher et al., 2013, 2015). Abnormal musical behaviors do not appear to be linked in any straightforward way to prior musical expertise or altered perception of music.

From a clinical perspective, abnormal valuation and emotional reactions to music in patients with diseases such as bvFTD and SD underscore the striking dependence of complex human behaviors on anterior frontotemporal and limbic network integrity: in these diseases, abnormal musical responsiveness signals a much broader repertoire of socioemotional dysfunction. On the other hand, for many people living with dementia, music provides an avenue to emotional engagement and continued participation in social activities long after their illness has closed many other such outlets. Retained musical competence is to some extent predictable in neurodegenerative diseases (such as AD) that spare the subcortical circuitry that sustains musical procedural memory; though we continue to be surprised by the sometimes remarkable musicality of individual patients with devastated extramusical cognition. Music may also focus patients' energies and help in managing troublesome behaviors, particularly in SD and bvFTD, though just occasionally obsessional craving for music may present a management issue in its own right.

A synthesis of musical phenotypes in major dementias

The profile of deficits across musical processing stages constitutes the "musical phenotype" of a particular dementia. Cardinal features of the musical phenotypes of the dementias we have been considering here are presented in Table 4.2 and their neuroanatomical profiles in Fig. 4.2. One important caveat is that diseases have generally not been assessed systematically in each domain of music processing, rather, particular musical functions have been targeted for study according to the symptoms patients commonly exhibit. This is potentially a source of bias in comparing musical phenotypes between diseases.

AD is characterized by impaired auditory scene analysis and musical episodic memory but relatively spared musical semantic and procedural memory; processing of "global" melodic contour patterns and harmonic relationships is also affected. This profile reflects the predominant involvement of posterior temporoparietal brain networks (see Fig. 4.2).

PD is often associated with deficits of temporal pattern perception and musical "executive function" (as indexed, e.g., by response inhibition); musical hallucinations are relatively more prominent than with other neurodegenerative diseases (though less common than other modalities of hallucinations), recognition of musical emotions may be affected and dopaminergic tone is likely to modulate deficits. These features are attributable to involvement of basal ganglia and corticosubcortical circuitry.

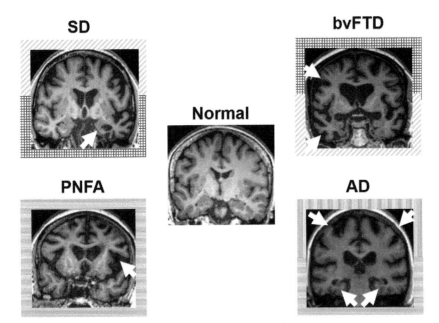

FIGURE 4.2 Musical phenotypes in some major dementia syndromes.
The panels show representative anatomical (T1-weighted) coronal brain MRI sections from patients with selected dementia syndromes and associated profiles of selective cerebral regional atrophy, in comparison to the brain of a healthy 61-year-old individual (normal, center). The left hemisphere is presented on the right in all sections; overlaid white arrows indicate the site of characteristic regional atrophy in each dementia syndrome. The frames for each clinical panel are coded following the shading convention corresponding to the cognitive operations principally affected in each syndrome, as delineated in the modular model of music processing represented in Fig. 4.1. Represented are typical AD, with medial temporal and parietal lobe atrophy symmetrically involving both cerebral hemispheres; PNFA, with predominantly left-sided atrophy involving peri-Sylvian cortices; SD, with predominantly left-sided anteromedial temporal lobe atrophy; and bvFTD, with frontal and temporal lobe atrophy more marked in the right hemisphere. *AD*, Alzheimer's disease; *bvFTD*, behavioral variant frontotemporal dementia; *MRI*, magnetic resonance imaging; *PNFA*, progressive nonfluent aphasia; *SD*, semantic dementia.

bvFTD characteristically affects the recognition of musical emotion with abnormal processing of musical reward and frequently, abnormal hedonic behaviors in response to music; there may be accompanying deficits of temporal and pitch pattern processing. These features reflect the prominent involvement of frontal lobe circuitry mediating socioemotional signal and reward processing, with more variable involvement of peri-Sylvian and posterior cortices (see Fig. 4.2).

SD produces a phenotype of impaired melody, musical instrument, and musical emotion recognition, frequently with abnormal musical hedonic processing and behavior; perception of musical patterns tends to be spared. This profile reflects the selective involvement of the anteromedial temporal lobes and adjacent orbitofrontal and insular cortices (see Fig. 4.2).

PNFA is associated with prominent deficits of pitch, temporal, and timbral pattern analysis which may be modulated by auditory working memory capacity; musical reward processing and hedonic behavior appear to be relatively unaffected. These features reflect the predominant involvement of peri-Sylvian cortices in this syndrome (see Fig. 4.2).

New formulations of music processing in dementia

Recent influential paradigms emerging from cognitive neuroscience promise to help us reformulate and better understand disorders of music processing in the dementias.

Universal hierarchical models of musical information processing proposed by Rohrmeier and Koelsch (Koelsch, 2011; Koelsch, Rohrmeier, Torrecuso, & Jentschke, 2013; Rohrmeier, Zuidema, Wiggins, & Scharff, 2015) emphasize structural "syntactic" relations (such as harmonic progressions and the nesting of melodic and rhythmic motifs) over different timescales. The processing of this syntactic hierarchy is computationally analogous to human language processing but also core to musical "meaning" (i.e., meaning that is purely musical and does not rely on extramusical associations); even musically untrained listeners implicitly acquire the relevant syntactic rules through exposure to the dominant musical culture. The important role of cognitive expectation in these syntactical models suggests that they may be reconciled with a very general paradigm of brain function that has gained wide currency: predictive coding. The predictive coding paradigm posits that the brain's fundamental computational task is to infer the state of its environment by making predictions about the world at large and bodily states that are then updated based on experience (Friston, Daunizeau, Kilner, & Kiebel, 2010; Friston & Kiebel, 2009; Koelsch, Vuust, & Friston, 2019). The essential computational module that supports predictive coding is repeated at each stage of the neural processing hierarchy: this module comprises an incoming (feedforward) or "update" signal, a stored template (expectation) corresponding to the predicted signal, and a top-down modulatory signal (feedback) that constrains the expectation.

The modular and iterative nature of these models suggests a generic mechanism by which neurodegenerative diseases that deposit pathogenic proteins in neural tissue may produce dynamic and widespread effects across large-scale brain networks. The effects of molecular pathology at the level of local neural microcircuits would be scaled and propagated up (and down) the predictive coding hierarchy, initially as dysfunctional information flow and (ultimately) as spreading pathogenic proteins. Music is an ideal probe of information flow in this system: it is built from acoustic regularities and establishes strong perceptual predictions based on "rules" internalized from past experience, but at the same time, it often violates or defers expectations to achieve its most salient effects ("chills" are a case in point: Huron, 2006).

The complexity of music further ensures that it samples the entire processing hierarchy, ranging from early perceptual analysis to the programming of complex behaviors (see Fig. 4.1).

A predictive coding framework might uncover common principles underpinning the rich phenomenology of disordered music processing in the dementias. Related approaches are already proving fruitful: examples include the modeling of musical hallucinosis as a disorder of overactive top-down predictions (Kumar et al., 2014) and in gait training for PD, a rationale for using rhythmic cues to reset dysfunctional feedback signaling (Pohl, Dizdar, & Hallert, 2013; Thaut et al., 1996; Thaut, McIntosh, McIntosh, & Hoemberg, 2001).

Conclusion and future directions

The study of music processing in dementia is at a crossroads. Considerable progress has been made in defining a spectrum of disorders and in applying sophisticated (especially, neuroimaging) techniques borrowed from basic neuroscience to elucidate the brain mechanisms by which neurodegenerative pathologies impact musicality. However, we lack validated neuropsychological instruments for quantifying deficits in cognitively impaired listeners from a range of musical backgrounds and the literature is still largely informed by studies in a single disease. Systematic evaluation of the modules of music cognition in larger patient cohorts representing a wider range of neurodegenerative pathologies will be required to redress this; particularly for rarer diseases, this may entail multicenter collaborative studies. Key unresolved issues concern the basis for individual variation within cohorts, the effects of prior musical expertise, and the longitudinal evolution of musical phenotypes. If such issues can be addressed, it is possible to envisage "musical biomarkers" that track the progress of neurodegeneration and (given the computational demands imposed by certain musical tasks) might constitute early diagnostic signals of disease. To date, appropriately, music psychologists have adopted a largely reductionist approach to the analysis of musical deficits, breaking music into its component cognitive parts to assess how these are affected by disease. However, music in the real world is a highly integrative phenomenon, and it is likely that a more complete picture of musical deficits and competencies in dementia will require an appreciation of the ways in which different dimensions of music (e.g., emotion, familiarity, and the musical autobiographical record) interact.

At present, our mapping of the musical brain in dementia is essentially static and piecemeal. Incorporation of dynamic neuroimaging and physiological tools that can capture the time course of processing and interactions between neural circuits will likely greatly enrich this picture. Defining network connectivity using functional MRI will take an important step toward this goal and magnetoencephalography is a particularly attractive proposition, both by virtue of its exquisite temporal resolution (which can track neuronal activity directly, without the latency imposed by the hemodynamic function) and its stratification of activity arising from different components of the cortical microcircuit. Alongside neuroimaging techniques, recording physiological markers of autonomic arousal (such as pupillary dilatation, heart rate, and electrodermal activity) may be highly pertinent to the study of music processing in neurodegenerative disease: such techniques provide objective indices of behavioral phenomena (such as hedonic valuation) that are difficult to measure and may also signal dissociations between cognitive and affective response (e.g., to musical familiarity) that would otherwise go undetected. Furthermore, autonomic recording techniques might extend the range of disease severity that can be meaningfully assessed, both in patients who can no longer perform pencil and paper tests and in very early stage disease before changes become apparent on conventional tests.

For those living with dementia, as well as clinicians, the ultimate purpose of understanding music processing in these diseases is to design effective music-based interventions that can improve patients' quality of life, adjustment to their illness, and perhaps cognitive function. For the first time, a rational approach to this challenge seems to be at hand, due in no small measure to the discovery that the musical brain can be remarkably resilient as well as vulnerable to the effects of neurodegenerative pathologies. The finding that musical semantic memory and emotional reactivity are relatively spared in AD, for example, gives a neurobiological impetus to the use of personalized playlists of favorite music to improve well-being (Garrido et al., 2018, 2019; Groussard et al., 2019). The use of rhythm cues to improve motor function in PD is another instance of a neurophysiological principle harnessed for therapeutic ends (Dauvergne et al., 2018; Dalla Bella et al., 2015; Hove & Keller, 2015; Murgia et al., 2018; Nombela et al., 2013; Volpe et al., 2013). Studies that directly examine the interaction of music with brain functional organization are potentially a powerful endorsement for the use of musical interventions and behavioral responses as a "proxy" for neural effects (King et al., 2019; Trost et al., 2018). It is clear that to be effective, music therapies cannot be "one-size-fits-all": rather, they should be customized, both to the particular illness and to the individual patient, taking account of psychosocial milieu, mood, and disease stage (Garrido et al., 2018). In FTD, for example, musical playlists are unlikely to benefit a person who has profound music aversion but may provide very useful behavioral regulation in someone else with musicophilia (Raglio et al., 2012). All in all, this is an exciting era for musical brain research in dementia, with grounds for optimism that the ancient hope of using music as medicine may finally be realized.

Acknowledgments

EB holds a Brain Research UK PhD Studentship. JDW receives grant support from the Alzheimer's Society, Alzheimer's Research UK, Wolfson Foundation, Association of

British Neurologists and Guarantors of Brain, Action on Hearing Loss, National Brain Appeal, and the NIHR UCL/UCLH Biomedical Research Centre.

References

Abe, M., Tabei, K.-I., Satoh, M., Fukuda, M., Daikuhara, H., Shiga, M., ... Tomimoto, H. (2018). Impairment of the missing fundamental phenomenon in individuals with Alzheimer's disease: A neuropsychological and voxel-based morphometric study. *Dementia and Geriatric Cognitive Disorders Extra*, *8*(1), 23−32. Available from https://doi.org/10.1159/000486331.

Abrams, D. A., Bhatara, A., Ryali, S., et al. (2011). Decoding temporal structure in music and speech relies on shared brain resources but elicits different fine-scale spatial patterns. *Cerebral Cortex*, *21*, 1507−1518.

Agustus, J. L., Golden, H. L., Callaghan, M. F., Bond, R. L., Benhamou, E., Hailstone, J. C., ... Warren, J. D. (2018). Melody processing characterizes functional neuroanatomy in the aging brain. *Frontiers in Neuroscience*, *12*, 815.

Agustus, J. L., Mahoney, C. J., Downey, L. E., Omar, R., Cohen, M., White, M. J., ... Warren, J. D. (2015). Functional MRI of music emotion processing in frontotemporal dementia. *Annals of the New York Academy of Sciences*, *1337*, 232−240.

Baird, A., Brancatisano, O., Gelding, R., & Thompson, W. F. (2018). Characterization of music and photograph evoked autobiographical memories in people with Alzheimer's disease. *Journal of Alzheimer's Disease*, *66*(2), 693−706.

Baird, A., & Samson, S. (2009). Memory for music in Alzheimer's disease: Unforgettable? *Neuropsychology Review*, *19*(1), 85−101. Available from https://doi.org/10.1007/s11065-009-9085-2.

Ballard, K. J., Savage, S., Leyton, C. E., Vogel, A. P., Hornberger, M., & Hodges, J. R. (2014). Logopenic and nonfluent variants of primary progressive aphasia are differentiated by acoustic measures of speech production. *PLoS One*, *9*(2), e89864. Available from https://doi.org/10.1371/journal.pone.0089864.

Barlett, J. C., Halpern, A. R., & Dowling, W. J. (1995). Recognition of familiar and unfamiliar melodies in normal aging and Alzheimer's disease. *Memory & Cognition*, *23*(5), 531−546.

Beatty, W. W. (1999). Preserved cognitive skills in dementia: Implications for geriatric medicine. *Journal of the Oklahoma State Medical Association*, *92*(1), 10−12.

Beatty, W. W., Rogers, C. L., Rogers, R. L., English, S., Testa, J. A., Orbelo, D. M., & Ross, E. D. (1999). Piano playingin Alzheimer's disease: Longitudinal study of a single case. *Neurocase*, *5*, 459−469.

Beatty, W. W., Winn, P., Adams, R. L., Allen, E. W., Wilson, D. A., Prince, J. R., ... Littleford, D. (1994). Preserved cognitive skills in dementia of the Alzheimer type. *Archives of Neurology*, *51*, 1040−1046.

Blood, A. J., & Zatorre, R. J. (2001). Intensely pleasurable responses to music correlate with activity in brain regions implicated in reward and emotion. *Proceedings of the National Academy of Sciences*, *98*(20), 11818−11823.

Blood, A. J., Zatorre, R. J., Bermudez, P., & Evans, A. C. (1999). Emotional responses to pleasant and unpleasant music correlate with activity in paralimbic brain regions. *Nature Neuroscience*, *2*(4), 382−387. Available from https://doi.org/10.1038/7299.

Boeve, B. F., & Geda, Y. E. (2001). Polka music and semantic dementia. *Neurology*, *57*(8), 1485.

Bora, E., Walterfang, M., & Velakoulis, D. (2015). Theory of mind in behavioural-variant frontotemporal dementia and Alzheimer's disease: A meta-analysis. *Journal of Neurology, Neurosurgery, and Psychiatry, 86*(7), 714–719.

Bregman, A. S. (1990). *Auditory scene analysis: The perceptual organization of sound.* Cambridge: MIT Press.

Brown, S., Martinez, M. J., & Parsons, L. M. (2004). Passive music listening spontaneously engages limbic and paralimbic systems. *Neuroreport, 15*(13), 2033–2037.

Burunat, I., Alluri, V., Toiviainen, P., Numminen, J., & Brattico, E. (2014). Dynamics of brain activity underlying working memory for music in a naturalistic condition. *Cortex, 57,* 254–269. Available from https://doi.org/10.1016/j.cortex.2014.04.012.

Cadena-Valencia, J., García-Garibay, O., Merchant, H., Jazayeri, M., & de Lafuente, V. (2018). Entrainment and maintenance of an internal metronome in supplementary motor area. *ELife,* 7. Available from https://doi.org/10.7554/eLife.38983.

Cameron, D. J., Pickett, K. A., Earhart, G. M., & Grahn, J. A. (2016). The effect of dopaminergic medication on beat-based auditory timing in Parkinson's disease. *Frontiers in Neurology, 7,* 19. Available from https://doi.org/10.3389/fneur.2016.00019.

Campanelli, A., Rendace, L., Parisi, F., D'Antonio, F., Imbriano, L., de Lena, C., & Trebbastoni, A. (2016). Musical cognition in Alzheimer's disease: Application of the Montreal Battery of Evaluation of Amusia. *Annals of the New York Academy of Sciences, 1375*(1), 28–37. Available from https://doi.org/10.1111/nyas.13155.

Chen, J. L., Zatorre, R. J., & Penhune, V. B. (2006). Interactions between auditory and dorsal premotor cortex during synchronization to musical rhythms. *NeuroImage, 32,* 1771–1781.

Chen, J. L., Penhune, V. B., & Zatorre, R. J. (2008). Listening to musical rhythms recruits motor regions of the brain. *Cerebral Cortex, 18,* 2844–2854.

Cho, H., Chin, J., Suh, M. K., Kim, H. J., Kim, Y. J., Ye, B. S., ... Na, D. L. (2015). Postmorbid learning of saxophone playing in a patient with frontotemporal dementia. *Neurocase, 21*(6), 767–772.

Clark, C. N., Downey, L. E., & Warren, J. D. (2014). Music biology: All this useful beauty. *Current Biology: CB, 24*(6), R234–R237. Available from https://doi.org/10.1016/j.cub.2014.02.013.

Clark, C. N., Golden, H. L., McCallion, O., Nicholas, J. M., Cohen, M. H., Slattery, C. F., ... Warren, J. D. (2018). Music models aberrant rule decoding and reward valuation in dementia. *Social Cognitive and Affective Neuroscience, 13*(2), 192–202. Available from https://doi.org/10.1093/scan/nsx140.

Clark, C. N., Golden, H. L., & Warren, J. D. (2015). Acquired amusia. *Handbook of Clinical Neurology, 129,* 607–631. Available from https://doi.org/10.1016/B978-0-444-62630-1.00034-2.

Cowles, A., Beatty, W. W., Nixon, S. J., Lutz, L. J., Paulk, J., Paulk, K., & Ross, E. D. (2003). Musical skill in dementia: A violinist presumed to have Alzheimer's disease learns to play a new song. *Neurocase, 9,* 493–503.

Cuddy, L. L., & Duffin, J. (2005). Music, memory, and Alzheimer's disease: Is music recognition spared in dementia, and how can it be assessed? *Medical Hypotheses, 64,* 229–235.

Cuddy, L. L., Duffin, J. M., Gill, S. S., Brown, C. L., Ritu, S., & Vanstone, A. D. (2012). Memory for melodies and lyrics in Alzheimer's disease. *Music Percept, 29,* 479–491.

Cuddy, L. L., Sikka, R., & Vanstone, A. (2015). Preservation of musical memory and engagement in healthy aging and Alzheimer's disease. *Annals of the New York Academy of Sciences, 1337,* 223–231. Available from https://doi.org/10.1111/nyas.12617.

Dalla Bella, S., Benoit, C.-E., Farrugia, N., Schwartze, M., & Kotz, S. A. (2015). Effects of musically cued gait training in Parkinson's disease: Beyond a motor benefit. *Annals of the New York Academy of Sciences, 1337*, 77–85.

Dauvergne, C., Bégel, V., Gény, C., Puyjarinet, F., Laffont, I., & Dalla Bella, S. (2018). Home-based training of rhythmic skills with a serious game in Parkinson's disease: Usability and acceptability. *Annals of Physical and Rehabilitation Medicinne, 61*(6), 380–385.

Delis, D. C., Massman, P. J., Butters, N., Salmon, D. P., Shear, P. K., Demadura, T., & Filoteo, J. V. (1992). Spatial cognition in Alzheimer's disease: Subtypes of global-local impairment. *Journal of Clinical and Experimental Neuropsychology, 14*(4), 463–477. Available from https://doi.org/10.1080/01688639208402838.

Downey, L. E., Blezat, A., Nicholas, J., Omar, R., Golden, H. L., Mahoney, C. J., ... Warren, J. D. (2013). Mentalising music in frontotemporal dementia. *Cortex, 49*(7), 1844–1855. Available from https://doi.org/10.1016/j.cortex.2012.09.011.

Drapeau, J., Gosselin, N., Gagnon, L., Peretz, I., & Lorrain, D. (2009). Emotional recognition from face, voice, and music in dementia of the Alzheimer type. *Annals of the New York Academy of Sciences, 1169*, 342–345.

El Haj, M., Fasotti, L., & Allain, P. (2012). The involuntary nature of music-evoked autobiographical memories in Alzheimer's disease. *Consciousness and Cognition, 21*(1), 238–246. Available from https://doi.org/10.1016/j.concog.2011.12.005.

El Haj, M., Antoine, P., Nandrino, J. L., Gély-Nargeot, M.-C., & Raffard, S. (2015). Self-defining memories during exposure to music in Alzheimer's disease. *International Psychogeriatrics, 27*(10), 1719–1730.

Eustache, F., Lechevalier, B., Viader, F., et al. (1990). Identification and discrimination disorders in auditory perception: A report on two cases. *Neuropsychologia, 28*, 257–270.

Eversfield, C. L., & Orton, L. D. (2018). Auditory and visual hallucination prevalence in Parkinson's disease and dementia with Lewy bodies: A systematic review and meta-analysis. *Psychological Medicine, 49*, 2342–2353.

Finke, C., Esfahani, N. E., & Ploner, C. J. (2012). Preservation of musical memory in an amnesic professional cellist. *Current Biology: CB, 22*(15), R591–R592. Available from https://doi.org/10.1016/j.cub.2012.05.041.

Fletcher, P. D., Clark, C. N., & Warren, J. D. (2014). Music, reward and frontotemporal dementia. *Brain, 137*(10), e300. Available from https://doi.org/10.1093/brain/awu145.

Fletcher, P. D., Downey, L. E., Golden, H. L., Clark, C. N., Slattery, C. F., Paterson, R. W., ... Warren, J. D. (2015). Auditory hedonic phenotypes in dementia: A behavioural and neuroanatomical analysis. *Cortex, 67*(Suppl. C), 95–105. Available from https://doi.org/10.1016/j.cortex.2015.03.021.

Fletcher, P. D., Downey, L., Witoonpanich, P., & Warren, J. (2013). The brain basis of musicophilia: Evidence from frontotemporal lobar degeneration. *Frontiers in Auditory Cognitive Neuroscience, 4*, 347.

Ford, J. H., Addis, D. R., & Giovanello, K. S. (2011). Differential neural activity during search of specific and general autobiographical memories elicited by musical cues. *Neuropsychologia, 49*(9), 2514–2526.

Fornazzari, L., Castle, T., Nadkarni, S., Ambrose, M., Miranda, D., Apana-siewicz, N., & Phillips, F. (2006). Preservation of episodic musical memory in a pianist with Alzheimer disease. *Neurology, 66*, 32–37.

Freitas, C., Manzato, E., Burini, A., Taylor, M. J., Lerch, J. P., & Anagnostou, E. (2018). Neural correlates of familiarity in music listening: A systematic review and a neuroimaging meta-analysis. *Frontiers in Neuroscience, 12*, 686.

Friston, K., & Kiebel, S. (2009). Predictive coding under the free-energy principle. *Philosophical Transactions of the Royal Society of London. Series B, Biological Sciences*, *364*(1521), 1211−1221. Available from https://doi.org/10.1098/rstb.2008.0300.

Friston, K. J., Daunizeau, J., Kilner, J., & Kiebel, S. J. (2010). Action and behavior: A free-energy formulation. *Biological Cybernetics*, *102*(3), 227−260. Available from https://doi.org/10.1007/s00422-010-0364-z.

Gagnon, L., Peretz, I., & Fülöp, T. (2009). Musical structural determinants of emotional judgments in dementia of the Alzheimer type. *Neuropsychology*, *23*(1), 90−97. Available from https://doi.org/10.1037/a0013790.

Garrido, S., Stevens, C. J., Chang, E., Dunne, L., & Perz, J. (2018). Music and dementia: Individual differences in response to personalized playlists. *Journal of Alzheimer's Disease: JAD*, *64*(3), 933−941.

Garrido, S., Stevens, C. J., Chang, E., Dunne, L., & Perz, J. (2019). Musical features and affective responses to personalized playlists in people with probable dementia. *American Journal of Alzheimer's Disease and Other Dementias*, *34*(4), 247−253. Available from https://doi.org/10.1177/1533317518808011.

Geiser, E., & Kaelin-Lang, A. (2011). The function of dopaminergic neural signal transmission in auditory pulse perception: Evidence from dopaminergic treatment in Parkinson's patients. *Behavioural Brain Research*, *225*(1), 270−275.

Geroldi, C., Metitieri, T., Binetti, G., Zanetti, O., Trabucchi, M., & Frisoni, G. B. (2000). Pop music and frontotemporal dementia. *Neurology*, *55*(12), 1935−1936. Available from https://doi.org/10.1212/wnl.55.12.1935.

Golden, E. C., & Josephs, K. A. (2015). Minds on replay: Musical hallucinations and their relationship to neurological disease. *Brain*, *138*(12), 3793−3802. Available from https://doi.org/10.1093/brain/awv286.

Golden, H. L., Agustus, J. L., Goll, J. C., Downey, L. E., Mummery, C. J., Schott, J. M., … Warren, J. D. (2015). Functional neuroanatomy of auditory scene analysis in Alzheimer's disease. *NeuroImage Clinical*, *7*, 699−708.

Golden, H. L., Agustus, J. L., Nicholas, J. M., Schott, J. M., Crutch, S. J., Mancini, L., & Warren, J. D. (2016). Functional neuroanatomy of spatial sound processing in Alzheimer's disease. *Neurobiology of Aging*, *39*, 154−164.

Golden, H. L., Clark, C. N., Nicholas, J. M., Cohen, M. H., Slattery, C. F., Paterson, R. W., … Warren, J. D. (2017). Music perception in dementia. *Journal of Alzheimer's Disease*, 1−18. Available from https://doi.org/10.3233/JAD-160359.

Golden, H. L., Downey, L. E., Fletcher, P. D., Mahoney, C. J., Schott, J. M., Mummery, C. J., … Warren, J. D. (2015). Identification of environmental sounds and melodies in syndromes of anterior temporal lobe degeneration. *Journal of the Neurological Sciences*, *352*(1−2), 94−98. Available from https://doi.org/10.1016/j.jns.2015.03.007.

Golden, H. L., Nicholas, J. M., Yong, K. X. X., Downey, L. E., Schott, J. M., Mummery, C. J., … Warren, J. D. (2015). Auditory spatial processing in Alzheimer's disease. *Brain: A Journal of Neurology*, *138*(Pt 1), 189−202.

Goll, J. C., Crutch, S. J., Loo, J. H. Y., Rohrer, J. D., Frost, C., Bamiou, D.-E., & Warren, J. D. (2010). Non-verbal sound processing in the primary progressive aphasias. *Brain*, *133*(1), 272−285. Available from https://doi.org/10.1093/brain/awp235.

Goll, J. C., Crutch, S. J., & Warren, J. D. (2010). Central auditory disorders: Toward a neuropsychology of auditory objects. *Current Opinion in Neurology*, *23*(6), 617−627. Available from https://doi.org/10.1097/WCO.0b013e32834027f6.

Goll, J. C., Kim, L. G., Hailstone, J. C., Lehmann, M., Buckley, A., Crutch, S. J., & Warren, J. D. (2011). Auditory object cognition in dementia. *Neuropsychologia, 49*(9), 2755−2765. Available from https://doi.org/10.1016/j.neuropsychologia.2011.06.004.

Goll, J. C., Kim, L. G., Ridgway, G. R., Hailstone, J. C., Lehmann, M., Buckley, A. H., ... Warren, J. D. (2012). Impairments of auditory scene analysis in Alzheimer's disease. *Brain: A Journal of Neurology, 135*(Pt 1), 190−200.

Grahn, J. A. (2012). Neural mechanisms of rhythm perception: Current findings and future perspectives. *Topics in Cognitive Science, 4*, 585−606.

Grahn, J. A., & Brett, M. (2007). Rhythm and beat perception in motor areas of the brain. *Journal of Cognitive Neuroscience, 19*(5), 893−906. Available from https://doi.org/10.1162/jocn.2007.19.5.893.

Grahn, J. A., & Brett, M. (2009). Impairment of beat-based rhythm discrimination in Parkinson's disease. *Cortex; A Journal Devoted to the Study of the Nervous System and Behavior, 45*(1), 54−61. Available from https://doi.org/10.1016/j.cortex.2008.01.005.

Griffiths, T. D. (2000). Musical hallucinosis in acquired deafness. Phenomenology and brain substrate. *Brain: A Journal of Neurology, 123*(Pt 10), 2065−2076. Available from https://doi.org/10.1093/brain/123.10.2065.

Griffiths, T. D., & Warren, J. D. (2002). The planum temporale as a computational hub. *Trends Neuroscience, 25*(7), 348−353.

Griffiths, T. D., & Warren, J. D. (2004). What is an auditory object? *Nature Reviews. Neuroscience, 5*(11), 887−892.

Griffiths, T. D., Johnsrude, I., Dean, J. L., et al. (1999). A common neural substrate for the analysis of pitch and duration pattern in segmented sound? *Neuroreport, 10*, 3825−3830.

Griffiths, T. D., Warren, J. D., Dean, J. L., & Howard, D. (2004). "When the feeling's gone": A selective loss of musical emotion. *Journal of Neurology, Neurosurgery, and Psychiatry, 75* (2), 344−345.

Grossman, M. (2012). The non-fluent/agrammatic variant of primary progressive aphasia. *Lancet Neurol, 11*, 545−555.

Groussard, M., Chan, T. G., Coppalle, R., & Platel, H. (2019). Preservation of musical memory throughout the progression of Alzheimer's disease? Toward a reconciliation of theoretical, clinical, and neuroimaging evidence. *Journal of Alzheimer's Disease: JAD, 68*(3), 857−883. Available from https://doi.org/10.3233/JAD-180474.

Groussard, M., La Joie, R., Rauchs, G., Landeau, B., Chételat, G., Viader, F., ... Platel, H. (2010). When music and long-term memory interact: Effects of musical expertise on functional and structural plasticity in the hippocampus. *PLoS One, 5*(10). Available from https://doi.org/10.1371/journal.pone.0013225.

Groussard, M., Rauchs, G., Landeau, B., Viader, F., Desgranges, B., Eustache, F., & Platel, H. (2010). The neural substrates of musical memory revealed by fMRI and two semantic tasks. *NeuroImage, 53*(4), 1301−1309.

Grube, M., Bruffaerts, R., Schaeverbeke, J., Neyens, V., De Weer, A.-S., Seghers, A., ... Vandenberghe, R. (2016). Core auditory processing deficits in primary progressive aphasia. *Brain, 139*(6), 1817−1829.

Grube, M., Cooper, F. E., & Griffiths, T. D. (2013). Auditory temporal-regularity processing correlates with language and literacy skill in early adulthood. *Cognitive Neuroscience, 4*(3−4), 225−230.

Guehl, D., Burbaud, P., Lorenzi, C., Ramos, C., Bioulac, B., Semal, C., & Demany, L. (2008). Auditory temporal processing in Parkinson's disease. *Neuropsychologia, 46*(9), 2326−2335.

Gutschalk, A., &. Dykstra, A. (2014). Functional imaging of auditory scene analysis. *Hearing Research, 307*, 98–110.

Hailstone, J. C., Crutch, S. J., Vestergaard, M. D., et al. (2010). Progressive associative phonagnosia: A neuropsychological analysis. *Neuropsychologia, 48*, 1104–1114.

Hailstone, J. C., Omar, R., Henley, S. M., et al. (2009). It's not what you play, it's how you play it: Timbre affects perception of emotion in music. *The Quarterly Journal of Experimental Psychology, 62*, 2141–2155.

Hailstone, J. C., Omar, R., & Warren, J. D. (2009). Relatively preserved knowledge of music in semantic dementia. *Journal of Neurology, Neurosurgery, and Psychiatry, 80*, 808–809.

Halpern, A. R., Golden, H. L., Magdalinou, N., Witoonpanich, P., & Warren, J. D. (2015). Musical tasks targeting preserved and impaired functions in two dementias. *Annals of the New York Academy of Sciences, 1337*(1), 241–248.

Hardy, C. J. D., Agustus, J. L., Marshall, C. R., Clark, C. N., Russell, L. L., Bond, R. L., ... Warren, J. D. (2017a). Behavioural and neuroanatomical correlates of auditory speech analysis in primary progressive aphasias. *Alzheimer's Research & Therapy, 9*. Available from https://doi.org/10.1186/s13195-017-0278-2.

Hardy, C. J. D., Agustus, J. L., Marshall, C. R., Clark, C. N., Russell, L. L., Brotherhood, E. V., ... Warren, J. D. (2017b). Functional neuroanatomy of speech signal decoding in primary progressive aphasias. *Neurobiology of Aging, 56*, 190–201.

Hellström, A., & Almkvist, O. (1997). Tone duration discrimination in demented, memory-impaired, and healthy elderly. *Dementia and Geriatric Cognitive Disorders, 8*, 49–54.

Hellström, A., Lang, H., Portin, R., & Rinne, J. (1997). Tone duration discrimination in Parkinson's disease. *Neuropsychologia, 35*(5), 737–740.

Henley, S. M. D., Downey, L. E., Nicholas, J. M., Kinnunen, K. M., Golden, H. L., Buckley, A., ... Crutch, S. J. (2014). Degradation of cognitive timing mechanisms in behavioural variant frontotemporal dementia. *Neuropsychologia, 65*, 88–101. Available from https://doi.org/10.1016/j.neuropsychologia.2014.10.009.

Herdener, M., Humbel, T., Esposito, F., et al. (2014). Jazz drummers recruit language-specific areas for the processing of rhythmic structure. *Cerebral Cortex, 24*, 836–843.

Herholz, K. (1995). FDG PET and differential diagnosis of dementia. *Alzheimer Dis Assoc Disord, 9*, 6–16.

Herholz, S. C., Halpern, A. R., & Zatorre, R. J. (2012). Neuronal correlates of perception, imagery, and memory for familiar tunes. *Journal of Cognitive Neuroscience, 24*(6), 1382–1397. Available from https://doi.org/10.1162/jocn_a_00216.

Honing, H. (2012). Without it no music: Beat induction as a fundamental musical trait. *Annals of the New York Academy of Sciences, 1252*, 85–91. Available from https://doi.org/10.1111/j.1749-6632.2011.06402.x.

Hove, M. J., & Keller, P. E. (2015). Impaired movement timing in neurological disorders: Rehabilitation and treatment strategies. *Annals of the New York Academy of Sciences, 1337*, 111–117. Available from https://doi.org/10.1111/nyas.12615.

Hsieh, S., Hornberger, M., Piguet, O., & Hodges, J. R. (2011). Neural basis of music knowledge: Evidence from the dementias. *Brain, 134*(9), 2523–2534. Available from https://doi.org/10.1093/brain/awr190.

Hsieh, S., Hornberger, M., Piguet, O., & Hodges, J. R. (2012). Brain correlates of musical and facial emotion recognition: Evidence from the dementias. *Neuropsychologia, 50*(8), 1814–1822. Available from https://doi.org/10.1016/j.neuropsychologia.2012.04.006.

Huron, D. B. (2006). *Sweet anticipation: Music and the psychology of expectation.* Cambridge, Mass: MIT Press.

Isenberg, A. L., Vaden, K. I., Saberi, K., et al. (2012). Functionally distinct regions for spatial processing and sensory motor integration in the planum temporale. *Human Brain Mapping, 33*, 2453–2463.

Jacobsen, J.-H., Stelzer, J., Fritz, T. H., Chételat, G., La Joie, R., & Turner, R. (2015). Why musical memory can be preserved in advanced Alzheimer's disease. *Brain: A Journal of Neurology, 138*(Pt 8), 2438–2450.

Janata, P., Birk, J. L., Van Horn, J. D., Leman, M., Tillmann, B., & Bharucha, J. J. (2002). The cortical topography of tonal structures underlying Western music. *Science (New York, N.Y.), 298*(5601), 2167–2170.

Johnson, J. K., Chang, C.-C., Brambati, S. M., Migliaccio, R., Gorno-Tempini, M. L., Miller, B. L., & Janata, P. (2011). Music recognition in frontotemporal lobar degeneration and Alzheimer disease. *Cognitive and Behavioral Neurology: Official Journal of the Society for Behavioral and Cognitive Neurology, 24*(2), 74–84.

Josephs, K. A., Duffy, J. R., Strand, E. A., Machulda, M. M., Senjem, M. L., Master, A. V., . . . Whitwell, J. L. (2012). Characterizing a neurodegenerative syndrome: Primary progressive apraxia of speech. *Brain: A Journal of Neurology, 135*(Pt 5), 1522–1536. Available from https://doi.org/10.1093/brain/aws032.

Juslin, P. N., & Laukka, P. (2003). Communication of emotions in vocal expression and music performance: Different channels, same code? *Psychological Bulletin, 129*(5), 770–814. Available from https://doi.org/10.1037/0033-2909.129.5.770.

Kerer, M., Marksteiner, J., Hinterhuber, H., Mazzola, G., Kemmler, G., Bliem, H. R., & Weiss, E. M. (2013). Explicit (semantic) memory for music in patients with mild cognitive impairment and early-stage Alzheimer's disease. *Experimental Aging Research, 39*, 536–564.

King, J. B., Jones, K. G., Goldberg, E., Rollins, M., MacNamee, K., Moffit, C., . . . Foster, N. L. (2019). Increased functional connectivity after listening to favored music in adults with Alzheimer dementia. *The Journal of Prevention of Alzheimer's Disease, 6*(1), 56–62. Available from https://doi.org/10.14283/jpad.2018.19.

Kleber, B., Veit, R., Birbaumer, N., Gruzelier, J., & Lotze, M. (2010). The brain of opera singers: Experience-dependent changes in functional activation. *Cerebral Cortex (New York, N. Y.: 1991), 20*(5), 1144–1152.

Koelsch, S. (2011). Toward a neural basis of music perception – a review and updated model. *Frontiers in Psychology, 2*. Available from https://doi.org/10.3389/fpsyg.2011.00110.

Koelsch, S. (2014). Brain correlates of music-evoked emotions. *Nature Reviews Neuroscience, 15*(3), 170.

Koelsch, S., Fritz, T., Schulze, K., Alsop, D., & Schlaug, G. (2005). Adults and children processing music: an fMRI study. *Neuroimage, 25*(4), 1068–1076.

Koelsch, S., Kilches, S., Steinbeis, N., & Schelinski, S. (2008). Effects of unexpected chords and of performer's expression on brain responses and electrodermal activity. *PLoS One, 3*(7), e2631. Available from https://doi.org/10.1371/journal.pone.0002631.

Koelsch, S., Rohrmeier, M., Torrecuso, R., & Jentschke, S. (2013). Processing of hierarchical syntactic structure in music. *Proceedings of the National Academy of Sciences of the United States of America, 110*(38), 15443–15448.

Koelsch, S., Vuust, P., & Friston, K. (2019). Predictive processes and the peculiar case of music. *Trends in Cognitive Sciences, 23*(1), 63–77. Available from https://doi.org/10.1016/j.tics.2018.10.006.

Konoike, N., Kotozaki, Y., Miyachi, S., et al. (2012). Rhythm information represented in the fronto-parieto-cerebellar motor system. *NeuroImage, 63*, 328–338.

Kumar, S., Sedley, W., Barnes, G. R., Teki, S., Friston, K. J., & Griffiths, T. D. (2014). A brain basis for musical hallucinations. *Cortex; A Journal Devoted to the Study of the Nervous System and Behavior, 52*, 86–97.

Kurylo, D. D., Corkin, S., Allard, T., Zatorre, R. J., & Growdon, J. H. (1993). Auditory function in Alzheimer's disease. *Neurology, 43*(10), 1893–1899. Available from https://doi.org/10.1212/wnl.43.10.1893.

Large, E. W., & Snyder, J. S. (2009). Pulse and meter as neural resonance. *Annals of the New York Academy of Sciences, 1169*, 46–57. Available from https://doi.org/10.1111/j.1749-6632.2009.04550.x.

Laskowska, I. P., Gawryś, L., Łęski, S., & Koziorowski, D. (2015). Emotional processing in Parkinson's disease and schizophrenia: Evidence for response bias deficits in PD. *Frontiers in Psychology, 6*, 1417.

Lehne, M., Rohrmeier, M., & Koelsch, S. (2014). Tension-related activity in the orbitofrontal cortex and amygdala: An fMRI study with music. *Social Cognitive and Affective Neuroscience, 9*(10), 1515–1523.

Liegeois-Chauvel, C., Peretz, I., Babai, M., et al. (1998). Contribution of different cortical areas in the temporal lobes to music processing. *Brain, 121*(Pt 10), 1853–1867.

Lim, I., van Wegen, E., de Goede, C., Deutekom, M., Nieuwboer, A., Willems, A., ... Kwakkel, G. (2005). Effects of external rhythmical cueing on gait in patients with Parkinson's disease: A systematic review. *Clinical Rehabilitation, 19*(7), 695–713. Available from https://doi.org/10.1191/0269215505cr906oa.

Lima, C. F., Brancatisano, O., Fancourt, A., Müllensiefen, D., Scott, S. K., Warren, J. D., & Stewart, L. (2016). Impaired socio-emotional processing in a developmental music disorder. *Scientific Reports, 6*, 34911.

Lima, C. F., Garrett, C., & Castro, S. L. (2013). Not all sounds sound the same: Parkinson's disease affects differently emotion processing in music and in speech prosody. *Journal of Clinical and Experimental Neuropsychology, 35*(4), 373–392. Available from https://doi.org/10.1080/13803395.2013.776518.

Massman, P. J., Delis, D. C., Filoteo, J. V., Butters, N., Salmon, D. P., & Demadura, T. L. (1993). Mechanisms of spatial impairment in Alzheimer's disease subgroups: Differential breakdown of directed attention to global-local stimuli. *Neuropsychology, 7*, 172–181.

Mathiak, K., Hertrich, I., Grodd, W., et al. (2004). Discrimination of temporal information at the cerebellum: Functional magnetic resonance imaging of nonverbal auditory memory. *NeuroImage, 21*, 154–162.

Matsumoto, E., Ohigashi, Y., Fujimori, M., & Mori, E. (2000). The processing of global and local visual information in Alzheimer's disease. *Behavioural Neurology, 12*, 119–125.

Matthews, B. R., Chang, C.-C., De May, M., Engstrom, J., & Miller, B. L. (2009). Pleasurable emotional response to music: A case of neurodegenerative generalized auditory agnosia. *Neurocase, 15*(3), 248–259. Available from https://doi.org/10.1080/13554790802632934.

McAdams, S., & Cunible, J. C. (1992). Perception of timbral analogies. *Philosophical Transactions of the Royal Society of London. Series B, Biological Sciences, 336*, 383–389.

Ménard, M.-C., & Belleville, S. (2009). Musical and verbal memory in Alzheimer's disease: A study of long-term and short-term memory. *Brain and Cognition, 71*(1), 38–45. Available from https://doi.org/10.1016/j.bandc.2009.03.008.

Mendez, M. F., & Geehan, G. R., Jr (1988). Cortical auditory disorders: Clinical and psychoacoustic features. *Journal of Neurology, Neurosurgery, and Psychiatry, 51*, 1–9.

Mendez, M. F., & Shapira, J. S. (2013). Hypersexual behavior in frontotemporal dementia: A comparison with early-onset Alzheimer's disease. *Archives of Sexual Behavior, 42*(3), 501–509. Available from https://doi.org/10.1007/s10508-012-0042-4.

Menon, V., & Levitin, D. J. (2005). The rewards of music listening: Response and physiological connectivity of the mesolimbic system. *NeuroImage, 28*(1), 175−184. Available from https://doi.org/10.1016/j.neuroimage.2005.05.053.

Miller, B. L., Boone, K., Cummings, J. L., Read, S. L., & Mishkin, F. (2000). Functional correlates of musical and visual ability in frontotemporal dementia. *The British Journal of Psychiatry: The Journal of Mental Science, 176*, 458−463.

Milner, B. (1962). Laterality effects in audition. In V. B. Mountcastle (Ed.), *Interhemispheric relations and cerebral dominance*. Baltimore, MD: Johns Hopkins University Press.

Moussard, A., Bigand, E., Clément, S., & Samson, S. (2008). Préservation des apprentissages implicites en musique dans le vieillissement normal et la maladie d'Alzheimer. *Revue de Neuropsychologie, Adrsc, 18*(2), 127−152.

Murgia, M., Pili, R., Corona, F., Sors, F., Agostini, T. A., Bernardis, P., & Pau, M. (2018). The use of footstep sounds as rhythmic auditory stimulation for gait rehabilitation in parkinson's disease: a randomized controlled trial. *Frontiers in Neurology, 9*, 348.

Nombela, C., Hughes, L. E., Owen, A. M., & Grahn, J. A. (2013). Into the groove: can rhythm influence Parkinson's disease? *Neuroscience Biobehaviour Review, 37*(10 Pt 2), 2564−2570.

Omar, R., Hailstone, J. C., Warren, J. E., Crutch, S. J., & Warren, J. D. (2010). The cognitive organization of music knowledge: A clinical analysis. *Brain: A Journal of Neurology, 133* (Pt 4), 1200−1213. Available from https://doi.org/10.1093/brain/awp345.

Omar, R., Henley, S. M. D., Bartlett, J. W., Hailstone, J. C., Gordon, E., Sauter, D. A., ... Warren, J. D. (2011). The structural neuroanatomy of music emotion recognition: Evidence from frontotemporal lobar degeneration. *NeuroImage, 56*(3), 1814−1821. Available from https://doi.org/10.1016/j.neuroimage.2011.03.002.

Overath, T., Kumar, S., von Kriegstein, K., & Griffiths, T. D. (2008). Encoding of spectral correlation over time in auditory cortex. *The Journal of Neuroscience: The Official Journal of the Society for Neuroscience, 28*(49), 13268−13273.

Overath, T., Kumar, S., Stewart, L., von Kriegstein, K., Cusack, R., Rees, A., & Griffiths, T. D. (2010). Cortical mechanisms for the segregation and representation of acoustic textures. *The Journal of Neuroscience: The Official Journal of the Society for Neuroscience, 30*(6), 2070−2076. Available from https://doi.org/10.1523/JNEUROSCI.5378-09.2010.

Patel, A. (2008). *Music, language and the brain*. Oxford: Oxford University Press.

Patterson, R. D., Uppenkamp, S., Johnsrude, I. S., & Griffiths, T. D. (2002). The processing of temporal pitch and melody information in auditory cortex. *Neuron, 36*(4), 767−776.

Pereira, C. S., Teixeira, J., Figueiredo, P., Xavier, J., Castro, S. L., & Brattico, E. (2011). Music and emotions in the brain: Familiarity matters. *PLoS One, 6*(11), e27241. Available from https://doi.org/10.1371/journal.pone.0027241.

Peretz, I. (1990). Processing of local and global musical information by unilateral brain-damaged patients. *Brain: A Journal of Neurology, 113*(Pt 4), 1185−1205. Available from https://doi.org/10.1093/brain/113.4.1185.

Peretz, I. (1996). Can we lose memory for music? A case of music agnosia in a nonmusician. *Journal of Cognitive Neuroscience, 8*(6), 481−496. Available from https://doi.org/10.1162/jocn.1996.8.6.481.

Peretz, I. (2006). The nature of music from a biological perspective. *Cognition, 100*(1), 1−32.

Peretz, I., & Coltheart, M. (2003). Modularity of music processing. *Nature Neuroscience, 6*(7), 688−691.

Perry, D. C., Sturm, V. E., Seeley, W. W., Miller, B. L., Kramer, J. H., & Rosen, H. J. (2014). Anatomical correlates of reward-seeking behaviours in behavioural variant frontotemporal dementia. *Brain, 137*(6), 1621−1626.

Platel, H., Baron, J.-C., Desgranges, B., Bernard, F., & Eustache, F. (2003). Semantic and episodic memory of music are subserved by distinct neural networks. *NeuroImage, 20*(1), 244–256.

Platel, H., & Groussard, M. (2010). La mémoire sémantique musicale: apport des données de la neuropsychologie clinique et de la neuro-imagerie fonctionnelle. *Revue de Neuropsychologie, 2,* 61–69.

Pohl, P., Dizdar, N., & Hallert, E. (2013). The Ronnie Gardiner Rhythm and Music Method—a feasibility study in Parkinson's disease. *Disability and Rehabilitation, 35*(26), 2197–2204. Available from https://doi.org/10.3109/09638288.2013.774060.

Polk, M., & Kertesz, A. (1993). Music and language in degenerative disease of the brain. *Brain and Cognition, 22,* 98–117.

Quoniam, N., Ergis, A.-M., Fossati, P., Peretz, I., Samson, S., Sarazin, M., & Allilaire, J.-F. (2003). Implicit and explicit emotional memory for melodies in Alzheimer's disease and depression. *Annals of the New York Academy of Sciences, 999,* 381–384.

Ragert, M., Fairhurst, M. T., & Keller, P. E. (2014). Segregation and integration of auditory streams when listening to multi-part music. *PLoS One, 9*(1), e84085. Available from https://doi.org/10.1371/journal.pone.0084085.

Raglio, A., Bellandi, D., Baiardi, P., Gianotti, M., Ubezio, M. C., & Granieri, E. (2012). Music therapy in frontal temporal dementia: A case report. *Journal of the American Geriatrics Society, 60*(8), 1578–1579.

Rohrer, J. D., Lashley, T., Schott, J. M., Warren, J. E., Mead, S., Isaacs, A. M., … Warren, J. D. (2011). Clinical and neuroanatomical signatures of tissue pathology in frontotemporal lobar degeneration. *Brain: A Journal of Neurology, 134*(Pt 9), 2565–2581. Available from https://doi.org/10.1093/brain/awr198.

Rohrer, J. D., Ridgway, G. R., Crutch, S. J., Hailstone, J., Goll, J. C., Clarkson, M. J., … Warren, J. D. (2010). Progressive logopenic/phonological aphasia: Erosion of the language network. *NeuroImage, 49,* 984–993.

Rohrer, J. D., Sauter, D., Scott, S., Rossor, M. N., & Warren, J. D. (2012). Receptive prosody in nonfluent primary progressive aphasias. *Cortex, 48*(3), 308–316.

Rohrmeier, M., Zuidema, W., Wiggins, G. A., & Scharff, C. (2015). Principles of structure building in music, language and animal song. *Philosophical Transactions of the Royal Society of London. Series B, Biological Sciences, 370*(1664), 20140097. Available from https://doi.org/10.1098/rstb.2014.0097.

Rossi, M., Cerquetti, D., & Merello, M. (2015). Piano playing festination as initial symptom of Parkinson's disease. *Parkinsonism & Related Disorders, 21*(4), 417–418. Available from https://doi.org/10.1016/j.parkreldis.2014.12.022.

Saenz, A., Doé de Maindreville, A., Henry, A., de Labbey, S., Bakchine, S., & Ehrlé, N. (2013). Recognition of facial and musical emotions in Parkinson's disease. *European Journal of Neurology, 20*(3), 571–577.

Salimpoor, V. N., Bosch, I., van den, Kovacevic, N., McIntosh, A. R., Dagher, A., & Zatorre, R. J. (2013). Interactions between the nucleus accumbens and auditory cortices predict music reward value. *Science, 340*(6129), 216–219.

Salimpoor, V. N., Zald, D. H., Zatorre, R. J., Dagher, A., & McIntosh, A. R. (2015). Predictions and the brain: How musical sounds become rewarding. *Trends in Cognitive Sciences, 19*(2), 86–91. Available from https://doi.org/10.1016/j.tics.2014.12.001.

Samson, S., Baird, A., Moussard, A., & Clément, S. (2012). Does pathological aging affect musical learning and memory? *Music Perception: An Interdisciplinary Journal, 29*(5), 493–500. Available from https://doi.org/10.1525/mp.2012.29.5.493.

Samson, S., Ehrlé, N., & Baulac, M. (2001). Cerebral substrates for musical temporal processes. *Annals of the New York Academy of Sciences, 930,* 166—178.

Samson, S., & Zatorre, R. J. (1994). Contribution of the right temporal lobe to musical timbre discrimination. *Neuropsychologia, 32,* 231—240.

Samson, S., Zatorre, R. J., & Ramsay, J. O. (2002). Deficits of musical timbre perception after unilateral temporal-lobe lesion revealed with multidimensional scaling. *Brain, 125,* 511—523.

Schuppert, M., Münte, T. F., Wieringa, B. M., & Altenmüller, E. (2000). Receptive amusia: Evidence for cross-hemispheric neural networks underlying music processing strategies. *Brain: A Journal of Neurology, 123*(Pt 3), 546—559.

Seeley, W. W., Matthews, B. R., Crawford, R. K., Gorno-Tempini, M. L., Foti, D., Mackenzie, I. R., & Miller, B. L. (2008). Unravelling Boléro: Progressive aphasia, transmodal creativity and the right posterior neocortex. *Brain: A Journal of Neurology, 131*(Pt 1), 39—49. Available from https://doi.org/10.1093/brain/awm270.

Sikka, R., Cuddy, L. L., Johnsrude, I. S., & Vanstone, A. D. (2015). An fMRI comparison of neural activity associated with recognition of familiar melodies in younger and older adults. *Frontiers in Neuroscience, 9,* 356.

Sivasathiaseelan, H., Marshall, C. R., Agustus, J. L., Benhamou, E., Bond, R. L., van Leeuwen, J. E. P., ... Warren, J. D. (2019). Frontotemporal dementia: A clinical review. *Seminars in Neurology, 39*(2), 251—263.

Slattery, C. F., Agustus, J. L., Paterson, R. W., McCallion, O., Foulkes, A. J. M., Macpherson, K., ... Warren, J. D. (2019). The functional neuroanatomy of musical memory in Alzheimer's disease. *Cortex; A Journal Devoted to the Study of the Nervous System and Behavior, 115,* 357—370. Available from https://doi.org/10.1016/j.cortex.2019.02.003.

Slavin, M. J., Mattingley, J. B., Bradshaw, J. L., & Storey, E. (2002). Local—global processing in Alzheimer's disease: An examination of interference, inhibition and priming. *Neuropsychologia, 40,* 1173—1186.

Steinbeis, N., & Koelsch, S. (2009). Understanding the intentions behind man-made products elicits neural activity in areas dedicated to mental state attribution. *Cerebral Cortex (New York, N.Y.: 1991), 19*(3), 619—623.

Stevens, M. C., Kiehl, K. A., Pearlson, G., & Calhoun, V. D. (2007). Functional neural circuits for mental timekeeping. *Human Brain Mapping, 28*(5), 394—408. Available from https://doi.org/10.1002/hbm.20285.

Stewart, L., Overath, T., Warren, J. D., Foxton, J. M., & Griffiths, T. D. (2008). fMRI evidence for a cortical hierarchy of pitch pattern processing. *PLoS One, 3*(1), e1470. Available from https://doi.org/10.1371/journal.pone.0001470.

Stewart, L., Von Kriegstein, K., Warren, J. D., & Griffiths, T. D. (2006). Music and the brain: disorders of musical listening. *Brain, 129,* 1—21.

Strouse, A. L., Hall, J. W., & Burger, M. C. (1995). Central auditory processing in Alzheimer's disease. *Ear and Hearing, 16*(2), 230—238.

Teki, S., Kumar, S., von Kriegstein, K., Stewart, L., Lyness, C. R., Moore, B. C. J., ... Griffiths, T. D. (2012). Navigating the auditory scene: An expert role for the hippocampus. *The Journal of Neuroscience: The Official Journal of the Society for Neuroscience, 32*(35), 12251—12257. Available from https://doi.org/10.1523/JNEUROSCI.0082-12.2012.

Thaut, M. H., McIntosh, G. C., Rice, R. R., Miller, R. A., Rathbun, J., & Brault, J. M. (1996). Rhythmic auditory stimulation in gait training for Parkinson's disease patients. *Movement Disorders: Official Journal of the Movement Disorder Society, 11*(2), 193—200. Available from https://doi.org/10.1002/mds.870110213.

Thaut, M. H., McIntosh, K. W., McIntosh, G. C., & Hoemberg, V. (2001). Auditory rhythmicity enhances movement and speech motor control in patients with Parkinson's disease. *Functional Neurology, 16*(2), 163−172.

Thavabalasingam, S., O'Neil, E. B., Tay, J., Nestor, A., & Lee, A. C. H. (2019). Evidence for the incorporation of temporal duration information in human hippocampal long-term memory sequence representations. *Proceedings of the National Academy of Sciences of the United States of America, 116*(13), 6407−6414. Available from https://doi.org/10.1073/pnas.1819993116.

Troche, J., Troche, M. S., Berkowitz, R., Grossman, M., & Reilly, J. (2012). Tone discrimination as a window into acoustic perceptual deficits in Parkinson's disease. *American Journal of Speech-Language Pathology, 21*(3), 258−263.

Trost, W., Leh, F., Houvenaghel, J. F., Choppin, S., Drapier, S., Sauleau, P., & Vérin, M. (2018). Subthalamic deep brain stimulation influences complex emotional musical experience in Parkinson's disease. *Neuropsychologia, 117*, 278−286.

Tsai, C.-G., & Li, C.-W. (2019). Increased activation in the left ventrolateral prefrontal cortex and temporal pole during tonality change in music. *Neuroscience Letters, 696*, 162−167. Available from https://doi.org/10.1016/j.neulet.2018.12.019.

van Tricht, M. J., Smeding, H. M., Speelman, J. D., & Schmand, B. A. (2010). Impaired emotion recognition in music in Parkinson's disease. *Brain and Cognition, 74*(1), 58−65.

Vanstone, A. D., & Cuddy, L. L. (2010). Musical memory in Alzheimer disease. *Neuropsychology, Development, and Cognition. Section B, Aging, Neuropsychology and Cognition, 17*(1), 108−128.

Vanstone, A. D., Cuddy, L. L., Duffin, J. M., & Alexander, E. (2009). Exceptional preservation of memory for tunes and lyrics: Case studies of amusia, profound deafness, and Alzheimer's disease. *Annals of the New York Academy of Sciences, 1169*, 291−294. Available from https://doi.org/10.1111/j.1749-6632.2009.04763.x.

Vikene, K., Skeie, G.-O., & Specht, K. (2019). Abnormal phasic activity in saliency network, motor areas, and basal ganglia in Parkinson's disease during rhythm perception. *Human Brain Mapping, 40*(3), 916−927.

Volpe, D., Signorini, M., Marchetto, A., Lynch, T., & Morris, M. E. (2013). A comparison of Irish set dancing and exercises for people with Parkinson's disease: A phase II feasibility study. *BMC Geriatrics, 13*, 54.

Warren, J. D., Fletcher, P. D., & Golden, H. L. (2012). The paradox of syndromic diversity in Alzheimer disease. *Nature Reviews Neurology, 8*(8), 451−464. Available from https://doi.org/10.1038/nrneurol.2012.135.

Warren, J. D., Jennings, A. R., & Griffiths, T. D. (2005). Analysis of the spectral envelope of sounds by the human brain. *NeuroImage, 24*(4), 1052−1057. Available from https://doi.org/10.1016/j.neuroimage.2004.10.031.

Warren, J. D., Rohrer, J. D., & Rossor, M. N. (2013). Frontotemporal dementia. *British Medical Journal, 347*, f4827.

Warren, J. D., Rohrer, J. D., Schott, J. M., Fox, N. C., Hardy, J., & Rossor, M. N. (2013). Molecular nexopathies: A new paradigm of neurodegenerative disease. *Trends in Neurosciences, 36*(10), 561−569.

Warren, J. D., & Schott, G. D. (2006). Musical hallucinations in a musician. *Journal of Neurology, 253*(8), 1097−1099.

Warren, J. E., Wise, R. J. S., & Warren, J. D. (2005). Sounds do-able: Auditory-motor transformations and the posterior temporal plane. *Trends in Neurosciences, 28*(12), 636−643. Available from https://doi.org/10.1016/j.tins.2005.09.010.

Watanabe, T., Yagishita, S., & Kikyo, H. (2008). Memory of music: Roles of right hippocampus and left inferior frontal gyrus. *NeuroImage, 39,* 483−491.

Weil, R. S., Schrag, A. E., Warren, J. D., Crutch, S. J., Lees, A. J., & Morris, H. R. (2016). Visual dysfunction in Parkinson's disease. *Brain, 139*(11), 2827−2843. Available from https://doi.org/10.1093/brain/aww175.

Weinstein, J., Koenig, P., Gunawardena, D., et al. (2011). Preserved musical semantic memory in semantic dementia. *Archives of Neurology, 68,* 248−250.

White, D. A., & Murphy, C. F. (1998). Working memory for nonverbal auditory information in dementia of the Alzheimer type. *Archives of Clinical Neuropsychology: The Official Journal of the National Academy of Neuropsychologists, 13*(4), 339−347.

Wiener, M., Turkeltaub, P., & Coslett, H. B. (2010). The image of time: A voxel-wise meta-analysis. *NeuroImage, 49*(2), 1728−1740. Available from https://doi.org/10.1016/j.neuroimage.2009.09.064.

Wilson, B. A., Baddeley, A. D., & Kapur, N. (1995). Dense amnesia in a professional musician following herpes simplex virus encephalitis. *Journal of Clinical and Experimental Neuropsychology, 17*(5), 668−681.

Woolley, J. D., Gorno-Tempini, M.-L., Seeley, W. W., Rankin, K., Lee, S. S., Matthews, B. R., & Miller, B. L. (2007). Binge eating is associated with right orbitofrontal-insular-striatal atrophy in frontotemporal dementia. *Neurology, 69*(14), 1424−1433. Available from https://doi.org/10.1212/01.wnl.0000277461.06713.23.

Zahn, R., Moll, J., Krueger, F., Huey, E. D., Garrido, G., & Grafman, J. (2007). Social concepts are represented in the superior anterior temporal cortex. *Proceedings of the National Academy of Sciences, 104*(15), 6430−6435.

Zahn, R., Moll, J., Paiva, M., Garrido, G., Krueger, F., Huey, E. D., & Grafman, J. (2009). The neural basis of human social values: Evidence from functional MRI. *Cerebral Cortex (New York, N.Y.: 1991), 19*(2), 276−283.

Zatorre, R. J., & Salimpoor, V. N. (2013). From perception to pleasure: Music and its neural substrates. *Proceedings of the National Academy of Sciences of the United States of America, 110*(Suppl. 2), 10430−10437.

Zhou, J., Greicius, M. D., Gennatas, E. D., Growdon, M. E., Jang, J. Y., Rabinovici, G. D., ... Seeley, W. W. (2010). Divergent network connectivity changes in behavioural variant frontotemporal dementia and Alzheimer's disease. *Brain, 133*(5), 1352−1367. Available from https://doi.org/10.1093/brain/awq075.

Zündorf, I. C., Lewald, J., & Karnath, H.-O. (2013). Neural correlates of sound localization in complex acoustic environments. *PLoS One, 8*(5), e64259. Available from https://doi.org/10.1371/journal.pone.0064259.

Chapter 5

Stroke and acquired amusia

Aleksi J. Sihvonen and Teppo Särkämö
Department of Psychology and Logopedics, University of Helsinki, Helsinki, Finland

Introduction

The rapid aging of the population across the world is leading to an increasing number of elderly persons living with a debilitating neurological disorder [World Health Organization (WHO), 2015]. Globally, neurological disorders are currently the leading cause of disability-adjusted life years (DALYs) and the second largest cause of death [Global Burden of Disease (GBD) 2016 Neurology Collaborators, 2019]. Societally, one of the most important such illnesses is stroke. In 2016 an estimated 13.7 million persons worldwide suffered a first-ever stroke, which is 78% more than in 1990, and stroke was clearly the largest contributor of neurological DALYs [Global Burden of Disease (GBD) 2016 Neurology Collaborators, 2019]. Over the period from 2010 to 2050, the number of incident strokes is expected to more than double, with the majority of the increase among the elderly (aged ≥ 75 years) and minority groups (Benjamin et al., 2019). Caused by interrupted blood supply to the brain resulting from either a blocked artery (ischemic stroke) or a ruptured blood vessel (hemorrhagic stroke), a stroke leads to permanent neural damage and a variety of neurological deficits, depending on the location and extent of the lesion. The most prevalent consequence of stroke is motor impairment of lower or upper extremity (hemiparesis), which affects approximately 80% of the patients (Rathore, Hinn, Cooper, Tyroler, & Rosamond, 2002). Importantly, more than 50% stroke patients also show signs of impairment in one or more cognitive domains, most often in attention and executive functioning, visuospatial cognition, reasoning, and memory (Hochstenbach, Mulder, van Limbeek, Donders, & Schoonderwaldt, 1998; Nys et al., 2007; Rasquin, Verhey, Lousberg, Winkens, & Lodder, 2002; Tatemichi et al., 1994). Aphasia, loss of speech production and/or comprehension ability, occurs in approximately 30% of stroke survivors (Engelter et al., 2006).

In addition to these motor, language, and cognitive deficits, a stroke can also cause a musical deficit known as amusia or tone (tune) deafness. By definition, amusia refers to the impairment of the perception, understanding,

Music and the Aging Brain. DOI: https://doi.org/10.1016/B978-0-12-817422-7.00005-5

151

or production of music which is not attributable to deficits in the peripheral auditory pathways or in the motor system (e.g., Clark, Golden, & Warren, 2015). There are two main types of amusias: *congenital amusia*, a developmental music deficit affecting approximately 1.5% of the population (see Peretz, 2016 for a review of congenital amusia), and *acquired amusia*, a music deficit caused by brain damage, most often as a result of stroke. Especially after a stroke to the middle cerebral artery (MCA) territory, the prevalence of acquired amusia is relatively high, ranging between 35% and 69% (Ayotte, Peretz, Rousseau, Bard, & Bojanowski, 2000; Särkämö et al., 2009; Schuppert, Münte, Wieringa, & Altenmüller, 2000), although studies with larger sample sizes are still needed to establish a more accurate and reliable prevalence estimate. Based on observed dissociations between the isolated loss and sparing of specific musical features in amusic patients, the symptoms of amusia can be broadly classified and different neurocognitive models have been put forth to account for amusias as disorders following a modular perceptual organization (Peretz & Coltheart, 2003) or, more recently, as disorders of cognitive information processing underpinned by selective dysfunction within brain networks (Clark et al., 2015). At the basic level, a distinction is most often made between amusias involving a deficit in the spectral (e.g., pitch, timbre) and temporal (e.g., rhythm, meter) musical domain.

During the past 20 years the development of modern magnetic resonance imaging (MRI)-based structural neuroimaging methods, such as voxel-based morphometry (VBM) and diffusion tensor imaging (DTI), as well as functional and neurophysiological neuroimaging methods, including electroencephalography and magnetoencephalography (EEG, MEG) and functional MRI (fMRI), have greatly increased our understanding of the large-scale music processing networks in the healthy brain (see Chapter 1: The musical brain). Importantly, they have also enabled mapping of the neural basis of congenital amusia by showing that it is associated with reduced white matter concentration and abnormalities in gray matter volume or cortical thickness in the inferior frontal gyrus (IFG) and the superior temporal gyrus (STG), predominantly in the right hemisphere (Albouy et al., 2013; Hyde, Zatorre, Griffiths, Lerch, & Peretz, 2006; Hyde et al., 2007) but also in the left hemisphere (Mandell, Schulze, & Schlaug, 2007), as well as reduced volume of the right arcuate fasciculus (AF), a key white matter tract connecting these two structures (Loui, Alsop, & Schlaug, 2009). Functionally, evidence from EEG, MEG, and fMRI studies suggests that in congenital amusia the right STG is normally responsive to pitch changes in music, but consciously attending to and cognitively analyzing this pitch information in right frontal regions, especially the IFG, fails due to reduced functional connectivity between these regions (Hyde, Zatorre, & Peretz, 2011; Leveque et al., 2016; Norman-Haignere et al., 2016; Peretz, Brattico, Järvenpää, & Tervaniemi, 2009; Peretz, Brattico, & Tervaniemi, 2005; Zendel, Lagrois, Robitaille, & Peretz, 2015).

Supplementing these advances, mapping the structural and functional neuroanatomy of acquired amusia can provide valuable information for answering both fundamental questions about the neural basis of music and clinical questions regarding stroke outcome and rehabilitation. First of all, while functional neuroimaging studies in healthy subjects provide largely correlational evidence due to methodological restrictions, lesion-based studies provide the valuable opportunity to explore causal relationships between lesioned brain areas and specific cognitive or motor functions (Adolphs, 2016; Rorden & Karnath, 2004). Compared to congenital amusia, which is developmental deficit in acquiring musical syntax and tonal representations that hampers the early development of the music processing network and leads to lifelong, often heterogeneous impairments with music (Omigie, Müllensiefen, & Stewart, 2012; Stewart, 2008), acquired amusia reflects a clear-cut transition from a previously normal to a deficient music processing system caused by a focal brain lesion. Therefore the dysfunction of the music processing network in acquired amusia creates a unique opportunity to examine and pin down the neural structures that are most critical—and causally linked—to music perception (Price & Friston, 2002; Rorden & Karnath, 2004). Second, from a clinical standpoint, uncovering which brain regions and networks typically underpin acquired amusia and its recovery can help in (1) the initial screening of stroke patients for more detailed diagnostic evaluation of acquired amusia, (2) establishing a prognosis of expected recovery of the deficit, (3) developing interventions targeted for its rehabilitation, and (4) deciding whether the patient could benefit from music-based rehabilitation for poststroke cognitive, verbal, motor, or emotional deficits (Magee, Clark, Tamplin, & Bradt, 2017; Sihvonen, Särkämö, Leo, et al., 2017).

With these considerations in mind, this chapter aims to provide an overview of older and more recent studies on the neural basis of poststroke acquired amusia and its recovery. Modern neuroimaging methods, including voxel-based lesion−symptom mapping (VLSM), VBM, DTI, and fMRI have been utilized in acquired amusia research only in recent years. Coupled with larger sample sizes and longitudinal follow-up, these methods have provided novel information of the neural basis of acquired amusia that is more spatially accurate and temporally precise than in previous studies. In this context, we specifically review the main findings of our recent four studies (Sihvonen et al., 2016; Sihvonen, Ripollés, Rodríguez-Fornells, Soinila, & Särkämö, 2017; Sihvonen, Ripollés, Särkämö, et al., 2017; Sihvonen, Särkämö, Ripollés, et al., 2017) in which the sample (total $N = 90$) consisted of two cohorts of stroke patients (all right-handed and nonmusicians) with a first-ever acute stroke in the left ($N = 43$) or right ($N = 47$) hemisphere, primarily in MCA territory. Both cohorts underwent amusia testing using a shortened version (Särkämö et al., 2009) of the Montreal Battery of Evaluation of Amusia (MBEA; Peretz, Champod, & Hyde, 2003) as well as structural MRI (sMRI) at the acute (<3 weeks poststroke) and 6-month poststroke stages. Additionally, the first cohort underwent an auditory MEG measurement at all time points and the second cohort underwent amusia testing at 3-month stage and s/fMRI at all time points. The Scale and Rhythm subtests of the MBEA were utilized as indices of musical pitch and rhythm perception deficits (referred to hereafter as pitch-amusia and rhythm-amusia, respectively).

Structural and functional neural correlates of acquired amusia

Descriptive lesion studies

Clinical interest in acquired amusia has a long and venerable history in neurology, with oldest case reports of amusic patients dating back to the end of the 19th century (Graziano & Johnson, 2015). The older descriptive studies of acquired amusia comprise *symptom-led* studies, presenting individual cases of amusic patients and reporting the locations of their lesions, as well as *lesion-led* studies, presenting small ($N \leq 20$) patient groups with lesions classified at gross (lobar, hemispheric) anatomical level and comparing them to other patients (and healthy control subjects) on music tests (for a review, see Stewart, von Kriegstein, Warren, & Griffiths, 2006). A summary of the number of case and group studies which reported acquired amusia, either in the spectral (e.g., pitch, timbre) or temporal (e.g., rhythm, meter) musical domain, after damage to a particular brain region is shown in Fig. 5.1. Spectral musical deficits have been reported mainly after right hemisphere damage (Griffiths et al., 1997; Hochman & Abrams, 2014; Johannes, Jobges, Dengler, & Münte, 1998; Kohlmetz, Altenmüller, Schuppert, Wieringa, & Münte, 2001; Kohlmetz, Muller, Nager, Münte, & Altenmüller, 2003; Mazzoni et al., 1993; McFarland & Fortin, 1982; Münte et al., 1998; Murayama, Kashiwagi, Kashiwagi, & Mimura, 2004; Rosslau et al., 2015; Särkämö et al., 2009; Satoh, Takeda, Nagata, Hatazawa, & Kuzuhara, 2003; Terao et al., 2006), but also after left hemisphere damage (Hofman, Klein, & Arlazoroff, 1993; Kohlmetz et al., 2001; Münte et al., 1998; Särkämö et al., 2009; Satoh et al., 2003; Schuppert et al., 2000). Similarly, temporal musical deficits have been reported after both left hemisphere damage (Di Pietro, Laganaro, Leemann, & Schnider, 2004; Kohlmetz et al., 2001; Mavlov, 1980; Münte et al., 1998; Särkämö et al., 2009; Schuppert et al., 2000) and right hemisphere damage (Griffiths et al., 1997; Johannes et al., 1998; Kohlmetz et al., 2001; Münte et al., 1998; Rosslau et al., 2015; Särkämö et al., 2009; Schuppert et al., 2000; Wilson, Pressing, & Wales, 2002; Yoo, Moon, & Pyun, 2016). Overall, the results regarding the type of musical deficit (spectral, temporal) associated with the laterality (left, right) and hemispheric location (temporal, frontal, parietal, occipital, subcortical) have been variable and inconsistent.

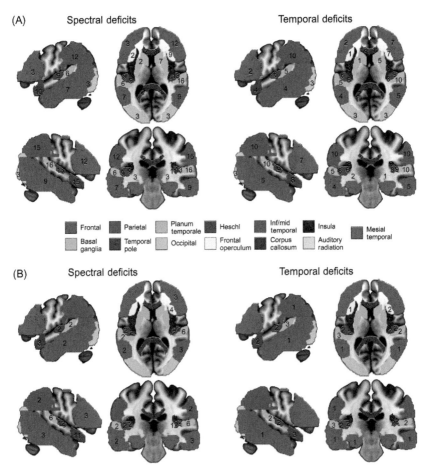

FIGURE 5.1 Symptom-led case studies (A) and lesion-led group studies (B) of acquired amusia. The number of single cases/group studies which reported acquired amusia after damage to a particular brain region is shown for both spectral (left) and temporal (right) deficits. The same number is reported in different slices (e.g., three case studies reported spectral deficits after damage to left frontal regions, so "3" is shown in the red region of interest in both axial and sagittal slices). Areas in which no deficit was reported have no number. Neurological convention is used with brain regions shown over a canonical template in MNI space. *MNI*, Montreal Neurological Institution. *Based on the data reported by Stewart, L., von Kriegstein, K., Warren, J. D., & Griffiths, T. D. (2006). Music and the brain: Disorders of musical listening. Brain, 129(Pt 10), 2533−2553 (Supplementary Tables 1 and 2) and updated by the authors for studies from 2006 to 2018.*

Structural neuroimaging studies

Voxel-based lesion−symptom mapping

Lesion−symptom relationships can be explored with VLSM, which uses the same voxel-based approach as other MRI neuroimaging techniques (Bates et al., 2003). Since 2004 VLSM has been successfully used in uncovering the lesion patterns of aphasia (Dronkers, Wilkins, Van Valin, Redfern, & Jaeger, 2004; Fridriksson, Fillmore, Guo, & Rorden, 2015; Henseler, Regenbrecht, & Obrig, 2014; Mirman et al., 2015), but it has been applied in acquired amusia only recently. In two studies of stroke patients, VLSM was used in conjunction with the Scale and Rhythm subtests of the MBEA (Sihvonen et al., 2016; Sihvonen, Ripollés, Rodríguez-Fornells, et al., 2017) and with a music (melodic) short-term memory task similar to the MBEA (Hirel et al., 2017). In their study of 20 chronic stroke patients, Hirel et al. (2017) found that lesions in the insula and inferior frontal areas were associated with deficits in performing the music task, but lesion laterality was not determined, as left and right lesions were combined in the VLSM analysis. Using a larger cohort ($N = 90$), Sihvonen et al. followed stroke patients with left ($N = 43$) and right ($N = 47$) lesions from the acute to 6-month poststroke stage. As shown in Fig. 5.2A, acquired amusia and lower MBEA scores were associated with a specific lesion pattern comprising the right STG, middle temporal gyrus (MTG), insula, IFG, basal ganglia, and hippocampus (Sihvonen et al., 2016; Sihvonen, Ripollés, Rodríguez-Fornells, et al., 2017). This is in line with previous small-scale group and case studies that have linked right MCA territory damage (Ayotte et al., 2000; Griffiths et al., 1997; Hochman & Abrams, 2014; Johannes et al., 1998; Kohlmetz et al., 2001, 2003; Mazzoni et al., 1993; McFarland & Fortin, 1982; Münte et al., 1998; Murayama et al., 2004; Rosslau et al., 2015; Särkämö et al., 2009; Satoh et al., 2003; Schuppert et al., 2000; Terao et al., 2006; Wilson et al., 2002; Yoo et al., 2016) and especially the right temporal lobe lesions (Ayotte et al., 2000; Griffiths et al., 1997; Hochman & Abrams, 2014; Kohlmetz et al., 2003; Mazzoni et al., 1993; McFarland & Fortin, 1982; Murayama et al., 2004; Särkämö et al., 2009; Satoh et al., 2003; Terao et al., 2006; Yoo et al., 2016) to acquired amusia. The lesion patterns for pitch-amusia and rhythm-amusia, indicated by poor performance in the MBEA Scale and Rhythm subtest, respectively, were largely overlapping, though lesions in the right basal ganglia were the most significant in rhythm-amusia (Sihvonen et al., 2016; Sihvonen, Ripollés, Rodríguez-Fornells, et al., 2017). Previously, studies in healthy subjects have linked basal ganglia closely to rhythm processing (Alluri et al., 2012; Grahn & Rowe, 2009; Penhune, Zattore, & Evans, 1998).

As shown in Fig. 5.2B, a comparison of nonamusics with amusics who showed or did not show behavioral recovery in the MBEA over a 6-month poststroke period indicated that lesions in the left IFG were associated with a better recovery of amusia, whereas lesions in the right STG, insula, and IFG were associated with a poor recovery (Sihvonen et al., 2016; Sihvonen, Ripollés, Rodríguez-Fornells, et al., 2017). These results are similar to the findings in congenital amusia (Albouy et al., 2013; Hyde et al., 2006, 2007) and suggest that the right superior temporal and inferior frontal regions are

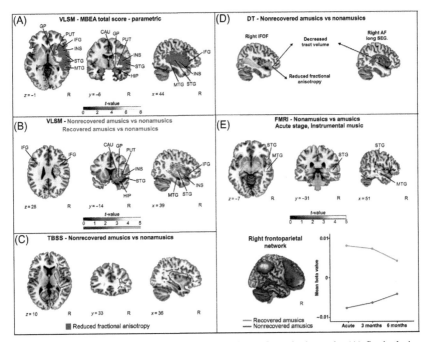

FIGURE 5.2 Structural and functional neural correlates of acquired amusia. (A) Stroke lesion pattern associated with lower MBEA total scores. (B) Lesion analyses comparing nonrecovered amusic versus nonmusic patients (red), and recovered amusic versus nonmusic patients (blue). (C) TBSS analysis comparing nonrecovered amusic versus nonmusic patients. (D) Main tractography findings in acute acquired amusia. (E) fMRI activation pattern comparison between nonmusic and amusic patients during instrumental music listening at acute stage and right frontoparietal network functional connectivity engagement comparison between recovered and nonrecovered amusic patients. *CAU*, Caudate; *DT*, deterministic tractography; *fMRI*, functional magnetic resonance imaging; *GP*, globus pallidus; *HIP*, hippocampus; *INS*, insula; *MBEA*, Montreal Battery of Evaluation of Amusia; *PUT*, putamen; *R*, right; *TBSS*, tract-based spatial statistics. *Adapted with permission from Sihvonen, A. J., Ripollés, P., Leo, V., Rodríguez-Fornells, A., Soinila, S., & Särkämö, T. (2016). Neural basis of acquired amusia and its recovery after stroke.* Journal of Neuroscience, 36(34), 8872−8881; Sihvonen, A. J., Ripollés, P., Rodriguez-Fornells, A., Soinila, S., & Särkämö, T. (2017). Revisiting the neural basis of acquired amusia: Structural changes underlying amusia recovery. *Frontiers in Neuroscience, 11, 426; Sihvonen, A. J., Ripollés, P., Särkämö, T., Leo, V., Rodriguez-Fornells, A., Saunavaara, J., et al. (2017). Tracting the neural basis of music: Deficient structural connectivity underlying acquired amusia.* Cortex, 97, 255−273; Sihvonen, A. J., Särkämö, T., Ripollés, P., Leo, V., Saunavaara, J., Parkkola, R., et al. (2017). Functional neural changes associated with acquired amusia across different stages of recovery after stroke. *Scientific Reports, 7(1), 11390.*

the core areas underlying severe, persistent acquired amusia. However, these results also indicate that damage to the left inferior frontal cortex may result in less severe, transient acquired amusia. Interestingly, there was virtually no overlap between the lesion patterns of amusia and aphasia, the latter being located in the left temporal cortex and insula (Sihvonen et al., 2016), which is generally in line with the findings of previous VLSM studies of aphasia (Dronkers et al., 2004; Fridriksson et al., 2015; Henseler et al., 2014; Mirman et al., 2015) and supports the classic dissociation of amusia and aphasia found in previous case studies (for a review, see Peretz & Coltheart, 2003).

Diffusion tensor imaging

Sihvonen et al. used DTI to determine white matter pathway deficits underlying acquired amusia in a sample of 42 stroke patients. Converging results from deterministic tractography (tract-level) and tract-based spatial statistics (voxel-level) analyses of acute stage data (see Fig. 5.2C and D) showed that nonrecovered amusic patients had damage to the right AF, inferior fronto-occipital fasciculus (IFOF), and uncinate fasciculus (UF), as well as to the corpus callosum compared to the nonamusics (Sihvonen, Ripollés, Särkämö, et al., 2017). In contrast, intact left AF was associated with recovery of amusia (Sihvonen, Ripollés, Särkämö, et al., 2017). Overall, these results converge with the right AF deficit observed in congenital amusia (Loui et al., 2009), but also implicate other right frontotemporal tracts as well as interhemispheric tracts in severe and persistent acquired amusia. Interestingly, these results also parallel recent findings on aphasia that damage not only to the left AF but also to the left IFOF and UF underlie deficits in speech processing, especially in language comprehension (Harvey, Wei, Ellmore, Hamilton, & Schnur, 2013; Ivanova et al., 2016; Kummerer et al., 2013).

Functional neuroimaging studies

Electroencephalography and magnetoencephalography

Using EEG, Münte et al. recorded event-related potentials (ERPs) in different auditory tasks in 12 stroke patients. Compared to nonamusic patients, amusic patients showed reduced P3a[1] responses to novel sounds within a repetitive sound sequence, reflecting an impairment in early attentional processing (Münte et al., 1998), as well as reduced mismatch negativity (MMN) responses to pitch changes within a repetitive sound sequence, indicating an impairment in auditory sensory memory for pitch (Kohlmetz et al., 2001). Similarly, using MEG, Särkämö et al. measured MMN responses to pitch and duration changes in a sample of 53 stroke patients (24 with left and 29 with right hemisphere damage) studied at acute, 3-month, and 6-month post-stroke stages. They reported that amusia caused by right hemisphere damage was more severe than amusia caused by left hemisphere damage and that the

---

1. The P3a is an ERP component that originates from stimulus-driven frontal attention mechanisms during task processing. It has been associated with brain activity related to the engagement of attention (especially orienting and involuntary shifts to changes in the environment) and the processing of novelty.

severity of amusia correlated with smaller MMN responses to pitch changes only in amusic patients with right hemisphere damage (Särkämö et al., 2010). Specifically, those amusic patients who had damage to the right auditory cortex showed worse recovery and also weaker MMN responses to both pitch and duration changes throughout the 6-month follow-up compared to nonamusic patients and amusic patients without auditory cortical damage (Särkämö et al., 2010).

Functional magnetic resonance imaging

Using fMRI in a sample of 41 stroke patients, Sihvonen et al. explored changes in activation patterns and functional connectivity in acquired amusia during passive listening to vocal (sung) and instrumental versions of familiar songs. At the acute poststroke stage (see Fig. 5.2E), amusic patients showed clearly reduced activation to instrumental music in the right STG and MTG compared to nonamusics (Sihvonen, Särkämö, Ripollés, et al., 2017). Functional connectivity analyses also indicated that the amusics with poor recovery showed reduced engagement of the right frontoparietal network during instrumental music listening (Sihvonen, Särkämö, Ripollés, et al., 2017), suggesting impaired allocation of attention to instrumental music, already at the acute stage. Interestingly, the amusics did not show decreased activations or functional connectivity deficits during the vocal music condition (Sihvonen, Särkämö, Ripollés, et al., 2017).

Longitudinal neural changes underlying the recovery of acquired amusia

Structural neuroimaging studies

Voxel-based morphometry

Sihvonen et al. utilized VBM in a sample of 90 stroke patients to explore gray and white matter volume changes associated with the longitudinal (acute to 6-month poststroke stage) outcome of acquired amusia. As summarized in Fig. 5.3A, poor versus good amusia recovery was associated with gray matter volume decrease in the right STG, MTG, and IFG as well as with white matter volume decrease in the right MTG, inferior temporal gyrus (ITG), basal ganglia, and hippocampus (Sihvonen et al., 2016; Sihvonen, Ripollés, Rodríguez-Fornells, et al., 2017), indicating that impaired amusia recovery is associated with atrophy in areas adjacent to the initial lesion. This atrophy pattern was somewhat different depending on amusia type: poor recovery was linked to the atrophy of the right posterior temporal and parietal regions in pitch-amusia and to the atrophy of the right anterior temporal cortex and hippocampus in rhythm-amusia (Sihvonen et al., 2016; Sihvonen, Ripollés, Rodríguez-Fornells, et al., 2017). Similar functional

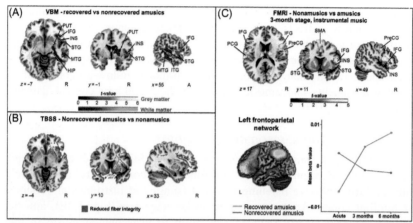

FIGURE 5.3 Longitudinal neural changes underlying the recovery of acquired amusia. (A) VBM analyses of gray (*red*) and white matter volume (*blue*) in recovered versus nonrecovered amusic patients. (B) TBSS analysis comparing nonrecovered amusic versus nonamusic patients. (C) fMRI activation pattern comparison between nonamusic and amusic patients during instrumental music listening at 3-month stage and left frontoparietal network functional connectivity engagement comparison between recovered and nonrecovered amusic patients. *HIP*, Hippocampus; *INS*, insula; *L*, left; *PCG*, postcentral gyrus; *PUT*, putamen; *R*, right; *TBSS*, tract-based spatial statistics; *VBM*, voxel-based morphometry. *Adapted with permission from Sihvonen, A. J., Ripollés, P., Leo, V., Rodríguez-Fornells, A., Soinila, S., & Särkämö, T. (2016). Neural basis of acquired amusia and its recovery after stroke.* Journal of Neuroscience, *36(34), 8872−8881; Sihvonen, A. J., Ripollés, P., Rodríguez-Fornells, A., Soinila, S., & Särkämö, T. (2017). Revisiting the neural basis of acquired amusia: Structural changes underlying amusia recovery.* Frontiers in Neuroscience, *11, 426; Sihvonen, A. J., Ripollés, P., Särkämö, T., Leo, V., Rodriguez-Fornells, A., Saunavaara, J., et al. (2017). Tracting the neural basis of music: Deficient structural connectivity underlying acquired amusia.* Cortex, *97, 255−273; Sihvonen, A. J., Särkämö, T., Ripollés, P., Leo, V., Saunavaara, J., Parkkola, R., et al. (2017). Functional neural changes associated with acquired amusia across different stages of recovery after stroke.* Scientific Reports, *7(1), 11390.*

dissociation of anterior versus posterior superior temporal regions has been found previously in both animals (Bendor & Wang, 2008) and humans (Jamison, Watkins, Bishop, & Matthews, 2006; Samson, Zeffiro, Toussaint, & Belin, 2011; Warren, Jennings, & Griffiths, 2005), with anterior regions showing greater sensitivity to changes in the temporal domain and posterior regions showing greater sensitivity to changes in the spectral domain. Structural abnormalities in the right STG have also been observed in congenital amusics (Albouy et al., 2013; Hyde et al., 2007).

Diffusion tensor imaging

The longitudinal DTI results of Sihvonen, Ripollés, Särkämö, et al. (2017) (see Fig. 5.3B) linked persistent, nonrecovering amusia to progressive white matter damage in the right ventral (IFOF, UF) and dorsal (AF) as well as in interhemispheric (corpus callosum) tracts. This degenerative pattern was similar in rhythm-amusia and pitch-amusia for the right frontotemporal tracts, but there were also some differences. In rhythm-amusia, poor recovery was additionally associated with white matter pathway damage in the left AF (Sihvonen, Ripollés, Särkämö, et al., 2017). In pitch-amusia, damage to the posterior (tapetum) part of the corpus callosum, which connects the left and right temporal lobes, was linked to poor recovery whereas lack of damage to the right AF was linked to good recovery (Sihvonen, Ripollés, Särkämö, et al., 2017), suggesting that preservation of this dorsal tract connecting the right frontoparietal cortices plays a role in the recovery of pitch-amusia. Interestingly, and in contrast with the deficient dorsal tract (AF) thought to underlie congenital amusia (Peretz, 2016), the ventral tract (IFOF) deficiency was the strongest predictor of acquired amusia. Both the IFOF and the AF have termination points in musically crucial brain regions, in right inferior frontal and inferior parietal areas (Burks et al., 2018; Catani, Jones, & Ffytche, 2005; Hau et al., 2016). It seems that as the white matter pathway degeneration progresses, the cortical terminals of the pathways become affected, leading to the gray matter atrophy observed in the VBM (Sihvonen et al., 2016; Sihvonen, Ripollés, Särkämö, et al., 2017).

Functional neuroimaging studies

Functional magnetic resonance imaging

The longitudinal data of the passive music listening task of Sihvonen et al. (see above) showed that in the instrumental music condition, amusia recovery was linked to increased activation in left and right frontoparietal regions at the 3-month stage and in right frontal areas at the 6-month stage as well as to increased functional connectivity in the left frontoparietal network (see Fig. 5.3C), especially during the first 3 months (Sihvonen, Särkämö, Ripollés, et al., 2017). This suggests that amusia recovery is underpinned by a dynamic shift characterized by a widespread recruitment of bilateral frontoparietal regions at the early stage and more focal right prefrontal regions at the later stage. This pattern was specific to instrumental music as similar changes were not observed in the vocal music condition, which also suggests that the observed effects cannot be due to deficits in general attentional orientation. Again, differing in lateralization, these results in the musical domain closely mirror those from the language domain, as aphasic stroke patients who recover have been reported to show upregulation of bilateral frontal region activity, especially in inferior frontal and supplementary motor areas, in a language task at the subacute stage, followed by normalization of activation with a reshift to the left hemisphere at the chronic stage (Saur et al., 2006).

Conclusions and future directions

Neural basis of acquired amusia

Functional neuroimaging studies in healthy subjects have shown that music perception engages a widespread network comprising bilateral temporal, frontal, parietal, and subcortical brain regions (for more information, see Chapter 1: The musical brain). As reviewed above, the current results from structural and functional neuroimaging studies of acquired amusia indicates that the deficit and its longitudinal recovery is likewise associated with a complex and widespread but consistent pattern of lesioned cortical and subcortical areas (indicated by VLSM), changes in gray and white matter structure (indicated by VBM and DTI), and changes in the functional activity and connectivity of cortical networks (indicated by EEG, MEG, and fMRI). This pattern follows the general organization principle of the brain that (1) spatially distributed areas subserving a cognitive function are connected both structurally and functionally to form a network that maximizes the processing, storage, and manipulation of information (Ross, 2010), and that (2) disruption of the neural network and its connections can lead to a disconnection syndrome and a cognitive-behavioral deficit (Catani & Mesulam, 2008; Thiebaut de Schotten et al., 2008), which has been postulated to be the core neural mechanism underlying also congenital amusia (Peretz, 2016). The converging findings obtained using multiple imaging modalities discussed above replicate and validate much of what has been observed in older symptom-led and lesion-led explorations of acquired amusia (see Stewart et al., 2006), while providing a more precise, spatially accurate, and comprehensive picture of the structural and functional neurobiological changes underpinning acquired amusia and its recovery. Crucially, these results enable modeling of the cascade of lesion-induced structural changes giving rise to acquired amusia and the structural and functional changes that either impair or facilitate its recovery (see Fig. 5.4).

Based on the VLSM results (Hirel et al., 2017; Sihvonen et al., 2016; Sihvonen, Särkämö, Ripollés, et al., 2017), the core of the lesion area causing acquired amusia is in the right insula and basal ganglia from where the lesion extends to temporal (STG/MTG), frontal (IFG), and limbic (hippocampus) areas. This core lesion area overlays crucial frontotemporal white matter pathways, including both dorsal (AF) and ventral (IFOF, UF) pathways, as well as the corpus callosum, reducing their volume and integrity at the acute stage (Sihvonen, Ripollés, Särkämö, et al., 2017). From ontogenetic and phylogenetic standpoints, the result linking the right IFOF to music perception is particularly interesting since in humans this tract is known to be present already at birth (Perani et al., 2011), but it is clearly less developed in monkeys (Thiebaut de Schotten, Dell'Acqua, Valabregue, & Catani, 2012). Functionally, the lesion also impairs the auditory encoding of lower-

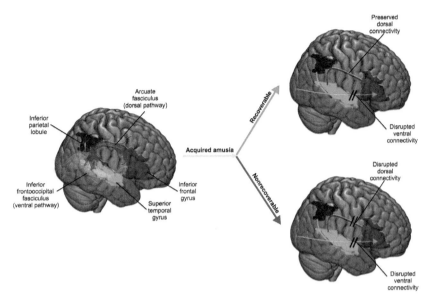

FIGURE 5.4   Dual-stream model of acquired amusia.

level acoustic features (e.g., pitch, duration) of music (Kohlmetz et al., 2001; Münte et al., 1998; Särkämö et al., 2010) and inhibits the engagement of the right STG/MTG, leading to reduced functional connectivity in the right frontoparietal attentional network when listening to music (Sihvonen, Särkämö, Ripollés, et al., 2017). The extent to which the lesion covers the key music processing cortical structures (right STG, IFG, and insula), disrupts the white matter pathways connecting them, and functionally impairs the activation and connectivity of right temporal, frontal, and parietal networks at the acute stage predicts poor recovery of amusia over the next 6 months. In contrast, damage to left frontal areas (IFG) or left AF causes a more transient form of acquired amusia that shows better recovery.

The longitudinal recovery process of acquired amusia is driven by a complex set of both positive (increased activation, preservation) and negative (atrophy, degeneration) structural and functional neural changes. Atrophy in the right temporal (STG, MTG, ITG), frontal (IFG), and subcortical (basal ganglia, hippocampus) areas adjacent to the lesion (Sihvonen et al., 2016; Sihvonen, Ripollés, Rodríguez-Fornells, et al., 2017) as well as degeneration of the right dorsal (AF) and ventral (IFOF, UF) tracts (Sihvonen, Ripollés, Särkämö, et al., 2017) are associated with poor amusia recovery. In contrast, the preservation of the right AF as well as the increased functional recruitment of frontoparietal regions, in both left and right hemisphere, during music processing are associated with good amusia recovery. In the language domain, two processing streams, the dorsal and ventral pathways, are thought to underlie the perception and production of speech (Hickok & Poeppel, 2007; Rauschecker, 2014; Rauschecker & Tian, 2000). A similar dual-stream model has been proposed to act in parallel in music processing, transferring crucial musical auditory information between the temporal, inferior parietal, and inferior frontal regions in the right hemisphere (Loui, 2015; Musso et al., 2015; Rauschecker, 2014; Sammler, Grosbras, Anwander, Bestelmeyer, & Belin, 2015; Zatorre, Belin, & Penhune, 2002). Of the two pathways, the dorsal pathway ("where" or "how") connecting temporal and inferior parietal regions with frontal areas is hypothesized to be important for evaluation of audiomotor movement and spatial information, whereas the ventral pathway ("what") is involved in categorizing sound to auditory objects (Rauschecker, 2014; Rauschecker & Scott, 2009; Rauschecker & Tian, 2000; Sammler et al., 2015). In aphasia, damage to the dorsal pathways (AF) is associated with speech production impairments, while speech comprehension impairments are associated with damage to the ventral pathway (IFOF) (Kummerer et al., 2013). In the musical domain, it is likewise possible that damage to individual pathways (dorsal or ventral) would manifest in different musical impairments (production vs perception) (Loui, 2015; Loui, Guenther, Mathys, & Schlaug, 2008; Sammler et al., 2015). In acquired amusia, the DTI results reviewed above suggest that if both the ventral and dorsal streams of the right hemisphere are damaged, recovery is unlikely, but if one of these streams in the right hemisphere is preserved, recovery is possible due to the cross-talk and shared functionalities of the streams, similar to what has been found in the language domain (Lopez-Barroso et al., 2011). Overall, the observed functional differences between the recovered and nonrecovered amusics most likely reflect longitudinal network reorganization associated with spontaneous recovery of function after stroke (Cramer, 2008; Saur et al., 2006).

In summary, current evidence suggests that acquired amusia is underpinned by a deficient network of right temporal, frontal, and subcortical areas and pathways, which show different neuroplasticity changes over time affecting the long-term outcome of acquired amusia. In future, neuroimaging studies with larger sample sizes are still warranted to compare in more detail the neural mechanisms underlying different types of acquired amusia (e.g., pitch vs rhythm) and also their comorbidity with aphasia and deficits in prosody perception. Moreover, exploring the neural correlates of music production versus perception deficits in acquired amusia would be highly interesting and increase our understanding of the auditory—motor coupling processes involved in music. From a methodological standpoint, the application of the latest multivoxel pattern analysis tools to the lesion data (Sperber, Wiesen, & Karnath, 2019) and functional data (Zavaglia et al., 2015) obtained from patients with acquired amusia would provide an even more precise view of the essential neural structures for music perception.

Clinical considerations

Aside from providing theoretical insight into the neural architecture crucial for music processing, the novel neuroimaging findings on acquired amusia reviewed above are important also from a clinical standpoint. Even though the prevalence of stroke is increasing in the aging population and acquired amusia is a relatively common deficit after stroke, especially at the acute poststroke stage (Ayotte et al., 2000; Särkämö et al., 2009; Schuppert et al., 2000; Sihvonen et al., 2016), it is unfortunate that in clinical practice acquired amusia is not routinely evaluated after stroke, for example during a neuropsychological assessment. Owing to the fact that the large right hemisphere lesions causing amusia often cause also unilateral spatial neglect (loss of awareness of left side of body or environment) and anosognosia (impaired self-awareness of illness or deficit) and that stroke patients are often not exposed to music at the acute poststroke stage, the patients themselves may well be unaware that they have acquired amusia. Unless the patient is a musician or is otherwise actively engaged with music vocationally, clinicians often do not consider amusia as their focus is on other poststroke cognitive, verbal, and motor deficits that present a more immediate barrier for everyday functioning. Thus acquired amusia is currently most likely underdiagnosed in the stroke population.

Clinically, the VLSM results suggest that a patient who has suffered a stroke located within the boundaries of the amusia lesion map (Fig. 5.2) should be behaviorally screened with a diagnostic music test, such as the MBEA, to determine if he/she has acquired amusia. The MBEA provides information about the perception and memory of music, but it is important also to assess musical production skills (e.g., singing ability), movement to music (entraining movements to the beat of music), and the hedonic qualities of music (pleasure and reward experienced from music). Amusia is often coupled also with problems in linguistic prosody (Liu, Patel, Fourcin, & Stewart, 2010) and affective prosody (Jafari, Esmaili, Delbari, Mehrpour, & Mohajerani, 2017; Lima et al., 2016; Thompson, Marin, & Stewart, 2012), which rely on the perception of subtle pitch, timbre, and intensity variations in speech. This can lead to difficulties in everyday communication and social interaction, making the detection of acquired amusia important in this regard as well. The results cited here also provide a prognostic tool for estimating the long-term outcome of acquired amusia. An accurate diagnosis and prognosis of acquired amusia is important also for the clinical application of music-based rehabilitation. The ability to perceive musical pitch and rhythm play a crucial role in many music-based rehabilitation methods, including Rhythmic Auditory Stimulation, where movements of the lower and upper extremities are trained with the help of rhythmic entrainment to the beat of music (Thaut, 2015); music-supported training, where musical instruments are used to train upper extremity movements (Ripollés et al., 2016;

Schneider, Münte, Rodriguez-Fornells, Sailer, & Altenmüller, 2010); and melodic intonation therapy, where the melody and rhythm of singing is used to train speech production in aphasic patients (Schlaug, Norton, Marchina, Zipse, & Wan, 2010; van der Meulen, van de Sandt-Koenderman, Heijenbrok-Kal, Visch-Brink, & Ribbers, 2014). Obtaining information about the severity of pitch and rhythm deficits can help in assessing whether the patient may benefit from music-based rehabilitation and for selecting the appropriate level of the musical stimuli used in the training.

Finally, there is also the important question of how acquired amusia itself could be rehabilitated. To date, there are no intervention studies on acquired amusia, but some recent evidence from congenital amusia suggests that singing may provide a useful tool in this regard. Persons with congenital amusia have been observed to be able vocalize pitch intervals in correct directions (Loui et al., 2008) and, crucially, a singing intervention has been found to improve both the vocal production of singing and music perception ability in congenital amusia (Anderson, Himonides, Wise, Welch, & Stewart, 2012; Wilbiks, Vuvan, Girard, Peretz, & Russo, 2016). Interestingly, the fMRI results of the music listening task by Sihvonen, Särkämö, Ripollés, et al. (2017) showed that while patients with acquired amusia displayed clearly reduced activation to instrumental music compared to nonamusic patients, vocal (sung) music, in turn, activated a more extensive network of bilateral frontoparietal and right temporal regions in amusics, suggesting that the processing of singing is at least partially preserved. As there were no significant differences between the amusic and nonamusic groups in the occurrence of poststroke aphasia, the observed results are unlikely due to differences in concurrent language deficits. Evidence from fMRI studies of healthy subjects indicates that vocal music activates frontotemporal and limbic areas more bilaterally and extensively compared to speech, which is more left-lateralized (Callan et al., 2006; Schön et al., 2010), or to instrumental music, which is more right-lateralized (Alluri et al., 2013; Brattico et al., 2011). Thus singing may provide a viable tool also in the rehabilitation of acquired amusia.

References

Adolphs, R. (2016). Human lesion studies in the 21st century. *Neuron, 90*(6), 1151–1153.

Albouy, P., Mattout, J., Bouet, R., Maby, E., Sanchez, G., Aguera, P. E., et al. (2013). Impaired pitch perception and memory in congenital amusia: The deficit starts in the auditory cortex. *Brain, 136*(Pt 5), 1639–1661.

Alluri, V., Toiviainen, P., Jääskeläinen, I. P., Glerean, E., Sams, M., & Brattico, E. (2012). Large-scale brain networks emerge from dynamic processing of musical timbre, key and rhythm. *NeuroImage, 59*(4), 3677–3689.

Alluri, V., Toiviainen, P., Lund, T. E., Wallentin, M., Vuust, P., Nandi, A. K., et al. (2013). From Vivaldi to Beatles and back: Predicting lateralized brain responses to music. *NeuroImage, 83*, 627–636.

Anderson, S., Himonides, E., Wise, K., Welch, G., & Stewart, L. (2012). Is there potential for learning in amusia? A study of the effect of singing intervention in congenital amusia. *Annals of the New York Academy of Sciences, 1252,* 345−353.

Ayotte, J., Peretz, I., Rousseau, I., Bard, C., & Bojanowski, M. (2000). Patterns of music agnosia associated with middle cerebral artery infarcts. *Brain, 123*(9), 1926−1938.

Bates, E., Wilson, S. M., Saygin, A. P., Dick, F., Sereno, M. I., Knight, R. T., et al. (2003). Voxel-based lesion-symptom mapping. *Nature Neuroscience, 6*(5), 448−450.

Bendor, D., & Wang, X. (2008). Neural response properties of primary, rostral, and rostrotemporal core fields in the auditory cortex of marmoset monkeys. *Journal of Neurophysiology, 100*(2), 888−906.

Benjamin, E. J., Muntner, P., Alonso, A., Bittencourt, M. S., Callaway, C. W., Carson, A. P., et al. (2019). Heart disease and stroke statistics-2019 update: A report from the American Heart Association. *Circulation, 139*(10), e56−e66.

Brattico, E., Alluri, V., Bogert, B., Jacobsen, T., Vartiainen, N., Nieminen, S., et al. (2011). A functional MRI study of happy and sad emotions in music with and without lyrics. *Frontiers in Psychology, 2,* 308.

Burks, J. D., Conner, A. K., Bonney, P. A., Glenn, C. A., Baker, C. M., Boettcher, L. B., et al. (2018). Anatomy and white matter connections of the orbitofrontal gyrus. *Journal of Neurosurgery, 128*(6), 1865−1872.

Callan, D. E., Tsytsarev, V., Hanakawa, T., Callan, A. M., Katsuhara, M., Fukuyama, H., et al. (2006). Song and speech: Brain regions involved with perception and covert production. *NeuroImage, 31*(3), 1327−1342.

Catani, M., Jones, D. K., & Ffytche, D. H. (2005). Perisylvian language networks of the human brain. *Annals of Neurology, 57*(1), 8−16.

Catani, M., & Mesulam, M. (2008). The arcuate fasciculus and the disconnection theme in language and aphasia: history and current state. *Cortex, 44*(8), 953−961.

Clark, C. N., Golden, H. L., & Warren, J. D. (2015). Acquired amusia. *Handbook of Clinical Neurology, 129,* 607−631.

Cramer, S. C. (2008). Repairing the human brain after stroke: I. Mechanisms of spontaneous recovery. *Annals of Neurology, 63*(3), 272−287.

Di Pietro, M., Laganaro, M., Leemann, B., & Schnider, A. (2004). Receptive amusia: Temporal auditory processing deficit in a professional musician following a left temporo-parietal lesion. *Neuropsychologia, 42*(7), 868−877.

Dronkers, N. F., Wilkins, D. P., Van Valin, R. D., Redfern, B. B., & Jaeger, J. J. (2004). Lesion analysis of the brain areas involved in language comprehension. *Cognition, 92*(1-2), 145−177.

Engelter, S. T., Gostynski, M., Papa, S., Frei, M., Born, C., Ajdacic-Gross, V., et al. (2006). Epidemiology of aphasia attributable to first ischemic stroke: Incidence, severity, fluency, etiology, and thrombolysis. *Stroke, 37*(6), 1379−1384.

Fridriksson, J., Fillmore, P., Guo, D., & Rorden, C. (2015). Chronic broca's aphasia is caused by damage to Broca's and Wernicke's areas. *Cerebral Cortex, 25*(12), 4689−4696.

Global Burden of Disease (GBD) 2016 Neurology Collaborators. (2019). Global, regional, and national burden of neurological disorders, 1990−2016: A systematic analysis for the Global Burden of Disease Study 2016. *Lancet Neurology, 18*(5), 459−480. Available from https://doi.org/10.1016/S1474-4422(18)30499-X.

Grahn, J. A., & Rowe, J. B. (2009). Feeling the beat: Premotor and striatal interactions in musicians and nonmusicians during beat perception. *Journal of Neuroscience, 29*(23), 7540−7548.

Graziano, A. B., & Johnson, J. K. (2015). Music, neurology, and psychology in the nineteenth century. *Progress in Brain Research*, *216*, 33−49.

Griffiths, T. D., Rees, A., Witton, C., Cross, P. M., Shakir, R. A., & Green, G. G. (1997). Spatial and temporal auditory processing deficits following right hemisphere infarction. A psychophysical study. *Brain*, *120*(Pt 5), 785−794.

Harvey, D. Y., Wei, T., Ellmore, T. M., Hamilton, A. C., & Schnur, T. T. (2013). Neuropsychological evidence for the functional role of the uncinate fasciculus in semantic control. *Neuropsychologia*, *51*(5), 789−801.

Hau, J., Sarubbo, S., Perchey, G., Crivello, F., Zago, L., Mellet, E., et al. (2016). Cortical termi-nations of the inferior fronto-occipital and uncinate fasciculi: Anatomical stem-based virtual dissection. *Frontiers in Neuroanatomy*, *10*, 58.

Henseler, I., Regenbrecht, F., & Obrig, H. (2014). Lesion correlates of patholinguistic profiles in chronic aphasia: Comparisons of syndrome-, modality- and symptom-level assessment. *Brain*, *137*(Pt 3), 918−930.

Hickok, G., & Poeppel, D. (2007). The cortical organization of speech processing. *Nature Reviews Neuroscience*, *8*(5), 393−402.

Hirel, C., Nighoghossian, N., Leveque, Y., Hannoun, S., Fornoni, L., Daligault, S., et al. (2017). Verbal and musical short-term memory: Variety of auditory disorders after stroke. *Brain and Cognition*, *113*, 10−22.

Hochman, M. S., & Abrams, K. J. (2014). Amusia for pitch caused by right middle cerebral artery infarct. *Journal of Stroke and Cerebrovascular Diseases*, *23*(1), 164−165.

Hochstenbach, J., Mulder, T., van Limbeek, J., Donders, R., & Schoonderwaldt, H. (1998). Cognitive decline following stroke: A comprehensive study of cognitive decline following stroke. *Journal of Clinical & Experimental Neuropsychology*, *20*(4), 503−517.

Hofman, S., Klein, C., & Arlazoroff, A. (1993). Common hemisphericity of language and music in a musician. A case report. *Journal of Communication Disorders*, *26*(2), 73−82.

Hyde, K. L., Lerch, J. P., Zatorre, R. J., Griffiths, T. D., Evans, A. C., & Peretz, I. (2007). Cortical thickness in congenital amusia: When less is better than more. *Journal of Neuroscience*, *27*(47), 13028−13032.

Hyde, K. L., Zatorre, R. J., Griffiths, T. D., Lerch, J. P., & Peretz, I. (2006). Morphometry of the amusic brain: A two-site study. *Brain*, *129*(10), 2562−2570.

Hyde, K. L., Zatorre, R. J., & Peretz, I. (2011). Functional MRI evidence of an abnormal neural network for pitch processing in congenital amusia. *Cerebral Cortex*, *21*(2), 292−299.

Ivanova, M. V., Isaev, D. Y., Dragoy, O. V., Akinina, Y. S., Petrushevskiy, A. G., Fedina, O. N., et al. (2016). Diffusion-tensor imaging of major white matter tracts and their role in language processing in aphasia. *Cortex*, *85*, 165−181.

Jafari, Z., Esmaili, M., Delbari, A., Mehrpour, M., & Mohajerani, M. H. (2017). Post-stroke acquired amusia: A comparison between right- and left-brain hemispheric damages. *NeuroRehabilitation*, *40*(2), 233−241.

Jamison, H. L., Watkins, K. E., Bishop, D. V., & Matthews, P. M. (2006). Hemispheric speciali-zation for processing auditory nonspeech stimuli. *Cerebral Cortex*, *16*(9), 1266−1275.

Johannes, S., Jobges, M. E., Dengler, R., & Münte, T. F. (1998). Cortical auditory disorders: A case of non-verbal disturbances assessed with event-related brain potentials. *Behavioural Neurology*, *11*(1), 55−73.

Kohlmetz, C., Altenmüller, E., Schuppert, M., Wieringa, B. M., & Münte, T. F. (2001). Deficit in automatic sound-change detection may underlie some music perception deficits after acute hemispheric stroke. *Neuropsychologia*, *39*(11), 1121−1124.

Kohlmetz, C., Muller, S. V., Nager, W., Münte, T. F., & Altenmüller, E. (2003). Selective loss of timbre perception for keyboard and percussion instruments following a right temporal lesion. *Neurocase, 9*(1), 86−93.

Kummerer, D., Hartwigsen, G., Kellmeyer, P., Glauche, V., Mader, I., Kloppel, S., et al. (2013). Damage to ventral and dorsal language pathways in acute aphasia. *Brain, 136*(Pt 2), 619−629.

Leveque, Y., Fauvel, B., Groussard, M., Caclin, A., Albouy, P., Platel, H., et al. (2016). Altered intrinsic connectivity of the auditory cortex in congenital amusia. *Journal of Neurophysiology, 116*(1), 88−97.

Lima, C. F., Brancatisano, O., Fancourt, A., Müllensiefen, D., Scott, S. K., Warren, J. D., et al. (2016). Impaired socio-emotional processing in a developmental music disorder. *Scientific Reports, 6*, 34911.

Liu, F., Patel, A. D., Fourcin, A., & Stewart, L. (2010). Intonation processing in congenital amusia: Discrimination, identification and imitation. *Brain, 133*(Pt 6), 1682−1693.

Lopez-Barroso, D., de Diego-Balaguer, R., Cunillera, T., Camara, E., Münte, T. F., & Rodriguez-Fornells, A. (2011). Language learning under working memory constraints correlates with microstructural differences in the ventral language pathway. *Cerebral Cortex, 21*(12), 2742−2750.

Loui, P. (2015). A dual-stream neuroanatomy of singing. *Music Perception, 32*(3), 232−241.

Loui, P., Alsop, D., & Schlaug, G. (2009). Tone deafness: A new disconnection syndrome? *Journal of Neuroscience, 29*(33), 10215−10220.

Loui, P., Guenther, F. H., Mathys, C., & Schlaug, G. (2008). Action-perception mismatch in tone-deafness. *Current Biology, 18*(8), R331−R332.

Magee, W. L., Clark, I., Tamplin, J., & Bradt, J. (2017). Music interventions for acquired brain injury. *Cochrane Database of Systematic Reviews, 1*, CD006787.

Mandell, J., Schulze, K., & Schlaug, G. (2007). Congenital amusia: An auditory-motor feedback disorder? *Restorative Neurology and Neuroscience, 25*(3−4), 323−334.

Mavlov, L. (1980). Amusia due to rhythm agnosia in a musician with left hemisphere damage: A non-auditory supramodal defect. *Cortex, 16*(2), 331−338.

Mazzoni, M., Moretti, P., Pardossi, L., Vista, M., Muratorio, A., & Puglioli, M. (1993). A case of music imperception. *Journal of Neurology, Neurosurgery, and Psychiatry, 56*(3), 322.

McFarland, H. R., & Fortin, D. (1982). Amusia due to right temporoparietal infarct. *Archives of Neurology, 39*(11), 725−727.

Mirman, D., Chen, Q., Zhang, Y., Wang, Z., Faseyitan, O. K., Coslett, H. B., et al. (2015). Neural organization of spoken language revealed by lesion-symptom mapping. *Nature Communications, 6*, 6762.

Münte, T. F., Schuppert, M., Johannes, S., Wieringa, B. M., Kohlmetz, C., & Altenmüller, E. (1998). Brain potentials in patients with music perception deficits: Evidence for an early locus. *Neuroscience Letters, 256*(2), 85−88.

Murayama, J., Kashiwagi, T., Kashiwagi, A., & Mimura, M. (2004). Impaired pitch production and preserved rhythm production in a right brain-damaged patient with amusia. *Brain and Cognition, 56*(1), 36−42.

Musso, M., Weiller, C., Horn, A., Glauche, V., Umarova, R., Hennig, J., et al. (2015). A single dual-stream framework for syntactic computations in music and language. *NeuroImage, 117*, 267−283.

Norman-Haignere, S. V., Albouy, P., Caclin, A., McDermott, J. H., Kanwisher, N. G., & Tillmann, B. (2016). Pitch-responsive cortical regions in congenital amusia. *Journal of Neuroscience, 36*(10), 2986−2994.

Nys, G. M., van Zandvoort, M. J., de Kort, P. L., Jansen, B. P., de Haan, E. H., & Kappelle, L. J. (2007). Cognitive disorders in acute stroke: Prevalence and clinical determinants. *Cerebrovascular Diseases*, 23(5-6), 408−416.

Omigie, D., Müllensiefen, D., & Stewart, L. (2012). The experience of music in congenital amusia. *Music Perception*, 30(1), 1−18.

Penhune, V. B., Zattore, R. J., & Evans, A. C. (1998). Cerebellar contributions to motor timing: A PET study of auditory and visual rhythm reproduction. *Journal of Cognitive Neuroscience*, 10(6), 752−765.

Perani, D., Saccuman, M. C., Scifo, P., Anwander, A., Spada, D., Baldoli, C., et al. (2011). Neural language networks at birth. *Proceedings of the National Academy of Sciences of the United States of America*, 108(38), 16056−16061.

Peretz, I. (2016). Neurobiology of congenital amusia. *Trends in Cognitive Sciences*, 20(11), 857−867.

Peretz, I., Brattico, E., Järvenpää, M., & Tervaniemi, M. (2009). The amusic brain: In tune, out of key, and unaware. *Brain*, 132(Pt 5), 1277−1286.

Peretz, I., Brattico, E., & Tervaniemi, M. (2005). Abnormal electrical brain responses to pitch in congenital amusia. *Annals of Neurology*, 58(3), 478−482.

Peretz, I., Champod, A. S., & Hyde, K. (2003). Varieties of musical disorders. The Montreal Battery of Evaluation of Amusia. *Annals of the New York Academy of Sciences*, 999, 58−75.

Peretz, I., & Coltheart, M. (2003). Modularity of music processing. *Nature Neuroscience*, 6(7), 688−691.

Price, C. J., & Friston, K. J. (2002). Degeneracy and cognitive anatomy. *Trends in Cognitive Sciences*, 6(10), 416−421.

Rasquin, S. M., Verhey, F. R., Lousberg, R., Winkens, I., & Lodder, J. (2002). Vascular cognitive disorders: Memory, mental speed and cognitive flexibility after stroke. *Journal of the Neurological Sciences*, 203-204, 115−119.

Rathore, S. S., Hinn, A. R., Cooper, L. S., Tyroler, H. A., & Rosamond, W. D. (2002). Characterization of incident stroke signs and symptoms: Findings from the atherosclerosis risk in communities study. *Stroke*, 33(11), 2718−2721.

Rauschecker, J. P. (2014). Is there a tape recorder in your head? How the brain stores and retrieves musical melodies. *Frontiers in Systems Neuroscience*, 8, 149.

Rauschecker, J. P., & Scott, S. K. (2009). Maps and streams in the auditory cortex: Nonhuman primates illuminate human speech processing. *Nature Neuroscience*, 12(6), 718−724.

Rauschecker, J. P., & Tian, B. (2000). Mechanisms and streams for processing of "what" and "where" in auditory cortex. *Proceedings of the National Academy of Sciences of the United States of America*, 97(22), 11800−11806.

Ripollés, P., Rojo, N., Grau-Sánchez, J., Amengual, J., Càmara, E., Marco-Pallarés, J., et al. (2016). Music supported therapy promotes motor plasticity in individuals with chronic stroke. *Brain Imaging and Behavior*, 10(4), 1289−1307.

Rorden, C., & Karnath, H. O. (2004). Using human brain lesions to infer function: A relic from a past era in the fMRI age? *Nature Reviews Neuroscience*, 5(10), 813−819.

Ross, E. D. (2010). Cerebral localization of functions and the neurology of language: Fact versus fiction or is it something else? *Neuroscientist*, 16(3), 222−243.

Rosslau, K., Steinwede, D., Schröder, C., Herholz, S. C., Lappe, C., Dobel, C., et al. (2015). Clinical investigations of receptive and expressive musical functions after stroke. *Frontiers in Psychology*, 6, 768.

Sammler, D., Grosbras, M. H., Anwander, A., Bestelmeyer, P. E., & Belin, P. (2015). Dorsal and ventral pathways for prosody. *Current Biology*, *25*(23), 3079–3085.

Samson, F., Zeffiro, T. A., Toussaint, A., & Belin, P. (2011). Stimulus complexity and categorical effects in human auditory cortex: An activation likelihood estimation meta-analysis. *Frontiers in Psychology*, *1*, 241.

Särkämö, T., Tervaniemi, M., Soinila, S., Autti, T., Silvennoinen, H. M., Laine, M., et al. (2009). Cognitive deficits associated with acquired amusia after stroke: A neuropsychological follow-up study. *Neuropsychologia*, *47*(12), 2642–2651.

Särkämö, T., Tervaniemi, M., Soinila, S., Autti, T., Silvennoinen, H. M., Laine, M., et al. (2010). Auditory and cognitive deficits associated with acquired amusia after stroke: A magnetoencephalography and neuropsychological follow-up study. *PloS One*, *5*(12), e15157.

Satoh, M., Takeda, K., Nagata, K., Hatazawa, J., & Kuzuhara, S. (2003). The anterior portion of the bilateral temporal lobes participates in music perception: A positron emission tomography study. *American Journal of Neuroradiology*, *24*(9), 1843–1848.

Saur, D., Lange, R., Baumgaertner, A., Schraknepper, V., Willmes, K., Rijntjes, M., et al. (2006). Dynamics of language reorganization after stroke. *Brain*, *129*(Pt 6), 1371–1384.

Schlaug, G., Norton, A., Marchina, S., Zipse, L., & Wan, C. Y. (2010). From singing to speaking: Facilitating recovery from nonfluent aphasia. *Future Neurology*, *5*(5), 657–665.

Schneider, S., Münte, T., Rodriguez-Fornells, A., Sailer, M., & Altenmüller, E. (2010). Music-supported training is more efficient than functional motor training for recovery of fine motor skills in stroke patients. *Music Perception*, *2010*(27), 271–280.

Schön, D., Gordon, R., Campagne, A., Magne, C., Astésano, C., Anton, J. L., et al. (2010). Similar cerebral networks in language, music and song perception. *NeuroImage*, *51*(1), 450–461.

Schuppert, M., Münte, T. F., Wieringa, B. M., & Altenmüller, E. (2000). Receptive amusia: Evidence for cross-hemispheric neural networks underlying music processing strategies. *Brain*, *123*(Pt 3), 546–559.

Sihvonen, A. J., Ripollés, P., Leo, V., Rodríguez-Fornells, A., Soinila, S., & Särkämö, T. (2016). Neural basis of acquired amusia and its recovery after stroke. *Journal of Neuroscience*, *36* (34), 8872–8881.

Sihvonen, A. J., Ripollés, P., Rodríguez-Fornells, A., Soinila, S., & Särkämö, T. (2017). Revisiting the neural basis of acquired amusia: Structural changes underlying amusia recovery. *Frontiers in Neuroscience*, *11*, 426.

Sihvonen, A. J., Ripollés, P., Särkämö, T., Leo, V., Rodriguez-Fornells, A., Saunavaara, J., et al. (2017). Tracting the neural basis of music: Deficient structural connectivity underlying acquired amusia. *Cortex*, *97*, 255–273.

Sihvonen, A. J., Särkämö, T., Leo, V., Tervaniemi, M., Altenmüller, E., & Soinila, S. (2017). Music-based interventions in neurological rehabilitation. *Lancet Neurology*, *16*(8), 648–660.

Sihvonen, A. J., Särkämö, T., Ripollés, P., Leo, V., Saunavaara, J., Parkkola, R., et al. (2017). Functional neural changes associated with acquired amusia across different stages of recovery after stroke. *Scientific Reports*, *7*(1), 11390.

Sperber, C., Wiesen, D., & Karnath, H. O. (2019). An empirical evaluation of multivariate lesion behaviour mapping using support vector regression. *Human Brain Mapping*, *40*(5), 1381–1390.

Stewart, L. (2008). Fractionating the musical mind: Insights from congenital amusia. *Current Opinion in Neurobiology*, *18*(2), 127–130.

Stewart, L., von Kriegstein, K., Warren, J. D., & Griffiths, T. D. (2006). Music and the brain: Disorders of musical listening. *Brain*, *129*(Pt 10), 2533–2553.

Tatemichi, T. K., Desmond, D. W., Stem, Y., Paik, M., Sano, M., & Bagiella, E. (1994). Cognitive impairment after stroke: Frequency, patterns, and relationship to functional abilities. *Journal of Neurology, Neurosurgery, and Psychiatry, 57*(2), 202–207.

Terao, Y., Mizuno, T., Shindoh, M., Sakurai, Y., Ugawa, Y., Kobayashi, S., et al. (2006). Vocal amusia in a professional tango singer due to a right superior temporal cortex infarction. *Neuropsychologia, 44*(3), 479–488.

Thaut, M. H. (2015). The discovery of human auditory-motor entrainment and its role in the development of neurologic music therapy. *Progress in Brain Research, 217*, 253–266.

Thiebaut de Schotten, M., Dell'Acqua, F., Valabregue, R., & Catani, M. (2012). Monkey to human comparative anatomy of the frontal lobe association tracts. *Cortex, 48*(1), 82–96.

Thiebaut de Schotten, M., Kinkingnehun, S., Delmaire, C., Lehericy, S., Duffau, H., Thivard, L., et al. (2008). Visualization of disconnection syndromes in humans. *Cortex, 44*(8), 1097–1103.

Thompson, W. F., Marin, M. M., & Stewart, L. (2012). Reduced sensitivity to emotional prosody in congenital amusia rekindles the musical protolanguage hypothesis. *Proceedings of the National Academy of Sciences of the United States of America, 109*(46), 19027–19032.

van der Meulen, I., van de Sandt-Koenderman, W. M., Heijenbrok-Kal, M. H., Visch-Brink, E. G., & Ribbers, G. M. (2014). The efficacy and timing of melodic intonation therapy in subacute aphasia. *Neurorehabilitation and Neural Repair, 28*(6), 536–544.

Warren, J. D., Jennings, A. R., & Griffiths, T. D. (2005). Analysis of the spectral envelope of sounds by the human brain. *NeuroImage, 24*(4), 1052–1057.

Wilbiks, J. M., Vuvan, D. T., Girard, P. Y., Peretz, I., & Russo, F. A. (2016). Effects of vocal training in a musicophile with congenital amusia. *Neurocase, 22*(6), 526–537.

Wilson, S. J., Pressing, J. L., & Wales, R. J. (2002). Modelling rhythmic function in a musician post-stroke. *Neuropsychologia, 40*(8), 1494–1505.

World Health Organization (WHO). (2015). *World report on ageing and health.* Retrieved on March 20, 2019 from <https://apps.who.int/iris/bitstream/handle/10665/186463/9789240694811_eng.pdf?sequence = 1>.

Yoo, H. J., Moon, H. I., & Pyun, S. B. (2016). Amusia after right temporoparietal lobe infarction: A case report. *Annals of Rehabilitation Medicine, 40*(5), 933–937.

Zatorre, R. J., Belin, P., & Penhune, V. B. (2002). Structure and function of auditory cortex: Music and speech. *Trends in Cognitive Sciences, 6*(1), 37–46.

Zavaglia, M., Forkert, N. D., Cheng, B., Gerloff, C., Thomalla, G., & Hilgetag, C. C. (2015). Mapping causal functional contributions derived from the clinical assessment of brain damage after stroke. *NeuroImage Clinical, 9*, 83–94.

Zendel, B. R., Lagrois, M. E., Robitaille, N., & Peretz, I. (2015). Attending to pitch information inhibits processing of pitch information: The curious case of amusia. *Journal of Neuroscience, 35*(9), 3815–3824.

Chapter 6

"Curious" cases of preservation of music compositional ability in the presence of organic brain disease: historical examples

Lola L. Cuddy[1] and Jacalyn M. Duffin[2]
[1]*Department of Psychology, Queen's University, Kingston, ON, Canada,* [2]*Professor Emerita, Hannah Chair of the History of Medicine, Queen's University, Kingston, ON, Canada*

Introduction

Previous chapters have documented music perception, cognition, and emotion in normal and pathological aging. Normal aging (see Halpern, this volume) may be accompanied by mild-to-moderate declines in sensory—motor coordination, attention, and short-term memory, all of which play a role in music processing. Moreover, diseases accompanying aging—brain injury following stroke (Sihvonen & Sarkamo, this volume) and neurodegenerative diseases (Benhamou & Warren, this volume)—typically have devastating effects on cognitive functions, resulting in language and musical impairments, known as aphasia and amusia, respectively. Yet, regarding brain disease, there are curious cases, curious in the sense of being neuroanatomical mysteries that do not fit the standard description of the disease process: they reveal remarkable preservation of musical functions in brain disorders. Cases, such as those described by the late Sacks (2008), have entertained and intrigued readers for many years.

In this chapter, we report instances of musical creations from composers who suffered from neurological disease with loss of cognitive and sensory—motor capacities. This exercise enters a well-trodden path that has explored the relationship of disease and artistic ability with questionable conclusions. For example, several decades ago, some authors were captivated by the idea that tuberculosis heightened creativity through a kind of exalted "spes phthisica" (Fraser, 1978; Jacobson, 1907, 1926; Ott, 1996, pp. 77−78). Well before Sontag (1978) complained about this movement in her famous

Music and the Aging Brain. DOI: https://doi.org/10.1016/B978-0-12-817422-7.00006-7
173

1978 book, *Illness as Metaphor*, the notion had been discredited. Why? Tuberculosis was the most common cause of death in the 19th century and it prevailed in impoverished settings; artists and musicians were often poor and were at least as likely as the average citizen to contract the prevalent disease. Their achievements were in spite of, not because of their maladies and they might well have created more had they lived (Chalke, 1962). Another movement that still continues to have some currency seeks to link creativity to mental illness, again emphasizing the link between the originality and insights of artistic geniuses to their psychic pathology (Andreasen, 2005, 2008). The flip side of this theory is to suggest that the creative brilliance is the cause of the mental disorder and that the flashes of genius are so intense that they distort reasoning. Again, along with many other authors (Trethowan, 1977, p. 400) we contend that these artists were successful *in spite of*, not because of their psychic ailments. Importantly, we do not believe that the cognitive damages outlined below actually produced the creativity—rather we view these cases as yet more examples of a natural experiment: persistence of musical ability in the face of devastating organic change.

In keeping with the focus of this book, we have selected examples of older composers afflicted with neurological disorders and excluded cases of younger composers similarly afflicted, such as Robert Schumann and George Gershwin. Similarly, we set aside the numerous, well-known examples of remarkable musical genius confronted with sensory disorders: blindness affected J.S. Bach, G. F. Handel, Ray Charles, and Stevie Wonder; deafness affected Ludwig van Beethoven, Gabriel Fauré, and Ralph Vaughan Williams.

We selected composition as representative of the highest form of musical art. Composition comprises a vast array of musical knowledge such as knowledge of the elements of music (individual notes, durations, dynamics, timbre), knowledge of the rules whereby elements may be combined within a given style, knowledge of voice and instrumentation, and so forth. This knowledge is then expressed and transcribed as an inspired creation that communicates musical ideas, structure, and emotion, a creation that passes the test of time. Musical composition is an intriguing example of brain function much more extensive than that involved in the memory of "how to do things," that is, procedural memory. While procedural memory may describe the automatic sensory—motor processes engaged in playing a scale on an instrument or singing a familiar song (Baird & Samson, 2009), musical composition suggests a more complex picture of the musical brain.

We selected cases for which there exists, first, a known record of compositions and performances during the course of the disease, and second, recorded medical/clinical observations. For the latter, the perils of retrospective diagnosis become evident. Not only did the neurological examination, as we know it today, evolve slowly across the 19th century and into the 20th, concepts of disease and of their causes also changed, the differences becoming ever more flagrant the further back we search, as the first example will illustrate. The most reliable symptom-based etiological categories, prior to chemical tests and brain imaging, are cerebrovascular conditions and various infections—which must include syphilis (from the 16th century). But because the evidence of infection was frequently glossed over by families and biographers wishing to protect the privacy and dignity of their subjects, the diagnosis is often presumptive.

Finally, we acknowledge the thoughtful efforts of others to trace changes in the quality of compositions during the course of the disease (e.g., Mazzucchi, Fanticini, Bellocchio, Petracchi, & Boller, 2017). Weiss (2013, 2016) links the composer Shebalin's loss of verbal language following stroke, and his poststroke compositional language. These are intriguing studies, but we must urge caution regarding the identification and interpretation of such changes for at least two reasons. The first concerns the difficulties of assessing creativity and shifts in creativity. There is no standard, universally agreed-upon metric on which to base judgment on the creative quality of a composition (Vempala, 2014). The second is that musical function in disease, whether preservation, change, or decline, has not yet been evaluated against a baseline control taking into account the effects of normal aging on the process of composition. Such control data are not available at this time and must be left to future research.

We now present seven short case histories, ranging from the 16th to the 20th century, of composers who provide examples of persistent compositional ability in the face of debilitating organic brain disease. They were well deserving of the attention garnered from their contemporaries as well as historians. Owing to the era in which they took place, or the absence of complete medical and autopsy reports, it is impossible to impose a contemporary neuroanatomical diagnosis. Nevertheless, they stand as a reminder and an inspiration to investigate how musical ability resides, resilient and irrepressible, in many damaged brains.

Following the biographical sketches, a final section revisits the limitations of the historical approach as well as its important implications and encouragement for future investigations.

Orlando de Lasso (c.1530—94)

Born in what is now Belgium, Lasso began his career in various Italian sites, but by 1536 he had joined the court of Albrecht V of Bavaria in Munich. He married Regina Wäckinger, daughter of a maid of honor in the court. It is owing to their letters and the fact that his physician is known that medical specialists have attempted to retrospectively diagnose the condition that marked his later years (Fig. 6.1).

FIGURE 6.1 Orlando di Lasso.

Following a voyage in autumn of 1585, Lasso was found to be tired and despondent. The fervent Catholic doctor, Thomas Mermann, was summoned. His treatments—likely diet, herbals, purgatives, and bleeding—were deemed to have been somewhat effective and Lasso dedicated his 1587 madrigals to his physician. But his health deteriorated. Out of concern for his wife, by November 1587, he had secured a pension that should continue after his death.

In late 1589 or early 1590, he returned from another journey gravely ill. His wife wrote that he would not speak to her or anyone. Others have interpreted her words to suggest that he had entered a kind of dementia (Fétis, 1867)—sad, dreaming, unable to recognize his spouse, and given to morose ideas. Dr. Mermann attended again. Some have labeled the diagnosis *melancholia hypochondriaca* (Pirro, 1940).

By 1592 Lasso had once again improved and was able to fill his *Kappelmeister* duties and accompany his master on official journeys. During the period of his illness, he composed his *Cantiones sacrae* (1594) for six voices and his *Lagrime di S. Pietro* (1595), said to be one of the most beautiful of his works. Lasso's dedication of the *Cantiones* reflected on the differences in the music composed in his youth with that of his older age aware of impending mortality. He died June 14, 1594.

It is difficult to judge Lasso's affliction in present-day terms, and melancholic syndromes have had many diagnostic categories (Jackson, 1986). Tempting though it may be to equate it with depression, the ancient diagnosis of *melancholia hypochondriaca*, as discussed by Mermann in Theirmair's

(1675) edition of his consultations, included numerous physical symptoms, and mental derangement that extended beyond sadness, to delirium, to stupor, and loss of reason—hinting at an organic brain disorder. Coeurdevey (2003) saw it as a "cerebral accident"—possibly a stroke—followed by depression. The content of the letters and the possible aphasia and agnosia have led several medical specialists to perceive signs of dementia through which Lasso remained "clearheaded for anything that touched on his art" (cited in Leuchtmann, 1976, p. 210; Pirro, 1940, p. 361).

Hugo Wolf (1860–1903)

Born in present-day Slovenia, Wolf lived most of his life in Vienna. A prodigy, he began to play piano and violin at the age of 4, but his irascible, temperamental personality meant that he was expelled from several schools. Despite great productivity as a composer, he relied heavily on various friends and benefactors for support, especially his friend, Heinrich Köchert, whose wife, Melanie, became Wolf's devoted mistress; their letters are an important source on his life. Inspired by Wagner and encouraged by Franz Liszt, he moved beyond songs to larger works including operas (Fig. 6.2).

Most of Wolf's biographers acknowledge that he had contracted syphilis at some point in his youth (Cooke, 1985; Walker, 1968). In neurosyphilis, no

FIGURE 6.2 Hugo Wolf.

part of the brain or nervous system is immune. The infection can destroy large parts of the brain in virtually every region through meningoencephalitis, cerebral vasculitis, and gummata that sometimes are mistaken for tumors. MRI studies reveal atrophy, hemorrhage, and edema (Zheng et al., 2011). Psychiatric symptoms are most common but cognitive difficulties and motor impairment are also possible. Recognized in the 1860s, the Argyll Robertson pupil, which accommodates (adjusts in diameter) to distance but does not contract with light, was thought to be diagnostic of syphilis. Initially considered to reflect mid-brain disease alone, this pupillary sign is now said to be pathognomonic for neurosyphilis either of the spinal cord in *tabes dorsalis* or of the brain, general paresis of the insane (GPI). The neuroanatomical features of GPI were already well-known, having first been described in an 1822 Paris thesis by Bayle (1822; see also Brown, 1994). But an Argyll Robertson pupil can also occur in conjunction with peripheral damage, and controversy remains over its pathophysiology (Thompson & Kardon, 2006).

By 1891 Wolf's syphilis was said to have caused symptoms of fever and sore throat and by 1896 a physician in Graz detected the Argyll Robertson pupil. At first, the diagnosis was kept from the composer. Wolf suffered episodes of "madness," delusions of grandeur, agitation, and depression, and was twice sent to asylums. First, he went to the Vienna asylum of Dr. Wilhelm Svetlin from October to November 1897, where he was said to have "astounded" his doctor by composing some entirely new music. Discharged in January 1898, he spent the summer in the care of the Köcherts, until he attempted suicide and lapsed again into "madness." From 1898 until his death in February 1903, he lived in the Lower Austrian Asylum. In 1899 he had a piano in his room and was able to play duets. By 1900 his speech was affected, although he continued to recognize friends, and in 1901 he developed paralysis. Almost blind and deaf, he was immobile, able only to lie in a cage bed (Newman, 1907/1966).

Bäzner and Hennerici (2010) have constructed a timeline showing that Wolf's periods of creativity and productivity persisted despite the onset of GPI. This author compared his symptoms to those of Robert Schumann, who also continued to compose in the face of advanced disease. Bäzner speculates that this madness did not result in creativity per se, but it marked the style of Wolf's music and the sense of impending doom may have prompted his feverish output before he lost his mind completely.

Frederick Delius (1862–1934)

Frederick Delius was born in Yorkshire, England, to German immigrant parents. Although he showed an aptitude for music, his father encouraged him to pursue a career in business. From 1884 to 1886 he managed an orange grove in Florida, where he was exposed to music of the American south and is alleged to have fathered an illegitimate child. Finally, his father relented, and Delius began musical studies in Leipzig. In 1888 he moved to Paris where he spent most of his adult life. In 1903 Delius married his longtime companion, artist Jelka Rosen, but he is said to have conducted many sexual affairs both before and after their marriage (Beecham, 1959/1975; Lee-Browne & Guinery, 2014) (Fig. 6.3).

By 1895 Delius is said to have been diagnosed with syphilis for which he was treated with iodine saltpeter, according to a history recorded in a clinic note in 1910 (Lederman, 2015). It is not known how the 1895 diagnosis was made. From 1909 or 1910 he displayed what has widely been acknowledged as the signs of neurosyphilis and for which he sought treatment from various specialists and at several sanatoria over the years.

Table 6.1 records a timeline of compositions and the stages of illness. It is our primary example of the interleaving of the two. Throughout the long saga of Delius's apparent neurosyphilis, he kept composing new works. Even toward the end, his mind was said to be active and he continued to compose relying on help with the physical act of writing from Jelka and a young amanuensis, Eric Fenby. In this manner, Delius produced a third *Sonata for Violin and Piano* and his *Songs of Farewell*, music for the poems of Walt Whitman, both in 1930. Some authors (Lederman, 2015) have considered the

FIGURE 6.3 Frederick Delius.

TABLE 6.1 Timeline of illness and compositions of Delius.

Year	Health	Composition begun
1907		*Brigg Fair*
1908		*In a Summer Garden*
1909	Depression—cure at Lake Constance	*Fennimore and Gerda* (Opera)
1910	Weakness and pain in limbs	
	Dr. W. Both, Weisser Hirsch sanatorium, Dresden	
	Sanatorium Switzerland 1910	
	Positive Wassermann test	
1911		*An Arabesque* (poems by Jens Peter Jacobsen)
		A Song of the High Hills
		Summer Night on the River
		On Hearing the First Cuckoo in Spring
1912		*Life's Dance*
1913		*North Country Sketches*
1914		*Sonata for Violin and Piano No. 1* (revision of 1905)
1914–16		*Requiem* (text by Heinrich Simon)
1915		*Double Concerto for Violin, Cello and Orchestra*
1916–17	Depression, limb weakness	*Concerto for Violin and Orchestra*
		Dance Rhapsody No. 2
		String Quartet
		Sonata for Cello and Piano
1917		*Eventyr* (Once Upon a Time)
1918		*A Song Before Sunrise*
1920–23		*Hassan* (incidental music for play)
1921–22	Cure in Wiesbaden	*Concerto for Cello and Orchestra*
1922	Loss of use of R hand	
1923	Limbs unsteady	*Sonata for Violin and Piano No. 2*
1925	Wheelchair	

(Continued)

TABLE 6.1 (Continued)

Year	Health	Composition begun
1928	Onset of blindness	
1929		*A Song of Summer*
1930		*Sonata for Violin and Piano No. 3*
		Songs of Farewell (poems by Walt Whitman)
1933	Bedridden and dies	

form of disease to have been *tabes dorsalis*—affecting the spinal cord rather than the brain because of the predominance of motor difficulties and the ability to keep composing; however, the frequent depression and advancing blindness suggest that he also suffered an organic brain syndrome.

As with the case of Hugo Wolf, this history has been complicated by the desire of friends and family to keep the diagnosis a secret. The positive Wasserman test in 1910 is interesting, given that it was relatively new, having been introduced in 1906 and known for numerous false positives and false negatives (Fleck, 1935/1979). Once again, we are left only with the observations of the clinical picture to hypothesize where and what were the neurological lesions that severely hampered Delius's quality of life without impairing his ability to compose.

Maurice Ravel (1875–1937)

Born to a French and Basque couple and raised in Paris, Ravel was encouraged in music by his parents and educated in piano at the prestigious Conservatoire de Paris from 1889. Following a successful start, he suffered a rocky trajectory in that institution, was expelled in 1895, and readmitted in 1897 to study composition with Gabriel Fauré. He admired the music of Nikolai Rimsky-Korsakoff and Claude Debussy. The animus against him by leaders of the Parisian musical establishment probably helped to generate public interest and sympathy for his compositional works, which began to draw attention by 1899. A slow but steady worker, he composed for piano and arranged for orchestra, producing ballets and operas. By 1918 and the death of Debussy, he was considered France's greatest living composer (Nichols, 2011) (Fig. 6.4).

Rejected by the army for physical frailty, Ravel enlisted in World War One as a truck driver, but he contracted amoebic dysentery and frostbite. He developed insomnia in 1918 and sought a cure in the Mégève for "senile involution" in 1919 at the age of 44 (Otte, De Bondt, Van De Wiele,

FIGURE 6.4 Maurice Ravel.

Audenaert, & Dierckx, 2003). Secretive and shy, Ravel never married, and his sexuality has been the subject of much conjecture: he was variously thought to have nurtured an unrequited heterosexual love, frequented brothels, or indulged in homosexual liaisons (Ivry, 2000).

By 1927 Ravel displayed signs of dysphasia and problems playing the piano owing to weakness and possibly apraxia. He consulted Dr. Pasteur Vallery-Radot whose recommendation, which he ignored, included rest. Nevertheless, Ravel's postwar output averaged about one composition a year and included his famous *Bolero* in 1928 and two piano concertos in each of 1929 and 1930.

A taxi accident in October 1932 resulted in loss of consciousness, broken teeth and ribs, followed by signs of concussion with difficulty concentrating. The relationship between this traumatic brain injury and the earlier symptoms has provoked a flurry of speculation over the exact nature of his neurological diagnosis both before and after the accident. Suggestions include cerebral amnesia, frontotemporal dementia (Pick's disease), primary progressive aphasia, Alzheimer's disease, Wernicke's encephalopathy, and corticobasal degeneration. Some authors have long sought to identify the impact of his undiagnosed preaccident neurological disease in these late compositions, *Bolero* and *Concerto for the Left Hand* (Alajouanine, 1948; Amaducci, Grassi, & Boller, 2002; Cybulska, 1997; Seeley et al., 2008). Others reject these connections between musical style and disease, perceiving the illness as the destruction of creative ability (Otte et al., 2003).

Suffice it to say that following the accident, Ravel's neurological condition worsened; his last public performance was in November 1933; his composing ceased; and he attended his last concert in November 1937. In December 1937 the French surgeon Clovis Vincent performed a craniotomy on Ravel, looking for a tumor or a clot—although he doubted one was present—and hypothesizing that the right hemisphere ought to be "inflated" to compensate for deficiencies of the left (Kanat, Kayaci, Yazar, & Yilmaz, 2010). Ravel died 10 days later. Syphilis serology was negative. There was no autopsy.

Sources for the clinical appearances are from memoirs of friends, the clinical notes of Theophile Alajouanine who followed the composer medically for 2 years and published his findings in 1948, and the notes of the surgeon, found in 1988 and published in a 1991 Paris medical thesis by B. Mercier (Alonso & Pascuzzi, 1999; Baeck, 1996, 2005). It is generally agreed that Ravel's preaccident condition represents some as yet undiagnosed progressive organic brain syndrome during which he was able to continue composing and produced some of his greatest works.

Aaron Copland (1900–90)

The Brooklyn-born, American Jewish composer and conductor Aaron Copland started writing music at the age of 8. His formal and informal education began in New York, but he spent 3 years in Paris in his early 20s. Upon returning to America, he taught at the New School and continued composing and, eventually, conducting to ever greater success. By 1963 he had conducted more than 100 orchestras (Fig. 6.5).

From the mid-1970s he had trouble with his short-term memory and by the late 1970s he was thought to have dementia, possibly of the Alzheimer's type. Opinion is divided on the impact of dementia on his musical abilities. Some contend that it slowed his compositional skills, although Copland's compositions had already declined in number after the 1950s and long before he developed memory problems.

As a composer, Copland was most productive from the 1930s to the 1960s. In an autobiography, written in collaboration with Vivian Perlis, he speculated on the music of the young and the old, describing the "creative impulse," as something separate from aging or disease. Referring to his work in the late 1970s, he wrote

The creative need, the impulse was no longer strong with me. That part of creativity is very mysterious. There are people who have every reason in the world to go on, but they just stop writing, while somebody else with no encouragement, no technique, no need—you can't stop him. Very strange. I was thinking of doing a study on the output of composers after the age of seventy. Of course, most earlier composers did not live long enough to have had to face the problem. (Copland & Perlis, 1989, pp. 387–388)

FIGURE 6.5 Aaron Copland.

A remarkable video of preparations and celebrations of his 80th birthday show him conducting with vigor and speaking of his life in music, notwithstanding the earlier diagnosis of dementia (https://www.youtube.com/watch?v = u7riNZZY1R4).

Copland's last composition, *Proclamation*, begun in 1973, was finished in 1982. Nevertheless, he continued to make public appearances—often to receive awards—to play and to conduct as his dementia advanced.

Alfred Garrievich Schnittke (1934–98)

Born in Engels of the Volga-German Soviet Socialist Republic, to a German-born Jewish father and a Russian-born German mother, educated in Vienna and Moscow, Schnittke's intellectual and musical influences included Mozart, Schostakovich, and a mystical form of Christianity to which he converted as a young man (Fig. 6.6).

In precarious health for most of his adult life, Schnittke suffered from migraine headaches, hypertension, and kidney problems. His first devastating stroke occurred at the age of 51 in June 1985, leaving him in a prolonged coma. When he awoke, he could speak only German, but by September he had recovered most of his faculties, although he tired quickly and could not use his right hand.

FIGURE 6.6   Alfred Schnittke.

Schnittke's biographers contend that his musical style changed following the stroke, but he was soon composing again, beginning his first cello concerto (1985−86) and completing the ballet *Peer Gynt*, planned before the stroke (1985−87). Many more compositions followed before a second cerebrovascular accident, in June 1991, rendered him unconscious once again. An urgent operation was performed on what was said to have been a cerebellar hemorrhage, from which he recovered, the only sequelae being walking difficulties. During 1993 and early 1994 his activity as a composer was considered amazingly high (Zagvazdin, 2015) as he produced more symphonies and concertos. A third stroke in 1994, said to have been a hemorrhage similar to the 1985 episode, left him almost completely paralyzed. The rehabilitation was slow, and he mostly stopped composing; however, in 1997 he completed some short works and his *Ninth Symphony*, the manuscript of which, owing to motor disability, is difficult to decipher and has led to several reconstructions.

   Given the known operative findings and the symptoms, neurological opinions locate Schnittke's strokes to the left hemisphere and the cerebellum. Zagvazdin (2015) carefully gathered the symptoms and the probable related anatomical lesions, not only of Schnittke but of several other composers (Haydn, Shebalin) to show that musical ability could sometimes persist following stroke and independent of aphasia.

Vissarion Shebalin (1902−63)

Born to schoolteacher parents in Omsk, Shebalin studied music in his home city and Moscow, graduating in 1928. He taught composition at the Moscow

Conservatory, where he was elected professor in 1941. Several distinguished composers were his students; Dmitri Shostakovich became his friend and admirer. Despite his compositions having won several Stalin prizes, in 1948 Shebalin was purged through the Stalinist Zhandov doctrine for creating works that did not conform to the party line. He was demoted and forced to teach at a lesser school but kept composing. In 1951 he was allowed to return as a director of the Moscow Conservatory; his full rehabilitation followed Stalin's death in March 1953 (Abraham, 1943/1970; Krebs, 1970) (Fig. 6.7).

Known to be hypertensive for several years, Shebalin suffered the first of three strokes on September 14, 1953. It resulted in incomplete right-sided sensory and motor impairment with severe aphasia, which persisted for several weeks before resolving. Only after the performance of his opera *Taming of the Shrew*, in 1957, did he achieve widespread acclaim in Russia.

On October 9, 1959 Shebalin suffered a second, more severe stroke with loss of consciousness for 36 hours and resultant hemiparesis involving right arm and leg and severe aphasia, including difficulty understanding speech. After 6 months, the motor symptoms improved but the severe dysphasia persisted. Nevertheless, he learned to write with his left hand and continued to compose many new works (Opus 51−60), and he revised several earlier works. He experienced two seizures in 1962 and 1963, and the third stroke on April 30, 1963, which, combined with a myocardial infarction a month later,

FIGURE 6.7   Vissarion Shebalin.

proved fatal. A postmortem examination showed massive "red softening of the left hemisphere of the brain in the left temporal and inferior parietal regions with a hemorrhagic cyst" (Luria, Tsvetkova, & Futer, 1965; Zagvazdin, 2015).

Unlike all the other case histories presented here, Shebalin's own physicians, Luria et al. (1965), published a detailed account of his history, dysphasia, and autopsy findings. His case is widely recognized as one of aphasia without amusia. Shebalin's disability was an inspiration to poet Tomas Transtromer (Iniesta, 2013). Several scholars, including Julliard doctoral graduate, Meta Weiss (2013, 2016), have attempted to identify changes in the mood of his compositions owing to his 1959 stroke.

Final comments: limitations, contributions, and future directions

Our goal in this chapter was to feature examples of accomplished composers who continued to produce music in spite of cognitive pathology, even if the apparent cognitive pathology has never been framed in 21st century terms. As such, this report has its limitations. There is the problem of the reliability and validity of historical sources. Moreover, we cannot generalize from these isolated and imperfectly documented historical examples of famous composers to the general population, certainly not to nonmusicians. Another limitation is that our collection above does not include a double dissociation between language and music; a double dissociation would yield theoretical support for the notion that language and music processing are isolable, or separable at the neural level. We deal with only one kind of dissociation between language and music—damaged speech and language skills, and preserved musical function—that is, aphasia without amusia. We do not have cases of the reverse dissociation, namely, damaged musical processing with otherwise preserved language skills, or amusia without aphasia. Amusia without aphasia has not to our knowledge been reported elsewhere among prominent composers (see Patel, 2008, p. 279) though evidence has been found in nonmusicians with brain damage (see the list of case reports, Peretz & Coltheart, 2003, Table 1).

At this point, many fascinating questions must remain unanswered—questions such as the relationship between musical style and pathology [e.g., see discussions over Ravel's *Bolero* (Warren, 2003); Shebalin's later works (Weiss, 2016)]. Can the structure and style of music reveal evidence of a pathological process? Or is the full creative genius revealed in compositions realized despite the disease process?

Notwithstanding unanswered questions, historical research provides a perspective on the context in which events occurred and the relative importance of, and attention paid to, events by medical contemporaries. The very existence of these case studies points to the possibility that, in some instances of neurodegenerative disease, the musical brain may be protected against assault. Regarding future directions, these and similar records of historical cases (e.g., Tzortzis, Goldblum, Dang, Forette, & Boller, 2000) point to the importance of pursuing research on at least three critical topics:

1. *The brains of musicians.* Putting aside the issue whether musician/non-musician brain differences reflect the influence of music training, genetic predisposition, or (quite probably) both, it is important to acknowledge that the brains of musicians and nonmusicians differ. Neuroimaging research has revealed structural and functional changes in brain organization that mirror the cognitive and physical demands of musical instrument playing (for a review, see Schlaug, 2015). For example, keyboard and string players differ in the size of cortical motor regions involved with the representation of hand and finger movement. Moreover, such differences are "dose-dependent," that is, they reflect the amount and intensity of musical training, thereby implicating the effects of musical practice. Thus according to Schlaug, musicians offer an excellent model for studying neural plasticity of the human brain. Could changes in musical brain organization account for the preservation of musical skill? What is the role of musical composition? To consider this question leads to our second topic for future directions.

2. *The neural basis of creativity in music.* A fair amount of research has addressed the neural basis of skilled musical performance (for a review, see Brown, Zatorre, & Penhune, 2015) and musical improvisation, or the spontaneous creation of music in real time (for a review, see Beaty, 2015). However, less is known about the neural basis of music composition. This may be partly so because musical composition, with its length and time-dependent course of realization, is less adaptable than improvisation to the technical demands of neuroimaging research (McPherson & Limb, 2019). To the extent that composition and improvisation share features of the same creative process, we may assume from improvisation studies that composition likely engages "dynamic interactions of distributed brain areas operating in large-scale networks" (Bressler & Menon, 2010, p. 278, see also Jacobson & Cuddy, 2019). Acquisition of the expertise underlying composition likely induces changes within, and connections between, such networks.[1]

---

1. Relevant networks include premotor and motor, executive (ECN), and default (DMN) networks. The ECN comprises the dorsolateral prefrontal cortex, the anterior cingulate cortex, and the anterior insula cortex and mediates three distinct cognitive mechanisms: working memory, inhibition (maintaining attention), and cognitive flexibility. The DMN comprises the ventromedial prefrontal cortex, the posterior cingulate cortex, and the medial temporal lobe. The DMN mediates future imagination and mind wandering. Recent studies have shown that in the generation of creative ideas process, the DMN activates (to generate an idea) and when the evaluation of the idea is required, the ECN activates. We thank Aydin Anic, McQuarrie University, for this brief summary and for helpful comments.

3. *Creativity in therapy.* Preservation of musical ability in the face of neurological disease has long been acknowledged by practitioners of music therapy. It is said to allow many people to revel in a spared capacity to appreciate, participate in, and even create musical arts, leading to an improved quality of life. Improvisation forms a part of neurological music therapy (see Thaut, this volume) but we do not yet know what specific benefits result from the addition of improvisational exercises to a program, nor how they might target specific brain regions. As we learn more about the brains of musicians and the neural basis of musical composition, we will be able in future to develop a rationale for including musical creativity in therapeutic programs, how best it may be implemented, and for whom it may be most beneficial.

Acknowledgment

The authors acknowledge the support of neurologist and medical historian Dr. T.J. (Jock) Murray, who kindly read and commented on a previous draft of this chapter.

References

Abraham, G. (1970). *Eight soviet composers*. Westport, CT: Greenwood Press. (Original work published 1943).

Alajouanine, T. (1948). Aphasia and artistic realization. *Brain: A Journal of Neurology, 71*(3), 229–241.

Alonso, R. J., & Pascuzzi, R. M. (1999). Ravel's neurological illness. *Seminars in Neurology, 19* (Suppl. 1), 53–57.

Amaducci, L., Grassi, E., & Boller, F. (2002). Maurice Ravel and right-hemisphere musical creativity: Influence of disease on his last musical works? *European Journal of Neurology, 9*(1), 75–82.

Andreasen, N. C. (2005). *The creating brain: The neuroscience of genius*. New York: Dana Press.

Andreasen, N. C. (2008). The relationship between creativity and mood disorders. *Dialogues in Clinical Neuroscience, 10*(2), 251–255.

Baeck, E. (1996). Was Maurice Ravel's illness a corticobasal degeneration? *Clinical Neurology and Neurosurgery, 98*(1), 57–61.

Baeck, E. (2005). The terminal illness and last compositions of Maurice Ravel. In J. Bogousslavsky, & F. Boller (Eds.), *Frontiers of neurology and neuroscience: vol 19. Neurological disorders in famous artists, Part 2* (pp. 132–140). Basel: Karger.

Baird, A., & Samson, S. (2009). Memory for music in Alzheimer's disease: Unforgettable? *Neuropsychology Review, 19*, 85–101.

Bayle, A. L. J. (1822). *Recherches sur les maladies mentales. Thèse médicale, no. 247*. Paris.

Bäzner, H., & Hennerici, M. G. (2010). Syphilis in German-speaking composers – 'Examination results are confidential'. In J. Bogousslavsky, M. G. Hennerici, H. Bäzner, & C. Bassetti (Eds.), *Frontiers of neurology and neuroscience, vol. 27: Neurological disorders in famous artists—Part 3* (pp. 61–83). Basel: KARGER.

Beaty, R. E. (2015). The neuroscience of musical improvisation. *Neuroscience & Biobehavioral Reviews, 51,* 108–117.

Beecham, T. (1975). *Frederick Delius.* London: Severn House. (Original work published 1959).

Bressler, S. L., & Menon, V. (2010). Large-scale brain networks in cognition: Emerging methods and principles. *Trends in Cognitive Sciences, 14*(6), 277–290.

Brown, E. M. (1994). French psychiatry's initial reception of Bayle's discovery of general paresis of the insane. *Bulletin of the History of Medicine, 68*(2), 235.

Brown, R. M., Zatorre, R. J., & Penhune, V. B. (2015). Expert music performance: Cognitive, neural, and developmental bases. *Progress in Brain Research, 217,* 57–88.

Chalke, H. D. (1962). The impact of tuberculosis on history, literature and art. *Medical History, 6*(4), 301–318.

Coeurdevey, A. (2003). *Roland de Lassus.* Paris: Fayard.

Cooke, D. (1985). *The New Grove late romantic masters: Bruckner, Brahms, Dvořák, Wolf.* London: W. W. Norton & Company.

Copland, A., & Perlis, V. (1989). *Copland since 1943.* New York: St. Martin's Press.

Cybulska, E. M. (1997). Boléro unravelled: A case of musical perseveration. *Psychiatric Bulletin, 21*(9), 576–577.

Fétis, F. J. (1867). In (2nd ed.). A. Pougin (Ed.), *Biographie universelle des musiciens et bibliographie générale de la musique* (Vol. 5). Paris: Firmin-Didot.

Fleck, L. (1979). In T. J. Trenn, & R. K. Merton (Eds.), *The genesis and development of a scientific fact.* Chicago, IL: University of Chicago Press. (Original work published 1935).

Fraser, I. (1978). Disease is good for you. *Ulster Medical Journal, 47*(2), 141–150.

Iniesta, I. (2013). Tomas Tranströmer's stroke of genius: Language but no words. *Progress in Brain Research, 206,* 157–167.

Ivry, B. (2000). *Maurice Ravel: A life.* New York: Welcome Rain.

Jackson, S. W. (1986). *Melancholia and depression: From Hippocratic times to modern times.* New Haven, CT: Yale University Press.

Jacobson, A. C. (1907). Tuberculosis and the creative mind. *Medical Library and Historical Journal, 5*(4), 225–249.

Jacobson, A. C. (1926). *Genius: Some reevaluations.* New York: Greenberg.

Jacobson, A. C., & Cuddy, L. L. (2019). Music training and transfer effects. In P. J. Rentfrow, & D. J. Levitin (Eds.), *Foundations in music psychology: Theory and research* (pp. 567–608). Cambridge, MA: MIT Press.

Kanat, A., Kayaci, S., Yazar, U., & Yilmaz, A. (2010). What makes Maurice Ravel's deadly craniotomy interesting? Concerns of one of the most famous craniotomies in history. *Acta Neurochirurgica, 152*(4), 737–742.

Krebs, S. D. (1970). *Soviet composers and the development of Soviet music.* London: Allen & Unwin.

Lederman, R. J. (2015). Frederick Delius: Controversies regarding his neurological disorder and its impact on his compositional output. *Progress in Brain Research, 216,* 217–232.

Lee-Browne, M., & Guinery, P. (2014). *Delius and his music.* Woodbridge: Boydell & Brewer Ltd.

Leuchtmann, H. (1976). *Orlando di Lasso* (2 Volumes). Wiesbaden: Breitkopf und Härtel.

Luria, A. R., Tsvetkova, L. S., & Futer, D. S. (1965). Aphasia in a composer. *Journal of the Neurological Sciences, 2*(3), 288–292.

Mazzucchi, A., Fanticini, F., Bellocchio, M. G., Petracchi, D., & Boller, F. (2017). The influence of brain lesion on musical masterpieces of famous composers. *Journal of Neurology and Neuroscience*, *8*(6), 1–13.

McPherson, M. J., & Limb, C. J. (2019). Improvisation: Experimental considerations, results, and future directions. In P. J. Rentfrow, & D. J. Levitin (Eds.), *Foundations in music psychology: Theory and research* (pp. 547–563). Cambridge, MA: MIT Press.

Newman, E. (1966). *Hugo Wolf*. Mineola, NY: Dover Publications, Inc. (Original work published 1907).

Nichols, R. (2011). *Ravel*. New Haven, CT: Yale University Press.

Ott, K. (1996). *Fevered lives: Tuberculosis in American culture since 1870*. Cambridge, MA: Harvard University Press.

Otte, A., De Bondt, P., Van De Wiele, C., Audenaert, K., & Dierckx, R. (2003). The exceptional brain of Maurice Ravel. *Medical Science Monitor: International Medical Journal of Experimental and Clinical Research*, *9*(6), 134–139.

Patel, A. D. (2008). *Music, language and the brain*. New York: Oxford University Press.

Peretz, I., & Coltheart, M. (2003). Modularity of music processing. *Nature Neuroscience*, *6*(7), 688–691.

Pirro, A. (1940). *Histoire de la musique, de la fin du XIVe siècle à la fin du XVIe*. Paris: Laurens.

Sacks, O. (2008). *Musicophilia: Tales of music and the brain*. Toronto: Vintage Canada.

Schlaug, G. (2015). Musicians and music making as a model for the study of brain plasticity. *Progress in Brain Research*, *217*, 37–55.

Seeley, W. W., Matthews, B. R., Crawford, R. K., Gorno-Tempini, M. L., Foti, D., Mackenzie, I. R., & Miller, B. L. (2008). Unravelling Boléro: Progressive aphasia, transmodal creativity and the right posterior neocortex. *Brain*, *131*(1), 39–49.

Sontag, S. (1978). *Illness as metaphor*. New York: Farrar, Straus and Giroux.

Theirmair, F. I. (Ed.), (1675). *Thomae Mermannii consultationes ac responsiones medicae*. Ingolstadt: J. P. Zinck.

Thompson, H. S., & Kardon, R. H. (2006). The Argyll Robertson pupil. *Journal of Neuro-Ophthalmology*, *26*(2), 134–138.

Trethowan, W. H. (1977). Music and mental disorders. In M. Herson, & R. H. Critchley (Eds.), *Music and the brain: Studies in the neurology of music* (pp. 398–432). London: Heinemann.

Tzortzis, C., Goldblum, M.-C., Dang, M., Forette, F., & Boller, F. (2000). Absence of amusia and preserved naming of musical instruments in an aphasic composer. *Cortex*, *36*(2), 227–242.

Vempala, N. N. (2014). Theories of musical creativity. In W. F. Thompson (Ed.), *Music in the social and behavioral sciences: An encyclopedia*. Thousand Oaks, CA: SAGE Publications, Inc.

Walker, F. (1968). *Hugo Wolf: A biography*. New York: Alfred A. Knopf.

Warren, J. (2003). Maurice Ravel's amusia. *Journal of the Royal Society of Medicine*, *96*(8), 424–424.

Weiss, M. (2013). *Is there a link between music and language? How loss of language affected the compositions of Vissarion Shebalin*. From Voices from the Sylff Community website: <http://www.sylff.org/news_voices/12911> Retrieved 25.10.18.

Weiss, M. (2016). *Vissarion Yakovlevich Shebalin: A study of his life, brain, and string quartets* (Unpublished doctoral dissertation). New York: Julliard School of Music.

Zagvazdin, Y. (2015). Stroke, music, and creative output: Alfred Schnittke and other composers. *Progress in Brain Research, 216*, 149−165.

Zheng, D., Zhou, D., Zhao, Z., Liu, Z., Xiao, S., Xing, Y., . . . Liu, J. (2011). The clinical presentation and imaging manifestation of psychosis and dementia in general paresis: A retrospective study of 116 cases. *The Journal of Neuropsychiatry and Clinical Neurosciences, 23*(3), 300−307.

Part 3

The Power of Music as Neuroprotection in Normal Aging

Chapter 7

Theories of cognitive aging: a look at potential benefits of music training on the aging brain

T.M. Vanessa Chan[1,2] **and Claude Alain**[1,2,3,4]
[1]Department of Psychology, University of Toronto, Toronto, ON, Canada, [2]Rotman Research Institute, Baycrest, Toronto, ON, Canada, [3]Institute of Medical Sciences, University of Toronto, Toronto, ON, Canada, [4]Faculty of Music, University of Toronto, Toronto, ON, Canada

Introduction

This chapter examines the extant literature on older adults and musicianship through the lens of theories of cognitive aging. Cognitive aging is a field of research that has been of much interest in recent years, especially with the growing older adult population around the world. It has been of interest for researchers, health care professionals, and citizens themselves to find interventions for the decline seen in cognition as people get older. What sorts of activities or treatments can individuals engage in as protective factors against age-related cognitive decline? What is the basis for the observed link between improved cognition in old age and lifestyle choices such as ongoing engagement in leisure activities (Dodge et al., 2008)?

Music training has been proposed as a method of promoting neuroplasticity and improving cognition across the life span, including for older adults (Schneider, Hunter, & Bardach, 2018). The use of music as an activity to promote healthy cognitive aging is attractive for several reasons: not only have older musicians outperformed matched nonmusicians on a variety of cognitive tests (Hanna-Pladdy & Gajewski, 2012; Hanna-Pladdy & MacKay, 2011; Strong & Mast, 2018), music is also generally an enjoyable pastime and frequently encountered. However, it is important that the observed effects of music making are examined in the lens of theories of cognitive aging, since these theories can in turn inform future directions of research on musicianship and the aging brain.

Music and the Aging Brain. DOI: https://doi.org/10.1016/B978-0-12-817422-7.00007-9
195

This chapter is separated into three sections: first, a review of some current theories of cognitive aging that account for effects of life experience; second, we examine how these align with the empirical findings of older musicians' cognitive function; third and lastly, we take a closer examination of recurring trends in what it is that older musicians perform better in, and tie it back to these theories of cognitive aging. We conclude with suggestions for future directions of research with regards to the mechanisms through which musical training can promote healthy cognitive aging.

Theories of cognitive aging

The field of cognitive aging has evolved significantly in the past 50 years, with major strides being made to account for age-related differences in cognition, particularly in attention and memory (Anderson & Craik, 2017; Park & Festini, 2017). Early theories examined different factors that could account for the decline observed in older adults, such as processing speed, or the speed at which cognitive functions can be executed (Salthouse, 1996), and inhibitory control, the ability to ignore goal-irrelevant information (Hasher & Zacks, 1988).

The advent of neuroimaging techniques allowed for the examination of some neural correlates that could underlie the differences in performance that were behaviorally observed. An observation of interest in early neuroimaging research of aging was an age-related change in visual perception, where there was a decline in occipital cortical activity but an increase in prefrontal activity (Grady et al., 1994), subsequently coined a posterior–anterior shift in aging (PASA; Dennis & Cabeza, 2008). In a similar vein, older adults showed a less asymmetric pattern of activity on cognitive tasks compared to younger adults, instead demonstrating more bilateral prefrontal activation, called a hemispheric asymmetry reduction in older adults (HAROLD; Cabeza, 2002).

These various models have been successful in describing age-related differences in cognitive function. Of interest to researchers now is developing models that can account for differences in cognitive aging, particularly when it comes to positive outcomes that result from differences in lifestyle. Here we discuss two models in particular that have considered the impact of lifestyle on the aging brain: cognitive reserve, and the scaffolding theory of aging and cognition (STAC).

Cognitive reserve

Cognitive reserve is a term used to characterize inter-individual differences in the susceptibility of cognitive abilities to decline as a result of age-related change, brain pathology, or other insult (Barulli & Stern, 2013; Stern et al., 2018). The concept of cognitive reserve can therefore be used to account for preservation of cognitive abilities, or a slower-than-expected decline, and is often referred to while discussing the efficacy of music in slowing cognitive aging. Cognitive reserve can be distinguished from a related concept, brain reserve, which is focused on quantitative measures of the brain such as the size of the brain, number of neurons, etc. (Barulli & Stern, 2013). Brain reserve can be considered a passive form of reserve, since in this model cognitive decline is inevitable when brain reserve capacity dips below a certain threshold. On the other hand, cognitive reserve may be viewed as an active model of reserve that allows for the alteration, though not the inevitability, of onset or rate of decline. In this way, two individuals expressing similar levels of pathology (or brain reserve) can have different functional outcomes, such as performance on a working memory task (see Figure 2 of Barulli & Stern, 2013, for an example). In other words, brain reserve is concerned with structural characteristics of the brain and structural integrity, while cognitive reserve considers the function of the brain, which can be discussed either as changes in behavioral outcomes of cognitive tasks or in the activity of the underlying neural networks (how the networks themselves are working, as opposed to how much they have changed in structure).

Two neural mechanisms through which cognitive reserve has been proposed to act—and thus can be further measured—are efficiency and compensation (Stern, 2006). Neural reserve is in relation to the efficiency of certain neural networks, such that at a similar level of neural pathology exhibited, those with higher neural reserve will require less activation of a given network to execute a cognitive function. In contrast, neural compensation is the involvement of additional networks not normally implicated in performing a certain task. Neural compensation is a phenomenon seen through changes in patterns of functional imaging such as PASA and HAROLD. Proxy measures of cognitive reserve (see below) have been associated with reduced functional activity in cognitive processing in healthy older adults, but increased functional activity in those with pathological aging (Solé-Padullés et al., 2009), implying increased efficiency in healthy populations as well as neural compensation when structural integrity is compromised. Furthermore, cognitive reserve proxies have been inversely related with plasma β-amyloid levels, a potential biomarker of Alzheimer's disease, and the relationship between plasma β-amyloid and cognitive decline was stronger for those with low levels of cognitive reserve (Yaffe et al., 2011).

Cognitive reserve, as a hypothetical construct, is not directly measured; it is operationalized with variables such as years of education and forms of crystallized intelligence, different proxies of lifetime accumulation of experiences and cognitive activity. Given some links between variables of musicianship and these proxies of cognitive reserve, it can be tempting to conclude that musicianship boosts cognitive reserve. However, there are issues with this conclusion; namely, this presumes that musicianship is correlated with improved cognitive function through mediating cognitive reserve, without establishing that it operates in this manner (Jones et al., 2011). With the rapid development of new neuroimaging technologies and methods of analysis, there is a high likelihood of eventually finding a functional measurement of cognitive reserve through neural reserve and/or neural compensation, such that it may be able to eventually resolve the issue.

Scaffolding theory of aging and cognition

Another important theory of cognitive aging is the STAC (Park & Reuter-Lorenz, 2009), and its revised version (STAC-r; Reuter-Lorenz & Park, 2014). The basis of STAC is that as people age, a high level of behavioral function is maintained with the aid of compensatory scaffolding, despite age-related neurological deterioration. This scaffolding takes the form of neural circuitry that aids and supplements the execution of a certain behavioral or cognitive outcome. Importantly, scaffolding is not framed as simply something that occurs at old age, but rather as a mechanism that is engaged throughout the life span as people encounter cognitively challenging situations.

Reuter-Lorenz and Park (2014) suggest that STAC is related to the concept of cognitive reserve in that individual differences in cognitive reserve may determine the amount and/or efficacy of scaffolding. The theory provides a mechanism through which differences in cognitive reserve could be expressed in improvements in cognitive outcomes. Similar to the cognitive reserve model's neural compensation account, STAC takes into consideration the increase in activity seen in bilateral prefrontal regions that is often observed in older adults and described in models such as PASA and HAROLD. It incorporates these prefrontal regions as examples of scaffolding in effect for older adults when their primary networks have begun to deteriorate. Scaffolding differs from neural compensation in that recruitment of scaffolding does not necessarily have to occur under conditions of neural degradation or age-related decline, but can occur at any time that the brain is cognitively challenged by the environment or the demands of a certain task.

STAC-r builds on the initial theory by adding that experiences across one's life span can interact with the aging process in a manner that affects brain structure and function. Experiences that promote the development of neural resources in a positive manner are considered as factors of neural resource enrichment. These experiences can be the same ones that confer cognitive or brain reserve. The effects and magnitude of a given source of neural resource enrichment will vary depending on the overall condition of a given brain, as well as the nature of the source itself, which can play out in terms of optimal time in life for a kind of enrichment or the optimal kind for a certain individual. In this framework, musicianship and musical training can be considered a source of neural resource enrichment if it has been shown to confer enhancements to brain structure and function.

The distinction between the reserve and scaffolding accounts of compensatory activity is in the age at which differences would manifest between those with increased reserve/scaffolding and those who do not have these increases. STAC would predict that, since the engagement of scaffolding is a lifelong mechanism that is not simply in response to neural degeneration but also overall cognitive challenge, those with enriched scaffolding should outperform those without such enrichment when tested on cognitively demanding tasks. Importantly, these differences should manifest upon commencing training, and be observed both in youth and old age. In contrast, a reserve model may suggest that even if there are no differences manifest in youth, there is a later onset of decline or decreased rate of decline in those with increased cognitive reserve.

Prefrontal dedifferentiation and brain maintenance

While a prefrontal increase in activity in older age has been often observed, whether it is a compensatory mechanism remains unclear. Morcom and Henson (2018) employed a multivariate analysis technique that assessed how much could be predicted about subsequent memory by looking at functional magnetic resonance imaging activity in certain regions of interest while participants did a memory task. This allowed them to compare models where the prefrontal cortex contained additional predictive information about success of memory retrieval on top of information from the posterior visual cortex, versus a model simply containing the visual cortex. They found that the increased involvement of prefrontal cortex did not contribute additionally to predictions of subsequent behavioral success in memory, which was taken as evidence against a model of prefrontal compensation. Instead, they discuss their findings in light of a prefrontal reduction, either in efficiency of activity (Nyberg et al., 2014; Rypma & D'Esposito, 2000) or in specificity of function (Carp, Park, Polk, & Park, 2011). It is possible that the lack of compensatory involvement indexed is restricted to the memory tasks tested, but these findings challenge the notion that additional prefrontal recruitment is indicative of behavioral functionality.

These results suggest that instead of theories of compensation, studies on cognitive aging may benefit from a perspective of brain maintenance (Nyberg, Lövdén, Riklund, Lindenberger, & Bäckman, 2012). Brain maintenance suggests that successful cognitive aging depends on keeping a youthful brain. Under this model, the more structural integrity that is preserved in aging, the more the pattern of brain activity should also look more like that of a younger adult's, and so more cognitive functions are also preserved when compared to performance at a younger age. In other words, the more an older adult's brain looks like a younger brain, the better their behavioral task performance; this pattern was indeed observed in several studies (Nagel et al., 2009, 2011).

Rogenmoser, Kernbach, Schlaug, and Gaser (2018) compared the brain structure of musicians and nonmusicians, using an algorithm to calculate an individual's "brain-age" based on anatomical correlates that varied with age. This "brain-age" was a score comparing the age of a person's brain, as calculated by the algorithm, to an individual's biological age, to determine whether their brain was classified as younger or older than that of their peers. On average, musicians displayed a younger brain age relative to matched controls, showing an association between musicianship and a maintained brain that looks more youth-like. Importantly, this analysis was done on structural data, which precludes any functional compensatory activity that could appear.

A brain maintenance model of music and cognitive aging would posit that musicianship in older adults is associated with both improved cognitive function and brain structural integrity, which are then both directly correlated with one another. To that effect, if music training were mitigating cognitive decline through maintaining the brain in a younger state, we would also expect to see a pattern of functional activity in older musicians that is similar to that of younger musicians, compared to a contrast of older versus younger nonmusicians, where the older nonmusicians would exhibit a steeper pattern of cognitive decline.

Examining the evidence: musicianship in older adults

As mentioned earlier, there is a wealth of research about the effects of music found on cognitive function. In young adult populations, musicians often outperform nonmusicians on various measures, including verbal memory (Franklin et al., 2008), verbal fluency (Zuk, Benjamin, Kenyon, & Gaab, 2014), nonverbal auditory working memory (Cohen, Evans, Horowitz, & Wolfe, 2011; George & Coch, 2011), and attentional control (Strait, Kraus, Parbery-Clark, & Ashley, 2010); such measures have been shown to be negatively impacted by aging (Park et al., 2002). Analogous benefits of musicianship have been found in cross-sectional studies of older adults, with studies citing musicianship conferring benefits in processing speed (Mansens, Deeg, & Comijs, 2018), nonverbal auditory memory (Hanna-Pladdy & Gajewski, 2012; Parbery-Clark, Strait, Anderson, Hittner, & Kraus, 2011) and verbal memory (Hanna-Pladdy & MacKay, 2011), as well as lower odds of developing mild cognitive impairment (MCI; Geda et al., 2011; Wilson, Boyle, Yang, James, & Bennett, 2015). It should be noted that there are also reports of no significant differences between musically trained and untrained adolescents on standard tests of working memory and verbal fluency (Saarikivi, Putkinen, Tervaniemi, & Huotilainen, 2016), and that longitudinal studies of musical training in children on verbal memory have also shown mixed results, with some studies showing improvements (Fujioka, Ross, Kakigi, Pantev, & Trainor, 2006; Schellenberg, 2004) and others not (Moreno et al., 2009).

Finally, the literature on visual memory in musicians compared to non-musicians is also inconclusive (see the "Specificity of transfer?" section for an expansion and discussion on modality-related limitations of cognitive benefits of training).

In support of the STAC account of neural resource enrichment, structural differences between musicians and nonmusicians have been shown (Gaser & Schlaug, 2003; Schlaug, Jancke, Huang, & Steinmetz, 1995), and musical training has been associated with accelerated cortical maturation in a sample of healthy youth 4–18 years of age (Hudziak et al., 2014). Support for the causal nature of music in effecting structural and functional change has been shown through several longitudinal studies that have tracked children receiving musical training, from a year to 15 months (Fujioka et al., 2006; Hyde et al., 2009) to 6 years (Putkinen, Tervaniemi, Saarikivi, Ojala, & Huotilainen, 2014). Furthermore, there is evidence to suggest that some functional changes due to musicianship can persist even after cessation of active musical engagement, with reports of enhanced auditory encoding in adults who received music training in their childhood but were no longer currently playing (Skoe & Kraus, 2012).

Like many skills, musical training confers more structural changes if one begins training earlier in life. Several comparisons have shown that those who started training prior to the age of 7 had more callosal connections (Schlaug, Jäncke, Huang, Staiger, & Steinmetz, 1995; Steele, Bailey, Zatorre, & Penhune, 2013), as well as increased gray matter in premotor regions (Bailey, Zatorre, & Penhune, 2014), compared to musicians who began training after. This suggests that any optimal time for music training to act as neural resource enrichment would be early in childhood; however, the association between age of music training onset and cognitive function, has not been uniformly found across modalities. A partition analysis showed that those who began playing music prior to the age of 9 had better verbal working memory as measured by the Letter-Number Span test of the WAIS-III, but this trend was not found for many of the other observed differences between the musically trained and untrained (Hanna-Pladdy & Gajewski, 2012).

A challenge of assessing the efficacy of music training as an intervention to promote healthy cognitive aging in light of these theories is the relative dearth of studies assessing behavioral, structural, and functional differences between older musicians and nonmusicians within the same experimental paradigm. Many studies have focused on the effect of training in childhood to early adulthood, and studies in older adults tend to report only behavioral results without functional or structural correlates. There is not enough evidence to support one model over another, and the results of the current literature can be interpreted in light of multiple models. Importantly, the aim here is to distinguish which of these models can better explain the findings of the musicianship and aging literature specifically.

One set of similar predictions could follow from accounts of brain maintenance and neural efficiency (Fig. 7.1A, left). In these models, if musicianship were to benefit cognitive aging, functional comparisons between musicians and nonmusicians should demonstrate a level of higher efficiency in musically trained older adults compared to the musically untrained when performing a certain task. In other words, even when musically trained and untrained older adults perform the same on a behavioral level for a given task, we would expect the musically trained older adults to show less neural activity in order to achieve that behavioral performance. For the brain maintenance model in particular, there is an underlying assumption that structural integrity in younger brains corresponds to preserved efficiency of activity; thus this difference in neural efficiency, as measured by a decrease in cortical activity relative to behavioral output, should also have a corresponding increase in structural integrity. The efficiency account of cognitive reserve appears less stringent in that regard, as cognitive reserve allows for an

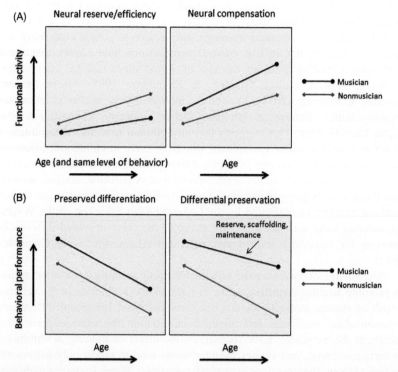

FIGURE 7.1 Illustration of trends in functional activity (A) or behavioral performance (B) as a function of increasing age, based on proposed methods of effectiveness seen in musical training. In all panels, musicians are indicated with dark blue lines and nonmusicians with light blue lines *Based on Alain, C., Zendel, B. R., Hutka, S., & Bidelman, G. M. (2014). Turning down the noise: the benefit of musical training on the aging auditory brain. Hearing Research, 308, 162–173.*

explanation of behavior and functional activity to be preserved in the face of structural decline.

The role of musical training in the development of compensatory function, however, is less clear. In the compensatory account, an increase in functional activity observed in the musically trained compared to the untrained in performing a challenging task could suggest musicians' being able to recruit nonprimary task regions to a greater extent. Implicit in this interpretation is that the increase in functional recruitment capacity also results in an increase in behavioral capacity, such that those with more to recruit from should see a correspondingly higher upper threshold of behavior. For any given cognitive task, musicians' ability to recruit more nonprimary regions should result in a corresponding improvement in processing speed, accuracy, or whatever other behavioral measure is being collected (Fig. 7.1A, right). An alternative explanation for increased functional activity in the musically trained is that nonprimary networks are more readily activated as a consequence of training, even if they are not necessary to achieve the required level of behavioral performance. This could explain any increase in functional activity in musicians in the absence of behavioral differences between groups, while still allowing for an overall higher capacity for recruiting nonprimary brain regions that leads to behavioral improvements (perhaps at other levels of difficulty than tested).

However, if music training improves the efficiency of these nonprimary networks that are being additionally recruited (rather than the overall recruitment capacity), musicians would show less brain activity compared to nonmusicians when they are both engaging additional networks to complete a task. This decrease should show up particularly in prefrontal areas that are thought to be additionally recruited in situations of cognitive challenge. This makes for an identical observation in both maintenance and compensation models if there is no method in place to quantify any potential gains in behavior that are associated with functional activity (Fig. 7.1A, left). In sum, maintenance and efficiency accounts overall would predict that musicians would show less brain activity compared to nonmusicians, if they are performing at the same level behaviorally, while a model where music training increases neural compensation would predict more brain activity in musicians compared to nonmusicians.

One further consideration is that even in examining differences in behavioral performance, differences observed between groups of older adults can be the result of either one or a combination of two patterns, as described by Salthouse (2006): preserved differentiation and differential preservation (Fig. 7.1B). In preserved differentiation, the differences observed in old age are a consequence of maintained differences from youth; in differential preservation, there may have been little to no difference between groups at youth, but one group maintained a more youth-like level of performance compared to the other. Here, a pattern of preserved differentiation (such as a main effect of Musicianship) could be an important contribution of musical training, by means of building reserve/scaffolding that puts the musically trained on a higher starting point in youth such that the impact of decline is mitigated; however, it is also possible that differences seen in this pattern are due to underlying differences between the groups that are not changed by the intervention. On the other hand, differential preservation (by way of an age $\times$ musicianship interaction) demonstrates a development that happened in the musically trained that sustains their cognitive performance over time (Zendel & Alain, 2012), though it is still possible that musicians who self-select into receiving musical training have differences unrelated to musical training that contribute to their preserved cognition in older age.

Observing different trends in the age and musicianship relationship can help shed light on the strength and longevity of various cognitive benefits associated with musical training, but as is already noted, there are other properties that could explain cognitive differences between the musically trained and untrained. Indeed, there is research suggesting that there are other properties, such as personality differences or preexisting differences in musical aptitude and intelligence, that influence whether an individual becomes a musician (Corrigall, Schellenberg, & Misura, 2013; Schellenberg, 2015; Swaminathan, Schellenberg, & Khalil, 2017). In light of these findings, it becomes much more difficult to interpret the results of studies where individuals self-select into musical training. With studies that incorporate random assignment into groups and longitudinal follow-ups, alternative explanations involving preexisting group differences can be mitigated.

When relating to cognitive aging, there are three ways to consider the potential influence of musical training: the effect of lifelong musicianship (starting in childhood and continuing into old age), the effect of early musicianship (starting in childhood without regular engagement in old age), and the effect of late training (starting in old age without previous experience). Examining the effect of starting—and discontinuing—regular musical activity and training at different times in life can be useful in defining the role of musical engagement as a preventative measure and as an intervention.

Effects of lifelong musicianship

Early studies of lifelong musicianship examined differences in performance on various neuropsychological tests between individuals who have limited encounters with music and those who have been actively engaged in music for significant portions of their life, including into old age. Together these are considered effects of lifelong musicianship in this section, although it is important to note that not all the studies distinguished between those currently playing and those not, instead grouping them based on the number of years of musical engagement.

Hanna-Pladdy and Mackay (2011) found that nonverbal recall was superior in their high activity musicians, classified as those with over 10 years of musical training and on average over 35 years of playing a musical instrument, compared to their nonmusician group. In a subsequent study, Hanna-Pladdy and Gajewski (2012) controlled for levels of general activity and found that, after controlling for level of general activity, musicians scored higher in verbal (but not nonverbal) recall, visuospatial ability, and cognitive flexibility. More recently using similar group classification metrics as above, Strong and Mast (2018) found effects of musicianship on inhibitory control, set-shifting, language, and visuospatial ability, results that also match a meta-analysis identifying musicianship-associated benefits in various domain-general cognitive processes such as processing speed, inhibition, attention, verbal memory, verbal fluency, and visuospatial ability (Román-Caballero, Arnedo, Triviño, & Lupiáñez, 2018).

In specifically looking at professional musicians, Amer, Kalender, Hasher, Trehub, and Wong (2013) found that their group of older adults (50−77 years of age) demonstrated superior visuospatial working memory, as well as measures of cognitive control such as the Simon task, reading with distraction, and the auditory Stroop task. That musicians outperformed nonmusicians on more measures in this study may not be surprising given that the musician group was made of professionals, although analysis of structural imaging suggests that amateur musicianship may confer more benefits than becoming a professional (Rogenmoser et al., 2018).

A recent study by Mansens et al. (2018) surveyed a group of Dutch older adults on their musical activity and performance on a battery of cognitive tasks. Participants were classified as musicians if they were engaged in musical activity at least once every 2 weeks; under this classification, the musicians performed superior to nonmusicians on the Letter Fluency test of the WAIS and the Dutch version of the Auditory Verbal Learning Test, even after taking into account how well musicians and nonmusicians performed in the other cognitive tests. Interestingly, among the musicians, the amount of time currently spent engaging in music was not a factor in task performance, which the authors suggested may be due to a larger contribution of early music-making compared to current engagement, a finding also observed by Hanna-Pladdy and MacKay (2011) in their nonverbal memory results.

Moving more specifically to changes related to auditory cognition, in a cross-sectional study of lifelong musicianship and central auditory cognition, Zendel and Alain (2012) found that, despite young adult musicians and nonmusicians exhibiting similar levels of proficiency in fine temporal processing and speech-in-noise perception, older musicians demonstrated better preservation of such skills compared to their nonmusician peers, with this difference growing larger as a function of the age being compared. Auditory skills such as speech-in-noise perception and auditory working memory (but not visual working memory) were found to be better in an older cohort

(45−65 years of age) in another study (Parbery-Clark et al., 2011). In a categorical vowel perception task where older adults were asked to classify vowels, older lifelong musicians were both faster at identifying vowels and showed both a better speech-tracking brainstem response as well as different attention-modulated responses depending on the speech sound (Bidelman & Alain, 2015). In younger adults, the finding of musicians benefiting on speech-in-noise tests is not as consistent (Parbery-Clark, Skoe, Lam, & Kraus, 2009; Ruggles, Freyman, & Oxenham, 2014; Zendel & Alain, 2012). Although together the studies cannot definitely point to a singular pattern, or whether one model of cognitive aging better fits the evidence on the relationship between speech-in-noise processing and musicianship, it is of note that the pattern seen in Zendel and Alain (2012) matches that of differential preservation.

Zendel and Alain (2013) compared lifelong musicians and nonmusicians' performance on a mistuned harmonic task, used as an index of listeners' ability to segregate concurrent auditory objects. They recorded event-related potentials while participants listened passively to auditory stimuli (no response required) or indicated whether they heard one or two sound objects. In both younger and older adult groups, musicians outperformed nonmusicians while there was no main effect of age; however, while younger musicians demonstrated a larger preattentive component (the object-related negativity), the older musicians displayed a modulation in the attentive component (the P400). This difference in functional activity suggests two different mechanisms at work between older and younger musicians to account for their behavioral improvements, a finding that was localized to the right auditory cortex in older musicians (Zendel & Alain, 2014). The attentive modulation in the older musicians, in the absence of the preattentive modulation in younger musicians, resembles a compensatory mechanism that arose to maintain a level of performance in older musicians similar to that of the young musicians.

There are a number of other studies that consider the impact of recent musicianship, particularly regarding its relationship with development of dementia; while not all of these studies specify lifelong musicianship, the questions asked of the participants implied prior musical experience earlier in life. Geda et al. (2011) asked about the cognitive leisure activities of older adults within the past year, and compared the odds ratio of developing MCI with these activities. Making music was associated with lower odds of developing MCI, although this was not a statistically significant relationship; however, it is in line with other work suggesting a protective relationship between musical activity and development of dementia. A twin study by Balbag, Pedersen, and Gatz (2014) found that in twins discordant for dementia, the twin who did not have dementia was more likely to have been engaged in musical activity in older adulthood, within 5 years of when the other twin developed dementia.

In a study of electrophysiological correlates of executive function, namely inhibitory control, Moussard, Bermudez, Alain, Tays, and Moreno (2016) compared electroencephalography (EEG) activity recorded between currently musically active older adults who began training in childhood and older adults with little to no regular musical activity. Participants performed a go/no-go task that required pressing a button in response to seeing a white shape, while withholding a press when seeing an occasional purple shape, meaning that participants had to stop the inclination to respond when seeing a purple shape. Older musicians exhibited more pronounced cognitive event-related potentials (i.e., N2 and P3 waves) in completion of the task, in addition to fewer no-go errors. Importantly, the P3 effect observed was correlated with not only age of musical instruction onset and years of instruction, but also current musical engagement as indexed by hours of regular practice over the last 2 years, suggesting contributions of both early training and current activity. Furthermore, the P3 in musicians was more significant over frontal scalp regions compared to nonmusicians, a pattern matching that of PASA. The increase in functional activity related to musical training is consistent with the neural compensation account outlined at the start of the "Examining the evidence: musicianship in older adults" section. Musicians also outperformed nonmusicians behaviorally; a compensation account would suggest that this represents a higher capacity for behavioral improvement in musicians, as a result of being able to recruit more frontal compensatory networks.

Interestingly, with a similar go/no-go paradigm, younger musicians were shown to have a reduced N2 compared to controls, which was interpreted as efficiency of sensorimotor networking and a reduction of necessary inhibition (Alain et al., 2018; Moreno, Wodniecka, Tays, Alain, & Bialystok, 2014). In the same study, young bilinguals showed an increased N2, possibly due to an increased sensitivity to conflict resolution. The older musicians in Moussard et al. (2016) show a pattern similar to the young bilinguals, distinct from that of young musicians, which could signify an age-related change in strategy or compensatory activity (but see Alain et al., 2019, where music training resulted in a reduced N2 similar to younger adults).

Together, these studies suggest that prolonged and continuous engagement with music throughout one's life span confers benefits in older age. However, from these studies it is unclear whether the early instruction is the impetus for benefit in old age, or whether the continuous activity into old age is necessary for such benefits to occur. The pattern of differential preservation observed suggests that there is something being conferred by musicianship beyond individual differences that existed prior to musical training. Based on the behavioral findings alone, one cannot distinguish which of the cognitive theories can best explain the pattern of benefits observed, although they can all account for why such benefits would be seen. Some of the electrophysiological findings suggest that there are different patterns of activity in old age due to lifelong musicianship, and some of these patterns are different from those seen in younger musicians as well, which lends support to compensatory models of activity.

Early musicianship's effects in old age

While the majority of studies on music training examine behavioral and neural changes during ongoing training or immediately posttraining, it is also of interest how long such changes can last once regular musical engagement has ceased. White-Schwoch, Carr, Anderson, Strait, and Kraus (2013) measured electrophysiological signals in older adults while they listened passively to a spoken syllable either in quiet or in noise, with three groups of participants varying on the amount of musical training attained in youth. Participants who reported a moderate amount of musical training (4—14 years) showed the fastest neural responses time-locked to the stimulus, compared to those who received a small amount of training (1—3 years) or no training at all; these moderately-trained musicians also showed more resilience to noise-related latency delays in encoding the transition between the consonant and vowel. These findings suggest that early training can contribute in a manner that enhances precognitive processing of sounds that are not necessarily musical in nature, and so can be a source of neural resource enrichment as outlined in STAC-r. It should be noted that since the groups were not assessed prior to the former musicians' onset of musical training, these differences in auditory processing may have existed prior to training.

In terms of potential cognitive benefits, a longitudinal study found that both foreign language instruction and music training prior to the age of 18 (for a minimum of 5 years) was associated with decreased incidence of MCI in a group of older adults (Wilson et al., 2015). In the same study, these two factors were also found to be associated with higher levels of global cognition as assessed at baseline, but rate of cognitive decline was the same in both groups across time. These results stand in contrast to those found in Zendel and Alain (2012), where measures of central auditory processing were preserved for aging musicians. While it appears that lifelong engagement in music may not be necessary for a reduction in cognitive decline, this is far from definitive; aside from these studies measuring different cognitive processes, Wilson et al. (2015) did not have data on how much their participants continued to engage in music or foreign language instruction in the years between their cutoff of 18 and the first longitudinal measurement taken.

Similarly, Gooding, Abner, Jicha, Kryscio, and Schmitt (2014) asked participants in a longitudinal study about their current musicianship, start and amount of musical training, and level of musical knowledge as measured by a music theory test, comparing these results to annual longitudinal assessments of performance on the Animal Naming Test (ANT) and the Wechsler

Logical Memory Story A Immediate Recall (LMI). Those sorted into having higher musical knowledge consistently performed better on both the ANT and the LMI over a 10-year period compared to those who had lower levels of musical knowledge, even after controlling for years of education and full scale IQ. In this sample, those who were classified as having higher musical knowledge also reported playing within the last year, suggesting that continuous musical engagement as a metric may interact with amount or intensity of training. The authors use their measure of musical knowledge as a proxy of amount or intensity of musical training in early- to midlife, and conclude that this early training contributes to preserved cognitive function. However, since higher knowledge appears to also be related to more current activity, it is possible that the increased musical knowledge could be attributed to continued practice rather than early training, although a relationship between current practice and their memory measures was not tested explicitly in their analysis.

To tackle specifically the question of what potential benefits of musical training are lost or preserved after one stops active musical engagement, Strong and Midden (2020) administered a similar test battery as in Strong and Mast (2018), comparing between nonmusicians, former musicians who no longer actively played, and active musicians who were regularly playing at the time of testing. They found that on several measures of executive function, active musicians outperformed both former musicians and nonmusicians, while former musicians did not differ from nonmusicians; however, for some other results in which there were group differences, such as the Boston Naming Test for testing language capacity, both groups of musicians outperformed nonmusicians. While the groups of former musicians and nonmusicians were smaller than that of the active musician group by half, making the group comparisons unbalanced, the findings point to a potential divergence between active and former musicians on the skills that may require ongoing musicianship to maintain, and benefits that remain even after active music participation has ceased.

Thus far, there is some evidence suggesting music training-related benefits in older adults, both when measured in people who report playing music in old age and when assessed with metrics of childhood training only. The accounts of increased structural change in musicians who began training earlier (see the "Scaffolding theory of aging and cognition" section) would support a view where early training plays an important role in conferring the cognitive benefits of musical training. Both compensatory and maintenance accounts of cognitive aging could predict these behavioral findings, although the functional underpinnings would look different for each. While compensatory accounts would predict distinct patterns between older and younger musicians as they outperform their nonmusician counterparts, maintenance accounts would expect a more similar pattern of activity between the musician groups due to preserved brain structure, while older and younger nonmusicians may differ more. More research is needed to specifically examine the effects of musical training for those who are no longer active musicians, in order to compare possibly dissociable contributions of early training and lifelong musicianship.

Music training in old age

If there are possible contributions of continuous musical engagement separate from early musical training, would beginning musical training late in life present any benefit? Several interventional studies have shown encouraging results in older adults regarding sustained engagement in activities and improvements in cognition (Carlson et al., 2008; Stine-Morrow, Parisi, Morrow, & Park, 2008). Park et al. (2014) in particular distinguished between different forms of engagement in their interventional study, finding that activities that promoted the learning of new skills and required a long sustainment of executive function were more effective than activities that used familiar skills or did not require new learning. These findings demonstrate the contribution of learning new skills, and point to a potential role of musical training in improvement in cognition. They also raise the question on whether learning to make music at old age—a new skill that is very cognitively demanding and requires many executive functions to successfully complete—would also show cognitive benefits.

To date, there have only been a few studies that have considered the impact of beginning music training at old age. Bugos, Perlstein, McCrae, Brophy, and Bedenbaugh (2007) examined the effects of individualized piano instruction on a group of older adults who had previously never received private musical instruction, evaluating them before and after instruction with a series of neuropsychological assessments. Participants were randomly assigned to either the instruction group or a no-action control group; when compared to the controls, older adults who received piano lessons for 6 months showed improvements posttraining on the Digit Symbol test, with a trend for improvement in the Trail Making Test-B as well. The authors hypothesized that their intervention was successful due to the attentional input of participants during lessons; however, as there was no active control, it was unclear as to whether this effect was limited to musical interventions.

Seinfeld, Figueroa, Ortiz-Gil, and Sanchez-Vives (2013) compared older adults who began piano lessons to another cohort of older adults who regularly engaged in other activities, such as physical exercise, computer lessons, and painting. Similar to Bugos et al. (2007), the authors found improvements in executive function and attention, although this time in the TMT-A and the Stroop task, which did not show benefit in the other study. Furthermore, this study reported improvements in mood and quality of life (QoL) in participants that were not observed in the control group. However, participants in the experimental group were not randomly assigned to doing the piano intervention after recruitment, and controls were recruited separately; this introduces potential effects of self-selection that could offer an alternative explanation for the better performance seen in the piano training group. Within the control group, activities were not characterized or standardized across participants in a way that was analogous to the experimental group, which also makes it difficult to conclude if the effects seen in the experimental group were due to the music training specifically, or the effects of a regimented training program.

Recently, Bugos and Kochar (2017) conducted a study on effects of music training on musically naïve older adults (<3 years of musical education), this time with an intensive short-term training paradigm. The dependent measures were specifically chosen to fit under the categories of verbal fluency, verbal memory, and processing speed. Compared to two pretraining sessions, older adults outperformed themselves posttraining on measures of verbal fluency and processing speed, but not verbal memory. Processing speed has been proposed as a mechanism through which age-related cognitive decline manifests (Salthouse, 1996), so improvements on processing speed could be indicative of transfer to other domains (although there may be limits to transferability; see below). Although the authors tried to mitigate the lack of a control group by demonstrating the absence of a test–retest effect between pretraining test sessions 1 and 2, which were separated by a week, it is still possible that the posttest improvements were due to doing the tests for a third time in the span of a month. Furthermore, the lack of a control group and random assignment into control or intervention means that to some extent, participants self-selected to do a music training study.

These studies demonstrate some benefits of taking up musical training in older age: not only were there observed improvements in executive function and attention, there were also reports of QoL improvement. QoL has been associated with measures of cognitive reserve, with the effects of reserve on QoL mediated by cognitive function, depression, and disability (Lara et al., 2017); this suggests that, outside of cognitive improvement, engagement in activities in old age can provide benefits to older adults in furthering their sense of autonomy. However, each of these studies has some limitations in their study design that makes the results they report somewhat inconclusive. More studies involving random assignment and well-designed active control interventions are needed in order to shed light on the specific contributions of starting music training in old age.

Indeed, researchers are already making strides to implement these elements of experimental design and using measures of functional neural activity to quantify training-induced changes, comparing between musical training and other control activities such as visual art training. Alain et al. (2019) employed a pseudorandom assignment of a group of minimally trained older adults to either music or visual art training and conducted testing before and after 3 months of training, as well as in a follow-up session (3 months later). These were compared against each other, as well as to a passive no-action control group. Behaviorally, the music group showed an improvement at posttest on the Stroop color-naming subtest that was retained at follow-up, supporting the previous research demonstrating training-related improvements in processing speed. Participants also conducted an auditory oddball task and visual go/no-go task, with both music and visual art training contributing to modulations in auditory and visual processing as well as neural correlates of cognitive control (as measured by EEG). Importantly, there were differences between the modulations conferred by music and art training, supporting an account of training-related benefits unique to music training (and to visual art training).

Specificity of transfer?

At a broad level, the findings in the field are in agreement: continued engagement in music-making at old age is associated with reduced likelihood of dementia and Alzheimer's disease (Balbag et al., 2014; Geda et al., 2011; Wilson et al., 2015). However, this effect is not exclusive to musicianship. Regarding what specifically is conferred in music training that could benefit cognitive aging, the lack of uniformity in the literature is somewhat under-standable, as each study uses slightly different criteria to define inclusion into their musician groups, and not all studies use the same tests to measure the same cognitive domain. However, despite this, there are some trends in what are generally observed and not observed that may hint at limitations to the transferability of music training on cognition. This raises the question of what a potential limitation is, and whether this can be accounted for in the theories of cognitive aging discussed.

STAC-r, in particular, introduces a mechanism that is employed across the life span as an answer to cognitive challenge, such as in learning a new skill. The question remains whether the widespread activations seen in early skill acquisition are functionally identical to the overactivation seen in older adults, or if the activity seen in these same regions is actually representative of two separate functions. Nevertheless, while there are allowances for neural resource enrichment opportunities to take place earlier in life, this does not mean that the enrichment will uniformly boost behavioral performance or even train all potential scaffolds that could be called upon. This can be explained using terms of transfer of learning and knowledge, or the ability to take a learned skill and apply it in another situation. Here, we are interested in looking at the extent to which skills learned in musicianship are trans-ferred to other activities that are either closely related to the skill originally learned (coined near transfer), or to activities that are more distantly related (coined far transfer). While there are some ambiguities regarding what is considered far transfer (see Barnett & Ceci, 2002, for a proposed taxonomy on how to distinguish between various dimensions of transfer), in our case a potential limitation of the effect of musicianship would constitute a degree of far transfer that can be reached on a certain dimension, after which musicianship would not have an effect on cognitive performance because of the dissimilarity in task demand. Moreno and Bidelman (2014) provide an example of classifying transfer dimensions with regards to music training.

So what are candidate limitations for the effects of musicianship on cognitive aging? One possible limitation is modality dependency. There has been extensive research on the effects of musical training on auditory processing and auditory-related tasks such as those measuring auditory attention and auditory memory (Cohen et al., 2011; George & Coch, 2011). Whether musicianship benefits the visual equivalents of these tasks has been tested as well, but the results are more disparate in younger adult populations, with some reporting benefits (George & Coch, 2011; Jakobson, Lewycky, Kilgour, & Stoesz, 2008) while others do not (Cohen et al., 2011; Hansen, Wallentin, & Vuust, 2013; Strait et al., 2010; Talamini, Carretti, & Grassi, 2016). Visuospatial judgments have been shown to be improved in older musicians compared to older nonmusicians (Hanna-Pladdy & Gajewski, 2012; Strong & Mast, 2018), suggesting some transferability of skill in an untimed task (the Benton Judgment of Line Orientation; but see Strong & Midden, 2020, for null findings in the JLO), and across several studies musicianship was found to have a large effect on visuospatial ability (Román-Caballero et al., 2018).

The cross-modal benefits have been suggested to allow musicianship to train domain-general executive functions, which then can support other cognitive activities; this view would match well with an enrichment of the brains of musicians, although it does not distinguish between whether this is training compensatory mechanisms specifically or if it is keeping brains more youthful. However, not all executive functions show benefits of musicianship. Furthermore, if enhanced executive functions were the source of transfer of cognitive enrichment, we would expect a global increase in the ability of older musicians compared to nonmusicians, or at least more benefits than reported, which has not been observed over several studies with extensive cognitive batteries. The benefits in visual processing observed could either be due to differences preexisting training that contributed to self-selection into musicianship, or a consequence of resources in reserve where the benefits only manifested in older age. However, the above studies are cross-sectional and do not compare across younger and older adults within the same design; to address differences in rate of change for performance on tasks would require a larger continuum of age in the same study.

Another possibility is that the benefits only manifest when the task at hand requires attentional input. Attentional benefits have been observed overall when comparing older musicians and nonmusicians (Román-Caballero et al., 2018), which raises the question of just how these domain-general functions are benefiting cognitive performance. In a study of young adults, auditory perceptual skills involving cognitive functions such as attention were selectively enhanced in musicians, while tasks that were more dependent on physiological features were not (Strait et al., 2010). Anderson, White-Schwoch, Parbery-Clark, and Kraus (2013) found that older adults who had received some form of musical training earlier in life tended to rely more on auditory cognitive mechanisms in speech-in-noise processing than those without, which also suggests a change in cognitive processing due to differential experience. In Mansens et al. (2018), associations of musicianship and attention were initially significant but were not after being corrected for the contributions of the other domains tested, which could either be due to effects of musicianship on attention being secondary to the memory and executive functions measured, or because any contributions of attention were already reflected in the other tasks and the task used to assess attention contributed nothing in addition.

In several EEG studies, the changes observed between older musicians and nonmusicians in task performance either did not manifest when the auditory stimuli were passively processed (Zendel & Alain, 2013, 2014) or only appeared in components associated with cognitive control (Moussard et al., 2016). In addition, Zendel and Alain (2013) found that, when comparing between older adult musicians and nonmusicians, the ERP component modulated by musical training in their active perceptual task was not the passively elicited component but the active one. So while the capacity and performance of auditory attention may or may not systematically differ between older musicians and nonmusicians in old age, its ability to contribute to performance on other tests may differ due to the training received by musicians.

One final consideration is that different theories of cognitive aging may apply better in musicianship depending on the domain being measured. Models of brain maintenance have been mostly considered in the domain of memory (Nyberg et al., 2012), but although structural data from younger adults supports the hypothesis that musicianship keeps the brain in a younger state (Rogenmoser et al., 2018), the evidence for musicianship's effects on episodic memory in older adults has been inconsistent or small in effect (Hanna-Pladdy & Gajewski, 2012; Hanna-Pladdy & MacKay, 2011; Strong & Mast, 2018). However, this does not preclude the possibility of older musicians preserving memory abilities in a manner consistent with brain maintenance, since to our knowledge there has been no study that examines musicianship's influence on brain structural integrity in old age. This construct could be particularly susceptible to individual variation and small sample sizes, since memory benefits to making music were found in a larger study (Mansens et al., 2018) as well as a meta-analysis (Román-Caballero et al., 2018).

On the other hand, the EEG research discussed above with regards to auditory cognition and executive function demonstrates functional changes in older musicians that are distinct from those of younger musicians, something that is predicted by compensatory models. Whether compensatory activity can explain other domain-general or cross-domain cognitive mechanisms will require further research into functional patterns of activity when performing such tasks. Even if there is no behavioral distinction between musicians and nonmusicians in healthy aging, the underlying brain networks performing the tasks could vary as a function of experience, which could be protective in pathological situations that are not even necessarily related to aging (as observed in reserve models).

Future directions

Thinking in a theoretical framework for musicianship and cognitive aging, there are a couple of questions that arise. First are the neural underpinnings of nonauditory cognitive benefits observed in older musicians. While the majority of neuroimaging work in musicianship has focused on the neural basis of improvements due to musical training in auditory cognitive aging, electrophysiological indices of effects of musicianship on nonauditory cognitive aging has been scant. Neuroimaging of older adults will be helpful in differentiating between compensatory and maintenance models depending on the cognitive task, especially in cross-sectional designs where the behavioral results predicted between musicianship membership would not differ between groups.

Secondly, the trends of age-related differences in cognition has been shown to differ between musicians and nonmusicians for some tasks, and even within a select set of tasks, different patterns of change were observed depending on the type of task (Zendel & Alain, 2012). This suggests that different cognitive domains may exhibit different rates of change and influence due to musical training. The prevailing study design to look at effects of musical training has been to either distinguish between older musicians and older nonmusicians, or to compare those two groups with younger musicians and nonmusicians; this categorization is useful for establishing initial patterns, but to further our understanding of how musicianship interacts across the life span, it will be beneficial to consider studies that evaluate cognition with age as a continuous variable, or construct longitudinal studies that observe the same population over an extended period of time. Observing different trends between musicians and nonmusicians in this type of study design will be useful in considering whether different cognitive theories may better explain the effects of musicianship in a certain cognitive function.

Finally, there is evidence to suggest that the benefit of continued musicianship extends into some cognitive domains, but not all (Strong & Midden, 2020). This is an interesting consideration that ties into the above notion that different aspects of cognitive aging are differentially impacted by musicianship. Some work has already suggested differences in training-related change between lifelong musicianship and short-term music training on measures of cognitive control (Alain et al., 2019; Moussard et al., 2016). Separating out the effects of early musical training and continued or late-life musical activity will be important for not only advocating an active lifestyle in old age that can improve QoL, but also in designing and implementing music-related interventions for older adults, while implementing more rigorous experimental designs that can more definitively allow for causal conclusions regarding music training and improvements in cognition.

References

Alain, C., Khatamian, Y., He, Y., Lee, Y., Moreno, S., Leung, A., & Bialystok, E. (2018). Different neural activities support auditory working memory in musicians and bilinguals. *Annals of New York Academy of Sciences, 1423*(1), 435–446.

Alain, C., Moussard, A., Singer, J., Lee, Y., Bidelman, G. M., & Moreno, S. (2019). Music and visual art training modulate brain activity in older adults. *Frontiers in Neuroscience, 13*, 182.

Alain, C., Zendel, B. R., Hutka, S., & Bidelman, G. M. (2014). Turning down the noise: the benefit of musical training on the aging auditory brain. *Hearing Research, 308*, 162–173.

Amer, T., Kalender, B., Hasher, L., Trehub, S. E., & Wong, Y. (2013). Do older professional musicians have cognitive advantages? *PLoS One, 8*(8), e71630.

Anderson, N. D., & Craik, F. I. (2017). 50 years of cognitive aging theory. *The Journals of Gerontology: Series B, 72*(1), 1–6.

Anderson, S., White-Schwoch, T., Parbery-Clark, A., & Kraus, N. (2013). A dynamic auditory-cognitive system supports speech-in-noise perception in older adults. *Hearing Research, 300*, 18–32.

Bailey, J. A., Zatorre, R. J., & Penhune, V. B. (2014). Early musical training is linked to gray matter structure in the ventral premotor cortex and auditory-motor rhythm synchronization performance. *Journal of Cognitive Neuroscience, 26*(4), 755–767.

Balbag, M. A., Pedersen, N. L., & Gatz, M. (2014). Playing a musical instrument as a protective factor against dementia and cognitive impairment: A population-based twin study. *International Journal of Alzheimer's Disease, 2014*, 836748.

Barnett, S. M., & Ceci, S. J. (2002). When and where do we apply what we learn?: A taxonomy for far transfer. *Psychological Bulletin, 128*(4), 612–637.

Barulli, D., & Stern, Y. (2013). Efficiency, capacity, compensation, maintenance, plasticity: Emerging concepts in cognitive reserve. *Trends in Cognitive Sciences, 17*(10), 502–509.

Bidelman, G. M., & Alain, C. (2015). Musical training orchestrates coordinated neuroplasticity in auditory brainstem and cortex to counteract age-related declines in categorical vowel perception. *Journal of Neuroscience, 35*(3), 1240–1249.

Bugos, J., & Kochar, S. (2017). Efficacy of a short-term intense piano training program for cognitive aging: A pilot study. *Musicae Scientiae, 21*(2), 137–150.

Bugos, J. A., Perlstein, W. M., McCrae, C. S., Brophy, T. S., & Bedenbaugh, P. (2007). Individualized piano instruction enhances executive functioning and working memory in older adults. *Aging and Mental Health, 11*(4), 464–471.

Cabeza, R. (2002). Hemispheric asymmetry reduction in older adults: The HAROLD model. *Psychology and Aging, 17*(1), 85.

Carlson, M. C., Saczynski, J. S., Rebok, G. W., Seeman, T., Glass, T. A., McGill, S., ... Fried, L. P. (2008). Exploring the effects of an "everyday" activity program on executive function and memory in older adults: Experience Corps®. *The Gerontologist, 48*(6), 793–801.

Carp, J., Park, J., Polk, T. A., & Park, D. C. (2011). Age differences in neural distinctiveness revealed by multi-voxel pattern analysis. *NeuroImage, 56*(2), 736−743.

Cohen, M. A., Evans, K. K., Horowitz, T. S., & Wolfe, J. M. (2011). Auditory and visual memory in musicians and nonmusicians. *Psychonomic Bulletin and Review, 18*(3), 586−591.

Corrigall, K. A., Schellenberg, E. G., & Misura, N. M. (2013). Music training, cognition, and personality. *Frontiers in Psychology, 4,* 222. Available from https://doi.org/10.3389/fpsyg.2013.00222.

Dennis, N. A., & Cabeza, R. (2008). Neuroimaging of healthy cognitive aging. *The Handbook of Aging and Cognition, 3,* 1−54.

Dodge, H. H., Kita, Y., Takechi, H., Hayakawa, T., Ganguli, M., & Ueshima, H. (2008). Healthy cognitive aging and leisure activities among the oldest old in Japan: Takashima study. *The Journals of Gerontology Series A: Biological Sciences and Medical Sciences, 63* (11), 1193−1200.

Franklin, M. S., Sledge Moore, K., Yip, C.-Y., Jonides, J., Rattray, K., & Moher, J. (2008). The effects of musical training on verbal memory. *Psychology of Music, 36*(3), 353−365.

Fujioka, T., Ross, B., Kakigi, R., Pantev, C., & Trainor, L. J. (2006). One year of musical training affects development of auditory cortical-evoked fields in young children. *Brain, 129,* 2593−2608.

Gaser, C., & Schlaug, G. (2003). Brain structures differ between musicians and non-musicians. *Journal of Neuroscience, 23*(27), 9240−9245.

Geda, Y. E., Topazian, H. M., Lewis, R. A., Roberts, R. O., Knopman, D. S., Pankratz, V. S., ... Ivnik, R. J. (2011). Engaging in cognitive activities, aging, and mild cognitive impairment: A population-based study. *The Journal of Neuropsychiatry and Clinical Neurosciences, 23*(2), 149−154.

George, E. M., & Coch, D. (2011). Music training and working memory: An ERP study. *Neuropsychologia, 49*(5), 1083−1094.

Gooding, L. F., Abner, E. L., Jicha, G. A., Kryscio, R. J., & Schmitt, F. A. (2014). Musical training and late-life cognition. *American Journal of Alzheimer's Disease & Other Dementias®, 29*(4), 333−343.

Grady, C. L., Maisog, J. M., Horwitz, B., Ungerleider, L. G., Mentis, M. J., Salerno, J. A., ... Haxby, J. V. (1994). Age-related changes in cortical blood flow activation during visual processing of faces and location. *Journal of Neuroscience, 14*(3), 1450−1462.

Hanna-Pladdy, B., & Gajewski, B. (2012). Recent and past musical activity predicts cognitive aging variability: Direct comparison with general lifestyle activities. *Frontiers in Human Neuroscience, 6,* 198.

Hanna-Pladdy, B., & MacKay, A. (2011). The relation between instrumental musical activity and cognitive aging. *Neuropsychology, 25*(3), 378.

Hansen, M., Wallentin, M., & Vuust, P. (2013). Working memory and musical competence of musicians and non-musicians. *Psychology of Music, 41*(6), 779−793.

Hasher, L., & Zacks, R. T. (1988). *Working memory, comprehension, and aging: A review and a new view,* . *Psychology of learning and motivation* (Vol. 22, pp. 193−225). Elsevier.

Hudziak, J. J., Albaugh, M. D., Ducharme, S., Karama, S., Spottswood, M., Crehan, E., ... Brain Development Cooperative Group. (2014). Cortical thickness maturation and duration of music training: Health-promoting activities shape brain development. *Journal of the American Academy of Child & Adolescent Psychiatry, 53*(11), 1153−1161, e1152.

Hyde, K. L., Lerch, J., Norton, A., Forgeard, M., Winner, E., Evans, A. C., & Schlaug, G. (2009). Musical training shapes structural brain development. *Journal of Neuroscience, 29* (10), 3019−3025.

Jakobson, L. S., Lewycky, S. T., Kilgour, A. R., & Stoesz, B. M. (2008). Memory for verbal and visual material in highly trained musicians. *Music Perception: An Interdisciplinary Journal, 26*(1), 41–55.

Jones, R. N., Manly, J., Glymour, M. M., Rentz, D. M., Jefferson, A. L., & Stern, Y. (2011). Conceptual and measurement challenges in research on cognitive reserve. *Journal of the International Neuropsychological Society, 17*(4), 593–601.

Lara, E., Koyanagi, A., Caballero, F., Domènech-Abella, J., Miret, M., Olaya, B., & Haro, J. M. (2017). Cognitive reserve is associated with quality of life: A population-based study. *Experimental Gerontology, 87*, 67–73.

Mansens, D., Deeg, D., & Comijs, H. (2018). The association between singing and/or playing a musical instrument and cognitive functions in older adults. *Aging & Mental Health, 22*(8), 964–971.

Morcom, A. M., & Henson, R. N. (2018). Increased prefrontal activity with aging reflects non-specific neural responses rather than compensation. *Journal of Neuroscience, 38*(33), 7303–7313.

Moreno, S., & Bidelman, G. M. (2014). Examining neural plasticity and cognitive benefit through the unique lens of musical training. *Hearing Research, 308*, 84–97.

Moreno, S., Marques, C., Santos, A., Santos, M., Castro, S. L., & Besson, M. (2009). Musical training influences linguistic abilities in 8-year-old children: More evidence for brain plasticity. *Cerebral Cortex, 19*(3), 712–723.

Moreno, S., Wodniecka, Z., Tays, W., Alain, C., & Bialystok, E. (2014). Inhibitory control in bilinguals and musicians: Event related potential (ERP) evidence for experience-specific effects. *PLoS One, 9*(4), e94169.

Moussard, A., Bermudez, P., Alain, C., Tays, W., & Moreno, S. (2016). Life-long music practice and executive control in older adults: An event-related potential study. *Brain Research, 1642*, 146–153.

Nagel, I. E., Preuschhof, C., Li, S.-C., Nyberg, L., Bäckman, L., Lindenberger, U., & Heekeren, H. R. (2009). Performance level modulates adult age differences in brain activation during spatial working memory. *Proceedings of the National Academy of Sciences of the United States of America, 106*(52), 22552–22557.

Nagel, I. E., Preuschhof, C., Li, S.-C., Nyberg, L., Bäckman, L., Lindenberger, U., & Heekeren, H. R. (2011). Load modulation of BOLD response and connectivity predicts working memory performance in younger and older adults. *Journal of Cognitive Neuroscience, 23*(8), 2030–2045.

Nyberg, L., Andersson, M., Kauppi, K., Lundquist, A., Persson, J., Pudas, S., & Nilsson, L.-G. (2014). Age-related and genetic modulation of frontal cortex efficiency. *Journal of Cognitive Neuroscience, 26*(4), 746–754.

Nyberg, L., Lövdén, M., Riklund, K., Lindenberger, U., & Bäckman, L. (2012). Memory aging and brain maintenance. *Trends in Cognitive Sciences, 16*(5), 292–305.

Parbery-Clark, A., Skoe, E., Lam, C., & Kraus, N. (2009). Musician enhancement for speech-in-noise. *Ear and Hearing, 30*(6), 653–661.

Parbery-Clark, A., Strait, D. L., Anderson, S., Hittner, E., & Kraus, N. (2011). Musical experience and the aging auditory system: Implications for cognitive abilities and hearing speech in noise. *PLoS One, 6*(5), e18082.

Park, D. C., & Festini, S. B. (2017). Theories of memory and aging: A look at the past and a glimpse of the future. *The Journals of Gerontology: Series B, 72*(1), 82–90.

Park, D. C., Lautenschlager, G., Hedden, T., Davidson, N. S., Smith, A. D., & Smith, P. K. (2002). Models of visuospatial and verbal memory across the adult life span. *Psychology and Aging*, *17*(2), 299.

Park, D. C., Lodi-Smith, J., Drew, L., Haber, S., Hebrank, A., Bischof, G. N., & Aamodt, W. (2014). The impact of sustained engagement on cognitive function in older adults: The synapse project. *Psychological Science*, *25*(1), 103–112.

Park, D. C., & Reuter-Lorenz, P. (2009). The adaptive brain: Aging and neurocognitive scaffolding. *Annual Review of Psychology*, *60*, 173–196.

Putkinen, V., Tervaniemi, M., Saarikivi, K., Ojala, P., & Huotilainen, M. (2014). Enhanced development of auditory change detection in musically trained school-aged children: A longitudinal event-related potential study. *Developmental Science*, *17*(2), 282–297.

Reuter-Lorenz, P. A., & Park, D. C. (2014). How does it STAC up? Revisiting the scaffolding theory of aging and cognition. *Neuropsychology Review*, *24*(3), 355–370.

Rogenmoser, L., Kernbach, J., Schlaug, G., & Gaser, C. (2018). Keeping brains young with making music. *Brain Structure and Function*, *223*(1), 297–305.

Román-Caballero, R., Arnedo, M., Triviño, M., & Lupiáñez, J. (2018). Musical practice as an enhancer of cognitive function in healthy aging—A systematic review and meta-analysis. *PLoS One*, *13*(11), e0207957.

Ruggles, D. R., Freyman, R. L., & Oxenham, A. J. (2014). Influence of musical training on understanding voiced and whispered speech in noise. *PLoS One*, *9*(1), e86980.

Rypma, B., & D'Esposito, M. (2000). Isolating the neural mechanisms of age-related changes in human working memory. *Nature Neuroscience*, *3*(5), 509.

Saarikivi, K., Putkinen, V., Tervaniemi, M., & Huotilainen, M. (2016). Cognitive flexibility modulates maturation and music-training-related changes in neural sound discrimination. *European Journal of Neuroscience*, *44*(2), 1815–1825.

Salthouse, T. A. (1996). The processing-speed theory of adult age differences in cognition. *Psychological Review*, *103*(3), 403.

Salthouse, T. A. (2006). Mental exercise and mental aging: Evaluating the validity of the "use it or lose it" hypothesis. *Perspectives on Psychological Science*, *1*(1), 68–87.

Schellenberg, E. G. (2004). Music lessons enhance IQ. *Psychological Science*, *15*(8), 511–514.

Schellenberg, E. G. (2015). Music training and speech perception: A gene–environment interaction. *Annals of the New York Academy of Sciences*, *1337*(1), 170–177.

Schlaug, G., Jäncke, L., Huang, Y., Staiger, J. F., & Steinmetz, H. (1995). Increased corpus callosum size in musicians. *Neuropsychologia*, *33*(8), 1047–1055.

Schlaug, G., Jancke, L., Huang, Y., & Steinmetz, H. (1995). In vivo evidence of structural brain asymmetry in musicians. *Science*, *267*(5198), 699–701.

Schneider, C. E., Hunter, E. G., & Bardach, S. H. (2018). Potential cognitive benefits from playing music among cognitively intact older adults: A scoping review. *Journal of Applied Gerontology*, *38*, 1763–1783, 0733464817751198.

Seinfeld, S., Figueroa, H., Ortiz-Gil, J., & Sanchez-Vives, M. V. (2013). Effects of music learning and piano practice on cognitive function, mood and quality of life in older adults. *Frontiers in Psychology*, *4*, 810.

Skoe, E., & Kraus, N. (2012). A little goes a long way: How the adult brain is shaped by musical training in childhood. *Journal of Neuroscience*, *32*(34), 11507–11510.

Solé-Padullés, C., Bartrés-Faz, D., Junqué, C., Vendrell, P., Rami, L., Clemente, I. C., ... Jurado, M. A. (2009). Brain structure and function related to cognitive reserve variables in normal aging, mild cognitive impairment and Alzheimer's disease. *Neurobiology of Aging*, *30*(7), 1114–1124.

Steele, C. J., Bailey, J. A., Zatorre, R. J., & Penhune, V. B. (2013). Early musical training and white-matter plasticity in the corpus callosum: Evidence for a sensitive period. *Journal of Neuroscience*, *33*(3), 1282–1290.

Stern, Y. (2006). Cognitive reserve and Alzheimer disease. *Alzheimer Disease & Associated Disorders*, *20*, S69–S74.

Stern, Y., Arenaza-Urquijo, E. M., Bartrés-Faz, D., Belleville, S., Cantilon, M., Chetelat, G., & Okonkwo, O. (2018). Whitepaper: Defining and investigating cognitive reserve, brain reserve, and brain maintenance. *Alzheimer's & Dementia*. Available from https://doi.org/10.1016/j.jalz.2018.07.219.

Stine-Morrow, E. A., Parisi, J. M., Morrow, D. G., & Park, D. C. (2008). The effects of an engaged lifestyle on cognitive vitality: A field experiment. *Psychology and Aging*, *23*(4), 778.

Strait, D. L., Kraus, N., Parbery-Clark, A., & Ashley, R. (2010). Musical experience shapes top-down auditory mechanisms: Evidence from masking and auditory attention performance. *Hearing Research*, *261*(1–2), 22–29.

Strong, J. V., & Mast, B. T. (2018). The cognitive functioning of older adult instrumental musicians and non-musicians. *Aging, Neuropsychology, and Cognition*, *26*, 367–386.

Strong, J. V., & Midden, A. (2020). Cognitive differences between older adult instrumental musicians: Benefits of continuing to play. *Psychology of Music*, *48*(1), 67–83.

Swaminathan, S., Schellenberg, E. G., & Khalil, S. (2017). Revisiting the association between music lessons and intelligence: Training effects or music aptitude? *Intelligence*, *62*, 119–124.

Talamini, F., Carretti, B., & Grassi, M. (2016). The working memory of musicians and nonmusicians. *Music Perception: An Interdisciplinary Journal*, *34*(2), 183–191.

White-Schwoch, T., Carr, K. W., Anderson, S., Strait, D. L., & Kraus, N. (2013). Older adults benefit from music training early in life: Biological evidence for long-term training-driven plasticity. *Journal of Neuroscience*, *33*(45), 17667–17674.

Wilson, R. S., Boyle, P. A., Yang, J., James, B. D., & Bennett, D. A. (2015). Early life instruction in foreign language and music and incidence of mild cognitive impairment. *Neuropsychology*, *29*(2), 292.

Yaffe, K., Weston, A., Graff-Radford, N. R., Satterfield, S., Simonsick, E. M., Younkin, S. G., ... Ding, J. (2011). Association of plasma β-amyloid level and cognitive reserve with subsequent cognitive decline. *JAMA*, *305*(3), 261–266.

Zendel, B. R., & Alain, C. (2012). Musicians experience less age-related decline in central auditory processing. *Psychology and Aging*, *27*(2), 410–417.

Zendel, B. R., & Alain, C. (2013). The influence of lifelong musicianship on neurophysiological measures of concurrent sound segregation. *Journal of Cognitive Neuroscience*, *25*(4), 503–516.

Zendel, B. R., & Alain, C. (2014). Enhanced attention-dependent activity in the auditory cortex of older musicians. *Neurobiology of Aging*, *35*(1), 55–63.

Zuk, J., Benjamin, C., Kenyon, A., & Gaab, N. (2014). Behavioral and neural correlates of executive functioning in musicians and non-musicians. *PLoS One*, *9*(6), e99868.

Chapter 8

Training-induced cognitive and neural changes in musicians: implications for healthy aging

Brenda Hanna-Pladdy and Miriam Menken
Center for Advanced Imaging Research, Department of Diagnostic Radiology & Nuclear Medicine, University of Maryland School of Medicine, Baltimore, MD, United States

Introduction

Cutting edge research that is focused on novel lifestyle activities offers promise for identifying various avenues of cognitive enrichment capable of enhancing healthy aging (Scarmeas & Stern, 2003). Recent studies tentatively suggest that sustained engagement in demanding mental tasks enhances cognitive functioning in older adults (Kramer, Bherer, Colcombe, Dong, & Greenough, 2004; Stine-Morrow et al., 2014). Although there is evidence that increased mental activity may protect against age-related cognitive declines, there are surprisingly few systematic investigations capable of isolating critical aspects of leisure activities that stimulate cognitive and neural changes (Scarmeas, Levy, Tang, Manly, & Stern, 2001; Stern & Munn, 2010). Mounting evidence supports the presence of training-induced brain changes from extended musical practice (Elbert, Pantev, Wienbruch, Rockstroh, & Taub, 1995; Gaser & Schlaug, 2003; Schlaug et al., 2009; Schlaug, Jancke, Huang, Staiger, & Steinmetz, 1995; Schneider et al., 2002; Sluming, Brooks, Howard, Downes, & Roberts, 2007; Steele, Bailey, Zatorre, & Penhune, 2013).

Intraindividual variability in cognitive aging may be explained by aspects of brain development such as genetic and environmental factors. The increase in life expectancy has heightened awareness of factors that impact brain and cognitive reserve that can buffer age-related functional declines. Consequently, there is growing interest in factors that bolster neural development and increase resilience to neuropathology later in life. This is evident in the extent of cognitive reserve available reflected in delay in the onset of noticeable clinical features of neurodegenerative disease. The conceptual

Music and the Aging Brain. DOI: https://doi.org/10.1016/B978-0-12-817422-7.00008-0

framework related to reserve and resilience is complex, and therefore the definitions across investigations may differ for cognitive and brain reserve highlighting the need for greater consensus as this research focus evolves in the future (Stern, Gazes, Razlighi, Steffener, & Habeck, 2018). These terms have previously referred to models of aging and Alzheimer's disease to describe variability in clinical presentation of age-related changes. The term cognitive reserve describes the dynamic adaptability to aging and pathology that is likely mediated by the flexibility of functional brain processes (Stern, Gazes, et al., 2018). Conversely, brain reserve is a term commonly used to describe the structural characteristics (number of neurons, etc.) that are more fixed. However, the structural basis of functional connectivity is an area of research that is early in evolution and additional research is required to investigate how structural changes impact cognitive reserve. Many factors can contribute to reserve including innate (genetic and in utero) conditions impacting general intelligence, education, exercise, and other life experiences (Stern, Arenaza-Urquijo, et al., 2018; Stern et al., 2003).

Theoretically, reserve can develop through intensive repetitive music training, but the specific mechanisms resulting in these advantages remain unspecified. Future studies are required to improve conceptualization of training-induced brain changes that can result in compensatory neural networks that can impact cognitive health outcomes across the life span (Bherer, 2015; Craik, Bialystok, & Freedman, 2010; Herholz & Zatorre, 2012; Jancke, 2009; Kramer et al., 2004; Munte, Altenmuller, & Jancke, 2002; Stine-Morrow et al., 2014; Wan & Schlaug, 2010; Zatorre & McGill, 2005).

In this chapter, we will consider controversies surrounding nature versus nurture in terms of cognitive and neural differences identified between musicians and nonmusicians. In considering evidence for and against innate and training-induced differences, we will review the neural basis of musical aptitude and theories of how individual characteristics and environment impact sustained musical engagement. Structural and functional brain changes in sensorimotor and auditory networks closely tied to critical aspects of musical instrumental activity will be discussed related to how training influences extent of neuroplasticity. Empirical support for music training effects on general cognitive capacities will be interpreted within a framework of how music impacts life span brain development. Finally, we will consider how our current knowledge of training-induced neuroplasticity from musical activity can guide future research to optimize models of cognitive stimulation.

Music as a model of cognitive stimulation across the life span

There is increased focus on exploration of viable options for cognitive stimulation with the goal of improving brain structure and function early in development and maintaining brain health across the life span (Anderson-Hanley, Maloney, Barcelos, Striegnitz, & Kramer, 2017; Fu, Belza, Nguyen, Logsdon, & Demorest, 2018; Geda et al., 2011; Gothe, Kramer, & McAuley, 2017). Previous research in this area has largely existed in isolation with segregated lines of research, focused either on early development and sensitive periods of enrichment, or preventive models designed to delay age-related cognitive declines (Hannon & Trainor, 2007; Schlaug et al., 2009; Schlaug, Norton, Overy, & Winner, 2005). Therefore there are few studies capable of characterizing brain changes across the life span to evaluate how early development can eventually impact cognitive capacity and reserve later in life (Bailey & Penhune, 2010; Cepeda, Kramer, & Gonzalez de Sather, 2001; Freedman et al., 2014; Schlaug, Jancke, Huang, Staiger, et al., 1995; Steele et al., 2013).

Additionally, while many models of neuroplasticity have been developed, previous studies have focused primarily on animal models, and functional recovery with reorganization offering limited translational potential for advancing mechanisms underlying human cognitive enrichment (Khan, Amatya, Galea, Gonzenbach, & Kesselring, 2017; Stewart & Cramer, 2017). Moreover, the human studies conducted have almost exclusively evaluated effective means of stimulating neuroplasticity and recovery of motor function following unilateral stroke (Pekna, Pekny, & Nilsson, 2012; Sarkamo & Soto, 2012; Sihvonen, Leo, Sarkamo, & Soinila, 2014; Taub et al., 1993). Research in motor recovery and neuroplasticity has yet to convert into intervention models of cognitive stimulation that can be applied to specific populations (Justice, Morrison, & Conway, 2013; Miao et al., 2018; Raffin & Hummel, 2018; Takeuchi & Izumi, 2015). Thus there is enormous potential in identifying the specific underlying mechanisms that mediate training-induced changes from music in order to develop practical methods that can enhance cognitive reserve. Critical to these investigations is the need to clarify the timing of initiation and duration of cognitive stimulation required for induction of neuroplastic changes that can be sustained over time. Controversy still remains as to the extent of neuroplasticity available beyond sensitive periods of development, and whether cognitive training can successfully yield functional reorganization in advanced age (Bherer, 2015; Bherer et al., 2005, 2006; Carlson et al., 2009). Therefore a focal issue relates to whether initiation of musical or other mentally stimulating activities is successful if initiated or maintained outside sensitive periods of development. To better understand the impact of sustained activity in advanced age, it is first important to understand the developmental literature in music instrumental activity and the impact of the timing of musical acquisition. Because of the implications of early music training on cognition in advanced age, the review of developmental impact of music training is critically important to set the stage for future research. That is, music acquisition and training in early development may be preventive in advanced age potentially, leading to reconceptualization of factors that impact variability in age-related cognitive decline. Therefore the main premise is that brain health prevention for cognitive aging may actually depend on early development. Thus models of cognitive, structural, and functional differences in early development demonstrating plasticity may be critical to understand this process.

Instrumental music training can induce exceptional neuroplasticity in both positive and negative directions, and allow for conceptualization of models of both motor and multisensory plasticity (Wan & Schlaug, 2010). The disorder musical dystonia provides a powerful illustration of precisely how intensive repetitive music training can dramatically alter brain plasticity and change functionality (Altenmuller & Furuya, 2016). In musical dystonia, overuse of motor skills results in aberrant task-specific cerebral plasticity primarily in sensorimotor control, eventually altering somatosensory receptive field representations (Chang & Frucht, 2013). Musical dystonia informs us of how intensive repetitive musical practice can have a detrimental effect on functional reorganization, and highlights individual variability in degree of plasticity. Musical dystonia has the highest prevalence of task-specific dystonia (1 in 100 musicians), and reflects how tasks demanding high spatiotemporal acuity (in addition to genetic and environmental risk factors) result in the highest risk for developing compensatory dysfunctional neural networks (Sadnicka, Kornysheva, Rothwell, & Edwards, 2018). Thus knowledge of intraindividual variability in plasticity and task demands in instrumental musical sequence acquisition, has potential to facilitate translation into formal applications that can develop compensatory networks to transform brain health.

Mounting evidence supports significant structural and functional changes secondary to music training, in brain regions closely tied to musical task demands (i.e., near transfer). However, it remains unclear the extent of far transfer effects that can impact nonmusical cognitive capacity. Further elucidation of mechanisms underlying cognitive and neural network changes secondary to intensive music training will provide unique insights into how experience shapes the brain across the life span (Moreno & Bidelman, 2014). In this chapter, we will focus on the features of instrumental musical acquisition and training that have the potential to impact cognitive reserve. The literature related to singing, passive listening, or emotional response to music is beyond the scope of this chapter and is addressed elsewhere in this volume.

Controversies surrounding nature versus nurture

Adult instrumental musicians display significant structural, functional, and cognitive changes when compared to nonmusicians, highlighting the role of music training in enrichment (Jancke, 2009; Munte et al., 2002; Wan & Schlaug, 2010). The relationship between cognitive capacity and history of music training has been well-established, but it has yet to be determined if this is the direct result of training-induced brain changes or innate abilities

(Schlaug, Jancke, Huang, & Steinmetz, 1995; Steinmetz, 1996). Consequently, many questions remain regarding the origin of these differences, and the extent to which they are driven by individual characteristics that sustain musical engagement, innate differences supporting musical aptitude, or training-induced brain changes (Abdul-Kareem, Stancak, Parkes, & Sluming, 2011; Mankel & Bidelman, 2018; Sala & Gobet, 2017; Schellenberg, 2019; Schlaug, Jancke, Huang, & Steinmetz, 1995; Sluming et al., 2002, 2007; Steinmetz, 1996).

The unique characteristics of instrumental musical activity include the high frequency of engagement in the general population, the early age of acquisition, and the number of years of sustained practice required for proficiency and resulting in functional alterations in cognitive or sensorimotor networks (Herholz & Zatorre, 2012; Wan & Schlaug, 2010). The extant literature has focused on how music alters motor and auditory networks. It is conceivable that the associated multisensory stimulation and overlap with language networks is critical for functional reorganization, but to date this has not been a focused area of research (Hannon & Trainor, 2007; Patel, 2008; Schellenberg & Peretz, 2008; Wan & Schlaug, 2010). In-depth exploration of the qualities of musical experience required to drive neuroplasticity will allow identification of aspects of nonacademic pursuits that create cognitive reserve similar to formal education, and inform us of the components of music training that can have a powerful impact on aging (Jung et al., 2018; Mungas et al., 2018; Munte et al., 2002; Thow et al., 2018).

Impact of intelligence and environment on musical engagement

The proponents of gene—environment theories argue that the intersection of genes with environmental circumstances determine which individuals will engage in musical activity. Strong advocates for this model argue that intelligence (IQ) and socioeconomic status (SES) predict who will successfully initiate and sustain music over time, as opposed to musical engagement directly changing neural networks (Norton et al., 2005). These types of investigations are in stark contrast to those that focus on the causal relationship between music lessons and nonmusical cognitive capacities to emphasize music educational benefits. Research on gene—environmental factors focus on whether children enrolled in music lessons arise from more educated and higher SES families, or if there are other factors independent of SES that might dictate musical participation such as early and frequent exposure to music (Corrigall & Schellenberg, 2015; Scarr & McCartney, 1983; Schellenberg & Peretz, 2008).

Specific individual characteristics that predict engagement of musical activity was explored in one large cross-sectional study across the life span with inclusion of both adults ($n = 118$) and children ($n = 167$) 10—12 years of age (Corrigall, Schellenberg, & Misura, 2013). After controlling for demographics and socioeconomic variables (parental education and household income), both cognitive capacity and personality profiles (i.e., *openness-to-experience*) predicted duration of musical engagement (Corrigall et al., 2013). However, a different study was not able to identify differences in cognitive, social, or neural measures prior to initiation of musical engagement (6- and 7-year-old children) (Habibi et al., 2014). The failure to clearly identify individual characteristics prior to initiation of formal music training was previously interpreted as supporting the absence of innate differences (Arnaud, Perlovsky, Bonniot-Cabanac, & Cabanac, 2013). Nonetheless, researchers have yet to resolve these complex issues in music cognition, and the explanation is likely multifactorial requiring more sophisticated study design and methods to unravel this controversy.

Ultimately, these questions can only be completely answered through studies of children before and following initiation of music training, and more importantly after sustained practice across the life span. The necessary investigations required to fully evaluate these questions are lacking because of the substantial financial and time resources required for long-term follow-up for at least a decade or more to capture the impact on cognitive reserve. Random assignment to musical and nonmusical groups can be addressed through study design, but the retention of subjects over time is likely related to individual and environmental circumstances. Even if these studies are feasible and conducted to completion, the results would be inconclusive despite random assignment because of selection factors affecting study maintenance versus attrition. Thus individual traits, skills, and environmental circumstances are still likely to account for who remains engaged in music over a sufficient duration to result in plastic brain changes.

Future investigations are likely to have greater probability of moving the field forward when there is consideration of multiple predictors characterizing the relative contribution from nature and nurture in predicting music engagement, and the cognitive and neural correlates of musical aptitude. The most parsimonious explanation is likely a gene−environment by training interaction, whereby genes determine musical aptitude but personality and cognitive capacity influence intensity and maintenance of activities. In combination, both innate and personality differences contribute to the likelihood of engaged and intensive practice over time, eventually impacting functional brain reorganization (Munte et al., 2002; Schellenberg, 2015). Clearly, the same characteristics that predict sustained and intense musical participation influence selection of other healthy behaviors, and so these should also be conceptualized in predictive models to exclude alternative hypotheses.

Innate differences predicting musical aptitude and engagement

There are documented innate differences associated with aspects of musical aptitude, in particular for individuals with exceptional musical abilities that predispose them to succeed in professional musical careers. Although professional musicians are more likely to have preexisting differences that predispose them to successful musical careers, they also engage in intense repetitive practice that can result in training-induced changes. To further tease apart contributions from nature or nurture, it is critical to evaluate both amateur and professional musicians in terms of cognitive and neuroimaging studies exploring differences in structure and function. One of the most compelling examples of innate differences is a stronger leftward planum temporale in professional musicians with absolute pitch documented by in vivo magnetic resonance morphometry (Schlaug, Jancke, Huang, & Steinmetz, 1995). The planum temporale is a brain region in the temporal lobe that corresponds to Wernicke's area involved in speech processing, with pitch processing representing nonlexical musical abilities (Geschwind & Levitsky, 1968; Schlaug, Jancke, Huang, & Steinmetz, 1995). Similar to sensitive periods for language development, training of pitch perception has a sensitive period early in development, although there are controversies surrounding to what extent training can impact pitch developmentally. The increased planum asymmetry present in musicians is predicted by genetic influences, with minimal impact based on the age of acquisition or early music training (Keenan, Thangaraj, Halpern, & Schlaug, 2001). In adulthood there is even less potential for improvement in pitch perception, with the exception of the blind population demonstrating increased plasticity in auditory function. Nonetheless, even in early blind individuals, the earlier the age of onset of blindness, the greater the pitch discrimination abilities consistent with early sensitive periods for auditory plasticity (Gougoux et al., 2004).

Additional controversy in the music literature surrounds the origin of these differences and is also fueled by the overlap between auditory and language processing networks. This is reflective of both preexisting advantages in musical skills, as well as structural enhancements secondary to musical practice (Abdul-Kareem et al., 2011; Alain, Zendel, Hutka, & Bidelman, 2014). Cross-sectional investigations have tried to disentangle the extent to which innate abilities versus training-induced brain changes account for the differences between musicians and nonmusicians. In comparing children exposed to music but not enrolling in music training with those beginning music training (5−7 years of age), there were no differences identified in cognitive, motor, or neural domains (Norton et al., 2005). However, correlations between auditory and visual pattern recognition were documented in 5- to 7-years-olds prior to music training, supporting the presence of shared neural substrates for music processing possibly related to innate abilities (Norton et al., 2005).

Consistent with these findings, a subgroup of nonmusicians displayed more adept skills in speech encoding as well as speech-in-noise benefits comparable to highly trained musicians (Mankel & Bidelman, 2018). Additional musical experience appears to boost neural encoding and speech perception, suggesting that in the absence of formal music training some individuals exhibit musician-like auditory function that can be further shaped by experience (Anderson-Hanley et al., 2018). Therefore musicianship is likely driven by both untrained aptitude reflecting innate abilities as well as training-related factors, both of which impact musical and nonmusical functional capacities (Scarr & McCartney, 1983; Schellenberg & Peretz, 2008). In the context of aging, the same controversy can arise with an unclear relationship between practice and enhanced performance. Active musical participation after the age of 65 was associated with modestly higher cognitive functioning in isolated domains theoretically linked to improved cognitive reserve (Hanna-Pladdy & Gajewski, 2012; Hanna-Pladdy & MacKay, 2011). However, the direction of the relationship is unclear, and another plausible explanation is that individuals with better cognition (with corresponding higher functionality) have the capacity to remain actively engaged in music in advanced age.

Training-induced structural and functional changes in instrumental musicians

Musical practice requires integration of motor and cognitive operations in the translation of musical symbols into coordinated precise movement sequences that create musical output with specified rhythmic and tonal properties. Instrumental musical practice allows for integration of multimodal information with sensorimotor integration, thereby providing an enriched environment transforming auditory—motor, visuomotor, and sensorimotor neural stimulations that alter associated brain regions (Gaser & Schlaug, 2003; Hyde et al., 2009b). Therefore the multisensory and integrative nature of musical engagement, coupled with intensive repetitive practice with auditory feedback for correction, provides an ideal environment for cognitive stimulation. This cognitive stimulation is capable of optimizing development of compensatory networks, or alternative networks that may be utilized in the event of neural compromise.

While many investigations have relied on professional to amateur musician comparisons as a model for differences in training intensity, the increased likelihood of innate differences often present in professional musicians should be considered. These studies have previously been interpreted as reflecting changes induced by intensive repetitive practice common to professional musicians, however, the findings are incapable of fully disambiguating preexisting differences from training-induced changes (Hyde et al., 2009a). Comparison of differences in instrumental musicians related to age of acquisition, practice intensity and duration, in addition to longitudinal studies, can help elucidate the extent to which learning versus innate differences can account for structural and functional brain differences.

Sensorimotor changes in instrumental musicians

Instrumental musical acquisition requires repetitive practice of sequential movements to reach precision so that a well-rehearsed musical performance can be produced. Musical movements are not only shaped by intense practice over time, but through a continuous feedback loop that provides online auditory shaping of the spatiotemporal properties of coordinated movements until they are efficient and automatic (Hyde et al., 2009a; Schlaug et al., 2005). Previous research exploring neural changes in musicians has not only focused on brain regions involved in auditory processing, but also regions involved in planning, execution, and sensorimotor control of movement (Amunts et al., 1997; Elbert et al., 1995; Gaser & Schlaug, 2003; Schlaug, Jancke, Huang, Staiger, et al., 1995; Steele et al., 2013). Given the bimanual and multimodal nature of instrumental musicianship, how practice and acquisition impact communication between the hemispheres has also been investigated (Schlaug et al., 2009; Schlaug, Jancke, Huang, Staiger, et al., 1995).

One of the seminal studies documenting structural changes in musicians was conducted by Elbert utilizing magnetic source imaging to characterize changes in cortical representations of the left hand of string players (Elbert et al., 1995). The findings revealed a larger left hand representation of string players relative to the right hand, and compared with controls. The extent of cortical reorganization in somatosensory cortex was not only related to musical experience, but also the age of musical initiation (Elbert et al., 1995). Other studies have corroborated structural changes in the premotor cortex and the corpus callosum based on the age of onset of music training, with the greatest differences evident for adults with musical initiation before the age of 7 (Amunts et al., 1997; Gaser & Schlaug, 2003; Schlaug, Jancke, Huang, Staiger, et al., 1995; Steele et al., 2013).

Developmental studies of music training effects versus preexisting differences

Studies attempting to resolve these issues have investigated preexisting neural, cognitive, and motor markers, but could not identify clear structural distinctions in expected brain regions in young children (≤ 7 years) prior to initiation of music or sports lessons (Habibi et al., 2014; Norton et al., 2005). Conversely, children with 4 years of music training (9−11 years) displayed larger sensorimotor cortices, implying that structural motor expansions can occur at a slightly later age demonstrating more of a sensitive period of enrichment as opposed to a critical age of plasticity (Schlaug et al., 2005).

The duration of training required for effective structural and functional changes has remained unclear without resolution, in part, because of methodological differences between studies. The developmental timing and duration of training needs to be further elucidated to clarify what is required for induction of cognitive, behavioral, and structural changes. In young children (mean age = 6 years), structural changes were evident 15 months after the commencement of musical instrumental training (Hyde et al., 2009a). Specifically, children displayed volume increases in the corpus callosum and motor cortex that correlated with music-associated motor and auditory skills (Hyde et al., 2009a, 2009b). These results are consistent with structural and task-related behavioral differences demonstrated between adult musicians and nonmusicians, implying that these changes are the direct result of music training.

Musical abilities rely on a specialized distributed network involving both hemispheres demonstrated by a larger corpus callosum secondary to sensorimotor integration and multisensory interhemispheric communication (Schlaug, Jancke, Huang, Staiger, et al., 1995; Sergent, Zuck, Terriah, & MacDonald, 1992; Woelfle & Grahn, 2013). Differences in interhemispheric communication related to sensorimotor areas in musicians provide evidence for increases in the anterior half of the corpus callosum, supporting a maturation period within the first decade of life (Schlaug, Jancke, Huang, Staiger, et al., 1995). Other support for training-induced structural brain plasticity has been demonstrated in motor and auditory regions following 15 months of music training in early childhood (Hyde et al., 2009a). It is important to note that there were no preexisting differences prior to training in behavioral or structural features when comparing instrumental or control groups similar to the study by Norton et al. in 2005 (Hyde et al., 2009a, 2009b). However, the 15-month duration of training may have been insufficient to result in far transfer effects.

Another developmental longitudinal study allowed for 30 weeks of training, and also controlled for practice intensity (Schlaug et al., 2009). Following music training, the instrumental musical group revealed increased volume in the areas of the corpus callosum associated with sensory and motor cortical regions (areas 3−6) and consistent with other investigations (Schlaug et al., 2009). Additionally, children that were characterized as "high-practicing musicians" (2−5 h/week) displayed greater changes than those characterized as "low-practicing musicians" (1−2 h/week). Practice intensity predicted structural changes in area 3 which was also correlated with behavioral measures of motor performance bilaterally (Schlaug et al., 2009). These findings were interpreted in the context of fiber tractography demonstrating this segment of the corpus callosum is connected to the prefrontal cortex, premotor, and supplementary motor areas, consistent with musical task demands that stimulate this region (Hofer & Frahm, 2006; Schlaug et al., 2009). Therefore this study highlights that in addition to timing of musical acquisition and duration of training as aspects of musical participation that predict plastic changes, the intensity of practice also plays a role in determining the extent of neuroplasticity.

Musical practice and nonmusical cognitive functions

The relationship between musical ability and nonmusical cognitive capacity has remained controversial. Specifically, it remains unclear whether musical skills or training are associated with or result in higher intelligence, enhanced language functions, mathematical abilities, visuospatial functions, and/or general academic functioning (Arnaud et al., 2013; Bialystok & Depape, 2009; Moreno et al., 2011; Schellenberg, 2011). Intense controversy surrounding these relationships has fueled a myriad of investigations to try and enhance our understanding of unresolved issues in music cognition. Multiregional gray matter volume differences have been identified in motor, auditory, and visuospatial brain regions when comparing professional musicians with a group of amateur musicians and nonmusicians (Gaser & Schlaug, 2003). However, despite clear documentation of these structural and functional differences between musicians and nonmusicians, the neural changes have not been directly tied to the cognitive advantages present in musicians. To fully evaluate the potential of music training to impact cognitive reserve and attenuate age-related cognitive declines, future investigations will need to closely tie neural network differences in musicians with orthogonal cognitive advantages.

Music and auditory networks

A related area of research that deserves focused attention in music processing is the expected auditory advantages of musicians. Auditory advantages in musicians have been documented in terms of morphologic changes in Heschl's gyrus and the left planum temporale, and developmentally in verbal and auditory cognitive functions, pitch and speech perception (Keenan et al., 2001; Schellenberg, 2019; Schlaug et al., 2005, 2009; Schneider et al., 2002). There is evidence for changes in auditory regions in longitudinal studies evaluating the critical timing of acquisition, but there is still a strong argument that it is inherent auditory advantages that propel individuals to engage in music as opposed to structural and neural changes resulting from training-induced changes (Mankel & Bidelman, 2018). Recent evidence has provided support that both inherent auditory skills as well as training-induced changes can impact auditory and speech processing networks (Abdul-Kareem et al., 2011; Mankel & Bidelman, 2018).

Structural and functional neuroimaging studies provide evidence for an enhanced left Broca's area in the inferior frontal gyrus, reflecting shared neural substrates of expressive music and language functions (Platel et al., 1997; Sluming et al., 2002). Also, based on pathological studies of amusia either secondary to vascular involvement or neurodevelopmental problems, there is elucidation of critical networks overlapping music, language, and speech processes. Examination of neural connectivity has demonstrated that the arcuate fasciculus (AF) is critical in music/speech processing, with lateralization implicating the left AF in speech and right AF in music (Miao et al., 2018). These findings suggest distinctive hemispheric processing between music and speech, but it is important to reconcile pathological conditions reflective of critical regions with the distributed network involved in music and speech/language processing.

Overlap between music and language networks

A growing focus in music cognition has been evaluating the overlap between language and music processing. Because of enhanced auditory regions conceptualized as innate and also auditory stimulation in response to music training, it is natural to consider the overlap between music and language networks. Previous research has primarily focused on auditory processing enhancements and detecting speech in noise (reviewed in other chapters) across the life span, instead of overlapping music and language networks (Alain et al., 2014; Bailey & Penhune, 2010; Coffey, Mogilever, & Zatorre, 2017; Parbery-Clark, Strait, Anderson, Hittner, & Kraus, 2011; Strait & Kraus, 2014). These auditory enhancements are often related to auditory focused attention in detecting signal from background noise, with some suggestion there is overlap with auditory working memory and executive functions (Clayton et al., 2016; Coffey et al., 2017).

Separate from auditory processing advantages related to music, there is evidence for overlapping music and language networks, and it is critical to characterize these overlapping networks to elucidate functional reorganization secondary to musical stimulation (Fedorenko, Patel, Casasanto, Winawer, & Gibson, 2009). Growing evidence supports a link between music and aspects of language processing, including syntactic, phonetic, and prosodic skills, but the underlying neural mechanisms remain unclear (Patel & Iversen, 2007). Investigations trying to unravel the underlying mechanisms have made parallels between Broca's aphasia related to syntactical processing involved in music and language, and subcortical processing of phonetic and prosodic skills and encoding of linguistic pitch patterns (Kunert, Willems, Casasanto, Patel, & Hagoort, 2015; Patel, 2003; Patel & Iversen, 2007).

Music and visuospatial advantages

The potential for far transfer effects secondary to musical participation has remained a difficult problem to reconcile. Pivotal to this controversy is the consideration of whether visuospatial advantages are present in musicians and if so, whether the underlying neural mechanisms mediating visuospatial enhancement are expected networks observed in nonmusicians or subserved by unique musical networks (Brochard, Dufour, & Despres, 2004; Sluming et al., 2002, 2007).

The role of the inferior frontal gyrus in music and language processing has been clearly depicted across a number of different investigations. However, it was surprising when exploration of the underlying mechanisms of visuospatial advantages in musicians demonstrated increased gray matter density in the left inferior frontal gyrus of professional musicians (Sluming et al., 2002). The linear relationship between years of instrumental participation and the density of gray matter in Broca's region as measured by voxel-based morphometry argues for use-dependent changes (Sluming et al., 2002). These structural differences were supported by functional differences evident on fMRI demonstrating that orchestral musicians not only revealed the same expected activations in the visuospatial network as nonmusicians, they also uniquely recruited additional regions (Broca's region) associated with language (Sluming et al., 2007).

Thus neurobehavioral, structural, and functional findings support enhancement of nonmusical cognitive capacities that are deemed far transfer based on expected neural basis of cognitive capacities, but indicate that from a neural perspective musical networks are uniquely utilized to enhance visuospatial functions in orchestral musicians (Brochard et al., 2004; Sluming et al., 2002, 2007). These findings highlight the critical importance of substantiating cognitive and behavioral outcomes with investigations of underlying neural mechanisms to explore how experience-dependent plasticity may alter functional reorganization (Herholz & Zatorre, 2012; Wan & Schlaug, 2010).

Musical acquisition across the life span: implications for plasticity and transfer of functions

Interindividual differences in cortical organization based on unique experiences can serve as a basis for developing targeted models of cognitive stimulation designed to optimize neural development that can be sustained across the life span. Many previous studies have posited that extended musical instrumental participation can result in experience-dependent changes, and there is evidence of delay in onset of age-related losses of neural encoding in speech perception and auditory working memory closely tied to musical task demands (Parbery-Clark, Anderson, Hittner, & Kraus, 2012; Parbery-Clark et al., 2011). However, it remains unclear whether there are experience-based neural changes that can be maintained across the life span to impact age-related cognitive declines that are not as closely tied to auditory musical stimulation such as executive and visuospatial processing.

Exploration of cognitive capacity in advanced age in amateur musicians relative to nonmusicians and in comparison to other cognitively stimulating leisure activities will elucidate long-term impact of music training on cognitive reserve. The focus on amateur musicians allows for minimization of innate or predisposing factors that might predict who might engage or sustain musical activities across the life span. Across two separate studies, we studied older amateur instrumental musicians to determine how the timing of musical engagement and the years of musical activity influence cognitive maintenance in advanced age (Hanna-Pladdy & Gajewski, 2012; Hanna-Pladdy & MacKay, 2011). A linear relationship between years of musical activity and cognitive capacity in aging was identified in a cross-sectional study of older amateur musicians (either 1−9 or >10 years of experience) versus nonmusicians (Hanna-Pladdy & MacKay, 2011). Neuropsychological findings across two different studies (140 community dwelling adults 59−83 years of age across two studies) demonstrated a positive impact of instrumental musical activity across the life span sustained over the age of 65 and independent of continued musical engagement in advanced age (Hanna-Pladdy & Gajewski, 2012; Hanna-Pladdy & MacKay, 2011).

Musicians who maintained at least 10 years of engagement at any time in their life span had better cognitive capacity in advanced age even when controlling for age, intelligence, and education (Hanna-Pladdy & Gajewski, 2012; Hanna-Pladdy & MacKay, 2011). Although musicians with some musical participation did demonstrate some cognitive advantages with a linear relationship between years of participation and cognitive capacity, those with at least 10 years outperformed those with less musical experience and nonmusicians (Hanna-Pladdy & MacKay, 2011). While the first study did not evaluate for other leisure activities, physical activity did account for unique variance in cognitive outcomes in advanced age. The contribution of other activities was further investigated in the second study with direct comparison of musical activity to general lifestyle activities. The findings revealed that cognitive functioning was predicted by lifelong musical activity, but not other nonmusical leisure activities (Hanna-Pladdy & Gajewski, 2012).

Our previous studies suggest the presence of cognitive and neural advantages in musicians with lifelong engagement maintained irrespective of continued engagement in advanced age. Cognitive functioning was less influenced by continued musical participation in advanced age as opposed to the age of acquisition and duration. The results revealed the critical importance of timing of engagement in terms of sensitive periods of enrichment, with enhanced auditory working memory in aging instrumental musicians with the age of acquisition before the age of 9 (Hanna-Pladdy & Gajewski, 2012). Nonetheless, continued musical engagement in advanced age buffered lower educational levels (<17 years) such that nonverbal cognition (visuo-perceptual functioning) was equivalent to individuals with higher levels of education. Continued musical engagement was also associated with better sensorimotor integration performance in individuals over the age of 70, and with lower levels of education (Hanna-Pladdy & Gajewski, 2012).

Education is the best known factor for yielding cognitive reserve, but other cognitively stimulating activities including artistic and musical pursuits have displayed decreased odds of developing mild cognitive deficits in advanced age (Geda et al., 2011). Despite the well documented early benefits of musical and other cognitively stimulating activities, there is optimism that training changes impact development across the lifespan into advanced age. The cognitive functions enhanced in older instrumental musicians across both studies included language functions, executive functions, memory, and visuospatial functions (Hanna-Pladdy & Gajewski, 2012; Hanna-Pladdy & MacKay, 2011). Each of these cognitive advantages in older musicians have been substantiated by a number of investigations (Fauvel et al., 2014; Gooding, Abner, Jicha, Kryscio, & Schmitt, 2014; Mansens, Deeg, & Comijs, 2018; Moussard, Bermudez, Alain, Tays, & Moreno, 2016; Roman-Caballero, Arnedo, Trivino, & Lupianez, 2018). The enhancement of language functions is in line with the lateralization subserving auditory and auditory−motor integration in music training that can have neuroprotective effects in aging (Parbery-Clark et al., 2011, 2012). Furthermore, converging evidence from music training and bilingualism investigations, which have overlapping networks, demonstrate executive enhancements as well as a potential delay in the onset of dementia in advanced age (Bialystok, Abutalebi, Bak, Burke, & Kroll, 2016; Bialystok & Depape, 2009; Bialystok & Viswanathan, 2009; Freedman et al., 2014).

Moreover, the skilled movement network in humans is subserved by a strong left lateralized cortical−subcortical network that mediates bilateral motor complexity in particular when semantics, auditory processing, and multisensory integration are involved (Hanna-Pladdy, Choi, Herman, & Haffey, 2018; Hanna-Pladdy, Heilman, & Foundas, 2001; Lewis et al., 2004; Schnider, Benson, Alexander, & Schnider-Klaus, 1994). The neural basis of visuoperceptual enhancements will require further investigation to uncover the structural and functional basis of visuoperceptual advantages in musicians. Given the previous work by Slumming and colleagues, it will be critical to determine whether visuoperceptual advantages in older musicians reflect far transfer effects of music training versus unique compensatory networks in the left hemisphere (Sluming et al., 2002, 2007). Finally, while most multisensory investigations have focused on obvious auditory−motor integration, visuomotor and auditory−visual investigations should also be explored given the task demands of musical sight-reading and musical performance.

Future directions to develop models of cognitive stimulation

Current evidence supports impressive structural and functional alterations associated with music training that can translate into enhanced neural networks common to music, skilled movements, auditory, language, and executive processes. Improved characterization of factors surrounding neuroplasticity from music training in terms of both positive (auditory and sensorimotor advantages) and negative outcomes (musical dystonia) can facilitate cognitive models of learning and plasticity. Ultimately, the knowledge gained of neuroplasticity in musicians across the life span can be utilized to develop hypothesis-driven models of cognitive stimulation designed to effectively harness neuroplasticity in advanced age.

These lines of investigation can be extended to evaluate how musical engagement may decrease risk of age-related cognitive declines in high-risk groups, such as those with lower educational levels, high vascular risk factors, family history of dementia, genetic, and other risk factors for neurodegeneration. Longitudinal studies will allow estimates of rate of change indices of cognition in older adults with and without musical experience, to allow estimation of attenuation in age-related cognitive declines. Evaluation of qualitative differences in cognitive, neural network, and protein deposition distribution between musicians and nonmusicians will improve conceptualization of protective mechanisms in aging.

The impact of instrumental musical practice on general cognition can be further examined by developing models of task-specific cognitive enrichment. Ideally, task-specific designs would fractionate critical aspects of music training to allow differentiation of how task demands in cognitive stimulation can alter differential neural networks. Eventually this knowledge can be utilized to develop focused models of cognitive stimulation able to capitalize on the most critical aspects of music training, and understand to what extent the multisensory demands drive plasticity. Furthermore, the unique and overlapping networks stimulated by aspects of music versus other stimulating activities should be better characterized. In turn, this can propel further exploration of domain-general and domain-specific cognitive enrichment optimally targeting enhanced neuroplasticity through multisensory stimulation. Comparison with older individuals with other experiences increasing cognitive reserve (education, bilingualism, and other cognitively stimulating activities) will allow improved understanding of the impact of life experiences on cognitive aging variability. Finally, future studies of at-risk populations should evaluate how music training impacts compensatory neural networks that have potential to alter rates of cognitive progression and/or delay the onset of the clinical features of dementia in the presence of neuropathology.

References

Abdul-Kareem, I. A., Stancak, A., Parkes, L. M., & Sluming, V. (2011). Increased gray matter volume of left pars opercularis in male orchestral musicians correlate positively with years of musical performance. *Journal of Magnetic Resonance Imaging, 33*(1), 24–32. Available from https://doi.org/10.1002/jmri.22391.

Alain, C., Zendel, B. R., Hutka, S., & Bidelman, G. M. (2014). Turning down the noise: The benefit of musical training on the aging auditory brain. *Hearing Research, 308*, 162–173. Available from https://doi.org/10.1016/j.heares.2013.06.008.

Altenmuller, E., & Furuya, S. (2016). Brain Plasticity and the concept of metaplasticity in skilled musicians. *Advances in Experimental Medicine and Biology, 957*, 197−208. Available from https://doi.org/10.1007/978-3-319-47313-0_11.

Amunts, K., Schlaug, G., Jancke, L., Steinmetz, H., Schleicher, A., Dabringhaus, A., & Zilles, K. (1997). Motor cortex and hand motor skills: Structural compliance in the human brain. *Human Brain Mapping, 5*(3), 206−215. Available from https://doi.org/10.1002/(SICI)1097-0193(1997)5:3 < 206::AID-HBM5 > 3.0.CO;2-7.

Anderson-Hanley, C., Maloney, M., Barcelos, N., Striegnitz, K., & Kramer, A. (2017). Neuropsychological benefits of neuro-exergaming for older adults: A pilot study of an Interactive Physical and Cognitive Exercise System (iPACES). *Journal of Aging Physical Activity, 25*(1), 73−83. Available from https://doi.org/10.1123/japa.2015-0261.

Anderson-Hanley, C., Stark, J., Wall, K. M., VanBrakle, M., Michel, M., Maloney, M., ... Kramer, A. F. (2018). The interactive Physical and Cognitive Exercise System (iPACES): Effects of a 3-month in-home pilot clinical trial for mild cognitive impairment and caregivers. *Clinical Interventions in Aging, 13*, 1565−1577. Available from https://doi.org/10.2147/CIA.S160756.

Arnaud, C., Perlovsky, L., Bonniot-Cabanac, M. C., & Cabanac, M. (2013). Music and academic performance. *Behavioural Brain Research, 256*, 257−260. Available from https://doi.org/10.1016/j.bbr.2013.08.023.

Bailey, J. A., & Penhune, V. B. (2010). Rhythm synchronization performance and auditory working memory in early- and late-trained musicians. *Experimental Brain Research, 204*(1), 91−101. Available from https://doi.org/10.1007/s00221-010-2299-y.

Bherer, L. (2015). Cognitive plasticity in older adults: Effects of cognitive training and physical exercise. *Annals of the New York Academy of Sciences, 1337*, 1−6. Available from https://doi.org/10.1111/nyas.12682.

Bherer, L., Kramer, A. F., Peterson, M. S., Colcombe, S., Erickson, K., & Becic, E. (2005). Training effects on dual-task performance: Are there age-related differences in plasticity of attentional control? *Psychology & Aging, 20*(4), 695−709. Available from https://doi.org/10.1037/0882-7974.20.4.695.

Bherer, L., Kramer, A. F., Peterson, M. S., Colcombe, S., Erickson, K., & Becic, E. (2006). Testing the limits of cognitive plasticity in older adults: Application to attentional control. *Acta Psychologica (Amst), 123*(3), 261−278. Available from https://doi.org/10.1016/j.actpsy.2006.01.005.

Bialystok, E., Abutalebi, J., Bak, T. H., Burke, D. M., & Kroll, J. F. (2016). Aging in two languages: Implications for public health. *Ageing Research Reviews, 27*, 56−60. Available from https://doi.org/10.1016/j.arr.2016.03.003.

Bialystok, E., & Depape, A. M. (2009). Musical expertise, bilingualism, and executive functioning. *Journal of Experimental Psychology: Human Perception and Performance, 35*(2), 565−574. Available from https://doi.org/10.1037/a0012735.

Bialystok, E., & Viswanathan, M. (2009). Components of executive control with advantages for bilingual children in two cultures. *Cognition, 112*(3), 494−500. Available from https://doi.org/10.1016/j.cognition.2009.06.014.

Brochard, R., Dufour, A., & Despres, O. (2004). Effect of musical expertise on visuospatial abilities: Evidence from reaction times and mental imagery. *Brain and Cognition, 54*(2), 103−109. Available from https://doi.org/10.1016/S0278-2626(03)00264-1.

Carlson, M. C., Erickson, K. I., Kramer, A. F., Voss, M. W., Bolea, N., Mielke, M., ... Fried, L. P. (2009). Evidence for neurocognitive plasticity in at-risk older adults: The experience corps program. *The Journals of Gerontology: Series A, Biological Sciences and Medical Sciences, 64*(12), 1275−1282. Available from https://doi.org/10.1093/gerona/glp117.

Cepeda, N. J., Kramer, A. F., & Gonzalez de Sather, J. C. (2001). Changes in executive control across the life span: Examination of task-switching performance. *Developmental Psychology, 37*(5), 715−730.

Chang, F. C., & Frucht, S. J. (2013). Motor and Sensory Dysfunction in Musician's Dystonia. *Current Neuropharmacology, 11*(1), 41−47. Available from https://doi.org/10.2174/157015913804999531.

Clayton, K. K., Swaminathan, J., Yazdanbakhsh, A., Zuk, J., Patel, A. D., & Kidd, G., Jr. (2016). Executive function, visual attention and the cocktail party problem in musicians and non-musicians. *PLoS One, 11*(7), e0157638. Available from https://doi.org/10.1371/journal.pone.0157638.

Coffey, E. B. J., Mogilever, N. B., & Zatorre, R. J. (2017). Speech-in-noise perception in musicians: A review. *Hearing Research, 352*, 49−69. Available from https://doi.org/10.1016/j.heares.2017.02.006.

Corrigall, K. A., & Schellenberg, E. G. (2015). Predicting who takes music lessons: Parent and child characteristics. *Frontiers in Psychology, 6*, 282. Available from https://doi.org/10.3389/fpsyg.2015.00282.

Corrigall, K. A., Schellenberg, E. G., & Misura, N. M. (2013). Music training, cognition, and personality. *Frontiers in Psychology, 4*, 222. Available from https://doi.org/10.3389/fpsyg.2013.00222.

Craik, F. I., Bialystok, E., & Freedman, M. (2010). Delaying the onset of Alzheimer disease: Bilingualism as a form of cognitive reserve. *Neurology, 75*(19), 1726−1729. Available from https://doi.org/10.1212/WNL.0b013e3181fc2a1c.

Elbert, T., Pantev, C., Wienbruch, C., Rockstroh, B., & Taub, E. (1995). Increased cortical representation of the fingers of the left hand in string players. *Science, 270*(5234), 305−307.

Fauvel, B., Groussard, M., Mutlu, J., Arenaza-Urquijo, E. M., Eustache, F., Desgranges, B., & Platel, H. (2014). Musical practice and cognitive aging: Two cross-sectional studies point to phonemic fluency as a potential candidate for a use-dependent adaptation. *Frontiers in Aging Neuroscience, 6*, 227. Available from https://doi.org/10.3389/fnagi.2014.00227.

Fedorenko, E., Patel, A., Casasanto, D., Winawer, J., & Gibson, E. (2009). Structural integration in language and music: Evidence for a shared system. *Memory & Cognition, 37*(1), 1−9. Available from https://doi.org/10.3758/MC.37.1.1.

Freedman, M., Alladi, S., Chertkow, H., Bialystok, E., Craik, F. I., Phillips, N. A., ... Bak, T. H. (2014). Delaying onset of dementia: Are two languages enough? *Behavioural Neurology, 2014*, 808137. Available from https://doi.org/10.1155/2014/808137.

Fu, M. C., Belza, B., Nguyen, H., Logsdon, R., & Demorest, S. (2018). Impact of group-singing on older adult health in senior living communities: A pilot study. *Archives of Gerontology & Geriatrics, 76*, 138−146. Available from https://doi.org/10.1016/j.archger.2018.02.012.

Gaser, C., & Schlaug, G. (2003). Brain structures differ between musicians and non-musicians. *Journal of Neuroscience, 23*(27), 9240−9245.

Geda, Y. E., Topazian, H. M., Roberts, L. A., Roberts, R. O., Knopman, D. S., Pankratz, V. S., ... Petersen, R. C. (2011). Engaging in cognitive activities, aging, and mild cognitive impairment: A population-based study. *The Journal of Neuropsychiatry and Clinical Neurosciences, 23*(2), 149−154. Available from https://doi.org/10.1176/appi.neuropsych.23.2.14910.1176/jnp.23.2.jnp149.

Geschwind, N., & Levitsky, W. (1968). Human brain: Left-right asymmetries in temporal speech region. *Science, 161*(3837), 186−187.

Gooding, L. F., Abner, E. L., Jicha, G. A., Kryscio, R. J., & Schmitt, F. A. (2014). Musical training and late-life cognition. *American Journal of Alzheimers Disease & Other Dementias, 29* (4), 333–343. Available from https://doi.org/10.1177/1533317513517048.

Gothe, N. P., Kramer, A. F., & McAuley, E. (2017). Hatha yoga practice improves attention and processing speed in older adults: Results from an 8-week randomized control trial. *Journal of Alternative and Complementary Medicine, 23*(1), 35–40. Available from https://doi.org/10.1089/acm.2016.0185.

Gougoux, F., Lepore, F., Lassonde, M., Voss, P., Zatorre, R. J., & Belin, P. (2004). Neuropsychology: Pitch discrimination in the early blind. *Nature, 430*(6997), 309. Available from https://doi.org/10.1038/430309a.

Habibi, A., Ilari, B., Crimi, K., Metke, M., Kaplan, J. T., Joshi, A. A., ... Damasio, H. (2014). An equal start: Absence of group differences in cognitive, social, and neural measures prior to music or sports training in children. *Frontiers in Human Neuroscience, 8*, 690. Available from https://doi.org/10.3389/fnhum.2014.00690.

Hanna-Pladdy, B., Choi, H., Herman, B., & Haffey, S. (2018). Audiovisual lexical retrieval deficits following left hemisphere stroke. *Brain Sciences, 8*(12). Available from https://doi.org/10.3390/brainsci8120206.

Hanna-Pladdy, B., & Gajewski, B. (2012). Recent and past musical activity predicts cognitive aging variability: Direct comparison with general lifestyle activities. *Frontiers in Human Neuroscience, 6*, 198. Available from https://doi.org/10.3389/fnhum.2012.00198.

Hanna-Pladdy, B., Heilman, K. M., & Foundas, A. L. (2001). Cortical and subcortical contributions to ideomotor apraxia: Analysis of task demands and error types. *Brain, 124*(Pt 12), 2513–2527.

Hanna-Pladdy, B., & MacKay, A. (2011). The relation between instrumental musical activity and cognitive aging. *Neuropsychology, 25*(3), 378–386. Available from https://doi.org/10.1037/a0021895.

Hannon, E. E., & Trainor, L. J. (2007). Music acquisition: Effects of enculturation and formal training on development. *Trends in Cognitive Science, 11*(11), 466–472. Available from https://doi.org/10.1016/j.tics.2007.08.008.

Herholz, S. C., & Zatorre, R. J. (2012). Musical training as a framework for brain plasticity: Behavior, function, and structure. *Neuron, 76*(3), 486–502. Available from https://doi.org/10.1016/j.neuron.2012.10.011.

Hofer, S., & Frahm, J. (2006). Topography of the human corpus callosum revisited—comprehensive fiber tractography using diffusion tensor magnetic resonance imaging. *NeuroImage, 32* (3), 989–994. Available from https://doi.org/10.1016/j.neuroimage.2006.05.044.

Hyde, K. L., Lerch, J., Norton, A., Forgeard, M., Winner, E., Evans, A. C., & Schlaug, G. (2009a). The effects of musical training on structural brain development: A longitudinal study. *Annals of the New York Academy of Sciences, 1169*, 182–186. Available from https://doi.org/10.1111/j.1749-6632.2009.04852.x.

Hyde, K. L., Lerch, J., Norton, A., Forgeard, M., Winner, E., Evans, A. C., & Schlaug, G. (2009b). Musical training shapes structural brain development. *Journal of Neuroscience, 29* (10), 3019–3025. Available from https://doi.org/10.1523/JNEUROSCI.5118-08.2009.

Jancke, L. (2009). Music drives brain plasticity. *F1000 Biology Reports, 1*, 78. Available from https://doi.org/10.3410/B1-78.

Jung, N. Y., Cho, H., Kim, Y. J., Kim, H. J., Lee, J. M., Park, S., ... Seo, S. W. (2018). The impact of education on cortical thickness in amyloid-negative subcortical vascular dementia: Cognitive reserve hypothesis. *Alzheimer's Research & Therapy, 10*(1), 103. Available from https://doi.org/10.1186/s13195-018-0432-5.

Justice, L. V., Morrison, C. M., & Conway, M. A. (2013). True and intentionally fabricated memories. *The Quarterly Journal of Experimental Psychology (Hove)*, *66*(6), 1196–1203. Available from https://doi.org/10.1080/17470218.2012.734832.

Keenan, J. P., Thangaraj, V., Halpern, A. R., & Schlaug, G. (2001). Absolute pitch and planum temporale. *NeuroImage*, *14*(6), 1402–1408. Available from https://doi.org/10.1006/nimg.2001.0925.

Khan, F., Amatya, B., Galea, M. P., Gonzenbach, R., & Kesselring, J. (2017). Neurorehabilitation: Applied neuroplasticity. *Journal of Neurology*, *264*(3), 603–615. Available from https://doi.org/10.1007/s00415-016-8307-9.

Kramer, A. F., Bherer, L., Colcombe, S. J., Dong, W., & Greenough, W. T. (2004). Environmental influences on cognitive and brain plasticity during aging. *The Journals of Gerontology, Series A: Biological Sciences and Medical Sciences*, *59*(9), M940–M957.

Kunert, R., Willems, R. M., Casasanto, D., Patel, A. D., & Hagoort, P. (2015). Music and Language syntax interact in Broca's area: An fMRI study. *PLoS One*, *10*(11), e0141069. Available from https://doi.org/10.1371/journal.pone.0141069.

Lewis, J. W., Wightman, F. L., Brefczynski, J. A., Phinney, R. E., Binder, J. R., & DeYoe, E. A. (2004). Human brain regions involved in recognizing environmental sounds. *Cerebral Cortex*, *14*(9), 1008–1021. Available from https://doi.org/10.1093/cercor/bhh061bhh061, [pii].

Mankel, K., & Bidelman, G. M. (2018). Inherent auditory skills rather than formal music training shape the neural encoding of speech. *Proceedings of the National Academy of Sciences United States of America*, *115*(51), 13129–13134. Available from https://doi.org/10.1073/pnas.1811793115.

Mansens, D., Deeg, D. J. H., & Comijs, H. C. (2018). The association between singing and/or playing a musical instrument and cognitive functions in older adults. *Aging & Mental Health*, *22*(8), 964–971. Available from https://doi.org/10.1080/13607863.2017.1328481.

Miao, P., Wang, C., Li, P., Wei, S., Deng, C., Zheng, D., & Cheng, J. (2018). Altered gray matter volume, cerebral blood flow and functional connectivity in chronic stroke patients. *Neuroscience Letters*, *662*, 331–338. Available from https://doi.org/10.1016/j.neulet.2017.05.066.

Moreno, S., Bialystok, E., Barac, R., Schellenberg, E. G., Cepeda, N. J., & Chau, T. (2011). Short-term music training enhances verbal intelligence and executive function. *Psychological Science*, *22*(11), 1425–1433. Available from https://doi.org/10.1177/0956797611416999.

Moreno, S., & Bidelman, G. M. (2014). Examining neural plasticity and cognitive benefit through the unique lens of musical training. *Hearing Research*, *308*, 84–97. Available from https://doi.org/10.1016/j.heares.2013.09.012.

Moussard, A., Bermudez, P., Alain, C., Tays, W., & Moreno, S. (2016). Life-long music practice and executive control in older adults: An event-related potential study. *Brain Research*, *1642*, 146–153. Available from https://doi.org/10.1016/j.brainres.2016.03.028.

Mungas, D., Gavett, B., Fletcher, E., Farias, S. T., DeCarli, C., & Reed, B. (2018). Education amplifies brain atrophy effect on cognitive decline: Implications for cognitive reserve. *Neurobiology of Aging*, *68*, 142–150. Available from https://doi.org/10.1016/j.neurobiolaging.2018.04.002.

Munte, T. F., Altenmuller, E., & Jancke, L. (2002). The musician's brain as a model of neuroplasticity. *Nature Reviews Neuroscience*, *3*(6), 473–478. Available from https://doi.org/10.1038/nrn843.

Norton, A., Winner, E., Cronin, K., Overy, K., Lee, D. J., & Schlaug, G. (2005). Are there pre-existing neural, cognitive, or motoric markers for musical ability? *Brain and Cognition, 59* (2), 124–134. Available from https://doi.org/10.1016/j.bandc.2005.05.009.

Parbery-Clark, A., Anderson, S., Hittner, E., & Kraus, N. (2012). Musical experience offsets age-related delays in neural timing. *Neurobiology & Aging, 33*(7), 1483.e1–1483.e4. Available from https://doi.org/10.1016/j.neurobiolaging.2011.12.015.

Parbery-Clark, A., Strait, D. L., Anderson, S., Hittner, E., & Kraus, N. (2011). Musical experience and the aging auditory system: Implications for cognitive abilities and hearing speech in noise. *PLoS One, 6*(5), e18082. Available from https://doi.org/10.1371/journal.pone.0018082.

Patel, A. (2008). *In music, language, and the brain.* Oxford: Oxford University Press.

Patel, A. D. (2003). Language, music, syntax and the brain. *Nature Neuroscience, 6*(7), 674–681. Available from https://doi.org/10.1038/nn1082.

Patel, A. D., & Iversen, J. R. (2007). The linguistic benefits of musical abilities. *Trends in Cognitive Science, 11*(9), 369–372. Available from https://doi.org/10.1016/j.tics.2007.08.003.

Pekna, M., Pekny, M., & Nilsson, M. (2012). Modulation of neural plasticity as a basis for stroke rehabilitation. *Stroke, 43*(10), 2819–2828. Available from https://doi.org/10.1161/STROKEAHA.112.654228.

Platel, H., Price, C., Baron, J. C., Wise, R., Lambert, J., Frackowiak, R. S., . . . Eustache, F. (1997). The structural components of music perception. A functional anatomical study. *Brain, 120*(Pt 2), 229–243.

Raffin, E., & Hummel, F. C. (2018). Restoring motor functions after stroke: Multiple approaches and opportunities. *Neuroscientist, 24*(4), 400–416. Available from https://doi.org/10.1177/1073858417737486.

Roman-Caballero, R., Arnedo, M., Trivino, M., & Lupianez, J. (2018). Musical practice as an enhancer of cognitive function in healthy aging - A systematic review and meta-analysis. *PLoS One, 13*(11), e0207957. Available from https://doi.org/10.1371/journal.pone.0207957.

Sadnicka, A., Kornysheva, K., Rothwell, J. C., & Edwards, M. J. (2018). A unifying motor control framework for task-specific dystonia. *Nature Reviews Neurology, 14*(2), 116–124. Available from https://doi.org/10.1038/nrneurol.2017.146.

Sala, G., & Gobet, F. (2017). Does far transfer exist? Negative evidence from chess, music, and working memory training. *Current Directions in Psychological Science, 26*(6), 515–520. Available from https://doi.org/10.1177/0963721417712760.

Sarkamo, T., & Soto, D. (2012). Music listening after stroke: Beneficial effects and potential neural mechanisms. *Annals of the New York Academy of Sciences, 1252*, 266–281. Available from https://doi.org/10.1111/j.1749-6632.2011.06405.x.

Scarmeas, N., Levy, G., Tang, M. X., Manly, J., & Stern, Y. (2001). Influence of leisure activity on the incidence of Alzheimer's disease. *Neurology, 57*(12), 2236–2242.

Scarmeas, N., & Stern, Y. (2003). Cognitive reserve and lifestyle. *Journal of Clinical and Experimental Neuropsychology, 25*(5), 625–633. Available from https://doi.org/10.1076/jcen.25.5.625.14576.

Scarr, S., & McCartney, K. (1983). How people make their own environments: A theory of genotype greater than environment effects. *Child Development, 54*(2), 424–435.

Schellenberg, E. G. (2011). Examining the association between music lessons and intelligence. *British Journal of Psychology, 102*(3), 283–302. Available from https://doi.org/10.1111/j.2044-8295.2010.02000.x.

Schellenberg, E. G. (2015). Music training and speech perception: A gene-environment interaction. *Annals of the New York Academy of Sciences, 1337,* 170−177. Available from https://doi.org/10.1111/nyas.12627.

Schellenberg, E. G. (2019). Music training, music aptitude, and speech perception. *Proceedings of the National Academy of Sciences United States of America.* Available from https://doi.org/10.1073/pnas.1821109116.

Schellenberg, E. G., & Peretz, I. (2008). Music, language and cognition: Unresolved issues. *Trends in Cognitive Sciences, 12*(2), 45−46. Available from https://doi.org/10.1016/j.tics.2007.11.005.

Schlaug, G., Forgeard, M., Zhu, L., Norton, A., Norton, A., & Winner, E. (2009). Training-induced neuroplasticity in young children. *Annals of the New York Academy of Sciences, 1169,* 205−208. Available from https://doi.org/10.1111/j.1749-6632.2009.04842.x.

Schlaug, G., Jancke, L., Huang, Y., Staiger, J. F., & Steinmetz, H. (1995). Increased corpus callosum size in musicians. *Neuropsychologia, 33*(8), 1047−1055.

Schlaug, G., Jancke, L., Huang, Y., & Steinmetz, H. (1995). In vivo evidence of structural brain asymmetry in musicians. *Science, 267*(5198), 699−701.

Schlaug, G., Norton, A., Overy, K., & Winner, E. (2005). Effects of music training on the child's brain and cognitive development. *Annals of the New York Academy of Sciences, 1060,* 219−230. Available from https://doi.org/10.1196/annals.1360.015.

Schneider, P., Scherg, M., Dosch, H. G., Specht, H. J., Gutschalk, A., & Rupp, A. (2002). Morphology of Heschl's gyrus reflects enhanced activation in the auditory cortex of musicians. *Nature Neuroscience, 5*(7), 688−694. Available from https://doi.org/10.1038/nn871.

Schnider, A., Benson, D. F., Alexander, D. N., & Schnider-Klaus, A. (1994). Non-verbal environmental sound recognition after unilateral hemispheric stroke. *Brain, 117*(Pt 2), 281−287.

Sergent, J., Zuck, E., Terriah, S., & MacDonald, B. (1992). Distributed neural network underlying musical sight-reading and keyboard performance. *Science, 257*(5066), 106−109.

Sihvonen, A. J., Leo, V., Sarkamo, T., & Soinila, S. (2014). [Effectiveness of music in brain rehabilitation. A systematic review]. *Duodecim, 130*(18), 1852−1860.

Sluming, V., Barrick, T., Howard, M., Cezayirli, E., Mayes, A., & Roberts, N. (2002). Voxel-based morphometry reveals increased gray matter density in Broca's area in male symphony orchestra musicians. *NeuroImage, 17*(3), 1613−1622.

Sluming, V., Brooks, J., Howard, M., Downes, J. J., & Roberts, N. (2007). Broca's area supports enhanced visuospatial cognition in orchestral musicians. *Journal of Neuroscience, 27*(14), 3799−3806. Available from https://doi.org/10.1523/JNEUROSCI.0147-07.2007.

Steele, C. J., Bailey, J. A., Zatorre, R. J., & Penhune, V. B. (2013). Early musical training and white-matter plasticity in the corpus callosum: Evidence for a sensitive period. *Journal of Neuroscience, 33*(3), 1282−1290. Available from https://doi.org/10.1523/JNEUROSCI.3578-12.2013.

Steinmetz, H. (1996). Structure, functional and cerebral asymmetry: In vivo morphometry of the planum temporale. *Neuroscience & Biobehavioral Review, 20*(4), 587−591.

Stern, C., & Munn, Z. (2010). Cognitive leisure activities and their role in preventing dementia: A systematic review. *International Journal of Evidenced Based Healthcare, 8*(1), 2−17. Available from https://doi.org/10.1111/j.1744-1609.2010.00150.x.

Stern, Y., Arenaza-Urquijo, E. M., Bartres-Faz, D., Belleville, S., Cantilon, M., Chetelat, G., ... Conceptual Frameworks, W. (2018). Whitepaper: Defining and investigating cognitive reserve, brain reserve, and brain maintenance. *Alzheimers Dementia.* Available from https://doi.org/10.1016/j.jalz.2018.07.219.

Stern, Y., Gazes, Y., Razlighi, Q., Steffener, J., & Habeck, C. (2018). A task-invariant cognitive reserve network. *NeuroImage*, *178*, 36−45. Available from https://doi.org/10.1016/j.neuroimage.2018.05.033.

Stern, Y., Zarahn, E., Hilton, H. J., Flynn, J., DeLaPaz, R., & Rakitin, B. (2003). Exploring the neural basis of cognitive reserve. *Journal of Clinical and Experimental Neuropsychology*, *25* (5), 691−701. Available from https://doi.org/10.1076/jcen.25.5.691.14573.

Stewart, J. C., & Cramer, S. C. (2017). Genetic variation and neuroplasticity: Role in rehabilitation after stroke. *Journal of Neurologic Physical Therapy*, *41*(Suppl. 3), S17−S23. Available from https://doi.org/10.1097/NPT.0000000000000180.

Stine-Morrow, E. A. L., Payne, B. R., Roberts, B. W., Kramer, A. F., Morrow, D. G., Payne, L., ... Parisi, J. M. (2014). Training versus engagement as paths to cognitive enrichment with aging. *Psychology & Aging*, *29*(4), 891−906. Available from https://doi.org/10.1037/a0038244.

Strait, D. L., & Kraus, N. (2014). Biological impact of auditory expertise across the life span: Musicians as a model of auditory learning. *Hearing Research*, *308*, 109−121. Available from https://doi.org/10.1016/j.heares.2013.08.004.

Takeuchi, N., & Izumi, S. (2015). Combinations of stroke neurorehabilitation to facilitate motor recovery: Perspectives on Hebbian plasticity and homeostatic metaplasticity. *Frontiers in Human Neuroscience*, *9*, 349. Available from https://doi.org/10.3389/fnhum.2015.00349.

Taub, E., Miller, N. E., Novack, T. A., Cook, E. W., III., Fleming, W. C., Nepomuceno, C. S., ... Crago, J. E. (1993). Technique to improve chronic motor deficit after stroke. *Archives of Physical Medicine Rehabilitation*, *74*(4), 347−354.

Thow, M. E., Summers, M. J., Saunders, N. L., Summers, J. J., Ritchie, K., & Vickers, J. C. (2018). Further education improves cognitive reserve and triggers improvement in selective cognitive functions in older adults: The Tasmanian Healthy Brain Project. *Alzheimers & Dementia Journal (Amst)*, *10*, 22−30. Available from https://doi.org/10.1016/j.dadm.2017.08.004.

Wan, C. Y., & Schlaug, G. (2010). Music making as a tool for promoting brain plasticity across the life span. *Neuroscientist*, *16*(5), 566−577. Available from https://doi.org/10.1177/1073858410377805.

Woelfle, R., & Grahn, J. A. (2013). Auditory and visual interhemispheric communication in musicians and non-musicians. *PLoS One*, *8*(12), e84446. Available from https://doi.org/10.1371/journal.pone.0084446.

Zatorre, R., & McGill, J. (2005). Music, the food of neuroscience? *Nature*, *434*(7031), 312−315. Available from https://doi.org/10.1038/434312a.

Chapter 9

Singing and choirs

Annabel J. Cohen

Department of Psychology, University of Prince Edward Island, Charlottetown, PE, Canada

Introduction

Singing provides older persons with opportunities to engage in music perfor-mance, whether or not they have done so in the past. It offers the esthetic pleasure of making music, but that may not be all. Singing in a group has been associated with enhanced social bonding (Pearce, Launay, & Dunbar, 2015), general feeling of well-being (Clift et al., 2010), sense of personal growth (Noice & Noice, 2009), reduced stress response (Gick, 2011), reduced pain (Balsnes, 2016; Weinstein, Launay, Pearce, Dunbar, & Stewart, 2016), reduced loneliness and increased interest in life (Johnson et al., 2018), and heightened immune function (Fancourt et al., 2016). The present chapter reviews research related to these findings focusing primarily on studies of choirs of healthy older persons. Attention is also directed to possible benefits of individual singing lessons for older adults. Comparisons with other leisure activities are drawn. Whereas studies have suggested that experience playing a musical instrument is associated with cognitive resilience in senior years (Strong & Mast, 2018; for review see Román-Caballero, Arnedo, Triviño, & Lupiáñez, 2018; Schneider, Hunger, & Bardach, 2018; Strong & Midden, 2018), few studies have considered the benefits of vocal training from this perspective. Such studies are needed to determine whether singing interven-tions hold promise as a cost-effective way to help maintain and increase health and well-being in even the oldest adults.

Singing, a complex, multidimensional behavior

Children learn to sing at the same time as they learn to speak (Stadler Elmer, 2011). Put another way, every older person sang as a child, and general abil-ity to sing a song is considered to be normally distributed (Dalla Bella, Giguère, & Peretz, 2007). Yet for some older people, singing may seem a daunting prospect. Indeed, many adults in the Western world classify them-selves as "nonsingers," believing they cannot sing or have no musical ability

Music and the Aging Brain. DOI: https://doi.org/10.1016/B978-0-12-817422-7.00009-2
245

(Knight, 2011, 2019; Numminen, Lonka, Rainio, & Ruismäki, 2015). If such self-described nonsingers have young children or grandchildren, they might pause to consider that the children are able to sing quite naturally while they as adults are not comfortable doing so. By chance, the present author met a new grandmother who spoke of plans to take voice lessons so as to feel at ease singing to her grandchild. Taking singing lessons in order to sing a lullaby? That might seem absurd, and skeptics could further question the possibility of improving one's singing at an advanced age. Before considering whether singing ability can improve later in life, it is well to step away from a Western European context and consider remarks of ethnomusicologist Aaron Carter-Ényì, who, in discussing sub-Saharan African vocal music and pedagogy, said: "Unlike North America and Europe, in Africa, one rarely hears the phrase "I cannot sing." (Yang, Carter-Ényì, Radhakrishanon, Grimmer, & Nix, 2019, p. 757).

A cross-cultural perspective, such as that provided by Carter-Ényì, implies that singing, just like speaking, is a behavior that is potentially available to persons of all ages. The present chapter takes this point of view and suggests that singing for many, if not most, people is an untapped human resource. Further, the chapter examines the proposal that singing can serve a unique role in "allaying the physical and cognitive effects of aging so that older adults can maintain good mental health and independence," quoting Lola Cuddy, Sylvie Belleville, and Aline Moussard, in the preface of this book.

Fundamentally, singing is an example of music performance. It is complex, multidimensional behavior, subject to many biological, psychological, and sociocultural influences (Cohen, 2019). Its complexity somewhat accounts for those who say "I can't sing" or who would take lessons in order to perform everyday activities involving singing. Singing in a choir differs from singing alone, but there are also many different kinds of choirs, as different as there are choir leaders and approaches to choral pedagogy (Abrahams & Head, 2017). Similarly, there are many kinds of solo singing and kinds of vocal pedagogy, and even a skilled voice teacher will offer different types of training depending on the behavior and proclivities of the student.

Fundamentals

Minimally, singing a melody entails producing extended vowels with pitches corresponding to a musical scale. Tacit knowledge of musical rules of a culture constrain the choice of pitch targets. For melodies with lyrics, phonetic, and syntactic rules also constrain the produced speech sounds. Tone languages, which characterize more than half of the world's languages, may have subtle influences on melodic pitch direction (e.g., Schellenberg & Gick, 2018). Suffice to say, much cognitive processing is activated in the singing of a simple nursery rhyme, let alone a more complex musical piece, even Happy Birthday or a national anthem.

Looking further at mental processing, singing entails a complex sensory–motor feedback system (Pfordresher et al., 2015; Tsang, Friendly, & Trainor, 2011). To sing a tune that will be recognizable to others entails that one first mentally represent the tune, which might be considered a sequential set of targeted pitches. Then one must activate the required muscle groups controlling the lungs and diaphragm, the vocal cords and the vocal tract in order to produce each targeted pitch with the expected frequency, intensity, and voice quality (Sundberg, 1987). Adjustments will be made depending on the degree of match between the produced and expected sound and the sensitivity of the singer to the mismatch. Singing can also mean vocalizing notes that go well with a tune, that is, singing in harmony.

Singing relies on memory. When singing a song, the singer must remember immediately preceding tones and phrases so as to position the next note appropriately. Memory for the overall higher order structure of the song can also provide cues. Singing a song without musical notation or printed lyrics is particularly taxing on memory. Every song that one has ever sung was at one time unfamiliar; therefore singing entails first learning the song and creating a long-term memory of it, if one is to sing it again. The remembered melody provides the mental model that guides vocal production.

Singing means subconsciously establishing a key in which to begin a song, retaining the key throughout the song, making sure that the primary notes that one sings are in the key, at least for simple tonal music. In certain cultures or musical styles, notes on nonfixed pitch instruments (like the voice or nonfretted stringed instruments) deviate from the key for esthetic reasons (e.g., North Indian Hindustani, Beijing opera, Middle Eastern cantillation, the blues).

In addition to the performance features learned by all musicians, such as lengthening and accentuating the first beat of a bar (Palmer, 1992), there are additional esthetic and stylistic principles associated with singing, such as controlling the musculature in such a way as to produce a uniform quality of the voice throughout its range ("to equalize vocal timbre throughout the great scale", Miller, 1996, p. 51), counteracting the physical constraints of the larynx and vocal tract that would normally lead to different timbres for different frequency ranges or different frequencies that fall in certain resonances of the vocal tract. Singing engages the entire body in appropriate posture to position and support the internal vocal instrument of the diaphragm, lungs, larynx, and vocal tract (Malde, Allen, & Zeller, 2013).

Neural basis of singing

Other chapters in this volume have described the neural underpinnings of music representation, showing that listening to music engages almost all parts of the human brain including motor areas. The distinction between the brain when performing music and when listening to it is not as great as one might expect, in part resulting from engagement of the motor system during listening. This motor engagement is found more in musicians than nonmusicians, and is to some extent instrument-specific.

From an evolutionary standpoint, the roots of singing go back to the time of the Neanderthals, between 200,000 and 35,000 BCE. According to Mithen (2005), their communication system was half-singing and half-speech that eventually bifurcated into the two vocal communication categories that we know today. Ontogenetically, singing is a natural behavior that is quite fully manifested in early childhood. The neural networks underlying singing and speech networks are partially overlapping (Kleber & Zarate, 2014). Overy and Molnar-Szakacs (2009) proposed the Shared Affective Motion Experience (SAME) theory which claims that listening to music engages the nervous system in a way that would also serve music performance. This model assumes that everyone is a performer, even if one has no formal training or ability on a musical instrument (other than the human voice, hand-clapping, toe-tapping, and body-swaying). In accordance with the SAME theory, listening to music may naturally engage the neural network underlying singing.

To an onlooker, singing may appear localized to activity of the mouth, but, as already mentioned, much of the body is involved, maintaining balanced posture, breathing, controlling the physical properties of the vocal folds to alter their vibration rate to change the pitch, activating the muscles that control articulation of vowels and consonants or influence the quality of the voice. Posture is important, as it is for playing most musical instruments. Breathing also plays a key role in performance of some musical instruments such as woodwinds and brass. But the control of the vocal cords is unique to singing.

The vocal folds are housed within the larynx. Their stiffness and length are controlled by the thyroarytenoid and cricothyroid muscles, affecting their vibration rate and consequent produced pitch, while other muscles control the starting and stopping of the pitch (adduction and abduction). All of these muscles are under control of neural activity thought to originate in the motor cortex dedicated to the larynx, as identified by Penfield and Rasmussen (1950). Brown, Ngan, and Liotti (2008) mapped the area more precisely (see also Belyk & Brown, 2017) naming it the larynx motor cortex (LMC), following evidence for its engagement in tasks of singing tasks (Brown, Martinez, Hodges, Fox, & Parsons, 2004) as well as auditory discrimination (Brown & Martinez, 2007). Recent efforts to map neural activity in the LMC that corresponds to the act of vocally producing a particular pitch have however met with disappointment. Whereas pitch height maps systematically onto the auditory cortex, the mapping of the relation between motor control and pitch production remains a mystery (Belyk, Lee, & Brown, 2018). The authors suggested that extra development of the LMC of highly trained choristers whose brains were studied may actually account for some of the challenges to finding a relation between the produced pitch and the command to produce it. Lesser trained singers might offer less dense neural networks whose connections might more readily be revealed.

As with practice on a musical instrument, vocal practice can change parts of the brain. Feedback studies which altered the vocally produced pitch by two semitones played back to singers and nonsingers during brain imaging (specifically functional magnetic resonance imagery, fMRI), have led to the proposal of a "singing network" that develops in trained singers. The network includes the posterior superior temporal sulcus, the intraparietal sulcus, the anterior insula, and the anterior cingulate cortex (Zarate & Zatorre, 2008; Zarate, 2013; Zarate, Wood, & Zatorre, 2010). Through extensive training, the singer becomes less reliant on auditory feedback (hearing one's own voice) and more able to trust the match between actual and expected motor activity. Studies entailing anesthetization of the vocal folds in singers and nonsingers showed reduced activity in the right anterior insula in singers and increased activity in nonsingers, while singers still maintained accurate performance due to reliance on a highly developed motor feedforward system (Kleber, Zeitouni, Friberg, & Zatorre, 2013). The importance of the right anterior insula in the singing network of the brain and the increased role of somatosensory as opposed to auditory feedback with increased vocal experience was further corroborated in a study in which a masking noise prevented the singers and non-singers from hearing their own singing (Kleber, Friberg, Zeitouni, & Zatorre, 2017).

A question that underlies much of this chapter is whether experience as a singer can equal that of a performer of a musical instrument, particularly in regard to neuroprotection and cognitive resilience. In addressing this question, it would be useful to know the extent of the similarity of the brain mechanisms underlying musical instrument performance and vocal performance, ideally when the amount of specialized training on each instrument was equal. A partial answer arises from the first study to compare brain networks engaged by singing and musical instrument playing. Segado, Hollinger, Thibodeau, Penhune, and Zatorre (2018) asked experienced cellists to produce notes on an MRI compatible cello and to sing the same notes while in an fMRI scanner. The similar range of the cello and voice and the continuous (versus discrete) pitch mapping of both instruments make the cello an ideal instrument for comparison with the singing voice. A further feature of similarity is the decoupling of pitch and timing production.

As summarized by Segado et al. (2018), current models of auditory–motor integration for music and speech entail a feedforward and a feedback system. The feedforward system comprises areas of the brain that control planning and implementation of motor responses. These areas are found in the motor cortex located primarily in the frontal lobe, anterior to the central sulcus separating the frontal and parietal lobes. Also included are the cerebellum and the periaqueductal gray (PAG) of the brainstem nuclei. The feedback system processes auditory and motor sensations and compares them to the expected output. This entails the auditory cortices in the temporal lobe, the anterior cingulate cortex (surrounding the frontal part of the corpus callosum with a specific function of error detection as well as interpretation of pain), the intraparietal sulcus, and the anterior insula.

The study compared brain activity under three conditions: Sing/Play, Listen, and Rest. In *Sing/Play*, the participant heard a *do, re, mi* pattern beginning on E_3 for the cello or E_3 or E_4 for the voice, depending on the voice range, and was asked either to sing or play it. In the *Listen* condition, participants simply listened, and in the *Rest* condition, there was no auditory stimulation.

Comparison of the fMRI results under the sing and play conditions revealed overlap in the majority of areas of the auditory–vocal network. In tune performance (vocal or cello) depended on the activation of this network. Activity in the auditory area is functionally connected with activity in the dorsal motor and premotor areas, and connectivity is positively correlated with accurate singing. Cellists who began playing before the age of 7 years showed significantly more activation of the larynx area during cello playing than did those who started at or after the age of 7 years. There was more activation in the motor larynx area for singing than for playing, and more activity in the hand areas for playing than for singing. Activation of the brainstem, particularly the PAG, was specific to singing, likely linked to vocal control and respiration.

The study showed that playing a musical instrument by persons who practice on average over 24 hours per week and have played on average for almost 15 years, activates the same auditory–vocal network for singing. Moreover, this auditory–vocal network is the same as found independently in brain-imaging studies of trained singers. While there are some differences arising from singing and playing, specifically the engagement of the brainstem and specific motor areas represented in the cerebellum, the results reinforce the notion that training on a musical instrument and on the singing voice, at least in part, activates the same auditory–vocal network. In the context of the present chapter, this would support the notion that if music training is neuroprotective so might be training of the singing voice in its coordination of many parts of the brain.

Diverse trajectories of singing acquisition

Yet the complexity of singing seems often overlooked in everyday perceptions as well as scholarly discourse. Perhaps this is because every child naturally engages in some elements of singing, and so singing may seem trivial, compared to performing on any other musical instrument, which requires deliberate training. In much the same way, a child naturally learns to talk but must be taught to read. There seems to be more excitement about children's first words than their first song fragments. Learning to talk and learning to sing begin in similar ways, each relying on exposure to the sound patterns of the culture in order to acquire the rules to which the vocalizations appropriate to the culture must adhere. Yet the long-term trajectories of the acquisition of singing and speaking are strikingly different. Learning to speak entails the integration of muscles commands, sensory−motor feedback, and knowledge of linguistic units and continues to early adulthood (Smith, 2006). For example, a first plateau in adult-like proficiency of lip and jaw coordination for speaking is achieved only by the age of 14 years (Smith & Zelaznik, 2004). But once satisfactory speech is acquired, a feat attained by every typically developing adult, it is retained and exercised throughout life. The trajectory for singing development across the life span is more variable among members of Western European cultures, possibly because singing is less essential than is speaking for successful functioning in adulthood.

In addition to musical predispositions or motivations, external influences of family, friends, and institutions impact both the development of the ability and the motivational vicissitudes associated with singing. The situation is similar to factors influencing individual trajectories in learning to play a musical instrument (Gaunt & Hallam, 2016) with the exception that for singing, the instrument is inside the body, or from some perspectives, the entire body is the instrument. As musicologist, social activist, and vocalist Shana Redmond (2020, p. 318) has put it: "To be the instrument, rather than to play it, lends itself to a very different engagement with one's environment and makes for a unique capacity for response in real time." Everyone, early in life, can use this inborn musical instrument, unlike any human-made musical instrument, but the levels of achievement attained on the adult vocal instrument, in comparison to the speaking voice, are widely varying.

Gender and historical considerations

A review of 21st century research literature on choral singing (Noble, 2020), revealed slightly less than three times as many females to males in choral groups in middle- and high-school levels. This phenomena known as "the problem of the missing males" (Freer, 2010) could be perpetuated as these boys get older. Male disenchantment with choral singing may in part stem from the dramatic changes in the adolescent vocal anatomy (e.g., increase in size of the vocal folds and lengthening of the larynx), changes that are unmatched in females (Kayes, 2019). The unpredictability of male vocalization during this time can lead to embarrassment and lack of confidence. It is no wonder that without suitable role models or encouragement, many boys will avoid choral singing. The negative attitude may filter down to male children who see few older males, be they family members or teachers, engaging in choral singing.

The idea that singing is an activity for females has origins that go beyond physiological differences in female and male vocal development. For example, more than two centuries ago, Rush (1787), a physician, early psychiatrist, and signer of the Declaration of Independence of the United States of America, recommended singing as essential to education of American women pioneers. That he was even thinking about educating women was advanced for the time. He advocated for a women's curriculum that included English literacy, mathematics and bookkeeping, geography and history, astronomy, natural philosophy, and reading about world "history, travels, poetry, and moral essays." Fifth in importance (before dancing, reading, Christian religion) was singing. The passage is worth quoting in full because of its resonance with contemporary thinking of the benefits of singing for resilience.

> *V. Vocal music should never be neglected in the education of a young lady in this country. Besides preparing her to join in that part of public worship which consists in psalmody it will enable her to soothe the cares of domestic life. The distress and vexation of a husband, the noise of a nursery, and even the sorrows that will sometimes intrude into her own bosom may all be relieved by a song, where sound and sentiment unite to act upon the mind. I hope it will not be thought foreign to this part of our subject to introduce a fact here which has been suggested to me by my profession, and that is, that the exercise of the organs of the breath by singing contributes very much to defend them from those diseases to which our climate, and other causes have of late exposed them. Our German fellow citizens are seldom afflicted with consumptions, nor have I ever known but one instance of a spitting of blood among them. This, I believe, is in part occasioned by the strength which their lungs acquire by exercising them frequently in vocal music, for this constitutes an essential branch of their education. The music master of our academy has furnished me with an observation still more in favor of this opinion. He informed me that he had known several instances of persons who were strongly disposed to the consumption who were restored to health by the moderate exercise of their lungs in singing. (p. 80 on-line publication of 1787 collection of writings of Benjamin Rush)[1]*

The passage is of interest because of its evidence that singing was valued but particularly for women, yet there are also intimations of gender-neutral benefits of singing from the standpoint of physical health, particularly lung disease. At that time, the life span at birth was 40 years, about half of what it is today. Given the relatively short life expectancy, Rush's insights into

---

1. I thank Gunter Kreutz (personal communication 2018) for directing my attention to a Dr. Rush's pioneering pronouncement regarding the benefits of singing.

the value of singing might be regarded as protective of aging well for that era. Similar ideas about the benefits of singing are prominent today, however, in this case they are applied to an older demographic, one nonexistent even a century ago.

The popular leisure activity

Singing in choirs is one of the most popular leisure activities in the Western world. Recently, a survey of a sample of over 5700 choral singers in the United States, and further surveys of more than 500 adults over the age of 18 and more than 500 over the age of 62 years, concluded that the percentage of Americans singing has increased from 14% in 2008 to 17% in 2018, with one in six Americans over the age of 18 singing in a chorus (Grunwald Associates LLC & Chorus America, 2019). Older choristers compared with older adults drawn from the general public had superior health status on several measures; the survey claimed to control for socioeconomic aspects. A national survey of Canadian participation in choirs estimated that Canadian choral singers represent roughly 10% of the population (Choral Canada, 2017). Of 861 choral organizations that completed the survey, 49% of them had members over the age of 65 years. In Europe, a survey of 21 countries was conducted between 2013 and 2015 under the supervision of the European Choral Association—Europa Cantat www.thevoiceproject.eu, (Bartel, 2015). It estimated that there were 1 million choirs or ensembles on the European continent equaling roughly 4.5% of the European population, ranging from 2% to 11% nationally. The social component was noted in 90% of the choirs. Although these estimates of European participation are lower than those for Canada and the United States, the conclusion was that for Europe "collective singing is a major cultural activity" (p. 8) and that its prevalence is unfortunately unknown to government policy makers and deserves recognition.[2] The three surveys also provided broad evidence for the inclusion of older adults (beyond retirement years) in these choirs.

Summary

In summary of this section, the demands of singing on engagement and coordination of sensory, cognitive, and motor functions indicate that singing is a highly complex task. Many biological and sociocultural factors lead to wide interindividual variability in attainment of proficiency as compared to

---

2. "This result should encourage policy makers and civil society stakeholders to support and foster and (sic) activity that is in essence both artistic and social, and that reaches out to a significance portion of the European population. It should also empower the singers and their organizations to be more 'vocal' about their own importance on the cultural policy scene … This global ignorance constitutes a 'blind spot' in the European and in most national cultural policies" (Bartel, 2015, p. 8).

learning to speak. Gender is one such factor, with singing often and historically associated more with females than males. Finally, American and European surveys reveal that group singing is one of the most popular leisure activities in the Western world, though still engaging a minority of the population.

Benefits of group singing

The ice-breaker effect

A social network is a contributing factor to physical, cognitive, and mental health. With age, social networks may shrink for a variety of reasons. Singing together builds trust quickly and can be a factor in establishing new friendships or a support network.

A series of original studies conducted in the United Kingdom provides evidence of a tendency for people to feel socially closer to strangers after singing together compared to when they have undertaken other group activities. The phenomenon is known as the *ice-breaker effect* (Pearce et al., 2015) and can extend to large groups of people on the order of 150 (Weinstein et al., 2016). Launay and Pearce (2020) suggest that singing with others may produce beta-endorphins, an endogenous (self-produced) opiate having similar effects to drugs like morphine causing mild euphoria. Endorphins are associated with the euphoria of the "runners' high" and have been found to relate to social bonding in primate species (Dunbar, 2010). To test the notion that singing can lead to the release of endorphins, the researchers measured the effect of group singing on pain thresholds before and after choir rehearsal. Pain was created with a blood pressure cuff, with which most of the participants were familiar from routine medical check-ups. After the choir rehearsal the choristers showed significantly higher pain tolerance levels. One explanation for this reduced sensitivity to pain is that endorphins resulting from the experience of singing together counteracted the normal feeling of pain. The authors however point out that in a study with older participants, rehearsals had no significant effect on the pain measurement. They suggested that the blood pressure cuff is not a suitable method for measuring pain in older participants who had various health conditions as well as negative reactions and associations to this procedure in some cases. Studies of the effect of playing in an orchestra or other instrumental ensemble on pain thresholds would also be of interest in order to determine whether group singing is special in raising thresholds for pain.

Further related to the impact of singing on social relations, Good and Russo (2016) report a study in which children who engaged in singing showed greater cooperation in a game than children engaged in other nonmusical activities. They suggest that the synchronized movement in singing is the key factor in enhancing empathy. Kirschner and Tomasello (2010) showed increased prosocial behavior in 4-year-old children who sang and danced together. It remains an open question whether singing together promotes empathetic responses at the older end of the life span.

Loneliness and interest in life

As one of the first arts-based randomized controlled trials for older adults, the Community of Voices Trial was conducted with the aim of determining cognitive, physical, and social benefits of a 6-month weekly choral activity that itself had cognitive, physical, and social dimensions (Johnson et al., 2018). The study was carried out in lower socioeconomic areas of San Francisco, with participants of average age 71 years, and 65% were non-white. After 6 months of weekly choral rehearsals, the choral group had significantly lower loneliness and greater interest in life than did a control group which had no intervention. There was no evidence of improved performance on the specific cognitive task chosen to measure cognition. Nor was improvement found on physical activity (preferred walking pace, and balance). The authors suggest that a longer period of choir involvement, more frequent rehearsals (e.g., two per week), or encouragement of daily practice could lead to greater benefits. Some other studies of choir members have concluded that choral singing was associated with increased well-being (Clift et al., 2010; Johnson, Louhivuori, & Siljander, 2016), however, participants in these studies have tended to be of higher socioeconomic status.

Linking musical and extramusical goals

Balsnes (2016) describes a case study of the Silver Voices choir of 150 persons all above the age of 62 years with an average of 70 years. The choir was initiated through the Kilden Performing Arts Centre in Norway which has as its mandate an outreach program with a vision of enriching and changing both people and society. Consistent with this mandate, the study was based on the premise that the potential for learning music does not diminish with age.

The two instructors, both with higher degrees in music education, report progress over the 4 years in the quality of the music, and "find it motivating that even at an advanced age it is possible to develop singers' voices and musicality" (p. 63). One part of the repertoire is classical choral works to be performed with the symphony orchestra associated with the Arts Center, and another part is lighter for less formal performances. Musical scores are provided for rehearsals, but for those who do not read music, recordings of the parts are provided.

The instructors direct their attention to the musical goals, which are their priority, but they are also engaged in managing the social dimension and understand its significance. There is a strong nonmusical social component to the choir. Coffee is served before the rehearsal starts. Members wear nametags and are reminded to greet new attendees. An annual trip including sightseeing and a joint concert with another local choir add to the activities. These seemingly insignificant details may be essential to the success of a choral singing intervention for older adults.

Among the benefits identified by interviewees were having something to look forward to and attend, and offering a sense of belonging and a purpose. Health benefits were also mentioned. A person with Parkinson's disease referred to the "joy of singing" being "the best medicine, a happy pill and pain reliever, a resource for physical relaxation and a counterbalance to depression." Another responder noted that learning about music and providing evidence that learning is possible (e.g., memorizing the material) is rewarding. Singing in four-part harmony was regarded as "an audible expression of fellowship and togetherness" (p. 64). The extent to which these comments represent the entire choir is unclear, because only seven members volunteered to offer their thoughts. Nevertheless the choir experience can offer such value at least to some if not all members. This choir achieves for its members the two goals of developing musically and reaping extramusical benefits. Desiring to perform music as beautifully as possible and nurturing personal well-being are intrinsically linked for this singing group. Similar findings regarding a small community choir in England tracked over a 4-year period were reported by Lamont, Murray, Hale, and Wright-Bevans (2018).

Intergenerational engagement

According to Erikson's (1959) psychosocial stages of development, the ages between 40 and 65 represent a stage of *generativity*, wanting to nurture those who are younger. Beyond the age of 65 is the final stage, *ego integrity*, during which life is reviewed and a sense of integrity rather than despair depends on the outcome of the reminiscence and review. Engagement with young children is often satisfying for older persons, but children can also benefit from interactions with older adults. Heydon & O'Neill (2016), Heydon, Beynon, O'Neill, Zhang, and Crocker (2013), and Heydon, McKee, and O'Neill (2020) studied the benefits of an intergenerational art program in a colocated facility, and then extended this work to include singing. Shared songs promote engagement in a joint activity. For older adults, an immediate sense of well-being and self-worth may result, consistent with Eriksonian theorizing. For young children, the experience may allow them to grow into adulthood having respect for older people. Initiatives involving university students and older adults in an intergenerational choir have also met with success (Harris & Caporella, 2018).

Multicultural engagement

About 40 years ago, several European immigrants in Calgary, Alberta, Canada who wanted to sing songs of their homelands formed a multicultural choir. The choir soon expanded and now boasts a membership reflecting 26 different nationalities. While there is no age restriction, the membership tends to be older adults. The professional choir leader aims to offer the experience of four-part harmony, a revered aspect of choral singing for many experienced choristers. It is appreciated that traditional Western harmony by definition is inconsistent with the notion of an all-embracing notion of multiculturalism. In acknowledging this, the choir has sung material based on themes of non-Western cultures that is nevertheless four-part harmony (sometimes commissioning such works). The multicultural aspect offers a new challenge to these choristers, some of whom belong to more than one choir and have been choristers all of their lives. The choir also offers the opportunity to meet people from many lands (See calgarymulticulturalchoir.ca).

In Australia, Jane Davidson and Samantha Dieckmann established a lullaby choir in collaboration with a community organization that provides support for newly arrived migrants, asylum seekers, and refugees. The staff of the organization was extremely diverse and formed the choir. Lullabies as content offered emotional, nostalgic, and cultural significance to the participants, all of whom were in the workforce. The model however might be applicable to older participants (Miller, 2018).

Research with schoolchildren has shown that learning the songs of the persons of a different culture can lead to reduced prejudice (Neto, Pinto, & Mullet, 2015). The singing program leading to this positive outcome was for an entire school term, however the effect was sustained for 2 years, the longest duration tested. Again, while this effect has been observed only for children, multicultural choirs for older adults could potentially lead to reduction of implicit bias and increased numbers of social ties. The principle may account for some of the social benefits of choral singing for older adults described earlier in this section, where choirs have had heterogeneous cultural membership.

Musical theater

Musical theater is typically much loved by audiences including older adults. One study explored whether combining the active singing engagement of an older adult audience might make the experience even more meaningful. In partnership with the Young at Heart Musical Theatre for Seniors performance group in Prince Edward Island, a study was conducted to explore the benefits of active singing versus listening on measures of psychological health of audiences living in senior residences (Beaton, Henderson, O'Brien, & Cohen, 2012). The musical theater performance entitled "Canada in Love" had been designed to interest older adults. It was professionally presented in two conditions differing only in whether the audience was encouraged to sing along to several songs. The performances were presented in eight different seniors residences, four of which encouraged active singing during the production. Following the presentation, audience members were asked to complete questionnaires regarding their enjoyment of the performance and their sense of well-being and their memory for material presented. Measures of degree of engagement were also made from audiovisual recordings. Even though audience members were encouraged to sing along on several occasions during the performance, only some of them did. The results of this pilot study suggested that willingness to engage in singing was associated with significantly higher measures of quality of life and scores on the memory test, and suggest the value of encouraging audience vocal participation in music theater performances directed toward a senior audience.

Summary

In summary of this section, studies of responses of members of choral groups for older singers have revealed that choral groups can lead to faster development of affiliation than other group activities, and can decrease loneliness and increase interest in life of members. Choral groups of older adults can appreciate striving for and attaining musical-esthetic goals while at the same time valuing the social aspects of associating with choir members during and beyond the choir rehearsals. Feelings of self-worth can be brought about through choral engagement with children or other younger generations, and special joy arises from sharing songs of one's own culture in a singing group whose members come from many cultures. Musical theater productions offer opportunities for active engagement in singing by an audience potentially adding to the enjoyment. It is noted that no study to date has shown cognitive benefits of group singing, although only one (Johnson et al., 2018) has looked for it.

Individual singing lessons

The experiences of choral singing and voice lessons are typically quite different. Choral singing entails blending one's voice with the voices of a group generally guided by the choir director. Private lessons focus on listening to your voice and focusing on your vocal apparatus (vocal tract, larynx, and lungs) and your body to create the best sound you can, with the help of a teacher whose entire focus is on you, rather than on multiple choristers (Murdock, 2015). There are no studies that compare the effects of choral singing versus voice lessons on cognitive or social aspects of well-being for persons of any age, let alone older adults.

Compared to choral singing for older adults, in everyday discourse and research, relatively little attention has been directed to individual voice training or solo singing in later life. This trend coincides with the fact that voice lessons, and music lessons in general, are typically considered the territory of the young. To my shame I remember my shocked reaction as a university student to my mother's idea of her resuming piano lessons after a gap of many decades. Years later, I was shocked again, this time by my own engagement in voice lessons in middle age, that taught me the appropriateness of music lessons for older adults. At any age, studying vocal music connects the student with the body, with emotion, with poetry, drama, languages, phonetics, and cultural history, in addition to all the musical matters, and the beauty of the music. While such experiences and learning can occur during choral singing, regular voice lessons over years with a fine teacher will assure that they take place.

Effects of voice training on brain development

Summarizing recent studies that compare persons with different degrees of vocal training (see also the "Neural basis of singing" section), singing entails a complex sensorimotor feedback system to support control of an extensive vocal apparatus for both gross (lungs, diaphragm) and fine motor (vocal folds, vocal tract) coordination. Both the anatomical and the neurophysiological systems underlying singing share many features with systems underlying speaking. Yet singing entails different constraints and demands in its simultaneous coordination of production of precise melodic, phonetic, and emotional information. At least for vocalists who have received extended training, there appears to be a "singing network" distinct from and perhaps in competition with a speaking network, but shared with the network engaged by performance of a musical instrument. Thus studies of highly trained compared to untrained or less-trained vocalists have revealed larger left-hemisphere arcuate fasciculus and reduced fractional anisotropy (Halwani, Loui, Rüber, & Schlaug, 2011); increased right hemisphere gray matter in somatosensory larynx S1, supramarginal gyrus (SMG) somatosensory S2, and primary auditory cortex, with increases in S1 and SMG varying with years of training after age 14 (Kleber et al., 2016); increased BOLD response in somatosensory S1 and parietal association areas (Kleber, Veit, Birbaumer, Gruzelier, & Lotze, 2010); more left hemisphere activity in covert (imagined) singing, and less overlap with the traditional language areas (Wilson, Abbott, Lusher, Gentle, & Jackson, 2011). The evidence that cortical laryngeal representation increases with vocal training after the age of 14 years leads to speculation regarding a critical period for development of motor control of singing that opens after the closure of the critical period for the development of sensorimotor articulatory competence underlying language acquisition. How long this window remains open is of interest from the perspective of aging. It should be noted that most of the studies referred to here have examined those for whom singing is a chosen musical activity. No studies, other than one by Schellenberg (2004) with children, have assigned study participants randomly to a condition of singing training to be compared with other participants in a group of performance on another musical instrument. It is possible that persons who have chosen to sing may have an innate predisposition for singing, and that results of studies would apply less to those with less predispositions toward singing.

Private lessons—a case study of an octogenarian

The learnability of singing throughout the life span is relevant to the discussion of the contribution of singing to mental and physical well-being in later life. To what extent can singing ability be retained and even augmented with training and practice throughout the course of normal aging? To this end, an opportunity arose to conduct a longitudinal single-case study with one older man who began voice lessons at the age of 84 years of age (Cohen & Pan, 2015). He continued with lessons on and off for 3 years. A previous exploration with four persons in their 80s revealed basic singing skills intact (Gallant, 2009). In this case study, the participant carried out the same vocal tasks on seven occasions, using the Advancing Interdisciplinary Studies in Singing Test Battery of Singing Skills (Cohen, 2015). The analysis focused on the stability of the pitch of 10 tonic-notes within one song that was repeated several times during the course of the test. Stability of the tonic within the piece over the 3 years of testing reflected stability of cognitive—motoric processes over this period during which data were collected. A systematic change of key following the change of prior tonal context suggested cognitive flexibility. Other components of the test, as yet unanalyzed, may also provide information about cognitive, motoric, and emotional processes. He reported practicing regularly, inspired by weekly voice lessons during this time. It is recognized that this is a case study of an unusually capable participant, a former clinical psychologist, independently living, who claimed to have little music training but who greatly enjoyed classical music and was a dedicated concert attender. The results however suggest the viability of voice lessons in later life, even if for the first time. His obituary several years after the final test session included the following: "He also indulged another lifelong passion by taking singing lessons; eventually he performed on stage, bringing down the house at the Bonshaw Ceilidh with his rendition of *Danny Boy*."[3]

Later life singing lessons survey

On a broader scale, there was a survey of older persons who had taken or were taking private voice lessons (Cohen & Kleinerman, 2010). The study

---

3. From the *Journal Pioneer* (January 25, 2019). P.E.I. psychologist, writer Dr. Sol Feldstein remembered for work with patients, cultural pursuits. https://www.journalpioneer.com/news/local/pei-psychologist-writer-dr-sol-feldstein-remembered-for-work-with-patients-cultural-pursuits-279048/.

explored singing as an avenue for personal growth and wellness with implications for understanding musical perceptual—cognitive development across the life span. The "later life singer" was defined as one who started private voice lessons at or after age 40 and continued consistently for at least 1 year. The study first entailed locating later life singers and determining their interest in sharing their experiences with the researchers. Primarily through contact with the National Association of Teachers of Singing and secondarily through a newspaper ad, approximately 75 students of voice responded (mean age 61.2 years, range 49.2—82.6 years). In the second and primary part of the study, an extensive online questionnaire was devised to provide specific information about experiences as older students of singing, including motivation, goals, the fit of singing into current and future endeavors, impact of participation in singing on their sense of health and general well-being, repertoire achievements, practice, lifestyle, and demographic information. Forty-six of the original respondents completed the questionnaire. Analysis of the open-ended questions (which is ongoing with Alexandra Smith) reveals emerging themes that show how singing lessons enhance the quality of life for older adults and contribute to individual well-being and development, both physically and psychologically, in addition to the intrinsic rewards of advancing one's musical performance skills. A relatively high socioeconomic status of the respondents suggested that the benefits of singing lessons may be currently open primarily to a privileged minority.

Cognitive benefits of vocal training compared with training on musical instruments

A few studies that have compared vocalists and musicians having comparable amounts of training have generally shown equal cognitive abilities of both groups and their superior level of cognitive abilities compared to persons who have had no musical training. For example, in a study with young adults, Bialystok and DePape (2009) examined the role of musical expertise and bilingualism on executive function in a spatial and auditory/verbal domain. Four groups of participants were compared: highly trained vocalists, highly trained musical instrumentalists, unilingual nonmusicians, and bilingual nonmusicians. Performance of singers and instrumentalists did not differ, and on the auditory task both musical groups exceeded performance of the other two groups lacking musical training. On the spatial task the performance of musicians and bilingual participants was equal and exceeded that of the unilingual nonmusicians. The study is consistent with the view that serious training on either the voice or a musical instrument produces cognitive advantages in both auditory/verbal and spatial realms. A similar finding arose for children who had taken either vocal or piano training and were compared with children who did not have such training and with children who had drama training (Schellenberg, 2004). In another study, vocalists, violinists, and nonmusicians were asked to indicate whether an acoustic signal was synchronous or asynchronous with their heartbeat (Schirmer-Mowka et al., 2015). Both groups of musicians showed superior sensitivity to their bodily sensations, known as *interoceptive accuracy*, as compared to nonmusicians. Thus similarities in the cognitive benefits of vocalists and performers of melodic instruments have been shown. But what about training on instruments that emphasize rhythm as compared to melody?

Slater and Kraus (2016) compared young male adult vocalists, percussionists, and nonmusicians on speech-in-noise perception and auditory working memory. On the auditory working memory task, musicians outperformed nonmusicians. On the sentence-in-noise task, musicians' performance exceeded that of nonmusicians, however, vocalists did not differ significantly from either percussionists or nonmusicians. On a test of musical competence, the musicians outperformed the nonmusicians on both melodic and rhythmic components, and vocalists were superior on the melodic task and percussionists were superior on the rhythm task. A further study examined performance on several other tasks by vocalists, percussionists, and nonmusicians, seeking nuances resulting from specialized musical experience (Slater, Azem, Nicol, Swedenborg, & Kraus, 2017). Compared to nonmusicians, vocalists had superior pitch discrimination and percussionists had superior rhythmic test performance, however vocalists and percussionists did not differ significantly from each other on these measures. In addition, brain wave recordings during presentation of speech sounds revealed greater sensitivity of vocalists than nonmusicians to the acoustical structure of vowels and greater sensitivity of percussionists than nonmusicians to the fast-changing acoustic transients characterizing speech consonants. Such results were consistent with the different foci of attention in performance of vocalists and percussionists. A serendipitous finding was that percussionists showed superior performance on a psychometric test (often used as one of many tests in diagnosis of attentional disorders) entailing accurately and quickly identifying whether a "1" is presented as opposed to a "2" in rapid sequences of the two items in blocks of visual and auditory trials. The test is known as a measure of "inhibitory control" which might have misleading connotations beyond the operationally defined meaning.

Patel (2011, 2014) has proposed that the high demands that music practice places on sensory and cognitive processes combined with emotional rewards can lead to enhancement of performance on other tasks. The proposal with the acronym OPERA highlights five brain-beneficial aspects of music training:

- Overlap between the mental processes underlying the musical and other activity.
- Precision required by musical training that may exceed that required by other tasks.

- Emotion derived through music that sustains the training associated with music learning.
- Repetition and practice required by music training that places rare demands on brain activity.
- Attention required and trained by music practice (e.g., sustained vs divided under high cognitive load).

Studies are needed that compare trained vocalists and trained instrumentalists with respect to these components. Is 1 hour of intensive, focused practice of singing equally beneficial to similar practice on another musical instrument? It is too soon to conclude that the benefits of vocal versus musical instrument practice, solo or in ensemble, are equivalent or that one is superior to the other. The rewarding nature of the activity may depend on individual differences in attitudes, and on contexts associated with available teachers and ensemble performance opportunities. The few studies that have been reviewed here are sufficient to support the view that serious vocal training may have equivalent benefits to similar study of another musical instrument. The engagement of muscular systems required for accurate, emotive singing can easily be overlooked because the motor action to move the vocal cords and vocal tract are less visible than moving fingers, hands, and arms required by other instruments. Further, visible orofacial movements may seem negligible 'in terms of their similarity in appearance to motions associated with everyday speech.

Summary

Private voice lessons can potentially have greater impact than choral singing due to the greater attentional focus on the coordination of sensorimotor aspects of vocal production aimed at creating the nearest match to the idealized model of the melody. This is not to underestimate the demands of choral singing, especially that of a very high performance level, and one requiring personal private practice. Yet the requirement for focused attention on various parts of the vocal instrument and on the music are more likely to be achieved through private instruction and the associated accountability for weekly practice. The case study of a man in his late 80s over a 3-year period indicates the potential feasibility of voice lessons at this age, as well as voice lessons as a means of monitoring perceptual−cognitive resilience. A survey of later life singers reveals that though rare, older adults do engage in voice lessons and find them to add meaning to their lives and to benefit from the standpoints of physical and mental health and social well-being. Although there are no tests comparing relative cognitive benefits of vocal versus instrumental training in later life, studies of younger adults have shown comparable cognitive benefits, though some nuances have been shown that may be instrument dependent.

Methodological considerations

Many practical challenges arise in conducting research with older adults, such as attrition in longitudinal studies (e.g., Solé, Mercadal-Brotons, Gallego, & Riera, 2010), mobility affecting participation, and perceptual deficits affecting communication of instructions. Attrition of course can be considered data in some cases, for example, providing information about the relevance of an activity to a participant. Several specific methodological issues are described in the following section.

Nonactive control groups

Control groups are regarded as valuable to a study design. Often, comparisons are made with a nonactive control group (i.e., with no control activity provided as part of the intervention). The nonactive control group however is insufficient for drawing conclusions about the effects of an intervention. For example, contrasting test performance of members of a choral group versus those of a nonactive control group does not distinguish whether observed benefits are attributable simply to the group-activity component rather than to the act of singing together. Studies with a nonactive control group showing increased quality of life scale scores following choral participation (Cohen et al., 2007; Coulton, Clift, Skingley, & Rodrigues, 2015; as discussed by Daykin et al., 2018) fall into this category.

Comparison interventions

When singing training is compared to another type of training, it is important that features of the two types of training are comparable on key dimensions, for example, equally meaningful and engaging. A study by Noice and Noice (2009) comparing singing and drama interventions offers an example for consideration in this light. Having previously gathered evidence that drama training led to cognitive benefits and increased sense of well-being in older adults, Noice and Noice compared effects of participation in a group singing class versus a drama class. They randomly assigned residents from subsidized senior housing complexes to either the theater training, singing training, or no-training control condition. Participants, who ranged in age between 68 and 93 years (mean age 81.7) attended eight classes, carried out related homework, and completed pre- and post-tests.

Theater training entailed increasingly demanding exercises that promoted becoming absorbed by a role, communicating as if one truly was the person in the particular fictional role. The singing training entailed breathing exercises and singing songs such as "Row, Row, Row Your Boat" and "America the Beautiful," familiar to most Americans. Complexity increased over the days, as "different groups sang different songs simultaneously, keeping their minds on their own melodies and lyrics" while maintaining coordinated rhythms. For the drama group, increased complexity was associated with increasingly deeper personal meaning.

Regarding the cognitive tests, the theater training was associated with significantly higher immediate word recall, verbal fluency, problem solving, delayed word recall, and delayed East Boston Memory Test scores than did the singing group and the nonactive control group. For the immediate East Boston Memory Test there was no difference with the singing group, and a marginal difference with the control group.[4] However, before concluding that theater training is more effective than group singing in augmenting cognition in the short-term, it is well to recognize that the singing training did not focus on personal meaning in the way that the drama training did. The study paves the way for one which does compare the benefits of meaningful and meaningless singing. A fairer comparison of theater and group singing training could have singers:

- focus on listening to each other, fully engage in the meaning of the lyrics, and bodily engage in the music;
- engage in a dramatic work, differing from theater training only by presenting words as lyrics of melodies, while at the same time engaging passionately with the meaning of the text, bolstered by the emotion conveyed by the music; or
- instead of singing different songs at the same beat as took place in the study, sing harmony, producing beauty at the same time as complexity.

In spite of the conclusion of Noice and Noice (2009) that drama training, as an intervention, outweighs the cognitive benefits that can be derived from singing, it is possible that the characteristics of singing in the study differed unnecessarily in a variety of ways from the theater training conditions. It therefore remains to be determined whether engagement in more emotionally and cognitively meaningful singing (with lyrics and melody and harmony), would have led to the same impressive benefits of the theater training.

Performance versus reception (listening)

The field of music perception and cognition has typically focused on reception rather than on production of music (Palmer, 1992). Studies of production

---

4. The statistical analysis entailed a multivariate analysis of covariance, with group membership as the independent variable (acting, singing, no-treatment), the eight cognitive variables at posttest as the dependent variables, and age, education, and pretest scores as covariates. There was a significant effect of treatment condition on the combined dependent variables. Subsequently univariate analysis of covariances were conducted on each dependent measure, leading to the five significant effects. Results for the digit span tasks and East Boston Memory test were not significant. Subsequently, planned comparisons (i.e., simple contrasts with acting as the reference category) were conducted on the posttest data.

are often more challenging to carry out, and the resulting continuous and multidimensional data are often more challenging to analyze. To suggest that singing has been disproportionately neglected by researchers may be unfair, as, in general, studies of performance on any musical instrument are rare, and studies of ensembles are rarer still.

Multidisciplinarity

In their study of the Silver Voices choir in Norway the author draws on the fields of music education, music therapy, community music, and social work, and suggests that "multidisciplinary perspectives can in fact contribute to developing new theories and practices" (Balsnes, 2016, p. 66). This is a good reminder of a key challenge to the study of the potential benefits of choral singing, individual lessons and practice, or solo singing as neuroprotective and a contributor to well-being in later life. To Balsnes' (2016) list of relevant disciplines we can add many branches of psychology (developmental, perceptual, cognitive, social, gerontological, cultural), and the field of voice sciences, including vocal pedagogy, voice acoustics, speech language pathology, fields additional to those usually considered for understanding the benefits of performing on a musical instrument. Progress therefore depends on collaboration and cooperation, and open-mindedness. An appeal for interdisciplinary collaboration in research on group singing has also been made by Dingle et al. (2019) with a focus on best practices for rigorous and replicable studies, including systematic, multi-site initiatives.

Summary

The challenges of dealing with issues of health, fragility, and mobility are general for all behavioral studies of older adults, but may be more profound in studies of singing where the body is the instrument. Inactive control groups are not ideal, but choice of active control requires careful decisions regarding comparability of conditions, for example, with regard to meaningfulness and degree of engagement of the activity. It is generally more difficult to collect and analyze data of performance as opposed to perception, and studies of singing in older adults relate to multiple disciplines and require the expertise and collaboration of multidisciplinary teams to overcome some of the challenges of conducting research on older adults in order to determine the neuroprotective benefits of singing. Past research has paved the way for much more to be done to determine the benefits of choral and solo singing in older adults.

Conclusions

The present chapter has presented singing as a complex human behavior demanding coordination of many brain mechanisms engaging the vocal tract, the vocal cords, breath support, and body-postural system. Development of the singing voice was discussed as subject to many biopsychosocial factors accounting for wide variability found in vocal skill and comfort with singing. The popularity of group singing as a leisure activity in the Western world was noted, but as well that this accounted for a minority of the population, and favored female over male participation. The small but growing body of research on benefits of choral singing for older adults was reviewed. The voice lesson was presented as providing musical and extramusical opportunities seldom taken by older adults. The comparison of benefits of singing versus performance on another musical instrument was also considered from the viewpoint of possible equivalence. Finally, methodological issues that challenge research in this area were reviewed. In the following we look to the future for addressing pressing questions that have emerged given the accessibility of singing for everyone.

Most brain-imaging research involving music is of young adult participants. There are no brain-imaging studies of older adults singing or playing an instrument. Brain-imaging studies of instrumentalists have the problem of simulating usual instruments with nonmagnetic materials that can be positioned outside of the magnet (which surrounds the head) and played while lying on one's back without head movements. The human voice is made of nonmagnetic material and can be used relatively well in any bodily position. Studies measuring brain activation and vocalization, similar to those conducted on younger adults by Steven Brown, Boris Kleber, Jean Mary Zarate, Robert Zatorre and their colleagues (e.g., Belyk et al., 2018; Brown et al., 2008; Kleber et al., 2010; Kleber et al., 2016; Zarate and Zatorre, 2008), among others, if carried out with older adults could illuminate understanding of development, maintenance, or atrophy of the singing network across the lifetime. Several research groups have begun to conduct brain-imaging studies of older adults listening to music (e.g., Sikka, Cuddy, Johnsrude, & Vanstone, 2015) suggesting the possibility of eventually adding a vocal production or vocal imaging (imagine singing along) component to such studies.

Comparisons of brain images of experienced and inexperienced young singers have revealed greater differentiation from the speech network on the part of young trained vocalists, yet still greater focus on the left hemisphere activity (Wilson et al., 2011). Would brain images of more mature experienced vocalists reveal even greater differentiation than that of younger experienced singers? And what of those who begin a serious interest in singing in older adult years? What evidence of neuroplasticity will be revealed in brain imagining studies? Such studies could provide concrete evidence of brain development in the later years of the life span. Also, in the context of cognitive reserve, another question is could we see different networks between musically trained and untrained people when they perform other (nonmusical) activities? Further, would neural efficiency or compensation mechanisms explain transfer effects?

A recent book entitled "Everybody sing!" (Morgan-Ellis, 2018) is subtitled "Community singing in the American picture palace." It describes a singing opportunity that was an integral part of going to the movies early in the 20th century. In the 1920s before the talkies, organist-led sing-alongs were part of the experience of attending the movie theater, known as the *picture palace*. The sing-alongs were sustained into the 1940s, even when the talkies arrived and replaced the silent film. During those decades, in the United States, archival attendance records suggest that the average person visited the picture palace at least once a week, and would have likely engaged in the 10-minute sing-along. This was not the only opportunity for community singing. Recorded music was much less accessible. People sang in church, and at home. We no longer sing at the movies, and one might wonder what else, from a mental and physical health standpoint, has been lost as a result.

Nationwide surveys, as referred to earlier, suggest that community choirs are flourishing in the 21st century, though participation may favor a demographic narrower than need be (Daykin et al., 2018). Much can be done from a policy standpoint to bring more people into the singing fold; however, research is still needed to show that choral singing is a cost-effective intervention that is worthy of government support (be it advertising, programs at libraries, sponsorship of choir directors, sponsorship of choir games for all ages, or support of intergenerational or multicultural choirs that would broaden the demographic).

Looking forward

The outcome of two well-designed longitudinal studies are a few years away. The Community of Voices Trial (Johnson et al., 2018), earlier discussed, has yet to report results for the second cohort of the participants, doubling the intervention's first 6-month sample, and extending the intervention eventually to 1 year, providing the opportunity to determine whether cognitive, social, and physical effects, as well as health cost savings, may arise, and whether the benefits of decreased loneliness and increased interest in life are replicated.

Tan et al. (2018) in Singapore are conducting a randomized controlled trial aiming to "evaluate the clinical efficacy and elucidate the possible underlying mechanisms of choral singing in dementia prevention." They are testing the hypothesis that choral singing can prevent cognitive decline among community-dwelling elderly at high risk of dementia. The extensive measures to be taken include cognitive tests, MRI, blood- and urine-based biomarkers, mental health, and sleep quality. The planned intervention is for 2 years of choral 1-hour choral singing focusing on the joy of choral singing. The control condition entails weekly 1-hour sessions for 2 years that focus on health-related topics. MRI data will provide information regarding whether the singing intervention group has a lower rate of structural change compared to the health-lecture control group. The study is designed to include participants in other countries than Singapore for the purpose of validation. The measures will provide information about the effects of involvement in choral singing as compared to an alternative positive active intervention. Fortunately, the protocol contains a measure of singing. Participants will be asked to listen to five short tunes and to hum each melody after hearing it. The melodies will be drawn from the music learned in the singing intervention. Ideally, a more extensive singing test battery might have been included. Data collection is expected to end in February 2020, with target number of participants being 360.

Tan et al. (2018) presented a model of the basis of effectiveness of choral singing as a means of slowing cognitive decline (see Fig. 9.1). This model is consistent with concepts presented in this chapter and is presented here for the purpose of consolidation of a vast amount of material.

Singing and aging—a new domain for research

Since the early days of research on aging, studies of language, including language production, have had an important role. The field explored speech production at the level of phonetics, semantics, and syntax, finding variations in working memory as a suspected cause of observed declines when compared to younger adults, noting large individual differences in the older populations. A recent review of behavioral and neuroimaging data shows that language systems remain stable across the life span and that "there is no robust evidence that core language processes are underpinned by different neural networks in younger and older adults" (Shafto & Tyler, 2014, p. 583). Suffice to say, comparable studies with older adults and singing would be of interest, given the wide variability in use of singing in later life. Psycholinguistic studies of older adults might also consider including individual differences in singing experience as a variable worthy of exploration or experimental control.

Unfortunately, no studies that have compared vocalists and other music-instrumentalists have examined older age groups. Studies comparing older adults who are trained vocalists, musical instrumentalists, and persons without music training are sorely needed. Meta-analyses or individual studies that have examined the cognitive benefits of music training have deliberately excluded vocalists in part because of the challenges of determining the extent of their training (e.g., Schneider et al., 2018; Strong & Mast, 2018). Credentials awarded by conservatories and university programs (including training for secondary school students) provide the criteria for characterizing trained older adult vocalists and instrumentalists, and enabling crucial experiments that can determine the relative benefits of vocal versus instrumental-music experience. And even if such studies were to show smaller benefits

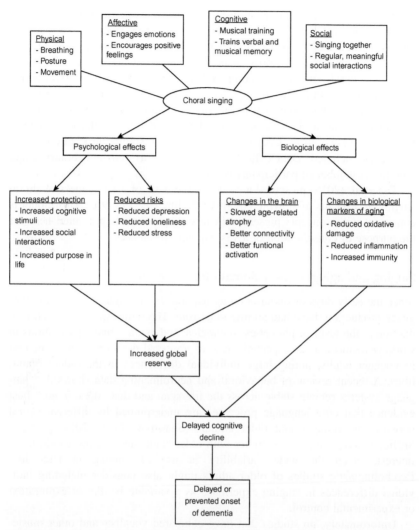

FIGURE 9.1 Theoretical model of the potential effectiveness of choral singing proposed by Tan et al. (2018) in slowing cognitive decline and preventing dementia. Choral singing is hypothesized to delay cognitive decline and prevent dementia by increasing protection of the brain and reducing the risk burdens of dementia. As a complex activity, its effects can be attributed to the cognitive, social, emotional, and physical aspects of choral singing. The biological mechanisms behind its effects may be observed from changes in brain structure and function and markers of biological aging. *Used with kind permission of J. Tan, F. H. M. Tsakok, E. K. Ow, B. Lanskey, K. S. D. Lim, L. G., Goh, C.-H Tan, I. K.-M. Cheah, A. Larbi, R. Foo, M. Loh, C. K. Y. Wong, J. Suckling, J. Li, R. Mahendran, E.-H. Kua, and L. Feng (copyright owners), from Figure 1 of their article (Tan et al., 2018). Study protocol for a randomized controlled trial of choral singing intervention to prevent cognitive decline in at-risk older adults living in the community. Frontiers in Aging Neuroscience, 10, 195. doi:10.3389/fnagi.2018.00195.*

from singing than playing a musical instrument (e.g., Mansens, Deeg, & Comijs, 2017), a finding of any benefit at all is of enormous importance because of the higher accessibility of vocal training and practice compared to that for other musical instruments.

In addition to the typical measurements in cognitive, social, and physical realms, measurements of singing achievement itself can inform our understanding of the link between singing and well-being. With the exception of the 2-year longitudinal study ongoing in Singapore (Tan et al., 2018), studies of the impact of singing on well-being rarely explore singing abilities. It is important to know how singing skills relate to other cognitive abilities, and how they are influenced by voice lessons or choral experience. If research on playing musical instruments is neuroprotective, there are many reasons to expect that the same is true for engagement in singing alone or with others. However, not everyone benefits from the same interventions. For some, voice lessons may be more beneficial than a community choir. Knowing more about the trajectories of singing ability itself in older ages may help define vocal opportunities that will be most beneficial to the well-being and resilience of individuals, communities, and society as a whole.

Acknowledgement

Appreciation is extended to the Social Sciences and Humanities Research Council of Canada (SSHRC) for the support of the Advancing Interdisciplinary Studies in Singing (AIRS) Major Collaborative Research Initiative (2009–17) and to Alexandra Smith for reviewing the manuscript. The careful review by the volume's editorial team is also gratefully acknowledged. In several places (e.g., reference to the work of A. Patel, discussion of nonactive control group) the specific suggestions of Aline Moussard were incorporated.

References

Abrahams, F., & Head, P. D. (Eds.), (2017). *The Oxford handbook of choral pedagogy*. Oxford, UK: Oxford University Press.

Balsnes, A. H. (2016). Hospitality in multicultural choral singing. *International Journal of Community Music, 9*, 171–189.

Bartel, R. (2015). *Singing Europe*. Bonn, Germany: European Choral Association Europa Cantat, file:///E:/B-05-26/2-Main%20Files_06/0%20Mscrpts/mscript%20progr/22.%20Book%20on%20Music%20and%20Aging/Europe%202015%20europe_report.pdf.

Beaton, D., Henderson, R., O'Brien, & Cohen, A. J. (2012). The effects of active singing versus passive listening on psychological health of senior citizens presented with a live musical theatre performance. In: *Annual meeting of the Canadian Psychological Association, Halifax, NS*.

Belyk, M., & Brown, S. (2017). The origins of the vocal brain in humans. *Neuroscience and Biobehavioral Reviews, 77*, 177–193.

Belyk, M., Lee, Y. S., & Brown, S. (2018). How does the human motor cortex regulate vocal pitch in singers? *Royal Society Open Science, 5*, 172208, https://doi.org/101098/rsos.172208.

Bialystok, E., & DePape, A. M. (2009). Musical expertise, bilingualism, and executive functioning. *Journal of Experimental Psychology: Human Perception and Performance*, *35*, 565–574.

Brown, S., & Martinez, M. J. (2007). Activation of premotor vocal areas during musical discrimination. *Brain & Cognition*, *63*, 59–69.

Brown, S., Martinez, M. J., Hodges, D. A., Fox, P. T., & Parsons, L. M. (2004). The song system of the human brain. *Cognitive Brain Research*, *20*, 363–375.

Brown, S., Ngan, E., & Liotti, M. (2008). A larynx area in the human motor cortex. *Cerebral Cortex*, *18*, 837–845.

Choral Canada. (2017). *Detailed national findings from Choral Canada's Survey of Choirs, Choruses, and Singing Groups in Canada*. Hamilton, ON: Hill Strategies Research Inc. <https://www.saskchoral.ca/images/file/Choral%20Canada/Census%202016-17/2017% 20Report%20-%20Complete.pdf>.

Clift, S., Hancox, G., Morrison, I., Hess, B., Kreutz, G., & Stewart, D. (2010). Choral singing and psychological wellbeing: Quantitative and qualitative findings from English choirs in a cross-national survey. *Journal of Applied Arts and Health*, *1*, 19–34.

Cohen, A. J. (2015). The AIRS Test Battery of Singing Skills: Rationale, item types, and life-span scope. *Musicae Scientiae*, *19*, 238–264.

Cohen, A. J. (2019). Singing. In P. J. Rentfrow, & D. J. Levitin (Eds.), *Foundations in Music Psychology: Theory & Research*. Cambridge, MA: MIT Press. (685-750).

Cohen, A. J., & Kleinerman, K. (2010). Transformative experience through voice lessons in later life. In: *11th International conference on music perception and cognition, Seattle, WA Abstract* (p. 115).

Cohen, A. J., & Pan, B.-Y. (2015). The singing octogenarian. In: *Talk presented at the annual meeting of the American Psychological Association, Toronto*.

Cohen, G. D., Perlstein, S., Chapline, J., Kelly, J., Firth, K., & Simmens, S. (2007). The impact of professionally conducted cultural programs on the physical health, mental health, and social functioning of older adults. *The Gerontologist*, *46*, 726–734.

Coulton, S., Clift, S., Skingley, S., & Rodrigues, J. (2015). Effectiveness and cost-effectiveness of community singing on mental health-related quality of life of older people: Randomised controlled trial. *British Journal of Psychiatry*, *207*, 250–255.

Dalla Bella, S., Giguère, J., & Peretz, I. (2007). Singing proficiency in the general population. *Journal of the Acoustical Society of America*, *121*(2), 1182–1189.

Daykin, N., Mansfield, L., Meads, C., Julier, G., Tomlinson, A., Payne, A., ... Victor, C. (2018). What words for wellbeing? A systematic review of wellbeing outcomes for music and singing in adults. *Perspectives in Public Health*, *138*, 39–46.

Dingle, G.A., Clift, S., Finn, S., Gilbert, R., Groarke, J.M., Irons, J.Y. ... Williams, E.J., An agenda for best practice research on group singing, health, and well-being. *Music & Science*, *2*, 1–15.

Dunbar, R. I. M. (2010). The social role of touch in humans and primates; behavioral function and neurobiological mechanisms. *Neuroscience Biobehavioral Review*, *34*, 260–268.

Erikson, E. H. (1959). *Identity and the life cycle*. New York: International Universities Press.

Fancourt, D., Williamon, A., Carvalho, L. A., Steptoe, A., Dow, R., & Lewis, I. (2016). Singing modulates mood, stress, cortisol, cytokine and neuropeptide activity in cancer patients and carers. *Ecancer*, *10*, 631. Available from https://doi.org/10.3332/ecancer.2016.631.

Freer, P. K. (2010). Two decades of research on possible selves and the "missing males" problem in choral music. *International Journal of Music Education*, *28*(1), 17–30.

Gallant, E. (2009). *Singing in elderly persons: Those who are healthy and those with Alzheimer's disease* (Unpublished honors thesis). University of Prince Edward Island.

Gaunt, H., & Hallam, S. (2016). Individuality in learning of musical skills. In S. Hallam, I. Cross, & G. Thaut (Eds.), *Handbook of music psychology* (2nd ed., pp. 463–477). Oxford, UK: Oxford University Press.

Gick, M. (2011). Singing, health and well-being: A health psychologist's review. *Psychomusicology: Music, Mind, & Brain, 21,* 176–207.

Good, A., & Russo, F. A. (2016). Singing promotes cooperation in a diverse group of children. *Social Psychology, 47,* 340–344.

Grunwald Associates LLC & Chorus America. (2019). *The Chorus Impact Study: Singing for a Lifetime.* Bethesda, MD: Grunwald Associates LLC.

Halwani, G. F., Loui, P., Rüber, T., & Schlaug, G. (2011). Effects of practice and experience on the arcuate fasciculus: Comparing singers, instrumentalists, and non-musicians. *Frontiers of Psychology, 2,* 1–9.

Harris, P. B., & Caporella, C. A. (2018). Making a university community more dementia friendly through participation in an intergenerational choir. *Dementia, 18,* 2556–2575, 1471301217752209.

Heydon, R., Beynon, C. A., O'Neill, S. A., Zhang, Z., & Crocker, W. (2013). Straining to hear the singing: Toward an understanding of successful intergenerational singing curriculum. *Journal of Intergenerational Relationships, 11*(2), 176–189.

Heydon, R., McKee, L., & O'Neill S., (2020). Connecting intergenerational voices: Curricula to foster the wellbeing of young children and elders.In: R. Heydon, D. Fancourt, & A. J. Cohen (Eds.). *Routledge companion to interdisciplinary studies in singing, Volume III: Wellbeing* (pp. 368-383). New York, NY: Routledge.

Heydon, R., & O'Neill, S. (2016). *Why multimodal literacy matters: (Re)conceptualizing literacy and wellbeing through singing-infused multimodal, intergenerational curricula.* Rotterdam, Netherlands: Sense.

Johnson, J. K., Louhivuori, J., & Siljander, E. (2016). Comparison of well-being of older adult choir singers and the general population of Finland: A case–control study. *Musicae Scientiae, 2,* 178–194.

Johnson, J. K., Stewart, A. L., Acree, M., Nápoles, A. M., Flatt, J. D., Max, W. B., & Gregorich, S. E. (2018). A community choir intervention to promote well-being among diverse older adults: Results from the Community of Voices Trial. *Journals of Gerontology: Psychological Sciences, 11,* 1–11. Available from https://doi.org/10.1093/geronb/gby132.

Kayes, G. (2019). Structure and function of the singing voice. In G. Welch, D. M. Howard, & J. Nix (Eds.), *The Oxford handbook of singing* (pp. 1–29). Oxford, UK: Oxford University Press.

Kirschner, S., & Tomasello, M. (2010). Joint music making promotes prosocial behavior in 4-year-old children. *Evolution and Human Behavior, 31,* 354–364.

Kleber, B., Veit, R., Birbaumer, N., Gruzelier, J., & Lotze, M. (2010). The brain of opera singers: Experience-dependent changes in functional activation. *Cerebral Cortex, 20,* 1144–1152.

Kleber, B., Veit, R., Moll, C. V., Gaser, C., Birmaumer, N., & Lotze, M. (2016). Voxel-based morphometry in opera singers: Increased gray-matter volume in right somatosensory and auditory cortices. *NeuroImage, 133,* 477–483.

Kleber, B. A., & Zarate, J. M. (2014). The neuroscience of singing. In G. Welch, & J. Nix (Eds.), *The Oxford handbook of singing.* Oxford, UK: Oxford University Press. Available from http://dx.doi.org/10.1093/oxfordhb/9780199660773.013.015.

Kleber, B., Zeitouni, A. G., Friberg, A., & Zatorre, R. J. (2013). Experience-dependent modulation of feedback integration during singing: Role of the right anterior insula. *Journal of Neuroscience, 33*, 6070–6080.

Knight, S. (2011). Adults identifying as "non-singers" in childhood: Cultural, social, and pedagogical implications. In A. Williamon, D. Edwards, & L. Bartel (Eds.), *Proceedings of the International Symposium on Performance Science-ISPS 2011* (pp. 117–122). Utrecht, NL: European Association of Conservatoires (AEC).

Knight, S. (2019). Addressing the needs of the adult "nonsinger" (NS). In G. F. Welch, D. M. Howard, & J. Nix (Eds.), *The Oxford Handbook of Singing* (pp. 621–650). Oxford, UK: Oxford University Press.

Lamont, A., Murray, M., Hale, R., & Wright-Bevans, K. (2018). Singing in later life: The anatomy of a community choir. *Psychology of Music, 46*, 424–439.

Launay, J., & Pearce., E. (2020). Singing as an evolved behavior for social bonding: the icebreaker effect, beta-endorphin, and groups of more than 150 people. In R. Heydon, D. Fancourt, & A. J. Cohen (Eds.), *Routledge companion to iterdisciplinary studies in singing, Volume III Well-being* (pp. 136–145). New York, NY: Routledge.

Malde, M., Allen, M. J., & Zeller, K.-A. (2013). *What every singer needs to know about the body*. San Diego, CA: Plural.

Mansens, D., Deeg, D. J. H., & Comijs, H. C. (2017). The association between singing and/or playing a musical instrument and cognitive functions in older adults. *Aging & Mental Health*. Available from https://doi.org/10.1080/13607863.2017.1328481.

Miller, E. (2018). Lullabies of our lives: Singing in multicultural harmony. <https://historiesofemotion.com/2018/06/15/lullabies-of-our-lives-singing-in-multicultural-harmony/>

Miller, R. (1996). *On the art of singing*. New York, NY: Oxford University Press.

Mithen, S. J. (2005). *The singing Neanderthals: The origins of music, language, mind and body*. London, UK: Weidenfield & Nicholson.

Morgan-Ellis, E. (2018). *Everybody sing!: Community singing in the American picture palace*. Atlanta, Georgia: University of Georgia Press.

Murdock, R. (2015). *Born to sing: A singer's journey toward mind-body unity*. Berkeley, CA: Mornum Time Press.

Neto, F., Pinto, M., & Mullet, E. (2015). Can music reduce anti-dark-skin prejudice? A test of a cross-cultural musical education programme. *Psychology of Music, 44*, 388–398.

Noble, J. (2020). Choral practice and research at the beginning of the 21st century. In: H. Gudmundsdottir, C. Beynon, K. Ludke, & A.J. Cohen (Eds.), *Routledge companion to interdisciplinary studies in singing, Volume II: Education* (pp 295-312). New York, NY: Routledge.

Noice, H., & Noice, T. (2009). An arts intervention for older adults living in subsidized retirement homes. *Aging, Neuropsychology and Cognition, 1*, 1–24. Available from https://doi.org/10.1080/13825580802223400.

Numminen, A., Lonka, K., Rainio, A. P., & Ruismäki, H. (2015). "Singing is no longer forbidden to me— It's like part of my human dignity has been restored." Adult non-singers learning to sing: An exploratory intervention study. *European Journal of Social and Behavioural Sciences, 12*, 1660–1674.

Overy, K., & Molnar-Szakacs, I. (2009). Being together in time: Musical experience and the mirror neuron system. *Music Perception: An Interdisciplinary Journal, 26*, 489–504.

Palmer, C. (1992). The role of interpretive preferences in music performance. In M. R. Jones, & S. Holleran (Eds.), *Cognitive bases of musical communication* (pp. 249−262). Washington, DC: American Psychological Association.

Patel, A. D. (2011). Why would musical training benefit the neural encoding of speech? The OPERA Hypothesis. *Frontiers in Psychology*, 2, 142. Available from https://doi.org/10.3389/fpsyg.2011.00142.

Patel, A. D. (2014). Can nonlinguistic musical training change the way the brain processes speech? The expanded OPERA hypothesis. *Hearing Research, 308*, 98−108.

Pearce, E., Launay, J., & Dunbar, R. I. (2015). The ice-breaker effect: Singing mediates fast social bonding. *Open Science, 2*(10), 1−9. Available from https://doi.org/10.1098/rsos.150221.

Penfield, W., & Rasmussen, T. (1950). *The cerebral cortex of man: A clinical study of localization of function*. New York: Macmillan.

Pfordresher, P. Q., Demorest, S. M., Dalla Bella, S., Hutchins, S., Loui, P., Rutkowski, J., & Welch, G. F. (2015). Theoretical perspectives on singing accuracy: An introduction to the special issue on singing accuracy (Part 1). *Music Perception, 32*, 227−231.

Redmond, S. (2020). Breathless: Singing and social justice in a time without air. In: R. Heydon, D. Fancourt, & A.J. Cohen (Eds.). *Routledge companion to interdisciplinary studies in singing, Volume III: Well-being* (pp. 316-326). New York, NY: Routledge.

Román-Caballero, R., Arnedo, M., Triviño, M., & Lupiáñez, J. (2018). Musical practice as an enhancer of cognitive function in healthy aging − A systematic review and meta-analysis. *PLoS ONE, 13*(11), e0207957. Available from https://doi.org/10.1371/journal.pone.0207957.

Rush, B. (1787). *Thoughts upon female education* (R. Bannister, Transcription). Boston. Rbannis1@swarthmore.edu. <http://www.swarthmore.edu/SocSci/rbannis1/AIH19th/female.html> (1995). Also found in Milson, A. J., Bohan, C. H., Glanzer, P. L., & Null, J. W. (Eds.). (2010). American educational thought: Essays from 1640-1940, rev. ed. 54-62.

Schellenberg, E. G. (2004). Music lessons enhance IQ. *Psychological Science, 15*, 511−514.

Schellenberg, M., & Gick, B. (2018). Microtonal variation in sung Cantonese. *Phonetica*. Available from https://doi.org/10.1159/000493755.

Schirmer-Mowka, K. L., Fard, P. R., Zamorano, A. M., Finkel, S., Birbaumer, N., & Kleber, B. A. (2015). Evidence for enhanced interoceptive accuracy in professional musicians. *Frontiers in Behavioral Neuroscience, 9*, 1−13. Available from https://doi.org/10.3389/fnbeh.2015.00349.

Schneider, C. E., Hunger, E. G., & Bardach, S. H. (2018). Potential benefits from playing music among cognitively intact older adults: A scoping review. *Journal of Applied Gerontology*, 1−22. Available from https://doi.org/10.1177/0733464817751198. (online first).

Segado, M., Hollinger, A., Thibodeau, J., Penhune, V., & Zatorre, R. J. (2018). Partially overlapping brain networks for singing and cello playing. *Frontiers in Neuroscience, 12*, 351. Available from https://doi.org/10.3389/fnins.2018.00351.

Shafto, M. A., & Tyler, L. K. (2014). Language in the aging brain: The network dynamics of cognitive decline and preservation. *Science, 346*, 583−587.

Sikka, R., Cuddy, L. L., Johnsrude, I. S., & Vanstone, A. D. (2015). An fMRI comparison on neural activity associated with recognition of familiar melodies in younger and older adults. *Frontiers in Neuroscience, 9*, 356. Available from https://doi.org/10.3389/fnins.2015.00356.

Slater, J., Azem, A., Nicol, T., Swedenborg, B., & Kraus, N. (2017). Variations on the theme of musical expertise: Cognitive and sensory processing in percussionists, vocalists and non-musicians. *European Journal of Neuroscience, 45*, 952−963.

Slater, J., & Kraus, N. (2016). The role of rhythm in perceiving speech in noise: A comparison of percussionists, vocalists and non-musicians. *Cognitive Processing, 17*, 79−87.

Smith, A. (2006). Speech motor development: Integrating muscles, movements, and linguistic units. *Journal of Communication Disorders, 39*, 331–349.

Smith, A., & Zelaznik, H. (2004). Development of functional synergies for speech motor coordination in childhood and adolescence. *Developmental Psychobiology, 45*, 22–33.

Solé, C., Mercadal-Brotons, M., Gallego, S., & Riera, M. (2010). Contributions of music to aging adults' quality of life. *Journal of Music Therapy, 47*, 264–281. Available from https://doi.org/10.1093/jmt/47.3.264.

Stadler Elmer, S. (2011). Human singing: Towards a developmental theory. *Psychomusicology: Music, Mind & Brain, 21*, 13–30.

Strong, J., & Midden, A. (2018). Cognitive differences between older adult instrumental musicians: Benefits of continuing to play. *Psychology of Music.* Available from https://doi.org/10.1177/0305735618785020.

Strong, J. V., & Mast, B. T. (2018). The cognitive functioning of older adult instrumental musicians and non-musicians. *Aging, Neuropsychology, and Cognition.* Available from https://doi.org/10.1080/13825585.2018.1448356.

Sundberg, J. (1987). *The science of the singing voice.* DeKalb, IL: Northern Illinois University Press.

Tan, J., Tsakok, F. H. M., Ow, E. K., Lanskey, B., Lim, K. S. D., Goh, L. G., , et al.. . . Feng, L. (2018). Study protocol for a randomized controlled trial of choral singing intervention to prevent cognitive decline in at-risk older adults living in the community. *Frontiers in Aging Neuroscience, 10*, 195. Available from https://doi.org/10.3389/fnagi.2018.00195.

Tsang, C. D., Friendly, R. H., & Trainor, L. J. (2011). Singing development as a sensorimotor interaction problem. *Psychomusicology: Music, Mind, & Brain, 21*, 45–53.

Weinstein, D., Launay, J., Pearce, E., Dunbar, R. I., & Stewart, L. (2016). Singing and social bonding: Changes in connectivity and pain threshold as a function of group size. *Evolution and Human Behavior, 37*(2), 152–158.

Wilson, S. J., Abbott, D. F., Lusher, D., Gentle, E. C., & Jackson, G. F. (2011). Finding your voice: A singing lesson from functional imaging. *Human Brain Mapping, 32*, 2115–2130.

Yang, Y., Carter-Ényì, A., Radhakrishanon, N., Grimmer, S., & Nix, J. (2019). Vocal music and pedagogy of Chinese African, and Indian Genres. In G. F. Welch, D. M. Howard, & J. Nix (Eds.), *The Oxford Handbook of Singing* (pp. 751–771). Oxford, UK: Oxford University Press.

Zarate, J. M. (2013). The neural control of singing. *Frontiers in Human Neuroscience, 7*, 1–12. Available from https://doi.org/10.3389/fnhum.2013.00237.

Zarate, J. M., Wood, S., & Zatorre, R. J. (2010). Neural networks involved in voluntary and involuntary vocal pitch regulation in experienced singers. *Neuropsychologia, 48*, 607–618. Available from https://doi.org/10.1016/j.neuropsychologia.2009.10.025.

Zarate, J. M., & Zatorre, R. J. (2008). Experience-dependent neural substrates involved in vocal pitch regulation during singing. *Neuroimage, 40*, 1871–1887. Available from https://doi.org/10.1016/j.neuroimage.2008.01.026.

Chapter 10

Effects on cognition of physical activity with or without music and of dance

David Predovan[1,2] and Louis Bherer[1,3,4]

[1]Centre de Recherche, Institut Universitaire de Gériatrie de Montréal, Montréal, QC, Canada,
[2]Département de Psychologie, Université du Québec à Montréal, Montréal, QC, Canada,
[3]Centre de Recherche, Institut de Cardiologie de Montréal, Montréal, QC, Canada,
[4]Département de Médecine, Université de Montréal, Montréal, QC, Canada

Introduction

Dementia presently affects 50 million people worldwide, and there are nearly 10 million new cases every year. There is no cure for dementia, but evidence suggests that lifestyle factors can help prevent it. Recent consensus statements from leading medical organizations, such as the Lancet Commission (Livingston et al., 2017), the American Academy of Neurology (Petersen et al., 2018), and the National Academies of Sciences, Engineering, and Medicine (United States) (National Academies of Sciences, Engineering, and Medicine; Health and Medicine Division; Board on Health Sciences Policy; Committee on Preventing Dementia and Cognitive Impairment, 2017) suggest that age-related cognitive decline, and potentially dementia, can be prevented through better lifestyle choices and management of medical risk factors. Physical activity, broadly defined, is consistently put forth as a lifestyle factor that can have a major impact on cognitive aging. In fact, evidence suggests that in older adults, physically active individuals have lower risks of developing dementia (Laurin, Verreault, Lindsay, MacPherson, & Rockwood, 2001). However, there is no clear statement as to which types of physical activity or exercise have the greatest impact on cognitive aging—some studies have shown improved cognition and brain functions following aerobic exercise, while others have reported benefits after motor coordination training regimens (Berryman et al., 2014; Nieman, Godde, & Voelcker-Rehage, 2014). In this chapter, we will explore the potentially positive impact of dance and dance-related interventions on cognition in older adults. After briefly reviewing evidence for the benefits

Music and the Aging Brain. DOI: https://doi.org/10.1016/B978-0-12-817422-7.00010-9
277

of physical activity, we will address the added benefits of music in exercise interventions. Finally, we will discuss the potential cognitive enhancement effects of dance and dance/movement therapy (D/MT) or programs based on this approach.

Physical activity and cognitive aging

Evidence suggests that physical activity and exercise have positive effects on cognition (Bherer, 2015). In cross-sectional studies, fitter individuals show better cognitive performances than their less fit counterparts (Dupuy et al., 2015; Renaud, Bherer, & Maquestiaux, 2010). Moreover, intervention studies suggest that an aerobic exercise program can lead to benefits in executive functions in healthy older adults (Predovan, Fraser, Renaud, & Bherer, 2012; Renaud, Maquestiaux, Joncas, Kergoat, & Bherer, 2010) and physically frail individuals (Langlois et al., 2013). Meta-analyses also support the benefits of exercise training to enhance cognitive performances in older adults, with executive control tasks being the most sensitive to training (Colcombe & Kramer, 2003).

In regards to brain imaging studies, physical exercise induces transient and long-lasting changes at the structural and functional organization of the brain (Bherer, Erickson, & Liu-Ambrose, 2013). For instance, Erickson et al. (2011) reported increased hippocampal volume bilaterally after a 1-year training program. Functional changes also occur with exercise. In a functional near-infrared spectroscopy study with healthy older women, it has been shown that cardiorespiratory fitness (VO_2 max) is positively linked to activation in the left dorsolateral prefrontal cortex during a Stroop task (Dupuy et al., 2015). The relationship between cardiorespiratory fitness and cognitive performances in cross-sectional studies, as well as associations between changes in cardiorespiratory fitness and cognitive enhancement in intervention studies, suggests that cardiovascular exercises and improvement in cardiovascular health mainly explain changes in cognition and brain function. However, other studies reported changes in hippocampal volume after motor coordination training (Voelcker-Rehage & Niemann, 2013) and resistance training (Liu-Ambrose et al., 2010), supporting the notion that the effects of exercise on brain structure and functions are complex and remain to be fully understood. More recent studies have focused on the use of different types of training regimens such as coordination exercises, yoga or other soft gym approaches. Increasing evidence suggests that dance can also induce cognitive enhancement effects, which would be partly related to the use of music. The next section focuses on the effect of music during physical activity programs on cognition.

Promoting physical activity with the use of music

Several studies have examined whether the use of music during physical activity can lead to additional benefits than physical exercise performed alone. One hypothesis is that music can facilitate gait patterns and therefore increase the level of physical activity. In a population of cardiac rehabilitation patients (Alter et al., 2015), participants were assigned to either a 3-month: (1) usual-care program with no music ($n = 11$), or (2) usual-care program with the use of tempo-pace synchronized audio-devices with personalized music playlists ($n = 23$). Participants assigned to the second group were further split into two subgroups; one in which the songs were calibrated for each participant to accentuate the tempo-pace synchrony [rhythmic auditory stimulation (RAS) (Chen, Zatorre, & Penhune, 2006)] and one in which the songs were left untouched. RAS is a technique to facilitate better synchronization of the gait movements to specific time cues (Thaut, Rice, Braun Janzen, Hurt-Thaut, & McIntosh, 2018). After completion of the respective intervention programs, larger improvements in terms of weekly volume of physical activity undertaken in the RAS subgroups were observed compared to the usual-care program with no music. In another intervention study (Clark, Baker, Peiris, Shoebridge, & Taylor, 2017), the proportion of participants achieving the recommended amounts of physical activity following a cardiac rehabilitation program was the same upon completion of either a usual-care program or a usual-care program with self-selected music (without any enhancement such as RAS) to support walking. Results of these two studies are inconclusive and do not fully support the notion that music helps promote physical activity. Future studies are needed to conclude about the benefit of adding music in an exercise program and in a cognitive enhancement perspective.

One possible benefit of integrating music during a physical activity could stand in the reduction of the perceived exertion. This was observed in a group of young adults (Potteiger, Schroeder, & Goff, 2000). After performing an initial graded exercise test to assess their cardiorespiratory fitness (VO_2 peak), participants performed four 20-minute exercise sessions on a cycle ergometer at 70% of their VO_2 peak. Each session represented a condition: upbeat music, classical music, self-selected music, and no music. The exercise sessions were conducted on nonconsecutive days (with a time interval of 2–7 days) and the order was counterbalanced. In comparison to the no-music condition, all the music conditions resulted in significantly lower ratings of perceived exertion, suggesting that music could play the role of a passive distractor from the unpleasant sensations associated with the physical demands. Similar findings were observed in a group of middle-aged women (Hayakawa, Miki, Takada, & Tanaka, 2000).

Another interpretation of the role of music listening in the decrease of the perceived exertion, may be due to "an illusionary experience in the sports performer that he or she exerts musical agency" (Fritz et al., 2013) in conditions where the synchronization between the movement and the musical structure is greater. According to this view, the sense of musical agency could possibly affect participants' subjective perception of fun during the physical activity, which could modulate the perceived exertion. Future research is needed to confirm this hypothesis.

Lastly, music induces several neurophysiological reactions in listeners, including the modulation of the activity of mesolimbic structures related to reward processing and dopamine release (Menon & Levitin, 2005), which could increase physical strength and thus reduce the sense of effort.

Does integrating music to physical activity improve cognitive performance?

Integrating music to short bouts of physical exercise has been shown to improve cognitive performance in older adults (Emery, Hsiao, Hill, & Frid, 2003). Performance on a verbal fluency test was assessed before and after a 10-minute bout of exercise on a treadmill at 85% of the participants' VO_2 max. Participants were tested in two conditions: treadmill exercise while listening to music (Vivaldi's Four Seasons) or not (blank tape). The exercise sessions were conducted on nonconsecutive days (with a time interval of 1 week) and the order was counterbalanced. In spite of a similar reduction in symptoms of depression, only participants in the music listening condition showed significant performance improvements on the verbal fluency test.

Satoh et al. (2014) assessed the integration of music during a longer physical exercise program (1 year of training in 1-hour session/week for a total of 40 sessions) in an older adult population. They observed an improvement in visuospatial function in the physical exercise intervention group where music listening (synthesizer-heavy dance pop music) was employed, compared to a similarly active group without the music listening (the participant only heard a percussive sound that counted the beat), or a passive nonexercise control group. The physical exercise program included a variety of exercises such as rhythmic walking, rhythmic exercises, muscle training, stretching, and respiration exercises. Using an identical physical exercise program and study design with a different sample of older adults, the same research group assessed the effect of the physical exercise intervention combined with music listening on brain volume (Tabei et al., 2017). Compared to the control group, older adults participating in the physical exercise intervention combined with music listening showed an increase in the volume of the right superior frontal gyrus, as well as a significant improvement in visuospatial function. Whether this effect is linked to stronger training-related gains or a stimulating effect of music needs to be further documented. Future studies should include a "music listening only" condition, to control for the effect of music listening per se. Also, one could compare the effect of a physical activity training with music listening to a similar physical activity training with a secondary nonmusic task, to better circumscribe the specific synergetic properties of music. Lastly, to further our understanding of the underlying mechanisms related to the synergetic effect of combined interventions, future studies should include outcomes such as exertion level and other variables assessing stimulating effects.

The effect of dance on cognition in older adults

Previous sections have reported studies suggesting that physical activity and physical exercise can help improve and maintain cognitive health over the life span and especially in elderly populations. Some studies also suggest that integrating music listening to a physical activity seems to offer even more cognitive benefits. These observations lead to the assumption that dance, which usually incorporates music to exercise or movement routines, would lead to some advantages on cognitive performances. Although being one of the most popular physical activities in American women aged 45 years and older (Fan, Kowaleski-Jones, & Wen, 2013), few studies have evaluated the impact of dance on cognition in healthy older adults. For the sake of this chapter, dancing is defined as "patterned, rhythmic movement in space and time" (Murrock & Graor, 2014). Some cognitive improvement has been observed in a prospective study (Verghese et al., 2003) and an advantage of dance on cognition has been reported in a cross-sectional study (Kattenstroth, Kolankowska, Kalisch, & Dinse, 2010). However, to establish a better quantification of the dose−response relationship between the participation in a dance activity and cognitive improvement, and to contribute to our understanding of the underlying mechanisms, appropriate experimental designs, such as the systematic evaluation of a formal dance program, are needed.

In a recent review, Predovan, Julien, Esmail, and Bherer (2018) investigated whether dance could be used as a promising alternative intervention to address physical inactivity, and to cognitively stimulate healthy older adults. Based on seven studies published between January 2000 and May 2018 ($n = 429$, 70% of women), dance interventions lasting between 10 weeks and 18 months were related to either the maintenance or the improvement of cognitive performance, particularly on tasks requiring either executive functions or visuospatial functions. These improvements appear in dance interventions regardless of dance style (e.g., tango, line dance, square dance, ballroom dancing, salsa, and rumba). However, cautious interpretation of these results is required as the methodological quality of many of the selected studies in this review (based on the Cochrane collaboration's tool for assessing risk of bias) present an unclear or high risk of bias.

To address the shortcomings in the existing literature, the review included the following future research avenues: (1) implementation of measurements at several time points to understand the evolution of performance changes, (2) extensive neuropsychological testing and use of computerized cognitive tasks, (3) consideration of vascular risk factors and other chronic diseases, (4) examination of biological sex effects, (5) comparison of adherence between different dance interventions, (6) inclusion of mood assessment and anxiety measurements, (7) exhaustive description of the program content to improve the reproducibility of the observed findings, (8) implementation of a randomized controlled trial design to reduce the selection bias and improve baseline comparability, (9) examination of gait performance, and (10) comparison of different types of dance programs [i.e., the different levels in complexity of the dance choreography, degree of improvisation, aerobic intensity, or the differing kinds of social interactions (alone, with a partner, or in a group)]. As mentioned by another review (Dhami, Moreno, & DeSouza, 2014), the potential of dance as an alternative therapy in the neurorehabilitation of populations affected by neurologic disease, such as Parkinson's disease, also requires further evaluation. Lastly, as for the other types of physical exercise interventions, earlier interventions may be beneficial for the prevention of cognitive decline associated with aging and, as such, dance interventions in a younger population could offer new avenues of research.

The effects of dance on cerebral health in older adults

Another research avenue is the use of neuroimaging techniques to further develop our comprehension of the underlying brain mechanisms by which dance and/or dance-related activities can help improve or maintain cognitive performance in older adults (Teixeira-Machado, Arida, & de Jesus Mari, 2018). Using a cross-sectional design, Niemann, Godde, and Voelcker-Rehage (2016) assessed the cognitive performance and brain volume in a group of older women (mean age = 72.92) with either long-term dance experience (of at least 5 years, at a minimum frequency of once a week) ($n = 28$) or no dance experience ($n = 29$). The groups were matched on numerous variables, including age, education, IQ score, cardiovascular fitness, motor fitness, and level of participation in other leisure activities. No significant difference in terms of cognitive performance, whole brain volume, or hippocampal volume was reported. These results are similar to another cross-sectional study (Verghese, 2006), comparing older social dancers to nondancers on different neuropsychological tests. No advantage was found for the dancers over the nondancers. The authors explain the lack of significant difference by addressing several limitations of their study, namely, that the "dose" of dancing in the social dancers group was not considered and that the sample size was small. Moreover, the lack of control for fitness condition and other types of physical exercise also limits the conclusion that can be drawn from this study. In the study by Niemann et al. (2016), the mean senior dancing experience was quantified as 13 years with a range of 5−34 years. As both groups presented similar lifestyles (e.g., level of participation in leisure activities other than dancing) and similar cardiorespiratory fitness, it is possible that overall, the association between dancing and cognitive gain and cerebral health [in the case of Niemann et al. (2016)] might have been precluded.

These mixed results highlight the importance of using interventional study designs as well. For instance, in a previous study, Burzynska et al. (2014) showed a relationship between physical activity, cardiorespiratory fitness, and white matter integrity. In a subsequent study, the authors used diffusion magnetic resonance imaging to investigate the change in white matter integrity related to the completion of four physical exercise programs (3×1-hour sessions per week for 6 months) in 174 cognitively healthy older adults (Burzynska et al., 2017). Participants were randomly assigned to either a Dance, Walking, Walking + Nutrition, or Active Control (stretching and toning) group. Upon evaluation at month 6, only the integrity of the fornix (based on fractional anisotropy, a measure of fiber orientation, coherence, and density) in the dance group increased, compared to a decline in the other groups. The fornix, which is part of the limbic system, is a major output tract of the hippocampus and is involved in episodic memory.

In another study, increased left hippocampal subfield volumes (CA1, CA2, subiculum) were respectively observed after an 18-month dancing intervention and after health fitness training (which comprised endurance training, strength−endurance training, and flexibility training) (Rehfeld et al., 2017). In addition, increases in the volume of the left dentate gyrus and the right subiculum were also observed in the dance group. Interestingly, the dentate gyrus is a region of the brain where neurogenesis (neural proliferation) presumably takes place. In mice, Angelucci, Ricci, Padua, Sabino, and Tonali (2007) showed that music exposure was also associated with the alteration of the brain-derived neurotrophic factor brain-derived neurotrophic factor (BDNF) levels in the hypothalamus. Based on the hypothesis of neurotrophic stimulation (Spirduso, 1980), physical exercise could also lead to the production of growth factors such as BDNF (Lledo, Alonso, & Grubb, 2006).

Moreover, the effects of an 18-month dance training program (compared to a strength−endurance training program of similar duration) on brain volume, plasma concentrations of BDNF, and cognitive health were examined in a group of older adults ($n = 22$) (Muller et al., 2017). At month 6, a significant increase in gray matter volume in the left precentral gyrus and an increase in BDNF levels were detected in the dance group, in comparison to the active control group. Furthermore, a similar pattern of cognitive improvement was reported in both groups, as performance on tasks requiring attention and verbal memory improved respectively after 6 and 18 months of training. After 18 months of dance training, the participants' BDNF levels returned to the pretreatment values and the parahippocampal region volume increased significantly. No change in cardiorespiratory fitness was reported in either intervention program. As the precentral gyrus is related to the control of voluntary motor functions, and the parahippocampal gyrus (part of the limbic system) is related to memory, the authors put forward particular features of the dance intervention, such as the learning of the choreography, multisensory integration, coordination of the body, and spatial navigation, to explain these effects.

In another study, Rehfeld et al. (2018) examined the effect of dance on BDNF plasma concentrations in older adults. A 6-month dance program (involving learning of novel and increasingly difficult choreographies) compared to a "sports intervention" (that included endurance training, strength—endurance training, and flexibility training) was shown to increase the volumes of multiple frontal and temporal cortical areas, as well as increase BDNF plasma concentration levels. It is to be noted that despite these group specific benefits, both interventions led to similar improvements in terms of physical fitness and performance on cognitive tasks requiring attention and spatial memory, respectively.

Lastly, Baniqued et al. (2018) assessed the brain network modularity (the degree to which the brain segments into independent networks) after the participation in different interventions including dance. They observed that older adults had no training-related gains in terms of cardiorespiratory fitness, and minimal changes in cognitive function for the dance group (based on a neuropsychological battery which included many tests from the Virginia Cognitive Aging Project). The authors raised the possibility that the lack of effect as a result of the dance intervention may have been due to the heterogeneity and lack of intensity of the dance sessions.

Overall, evidence indicates potential brain plasticity in older adults following participation in a dance program, such as increases in the integrity of the fornix (Burzynska et al., 2014), in the left hippocampal subfield volumes (Rehfeld et al., 2017), in gray matter volume in the left precentral gyrus (Muller et al., 2017), and an increase of the volumes of multiple frontal and temporal cortical areas (Rehfeld et al., 2018). More studies are needed to better delimit the specific effects of music and other components of the dancing activity (e.g., different types of dances, done in groups or individually) and investigate whether changes in brain plasticity are related to changes in cardiorespiratory fitness or other physical adaptations induced by the program.

The effect of dance/movement therapy on cognition in older adults

Another relevant stream of research has looked at the potential benefits of D/MT. D/MT is defined by the American Dance Therapy Association as the therapeutic use of movement in order to promote the integration of physical and emotional aspects of the human being, working to harmonize the physical, mental, and spiritual dimensions. Adapted to the needs of a vulnerable population, it is used as a complement to other medical treatments

(Hokkanen et al., 2008; Nystrom & Lauritzen, 2005). For example, it may be used in psychotherapy within the context of a process of growth and well-being. D/MT promotes socialization in populations often isolated by their conditions, and stimulates their creativity. A recent meta-analysis by Koch, Kunz, Lykou, and Cruz (2014) states that current studies on this subject have several methodological shortcomings, namely, lack of control groups, small sample sizes, and inadequate experimental designs. Similar statements are also found in literature reviews measuring the effects of D/MT on patients with chronic heart failure (Gomes Neto, Menezes, & Oliveira Carvalho, 2014), cancer (Bradt, Goodill, & Dileo, 2011), schizophrenia (Ren & Xia, 2013), and Parkinson's disease (Earhart, 2009).

In healthy older adults, Esmail et al. (2019) examined the effects of D/MT on cognition, physical fitness and health-related quality of life. Older adults were randomly assigned to either a 3-month (3 × per week, 1 h/session) D/MT program, an aerobic exercise program, or a waiting list. Improvements in composite scores of executive and nonexecutive cognitive tests and mobility (based on the 10-m walk test and Time-Up and Go) were observed, but these changes were not group-dependent, which suggests that D/MT did not have a specific effect on these performances. In the same study, cortisol awakening response (a marker of chronic stress), was also measured (Vrinceanu et al., 2019). Saliva samples were collected (at 0, 30, and 60 minutes after awakening) on three nonconsecutive weekdays during the pre- and posttest periods. Interestingly, the D/MT group showed lower salivary cortisol values posttraining, compared to the group that followed an exercise intervention or the waiting-list group.

In a randomized controlled trial, Ho et al. (2018) evaluated the effect of a 3-month D/MT intervention (24 × 1-hour sessions) in older adults with mild dementia. Compared to a passive control group (a wait list), participants who had completed the D/MT intervention showed less depressive symptoms, loneliness, and negative mood, in addition to enhanced daily functioning (as measured by the Instrumental Activities of Daily Living) and decreased diurnal cortisol slope (interpreted as an improvement of neuroendocrine functioning). A follow-up evaluation 3 months after the completion of the intervention showed an improvement in memory performances for the D/MT intervention compared to the passive control group. A subsequent evaluation 6 months after the completion of the intervention showed that the improvements in daily functioning and diurnal cortisol slope observed at month 3 in the D/MT group were maintained. These studies suggest that D/MT has the potential to be an accessible type of intervention to maintain daily functioning, reduce stress, and potentially improve cognition in older adults (Guzman-Garcia, Hughes, James, & Rochester, 2013). More studies, including studies with active control groups, are needed to confirm these observations and identify the mechanisms by which D/MT induces these benefits.

Discussion and conclusion

This chapter presents an overview of recent studies supporting the notion that physical activity, with or without music, dance, and D/MT could help alleviate negative symptoms associated with aging, with a more specific emphasis on age-related cognitive decline. Overall, these activities seem to have a positive effect on cognition and help enhance cognitive performances in older adults. Moreover, additional benefits of the use of music during physical activity have been observed such as the facilitation of gait patterns, the reduction of the perceived exertion during exercise and the capacity to arouse the individual. Over either short bouts of exercise or longer intervention programs, integrating music with physical activity leads to small but significant improvements in cognitive functioning.

As a type of physical activity, dance often incorporates music. Researchers have investigated the benefits of dance in older adults. A review of the literature suggests that dance interventions in older adults lead to maintenance or improvement of cognitive performance, particularly with regard to tasks requiring executive functions or visuospatial functions. These improvements are most likely the result of a multitude of interacting mechanisms. Neuroimaging techniques highlight some possible mechanisms, such as an increase in white matter integrity and an increase in some brain structure volumes (e.g., the hippocampal subfield). Another mechanism by which participation in dance activity could have an effect on cognition and brain health is through an increase in BDNF plasma concentrations. With regard to the effect of D/MT on cognitive aging, a recent study (Vrinceanu et al., 2019) in healthy older adults shows a lower total concentration of cortisol released during the first hour after awakening, a marker of chronic stress, but no change in terms of cognitive functioning and mobility measurements. In older adults with dementia, a D/MT intervention (compared to a wait-list condition) has been shown to induce some cognitive improvements (Ho et al., 2018).

With regard to an older adult population, many research avenues remain to be explored, such as the ergogenic effect of music listening prior to exercise or its role during postexercise recuperation (Karageorghis & Priest, 2012a, 2012b). In the context of the self-determination theory (Ryan & Deci, 2000), the benefits of self-selected music during a physical activity could also be explored as a way to increase participant engagement and adherence to a program. Another avenue is to explore which factors increase the benefit of music listening during physical activity, such as personality types, or physical activity intensities and duration. In some cases, listening to music could be counterproductive, as some individuals prefer to "listen to their bodies" while exercising, instead of listening to music (Karageorghis & Priest, 2012a, 2012b).

Increasing the range of physical activities available for older adults that can be carried out alone, in groups or with a partner, is important. This review examined the most recent evidence regarding the impact of dancing and D/MT on cognitive performance and brain health in older adults. Some evidence suggests that dance as an intervention for older adults can improve and help maintain cognition and that these changes could be the results of structural brain changes. These studies are part of a common endeavor which is to better understand how to achieve successful aging by promoting the development of strategies and interventions for older adults so that they can continue to function at a high level and contribute to society.

Acknowledgments

This research was supported in part by a fellowship (36126) from the Fonds de recherche du Québec-Santé (FRQS) and Réseau Québécois de Recherche sur le Vieillissement (RQRV) (DP) and the Mirella and Lino Saputo Research Chair in Cardiovascular health and the prevention of cognitive decline from University of Montreal at the Montreal Heart Institute (LB).

Conflict of interest

The authors declare that there are no conflicts of interest.

References

Alter, D. A., O'Sullivan, M., Oh, P. I., Redelmeier, D. A., Marzolini, S., Liu, R., ... Bartel, L. R. (2015). Synchronized personalized music audio-playlists to improve adherence to physical activity among patients participating in a structured exercise program: A proof-of-principle feasibility study. *Sports Medicine—Open*, *1*(1), 23. Available from https://doi.org/10.1186/s40798-015-0017-9.

Angelucci, F., Ricci, E., Padua, L., Sabino, A., & Tonali, P. A. (2007). Music exposure differentially alters the levels of brain-derived neurotrophic factor and nerve growth factor in the mouse hypothalamus. *Neuroscience Letters*, *429*(2−3), 152−155. Available from https://doi.org/10.1016/j.neulet.2007.10.005.

Baniqued, P. L., Gallen, C. L., Voss, M. W., Burzynska, A. Z., Wong, C. N., Cooke, G. E., ... D'Esposito, M. (2018). Brain network modularity predicts exercise-related executive function gains in older adults. *Frontiers in Aging Neuroscience*, *9*. Available from https://doi.org/10.3389/fnagi.2017.00426.

Berryman, N., Bherer, L., Nadeau, S., Lauziere, S., Lehr, L., Bobeuf, F., & Bosquet, L. (2014). Multiple roads lead to Rome: combined high-intensity aerobic and strength training vs. gross motor activities leads to equivalent improvement in executive functions in a cohort of healthy older adults. *Age (Dordr)*, *36*, 9710. Available from https://doi.org/10.1007/s11357-014-9710-8.

Bherer, L. (2015). Cognitive plasticity in older adults: Effects of cognitive training and physical exercise. *Annals of the New York Academy of Sciences*, *1337*, 1−6. Available from https://doi.org/10.1111/nyas.12682.

Bherer, L., Erickson, K. I., & Liu-Ambrose, T. (2013). Physical exercise and brain functions in older adults. *Journal of Aging Research*, *2013*, 197326. Available from https://doi.org/10.1155/2013/197326.

Bradt, J., Goodill, S. W., & Dileo, C. (2011). Dance/movement therapy for improving psychological and physical outcomes in cancer patients. *Cochrane Database of Systematic Reviews, 10*, CD007103. Available from https://doi.org/10.1002/14651858.CD007103.pub2.

Burzynska, A. Z., Chaddock-Heyman, L., Voss, M. W., Wong, C. N., Gothe, N. P., Olson, E. A., ... Kramer, A. F. (2014). Physical activity and cardiorespiratory fitness are beneficial for white matter in low-fit older adults. *PLoS One, 9*(9), e107413. Available from https://doi.org/10.1371/journal.pone.0107413.

Burzynska, A. Z., Jiao, Y., Knecht, A. M., Fanning, J., Awick, E. A., Chen, T., ... Kramer, A. F. (2017). White matter integrity declined over 6-months, but dance intervention improved integrity of the fornix of older adults. *Frontiers in Aging Neuroscience, 9*, 59. Available from https://doi.org/10.3389/fnagi.2017.00059.

Chen, J. L., Zatorre, R. J., & Penhune, V. B. (2006). Interactions between auditory and dorsal premotor cortex during synchronization to musical rhythms. *Neuroimage, 32*(4), 1771−1781. Available from https://doi.org/10.1016/j.neuroimage.2006.04.207.

Clark, I. N., Baker, F. A., Peiris, C. L., Shoebridge, G., & Taylor, N. F. (2017). Participant-selected music and physical activity in older adults following cardiac rehabilitation: A randomized controlled trial. *Clinical Rehabilitation, 31*(3), 329−339. Available from https://doi.org/10.1177/0269215516640864.

Colcombe, S., & Kramer, A. F. (2003). Fitness effects on the cognitive function of older adults: A meta-analytic study. *Psychological Science, 14*(2), 125−130. Available from https://doi.org/10.1111/1467-9280.t01-1-01430.

Dhami, P., Moreno, S., & DeSouza, J. F. (2014). New framework for rehabilitation—Fusion of cognitive and physical rehabilitation: The hope for dancing. *Frontiers in Psychology, 5*, 1478. Available from https://doi.org/10.3389/fpsyg.2014.01478.

Dupuy, O., Gauthier, C. J., Fraser, S. A., Desjardins-Crepeau, L., Desjardins, M., Mekary, S., ... Bherer, L. (2015). Higher levels of cardiovascular fitness are associated with better executive function and prefrontal oxygenation in younger and older women. *Frontiers in Human Neuroscience, 9*, 66. Available from https://doi.org/10.3389/fnhum.2015.00066.

Earhart, G. M. (2009). Dance as therapy for individuals with Parkinson disease. *European Journal of Physical and Rehabilitation Medicine, 45*(2), 231−238.

Emery, C. F., Hsiao, E. T., Hill, S. M., & Frid, D. J. (2003). Short-term effects of exercise and music on cognitive performance among participants in a cardiac rehabilitation program. *Heart and Lung, 32*(6), 368−373. Available from https://doi.org/10.1016/s0147.

Erickson, K. I., Voss, M. W., Prakash, R. S., Basak, C., Szabo, A., Chaddock, L., ... Kramer, A. F. (2011). Exercise training increases size of hippocampus and improves memory. *Proceedings of the National Academy of Sciences of the United States of America, 108*(7), 3017−3022. Available from https://doi.org/10.1073/pnas.1015950108.

Esmail, A., Vrinceanu, T., Lussier, M., Predovan, D., Berryman, N., Houle, J., ... Bherer, L. (2019). Effects of dance/movement training vs. aerobic exercise training on cognition, physical fitness and quality of life in older adults: A randomized controlled trial. *Journal of Bodywork and Movement Therapies*. Available from https://doi.org/10.1016/j.jbmt.2019.05.004.

Fan, J. X., Kowaleski-Jones, L., & Wen, M. (2013). Walking or dancing: Patterns of physical activity by cross-sectional age among U.S. women. *Journal of Aging and Health, 25*(7), 1182−1203. Available from https://doi.org/10.1177/0898264313495561.

Fritz, T. H., Hardikar, S., Demoucron, M., Niessen, M., Demey, M., Giot, O., ... Leman, M. (2013). Musical agency reduces perceived exertion during strenuous physical performance. *Proceedings of the National Academy of Sciences of the United States of America, 110*(44), 17784−17789. Available from https://doi.org/10.1073/pnas.1217252110.

Gomes Neto, M., Menezes, M. A., & Oliveira Carvalho, V. (2014). Dance therapy in patients with chronic heart failure: A systematic review and a meta-analysis. *Clinical Rehabilitation*, *28*(12), 1172−1179. Available from https://doi.org/10.1177/0269215514534089.

Guzman-Garcia, A., Hughes, J. C., James, I. A., & Rochester, L. (2013). Dancing as a psychosocial intervention in care homes: A systematic review of the literature. *International Journal of Geriatric Psychiatry*, *28*(9), 914−924. Available from https://doi.org/10.1002/gps.3913.

Hayakawa, Y., Miki, H., Takada, K., & Tanaka, K. (2000). Effects of music on mood during bench stepping exercise. *Perceptual and Motor Skills*, *90*(1), 307−314. Available from https://doi.org/10.2466/pms.2000.90.1.307.

Ho, R. T. H., Fong, T. C. T., Chan, W. C., Kwan, J. S. K., Chiu, P. K. C., Yau, J. C. Y., & Lam, L. C. W. (2018). Psychophysiological effects of Dance Movement Therapy and physical exercise on older adults with mild dementia: A randomized controlled trial. *Journals of Gerontology: Series B: Psychological Sciences and Social Sciences*. Available from https://doi.org/10.1093/geronb/gby145.

Hokkanen, L., Rantala, L., Remes, A. M., Harkonen, B., Viramo, P., & Winblad, I. (2008). Dance and movement therapeutic methods in management of dementia: A randomized, controlled study. *Journal of the American Geriatrics Society*, *56*(4), 771−772. Available from https://doi.org/10.1111/j.1532-5415.2008.01611.x.

Karageorghis, C. I., & Priest, D. L. (2012a). Music in the exercise domain: A review and synthesis (Part I). *International Review of Sport and Exercise Psychology*, *5*(1), 44−66. Available from https://doi.org/10.1080/1750984X.2011.631026.

Karageorghis, C. I., & Priest, D. L. (2012b). Music in the exercise domain: A review and synthesis (Part II). *International Review of Sport and Exercise Psychology*, *5*(1), 67−84. Available from https://doi.org/10.1080/1750984X.2011.631027.

Kattenstroth, J. C., Kolankowska, I., Kalisch, T., & Dinse, H. R. (2010). Superior sensory, motor, and cognitive performance in elderly individuals with multi-year dancing activities. *Frontiers in Aging Neuroscience*, *2*. Available from https://doi.org/10.3389/fnagi.2010.00031.

Koch, S., Kunz, T., Lykou, S., & Cruz, R. (2014). Effects of dance movement therapy and dance on health-related psychological outcomes: A meta-analysis. *The Arts in Psychotherapy*, *41*(1), 46−64. Available from https://doi.org/10.1016/j.aip.2013.10.004.

Langlois, F., Vu, T. T., Chasse, K., Dupuis, G., Kergoat, M. J., & Bherer, L. (2013). Benefits of physical exercise training on cognition and quality of life in frail older adults. *Journals of Gerontology, Series B: Psychological Sciences and Social Sciences*, *68*(3), 400−404. Available from https://doi.org/10.1093/geronb/gbs069.

Laurin, D., Verreault, R., Lindsay, J., MacPherson, K., & Rockwood, K. (2001). Physical activity and risk of cognitive impairment and dementia in elderly persons. *Archives of Neurology*, *58*(3), 498−504.

Liu-Ambrose, T., Nagamatsu, L. S., Graf, P., Beattie, B. L., Ashe, M. C., & Handy, T. C. (2010). Resistance training and executive functions: A 12-month randomized controlled trial. *Archives of Internal Medicine*, *170*(2), 170−178. Available from https://doi.org/10.1001/archinternmed.2009.494.

Livingston, G., Sommerlad, A., Orgeta, V., Costafreda, S. G., Huntley, J., Ames, D., ... Mukadam, N. (2017). Dementia prevention, intervention, and care. *Lancet*, *390*(10113), 2673−2734. Available from https://doi.org/10.1016/S0140-6736(17)31363-6.

Lledo, P. M., Alonso, M., & Grubb, M. S. (2006). Adult neurogenesis and functional plasticity in neuronal circuits. *Nature Reviews Neuroscience*, *7*(3), 179−193. Available from https://doi.org/10.1038/nrn1867.

Menon, V., & Levitin, D. J. (2005). The rewards of music listening: Response and physiological connectivity of the mesolimbic system. *Neuroimage, 28*(1), 175−184. Available from https://doi.org/10.1016/j.neuroimage.2005.05.053.

Muller, P., Rehfeld, K., Schmicker, M., Hokelmann, A., Dordevic, M., Lessmann, V., ... Muller, N. G. (2017). Evolution of neuroplasticity in response to physical activity in old age: The case for dancing. *Frontiers in Aging Neuroscience, 9*, 56. Available from https://doi.org/10.3389/fnagi.2017.00056.

Murrock, C. J., & Graor, C. H. (2014). Effects of dance on depression, physical function, and disability in underserved adults. *Journal of Aging and Physical Activity, 22*(3), 380−385. Available from https://doi.org/10.1123/japa.2013-0003.

National Academies of Sciences, Engineering, and Medicine; Health and Medicine Division; Board on Health Sciences Policy; Committee on Preventing Dementia and Cognitive Impairment. (2017). In A. Downey, C. Stroud, S. Landis, & A. I. Leshner (Eds.), *Preventing cognitive decline and dementia: A way forward*. Washington, DC: National Academies Press (US), Copyright 2017 by the National Academy of Sciences. All rights reserved.

Niemann, C., Godde, B., & Voelcker-Rehage, C. (2014). Not only cardiovascular, but also coordinative exercise increases hippocampal volume in older adults. *Front Aging Neurosci, 4*(6), 170. Available from https://doi.org/10.3389/fnagi.2014.00170.

Niemann, C., Godde, B., & Voelcker-Rehage, C. (2016). Senior dance experience, cognitive performance, and brain volume in older women. *Neural Plasticity, 2016*, 9837321. Available from https://doi.org/10.1155/2016/9837321.

Nystrom, K., & Lauritzen, S. O. (2005). Expressive bodies: Demented persons' communication in a dance therapy context. *Health (London), 9*(3), 297−317. Available from https://doi.org/10.1177/1363459305052902.

Petersen, R. C., Lopez, O., Armstrong, M. J., Getchius, T. S. D., Ganguli, M., Gloss, D., ... Rae-Grant, A. (2018). Practice guideline update summary: Mild cognitive impairment: Report of the Guideline Development, Dissemination, and Implementation Subcommittee of the American Academy of Neurology. *Neurology, 90*(3), 126−135. Available from https://doi.org/10.1212/WNL.0000000000004826.

Potteiger, J. A., Schroeder, J. M., & Goff, K. L. (2000). Influence of music on ratings of perceived exertion during 20 minutes of moderate intensity exercise. *Perceptual and Motor Skills, 91*(3 Pt 1), 848−854. Available from https://doi.org/10.2466/pms.2000.91.3.848.

Predovan, D., Fraser, S. A., Renaud, M., & Bherer, L. (2012). The effect of three months of aerobic training on stroop performance in older adults. *Journal of Aging Research, 2012*, 269815. Available from https://doi.org/10.1155/2012/269815.

Predovan, D., Julien, A., Esmail, A., & Bherer, L. (2018). Effects of dancing on cognition in healthy older adults: A systematic review. *Journal of Cognitive Enhancement*. Available from https://doi.org/10.1007/s41465-018-0103-2.

Rehfeld, K., Luders, A., Hokelmann, A., Lessmann, V., Kaufmann, J., Brigadski, T., ... Muller, N. G. (2018). Dance training is superior to repetitive physical exercise in inducing brain plasticity in the elderly. *PLoS One, 13*(7), e0196636. Available from https://doi.org/10.1371/journal.pone.0196636.

Rehfeld, K., Müller, P., Aye, N., Schmicker, M., Dordevic, M., Kaufmann, J., ... Müller, N. G. (2017). Dancing or fitness sport? The effects of two training programs on hippocampal plasticity and balance abilities in healthy seniors. *Frontiers in Human Neuroscience, 11*, 305. Available from https://doi.org/10.3389/fnhum.2017.00305.

Ren, J., & Xia, J. (2013). Dance therapy for schizophrenia. *Cochrane Database of Systematic Reviews, 10*, CD006868. Available from https://doi.org/10.1002/14651858.CD006868.pub3.

Renaud, M., Bherer, L., & Maquestiaux, F. (2010). A high level of physical fitness is associated with more efficient response preparation in older adults. *Journals of Gerontology, Series B: Psychological Sciences and Social Sciences*, 65b(3), 317−322. Available from https://doi. org/10.1093/geronb/gbq004.

Renaud, M., Maquestiaux, F., Joncas, S., Kergoat, M. J., & Bherer, L. (2010). The effect of three months of aerobic training on response preparation in older adults. *Frontiers in Aging Neuroscience*, 2, 148. Available from https://doi.org/10.3389/fnagi.2010.00148.

Ryan, R. M., & Deci, E. L. (2000). Self-determination theory and the facilitation of intrinsic motivation, social development, and well-being. *American Psychologist*, 55(1), 68−78.

Satoh, M., Ogawa, J., Tokita, T., Nakaguchi, N., Nakao, K., Kida, H., & Tomimoto, H. (2014). The effects of physical exercise with music on cognitive function of elderly people: Mihama-Kiho project. *PLoS One*, 9(4), e95230. Available from https://doi.org/10.1371/journal.pone.0095230.

Spirduso, W. W. (1980). Physical fitness, aging, and psychomotor speed: A review. *Journal of Gerontology*, 35(6), 850−865.

Tabei, K. I., Satoh, M., Ogawa, J. I., Tokita, T., Nakaguchi, N., Nakao, K., ... Tomimoto, H. (2017). Physical exercise with music reduces gray and white matter loss in the frontal cortex of elderly people: The Mihama-Kiho Scan Project. *Frontiers in Aging Neuroscience*, 9, 174. Available from https://doi.org/10.3389/fnagi.2017.00174.

Teixeira-Machado, L., Arida, R. M., & de Jesus Mari, J. (2018). Dance for neuroplasticity: A descriptive systematic review. *Neuroscience and Biobehavioral Reviews*, 96, 232−240. Available from https://doi.org/10.1016/j.neubiorev.2018.12.010.

Thaut, M. H., Rice, R. R., Braun Janzen, T., Hurt-Thaut, C. P., & McIntosh, G. C. (2018). Rhythmic auditory stimulation for reduction of falls in Parkinson's disease: A randomized controlled study. *Clinical Rehabilitation*. Available from https://doi.org/10.1177/0269215518788615, 269215518788615.

Verghese, J. (2006). Cognitive and mobility profile of older social dancers. *Journal of the American Geriatrics Society*, 54(8), 1241−1244. Available from https://doi.org/10.1111/j.1532-5415.2006.00808.x.

Verghese, J., Lipton, R. B., Katz, M. J., Hall, C. B., Derby, C. A., Kuslansky, G., ... Buschke, H. (2003). Leisure activities and the risk of dementia in the elderly. *New England Journal of Medicine*, 348(25), 2508−2516. Available from https://doi.org/10.1056/NEJMoa022252.

Voelcker-Rehage, C., & Niemann, C. (2013). Structural and functional brain changes related to different types of physical activity across the life span. *Neuroscience and Biobehavioral Reviews*, 37(9 Pt B), 2268−2295. Available from https://doi.org/10.1016/j.neubiorev.2013.01.028.

Vrinceanu, T., Esmail, A., Berryman, N., Predovan, D., Vu, T. T. M., Villalpando, J. M., ... Bherer, L. (2019). Dance your stress away: Comparing the effect of dance/movement training to aerobic exercise training on the cortisol awakening response in healthy older adults. *Stress (Amsterdam, Netherlands)*, 1−9. Available from https://doi.org/10.1080/10253890.2019.1617690.

Chapter 11

Toward music-based auditory rehabilitation for older adults

Benjamin Rich Zendel[1,2] and Sarah Sauvé[1]

[1]*Faculty of Medicine, Memorial University of Newfoundland, St. John's, NL, Canada,*
[2]*Aging Research Centre - Newfoundland and Labrador, Grenfell Campus, Memorial University,
Corner Brook, NL, Canada*

---

*Musical training is a more potent instrument than any other, because rhythm
and harmony find their way into the inward places of the soul, on which they
mightly fasten, imparting grace, and making the soul of him who is rightly
educated graceful....*

Socrates, iv. Benjamin Jowett (trans.), The Republic of Plato (Oxford Clarendon
Press, 1888): 88.

Introduction

One of the most common hearing difficulties reported by older adults is difficulty understanding speech in the presence of background noise (Pichora-Fuller et al., 2016; Pichora-Fuller & Souza, 2003; Schneider, Pichora-Fuller, & Daneman, 2010). This difficulty is often associated with requiring greater listening effort (Gosselin & Gagné, 2011) and consequently, this greater listening effort can take away cognitive resources from other cognitive domains, such as the ability to remember the content of the speech (Pichora-Fuller, Schneider, & Daneman, 1995). The more effort required for understanding speech, the more tiring this seemingly innocuous task becomes and this can have a negative impact on older adults' social life, becoming a driver of isolation and loneliness.

We also know that overall, musicians have better listening skills than nonmusicians (e.g., Parbery-Clark, Skoe, Lam, & Kraus, 2009; Zendel & Alain, 2009). This benefit persists into old age (e.g., Parbery-Clark, Strait, Anderson, Hittner, & Kraus, 2011; Zendel & Alain, 2012, 2013, 2014), and has driven interest in using music to improve hearing abilities in older adults. Recent work has shown that short-term music training can improve hearing abilities in older adults (Zendel, West, Belleville, & Peretz, 2019; Fleming, Belleville, Peretz, West, & Zendel, 2019; Dubinsky, Nespoli, & Russo, 2019).

Music and the Aging Brain. DOI: https://doi.org/10.1016/B978-0-12-817422-7.00011-0

The goal of this chapter is to integrate findings about musicianship and musical training in younger and older adults in order to highlight the putative mechanisms which drive the neuroplasticity that supports enhanced hearing in older adult musicians or those who have done short-term music training. Given how many older adults experience some degree of hearing loss, understanding the potential benefits of music training on hearing abilities is of critical importance. In this chapter we will focus on two mechanisms that may serve as cognitive scaffolds that could support the preservation or enhancement of hearing abilities. Introduced in Chapter 3, Age-related hearing loss (Chan & Alain, 2020), the scaffolding theory of aging and cognition (STAC) was first described by Park and Reuter-Lorenz (2009), and updated in 2014 (Reuter-Lorenz & Park, 2014). STAC consists of five major sources of influence on cognitive function in older adults: neural challenges, functional deterioration, neural resources depletion, neural resource enrichment, and cognitive scaffolding. While the first three indicate loss or decline in cognitive function, cognitive scaffolding mitigates these losses via neural resource enrichment. Neural resource enrichment refers to positive contributions to the cognitive scaffold including education, physical activity, and training, while neural resource depletion refers to negative contributions to the cognitive scaffold such as strokes, smoking, and normal aging (Reuter-Lorenz & Park, 2014).

The first cognitive scaffold we will explore is based on the idea that the motor planning system is relatively preserved in normal aging, and that auditory information, particularly speech, is often processed in parallel in parts of the motor planning system. It has been demonstrated that music training strengthens the integration of the auditory and motor systems. Music training enhances the motor responses to auditory stimuli because skilled music performance requires auditory—motor integration. This strengthened auditory—motor connection likely leads to enhanced processing of speech via the speech—motor system. The speech—motor system aids in speech understanding by making inferences about how the motor system would move speech articulators (i.e., lips and tongue) to produce the incoming speech. This strengthened auditory—motor connectivity likely drives lower level plasticity of the auditory system by continually refining both cortical and subcortical responses to incoming acoustic information. This increased refinement in responses leads to better inferences about the underlying motor gestures that produced the incoming speech and therefore aids in comprehension.

The second potential scaffold that may support the development of enhanced hearing abilities is through music perception. Emerging evidence suggests that music perception is relatively preserved in older adults, particularly the ability to process the tonal structure of music. Thus, preserved processing of musical stimuli could be used as a cognitive scaffold on which other cognitive tasks could be learned. By scaffolding speech perception onto the music perception system, it may be possible to mitigate age-related decline in the ability to understand speech in noisy environments.

For both the music perception and motor scaffolds, similar neurophysio-logical mechanisms likely contribute to the music training-related enhance-ment to understanding speech in noise. The first putative mechanism is related to enhanced neural synchrony with incoming acoustic information at the level of the brain stem. Enhanced neural synchrony would create a more robust representation of the incoming speech signal, which would facilitate the ability to understand the incoming speech. The second putative mecha-nism is via an improved ability to "listen" attentively to speech. Interestingly, the scant research in this field provides some evidence for both of these accounts, suggesting that music training could improve both mechanisms individually, could improve neural synchrony, which would then facilitate listening effort, or could facilitate listening effort, which could refine neural synchrony via top-down neuronal projections either online or through neuroplastic changes to subcortical structures. The rest of the chapter is divided into two sections: the case for the auditory−motor scaffold, and the case for the music perception scaffold. We then present some concluding remarks and suggestions for future research.

The case for an auditory−motor scaffold

One of the most ubiquitous daily listening tasks is understanding speech when there is background noise. This task has been referred to as the cocktail party problem and was first described by Cherry (1953). In the past decade, several studies have shown a musician advantage for various speech-in-noise tasks. For instance, one of the first studies to compare musicians and nonmu-sicians on a speech-in-noise task found that musicians outperformed nonmu-sicians on two standardized clinical assessments of the ability to understand speech in noise (i.e., QuickSIN: Killion, Niquette, Gudmundsen, Revit, & Banerjee, 2004 and HINT: Nilsson, Soli, & Sullivan, 1994; Parbery-Clark, Skoe, & Kraus, 2009). In these preliminary studies, this enhanced ability in musicians was related to both frequency discrimination (identify the higher tone) and working memory (Woodcock−Johnson III Cognitive test: Woodcock, Mather, McGrew, & Wendling, 2001) performance.

In a recent review, Coffey, Mogilever, and Zatorre (2017), examined research comparing musicians and nonmusicians on the ability to understand speech in noise and other auditory tasks that involved detecting a signal embedded in a masker. The results of this review were equivocal. Of the 29 papers included, 27 reported at least one condition where musicians out-performed nonmusicians, or musicians exhibited different neurophysiological responses using electroencephalography (EEG) or magnetoencephalography compared to nonmusicians on speech/signal-in-noise tasks. There were, how-ever, some inconsistencies in the findings across the studies. That is, many papers reported null effects in conditions where other papers report signifi-cant effects. Coffey et al. (2017) produced a chart summarizing significant and nonsignificant musician advantages across all combinations of target signals (e.g., sentence, word, phoneme, or tone) and maskers [e.g., none, broadband noise, tone, speech-like (but not comprehensible) noise, single-talker noise, and multitalker babble noise] used among the reviewed papers. A few interesting patterns emerged from this chart. First, all studies that examined neuroelectric/magnetic responses reported differences in brain activity between musicians and nonmusicians when processing words, phonemes, and tones when no background noise was present. Second, most of the studies that found a behavioral advantage for understanding sentences, words, or phonemes in musicians did so when the masking noise was multitalker babble. This pattern of results suggests that the musician advantage for understanding speech in noise is not just due to their improved ability to process the target speech, but also their improved ability to process the background noise when the noise is speech that can be comprehended or predicted (i.e., there is informational masking present). This enhanced processing of background speech could be due to an enhanced ability to inhibit the background speech, or to successfully divide attention and comprehend both the target speech and the background speech.

Speech in noise, rhythm, and the motor system

Emerging evidence suggests that rhythmic skills are related to the ability to understand speech in noise (Slater & Kraus, 2016). This connection is likely due to the importance of synchronizing to the rhythm/prosody of speech during speech perception. When understanding speech in background noise, an enhanced ability to entrain to the temporal envelope of speech rhythms embedded in noise would allow the listener to better guide their attention to critical acoustic features in the speech signal. Moreover, this connection could facilitate the suppression of background noise when it contains information that can be modeled by the speech−motor system (i.e., by being periodic or by containing speech with an identifiable prosody). Accordingly, the musician advantage for understanding speech-in-noise could be due to enhanced abilities in perceiving rhythm via the motor system. There is now significant evidence that the perception of rhythm involves brain structures that form the motor system (Fujioka, Zendel, & Ross, 2010; Grahn & Brett, 2007; Zatorre, Chen, & Penhune, 2007).

The motor system has long been considered an integral part of the speech perception system. Liberman and Mattingly (1985) proposed that phonetic information is perceived in a neural module that was specialized to detect the intended vocal articulations of the talker. Functional neuroimaging studies have confirmed that brain regions that were traditionally thought to be associated only with speech production are also involved in speech perception. For example, Broca's area, in the left inferior frontal gyrus, is critical for both the production and perception of speech sounds (Nishitani, Amunts,

& Hari, 2005; Watkins & Paus, 2004). Other parts of the motor system have also been shown to be involved in speech perception. For example, regions in the precentral gyrus, extending into the anterior portion of the central sulcus, are active for both the production and perception of speech sounds (Wilson, Saygin, Sereno, & Iacoboni, 2004). Further support for this claim comes from studies that have shown that lip regions of the motor cortex are activated when perceiving a [p] sound, and tongue regions of the motor cortex are activated when perceiving a [t] sound (Pulvermüller et al., 2006), as the place of articulation for producing a [p] is the lips, and for a [t] is the tongue.

Not surprisingly, the speech−motor system becomes more active in processing speech when there is background noise (Du, Buchsbaum, Grady, & Alain, 2014). Multivoxel pattern analysis using functional magnetic resonance imaging (fMRI) data revealed that specific speech tokens were discriminated better in the ventral premotor regions and in Broca's area when background noise was −6 dB SNR (speech-to-noise ratio) or above (Du et al., 2014). A similar analysis in auditory regions along the superior temporal plane was only reliable when the SNR was much higher at +8 dB SNR (i.e., quieter background noise and easier to understand; Du et al., 2014). Clearly the speech−motor system is involved in the perception of speech and it is activated to a greater extent in challenging listening situations.

When examining the benefit of musical training for speech-in-noise perception, a recent study revealed that the musician advantage for understanding speech-in-noise was related to enhanced activity in both Broca's area and in right auditory regions (Du & Zatorre, 2017). Moreover, musicians exhibited higher discriminability of speech phonemes in background noise in Broca's area and its right hemisphere homologue, the left and right premotor areas, and in auditory regions along the superior temporal plane (Du & Zatorre, 2017). Finally, functional connectivity between auditory and motor regions was found to be enhanced in musicians (Du & Zatorre, 2017). Overall this pattern of results suggests that at least part of the musician advantage for processing speech in noise comes from enhanced activation and connectivity in the speech−motor system.

One possible explanation for the connection between the speech−motor system and the musician advantage for speech processing is due to music training itself. Learning to play music requires tight coupling between the auditory and motor systems. Support for this proposal comes from longitudinal studies that compared auditory−motor training to auditory-only training in terms of cortical brain plasticity. In these studies, nonmusicians were randomly assigned to either learn to play a musical sequence on a piano (i.e., auditory−motor condition), or to listen to sequences and to detect errors in their production (i.e., auditory-only condition) over the course of 2 weeks (Lappe, Herholz, Trainor, & Pantev, 2008; Lappe, Trainor, Herholz, & Pantev, 2011). Each participant in the auditory-only condition was paired with a participant in the auditory—motor condition so that both groups were exposed to the exact same stimuli during the training. The only difference was that the auditory—motor group produced the melodies with specific finger sequences, while the auditory-only group listened to these recorded sequences and detected errors in them (Lappe et al., 2008, 2011). After the training sessions concluded, auditory abilities were assessed by using an oddball paradigm, where participants listen to sequences of tones with occasional deviants while their brain activity was monitored using EEG. The deviant tones evoke a mismatch negativity (MMN), a negative deflection automatically generated in response to a deviant, or unexpected, tone. In both studies, the auditory—motor group had greater training-related enhancements in their ability to detect errors, and greater enhancements to the MMN (Lappe et al., 2008, 2011). This suggests that one of the critical components of music training is the motor component and supports the idea that plasticity in the auditory—motor pathway can lead to enhanced speech perception in musicians. Evidence for such plasticity is discussed next.

Auditory—motor plasticity

At the neurophysiological level, using the frequency following response, it has been shown that the subcortical encoding of speech presented in background noise is more robust in musicians compared to nonmusicians (Musacchia, Sams, Skoe, & Kraus, 2007; Parbery-Clark et al., 2009; Russo, Nicol, Zecker, Hayes, & Kraus, 2005; Wong, Skoe, Russo, Dees, & Kraus, 2007; see Chandrasekaran & Kraus, 2010; Kraus & Chandrasekaran, 2010 for reviews). Although these enhancements are at the subcortical level, it is thought that they are due to top-down control or changes in long-term potentiation, which arise via the corticofugal pathway (Sörqvist, Stenfelt, & Rönnberg, 2012; Suga, 2008; Suga & Ma, 2003; Tzounopoulos & Kraus, 2009). This idea was based on the reverse hierarchy theory, which states that perceptual learning is a top-down process, and as perceptual learning progresses, the associated neural plasticity will move to lower level brain structures (Ahissar & Hochstein, 2004). Short-term music training (2 weeks) that involved both an auditory and motor component was found to improve auditory processing abilities and enhance cortical responses to auditory oddballs (Lappe et al., 2008, 2011). It is therefore possible that music training first impacts the connection between the auditory—motor system at the cortical level, and then as music training continues, neuronal connections in subcortical structures are refined via top-down mechanisms.

Accordingly, enhancements to speech perception due to music training could start at the level of the motor system in the cortex. For the information from the motor system to descend the corticofugal pathway and impact auditory neurons, there would have to be a consistent mapping of specific motor activations to specific acoustic information. Indeed, the shape of the vocal tract, especially the shape and orientation of the tongue is directly correlated with the frequency of the first three formants (F1, F2, F3) in vowel sounds (Ladefoged, Harshman, Goldstein, & Rice, 1978). For instance, higher tongue positions are associated with a lower frequency F1, while lower tongue positions are associated with a higher frequency F1. Similarly, forward tongue positions are associated with a higher frequency F2, while back tongue positions are associated with a lower frequency F2. Thus production of any vowel sound is associated with a specific tongue position. Interestingly, when speech is presented in background noise, the place of articulation that leads to variability in F2 is the most difficult feature to detect based on acoustic features alone; however, it is one of the easier features to detect based on the movement of a talker's lips (Miller & Nicely, 1955). Interestingly, musicians have greater neural differentiation of the F2 consonant to vowel transition compared to nonmusicians (Parbery-Clark, Tierney, Strait, & Kraus, 2012). Older musicians exhibited a similar advantage compared to older nonmusicians (Parbery-Clark, Anderson, Hittner, & Kraus, 2012). Importantly, the differences between musicians and nonmusicians were further enhanced when speech material was presented with corresponding videos of lip movements (Musacchia et al., 2007). This pattern of results suggests that the observation of motor movements can further facilitate speech processing in musicians. Over time, this strengthened auditory–motor connection could give rise to neuroplastic modulations that extend to the level of the brain stem via the corticofugal pathway. This plasticity, while based on a visual input, would not require a visual input for support, as it would be related to an enhanced encoding of acoustic features that relate to a specific pattern of articulation. If observing motor movements is a critical part of this plasticity, then it is possible that musician advantages for auditory processing are driven by stronger integration between the auditory and motor systems.

The motor system as a scaffold

In younger adults, the association of musicianship to enhanced processing of speech appears to be related to enhanced activity in the speech–motor system (Du & Zatorre, 2017). In older adults, preliminary evidence suggests that short-term music training improves the ability to process speech due to functional enhancements in brain regions involved in the speech–motor system (Fleming et al., 2019; Zendel et al., 2019). At the same time, research examining age-related changes in speech production revealed no significant age effects in motor or premotor regions (Sörös, Bose, Sokoloff, Graham, & Stuss, 2011; Tremblay, Dick, & Small, 2013). If the motor system that supports speech production is relatively preserved in older adults, then the motor system may be a candidate to develop cognitive scaffolds from which other abilities can be refined, such as speech perception.

This motor system scaffold could develop automatically due to the intrinsic connections between the auditory, sensory, and motor systems. The representation of incoming auditory information is enhanced in belt areas around the primary auditory cortex, when it is paired with tactile sensory information (Foxe et al., 2002; Kayser, Petkov, Augath, & Logothetis, 2005). This pairing would occur naturally when playing piano, and would provide a more robust representation of the auditory information as it is processed. This enhancement is critical, as developing a motor skill (e.g., playing a musical instrument) requires gathering and processing of sensory information related to the action (Wolpert, Diedrichsen, & Flanagan, 2011). Thus when learning to play a musical instrument, the learner must integrate the auditory information in order to refine the associated motor action in the future. Over time, this leads to a greater connectivity between the auditory and motor systems and may lead to plasticity in motor and premotor cortices and regions that connect the auditory and motor systems. Given that age-related changes in the peripheral auditory system decrease the quality of the incoming acoustic signal, this strengthened pathway might be exploited to help refine this impoverished incoming auditory information. Indeed, integration of multiple modalities can improve the processing of a single sensory modality (Ernst & Bülthoff, 2004). In music training, the constant pairing of an auditory input with both a motor command and sensory feedback via the finger (e.g., in the case of playing piano) would increase the cortical representation of the auditory signal. After training, the strengthened auditory—motor system may better process speech information. Given that the motor system is naturally involved in speech perception the enhancement would occur automatically. The result would be that speech processing is enhanced by music training.

Applying the speech—motor system scaffold

There is already some evidence that instrumental training leads to improved speech-in-noise perception in older adults due to neuroplasticity in auditory—motor regions. Zendel et al. (2019) and Fleming et al. (2019) randomly assigned older adults to receive piano lessons, video game training, or no activity for a period of 6 months and evaluated speech-in-noise performance (word detection in silence, and quiet and loud multi-talker babble background noise) as well as late positive event-related potential (ERP) components extracted from EEG data before, half-way, and after training (or no training in the case of the no-contact controls). Performance when background noise was loudest improved only in the group that received music training (Zendel et al., 2019). That is, 6 months of music lessons improved the ability to understand speech in noise in older adults. In terms of cortical effects, participants in the music group showed an increased positivity over fronto-left electrodes that were related to their increased ability to understand speech in noise (Zendel et al., 2019). A source analysis of the ERP data

(Zendel et al., 2019) and fMRI data collected in parallel (Fleming et al., 2019) suggest that these enhancements were related to structures in the speech—motor system, including the left inferior frontal gyrus (Broca's area), bilateral middle frontal gyrus (including the supplementary motor area), the supramarginal gyrus, and the cerebellum (Fleming et al., 2019; Zendel et al., 2019). Training-related change in these regions was associated with enhanced ability to understand speech across all levels of background noise, supporting the connection between speech understanding and the speech—motor system (Fleming et al., 2019). Moreover, other research has identified these regions as being critical for both speech production and speech perception tasks, further supporting the idea that they are part of the speech—motor system (Vigneau et al., 2006).

These results are encouraging, demonstrating an improvement in speech-in-noise perception and neural processing in older listeners due to a late-life musical training program. Such training programs could be developed for various instruments such as piano, guitar, ukulele, bass, percussion, or singing. These instruments are suggested as they are relatively accessible in terms of fine motor movement and cost (as opposed to the violin for example) and are likely to attract interest. Training programs should continue to be implemented and evaluated, focusing on using cognitive scaffolding through motor tasks which can be paired with auditory processing, memory, attention, or executive functions. These cognitive abilities have all been associated with understanding speech in noise, and enhancing them could also improve the ability to understand speech.

The case for a music perception scaffold

There is a long history of examining auditory processing abilities in musicians. Many early studies demonstrated that musicians performed better than nonmusicians on music-based auditory perceptual tasks. One of the earliest studies found that musicians were better than nonmusicians at recognizing melodies presented earlier in the experiment when melodies were presented monaurally to the right ear (Bever & Chiarello, 1974). Given that the left hemisphere was thought to be the center of language processing, a right ear advantage[1] suggested that musicians treat music like a language (Bever & Chiarello, 1974). This finding provided the foundation for many studies on the impact of music training on hearing abilities such as pitch, rhythm, harmony, and timbre perception, as well as auditory streaming and attentional allocation.

Over the next decades, numerous studies demonstrated that musicians had better auditory processing abilities in both musical and nonmusical

---

1. Due to brain lateralization, sensory input is processed in the opposite hemisphere of the brain: all input from the right side of the body is processed in the left hemisphere and vice versa.

situations. For example, musicians, compared to nonmusicians, perceived differences in pitch more categorically, like notes in a musical scale (e.g., like a language where pitch is a unit; Zatorre & Halpern, 1979); musicians could identify tone intervals better than nonmusicians (Siegel & Siegel, 1977); musicians could identify the emotional content of a speech prosody better than nonmusicians (Nilsonne & Sundberg, 1985); musicians could identify chord changes better than nonmusicians (Morais, Peretz, Gudanski, & Guiard, 1982); and musicians were better than nonmusicians at identifying tempo changes in musical sequences (Madsen, 1979). Subsequent research revealed that even some very basic auditory processing abilities were enhanced in musicians compared to nonmusicians. For example, auditory streams persist longer in musicians (Beauvois & Meddis, 1997); musicians are less susceptible to timbral influences on pitch perception (Pitt, 1994); musicians have enhanced frequency discrimination abilities (Besson, Schön, Moreno, Santos, & Magne, 2007; Micheyl, Delhommeau, Perrot, & Oxenham, 2006); and musicians have enhanced sound duration discrimination abilities (Jeon & Fricke, 1997), when compared to nonmusicians. This list is not exhaustive and only highlights the earliest investigations into the auditory advantages observed in musicians.

There is now a small, but significant body of literature highlighting the benefits of musical training on hearing abilities for nonmusical material in older adults (Alain, Zendel, Hutka, & Bidelman, 2014; Kraus & Chandrasekaran, 2010). Two of the first studies that examined hearing abilities in older adult musicians found advantages for lifelong musicians (Parbery-Clark et al., 2011; Zendel & Alain, 2012). Parbery-Clark et al. (2011) compared older (i.e., 45–65 years) musicians and nonmusicians on three speech-in-noise tasks: QuickSIN (Killion et al., 2004), HINT (Nilsson et al., 1994), and WIN (Wilson, 1993). They found a musician advantage across all three tasks that was related to both auditory working memory (subtest of the Woodcock–Johnson III Test of Cognitive Abilities; Woodcock et al., 2001) and auditory temporal acuity (backwards masking subtest of the IHR Multicenter Battery for Auditory Processing; Moore, Ferguson, Edmondson-Jones, Ratib, & Riley, 2010). Zendel and Alain (2012) compared musicians and nonmusicians who ranged in age from 18–91 years, on the QuickSIN test and found slower rates of age-related decline on the QuickSIN in musicians compared to nonmusicians. In this study, the average 70-year-old musician performed as well as the average 50-year-old nonmusician on the QuickSIN test. Zendel and Alain (2012) also reported that older musicians were better than older nonmusicians at segregating concurrent sounds based on harmonic structure, and detecting a small silent gap.

Neurophysiological evidence

At the level of the cortex, auditory processing can be assessed by scalp-recorded brain potentials (i.e., ERPs). One interesting pattern that has come out of this work is that aging impacts how acoustic information is processed. In general, older adults are able to rely on attention-dependent processing (i.e., using knowledge to make predictions, focusing on acoustic features relevant to the task, etc.) to overcome age-related decline in the transduction and encoding of acoustic information. In other words, while hearing abilities decline in older adults, their listening skills improve to compensate (Pichora-Fuller et al., 2016). This "listening" benefit is likely further enhanced in musicians or by musical training, which explains why older musicians can understand speech in noise better than older nonmusicians (Alain et al., 2014).

One way to observe how music is processed is to use ERPs. ERPs represent phase-locked neural responses to an auditory stimulus. ERP responses from around 50 ms poststimulus onset until about 250 ms are thought to represent activity from the primary auditory cortex, and secondary auditory regions along the superior temporal plane (Näätänen & Picton, 1987). The peaks of these responses are referred to by their electrical polarity ([P]ositive or [N]egative), and the order in which the peak occurs. Typically, a transient acoustic stimulus will evoke a P1−N1−P2 response, regardless of the attentional state of the listener. A P3 response is usually evoked when a listener is asked to attend to the stimulus and make some sort of a judgment (Polich, 2007). In older adults, there have only been a few studies that have investigated how musicianship moderates the auditory evoked response. Aging tends to increase the amplitude of the P1−N1−P2 component of the auditory evoked response, and this enhancement is thought to be related to a decrease in frontal inhibitory activity (Alho, Woods, Algazi, Knight, & Naatanen, 1994; Knight, Hillyard, Woods, & Neville, 1980; Zendel & Alain, 2014). This creates a challenge when interpreting the results of auditory ERP studies comparing older and younger musicians and nonmusicians because many studies comparing younger musicians to nonmusicians report enhanced auditory evoked responses that are associated with enhanced hearing due to neuroplasticity (Koelsch, Schröger, & Tervaniemi, 1999; Shahin, Bosnyak, Trainor, & Roberts, 2003; Shahin, Roberts, Pantev, Trainor, & Ross, 2005). In other words, when comparing older adults to younger adults, the larger P1−N1−P2 in older adults is usually associated with a decline in hearing abilities due to decreased frontal inhibition, whereas when comparing younger musicians to nonmusicians, the enhanced P1−N1−P2 in musicians is associated with improved hearing abilities due to neuroplasticity associated with music training. These neuroelectric brain responses are usually evoked by short transient tones, and thus are thought to represent the synchronized neural activity evoked by a transient tone.

A study examining concurrent sound segregation, or the ability to separate simultaneously occurring sounds, found that the older musician advantage was related to attention-dependent processing (Zendel & Alain, 2013). In this study, participants were presented with a harmonic complex, where the third harmonic could either be in-tune with the complex, or mistuned by 1%, 2%, 4%, 8%, or 16%. EEG data was collected while participants indicated whether they perceived one or two distinct sounds, where greater mistuning resulted in an increased likelihood of perceiving a complex tone and a pure tone simultaneously rather than a single complex tone (Moore, Glasberg, & Peters, 1986). Older and younger musicians were more likely to report hearing a second tone when the harmonic complex was mistuned by above 2% (Zendel & Alain, 2013). Despite the similarities between older and younger musicians in terms of their perceptual judgments, the electrophysiological data revealed a different pattern of results. During passive listening, a mistuned harmonic complex evoked an object-related negativity (ORN) that overlapped the N1 (Alain, Arnott, & Picton, 2001). During active listening, where participants made a perceptual judgment, the ORN was followed by a positive deflection that occurred around 400 ms (P400) (Alain, Arnott, et al., 2001). This pattern suggests that the ORN represents the automatic detection of acoustic features that suggest two simultaneous sound sources, while the P400 represents the perception of two simultaneous sound sources. In younger adults, both the ORN and P400 were enhanced in musicians compared to nonmusicians (Zendel & Alain, 2009, 2013). In older adults, the ORN was similar between musicians and nonmusicians, but the P400 was enhanced in older musicians compared to the other three groups (Zendel & Alain, 2013). Given that the P400 is thought to index the conscious perception of two separate sound objects, the results suggest that older musicians overcome age-related decline in the early stages of auditory processing through enhanced listening.

In another study that examined the cortical response to a harmonic complex, an age-related increase in P1 amplitude was observed, but musicians, both older and younger, had a reduced P1 amplitude compared to age-matched nonmusicians (Zendel & Alain, 2014). Interestingly, this difference was observed only during a passive listening task, and was eliminated when participants were asked to make a judgment about the incoming acoustic stimulus (i.e., active listening task). During active listening, late positive activity from right auditory regions, along the superior temporal plane, was enhanced in older musicians compared to older nonmusicians, younger musicians, and younger nonmusicians (Zendel & Alain, 2014). Activity in the right auditory cortex is associated with processing spectral information from the incoming acoustic stimulus (Warrier et al., 2009; Zatorre, 1988), suggesting that older musicians are better able to focus their listening to acoustic features that are critical for the task being performed. The underlying cause of this enhanced listening could be due to either long-term neuroplasticity in conscious auditory perception, or to enhanced motivation of older musicians to perform well on hearing tests.

The preservation of music perception

In addition to enhanced "listening" abilities in older adults, which appears to be further enhanced in older musicians, music perception also seems to be relatively preserved in older adults. To date, there have only been a few studies that examined how music perception is affected by age. Investigations of tonal structure using a classic probe tone paradigm (Krumhansl & Kessler, 1982) in older listeners indicated that the perceived stability of tonic chord tones compared to scale tones and chromatic tones is sharpened in older adults (Halpern, Kwak, Bartlett, & Dowling, 1996). A study by Lynch and Steffens (1994) compared mistuning detection abilities in tonal and atonal music in younger and older listeners and found that older listeners' performance was only worse than younger listeners' performance in atonal music, but similar for tonal music. Neurophysiological investigations of tonal processing have revealed that electrical brain responses and the ability to classify or detect unexpected, or out-of-tune notes in a melody are similar in both older and younger adults (Halpern et al., 2017; Lagrois, Peretz, & Zendel, 2018).

The study of musical memory generally finds adverse effects of age on memory performance for music (Andrews, Dowling, Bartlett, & Halpern, 1998; Bartlett, Halpern, & Dowling, 1995; Dowling, Bartlett, Halpern, & Andrews, 2008; Halpern & Bartlett, 2002; Halpern, Bartlett, & Dowling, 1995, 1998), where older adults achieve fewer hits and more false alarms on same/different and recognition tasks where contour, tempo, and source identification are manipulated. However, one study investigated similarity judgements between melodies that were manipulated in terms of mode, rhythm, and contour found that older and younger listeners perceived similarity in the same way, where melodies that differed in mode were perceived as more similar than melodies that differed in contour, which in turn were perceived as more similar than melodies that differed in rhythm (Halpern et al., 1998). The only exception to this pattern were older musicians, who found melodies differing in rhythm more similar than melodies differing in contour (Halpern et al., 1998). Older listeners were also no different from younger listeners at identifying very slow melodies, though they could not recognize these melodies when played at a tempo as fast as could be recognized by younger listeners (Andrews et al., 1998; Dowling et al., 2008). This body of literature suggests that given enough time to "digest" the musical material being presented, older adults can perform memory and recognition tasks just as well as younger listeners when using musical stimuli. Importantly, most real-world music is within these parameters. Furthermore, while episodic memory suffers with age, older adults appear to have preserved semantic memory for music, even in older adults with mild-to-severe dementia (Cuddy et al., 2012; Vanstone et al., 2012). Although there is a general cognitive slowing with age, pairing preserved cognitive abilities with music perception tasks that are most similar to real music may be the key to training programs designed to improve day-to-day hearing abilities in older adults.

Applying the music perception scaffold

Having discussed how lifelong musical training can slow the decline of auditory—cognitive abilities and how music perception seems to be generally preserved in old age, we can offer some suggestions for how a music-based training program could improve listening abilities in older adults. Since basic music perception skills such as pitch, time, mode, contour, and harmony perception seem preserved in older adults, we can use this existing scaffold to train and improve higher-level listening skills. After all, evidence suggests that while older musicians' hearing declines equally to nonmusicians', musical experience trains them to be better *listeners* (Alain et al., 2014). The goal is that focusing on refining these skills in a training program will have a similar effect to formal musical training. The listening skills we will discuss are auditory stream segregation and musical memory.

Assuming a training program spanning several weeks, training could be divided into multiple types of tasks to provide variation with varying levels of difficulty within each task. In the case of auditory stream segregation, one type of task could be to detect a deviant (e.g., timbre or pitch) in a familiar melody interleaved with distractor tones (Dowling, 1973). Within this task, difficulty can be adaptively adjusted to each individual by modifying the similarity between the distractor tones and the familiar melody, where more similarity equates to more difficulty. Familiar melodies could be tailored to each individual for a more engaging experience that is also easier as there is no need to learn new material. There is also evidence that older adults perceive speech in music better when music is familiar than when it is unfamiliar (Russo & Pichora-Fuller, 2008). A variation of this task could be to perform the same deviant detection with unfamiliar melodies written for the training program. This would not only engage streaming skills but also memory for new content.

A task with more ecological stimuli might be to focus on a particular instrument or voice in a piece of music. For example, in a string quartet it would almost always be easier to focus on the violins but more difficult to pick out the cello line (picking out the viola line could be left for extra keen individuals!). Orchestral works provide a much wider range of instruments to choose from. Again, working with familiar and loved works, the individual could either follow program suggestions of easy/medium or difficult instruments to focus on, or choose their own desired level of challenge. While this task does not provide any objective measurement of performance, it is designed to be enjoyable, engaging, and challenging while focusing on developing auditory stream segregation skills. As older adults succeed at this task, speech could be used in place of instruments as targets and background in order to scaffold speech perception onto music perception abilities.

Turning to musical memory, a straightforward task could be to either have the individual sing or playback a given novel melody, where that melody is adaptively modified in terms of complexity. Complexity can be manipulated in terms of length of the melody (longer = complex), number of contour changes (more = complex), degree of tonality (low = complex), and interval patterns (leaps = complex). This type of task would require transcription software capable of measuring the degree of success of the singing or playback. If this is not possible, a same/different or deviant detection task can also be applied here.

The tasks described above are only a few suggestions for the application of the music perception scaffold to improve listening skills in older adults. Given that music perception is preserved and music listening is still widely enjoyed in older adults, narrowly training specific listening skills that musicians develop throughout their own training should impart similar benefits. The auditory streaming tasks mirror musicians' transcription and ensemble listening skills while the musical memory tasks mirror both transcription and performance memorization skills. We hope that these suggestions provide some exciting research avenues, or at the very least, productive discussions in the field.

Summary and conclusion

It is likely that hearing abilities in older adults can be improved using music as a cognitive scaffold. The two potential cognitive scaffolds are the speech−motor system and music perception, both of which demonstrate preservation in older age. Since they are preserved, these mechanisms could potentially act as cognitive scaffolds through which older adults can develop better listening skills that can in turn improve their speech-in-noise perception. New forms of auditory rehabilitation could be examined based on this cognitive scaffold model. While the speech−motor-based training strengthens connectivity in the speech−motor system through music performance, the music perception-based training targets high-level listening skills through music listening. These types training programs could be combined, with some performance and some listening, or implemented alone. The choice of training program could also depend on the individual seeking training. For example, motor abilities could be an important factor to consider when choosing a training program. Restricted motor abilities may exclude instrumental performance but could be integrated into the listening-based training program by developing tasks that include tapping or conducting for example. Other individual factors may also play a role, for example, cognitive abilities, education level, or hearing abilities could impact success in the proposed training programs. Another important factor to consider is the length of these training programs. Current studies range from 2 weeks of training (Lappe et al., 2008) to 6 months of training (Zendel et al., 2019) with positive results. However, whether these positive effects are maintained in the long term is unknown and future research will need to explore length and intensity (i.e., hours per week) of training for best results. As research answers these questions, individualized forms of music-based auditory rehabilitation could become important at preserving quality of life for older adults.

References

Ahissar, M., & Hochstein, S. (2004). The reverse hierarchy theory of visual perceptual learning. *Trends in Cognitive Sciences*, *8*(10), 457−464. Available from https://doi.org/10.1016/j.tics.2004.08.011.

Alain, C., Arnott, S. R., & Picton, T. W. (2001). Bottom−up and top−down influences on auditory scene analysis: Evidence from event-related brain potentials. *Journal of Experimental Psychology: Human Perception and Performance*, *27*(5), 1072.

Alain, C., Zendel, B. R., Hutka, S., & Bidelman, G. M. (2014). Turning down the noise: The benefit of musical training on the aging auditory brain. *Hearing Research*, *308*. Available from https://doi.org/10.1016/j.heares.2013.06.008.

Alho, K., Woods, D. L., Algazi, A., Knight, R. T., & Naatanen, R. (1994). Lesions of frontal cortex diminish the auditory mismatch negativity. *Electroencephalography and Clinical Neurophysiology*, *91*, 353−362.

Andrews, M. W., Dowling, W. J., Bartlett, J. C., & Halpern, A. R. (1998). Identification of speeded and slowed familiar melodies by younger, middle-aged, and older musicians and nonmusicians. *Psychology and Aging*, *13*(3), 462−471. Available from https://doi.org/10.1037/0882-7974.13.3.462.

Bartlett, J. C., Halpern, A. R., & Dowling, W. J. (1995). Recognition of familiar and unfamiliar melodies in normal aging and Alzheimer's disease. *Memory & Cognition*, *23*(5), 531−546.

Beauvois, M., & Meddis, R. (1997). Time decay of auditory stream biasing. *Perception & Psychophysics*, *59*(1), 81−86.

Besson, M., Schön, D., Moreno, S., Santos, A., & Magne, C. (2007). Influence of musical expertise and musical training on pitch processing in music and language. *Restorative Neurology and Neuroscience*, *25*(3−4), 399−410.

Bever, T., & Chiarello, R. (1974). Cerebral dominance in musicians and nonmusicians. *Science*, *185*(4150), 537−539.

Chan, T.M.V., & Alain, C. (2020). Theories of cognitive aging: A look at potential benefits of music training on the aging brain. In L.L. Cuddy, S. Belleville, and A. Moussard (Eds.), *Music and the Aging Brain* (In press).

Chandrasekaran, B., & Kraus, N. (2010). The scalp-recorded brainstem response to speech: Neural origins and plasticity. *Psychophysiology*, *47*(2), 236−246. Available from https://doi.org/10.1111/j.1469-8986.2009.00928.x.

Cherry, E. C. (1953). Some experiments on the recognition of speech with on and with two ears. *The Journal of the Acoustical Society of America*, *25*(5), 975−979. Available from https://doi.org/10.1121/1.1907373.

Coffey, E. B. J., Mogilever, N. B., & Zatorre, R. J. (2017). Speech-in-noise perception in musicians: A review. *Hearing Research*, *352*, 49−69. Available from https://doi.org/10.1016/j.heares.2017.02.006.

Cuddy, L. L., Duffin, J. M., Gill, S. S., Brown, C. L., Sikka, R., & Vanstone, A. D. (2012). Memory for melodies and lyrics in Alzheimer's disease. *Music Perception: An Interdisciplinary Journal, 29*(5), 479−491.

Dowling, W. J. (1973). The perception of interleaved melodies. *Cognitive Psychology, 5*(3), 322−337.

Dowling, W. J., Bartlett, J. C., Halpern, A. R., & Andrews, M. W. (2008). Melody recognition at fast and slow tempos: Effects of age, experience, and familiarity. *Perception & Psychophysics, 70*(3), 496−502. Available from https://doi.org/10.3758/PP.

Du, Y., Buchsbaum, B. R., Grady, C. L., & Alain, C. (2014). Noise differentially impacts phoneme representations in the auditory and speech motor systems. *Proceedings of the National Academy of Sciences of the United States of America, 111*(19), 7126−7131. Available from https://doi.org/10.1073/pnas.1318738111.

Du, Y., & Zatorre, R. J. (2017). Musical training sharpens and bonds ears and tongue to hear speech better. *Proceedings of the National Academy of Sciences of the United States of America*, 12223. Available from https://doi.org/10.1073/pnas.1712223114.

Dubinsky, E., Wood, E. A., Nespoli, G., & Russo, F. A. (2019). Short-term choir singing supports speech-in-noise perception and neural pitch strength in older adults with age-related hearing loss. *Frontiers in Neuroscience, 13*.

Ernst, M. O., & Bülthoff, H. H. (2004). Merging the senses into a robust percept. *Trends in Cognitive Sciences, 8*(4), 162−169. Available from https://doi.org/10.1016/j.tics.2004.02.002.

Fleming, D., Belleville, S., Peretz, I., West, G. L., & Zendel, B. R. (2019). The effects of short-term musical training on the neural processing of speech-in noise in older adults. *Brain and Cognition, 136*(103592), 1−12.

Foxe, J. J., Wylie, G. R., Martinez, A., Schroeder, C. E., Javit, D. C., Guilfoyle, D., ... Murray, M. M. (2002). Auditory-somatosensory multisensory processing in auditory association cortex: An fMRI study. *Journal of Neurophysiology, 88*, 540−543. Available from https://doi.org/10.1152/jn.00694.2001.

Fujioka, T., Zendel, B. R., & Ross, B. (2010). Endogenous neuromagnetic activity for mental hierarchy of timing. *Journal of Neuroscience, 30*(9). Available from https://doi.org/10.1523/JNEUROSCI.3086-09.2010.

Gosselin, P. A., & Gagné, J. (2011). Older adults expend more listening effort than young adults recognizing speech in noise. *Journal of Speech, Language, and Hearing Research, 54*, 944−958. Available from https://doi.org/10.1044/1092-4388(2010/10-0069)a.

Grahn, J. A., & Brett, M. (2007). Rhythm and beat perception in motor areas of the brain. *Journal of Cognitive Neuroscience, 19*(5), 893−906.

Halpern, A. R., & Bartlett, J. C. (2002). Aging and memory for music: A review. *Psychomusicology, 18*(1−2), 10−27. Available from https://doi.org/10.1037/h0094054.

Halpern, A. R., Bartlett, J. C., & Dowling, W. J. (1995). Aging and experience in the recognition of musical transpositions. *Psychology and Aging, 10*(3), 325−342.

Halpern, A. R., Bartlett, J. C., & Dowling, W. J. (1998). Perception of mode, rhythm, and contour in unfamiliar melodies: Effects of age and experience. *Music Perception, 15*(4), 335−355.

Halpern, A. R., Kwak, S., Bartlett, J. C., & Dowling, W. J. (1996). Effects of aging and musical experience on the representation of tonal hierarchies. *Psychology and Aging, 11*(2), 235−246.

Halpern, A. R., Zioga, I., Shankleman, M., Lindsen, J., Pearce, M. T., & Bhattarcharya, J. (2017). That note sounds wrong! Age-related effects in processing of musical expectation. *Brain and Cognition, 113*, 1−9. Available from https://doi.org/10.1016/j.bandc.2016.12.006.

Jeon, J. Y., & Fricke, F. R. (1997). Duration of perceived and performed sounds. *Psychology of Music, 25*(1), 70−83. Available from https://doi.org/10.1177/0305735697251006.

Kayser, C., Petkov, C. I., Augath, M., & Logothetis, N. K. (2005). Integration of touch and sound in auditory cortex. *Neuron, 48*(2), 373−384. Available from https://doi.org/10.1016/j.neuron.2005.09.018.

Killion, M. C., Niquette, P. A., Gudmundsen, G. I., Revit, L. J., & Banerjee, S. (2004). Development of a quick speech-in-noise test for measuring signal-to-noise ratio loss in normal-hearing and hearing-impaired listeners. *The Journal of the Acoustical Society of America, 116*(4), 2395−2405.

Knight, R. T., Hillyard, S. A., Woods, D. L., & Neville, H. J. (1980). The effects of frontal and temporal-parietal lesions on the auditory evoked potential in man. *Electroencephalography and Clinical Neurophysiology, 50*, 112−124.

Koelsch, S., Schröger, E., & Tervaniemi, M. (1999). Superior pre-attentive auditory processing in musicians. *Neuroreport, 10*(6), 1309−1313.

Kraus, N., & Chandrasekaran, B. (2010). Music training for the development of auditory skills. *Nature Reviews Neuroscience, 11*(8), 599−605. Available from https://doi.org/10.1038/nrn2882.

Krumhansl, C. L., & Kessler, E. J. (1982). Tracing the dynamic changes in perceived tonal organization in a spatial representation of musical keys. *Psychological Review, 89*(4), 334−368.

Ladefoged, P., Harshman, R., Goldstein, L., & Rice, L. (1978). Generating vocal tract shapes from formant frequencies. *The Journal of the Acoustical Society of America, 64*(4), 1027−1035. Available from https://doi.org/10.1121/1.382086.

Lagrois, M.-É., Peretz, I., & Zendel, B. R. (2018). Neurophysiological and behavioral differences between older and younger adults when processing violations of tonal structure in music. *Frontiers in Neuroscience, 12*(54), 1−15. Available from https://doi.org/10.3389/fnins.2018.00054.

Lappe, C., Herholz, S. C., Trainor, L. J., & Pantev, C. (2008). Cortical plasticity induced by short-term unimodal and multimodal musical training. *Journal of Neuroscience, 28*(39), 9632−9639. Available from https://doi.org/10.1523/JNEUROSCI.2254-08.2008.

Lappe, C., Trainor, L. J., Herholz, S. C., & Pantev, C. (2011). Cortical plasticity induced by short-term multimodal musical rhythm training. *PLoS One, 6*(6). Available from https://doi.org/10.1371/journal.pone.0021493.

Liberman, A. M., & Mattingly, I. G. (1985). The motor theory of speech perception revised. *Cognition, 21*(1), 1−36.

Lynch, M. P., & Steffens, M. L. (1994). Effects of aging on processing of novel musical structure. *Journal of Gerontology, 49*(4), P165−P172.

Madsen, C. K. (1979). Modulated beat discrimination among musicians and nonmusicians. *Journal of Research in Music Education, 27*(2), 57−67.

Micheyl, C., Delhommeau, K., Perrot, X., & Oxenham, A. J. (2006). Influence of musical and psychoacoustical training on pitch discrimination. *Hearing Research, 219*(1−2), 36−47. Available from https://doi.org/10.1016/j.heares.2006.05.004.

Miller, G. A., & Nicely, P. E. (1955). An analysis of perceptual confusions among some English consonants. *The Journal of the Acoustical Society of America, 27*(2), 338−352. Available from https://doi.org/10.1121/1.1907526.

Moore, B. C., Glasberg, B. R., & Peters, R. W. (1986). Thresholds for hearing mistuned partials as separate tones in harmonic complexes. *The Journal of the Acoustical Society of America, 80*(2), 479−483.

Moore, D. R., Ferguson, M. A., Edmondson-Jones, A. M., Ratib, S., & Riley, A. (2010). Nature of auditory processing disorder in children. *Pediatrics, 126*(2), e382−e390.

Morais, J., Peretz, I., Gudanski, M., & Guiard, Y. (1982). Ear asymmetry for chord recognition in musicians and nonmusicians. *Neuropsychologia, 20*(3), 351−354.

Musacchia, G., Sams, M., Skoe, E., & Kraus, N. (2007). Musicians have enhanced subcortical auditory and audiovisual processing of speech and music. *Proceedings of the National Academy of Sciences of the United States of America, 104*(40), 15894−15898. Available from https://doi.org/10.1073/pnas.0701498104.

Näätänen, R., & Picton, T. (1987). The N1 wave of the human electric and magnetic response to sound: A review and an analysis of the component structure. *Psychophysiology, 24*(4), 375−425.

Nilsson, M., Soli, S. D., & Sullivan, J. A. (1994). Development of the Hearing in Noise Test for the measurement of speech reception thresholds in quiet and in noise. *The Journal of the Acoustical Society of America, 95*(2), 1085−1099.

Nilsonne, Å., & Sundberg, J. (1985). Differences in ability of musicians and nonmusicians to judge emotional state from the fundamental frequency of voice samples. *Music Perception, 2*(4), 507−516.

Nishitani, N., Amunts, K., & Hari, R. (2005). Broca's region: From action to language. *Physiology, 20*, 60−69.

Parbery-Clark, A., Anderson, S., Hittner, E., & Kraus, N. (2012). Musical experience offsets age-related delays in neural timing. *Neurobiology of Aging, 33*(7), 1483.e1−1483.e4. Available from https://doi.org/10.1016/j.neurobiolaging.2011.12.015.

Parbery-Clark, A., Skoe, E., & Kraus, N. (2009). Musical experience limits the degradative effects of background noise on the neural processing of sound. *The Journal of Neuroscience, 29*(45), 14100−14107. Available from https://doi.org/10.1523/JNEUROSCI.3256-09.2009.

Parbery-Clark, A., Skoe, E., Lam, C., & Kraus, N. (2009). Musician enhancement for speech-in-noise. *Ear and Hearing, 30*(6), 653−661. Available from https://doi.org/10.1097/AUD.0b013e3181b412e9.

Parbery-Clark, A., Strait, D. L., Anderson, S., Hittner, E., & Kraus, N. (2011). Musical experience and the aging auditory system: Implications for cognitive abilities and hearing speech in noise. *PLoS One, 6*(5). Available from https://doi.org/10.1371/journal.pone.0018082.

Parbery-Clark, A., Tierney, A., Strait, D. L., & Kraus, N. (2012). Musicians have fine-tuned neural distinction of speech syllables. *Neuroscience, 219*, 111−119. Available from https://doi.org/10.1016/j.neuroscience.2012.05.042.

Park, D. C., & Reuter-Lorenz, P. (2009). The adaptive brain: Aging and neurocognitive scaffolding. *Annual Review of Psychology, 60*, 173−196. Available from https://doi.org/10.1146/annurev.psych.59.103006.093656.

Pichora-fuller, M. K., Kramer, S. E., Eckert, M. A., Edwards, B., Hornsby, B. W. Y., Humes, L. E., ... Wingfield, A. (2016).). Hearing impairment and cognitive energy: The framework for understanding effortful listening (FUEL). *Ear and Hearing, 37*(S1), 5−27.

Pichora-Fuller, M. K., Schneider, B. A., & Daneman, M. (1995). How young and old adults listen to and remember speech in noise. *The Journal of the Acoustical Society of America, 97*(1), 593−608.

Pichora-Fuller, M. K., & Souza, P. E. (2003). Effects of aging on auditory processing of speech effects of aging on auditory processing of speech. *International Journal of Audiology, 42*(2), s11−s16. Available from https://doi.org/10.3109/14992020309074638.

Pitt, M. (1994). Perception of pitch and timbre by musically trained and untrained listeners. *Journal of Experimental Psychology: Human Perception and Performance, 20*(5), 976.

Polich, J. (2007). Updating P300: An integrative theory of P3a and P3b. *Clinical Neurophysiology*, *118*(10), 2128–2148. Available from https://doi.org/10.1016/j. clinph.2007.04.019.

Pulvermüller, F., Huss, M., Kherif, F., Martin, F., Hauk, O., & Shtyrov, Y. (2006). Motor cortex maps articulatory features of speech sounds. *Proceedings of the National Academy of Sciences of the United States of America*, *103*(20), 7865–7870.

Reuter-Lorenz, P. A., & Park, D. C. (2014). How does it STAC Up? Revisiting the scaffolding theory of aging and cognition. *Neuropsychology Review*, *24*(3), 355–370. Available from https://doi.org/10.1007/s11065-014-9270-9.

Russo, F. A., & Pichora-Fuller, M. K. (2008). Tune in or tune out: Age-related differences in listening to speech in music. *Ear and Hearing*, *29*(5), 746–760.

Russo, N. M., Nicol, T. G., Zecker, S. G., Hayes, E. A., & Kraus, N. (2005). Auditory training improves neural timing in the human brainstem. *Behavioural Brain Research*, *156*(1), 95–103. Available from https://doi.org/10.1016/j.bbr.2004.05.012.

Schneider, B. A., Pichora-Fuller, M. K., & Daneman, M. (2010). Effects of senescent changes in audition and cognition on spoken language comprehension. In S. Gordon-Salant, R. D. Frisina, & A. N. Popper (Eds.), *Aging auditory system* (pp. 167–210). Springer, New York, NY.

Shahin, A., Bosnyak, D. J., Trainor, L. J., & Roberts, L. E. (2003). Enhancement of neuroplastic P2 and N1c auditory evoked potentials in musicians. *The Journal of Neuroscience*, *23*(13), 5545–5552.

Shahin, A., Roberts, L. E., Pantev, C., Trainor, L. J., & Ross, B. (2005). Modulation of P2 auditory-evoked responses by the spectral complexity of musical sounds. *Neuroreport*, *16* (16), 1781–1785.

Siegel, J. A., & Siegel, W. (1977). Absolute identification of notes and intervals by musicians. *Perception & Psychophysics*, *21*(2), 143–152.

Slater, J., & Kraus, N. (2016). The role of rhythm in perceiving speech in noise: A comparison of percussionists, vocalists and nonmusicians. *Cognitive Processing*, *17*(1), 79–87. Available from https://doi.org/10.1007/s10339-015-0740-7.

Sörös, P., Bose, A., Sokoloff, L. G., Graham, S. J., & Stuss, D. T. (2011). Age-related changes in the functional neuroanatomy of overt speech production. *Neurobiology of Aging*, *32*(8), 1505–1513.

Sörqvist, P., Stenfelt, S., & Rönnberg, J. (2012). Working memory capacity and visual–verbal cognitive load modulate auditory–sensory gating in the brainstem: Toward a unified view of attention. *Journal of cognitive neuroscience*, *24*(11), 2147–2154.

Suga, N. (2008). Role of corticofugal feedback in hearing. *Journal of Comparative Physiology A*, *194*(2), 169–183. Available from https://doi.org/10.1007/s00359-007-0274-2.

Suga, N., & Ma, X. (2003). Multiparametric corticofugal modulation and plasticity in the auditory system. *Nature Reviews Neuroscience*, *4*(10), 783–794. Available from https://doi.org/ 10.1038/nrn1222.

Tremblay, P., Dick, A. S., & Small, S. L. (2013). Functional and structural aging of the speech sensorimotor neural system: Functional magnetic resonance imaging evidence. *Neurobiology of Aging*, *34*(8), 1935–1951. Available from https://doi.org/10.1016/j. neurobiolaging.2013.02.004.

Tzounopoulos, T., & Kraus, N. (2009). Learning to encode timing: Mechanisms of plasticity in the auditory brainstem. *Neuron*, *62*(4), 463–469. Available from https://doi.org/10.1016/j. neuron.2009.05.002.

Vanstone, A. D., Sikka, R., Tangness, L., Sham, R., Garcia, A., & Cuddy, L. L. (2012). Episodic and semantic memory for melodies in Alzheimer's disease. *Music Perception: An Interdisciplinary Journal, 29*(5), 501−507.

Vigneau, M., Beaucousin, V., Herve, P. Y., Duffau, H., Crivello, F., Houde, O., . . . Tzourio-Mazoyer, N. (2006). Meta-analyzing left hemisphere language areas: phonology, semantics, and sentence processing. *Neuroimage, 30*(4), 1414−1432.

Warrier, C., Wong, P., Penhune, V., Zatorre, R., Parrish, T., Abrams, D., et al. (2009). Relating structure to function: Heschl's gyrus and acoustic processing. *Journal of Neuroscience, 29*, 61−69.

Watkins, K., & Paus, T. (2004). Modulation of motor excitability during speech perception: The role of Broca's area. *Journal of Cognitive Neuroscience, 16*(6), 978−987. Available from https://doi.org/10.1364/OE.21.015530.

Wilson, R. H. (1993). Development and use of auditory compact discs in auditory evaluation. *Journal of Rehabilitation Research and Development, 30*, 342.

Wilson, S. M., Saygin, A. P., Sereno, M. I., & Iacoboni, M. (2004). Listening to speech activates motor areas involved in speech production. *Nature Neuroscience, 7*(7), 701−702. Available from https://doi.org/10.1038/nn1263.

Wolpert, D. M., Diedrichsen, J., & Flanagan, J. R. (2011). Principles of sensorimotor learning. *Nature Reviews Neuroscience, 12*(12). Available from https://doi.org/10.1038/nrn3112.

Wong, P. C. M., Skoe, E., Russo, N. M., Dees, T., & Kraus, N. (2007). Musical experience shapes human brainstem encoding of linguistic pitch patterns. *Nature Neuroscience, 10*(4), 420−422. Available from https://doi.org/10.1038/nn1872.

Woodcock, R. W., Mather, N., McGrew, K. S., & Wendling, B. J. (2001). *Woodcock-Johnson III tests of cognitive abilities* (pp. 371−401). Itasca, IL: Riverside Publishing Company.

Zatorre, R. J. (1988). Pitch perception of complex tones and human temporal-lobe function. *Journal of the Acoustical Society of America, 84*, 566−572.

Zatorre, R. J., Chen, J. L., & Penhune, V. B. (2007). When the brain plays music: Auditory−motor interactions in music perception and production. *Nature Reviews Neuroscience, 8*(7), 547.

Zatorre, R. J., & Halpern, A. R. (1979). Identification, discrimination, and selective adaptation of simultaneous musical intervals. *Perception & Psychophysics, 26*(5), 384−395.

Zendel, B. R., & Alain, C. (2009). Concurrent sound segregation is enhanced in musicians. *Journal of Cognitive Neuroscience, 21*(8), 1488−1498. Available from https://doi.org/10.1162/jocn.2009.21140.

Zendel, B. R., & Alain, C. (2012). Musicians experience less age-related decline in central auditory processing. *Psychology and Aging, 27*(2). Available from https://doi.org/10.1037/a0024816.

Zendel, B. R., & Alain, C. (2013). The influence of lifelong musicianship on neurophysiological measures of concurrent sound segregation. *Journal of Cognitive Neuroscience, 25*(4), 503−516. Available from https://doi.org/10.1162/jocn_a_00329.

Zendel, B. R., & Alain, C. (2014). Enhanced attention-dependent activity in the auditory cortex of older musicians. *Neurobiology of Aging, 35*(1), 55−63. Available from https://doi.org/10.1016/j.neurobiolaging.2013.06.022.

Zendel, B. R., West, G. L., Belleville, S., & Peretz, I. (2019). Music training improves the ability to understand speech-in-noise in older adults. *Neurobiology of Aging, 82*, 102−115. Available from https://doi.org/10.1101/196030.

Part 4

The Power of Music in Rehabilitation and Care in Disordered Aging

Chapter 12

Benefits and limits of musical interventions in pathological aging

Hervé Platel and Mathilde Groussard

Normandy Univ, UNICAEN, PSL Research University, EPHE, INSERM, U1077, CHU de Caen, Cyceron, Caen, France

Introduction

In the absence of pharmacological treatment, most government health agencies support psychosocial interventions in patients with neurodegenerative diseases such as Alzheimer's disease. Thus for the past 10 years, nonpharmacological interventions using artistic media, and particularly music, have been largely supported and promoted. Many specialists in gerontology, from clinicians to researchers, are now recommending these strategies, finally lending credibility to years of empirical practice. Despite lack of solid scientific work and validated methods to support the relevance of these approaches, patients and their families report very positive feedback—creating an ambiguous situation. In their daily work, practitioners are clearly getting convinced of the interest and positive effects of artistic practices in supporting the autonomy loss of elderly persons in a fragile state. By interviewing patients living at home or in institutions, Sixmith and Gibson (2007) highlighted the importance of music in their daily lives. As an activity with multiple components, music is demonstrated to be very stimulating because, while providing a feeling of well-being, it facilitates social interactions, communication, and the evocation of autobiographical memories. However, the great diversity (not to say the heterogeneity) of proposals and application contexts, as well as the lack of scientific validation of these practices, have produced an understandable distrust of these nonpharmacological approaches.

Music and the Aging Brain. DOI: https://doi.org/10.1016/B978-0-12-817422-7.00012-2
317

Diversity and heterogeneity of musical interventions

It is crucial to specify the different kinds of musical interventions proposed to patients with neurodegenerative pathology. First, many of these interventions are presented as "music therapy." The word "therapy" brings already much confusion and raises numerous questions for family caregivers who may believe that musical interventions can heal. In the context of neurodegenerative diseases this word clearly connotes to "manage," "support," or "take care," rather than to "treat" or "cure." Thus in gerontology, to "take care" is an important part of the therapeutic program and support for wellness, better health, or vitality.

Music therapy is defined by the World Federation of Music Therapy (WFMT) as the use of music and/or its musical elements (sound, rhythm, melody, and harmony) by a qualified music therapist, with a client or group, in a process designed to facilitate and promote communication, relationships, learning, mobilization, expression, organization, and other relevant therapeutic objectives in order to meet physical, emotional, mental, social, and cognitive needs.

Music therapy interventions can thus be extremely diverse. There is also a traditional differentiation between two main techniques: active music therapy, which consists of using sound-producing objects, musical instruments or the voice, and receptive (or passive) music therapy, based on listening to music (Raglio & Gianelli, 2009). However, in practice, it has been found that music therapists tend to combine both techniques.

As we can see, there is no standard protocol for musical intervention for elderly patients. Similarly, the objectives of these interventions are very diverse: music is sometimes used to enable the expression of emotions and to stimulate the patient's ability to communicate; other times to help patients remember old memories (reminiscence therapy). One can even expect that the music listened to, played, or sung decreases behavioral disorders (depression, anxiety, agitation, apathy, etc.). Thus most of the studies published in scientific journals mainly address social, psychological, and behavioral disorders, essentially using well-being scales and questionnaires. In contrast, very few studies address cognitive assessment (motor and emotional responses, language skills, memory, executive functions, etc.). Similarly, biological and neurological processes have been paradoxically often missing from the concerns of music therapists for a very long time, even though the musical experience largely implies sensory, physiological, and neurological mechanisms. Consequently, it is clear that a lack of knowledge regarding the underlying mechanisms and the considerable heterogeneity of the methodologies employed have considerably reduced the scientific value of these clinical approaches. Thanks to the progress of the last 25 years in neurocognitive research in the field of music cognition, notably using brain-imaging techniques, the better understanding of the neuropsychological mechanisms at work while listening to or practicing music has brought a renewal of music therapy practices and art-therapy in general. This scientific work has shed light on the active ingredient underlying the benefits of musical interventions. Thus thanks to neuropsychological knowledge, music therapists should now be able to build interventions with specific driven goals and validated methods in order to clearly demonstrate the impact of their music therapy approach.

In sum, interventions named as "musical therapy" still lack clear methods and objectives, and are highly heterogeneous, in terms of approaches, therapeutic goals, levels of expertise, and qualifications of interveners. These ambiguities prompt some professionals to avoid using the term "music therapy" but rather to speak of "musical interventions," "music medicine," or even "neurologic music therapy" to account for certain types of music-based practices. Clements-Cortes and Bartel (2018) distinguish music therapy and music medicine. This distinction mainly refers to the inclusion and central role of the therapist in music therapy, and on the focus that is brought on the neurophysiological mechanisms induced by the music itself in music medicine: "Music therapy looks at treating the whole person, and is broader than music medicine which can be considered to be more of a prescribed approach to music applications" (Clements-Cortes & Bartel, 2018). In other words, "music medicine" or "neurologic music therapy" are based on scientific data and models and aim to target specific behavioral disturbances or cognitive mechanisms, with predictions about the mechanisms in action supporting the expected effects (Thaut, 2010; this volume), compared to a more intuitive and broad approach for "music therapy" that classically seeks to increase the overall well-being and self-esteem of patients. Consequently, bearing in mind the heterogeneity of definitions, we must now take into account all clinical interventions and scientific studies using music without necessarily referring to the term "music therapy" in its traditional sense. Thus it is difficult to render a global and accurate vision of the literature.

Clinical trials results and methodological considerations

The benefit of musical intervention is often difficult to demonstrate on the basis of scientific research. As Guetin et al. (2013) point out in a review on the impact of musical interventions in Alzheimer's disease, this literature revealed many limitations regarding the methods used in music-based trials. In the context of the Cochrane Database review of 2011 (Vink, Bruinsma, & Scolten, 2011), strict criteria were applied when selecting the studies to be included: they had to be randomized and controlled; the implementation of randomization was verified; it was necessary for treatment to be allocated by an independent professional; and the groups needed to be comparable, with clearly specified criteria for inclusion and exclusion. In addition, the studies had to be performed under double-blind conditions, which means that neither the participants nor the experimenters know who is receiving a particular treatment so the data are not biased by participants' or assessors' expectations. Quantitative measurements of the results (including frequencies, means, or medians, and 95% confidence intervals) were necessary for continuous variables and the number of subjects required to reach a conclusion had to be specified. Finally, all statistical analyses had to be performed on the "intent to treat" population. An intention-to-treat analysis consists of analyzing all available data of patients that have been randomized, ignoring noncompliance, protocol deviations, withdrawal, and anything that happens after randomization (Gupta, 2011). In the context of this review, only 10 clinical studies met the criteria fixed by the authors. After statistical reanalysis of the data of the selected studies, the authors of this meta-analysis (Vink et al., 2011) concluded that the statistical significance of effects was globally poor and that these studies showed conflicting results.

Since then, much more work has been published, with the willingness of many clinical teams to improve the methodological quality of their trials. In the latest update of the review for the Cochrane Database (van der Steen et al., 2017), researchers perform a meta-analysis on the basis of 17 studies, including 620 participants. All individuals in these trials were living in care homes and all severities of dementia were included. These trials included any music-based interventions, either active or receptive, delivered to individuals or groups. van der Steen et al. (2017) required a minimum of five sessions in order to ensure that a therapeutic intervention could have taken place. The music-based interventions were compared with any other type of therapy or no therapy, but control groups could not receive any music-based therapeutic intervention (even if fewer sessions than the intervention group). Two reviewers independently assessed risk of bias for the included studies of this Cochrane meta-analysis, according to the guidelines in the Cochrane Handbook for Systematic Reviews of Interventions, and using the "Risk of bias" assessment tool (Higgins & Green, 2011). They looked at the following elements of study quality: selection bias (random sequence generation, allocation concealment); performance bias (blinding of participants and personnel); detection bias (blinding of outcome assessment, which means that collection and analysis of data is not achieved by the same person); attrition bias (incomplete outcome data); reporting bias (selective reporting); and other potential threats to validity. They assessed performance, detection, and attrition bias for each outcome. While some studies are successful in limiting selection, detection, or attrition bias, no study can solve the performance bias, and the authors of the review admitted that blinding of therapists and participants to the intervention is not easy in this particular case. However, even though participants will always be aware of the type of activity they are engaged in (e.g., music or drama lessons), it could be possible that they nonetheless ignore whether their group is a therapy or control group (or just believe they both are intervention), or what the predicted outcomes are (what this therapy targets). In that case, all participants and teachers (from intervention and active control groups) are provided with the same information of the study goals, which make them as blind as they can be. Finally, van der Steen et al.'s (2017) conclusions are that music-based therapeutic intervention probably reduces depressive symptoms but has little or no effect on agitation or aggression. There may also be little or no effect on emotional well-being or quality of life, overall behavioral problems, and cognition. Moreover, the heterogeneity of the methods used in the selected studies does not make it possible to account for the durability of the observed effects; at the very most it is possible to conclude that the benefits are visible at the time of the interventions. Again, these conclusions are rather disappointing, even though the studies selected in this meta-analysis are those that respect precisely the highest criteria of methodological quality expected for a clinical trial. Whether it is relevant to use the clinical trials' criteria of the evidence-based medicine in order to account for the therapeutic effects of musical interventions is still an open question among clinicians and researchers. Some authors have suggested that it may not be relevant to use the same criteria as pharmacological clinical trials (e.g., double-blind approach and full randomization of groups) for the validation of nonpharmacological interventions (Hoemberg, 2014). van der Steen et al. (2017) have likewise discussed the divergences between their meta-analysis and recent literature reviews that have concluded that musical interventions are beneficial: they argued that this divergence of conclusion is due to the fact that these literature reviews did not propose any meta-analysis of the data, nor did they consider statistical measures of the effect size.

The Cochrane publication is not the only meta-analysis using stringent criteria for the selection of studies focusing on the effect of musical interventions in dementia. The meta-analysis performed by Zhang et al. (2017) is interesting since it is based on the use of two scales to assess the methodological quality of the included studies: the Physiotherapy Evidence Database (PEDro) scale score (Maher, Sherrington, Herbert, Moseley, & Elkins, 2003), and the Critical Appraisal Skills Program scale score (Guyatt, Sackett, & Cook, 1993). From 353 identified papers, 34 studies were finally included in this meta-analysis, corresponding to 1757 participants allocated to music intervention or control. Overall, 16 studies were randomized controlled trials (RCTs), 10 were controlled clinical trials, and the other 8 were randomized crossover trials (RCT/crossover, before–after studies without control groups). Of the 34 studies, 7 reported on patients with Alzheimer's disease, 18 were based on elderly patients with mixed dementia, and nine were based on other types of dementia. Standardized mean difference, odds ratio, and meta-regression analyses show that music therapy had positive effects on disruptive behavior and anxiety and a positive trend for cognitive function, depression, and quality of life. These results are quite in line with other previous reviews (Chang et al., 2015; Li, Wang, Chou, & Chen, 2015;

Ueda, Suzukamo, Sato, & Izumi, 2013), showing a modest but real positive effect of musical interventions in dementia.

A review by Gómez-Romero et al. (2017), also using the PEDro scale to assess the methodological value of the included studies, equally concluded that music intervention is beneficial for improving behavior problems, anxiety, and agitation in patients with dementia. Along with the often underlined limitations, another is that most music interventions are held for a very short period and a low number of sessions. Moreover, they do not include reassessments beyond 1 month after the intervention, thus limiting the possibility to observe long-term effects and maintenance of the benefits of music interventions.

Thus if we refer to these analyses of the literature, the scientific evidence of the effectiveness of musical interventions in the context of dementia is still fragile. It would be too easy to denigrate these conclusions and consider them as not reflecting the reality of these clinical practices because the benefits of the latter are not objectively or scientifically quantifiable. On the contrary, we must think of the difficulties encountered in demonstrating the benefits of musical interventions and understand more precisely why we still have such a lack of consensus regarding these clinical trials.

Go beyond the limits: recommendations for future studies

We should not conclude by these weaknesses that all the results of this literature are irrelevant. Similarly, the difficulty of reaching the clinical trials methodological requirements should not discourage researchers and clinicians from working together on innovating studies to objectively highlight the requirements, rather to demonstrate a therapeutic impact. Moreover, in the reviews and meta-analyses already mentioned, dozens of studies are currently considered to be of good methodological quality.

Among the weaknesses often mentioned in these studies are the limited numbers of patient sample size, the absence of control groups, and especially the absence of blind studies (subjects, therapists, and assessors blinding). Although treating a psychosocial situation such as musical interventions in double-blind is barely possible, it is quite easy to increase the number of participants in the patient samples and to find control conditions, while being attentive to maintaining fairness of the patient's care conditions. It would indeed be unethical to limit the global care management of some patients living in institutions just to create a control group "without activity." The ethical solution is generally to have a control group with regular management plus a novel nonmusical activity started at the same time as the musical intervention proposed to the experimental group.

Apart from these common methodological and statistical limits, we wish to stress other difficulties which undoubtedly explain the lack of consensus in the results of the literature. First, it is necessary to mention the important diversity of the assessment tools that are used, each team using their usual or preferred clinical scales (Zhang et al., 2017). Thus disruptive behaviors are classically evaluated by the Cohen-Mansfield Agitation Inventory (Cohen-Mansfield, 1986), the Behavioral Symptomatology in Alzheimer's disease scale (BEHAVE-AD) (Reisberg et al., 1987), the Neuropsychiatric Inventory (NPI) (Cummings et al., 1994), and the NPI—Brief Questionnaire Form (Kaufer et al., 2000). Cognitive functions are very often evaluated by the Mini—Mental State Examination (MMSE) (Folstein, Folstein, & McHugh, 1975), the Hasegawa's Dementia Scale—revised (Hasegawa, 1974), or the Self-Administered Gerocognitive Examination (Scharre et al., 2010). Depressive symptoms are assessed by the Geriatric Depression Scale (Yesavage et al., 1982) and the Cornell Scale Depression in Dementia (Alexopoulos, Abrams, Young, & Shamoian, 1988). Anxiety is evaluated by the Rating Anxiety in Dementia scale (Shankar, Walker, Frost, & Orrell, 1999) and the State—Trait Anxiety Inventory for Adults (Spielberger, 1983). Quality of life is evaluated by the Quality of Life—Alzheimer's Disease (Logsdon & Gibbons, 1999). In addition, many scale scores, such as the NPI, and BEHAVE-AD subscales, are considered measures of "other indicators" and are then combined in the analyses with other nonsubscale scores, thus creating analysis issues. First, scales and scores differ from one study to another. Second, it is necessary to underline the poverty of cognitive assessments. Most studies use global scales such as the MMSE, that are not very sensitive and do not bring out subtle cognitive performance changes such as language and communication, memory, attention, or executive functions. Therefore more subtle cognitive assessments of patients receiving music interventions are necessary. While it is generally true that patients with neurodegenerative diseases have significant cognitive impairments that cannot be rehabilitated per se, it is nonetheless interesting to assess qualitative changes in cognitive functioning following interventions, as those changes can significantly impact quality of life. For example, studies focusing on the impact of an intervention with or without music could include assessments of verbal fluency, communication ability, or of the richness of evoked memories.

Another major limitation of this literature is the heterogeneity of patients included in the experimental groups. Patients with different etiology are mixed together: Alzheimer's patients with individuals showing a vascular dementia or a frontotemporal dementia, groups of participants with cognitive and/or behavioral disorders are mixed without knowing precisely their specific neuropsychological diagnosis. In addition, many studies systematically mix patients at various stages of the disease severity, masking the statistical effects, and complicating the interpretation of any positive results that might occur. Neurodegenerative diseases such as Alzheimer's are progressive and characterized by growing memory deficits that affect episodic memory early, which are soon accompanied by the deterioration of other functions such as language, temporospatial orientation, executive functions, motor and perceptual skills. Several stages are classically distinguished to reflect this evolution: mild stage ($21 \leq \text{MMSE} \leq 26$), moderate stage ($16 \leq \text{MMSE} \leq 20$), and severe stage ($\text{MMSE} \leq 15$; Functional Assessment Staging; Reisberg, 1988; Sclan & Reisberg, 1992). Beside the evolution of cognitive disorders, behavioral disorders also evolve with the severity of the disease, with more anxiety and depression at the onset of illness, and more apathy and wandering at severe stages. Homogenizing the stages of severity of the disease in each experimental group is crucial since the expected impacts of musical interventions might differ throughout the different stages of severity.

Finally, the heterogeneity of patients in the samples is generally combined with a lack of treatment indications and guidelines, resulting from a lack of specific therapeutic goals and thus of targeted approaches. Indeed, too many researchers do not define their expectations or objectives for their proposed musical intervention. It is regrettable from a scientific validation point of view, because it decreases the statistical power of the studies that remain at a global exploratory stage. From a clinical point of view, this lack of treatment indication blurs the distinction between a musical intervention aiming at a specific therapeutic effect on a targeted dimension (such as the decrease of behavioral disorders or the stimulation of cognitive function), and a cultural animation with the global objective to bring some pleasure and to increase well-being. Knowing why and for what purpose a specific therapeutic technique must be recommended to a patient, even psychosocially, as well as possible contraindications of these approaches is crucial. Indeed, some patients might not be receptive to certain types of musical intervention, and this is too seldom taken into account in the literature. Beyond an assessment of the auditory perception, it is important to estimate if music stimulation conveys positive emotions and therefore potentially represents a "reward" for a participant. Before recommending a musical intervention, using a scale like the Barcelona Music Reward Questionnaire could be very relevant in order to measure whether music is an area of interest for the patient (Mas-Herrero, Marco-Pallares, Lorenzo-Seva, Zatorre, & Rodriguez-Fornells, 2013).

Understanding the mechanisms in action

In order to improve the specificity of approaches, it is crucial to better understand the underlying mechanisms that lead to the positive effects of music interventions. This section will propose different hypotheses for these mechanisms, aiming to help researchers and clinicians to optimally design music interventions according to their therapeutic targets.

Since the 1990s, numerous research teams working in the fields of cognitive psychology, neuropsychology and general neurosciences have been involved in studying the brain and its response to music. Their findings now provide a clearer understanding of the cognitive and neural mechanisms mediating the beneficial effects of music interventions.

1. An important aspect is that music processing seems to be relatively well-preserved in dementia. Alzheimer's patients are able to perceive and understand the emotional connotations of musical material and to react to its listening. These patients usually maintain their sensory and emotional musical appreciation when other cognitive (especially verbal) abilities are completely impaired, even in the severe stages of the disease (Norberg, Melin, & Asplund, 2003). Although there is a debate about the alteration of the perception of emotions in neurodegenerative diseases (Elferink, van Tilborg, & Kessels, 2015; Klein-Koerkamp, Beaudoin, Baciu, & Hot, 2012), esthetic judgment and emotional appreciation seem largely preserved in dementia, especially in Alzheimer's disease (Halpern, Ly, Elkin-Frankston, & O'Connor, 2008). Therefore the professionals and families' empirical observations appear to be confirmed by these studies: despite a possible emotional blunting and behavioral disorders such as apathy, the vast majority of Alzheimer's patients take pleasure in hearing music. This preserved responsiveness to music allows using the well-known emotional and neurophysiological effects of music on mood and behavior. For example, it has been well established that lively music has an arousing effect, associated with dopamine release (Ferreri et al., 2019; Salimpoor, Benovoy, Larcher, Dagher, & Zatorre, 2011), which awakens people and makes them temporarily more efficient in different kinds of tasks (Schellenberg, Nakata, Hunter, & Tamoto, 2007). This could explain why music can sometimes alleviate apathy in dementia patients. It can also lead to temporary improvement in cognition and explain benefits in patients' reactiveness, orientation, and communication. On the other hand, calm music has been shown to reduce our feeling of stress, as well as the body's physiological response to stress (e.g., decrease of cortisol; Linnemann, Ditzen, Strahler, Doerr, & Nater, 2015). This could contribute to explain why music may have a soothing effect and decrease anxiety and aggressive behaviors of dementia patients. Thus the emotions driven by music could also explain why music could facilitate the encoding of new information (Samson, Dellacherie, & Platel, 2009; Simmons-Stern, Budson, & Ally, 2010; Simmons-Stern et al., 2012). Therefore more work is definitely needed to understand the relationship between emotions and musical memory, and would provide the key to understand discrepancies between research findings and fieldwork regarding musical memory. However, using music in experimental conditions may dispossess it of the emotions it conveys, which is one of its most important dimensions, and can largely influence memories attached to it. To fix that important issue, alternative ways of testing music memory in more ecologically valid settings should be developed to encompass every parameter of music listening, including emotions.

2. The memory of old songs and tunes listened to in their youth is very resistant to amnesia, and semantic memory has been shown to be relatively well-preserved, even at severe stages of the illness (Baird & Samson, 2015; Cuddy, Sikka, & Vanstone, 2015; Groussard, Chan, Coppalle, & Platel, 2019; Samson et al., 2009; Vanstone et al., 2012). This could enlighten why music is a preferred material to use in reminiscence therapy, to trigger autobiographical memories and engage patients in reconnecting with their past and identity, which could in turn contribute to diminishing anxiety or depression. How can we explain these preserved musical abilities in most dementia syndromes and particularly in Alzheimer's disease? Peretz (1994) proposed the existence of a system of perceptual representation, specific to musical material. The multiple neuropsychological dissociations observed between language and music led this author to suggest a functional independence between the "verbal lexicon" and a "musical lexicon." The latter would store all the perceptual representations of all the musical pieces heard since the beginning of our existence, and this independently of the linguistic knowledge that can be associated to music. In Alzheimer's disease, the "verbal lexicon" would be mainly affected, while the "musical lexicon" would be more preserved (Peretz & Coltheart, 2003). The results of neuroimaging work, performed in healthy young nonmusicians, tend to confirm that there is possible neurofunctional independence for the complex processes of long-term musical and verbal memory. For example, our neuroimaging studies have shown two partially distinct brain networks during memory retrieval of musical and verbal material (Groussard, Rauchs, et al., 2010; Groussard, Viader, et al., 2010). Yet, more work ought to be done to understand the disease pathogenesis and why some brain networks are preferentially spared.

3. Music could be used as a mnemonic proxy to decrease the difficulties of verbal learning. Many studies have explored the strong associations between verbal and musical memory abilities in order to retrieve otherwise inaccessible verbal semantic or even episodic memories (Baird, Samson, Miller, & Chalmers, 2017; Moussard, Bigand, Belleville, & Peretz, 2014; Prickett & Smoore, 1991; Simmons-Stern et al., 2010, 2012; Wallace, 1994). Some authors suggest that it merely provides an arousal effect, heightening our attention and priming our perceptual systems to encode and store the memories with more precision. Globally, this would suggest that any arousing material would have the same end, but the suggestion is misleading: musically accompanied text is better retained than when it is associated with nonmusical sound or video (Palisson et al., 2015), which shows that music produces a particularly effective arousal effect compared to other sensory stimuli.

4. Finally, music is often a very social activity. Even when listening to music by ourselves, it often triggers our sense of belonging to a social

group or reminds us of our relationships. This social aspect of music may be crucial in supporting the communication and connection between dementia patients and their family or caregivers (see Chapter 14: Neurorehabilitation in aging through neurologic music therapy, Hobeika & Samson, this volume).

To sum up the actual neuropsychological literature about musical intervention in neurodegenerative disorders: during the first stage of the disease, when distress, depression, and anxiety are associated with the fall of cognitive performances, receptive musical therapy as a psychomusical relaxation technique is very useful to reduce these disorders. Indeed, at all stages of the disease, using preserved abilities is often a pillar of care for people with neurodegenerative disease (Sauer, Fopma-Loy, Kinney, & Lokon, 2016). By gathering information about patients' tastes, it is possible to easily set up activities where they can comment and evoke autobiographical memories about music with or without lyrics (e.g., Cuddy, Sikka, Silveira, Bai, & Vanstone, 2017; El Haj, Clément, Fasotti, & Allain, 2013; El Haj, Postal, & Allain, 2012). During the Alzheimer's severe stage, when verbal communication decreases and apathy becomes the biggest behavioral disorder to handle, music intervention, such as singing workshops, is very pertinent to fight against the apathy and to stimulate verbal communication. Relying upon semantic memory and creating a sense of familiarity seem to be the two most beneficial options whenever trying to use music with patients at the severe stage. Thus at all stages of severity of the disease, receptive or active musical interventions have complementary impacts. Music can be relaxing or stimulating, and this dual quality brings an undeniable interest in music intervention for neurodegenerative pathologies.

For now, most of the scientific studies have focused on Alzheimer's pathology, so the literature regarding other dementias or other neurological pathologies is scarcer. Work on semantic (Hailstone, Omar, & Warren, 2009; Weinstein et al., 2011) and frontotemporal dementia (Downey et al., 2013; Geroldi et al., 2000; Omar et al., 2011) continues to emerge and may be able to provide additional understanding of music's benefit for patients suffering from neurological diseases (see Chapter 4: Disorders of music processing in dementia, Benhamou & Warren, this volume).

Conclusion

What is music? For humans, it clearly corresponds to the cultural transformation of the sound world. Even listening or in solitary production, music for humans is first and foremost a social experience. Newborns hear the songs of their mother and the music of their culture and build an understanding of these objects, and experience those as an individual reward. Thus our knowledge of music was built through relationships and social education; which is probably one of the main reasons why it has such an impact on our mood, well-being, and ability to connect with our peers. This gives music a huge potential to be used in dementia care.

Nonetheless, there is no "one size fits all" approach in the context of dementia care. To optimally alleviate patients' and caregivers' burdens, we have to rely on theoretical models of musical interventions and a better understanding of the mechanisms underlying the observed effects, which will help propose specific approaches for targeted goals. To that purpose, we believe that music interventions should be designed and delivered by a music therapist, that is, a professional who masters the use of music as a tool (i.e., with strong musical training, as well as training on how teach or use music in therapy) and who is trained in the cognitive and psychomedical dimensions of the clinical population, which allows them to optimally interact with the patients and understand their needs. Therefore a session of passive listening to music can only be considered as a music therapy intervention if this latter is prescribed in a clear framework of care (in an institution or at home), ideally in connection with a care project validated by a medical team. Even such a receptive musical intervention (listening to music in a care unit) would be preferably mediated by a professional music therapist, who can customize the music to be listened to according to the tastes and cognitive difficulties of each participant. Like the prescription of a drug requiring the prescription and the expertise of a medical doctor and a pharmacist (dosage, frequency, contraindications, etc.), setting up a music session implies a personalization of the intervention to optimize the expected impact and prevent possible adverse effects like anxiety. Without these conditions, we can only talk at best about "musical animation," but not music therapy or interventions. Today's music therapy practices can, thanks to the contributions of scientific research, be part of a rational, technical, and objective approach while remaining fundamentally human. In dementia care, this is what we need to bring to patients and their families.

Acknowledgments

We warmly thank the editors and reviewers, especially Aline Moussard, for their suggestions and their very helpful comments. We also thank Camille Chapot for her proofreading of the English version of this manuscript.

References

Alexopoulos, G. S., Abrams, R. C., Young, R. C., & Shamoian, C. A. (1988). Cornell scale for depression in dementia. *Biological Psychiatry, 23*(3), 271−284.
Baird, A., & Samson, S. (2015). Music and dementia. *Progress in Brain Research, 217,* 207−235.

Baird, A., Samson, S., Miller, L., & Chalmers, K. (2017). Does music training facilitate the mnemonic effect of song? An exploration of musicians and nonmusicians with and without Alzheimer's dementia. *Journal of Clinical and Experimental Neuropsychology*, *39*, 9−21.

Chang, Y. S., Chu, H., Yang, C. Y., Tsai, J. C., Chung, M. H., Liao, Y. M., ... Chou, K. R. (2015). The efficacy of music therapy for people with dementia: A meta-analysis of randomised controlled trials. *Journal of Clinical Nursing*, *24*(23−24), 3425−3440.

Clements-Cortes, A., & Bartel, L. (2018). Are we doing more than we know? Possible mechanisms of response to music therapy. *Frontiers in Medicine.*, *5*, 255. Available from https://doi.org/10.3389/fmed.2018.00255.

Cohen-Mansfield, J. (1986). Agitated behaviors in the elderly: II. Preliminary results in the cognitively deteriorated. *Journal of the American Geriatrics Society*, *34*(10), 722−727.

Cuddy, L. L., Sikka, R., Silveira, K., Bai, S., & Vanstone, A. (2017). Music-evoked autobiographical memories (MEAMs) in Alzheimer disease: Evidence for a positivity effect. *Cogent Psychology*, *4*, 1. Available from https://doi.org/10.1080/23311908.2016.1277578.

Cuddy, L. L., Sikka, R., & Vanstone, A. (2015). Preservation of musical memory and engagement in healthy aging and Alzheimer's disease. *Annals of the New York Academy of Sciences*, *1337*, 223−231.

Cummings, J. L., Mega, M., Gray, K., Rosenberg-Thompson, S., Carusi, D. A., & Gornbein, J. (1994). The Neuropsychiatric Inventory: Comprehensive assessment of psychopathology in dementia. *Neurology*, *44*(12), 2308−2314.

Downey, L. E., Blezat, A., Nicholas, J., Omar, R., Golden, H. L., Mahoney, C. J., ... Warren, J. D. (2013). Mentalising music in frontotemporal dementia. *Cortex; A Journal Devoted to the Study of the Nervous System and Behavior*, *49*, 1844−1855.

Elferink, M. W., van Tilborg, I., & Kessels, R. P. (2015). Perception of emotions in mild cognitive impairment and Alzheimer's dementia: Does intensity matter? *Translational Neuroscience*, *6*(1), 139−149. Available from https://doi.org/10.1515/tnsci-2015-0013.

El Haj, M., Clément, S., Fasotti, L., & Allain, P. (2013). Effects of music on autobiographical verbal narration in Alzheimer's disease. *Journal of Neurolinguistics*, *26*(6), 691−700.

El Haj, M., Postal, V., & Allain, P. (2012). Music enhances autobiographical memory in mild Alzheimer's disease. *Educational Gerontology*, *38*(1), 30−41.

Ferreri, L., Mas-Herrero, E., Zatorre, R. J., Ripollés, P., Gomez-Andres, A., Alicart, H., ... Riba, J. (2019). Dopamine modulates the reward experiences elicited by music. *Proceedings of the National Academy of Sciences of the United States of America*, *116*(9), 3793−3798.

Folstein, M. F., Folstein, S. E., & McHugh, P. R. (1975). Mini-mental state: A practical method for grading the cognitive state of patients for the clinician. *Journal of Psychiatric Research*, *12*(3), 189−198.

Geroldi, C., Metitieri, T., Binetti, G., Zanetti, O., Trabucchi, M., & Frisoni, G. B. (2000). Pop music and frontotemporal dementia. *Neurology*, *55*, 1935−1936.

Gómez-Romero, M., Jiménez-Palomares, M., Rodríguez-Mansilla, J., Flores-Nieto, A., Garrido-Ardila, E. M., & González-López-Arza, M. V. (2017). Benefits of music therapy on behaviour disorders in subjects diagnosed with dementia: A systematic review. *Neurología*, *32*, 253−263.

Groussard, M., Chan, T., Coppalle, R., & Platel, H. (2019). Preservation of musical memory throughout the progression of Alzheimer's disease? Toward a reconciliation of theoretical, clinical and neuroimaging evidences. *Journal of Alzheimer's Disease*, *68*(3), 857−883.

Groussard, M., Rauchs, G., Landeau, B., Viader, F., Desgranges, B., Eustache, F., & Platel, H. (2010). The neural substrates of musical memory revealed by fMRI and two semantic tasks. *Neuroimage*, *53*, 1301−1309.

Groussard, M., Viader, F., Hubert, V., Landeau, B., Abbas, A., Desgranges, B., ... Platel, H. (2010). Musical and verbal semantic memory: Two distinct neural networks? *Neuroimage, 49,* 2764−2773.

Guetin, S., Charras, K., Berard, A., Arbus, C., Berthelon, P., Blanc, F., ... Leger, J. M. (2013). An overview of the use of music therapy in the context of Alzheimer's disease: A report of a French expert group. *Dementia (Basel, Switzerland), 12*(5), 619−634, *28.*

Gupta, S. K. (2011). Intention-to-treat concept: A review. *Perspectives in Clinical Research, 2* (3), 109−112. Available from https://doi.org/10.4103/2229-3485.83221.

Guyatt, G. H., Sackett, D. L., & Cook, D. J. (1993). Users' guides to the medical literature: II. How to use an article about therapy or prevention. A. Are the results of the study valid? Evidence-based medicine Working Group. *The Journal of the American Medical Association, 270*(21), 2598−2601.

Hailstone, J. C., Omar, R., & Warren, J. D. (2009). Relatively preserved knowledge of music in semantic dementia. *Journal of Neurology, Neurosurgery, and Psychiatry, 80,* 808−809.

Halpern, A. R., Ly, J., Elkin-Frankston, S., & O'Connor, M. G. (2008). "I know what I like": Stability of aesthetic preference in Alzheimer's patients. *Brain and Cognition, 66*(1), 65−72.

Hasegawa, K. (1974). Assessment scale of elderly people. *The Journal of Clinical Psychiatry, 16,* 965−969.

Higgins, J. P. T., & Green, S. (2011). *Cochrane handbook for systematic reviews of interventions version 5.1.0.* The Cochrane Collaboration. Available from <handbook.cochrane.org> Updated March 2011.

Hoemberg, V. (2014). A neurologist's view for neurologic music therapy. In M. Thaut, & V. Hoemberg (Eds.), *Handbook of neurologic music therapy.* Oxford University Press (UK).

Kaufer, D. I., Cummings, J. L., Ketchel, P., Smith, V., MacMillan, A., Shelley, T., ... DeKosky, S. T. (2000). Validation of the NPI-Q, a brief clinical form of the Neuropsychiatric Inventory. *The Journal of Neuropsychiatry and Clinical Neurosciences, 12*(2), 233−239.

Klein-Koerkamp, Y., Beaudoin, M., Baciu, M., & Hot, P. (2012). Emotional decoding abilities in Alzheimer's disease: A meta-analysis. *Journal of Alzheimer's Disease: JAD, 32*(1), 109−125.

Li, H. C., Wang, H. H., Chou, F. H., & Chen, K. M. (2015). The effect of music therapy on cognitive functioning among older adults: A systematic review and meta-analysis. *Journal of the American Medical Directors Association, 16*(1), 71−77.

Linnemann, A., Ditzen, B., Strahler, J., Doerr, J. M., & Nater, U. M. (2015). Music listening as a means of stress reduction in daily life. *Psychoneuroendocrinology, 60,* 82−90.

Logsdon, R. G., & Gibbons, L. E. (1999). Quality of life in Alzheimer's disease: Patient and caregiver reports. *Journal of Mental Health and Aging, 5*(1), 21−32.

Maher, C. G., Sherrington, C., Herbert, R. D., Moseley, A. M., & Elkins, M. (2003). Reliability of the PEDro scale for rating quality of randomized controlled trials. *Physical Therapy, 83* (8), 713−721.

Mas-Herrero, E., Marco-Pallares, J., Lorenzo-Seva, U., Zatorre, R. J., & Rodriguez-Fornells, A. (2013). Individual differences in music reward experiences. *Music Perception, 31,* 118−138. Available from https://doi.org/10.1525/mp.2013.31.2.118.

Moussard, A., Bigand, E., Belleville, S., & Peretz, I. (2014). Learning sung lyrics aids retention in normal ageing and Alzheimer's disease. *Neuropsychological Rehabilitation, 24,* 894−917.

Norberg, A., Melin, E., & Asplund, K. (2003). Reactions to music, touch and object presentation in the final stage of dementia: An exploratory study. *International Journal of Nursing Studies*, *40*(5), 473−479.

Omar, R., Henley, S. M. D., Bartlett, J. W., Hailstone, J. C., Gordon, E., Sauter, D. A., ... Warren, J. D. (2011). The structural neuroanatomy of music emotion recognition: Evidence from frontotemporal lobar degeneration. *Neuroimage*, *56*, 1814−1821.

Palisson, J., Roussel-Baclet, C., Maillet, D., Belin, C., Ankri, J., & Narme, P. (2015). Music enhances verbal episodic memory in Alzheimer's disease. *Journal of Clinical and Experimental Neuropsychology*, *37*, 503−517.

Peretz, I. (1994). Les agnosies auditives. In X. Seron, & M. Jeannerod (Eds.), *Neuropsychologie humaine* (pp. 205−216). *Mardaga: Liège*.

Peretz, I., & Coltheart, M. (2003). Modularity of music processing. *Nature Neuroscience*, *6*(7), 688.

Prickett, C. A., & Smoore, R. (1991). The use of music to aid memory of Alzheimer's patients. *Journal of Music Therapy*, *28*, 101−110.

Raglio, A., & Gianelli, M. V. (2009). Music therapy for individuals with dementia: Areas of interventions and research perspectives. *Current Alzheimer Research*, *6*, 293−301.

Reisberg, B. (1988). Functional assessment staging (FAST). *Psychopharmacology*, *24*, 653−659.

Reisberg, B., Borenstein, J., Salob, S. P., Ferris, S. H., Franssen, E., & Georgotas, A. (1987). Behavioral symptoms in Alzheimer's disease: Phenomenology and treatment. *The Journal of Clinical Psychiatry*, *48*(Suppl), 9−15.

Salimpoor, V. N., Benovoy, M., Larcher, K., Dagher, A., & Zatorre, R. J. (2011). Anatomically distinct dopamine release during anticipation and experience of peak emotion to music. *Nature Neuroscience*, *14*(2), 257.

Samson, S., Dellacherie, D., & Platel, H. (2009). Emotional power of music in patients with memory disorders: Clinical implications of cognitive neuroscience. *Annals of the New York Academy of Sciences*, *1169*, 245−255.

Sauer, P. E., Fopma-Loy, J., Kinney, J. M., & Lokon, E. (2016). "It makes me feel like myself": Person-centered versus traditional visual arts activities for people with dementia. *Dementia (Basel, Switzerland)*, *15*, 895−912.

Scharre, D. W., Chang, S. I., Murden, R. A., Lamb, J., Beversdorf, D. Q., Kataki, M., & Bornstein, R. A. (2010). Self-Administered Gerocognitive Examination (SAGE): A brief cognitive assessment instrument for mild cognitive impairment (MCI) and early dementia. *Alzheimer Disease and Associated Disorders*, *24*(1), 64−71.

Schellenberg, E. G., Nakata, T., Hunter, P. G., & Tamoto, S. (2007). Exposure to music and cognitive performance: Tests of children and adults. *Psychology of Music*, *35*(1), 5−19.

Sclan, S. G., & Reisberg, B. (1992). Functional assessment staging (FAST) in Alzheimer's disease: Reliability, validity, and ordinality. *International Psychogeriatric Association*, *4* (Suppl. 1), 55−69.

Shankar, K. K., Walker, M., Frost, D., & Orrell, M. W. (1999). The development of a valid and reliable scale for Rating Anxiety in Dementia (raid). *Aging and Mental Health*, *3*(1), 39−49.

Simmons-Stern, N. R., Budson, A. E., & Ally, B. A. (2010). Music as a memory enhancer in patients with Alzheimer's disease. *Neuropsychologia*, *48*, 3164−3167.

Simmons-Stern, N. R., Deason, R. G., Brandler, B. J., Frustace, B. S., O'Connor, M. K., Ally, B. A., & Budson, A. E. (2012). Music-based memory enhancement in Alzheimer's disease: Promise and limitations. *Neuropsychologia*, *50*, 3295−3303.

Sixmith, A., & Gibson, G. (2007). Music and the wellbeing of people with dementia. *Ageing and Society*, *27*, 127−145.

Spielberger, C. D. (1983). *Manual for the state-trait anxiety inventory STAI (form Y) (self-evaluation questionnaire)*. Consulting Psychologists Press Inc.

Thaut, M. H. (2010). Neurologic music therapy in cognitive rehabilitation. *Music Perception, 27* (4), 281−285.

Ueda, T., Suzukamo, Y., Sato, M., & Izumi, S. I. (2013). Effects of music therapy on behavioral and psychological symptoms of dementia: A systematic review and meta-analysis. *Ageing Research Reviews, 12*(2), 628−641.

van der Steen, J. T., van Soest-Poortvliet, M. C., van der Wouden, J. C., Bruinsma, M. S., Scholten, R. J. P. M., & Vink, A. C. (2017). Music-based therapeutic interventions for people with dementia. *Cochrane Database of Systematic Reviews, 5*. Available from https://doi.org/10.1002/14651858.CD003477.pub3, *Art. No.: CD003477.*

Vanstone, A. D., Sikka, R., Tangness, L., Sham, R., Garcia, A., & Cuddy, L. L. (2012). Episodic and semantic memory for melodies in Alzheimer's disease. *Music Perception, 29*, 501−507.

Vink, A. C., Bruinsma, M. S., & Scolten, R. J. P. M. (2011). Music therapy for people with dementia (review). *Cochrane Database Systematic Reviews, 3*, CD003477.

Wallace, W. T. (1994). Memory for music: Effect of melody on recall of text. *Journal of Experimental Psychology: Learning, Memory, and Cognition, 20*, 1471−1485.

Weinstein, J., Koenig, P., Gunawardena, D., McMillan, C., Bonner, M., & Grossman, M. (2011). Preserved musical semantic memory in semantic dementia. *Archives of Neurology, 68*, 248−250.

Yesavage, J. A., Brink, T. L., Rose, T. L., Lum, O., Huang, V., Adey, M., & Leirer, V. O. (1982). Development and validation of a geriatric depression screening scale: A preliminary report. *Journal of Psychiatric Research, 17*(1), 37−49.

Zhang, Y., Cai, J., An, L., Hui, F., Ren, T., Ma, H., & Zhao, Q. (2017). Does music therapy enhance behavioral and cognitive function in elderly dementia patients? A systematic review and meta-analysis. *Ageing Research Reviews, 35*, 1−11.

Chapter 13

Why do music-based interventions benefit persons with neurodegenerative disease?

Lise Hobeika[1,2] and Séverine Samson[1,3]

[1]Université de Lille, EA 4072 – PSITEC – Psychologie: Interactions, Temps, Emotions, Cognition, Equipe Neuropsychologie et Audition, Lille, France, [2]Sciences et Technologies de la Musique et du Son, IRCAM, CNRS, Sorbonne Université, Paris, France, [3]AP-HP, GHU Pitié-Salpêtrière-Charles Foix, Unité d'épilepsie, Paris, France

Introduction

For a long time, musical practices with a therapeutic vocation have existed and their use in this context has considerably increased during recent decades (Sihvonen et al., 2017; van der Steen et al., 2018). Widely relayed by the media, music-based interventions have shown growing success in persons with neurodegenerative disease and their caregivers. An important field of application of these methods concerns the management of psychological and behavior symptoms in Alzheimer's disease (AD) and related diseases from mild to severe stages. Considering the limited impact of pharmacological treatments with the iatrogenic effects of medication in these patients, several health institutions have recommended in parallel the development of non-pharmacological approaches to alleviate some symptoms (National Institute for Health and Care Excellence, 2018).

AD is a neurodegenerative disorder that is associated with several cognitive and emotional deficits. Symptoms usually include memory impairment (Hodges, 2000), mood dysfunction (Christensen, Griffiths, Mackinnon, & Jacomb, 1997), and, in particular, depression and anxiety (Chu et al., 2014). These deficits have been associated with behavioral disorders such as agitation, and sometimes aggressiveness, which are the main causes of patients' institutionalization (Luppa, Luck, Brähler, König, & Riedel-Heller, 2008; Toot, Swinson, Devine, Challis, & Orrell, 2017), and are also at the root of caregivers' suffering (Black & Almeida, 2004). Altogether, these difficulties lead to a progressive social deterioration, including a loss of sense of self

Music and the Aging Brain. DOI: https://doi.org/10.1016/B978-0-12-817422-7.00013-4

and identity (Caddell & Clare, 2010), and weakening of interpersonal relationships that may stem from a decline in emotional comprehension (Shimokawa et al., 2001), and communication difficulties (Feyereisen & Hupet, 2007; Potkins et al., 2003). Such social dysfunctions, which can have a strong impact on the organization of clinical units and staff, might be aggravated by patients' decline of verbal function. The most common language deficits are lexical access, as well as speech disfluencies such as aposiopesis (sentences left unfinished), logorrhea (excessive wordiness with incoherent talkativeness), palilalia (repetition of syllables, words, or phrases; Hier, Hagenlocker, & Shindler, 1985), abnormal turn-taking (Perkins, Whitworth, & Lesser, 1998; Ripich, Vertes, Whitehouse, Fulton, & Ekelman, 1991), and empty discourse (Nicholas, Obler, Albert, & Helm-Estabrooks, 1985). In more severely deteriorated patients, language can be totally absent (Caramelli, Mansur, & Nitrini, 1998). Thus AD patients' attempts to share their thoughts or engage in dialog for social purposes may go unnoticed because of their verbal communication deficits (Potkins et al., 2003; Small, Geldart, Gutman, Ann, & Scott, 1998). The combination of memory, mood, and communication disorders increases social isolation, therefore reducing the quality of life of patients with neurodegenerative diseases (Klimova, Maresova, Valis, Hort, & Kuca, 2015). However, while verbal communication is impaired, nonverbal communication appears to be relatively spared at least in mild to moderate stages of the disease (Tzortzis, Goldblum, Dang, Forette, & Boller, 2000; Warren, Warren, Fox, & Warrington, 2003). It has therefore been proposed that nonverbal skills might compensate verbal difficulties in these patients (Schiaratura, Di Pastena, Askevis-Leherpeux, & Clément, 2015).

Musical interventions are thought to improve mood regulation, social functioning, and cognition of patients with AD and related diseases, as well as the well-being of their caregivers. However, the factors that explain their therapeutic efficacy are not yet clarified. In our chapter, we want to shed light on the intervention elements that appear to benefit patients from mild to severe stages of the disease, and will discuss the idea that synchronization to music, which is relatively spared even in advanced stages of the disease, can enhance interpersonal coordination, and thus can improve social functioning and sustain nonverbal communication skills. For this purpose, we will also review the evidence from psychology, neuroscience, and embodied music cognition that may have important implications to understand and to improve the efficacy of music-based interventions in patients with AD.

Music-based interventions in patients with Alzheimer's disease

There are several reasons to justify the use of music as a privileged support for therapy. Appreciated by patients of all ages, backgrounds, and sociocultural levels, music is widely accessible, easy to utilize, enjoyed by the majority of people, and thus a potentially playful and motivating tool for rehabilitation. Indeed, music naturally conveys strong emotions (Koelsch, 2014), induces extremely pleasurable experiences and physiological reactions such as chills or goosebumps (Blood & Zatorre, 2001; Pankseep, 1995). It seems that patients with AD retain an intriguing sensitivity to music, even at advanced stages (Baird & Samson, 2015; Cuddy & Duffin, 2005; Johnson et al., 2011). Music can trigger memory, or more specifically autobiographical memory (Baird & Samson, 2014; Cuddy, Sikka, Silveira, Bai, & Vanstone, 2017; El Haj, Postal, & Allain, 2012). As demonstrated by neuroimaging and pharmacological studies in healthy participants, music can modulate emotional state and motivation (Ferreri et al., 2019; Mas-Herrero, Dagher, & Zatorre, 2018; Salimpoor et al., 2013; Salimpoor, Zald, Zatorre, Dagher, & McIntosh, 2015). Its unique ability to elicit both emotions and memories means that it can potentially provide a link to the person's past. Furthermore, music can be a social activity. It is commonly used for communication (Mehr, Singh, York, Glowacki, & Krasnow, 2018) and thus may promote feelings of interconnectedness among patients and between patients and their caregivers. Overall, music appears as an ideal media to present to persons with potential memory and mood disorders and diminished social interactions. Some studies even suggest that by reducing agitation, music interventions might limit the use of medication (fewer side effects) and, consequently, the cost of care in patients with AD (Kali et al., 2017; Ridder, Stige, Qvale, & Gold, 2013). However, the lack of another intervention group (or nonmusic group) in these studies to control for changes due to patients' stimulation limits the interpretation of the results. It remains therefore difficult to dissociate the specific impact of a music intervention from the social impact of group activities. Although such results would be a major improvement for patients' health, further studies are still necessary to confirm these promising findings.

Music-based interventions involve a large variety of activities that can be divided in two types: passive (or receptive) or active (or participatory) interventions. In receptive interventions, patients listen to music or songs performed by musicians, caregivers or from audio or video recordings. In participatory interventions, patients are encouraged to join the music-making by singing, playing simple instruments, dancing, or simply moving with the beats. Those musical activities can be performed individually or more frequently in groups with the presence of another person (caregiver or therapist) or other persons (i.e., patients' group). Since it remains difficult to induce passive listening without any active processes, passive and active sessions are generally combined during music-based interventions. However, the few studies examining active and passive music-based interventions as compared to a control group with usual care suggest that participatory activities bring greater benefits than passive listening to music (Sakamoto, Ando, & Tsutou, 2013; Särkämö et al., 2014). In a study in which short- and long-term effects of such interventions were assessed, Sakamoto et al. (2013) showed that the active interventions requiring patients to sing and to dance to music led to the greatest improvement in emotional state and better long-term reduction of behavioral problems. In another study, Särkämö et al. also demonstrated that both types of music interventions improved mood and remote episodic memory. However, only the active interventions enhanced short-term and working memory, and caregiver well-being (Särkämö et al., 2014). Taken together, these findings support the idea that musical interventions requiring patients to actively participate at the motor level may provide most important benefits.

A potential explanation of the advantage of active intervention is first the emotional content. We know that moving to the rhythm of music provides pleasure (Janata, Tomic, & Haberman, 2012). The audiomotor coupling and the temporal expectations produced by the perception of the musical beat would stimulate the reward brain network, therefore inducing pleasure (Salimpoor, Benovoy, Larcher, Dagher, & Zatorre, 2011). Moreover, another important component of those interventions is the social aspect. Some studies suggest that the social context modifies music perception. Thus the presence of a singer—which is often the case in active interventions—can improve the engagement of patients in the musical task compared to a music recording (Holmes, Knights, Dean, Hodkinson, & Hopkins, 2006; Lesaffre, Moens, & Desmet, 2017; Sherratt, Thornton, & Hatton, 2004). Moreover, sharing a musical rhythm with others may be a way to connect with them and share positive emotions (Tarr, Launay, & Dunbar, 2014). Therefore we propose that the therapeutic benefits of music lie in its hedonic and emotional component coupled with its role in communication and in the creation of social bonds (social bonding), which patients are often lacking. However, the mechanisms underlying the beneficial impacts of music in these patients and the extent to which the efficacy of music seems to surpass that of other pleasant activities need to be further explored.

Interpersonal coordination in music to improve social functioning

Motor behaviors and social bonding

When verbal communication is impaired, patients with AD may rely on nonverbal communication to connect with others (Schiaratura et al., 2015). Nonverbal communication describes conscious or unconscious behaviors that share information about our mental state to others without the use of language. Nonverbal communication can take various forms such as facial expressions, body postures, interpersonal distances, or eye gaze contact. These behaviors can be used to communicate to others information about our intentions, our emotional state, or our willingness to bond with them.

Other nonverbal communication behaviors rely on the coordination of movements with others in time and space, that is, interpersonal coordination. Interpersonal coordination is at the core of social life, as it is necessary for most social interactions to succeed: such as doing collective sports, moving a piece of furniture with a friend, or even having a conversation. In the musical domain, interpersonal coordination such as singing, dancing, or music playing in group are activities that allow communicating to others the willingness to bond. Anthropologists suggest that those musical activities, found in churches, in armies, or in sport teams, create a feeling of cohesion between individuals by weakening the boundaries between the self and the group (Ehrenreich, 2007; Radcliffe-Brown, 1952). It has also been shown that individuals singing in unison, or moving together on musical beats have a higher tendency to cooperate with each other (Hove & Risen, 2009; Mogan, Fischer, & Bulbulia, 2017). This effect is not specific to musical interaction. Moving together by simply walking in step, rocking chairs synchronously, or tapping to a metronome beat with others can promote social cohesion (Demos, Chaffin, Begosh, Daniels, & Marsh, 2012; Reddish, Fischer, & Bulbulia, 2013; Wiltermuth & Heath, 2009). Thus singing or music-making can be a form of nonverbal communication between individuals, promoting cohesion and cooperation between individuals.

At the physiological level, the social effect of interpersonal coordination seems to be associated with the release of oxytocin. As reported by several authors, this neurohormone is known for its role in social behaviors, as it induces increase in trust (Kosfeld, Heinrichs, Zak, Fischbacher, & Fehr, 2005), cooperation (Zhang, Gross, De Dreu, & Ma, 2018), and empathy (Domes, Heinrichs, Michel, Berger, & Herpertz, 2007). Synchronized behaviors could also stimulate the endogenous opioid system and particularly endorphins, which are neurohormones associated with pleasure and wellbeing, and have a role in social bonding in human and nonhuman primates (Cohen, Ejsmond-frey, Knight, & Dunbar, 2010; Martel, Nevison, Simpson, & Keverne, 1995; Schino & Troisi, 1992; Tarr et al., 2014). We can therefore suggest that physiological responses resulting from interpersonal coordination activities could, at least in part, mediate the impact of musical interventions on social interactions.

In active musical interventions, patients with AD spontaneously sing or move with the musical rhythm while engaging with others (i.e., therapist, other patients, or caregivers). We hypothesize that the success of those interventions may in part rely on their benefits on social behaviors. Moving to music with others could induce patients with AD to interact positively with others, to feel included in a group, and thus to improve social functioning. It could also increase trust and collaboration with the surroundings and with the caregivers. This interpretation, based on hypotheses raised by the study of healthy young adults, deserves to be tested in aged populations. Although it seems in agreement with the fact that participatory musical interventions have greater efficacy than receptive ones on the well-being of patients with AD (see the "Introduction" section), further research is still needed to better understand the social cognitive functioning of these patients, and their communication behaviors.

Social cognition abilities

The few studies investigating social cognitive abilities in patients with AD found a decrease in theory of mind (Fernandez-Duque, Baird, & Black, 2009; Gregory et al., 2002), emotion recognition (Albert, Cohen, & Koff, 1991; Bediou et al., 2009), and empathy (Fernandez-Duque, Hodges, Baird, & Black, 2010). These high-order social cognitive functions allow the understanding of others and support nonverbal communication. By using active music interventions in pathological as well as in physiological aging, we can expect to stimulate social cognitive abilities and to maintain these skills as long as possible. Since no study has addressed the relationship between interpersonal coordination and social cognitive abilities in AD, we will report evidence obtained in individuals with typical and atypical development.

According to a large literature, the development of social cognition skills is partially linked to interpersonal coordination, synchronization, and imitation (Asendorpf & Baudonnière, 1993; Feldman, 2007a, 2007b; Harrist & Waugh, 2002). By testing the development of empathy in a longitudinal study, Feldman (2007a) found an association between mother—infant synchrony at 3 months and empathy capacities of adolescents at 13 years (Feldman, 2007a). In line with this result, recent evidence obtained for individuals with atypical development showed that training programs focusing on interpersonal synchronization and imitation (i.e., dance and movements) improved social abilities (Koehne, Behrends, Fairhurst, & Dziobek, 2016). The link between interpersonal synchronization and social cognition abilities reported in these studies is usually explained by the fact that the understanding of others' actions may be based on motor resonance, that is, the mapping of others' action in our own motor repertoire (Panasiti, Porciello, & Aglioti, 2017). The so-called mirror system is activated during both the observation and the realization of the same action (Aglioti, Cesari, Romani, & Urgesi, 2008; Calvo-Merino, Glaser, Grèzes, Passingham, & Haggard, 2005). If interpersonal coordination, synchronization, and imitation may be effective in developing and improving social cognition skills in typical and atypical development, we can suggest that it might also help to restore these abilities in pathological aging. Engaging individuals in interpersonal synchronization may be an appropriate way to stimulate this association between observation and motor resonance, boosting therefore the ability to understand others' action.

Interestingly, music interventions appear as perfect situations to engage in interpersonal synchronization. In participatory musical interventions, individuals can easily and naturally synchronize their movements thanks to the presence of musical rhythm. It would also be interesting to test if the success of those interventions can be linked to an improvement in social cognitive functioning of patients with AD, and particularly to an amelioration of empathy, emotions' recognition, and theory of mind. However, to provide support to these findings or interpretations, appropriate evaluating tools and methods to measure synchronization to music and to others should be designed.

Methodological aspects related to the impact of musical intervention in patients with Alzheimer's disease

A large number of studies claim positive effects of music-based interventions on emotions, well-being, social functioning, and even sometimes on cognition in patients with AD, as well as on caregivers' well-being (Choi, Lee, Cheong, & Lee, 2009; Raglio et al., 2012; Svansdottir & Snaedal, 2006; Ueda, Suzukamo, Sato, & Izumi, 2013). Yet, those conclusions need to be interpreted with caution. As recently discussed in a meta-analysis (van der Steen et al., 2018), the validity of such positive effects can be questioned by considering methodological biases that weaken the conclusions. Such biases include small sample sizes, lack of blind assessors, lack of randomization, and the absence of a control group with no intervention (i.e., with treatment as usual) or with a nonmusical intervention. This latter group is necessary to control for social stimulation and hedonic factors, to determine whether or not any pleasant social activity could have effects similar to music interventions. Moreover, the potency of the treatment varies considerably between individuals, thus emphasizing the necessity to further investigate the factors that might be associated with the efficacy of music in patients with AD and related disease.

As already mentioned, the proposed musical activities in those prior studies cover a large variety of skills from music listening individually to music playing in groups. Therefore it is not surprising that the reported studies lead to inconsistent results. Two main characteristics of those interventions can impact their potential effects: the social context (alone or in social presence) and as mentioned above, the type of intervention (passive or active intervention) (see Fig. 13.1). These characteristics can change patients' engagement during the interventions, the pleasure felt but also the impact of such interventions on the social, emotional, and cognitive functioning. To disentangle the influence of those factors and to understand the mechanisms underlying the positive impact of musical interventions, well-controlled studies using multimodal measures, such as cognitive, emotional, social, or psychophysiological data, are necessary.

Usually, the evaluation of a musical intervention's impacts includes the assessment of patients' moods and behavior, as well as caregivers' quality of life. These evaluations are often performed using questionnaires filled by the patient (self-reported evaluation) or by a family or medical caregiver

FIGURE 13.1 Musical-based interventions can be classified according to the social context (alone or in social presence) and the motor engagement (passive or active).

(hetero evaluation), depending on the disease progression. Frequently used questionnaires are the Behavior Pathology in Alzheimer's Disease Ratings Scale that rates behavioral problems of dementia (Reisberg, Auer, & Monteiro, 1997), the Cohen-Mansfield Agitation Inventory that rates agitated behaviors (Cohen-Mansfield, Marx, & Rosenthal, 1989), the State-Trait Anxiety Inventory for Adults that assesses mood and anxiety (Spielberger, Gorsuch, Lushene, Vagg, & Jacobs, 1983), and the Neuropsychiatric Inventory that evaluates the severity and frequency of several behavioral functioning (e.g., delusions, hallucinations, agitation, disinhibition, sleep abnormalities) as well as caregivers distress (Sisco et al., 2000).

The questionnaires can be completed by objective measures such as the evaluation of physiological changes induced by musical intervention. Indeed, measures of cortisol level can be a marker of patients' stress levels (Kirschbaum & Hellhammer, 1994). Heart rate and blood pressure can also constitute an interesting marker of patients' affective state (de Witte, Spruit, van Hooren, Moonen, & Stams, 2019; Sakamoto et al., 2013). However, we still need additional studies to confirm their relevance to examine the effect of music-based interventions on psychophysiological responses in patients with AD.

Quantitative measures of patients' engagement should also be considered to study the benefits of music-based interventions. Engagement in the musical activity can be analyzed at the motor, the emotional, or the social level. Motor engagement is evaluated by the spontaneous motor reaction with music. Music is built on a strong regular rhythm that elicits spontaneous motor responses in listeners (Fraisse, 1982): people have the tendency to move in synchrony with musical beats (Leman & Buhmann, 2017;

Repp, 2005). The production of behaviors like singing, clapping, or the global quantity of body movements can provide measures of patients' rhythmic entrainment with the music (Ghilain et al., n.d.; Holmes et al., 2006; Lesaffre et al., 2017; Sherratt et al., 2004). Emotional engagement can be evaluated using methods from social psychology (Schiaratura, 2008). The production of nonverbal behaviors in patients with dementia have already been successfully measured in studies that have found benefits of music interventions (Narme et al., 2014). The measurements of the production of emotional facial or vocal expressions, or of body postures and gestures seem to be very promising markers of patients' emotional state. They can be decoded from video recordings of the participants, providing information related to the quality of nonverbal behaviors produced in response to music listening or practicing.

Music-based interventions in groups can be analyzed as a joint action supported by the presence of music. The degree of synchronization between participants' behaviors reflects social engagement. As already mentioned, individuals tend to synchronize their behaviors with others', and especially rhythmic movements when they are in a group. This spontaneous interpersonal synchronization, called motor entrainment or alignment, has been observed in laboratory studies, in which dyads of participants unconsciously or voluntarily synchronized their finger tapping (Oullier, Guzman, De Jantzen, Lagarde, & Kelso, 2008), their steps while walking side by side (van Ulzen, Lamoth, Daffertshofer, Semin, & Beek, 2008), or the rhythm of rocking chair sways (Richardson, Marsh, Isenhower, Goodman, & Schmidt, 2007). We can therefore propose that interpersonal synchronization of rhythmic movements might provide relevant indexes to measure patients' engagement with others in a musical context (Ghilain, Schiaratura, Singh, Lesaffre, & Samson, 2019). In addition, the synchronization of individuals' posture, gestures, facial expression, and eye gaze, which have long been regarded as the regulators of social interaction, are notably important for the development of rapport and personal relationships (Lakin, Jefferis, Cheng, & Chartrand, 2003). Rigorous measures to quantify the production of rhythmic joint actions in musical activities should be developed to examine their relationships with social cognitive abilities.

Finally, patients' rhythmic abilities can also be measured by asking participants to tap along with the musical beat. Sensorimotor precision in tapping tasks gives a measure of individuals' prediction and adaptive abilities (Keller, Novembre, & Hove, 2014). The variability of the tapping can be provided by assessing the sensorimotor consistency (Dalla Bella et al., 2016). Usually, such rhythmic behaviors are measured in tasks involving finger or hand tapping with music or metronome beats. Very few studies examined this type of rhythmic abilities in patients with AD or mild cognitive impairment (Kluger, Gianutsos, Golomb, Ferris, & Reisberg, 1997; Suzumura et al., 2016). Even if gross motor skills appear clinically normal at the early stage of AD, motor control deficits may be associated with disease progression (Bangert & Balota, 2012; Kluger et al., 1997; Suzumura et al., 2016). Yet they often pass undetected in comparison to cognitive impairments and decline in daily living activities (de Paula et al., 2016; Yan, Rountree, Massman, Doody, & Li, 2008). A careful examination of the accuracy and the variability of sensorimotor synchronization with musical rhythms might offer additional and relevant behavioral markers of interpersonal coordination and deserve to be examined in patients with AD disease.

Conclusion

Music is a universal human activity that can play a key role in communication, social interaction, and mood regulation. The richness of music on emotional, motor, and social stimulation might explain the success of music-based interventions as a nonpharmacological treatment for patients with AD. Among the different musical activities responsible for their effectiveness, the synchronization of movements to the musical rhythm, which is relatively spared even in advanced stages of AD, is largely used. It seems to induce a lot of pleasure, improve emotion regulation and stimulate motor control and social functioning. However, more specific and control studies with appropriate and innovative tools need to be developed to assess and to train elderly persons. Such technical and scientific progress that combines methods from psychology, neuroscience, and embodied music cognition will allow a better understanding of the factors that contribute to the positive effect of music-based interventions in patients with AD. This knowledge will help to design rhythmic training programs. By adapting the musical activities to the patients' needs, personalized training sessions will be proposed to reduce social isolation and to improve the quality of life of elderly people and of their family and medical caregivers.

Acknowledgments

Grant support was provided by the Institut Universitaire de France and the French Foundation France Alzheimer to Séverine Samson.

References

Aglioti, S. M., Cesari, P., Romani, M., & Urgesi, C. (2008). Action anticipation and motor resonance in elite basketball players. *Nature Neuroscience*, *11*(9), 1109−1116. Available from https://doi.org/10.1038/nn.2182.

Albert, M. S., Cohen, C., & Koff, E. (1991). Perception of affect in patients with dementia of the Alzheimer type. *Archives of Neurology*, *48*(8), 791−795. Available from https://doi.org/10.1001/archneur.1991.00530200027013.

Asendorpf, J. B., & Baudonnière, P. M. (1993). Self-awareness and other-awareness: Mirror self-recognition and synchronic imitation among unfamiliar peers. *Developmental Psychology*, *29*(1), 88−95. Available from https://doi.org/10.1037/0012-1649.29.1.88.

Baird, A., & Samson, S. (2014). Music evoked autobiographical memory after severe acquired brain injury: Preliminary findings from a case series. *Neuropsychological Rehabilitation*, *24* (1), 125−143. Available from https://doi.org/10.1080/09602011.2013.858642.

Baird, A., & Samson, S. (2015). Music and dementia. In *Progress in brain research* (Vol. 217, pp. 207−235). <https://doi.org/10.1016/bs.pbr.2014.11.028>

Bangert, A. S., & Balota, D. A. (2012). Keep up the pace: Declines in simple repetitive timing differentiate healthy aging from the earliest stages of Alzheimer's disease. *Journal of the International Neuropsychological Society*, *18*(6), 1052−1063. Available from https://doi.org/10.1017/S1355617712000860.

Bediou, B., Ryff, I., Mercier, B., Milliery, M., Hanaff, M. A., D'Amato, T., et al. (2009). Impaired social cognition in mild Alzheimer disease. *Journal of Geriatric Psychiatry and Neurology*, *22*(2), 130−140. Available from https://doi.org/10.1177/0891988709332939.

Black, W., & Almeida, O. P. (2004). A systematic review of the association between the behavioral and psychological symptoms of dementia and burden of care. *International Psychogeriatrics*, *16*(3), 295−315. Available from https://doi.org/10.1017/s1041610204000468.

Blood, A. J., & Zatorre, R. J. (2001). Intensely pleasurable responses to music correlate with activity in brain regions implicated in reward and emotion. *Proceedings of the National Academy of Sciences of the United States of America*, *98*(20). Available from https://doi.org/10.1073/pnas.191355898.

Caddell, L. S., & Clare, L. (2010). The impact of dementia on self and identity: A systematic review. *Clinical Psychology Review*, *30*(1), 113−126. Available from https://doi.org/10.1016/j.cpr.2009.10.003.

Calvo-Merino, B., Glaser, D. E., Grèzes, J., Passingham, R. E., & Haggard, P. (2005). Action observation and acquired motor skills: An FMRI study with expert dancers. *Cerebral Cortex (New York, N.Y.: 1991)*, *15*(8), 1243−1249. Available from https://doi.org/10.1093/cercor/bhi007.

Caramelli, P., Mansur, L. L., & Nitrini, R. (1998). *Language and communication disorders in dementia of the Alzheimer type. Handbook of neurolinguistics* (pp. 463−473). Academic Press. Woodhead Publishing Limited. Available from https://doi.org/10.1016/B978-012666055-5/50036-8.

Choi, A. N., Lee, M. S., Cheong, K. J., & Lee, J. S. (2009). Effects of group music intervention on behavioral and psychological symptoms in patients with dementia: A pilot-controlled trial. *International Journal of Neuroscience*, *119*(4), 471−481. Available from https://doi.org/10.1080/00207450802328136.

Christensen, H., Griffiths, K., Mackinnon, A., & Jacomb, P. (1997). A quantitative review of cognitive deficits in depression and Alzheimer-type dementia. *Journal of the International Neuropsychological Society: JINS*, *3*(6), 631−651.

Chu, H., Yang, C. Y., Lin, Y., Ou, K. L., Lee, T. Y., O'Brien, A. P., et al. (2014). The impact of group music therapy on depression and cognition in elderly persons with dementia: A randomized controlled study. *Biological Research for Nursing*, *16*(2), 209−217. Available from https://doi.org/10.1177/1099800413485410.

Cohen, E., Ejsmond-frey, R., Knight, N., & Dunbar, R. I. M. (2010). Rowers' high: Behavioural synchrony is correlated with elevated pain thresholds. *Biology Letters*, *6*(1), 106−108. Available from https://doi.org/10.1098/rsbl.2009.0670.

Cohen-Mansfield, J., Marx, M. S., & Rosenthal, A. S. (1989). A description of agitation in a nursing home. *Journals of Gerontology, 44*(3). Available from https://doi.org/10.1093/geronj/44.3.M77.

Cuddy, L. L., & Duffin, J. (2005). Music, memory, and Alzheimer's disease: Is music recognition spared in dementia, and how can it be assessed? *Medical Hypotheses, 64*(2), 229−235. Available from https://doi.org/10.1016/j.mehy.2004.09.005.

Cuddy, L. L., Sikka, R., Silveira, K., Bai, S., & Vanstone, A. (2017). Music-evoked autobiographical memories (MEAMs) in Alzheimer disease: Evidence for a positivity effect. *Cogent Psychology, 4*(1), 1−20. Available from https://doi.org/10.1080/23311908.2016.1277578.

Dalla Bella, S., Farrugia, N., Benoit, C., Begel, V., Verga, L., Harding, E., et al. (2016). BAASTA: Battery for the Assessment of Auditory Sensorimotor and Timing Abilities. *Behavior Research Methods, 49*(3), 1128−1145. Available from https://doi.org/10.3758/s13428-016-0773-6.

Demos, A. P., Chaffin, R., Begosh, K. T., Daniels, J. R., & Marsh, K. L. (2012). Rocking to the beat: Effects of music and partner's movements on spontaneous interpersonal coordination. *Journal of Experimental Psychology: General, 141*(1), 49−53. Available from https://doi.org/10.1037/a0023843.

Domes, G., Heinrichs, M., Michel, A., Berger, C., & Herpertz, S. C. (2007). Oxytocin improves "mind-reading" in humans. *Biological Psychiatry, 61*(6), 731−733. Available from https://doi.org/10.1016/j.biopsych.2006.07.015.

Ehrenreich, B. (2007). *Dancing in the streets: A history of collective joy.* New York: Metropolitan Books.

Feldman, R. (2007a). Mother-infant synchrony and the development of moral orientation in childhood and adolescence: Direct and indirect mechanisms of developmental continuity. *American Journal of Orthopsychiatry, 77*(4), 582−597.

Feldman, R. (2007b). Parent-infant synchrony and the construction of shared timing; physiological precursors, developmental outcomes, and risk conditions. *Journal of Child Psychology and Psychiatry, and Allied Disciplines, 48*, 329−354. Available from https://doi.org/10.1111/j.1469-7610.2006.01701.x.

Fernandez-Duque, D., Baird, J. A., & Black, S. E. (2009). False-belief understanding in frontotemporal dementia and Alzheimer's disease. *Journal of Clinical and Experimental Neuropsychology, 31*(4), 489−497. Available from https://doi.org/10.1080/13803390802282688.

Fernandez-Duque, D., Hodges, S. D., Baird, J. A., & Black, S. E. (2010). Empathy in frontotemporal dementia and Alzheimer's disease. *Journal of Clinical and Experimental Neuropsychology, 32*(3), 289−298.

Ferreri, L., Mas-Herrero, E., Zatorre, R. J., Ripollés, P., Gomez-Andres, A., Alicart, H., et al. (2019). Dopamine modulates the reward experiences elicited by music. *Proceedings of the National Academy of Sciences of the United States of America, 116*(9), 3793−3798. Available from https://doi.org/10.1073/pnas.1811878116.

Feyereisen, P., & Hupet, M. (2007). Pragmatic skills in the early stages of Alzheimer's disease: An analysis by means of a referential communication task. *International Journal of Language, 42*(1), 1−17. Available from https://doi.org/10.1080/13682820600624216.

Fraisse, P. (1982). Rhythm and tempo. In *Psychology of music* (pp. 149−180).

Ghilain, M., Schiaratura, L., Lesaffre, M., Six, J., Clément, S., & Samson, S. (in rev). Does a life performance impacts rhythmic synchronization to music and metronome in Alzheimer disease?

Ghilain, M., Schiaratura, L., Singh, A., Lesaffre, M., & Samson, S. (2019). Is music special for people with dementia. In A. Baird, S. Garrido, & J. Tamplin (Eds.), *Music and dementia: From cognition to therapy.* (Oxford University).

Gregory, C., Lough, S., Stone, V., Erzinclioglu, S., Martin, L., Baron-Cohen, S., et al. (2002). Theory of mind in patients with frontal variant frontotemporal dementia and Alzheimer's disease: Theoretical and practical implications. *Brain, 125*, 752−764.

El Haj, M., Postal, V., & Allain, P. (2012). Music enhances autobiographical memory in mild Alzheimer's disease. *Educational Gerontology, 38*(1), 30−41. Available from https://doi. org/10.1080/03601277.2010.515897.

Harrist, A. W., & Waugh, R. M. (2002). Dyadic synchrony: Its structure and function in children's development. *Developmental Review, 22*, 555−592.

Hier, D. B., Hagenlocker, K., & Shindler, A. G. (1985). Language disintegration in dementia: Effects of etiology and severity. *Brain and Language, 25*(1), 117−133. Available from https://doi.org/10.1016/0093-934X(85)90124-5.

Hodges, J. R. (2000). Memory in the dementias. In *The Oxford handbook of memory* (pp. 441−459).

Holmes, C., Knights, A., Dean, C., Hodkinson, S., & Hopkins, V. (2006). Keep music live: Music and the alleviation of apathy in dementia subjects. *International Psychogeriatrics, 18* (4), 623−630. Available from https://doi.org/10.1017/s1041610206003887.

Hove, M. J., & Risen, J. L. (2009). It's all in the timing: Interpersonal synchrony increases affiliation. *Social Cognition, 27*(6), 949−960. Available from https://doi.org/10.1521/ soco.2009.27.6.949.

Janata, P., Tomic, S. T., & Haberman, J. M. (2012). Sensorimotor coupling in music and the psychology of the groove. *Journal of Experimental Psychology: General, 141*(1), 54−75. Available from https://doi.org/10.1037/a0024208.

Johnson, J. K., Chang, C.-C., Brambati, S. M., Migliaccio, R., Gorno-Tempini, M. L., Miller, B. L., et al. (2011). Music recognition in frontotemporal lobar degeneration and Alzheimer disease. *Cognitive and Behavioral Neurology: Official Journal of the Society for Behavioral and Cognitive Neurology, 24*(2), 74−84.

Kali, T., Baier, R., Kosar, C., Ogarek, J., Trepman, A., & Mor, V. (2017). Individualized music program is associated with improved outcomes for U.S. nursing home residents with dementia. *The American Journal of Geriatric Psychiatry, 25*(9), 931−938.

Keller, P. E., Novembre, G., & Hove, M. J. (2014). Rhythm in joint action: Psychological and neurophysiological mechanisms for real-time interpersonal coordination. *Philosophical Transactions of the Royal Society B: Biological Sciences, 369*.

Kirschbaum, C., & Hellhammer, D. H. (1994). Salivary cortisol in psychoneuroendocrine research: Recent developments and applications. *Psychoneuroendocrinology, 19*(4), 313−333.

Klimova, B., Maresova, P., Valis, M., Hort, J., & Kuca, K. (2015). Alzheimer's disease and language impairments: Social intervention and medical treatment. *Clinical Interventions in Aging, 10*, 1401.

Kluger, A., Gianutsos, J. G., Golomb, J., Ferris, S. H., & Reisberg, B. (1997). Motor/psychomotor dysfunction in normal aging, mild cognitive decline, and early Alzheimer's disease: Diagnostic and differential diagnostic features. *International Psychogeriatrics, 9*(S1), 307−316. Available from https://doi.org/10.1017/s1041610297005048.

Koehne, S., Behrends, A., Fairhurst, M. T., & Dziobek, I. (2016). Fostering social cognition through an imitation- and synchronization-based dance/movement intervention in adults with autism spectrum disorder: A controlled proof-of-concept study. *Psychotherapy and Psychosomatics, 85*(1), 27−35. Available from https://doi.org/10.1159/000441111.

Koelsch, S. (2014). Brain correlates of music-evoked emotions. *Nature Reviews Neuroscience, 15*(3), 170. Available from https://doi.org/10.1038/nrn3666.

Kosfeld, M., Heinrichs, M., Zak, P. J., Fischbacher, U., & Fehr, E. (2005). Oxytocin increases trust in humans. *Nature, 435*, 673−676. Available from https://doi.org/10.1038/nature03701.

Lakin, J. L., Jefferis, V. E., Cheng, C. M., & Chartrand, T. L. (2003). The chameleon effect as social glue: Evidence for the evolutionary significance of nonconscious mimicry. *Journal of Nonverbal Behavior, 27*(3), 145−162.

Leman, M., & Buhmann, J. (2017). *The empowering effects of being locked into the beat of the music. Body, sound and space in music and beyond: Multimodal explorations* (pp. 11−28). Routledge.

Lesaffre, M., Moens, B., & Desmet, F. (2017). *Monitoring music and movement interaction in people with dementia. The Routledge companion to embodied music interaction* (pp. 294−303). Routledge.

Luppa, M., Luck, T., Brähler, E., König, H. H., & Riedel-Heller, S. G. (2008). Prediction of institutionalisation in dementia: A systematic review. *Dementia and Geriatric Cognitive Disorders, 26*(1), 65−78. Available from https://doi.org/10.1159/000144027.

Martel, F. L., Nevison, C. M., Simpson, M. J. A., & Keverne, E. B. (1995). Effects of opioid receptor blockade on the social behavior of rhesus monkeys living in large family groups. *Developmental Psychobiology, 28*(2), 71−84. Available from https://doi.org/10.1002/dev.420280202.

Mas-Herrero, E., Dagher, A., & Zatorre, R. J. (2018). Modulating musical reward sensitivity up and down with transcranial magnetic stimulation. *Nature Human Behaviour, 2*(1), 27−32. Available from https://doi.org/10.1038/s41562-017-0241-z.

Mehr, S. A., Singh, M., York, H., Glowacki, L., & Krasnow, M. M. (2018). Form and function in human song. *Current Biology, 28*(3), 356−368.e5. Available from https://doi.org/10.1016/j.cub.2017.12.042.

Mogan, R., Fischer, R., & Bulbulia, J. A. (2017). To be in synchrony or not? A meta-analysis of synchrony's effects on behavior, perception, cognition and affect. *Journal of Experimental Social Psychology, 72*(September), 13−20. Available from https://doi.org/10.1016/j.jesp.2017.03.009.

Narme, P., Clément, S., Ehrlé, N., Schiaratura, L., Vachez, S., Courtaigne, B., et al. (2014). Efficacy of musical interventions in dementia: Evidence from a randomized controlled trial. *Journal of Alzheimer's Disease, 38*, 359−369. Available from https://doi.org/10.3233/JAD-130893.

National Institute for Health and Care Excellence. (2018). *Dementia: Assessment, management and support for people living with dementia and their carers.* https://doi.org/10.1007/978-1-349-95810-8_867.

Nicholas, M., Obler, L. K., Albert, M. L., & Helm-Estabrooks, N. (1985). Empty speech in Alzheimer's disease and fluent aphasia. *Journal of Speech and Hearing Research, 28*, 405−410.

Oullier, O., Guzman, G. C., De Jantzen, K. J., Lagarde, J., & Kelso, J. A. S. (2008). Social coordination dynamics: Measuring human bonding. *Social Neuroscience, 3*(2), 178−192. Available from https://doi.org/10.1080/17470910701563392.

Panasiti, M. S., Porciello, G., & Aglioti, S. M. (2017). The bright and the dark sides of motor simulation. *Neuropsychologia, 105*, 92−100. Available from https://doi.org/10.1016/j.neuropsychologia.2017.05.020.

Pankseep, J. (1995). The emotional sources of "chills" induced by music. *Music Perception: An Interdisciplinary Journal, 13*(2), 171−207.

de Paula, J. J., Albuquerque, M. R., Lage, G. M., Bicalho, M. A., Romano-Silva, M. A., & Malloy-Diniz, L. F. (2016). Impairment of fine motor dexterity in mild cognitive impairment and Alzheimer's disease dementia: Association with activities of daily living. *Revista Brasileira de Psiquiatria, 38*(3), 235−238. Available from https://doi.org/10.1590/1516-4446-2015-1874.

Perkins, L., Whitworth, A., & Lesser, R. (1998). Conversing in dementia: A conversation analytic approach. *Journal of Neurolinguistics*, *11*(1−2), 33−53. Available from https://doi.org/10.1016/S0911-6044(98)00004-9.

Potkins, D., Myint, P., Bannister, C., Tadros, G., Chithramohan, R., Swann, A., et al. (2003). Language impairment in dementia: Impact on symptoms and care needs in residential homes. *International Journal of Geriatric Psychiatry*, *18*(11), 1002−1006. Available from https://doi.org/10.1002/gps.1002.

Radcliffe-Brown, A. R. (1952). *Structure and function in primitive society*. Glencoe, IL: The Free Press.

Raglio, A., Bellelli, G., Mazzola, P., Bellandi, D., Giovagnoli, A. R., Farina, E., et al. (2012). Music, music therapy and dementia: A review of literature and the recommendations of the Italian Psychogeriatric Association. *Maturitas*, *72*(4), 305−310. Available from https://doi.org/10.1016/j.maturitas.2012.05.016.

Reddish, P., Fischer, R., & Bulbulia, J. (2013). Let's dance together: Synchrony, shared intentionality and cooperation. *PLoS One*, *8*(8), e71182. Available from https://doi.org/10.1371/journal.pone.0071182.

Reisberg, B., Auer, S. R., & Monteiro, I. M. (1997). Behavioral pathology in Alzheimer's disease (BEHAVE-AD) rating scale. *International Psychogeriatrics*, *8*(3), 301−308.

Repp, B. H. (2005). Sensorimotor synchronization: A review of the tapping literature. *Psychonomic Bulletin & Review*, *12*(6), 969−992.

Richardson, M. J., Marsh, K. L., Isenhower, R. W., Goodman, J. R. L., & Schmidt, R. C. (2007). Rocking together: Dynamics of intentional and unintentional interpersonal coordination. *Human Movement Science*, *26*, 867−891. Available from https://doi.org/10.1016/j.humov.2007.07.002.

Ridder, H. M. O., Stige, B., Qvale, L. G., & Gold, C. (2013). Individual music therapy for agitation in dementia: An exploratory randomized controlled trial. *Aging and Mental Health*, *17*(6), 667−678. Available from https://doi.org/10.1080/13607863.2013.790926.

Ripich, D. N., Vertes, D., Whitehouse, P., Fulton, S., & Ekelman, B. (1991). Turn-taking and speech act patterns in the discourse of senile dementia of the Alzheimer's type patients. *Brain and Language*, *40*(3), 330−343. Available from https://doi.org/10.1016/0093-934X(91)90133-L.

Sakamoto, M., Ando, H., & Tsutou, A. (2013). Comparing the effects of different individualized music interventions for elderly individuals with severe dementia. *International Psychogeriatrics*, *25*(5), 775−784. Available from https://doi.org/10.1017/s1041610212002256.

Salimpoor, V. N., Benovoy, M., Larcher, K., Dagher, A., & Zatorre, R. J. (2011). Anatomically distinct dopamine release during anticipation and experience of peak emotion to music. *Nature Neuroscience*, *14*(2), 257−262. Available from https://doi.org/10.1038/nn.2726.

Salimpoor, V. N., Van Den Bosch, I., Kovacevic, N., McIntosh, A. R., Dagher, A., & Zatorre, R. J. (2013). Interactions between the nucleus accumbens and auditory cortices predict music reward value. *Science (New York, N.Y.)*, *340*(6129), 216−219. Available from https://doi.org/10.1126/science.1231059.

Salimpoor, V. N., Zald, D. H., Zatorre, R. J., Dagher, A., & McIntosh, A. R. (2015). Predictions and the brain: How musical sounds become rewarding. *Trends in Cognitive Sciences*, *19*(2), 86−91. Available from https://doi.org/10.1016/j.tics.2014.12.001.

Särkämö, T., Tervaniemi, M., Laitinen, S., Numminen, A., Kurki, M., Johnson, J. K., et al. (2014). Cognitive, emotional, and social benefits of regular musical activities in early dementia: Randomized controlled study. *The Gerontologist*, *54*(4), 634−650. Available from https://doi.org/10.1093/geront/gnt100.

Schiaratura, L. T. (2008). Non-verbal communication in Alzheimer's disease. *La Communication Non Verbale Dans La Maladie d'Alzheimer*, *6*(3), 183−188. Available from https://doi.org/10.1684/pnv.2008.0140.

Schiaratura, L. T., Di Pastena, A., Askevis-Leherpeux, F., & Clément, S. (2015). Expression verbale et gestualité dans la maladie d'Alzheimer: une étude en situation d'interaction sociale. *Geriatrie et Psychologie Neuropsychiatrie Du Vieillissement*, *13*(1), 97−105. Available from https://doi.org/10.1684/pnv.2014.0514.

Schino, G., & Troisi, A. (1992). Opiate receptor blockade in juvenile macaques: Effect on affiliative interactions with their mothers and group companions. *Brain Research*, *576*(1), 125−130. Available from https://doi.org/10.1016/0006-8993(92)90617-I.

Sherratt, K., Thornton, A., & Hatton, C. (2004). Music interventions for people with dementia: A review of the literature. *Aging and Mental Health*, *8*(1), 3−12. Available from https://doi.org/10.1080/13607860310001613275.

Shimokawa, A., Yatomi, N., Anamizu, S., Torii, S., Isono, H., Sugai, Y., et al. (2001). Influence of deteriorating ability of emotional comprehension on interpersonal behavior in Alzheimer-type dementia. *Brain and Cognition*, *47*(3), 423−433. Available from https://doi.org/10.1006/brcg.2001.1318.

Sihvonen, A. J., Särkämö, T., Leo, V., Tervaniemi, M., Altenmüller, E., & Soinila, S. (2017). Music-based interventions in neurological rehabilitation. *The Lancet Neurology*, *16*(8), 648−660. Available from https://doi.org/10.1016/S1474-4422(17)30168-0.

Sisco, F., Taurel, M., Lafont, V., Bertogliati, C., Baudu, C., Giordana, J. Y., et al. (2000). Les troubles du comportement chez le sujet dément en institution: évaluation à partir de l'inventaire neuropsychiatrique pour les équipes soignantes (NPI/ES). *L'Année Gérontologique*, *14*, 151−173.

Small, J. A., Geldart, K., Gutman, G., Ann, M., & Scott, C. (1998). The discourse of self in dementia. *Ageing and Society*, *18*.

Spielberger, C. D., Gorsuch, R., Lushene, R. E., Vagg, P. R., & Jacobs, G. A. (1983). *Manual for the state-trait anxiety inventory*. Palo Alto, CA: Consulting Psychologists Press.

van der Steen, J. T., Van Soest-Poortvliet, M. C., Van Der Wouden, J. C., Bruinsma, M. S., Scholten, R. J., & Vink, A. C. (2018). Music-based therapeutic interventions for people with dementia (review). *Cochrane Database of Systematic Reviews*, *7*. Available from https://doi.org/10.1002/14651858.CD003477.pub3.

Suzumura, S., Osawa, A., Nagahama, T., Kondo, I., Sano, Y., & Kandori, A. (2016). Assessment of finger motor skills in individuals with mild cognitive impairment and patients with Alzheimer's disease: Relationship between finger-to-thumb tapping and cognitive function. *Japanese Journal of Comprehensive Rehabilitation*, *7*, 19−28.

Svansdottir, H. B., & Snaedal, J. (2006). Music therapy in moderate and severe dementia of Alzheimer's type: A case-control study. *International Psychogeriatrics*, *18*(4), 613−621. Available from https://doi.org/10.1017/S1041610206003206.

Tarr, B., Launay, J., & Dunbar, R. I. M. (2014). Music and social bonding: "Self-other" merging and neurohormonal mechanisms. *Frontiers in Psychology*, *5*(1096). Available from https://doi.org/10.3389/fpsyg.2014.01096.

Toot, S., Swinson, T., Devine, M., Challis, D., & Orrell, M. (2017). Causes of nursing home placement for older people with dementia: A systematic review and meta-analysis. *International Psychogeriatrics*, *29*(2), 195−208. Available from https://doi.org/10.1017/S1041610216001654.

Tzortzis, C., Goldblum, M. C., Dang, M., Forette, F., & Boller, F. (2000). Absence of amusia and preserved naming of musical instruments in an aphasic composer. *Cortex; A Journal Devoted to the Study of the Nervous System and Behavior*, *36*(2), 227−242. Available from https://doi.org/10.1016/S0010-9452(08)70526-4.

Ueda, T., Suzukamo, Y., Sato, M., & Izumi, S. I. (2013). Effects of music therapy on behavioral and psychological symptoms of dementia: A systematic review and meta-analysis. *Ageing Research Reviews*, *12*(2), 628–641. Available from https://doi.org/10.1016/j.arr.2013.02.003.

van Ulzen, N. R., Lamoth, C. J. C., Daffertshofer, A., Semin, G. R., & Beek, P. J. (2008). Characteristics of instructed and uninstructed interpersonal coordination while walking side-by-side. *Neuroscience Letters*, *432*(2), 88–93. Available from https://doi.org/10.1016/j.neulet.2007.11.070.

Warren, J. D., Warren, J. E., Fox, N. C., & Warrington, E. K. (2003). Nothing to say, something to sing: Primary progressive dynamic aphasia. *Neurocase: Case Studies in Neuropsychology, Neuropsychiatry, and Behavioural Neurology*, *9*(2), 140–155. Available from https://doi.org/10.1076/neur.9.2.140.15068.

Wiltermuth, S. S., & Heath, C. (2009). Synchrony and cooperation. *Psychological Science*, *20*(1), 1–5. Available from https://doi.org/10.1111/j.1467-9280.2008.02253.x.

de Witte, M., Spruit, A., van Hooren, S., Moonen, X., & Stams, G.-J. (2019). Effects of music interventions on stress-related outcomes: A systematic review and two meta-analyses. *Health Psychology Review*, 1–31. Available from https://doi.org/10.1080/17437199.2019.1627897.

Yan, J. H., Rountree, S., Massman, P., Doody, R. S., & Li, H. (2008). Alzheimer's disease and mild cognitive impairment deteriorate fine movement control. *Journal of Psychiatric Research*, *42*(14), 1203–1212. Available from https://doi.org/10.1016/j.jpsychires.2008.01.006.

Zhang, H., Gross, J., De Dreu, C., & Ma, Y. (2018). Oxytocin promotes synchronized out-group attack during intergroup conflict in humans. *eLife*, *8*, e40698. Available from https://doi.org/10.7554/eLife.40698.

Chapter 14

Neurorehabilitation in aging through neurologic music therapy

Michael Thaut and Yuko Koshimori
Music and Health Research Collaboratory, University of Toronto, Toronto, ON, Canada

Neurorehabilitation in aging through neurologic music therapy

Neurologic music therapy (NMT) has been developed as a standardized, music-based rehabilitation technique in the field of sensorimotor, speech and language, and cognitive rehabilitation, pursuant to the neuroscientific findings regarding the effects of rhythm and music on brain structure and function. It stands apart from the traditional role of music in therapy in which music has been primarily attributed to the field of social science as an effective facilitator for psychological well-being, regulation of emotional responses, and relationship building (Thaut & McIntosh, 2014).

Recent advancements in neuroimaging techniques have uncovered that the auditory areas have widely distributed connections to other functional brain areas including regions for motor control, cognition, emotion, and motivation. This suggests that rhythm and music can stimulate nonauditory brain regions including those affected by neurological diseases and psychiatric disorders (e.g., stimulating the residual/spared neural resources in the affected brain regions) and/or can stimulate unaffected (e.g., homologous) areas that can compensate for impaired functions. In fact, preliminary behavioral studies combined with neuroimaging techniques have started to show such data. Therefore rhythm and music are a potentially powerful modality for recovery of brain dysfunction. This neuroscientific pursuit of music-based interventions is essential to facilitate further development of the interventions in the field of health and medicine.

As populations are growing old, age-associated neurological disorders and injuries have become prevalent. Aging is one of the important risk factors for devastating neurodegenerative diseases such as Alzheimer's disease

Music and the Aging Brain. DOI: https://doi.org/10.1016/B978-0-12-817422-7.00014-6

(AD; the most common form of dementia), followed by Parkinson's disease (PD). AD and dementia in general present memory impairment and executive dysfunction interfering with daily life activities (Scheltens et al., 2016). PD produces cardinal motor symptoms such as resting tremor, rigidity, bradykinesia (slowness of movement), and postural instability, secondary motor symptoms such as speech disorders, as well as nonmotor symptoms such as cognitive impairment. To date, there is no cure and effective preventive measures for these diseases. In addition to these chronic neurological diseases, stroke is prevalent in older adults, showing a disproportionately higher incidence compared to younger adults aged ≤ 45 (O'Donnell et al., 2010). Stroke often causes impairments in motor behaviors such as walking (Mehrholz, Thomas, & Elsner, 2017). However, depending on the location of the stroke, it can also cause various impairments such as hemispatial neglect and nonfluent aphasia. NMT techniques have been applied to alleviate the symptomology from motor, language and speech, to cognitive impairments. This chapter introduces NMT techniques for motor, language and speech, and cognitive rehabilitation, with emphasis for those with aging-associated neurological disorders such as PD, stroke, and dementia, summarizing the behavioral and neuroimaging research data, as well as presenting future directions for research in the field of music and neuroscience.

Motor rehabilitation

Rhythmic auditory stimulation

Rhythmic auditory stimulation (RAS) is one of the most researched and established neurorehabilitation techniques of NMT. RAS is applied in a form of repetitive isochronous auditory pulses such as metronome clicks or metrical acoustical beats embedded in music (usually in 2/4 or 4/4 m) to "entrain" an individual's cadence (steps per minute) in time to the rhythmic cues, resulting in stable and consistent gait kinematic parameters as well as amplitude and time variability of muscle activation patterns (Thaut, Kenyon, Hurt, McIntosh, & Hoemberg, 2002).

Entrainment in physics refers to a phenomenon in which two different oscillating bodies resonate in the same coupled frequencies (Thaut, 2015) and frequency or period entrainment induced by RAS (Large, Fink, & Kelso, 2002; Nozaradan, Peretz, Missal, & Mouraux, 2011; Thaut & Kenyon, 2003) drives the steady-state tracking strategy to improve motor control. More specifically, the period entrainment gives the brain an interval reference with which velocity and acceleration are computed to help plan movements and map them on the temporal rhythmic template (Kenyon & Thaut, 2000; Prassas, Thaut, McIntosh, & Rice, 1997; Thaut, Tian, & Azimi-Sadjadi, 1998). Therefore auditory rhythm via physiological period entrainment of the motor system can facilitate the elements required for motor control (Thaut, 2015).

The most pronounced entrainment effects during finger tapping were demonstrated with frequencies ranging from 1 to 4 Hz (e.g., Braunlich et al., 2018; Crasta, Thaut, Anderson, Davies, & Gavin, 2018; Molinari et al., 2005; Rao et al., 1997; Repp, 2005; Stephan et al., 2002; Thaut & Kenyon, 2003; Thaut, Miller, & Schauer, 1998; Thaut, Tian, et al., 1998).

Neural entrainment of auditory rhythms is not fully understood (Large et al., 2002; Nozaradan, 2014; Patel & Iversen, 2014; Rajendran & Schnupp, 2019). However, a series of EEG studies showed that the periodicity in neural response in the auditory system exactly corresponded to the frequency of an auditory beat (Crasta et al., 2018; Nozaradan et al., 2011; Nozaradan, Peretz, & Mouraux, 2012a; 2012b). An MEG study showed that changes in rhythmic interval durations linearly changes the amplitude of the M100 component of auditory evoked filed potential (Tecchio, Salustri, Thaut, Pasqualetti, & Rossini, 2000). In another MEG study, listening to isochronous auditory rhythms without producing movements induced modulations in beta-band oscillations in bilateral primary auditory cortices according to the periodicity of the stimuli, as well as temporally correlated beta modulation between auditory and motor areas (Fujioka, Trainor, Large, & Ross, 2012).

The auditory—motor entrainment via RAS also entails two important mechanisms to improve motor behavior: priming and anticipation. Priming is the ability of external auditory rhythms to promote recruitment of the motor system for readiness to move (Crasta et al., 2018; Thaut, 2015; Thaut, McIntosh, Prassas, & Rice, 1992; Thaut, Schleiffers, & Davis, 1991). Priming effects were demonstrated by early landmark studies (Paltsev & E-lner, 1967; Rossignol & Jones, 1976). Auditory—motor entrainment also provides the brain with the precise anticipatory time periods to plan movements (Thaut, 2015; Thaut, Kenyon, Schauer, & McIntosh, 1999). This anticipatory nature of rhythmic tracking is usually observed as a motor response slightly ahead of the stimulus (Aschersleben & Prinz, 1995; Thaut, Rathbun, & Miller, 1997). These mechanisms may also be exemplified by more recent neuroimaging studies demonstrating that merely listening to auditory rhythms without producing movements activates motor areas such as the supplementary motor area (SMA), premotor area, basal ganglia (BG), and cerebellum (Chen, Penhune, & Zatorre, 2008; Fujioka et al., 2012; Fujioka, Trainor, Large, & Ross, 2009; Grahn & Brett, 2007; Grahn & Rowe, 2013).

Rhythms can be presented using other sensory systems (i.e., visual and tactile systems). However, the auditory system is faster and more precise to detect a temporal structure than the visual and tactile systems (Comstock, Hove, & Balasubramaniam, 2018; Shelton & Kumar, 2010). These superior features of auditory rhythm for motor rehabilitation were demonstrated in studies by Thaut et al. showing that auditory—motor entrainment occurred without practice or learning and remained locked to frequency modulations even when subliminal changes were induced (Thaut et al., 2002; Thaut, Tian, et al., 1998).

RAS-induced improvement on gait parameters such as velocity, cadence, stride length, and timing variability was first demonstrated in a series of seminal experimental studies and randomized controlled trials (RCTs) in healthy older adults as well as persons with stroke and PD (McIntosh, Brown, Rice, & Thaut, 1997; Prassas et al., 1997; Thaut et al.,1992, 1993, 2007; Thaut, McIntosh, & Rice, 1997). Subsequent controlled clinical trials and RCTs, including four RCTs in stroke (Cha, Kim, Hwang, & Chung, 2014; Jeong & Kim, 2007; Lee, Lee, & Song, 2018; Schauer & Mauritz, 2003) and seven RCTs in PD (de Bruin et al., 2010; Elston, Honan, Powell, Gormley, & Stein, 2010; Harro et al., 2014; Nieuwboer et al., 2007, 2009; Rochester, Baker, Nieuwboer, & Burn, 2011) that involved more than 20 participants, as well as one large-scale RCT in 134 healthy older adults (Trombetti et al., 2011), consistently support the initial findings in these populations (Ghai & Ghai, 2019; Ghai, Ghai, Schmitz, & Effenberg, 2017; Ghai, Ghai, Schmitz, & Effenberg, 2018; Koshimori & Thaut, 2018; Sihvonen et al., 2017). The RAS-induced benefits persisted 3 months after the completion of a 6-week intervention in PD (Harro et al., 2014) and 6 months after the completion of a 6-month intervention in healthy older adults (Trombetti et al., 2011). A clinical dosage of three to five 20–40-min sessions per week is most effective for the clinical populations (Ghai & Ghai, 2019; Ghai, 2018). In addition to improvement of the gait parameters, a more recent RCT including 60 persons with PD demonstrated that an 8-week RAS training significantly reduced incidences of falls (Thaut, Rice, Braun Janzen, Hurt-Thaut, & McIntosh, 2019). Interestingly, another RCT including 41 persons with PD showed that finger tapping with RAS led to immediate improvement in gait parameters, suggesting possible priming across effector systems (Braun Janzen, Haase, & Thaut, 2019). Additionally, the RAS research has extended to investigate the modified applications for its greater effectiveness in a rehabilitation setting (e.g., RCTs on a combination of RAS and treadmill training in stroke by Mainka, Wissel, Völler, & Evers, 2018; in PD by Calabrò et al., 2019); an RCT on ecological RAS in PD by Murgia et al. (2018).

Neuromodulation of RAS can be investigated in task-based functional neuroimaging studies using a synchronization paradigm. In this paradigm, a participant performs a simple motor task such as finger tapping cued by auditory rhythm with the frequencies between 1 and 4 Hz (Thaut, Miller, et al., 1998; Thaut, Tian, et al., 1998). To elucidate the facilitating effects of auditory rhythm on motor responses, the neural activity in the synchronization paradigm can be contrasted to that in a continuation paradigm in which a participant performs the same motor task without auditory rhythmic cues (Braunlich et al., 2018; Koshimori & Thaut, 2018; Koshimori et al., 2019; Teghil et al., 2019). The neural modulations during finger tapping with RAS may be able to shed light on the neural plasticity that has occurred after RAS gait training because behavioral studies demonstrated a transfer effect between walking and finger tapping using RAS (Braun Janzen et al., 2019; del Olmo, Arias, Furio, Pozo, & Cudeiro, 2006).

One fMRI study using the synchronization—continuation paradigm showed that both older healthy control and medicated PD groups behaviorally benefitted from RAS and that the PD group showed weaker intranetwork connectivity in the auditory, salience, motor/inferior frontal gyrus (IFG), BG/thalamus, and motor/cerebellar networks but greater compensatory internetwork connectivity between auditory and executive control as well as between executive control and motor/cerebellar networks during both synchronization and continuation tasks compared to the control group. When the neural activity during the synchronization task was contrasted with that of the continuation task, it showed greater activation in only the auditory network consisting of bilateral auditory areas (Braunlich et al., 2018).

In addition to this experimental paradigm during a functional neuroimaging scan, neural plasticity induced by RAS training can be investigated by contrasting neuroimaging data between pre- and postintervention. One study used PET to investigate the behavioral and neural changes pre- and post-RAS training in medicated persons with PD (del Olmo et al., 2006). The PD group received gait and repetitive arm training using RAS for 1 hour daily for 5 days a week over a period of 4 weeks. Following the training, the PD group showed significantly reduced temporal variabilities of both gait and finger tapping, which became compatible to those observed in the healthy control group. These patients also showed significantly increased activity in the right anterior cerebellum and the right parietal and temporal lobes (BA 22, 42, 43) posttraining compared to pretraining. This study suggests that strengthened right-lateralized auditory and corticocerebellar activity may present compensatory/adaptive responses that emerged after the training in PD.

These two studies demonstrated the functional changes in the cerebellum, which is consistent with the externally triggered explicit timing tasks (Coull & Nobre, 2008) recruiting the cerebellothalamocortical circuit (Avanzino et al., 2016; Nombela, Hughes, Owen, & Grahn, 2013). The greater involvement of the executive control network consisting of bilateral prefrontal, inferior parietal, and medical frontal areas during finger tapping task with RAS observed in the PD group (Braunlich et al., 2018) may be partly associated with the recruitment of associative BG and thalamocortical circuitry by externally triggered explicit timing tasks (Avanzino et al., 2016).

Both BG and cerebellar circuits are associated with timing control, and closely communicate with each other through their anatomical connections not only on the thalamocortical level but also on BG—cerebellum levels (Bostan, Dum, & Strick, 2010; Hoshi, Tremblay, Féger, Carras, & Strick, 2005; Milardi et al., 2016; Pelzer et al., 2013). BG and cerebellum are involved in timing processes in a distinct way, but their contributions to the function may be interchangeable depending on task conditions or damage to their circuits (Petter, Lusk, Hesslow, & Meck, 2016). Further studies are needed in drug-naïve and unmedicated persons with PD to clarify how RAS interacts with motor and other networks when BG and thalamocortical circuits and dopaminergic function are compromised.

Patterned sensory enhancement and therapeutic instrumental music playing

While RAS is primarily used for the rehabilitation of gait movement, there are two NMT techniques to improve whole body movements and functional movements of daily activities, such as reaching, grasping, and sit-to-stand transfers, involving the upper extremities and full body that are not intrinsically rhythmic by nature (Mertel, 2014; Thaut & McIntosh, 2014; Thaut, 2014a). These include patterned sensory enhancement (PSE) and therapeutic instrumental music playing (TIMP) in which the functional movements are practiced via cyclical repetitive movement patterns that can also be cued by rhythmic stimuli. In the PSE technique, the rhythmic, melodic, harmonic, and dynamic acoustical elements of music serve as temporal, spatial, and force-dynamic components of movement kinematics, similar to sonification (Ghai, 2018), to assemble single discrete motions with feedback and feedforward regulation to enhance motor control. PSE is also effective to increase physical strength and endurance, and to improve posture and balance (Thaut, 2005). The TIMP technique uses mapping functional movements onto musical instruments such as percussion, keyboard, or digital sound surfaces.

Both techniques create an enriched sound environment that primes the motor system. TIMP particularly provides auditory feedback for spatial movement control via sounds produced from striking the instrument or digital sound device correctly. It also provides an anticipatory timing structure for movement, which actually integrates rhythmic feedforward information with the acoustical feedback information generated by the movement itself.

These techniques have been mostly applied to stroke rehabilitation (Ghai, 2018; Thaut & McIntosh, 2014). The beneficial effects that have been demonstrated in multiple controlled clinical trials and RCTs include increases in ranges of motion with increases in isometric arm-joint strength and significant improvements on several standardized tests of arm function, decreases in variability and increases in speed of movement times, and smoothing of trajectory variability during reaching movements. TIMP has also been shown to be more effective compared to conventional physical therapy in persons with subacute stroke (Altenmüller, Marco-Pallare, Münte, & Schneider, 2009; Schneider, Müünte, Rodriguez-Fornells, Sailer, & Altenmüller, 2010; Schneider, Schönle, Altenmüller, & Müünte, 2007). In addition to the improvement of functional movements, recent RCTs showed that TIMP has a positive effect on patients' motivation (Grau-Sánchez et al., 2018; Street et al., 2018). Furthermore, neuroimaging studies showed that improved functional movements were accompanied by neuroplasticity in the affected hemisphere such as greater EEG coherence (Altenmüller et al., 2009), altered excitability in the motor cortex (Grau-Sánchez et al., 2013), an increase in activity and connectivity between auditory and motor regions (Ripollés et al., 2016), as well as a normalization of somatotopic organization with recovered digit separation and increased gamma synchrony in the somatosensory cortex (Jamali & Ross, 2013).

There are also two studies in PD. One study employed all of the three NMT motor techniques (i.e., RAS, PSE, and TIMP) to assess their benefits on spatiotemporal gait parameters (stance and swing phase, double support, stride time and cadence, step and stride length, velocity and step width) and postural stability in 30 persons with PD (Bukowska, Krężałek, Mirek, Bujas, & Marchewka, 2016). The PD group who underwent the NMT training consisting of a 45-minutes training session four times per week for 4 weeks showed significant improvement on all the parameters except the step width posttraining compared to pretraining. Similar benefits were also observed when the group was compared to a control group consisting of 25 persons with PD who was asked to continue to be active and perform their daily activities such as walking, walking stairs, and changing of position. The authors interpreted no improvement in step width as indicating that it might reflect a compensatory behavior for increasing balance disorders in the control group. Benefits of the training in stability were limited with a lesser extent compared to those in gait parameters. Another PD study was a case study using MEG (Buard, Dewispelaere, Thaut, & Kluger, 2019). Three persons with PD received a TIMP training administered by an NMT-certified music therapist three times per week for 5 weeks. This study provides preliminary evidence that TIMP alleviated the severity of motor symptoms measured on the motor part of Unified Parkinson's Disease Rating Scale (UPDRS III) and strengthened neurophysiological connectivity between cortical auditory and motor areas during finger tapping.

Speech and language rehabilitation

Melodic intonation therapy

Melodic intonation therapy (MIT) was originally developed in the early 1970s to assist speech and language rehabilitation in nonfluent aphasia (Albert, Sparks, & Helm, 1973; Sparks & Holland, 1976; Sparks, Helm, & Albert, 1974) and has been continuously modified by clinicians and researchers. Nonfluent aphasia results from lesions primarily in the left frontal lobe including Broca's area or lesions in the arcuate fasciculus—a white matter tract connecting frontal and temporal lobes (Schlaug, 2016). MIT is the most commonly used speech/language therapy technique in many right-handed persons with stroke (Thaut & McIntosh, 2014).

The NMT protocol follows the original hierarchical structure of MIT, but it has been compressed into a shorter process for clinical efficacy (Thaut, Thaut, & McIntosh, 2014). Briefly, patients intone or sing functional phrases along with left-hand rhythmic tapping, gradually shifting their vocalizations from singing to speech. Functional phrases or brief statements/utterances are sung or intoned, whereby the musical prosody should be modeled closely to the normal speech inflection patterns of the verbal utterance (Thaut et al., 2014). The relative contribution of rhythm and melody to the beneficial effect of MIT is unknown (Schlaug, 2016). However, rhythm may play an equal or more important role than melody in MIT (Stahl, Kotz, Henseler, Turner, & Geyer, 2011).

MIT utilizes differences and commonalities between speaking and singing (Merrett, Peretz, & Wilson, 2014). Earlier studies reported double-dissociation and laterality of speaking and singing: right-handed persons with nonfluent aphasia due to the left frontal damage could sing without much deficit (Hébert, Racette, Gagnon, & Peretz, 2003; Jacome, 1984; Yamadori, Osumi, Masuhara, & Okubo, 1977), while those with the right frontal damage who lost musical ability showed little deficit in speech (Peretz, Belleville, & Fontaine, 1997). However, later neuroimaging studies showed that singing was associated with more distributed regions than restricted right frontal regions (Callan et al., 2006; Jeffries, Fritz, & Braun, 2003; Stewart, Walsh, Frith, & Rothwell, 2010). In contrast to the functional dissociation, there are two important functions shared between speaking and singing: acoustical perception and production features as well as the ability of both systems to embed communicative functions in the auditory modality (Thaut & McIntosh, 2014; Thaut, 2015).

The potential of MIT as a clinical therapy has been demonstrated in multiple controlled clinical studies, but frequently with small sample sizes. The first RCT in 27 persons with aphasia in the subacute stage of stroke showed that those who received MIT benefited significantly on language repetition on trained items with mixed results on untrained items and verbal communication (Van Der Meulen, Van De Sandt-Koenderman, Heijenbrok-Kal, Visch-Brink, & Ribbers, 2014). Subsequently, the same research group conducted a pilot RCT in 17 persons with aphasia in the chronic stage of stroke and reported a significant, but transient MIT benefit on language repetition on trained items without a transfer benefit onto untrained material or functional communication (Van Der Meulen, Van De Sandt-Koenderman, Heijenbrok, Visch-Brink, & Ribbers, 2016). The authors concluded that the benefit of MIT to chronic aphasia was more restricted because it was limited to therapeutic session applications and did not entail training and guidance for use of MIT to transfer to activities of daily living. The latter point receives more and more attention to consider MIT as a key to unlock intact speech circuitry, which has to be trained in a more comprehensive MIT approach in ecologically salient environments (Thaut, Thaut, et al., 2014). The findings of both RCTs, however, need to be interpreted with caution as they were underpowered. Future RCTs with large sample sizes are warranted to establish its clinical efficacy.

Neuroimaging studies reported that MIT leads to neuroplasticity in the damaged left hemisphere (Belin et al., 1996; Breier, Randle, Maher, &

Papanicolaou, 2010). There is also evidence that MIT leads to greater activation in the right fronto-temporal regions (Belin et al., 1996; Özdemir, Norton, & Schlaug, 2006; Schlaug, Marchina, & Norton, 2008), altered right AF (Schlaug et al., 2009), and increased functional connectivity between motor and right homologous language regions (Bitan et al., 2018). These findings suggest that MIT can recruit intact homologous circuitry, compensating for affected speech function and facilitate functional recovery of the affected region.

The following elements in MIT may be considered the main mechanisms engaging preferentially right hemispheric networks for speech production. First, in melodic−rhythmic intonation, vocal output is slower than when spoken. Singing is characterized by syllables being lengthened, chunked, and patterned, contributing to speed reduction in vocal output. The right hemisphere is better suited to process slowly modulating signals. Thus translating spoken language into musical prosody preferentially activates homologous networks of the right hemisphere (Patel, 2008). Second, processing of music engages the right hemisphere (Zatorre, Chen, & Penhune, 2007), thus helping to bypass damaged language networks in the left hemisphere. Third, rhythmic pacing and entrainment predominantly engages networks involving auditory, prefrontal, and parietal regions of the right hemisphere (Stephan et al., 2002). Lastly, left-hand tapping activates homologous networks in the right hemisphere because spoken language and arm gestures are controlled by the same motor control network (Gentilucci & Dalla Volta, 2008).

Rhythmic speech cueing and vocal intonation therapy

Rhythmic speech cueing is used to improve temporal characteristics of speech such as fluency, articulatory rate, pause time, and intelligibility using auditory rhythm (Mainka & Mallien, 2014). It primarily targets dysarthria characterized by slow or hastened, weak, uncoordinated movements of the articulatory muscles, resulting in reduced speech intelligibility and communicative difficulties. Dysarthria is frequently observed in persons with PD (Jankovic, 2008). Thaut, McIntosh, McIntosh, and Hoemberg (2001) investigated the effectiveness of different types of rhythmic components to improve speech intelligibility in 20 persons with PD who had hypokinetic dysarthria. Both metered (using a pulsed auditory stimulation) and patterned (using a prestructured rhythmic sentence at a given tempo) rhythmic cueing led to significant improvement in speech intelligibility rates. However, the positive effects were primarily observed in the severely impaired speakers.

PD also presents speech disorders characterized by monotonous, soft, and breathy speech with short phonation time (Jankovic, 2008; Thaut, 2014b). Vocal intonation therapy (VIT) can be used to improve the symptoms. VIT uses vocal exercises similar to those used by a choir director to warm up and practice vocal control with a choir (Thaut, 2014b). The benefits of vocal exercises have been demonstrated in neurological disorders including PD (De Swart, Willemse, Maassen, & Horstink, 2003; Han, Yun, Chong, & Choi, 2018; Ramig, Bonitati, Lemke, & Horii, 1994).

Cognitive rehabilitation

Musical neglect training

Stroke can cause hemispatial neglect when the insult occurs in the middle cerebral artery of the right parietal, temporal, and frontal cortices (Li & Malhotra, 2015). Hemispatial neglect is characterized by an inability to perceive and orient to sensory events toward one side of space contralateral to the lesioned side (Heilman, Watson, & Valenstein, 1984). The clinical manifestations are most likely due to the damage of the right lateral hemisphere that plays an important role in the attentional process (Li & Malhotra, 2015). As a result, persons with hemispatial neglect may eat food only from one side of the plate or groom (e.g., shave or apply makeup) on one side of the face.

Musical neglect training (MNT) uses active performance exercises on musical instruments (e.g., scale playing on tone bars or keyboards) that are set up in appropriate spatial configurations to focus attention to the neglected visual field (Thaut, 2005). In these exercises, participants are asked to play familiar musical (melodic or rhythmic) patterns on musical instruments that are increasingly extended into the neglect field to drive the attentional search to find and complete all musical events (Abiru, 2014). Another MNT technique uses receptive music listening while engaging in exercises addressing neglect or inattention. One study demonstrated that music stimuli were superior to other sensory stimuli, such as tactile cues and cognitive cues, such as instructions and speech in neglect, because they could alter arousal levels (Hommel et al., 1990).

Several studies demonstrated that music-based intervention techniques improved neglect. Using the active MNT protocols, one study demonstrated that sounds produced by playing decreasing scales on the piano keyboard facilitated spatial exploration in 11 persons with hemispatial neglect, compared to two control conditions: a silent keyboard and a keyboard producing random pitches (Bernardi et al., 2017). In one case study, two persons with chronic stroke received four 30-minute weekly training sessions consisting of learning to play the chime-bar instrument, first by striking all bars moving from the right to the left and then practicing familiar simple melodies. They showed significant improvement on one of the clinical tests immediately and 1 week after postintervention (Bodak, Malhotra, Bernardi, Cocchini, & Stewart, 2014). An immediate effect of NMT training was also supported by another case study including two persons with stroke who had chronic, persistent neglect (Kang & Thaut, 2019).

MNT may be able to modulate the brain activity in the attentional networks: dorsal and ventral attention networks (DAN and VAN, respectively) (Fox, Corbetta, Snyder, Vincent, & Raichle, 2006). DAN is bilateral, including the frontal eye fields and intraparietal sulcus, and is involved in spatial attention, while VAN is right-lateralized, including the anterior IFG and temporoparietal junction, and is involved in sustained attention and arousal, as well as reorientation of attention. In hemispatial neglect, the VAN is structurally damaged while the DAN is structurally intact but functionally disrupted (Baldassarre et al., 2014; Corbetta & Shulman, 2011). Brain connectivity between DAN and the motor network was also disrupted (Baldassarre et al., 2014, 2016; Barrett, Boukrina, & Saleh, 2019). MNT may be able to normalize the functionality in DAN, and/or stimulate the spared area in VAN via connectivity between cortical auditory areas, and these attentional networks as cortical auditory areas are extensively connected to the prefrontal, inferior parietal, and occipital lobes (Hackett, 2015).

Some studies also showed that listening to preferred/pleasant music improved neglect (Chen, Tsai, Huang, & Lin, 2013; Soto et al., 2009; Tsai, Chen, Huang, & Lin, 2013; Tsai, Chen, Huang, Lin, et al., 2013). In addition, the case study of three persons with neglect conducted by Soto et al. (2009) demonstrated that the improved performance on a detection task with preferred music compared to unpreferred music was accompanied with enhanced coupling between emotional and attentional areas. Furthermore, the study by Chen et al. (2013) demonstrated that listening to preferred, pleasant music chosen by the participants resulted in improvement of the performance on clinical assessments and on a functional visual exploration task, as well as eye movements in a group of 19 participants (acute and chronic stages combined) compared to listening to participant-chosen unpleasant music and white noise. Furthermore, the participants rated their mood as more positive and arousal as higher (but not reflected in the measurements of heart rate or galvanic skin response) with preferred music. The same research group also reported in a case study of two persons with chronic stroke that the positive effects of repetitive listening to preferred, pleasant music persisted for 2 weeks postintervention (Tsai, Chen, Huang, & Lin, 2013). Using a similar design to the one employed by Chen et al. (2013), Tsai, Chen, Huang, and Lin (2013), Tsai, Chen, Huang, Lin, et al. (2013) compared investigator-chosen classical music to white noise and silence in 16 persons with neglect. The study did not find any statistically significant differences among three conditions although the classical music condition tended to show higher scores on clinical tests compared to two other conditions.

The inconsistent results may be due to the difference in music (i.e., participant- vs investigator-chosen music). The effectiveness of preferred/pleasant music may be because it produces positive affect, which in turn, improves attention (Rowe, Hirsh, & Anderson, 2006) via enhanced activity in the orbitofrontal cortex and cingulate gyrus (Soto et al., 2009). Repetitive listening to participant-chosen preferred music was also demonstrated to improve focused attention and emotion (with less depression and confusion) in 19 persons with acute stroke (Särkämö et al., 2008).

Musical executive function training

Musical executive function training (MEFT) aims to improve executive skills—decision-making, problem-solving, reasoning, comprehending, planning, initiating, inhibiting, etc.—through functional music-based exercises, involving improvisation and composition tasks, in a group or individually (Thaut, 2005). The level of complexity in the music exercises can vary. In one training setting, a therapist may prepare several songs with missing key words to be filled by the client group to promote creative problem-solving, initiating interactions, and address executive motivation in enjoyable learning environments (Gardiner and Thaut, 2014). In a more advanced exercise, a therapist may guide the client or the group through each step of the spontaneous process of creating and performing a piece of music using easily accessible instruments such as percussion or keyboard. This exercise involves executive functions such as decision-making, problem-solving, reasoning, comprehending, organizing, evaluating, and creative thinking. More specifically, the client or the group is required to plan and decide how to build a spontaneous composition, ideas to express in the music, instruments (pitched and nonpitched percussion instruments, keyboards, and sound tablets), and sound types (melodies, sound clusters, rhythms, tempi, etc.). Finally, the client or the group performs on live instruments (or digital devices due to physical movement constraints) to integrate the process and product in real time.

Musical attention control training

Musical attention control training focuses on the rehabilitation of attention skills including attention control/switching and selective attention/executive control skills (Thaut and Gardiner, 2014). In one exercise targeting selective attention, the therapist and the client may play together following a basic improvisational scheme and the client has to respond musically to a specific musical cue that appears in a random sequence. In order to succeed, the client has to select and respond to one distinct auditory event selected from a large array of the musical events. Music contains the most comprehensive array and combinatorial richness of acoustical elements of any auditory "language" that can be manipulated to create diverse auditory patterns with a wide range of different degrees of complexity. In another training exercise targeting divided attention, the client may have to track and respond to two different musical cues; for example, one cue signaling play/no play and the other cue signaling to switch from a high to a low pitch register. Similarly, active music making can train alternating attention, during which the client shift his/her attention between two or more different musical cues and follow them and train sustained attention, in which the client follows and responds continuously on his/her instrument to the changing musical cues—for example, in pitch, loudness, tempo, rhythms—provided by a therapist's playing. One frequently used assessment tool for improvement of attention and executive control following the training has been the Trail Making Test B, which is very sensitive to detect impairments in multiple cognitive domains but especially in cognitive shifts and flexibility (Kortte, Horner, & Windham, 2002).

Using MEFT, Thaut et al. (2009) demonstrated that one 30-min training session improved mental flexibility in persons with acquired brain dysfunction. The training session included group improvisation projects requiring decision-making, problem-solving, comprehension, and reasoning with a specific emphasis on switching attention to two rapidly alternating musical cues. Mental flexibility assessed using the Trail Making Test B was significantly improved postintervention compared to preintervention with a large effect size. In addition, the MEFT group significantly increased their confidence in that ability. The control group without any intervention did not show any improvement on the test as expected.

In one RCT, 14 persons with chronic stroke received a 30-hour NMT-based therapy consisting of mapping functional movements on playing musical instruments and creating music over a 10-week period and showed significantly improved performance on the Trail Making Test B in the mid-intervention (Fujioka et al., 2018). On the other hand, a control group of 14 persons with stroke who had received conventional physical training showed similar improvement on the test postintervention.

Since many cognitive NMT techniques involve functional musical improvisation-based tasks, the brain activity during musical improvisation may shed light on the neural mechanisms to enhance executive function. Musical improvisation is a domain-specific creative phenomenon. However, it also uses domain-general processes or general cognitive flexibility (de Manzano & Ullén, 2012; Dreisbach, 2006). A direct link between musical improvisation and executive function is still unknown. However, musical improvisators with more than 5 years of experience ranked above the 80th percentile in the normative data of executive function (Liu et al., 2012). Musical improvisation also modulates brain activity in the prefrontal regions including dorsal premotor cortex, presupplementary motor area (pre-SMA), medial prefrontal cortex (MPFC), dorsolateral prefrontal cortex, anterior cingulate cortex, and inferior frontal cortex (Beaty, 2015; Loui, 2018). Furthermore, there are studies reporting differential prefrontal activity between medial and lateral prefrontal areas during musical improvisation (Boasen, Takeshita, Kuriki, & Yokosawa, 2018; Limb and Braun, 2008; Liu et al., 2012). It may reflect an interaction between executive control and default mode networks (Beaty, 2015) and the coupling between two networks may be manifested differently depending on the degree of goal-directedness of a given task (Beaty, 2015; Pinho, Ullén, Castelo-Branco, Fransson, & de Manzano, 2016) and/or the level of improvisational training (Limb and Braun, 2008). For example, the total hours of musical improvisation experience was negatively associated with activity in frontoparietal cortical areas in 39 professional pianists, suggesting that more experience may be characterized by spared executive function load (Pinho, de Manzano, Fransson, Eriksson, & Ullén, 2014). The existing research studies suggest that musical improvisation modulates the prefrontal regions associated with executive function. However, they have been primarily conducted in musicians. Therefore these findings need to be interpreted with caution. Investigations on the neural correlates of musical improvisation exercises/training in nonmusicians are warranted.

Music-based memory interventions

Aging and dementia are often associated with impairment in episodic memories (EMs). EM is defined as a cognitive system in which an individual encodes, stores, and retrieves information about personal experiences, accompanied with their temporal and spatial contexts (Tulving, 1972). Encoding is associated with the primary sensory and motor cortices, prefrontal cortex (PFC), and medial temporal lobe (MTL), including the perirhinal, entorhinal, and parahippocampal cortices, as well as the hippocampus. The contextual details of a specific episode are processed in a widely distributed area of brain (Squire, 1992), converging in the hippocampus via other MTL structures (Kessels, Hobbel, & Postma, 2007; Lekeu et al., 2002; Piolino et al., 2010). Consolidation of the encoded information occurs in the hippocampus and neocortex. To retrieve the information, the MTL structures are involved along with the MPFC, angular gyrus (AG), retrosplenial cortex, and posterior cingulate cortex (Tromp, Dufour, Lithfous, Pebayle, & Després, 2015).

In AD, EM impairment is more associated with encoding and storage problems resulting from MTL atrophy, which is therefore thought to be a memory disorder (Eustache et al., 2006), although AD also shows impairment in retrieval (Tromp et al., 2015). On the other hand, some persons with PD show a problem in retrieval, which is likely due to attentional and executive dysfunction, underpinned by the frontostriatal dysfunction (Costa et al., 2014; Emre et al., 2007). Similarly, normal aging decline in memory function is more associated with structural and functional alternation in PFC and thus may be related to impairment in executive function, attention, and processing speed (Tromp et al., 2015). These findings suggest that it is important to understand both neuropathology underlying memory impairment and neural mechanisms of music-based interventions to be employed.

Musical mnemonics training

Musical mnemonics training uses music as mnemonics or auditory scaffold to enhance both encoding and retrieval of information by chunking, sequencing, and organizing information and by potentially adding meaning, pleasure, emotion, and motivation (Thaut, 2005). A series of experimental studies demonstrated that verbal information learned by singing was better learned and recalled compared to the information learned by speaking in persons with a neurological disorder (Thaut, Peterson, & McIntosh, 2005; Thaut, Peterson, McIntosh, & Hoemberg, 2014). Musical verbal learning was primarily characterized by enhanced coherent bilateral frontal oscillations in healthy individuals (Thaut et al., 2005) as well as persons with a neurological disorder (Peterson & Thaut, 2007; Thaut et al., 2014).

The benefit of learning verbal information by singing has also been reported in the AD literature. Recognition accuracy was improved when the verbal information had been learned by singing to an unfamiliar song compared to speaking in persons with probable AD (Simmons-Stern et al., 2012; Simmons-Stern, Budson, & Ally, 2010) and older healthy controls (Simmons-Stern et al., 2012), but this benefit was observed for recognition, not for recall (Simmons-Stern et al., 2012). However, another study showed that sung texts using preselected familiar music were better encoded, learned, and retrieved on free recall than spoken texts in both older healthy control and mild AD groups (Palisson et al., 2015). The better recall was observed immediately and at 5-minute delay. The inconsistent results among these studies may be partly due to a number of materials to be learned, the familiarity of the songs used, and encoding procedures employed. One study included three sung conditions with unfamiliar, low-familiar, and high-familiar songs (Moussard, Bigand, Belleville, & Peretz, 2014). The benefit of the song familiarity on a 10-minute delayed recall was observed in only the control group while the mild AD group benefitted from all sung conditions.

Music exposure and autobiographical memory

Several studies showed that exposure to investigator-chosen music (Vivaldi's Spring first movement from the Four Seasons) (Irish et al., 2006), investigator-chosen familiar and novel music (Vivaldi's "Winter" first movement from "Four Seasons" and Fitkin's "Hook," respectively) (Foster & Valentine, 2001), as well as participant-chosen favorite music (El Haj, Postal, & Allain, 2012), enhanced autobiographical recalls compared to the silence condition in persons with AD.

Furthermore, two studies compared investigator-chosen familiar/popular music with visual familiar stimuli such as photographs of famous faces (Belfi, Karlan, & Tranel, 2016) and famous events (Baird, Brancatisano, Gelding, & Thompson, 2018). The photographs evoked a greater number of memories than the music while the music evoked more vivid descriptions of memories than the photographs in healthy adults with approximately 30% of the stimuli evoking memories (Belfi et al., 2016). In another study, older healthy controls reported that picture-evoked autobiographical memories (PEAMs) occurred more frequently than music-evoked autobiographical memories (MEAMs) while persons with probable AD reported no difference (Baird et al., 2018). The control group rated the photographic stimuli as significantly more familiar than the music stimuli and both groups rated the stimuli that evoked autobiographic memories as more familiar, suggesting a close link between memory and familiarity of the stimuli/cues. The frequency of MEAMs was similar in both groups and the AD group did not report any difference in the frequency of MEAMs and PEAMs. However, in only the AD group, MEAMs occurred significantly more frequently in response to songs from when the participants were 10−30 years old compared to when they were older. This was not observed using the picture stimuli, suggesting that familiar music may be a more effective cue on retrieval of some preserved memory in AD.

Neuroimaging studies in healthy adults have shown that familiar music modulates a distributed area of the brain. An fMRI study showed that greater familiarity of music (mean: 56.2% and range: 20%−80% of the music judged to be familiar by the participants) was associated with greater brain activation in a number of regions including pre-SMA/SMA, bilateral IFG, inferior frontal sulcus, medial frontal gyrus (MFG), superior frontal gyrus (SFG), cingulate sulcus, anterior insula, posterior superior temporal gyrus, medial temporal gyrus, posterior cingulate, thalamus, and cerebellum (Janata, 2009). A meta-analysis of 11 neuroimaging studies reported that familiar music showed more activation in the lateral and medial SFG and thalamus compared to unfamiliar music (Freitas et al., 2018). Another study showed that familiarity of music (familiar vs unfamiliar) modulated more areas than liking (liked vs disliked) of music in MPFC, BG, and limbic structures (Pereira et al., 2011). Furthermore, the contrast of familiar versus unfamiliar music showed more modality-specific activations compared to the contrast of familiar versus unfamiliar odors (Plailly, Tillmann, & Royet, 2007). The activated areas specific to the familiar music included the SFG, MFG, and precentral gyrus, the superior temporal sulcus, posterior part of CG, and supramarginal gyrus in the left hemisphere and the right AG.

Taken together, familiar music plays an important role in evoking autobiographical memories, which is likely to be associated with its modulatory effect on brain activity in a distributed area. However, the familiar music used in these studies was chosen by investigators and thus the familiarity varied within participants. El Haj et al. (2012) demonstrated that participant-chosen music evoked more autobiographical memories relative to both investigator-chosen music and silence in persons with mild AD.

One study employed 1-hour daily listening to autobiographically salient, long-known music (known for 20 years) over a period of 3 weeks as an intervention method to reduce memory dysfunction in persons with mild AD/MCI and demonstrated that the intervention led to better scores on the memory section of the Montreal Cognitive Assessment (Nasreddine et al., 2005) in these participants (Thaut et al., 2018). This study also showed that the long-known music activated more spatially extensive and bilateral networks compared to the recently heard music (1-hour before an MRI scan). When contrasting the brain images between two listening conditions, the long-known music preferentially activated the MPFC, AC, precuneus, anterior insula, BG, hippocampus, and amygdala. In addition, decreased brain activation was found postintervention in the IFG, SMA, insula, and putamen compared to preintervention. The authors interpreted the result as indicating that decreased activation may have resulted from improved neural efficiency and concluded that the 3-week structured music listening regimen to long-known, preferred music could induce brain plasticity mechanisms that result in more efficient networks to improve memory performance. Further research and RCTs are warranted to replicate the findings.

In one RCT, 89 persons with mild to moderate dementia were randomly assigned to a music listening, singing, or usual care group (Särkämö, Tervaniemi, et al., 2014). The intervention was group-based and lasted for 10 weeks with a 1.5-hour daily session. In the music groups, music was chosen by the participants and 6–10 songs were used in each session. Both music groups showed improvement on personal EM compared to the usual care group. The singing group additionally showed improvement on short-term and working memory.

In another RCT, 54 persons with stroke were randomly assigned to a music listening, an audiobook-listening, or a no-listening group. The listening session was held daily on an individual basis for at least 1 hour over a period of 2 months and the music was a participant-chosen favorite song. The music group showed significant improvement on verbal memory in addition to focused attention at 3- and 6-month follow-ups (Särkämö et al., 2008). The subsequent neuroimaging study also showed that the improvement on verbal memory was significantly correlated with an increase in gray matter volume in bilateral SFG in persons with left hemisphere stroke (Särkämö, Ripollés et al., 2014).

The beneficial effects of music-based interventions on memory retrieval in persons with dementia may be because music serves as a cue to elicit stored memory (Leggieri et al., 2019), modulating brain activity in the EM-associated regions. Musical memory and associated brain structure and function (e.g., MPFC) are relatively spared in dementia (Cuddy, Sikka, & Vanstone, 2015; Jacobsen et al., 2015; Scahill, Schott, Stevens, Rossor, & Fox, 2002). MPFC is closely interacted with the hippocampus and plays a crucial role in the EM system (Preston & Eichenbaum, 2013).

Discussion

In this chapter, we discussed several training techniques of NMT for motor, speech/language, and cognitive rehabilitation and presented encouraging data of NMT and other music-based interventions in aging with disorders. The periodicity of auditory rhythmic patterns assists in improving movement impairment in persons with PD and stroke. In addition, rhythm has been extended into applications in speech and language rehabilitation, demonstrating its important role in music-based interventions. The role of music in cognitive rehabilitation emerged as the last rehabilitation domain in NMT and thus more clinical studies, particularly RCTs with large sample sizes, are warranted to confirm the efficacy of the techniques. In addition, more research is needed to develop specific protocols for cognitive rehabilitation such as type and length of intervention, type of music, group size, and targeted disease characteristics. Combined with neuroimaging tools, future research will be able to reveal the neural mechanisms and neural plasticity induced by rhythm and music as well as by specific music-based interventions including NMT. It is important to demonstrate whether rhythm and music can modulate the residual neural resources in the deteriorating brain areas affected by aging and disorders and/or in the unaffected brain areas to compensate for affected function. Such studies also can help to refine NMT and other music-based interventions as well as to generate more specific clinical/training applications to be combined with existing pharmacological and other nonpharmacological therapies and to counteract declining motor and cognitive functions associated with normal aging.

The neural mechanisms of rhythm/music and music-based interventions have been investigated primarily using fMRI and PET. Considering that music extensively modulates prefrontal activity and that anatomical and functional connectivity between auditory association areas and striatum, music-induced dopaminergic responses and changes in the frontostriatal circuits associated with motor, cognitive, and emotional functions are of interest. Only a few studies have investigated dopaminergic function using PET and dopamine radioligands (Koshimori et al., 2019; Salimpoor, Benovoy, Larcher, Dagher, & Zatorre, 2011). Furthermore, functional near-infrared spectroscopy can be used to investigate the neural activity during active music-based interventions. It can be combined with other physiological and neurobehavioral measures, including EEG, eye tracking, pupil reflex, heart rate variability, respiration, and electrodermal activity to further elucidate the underlying mechanisms.

Music can modulate brain activity in a distributed area, covering multiple functional areas (i.e., motor control, cognition, and emotion) simultaneously, which potentially allows for a broad clinical application. In fact, some studies demonstrated improvement in emotional function in addition to cognitive function (e.g., Fujioka et al., 2018; Särkämö, Tervaniemi, et al., 2014). However, neuropathology and the resultant symptoms as well as other disease characteristics (e.g., acute or chronic, and reversible or irreversible) should be carefully considered when music-based interventions are employed.

Music-based interventions are inexpensive, easily implemented, and enjoyable (Leggieri et al., 2019). The benefits of the interventions have been demonstrated regardless of an individual's musical expertise or regular music listening/engagement (Baird et al., 2018; Palisson et al., 2015; Särkämö, Tervaniemi, et al., 2014). Therefore rhythm and music have great potential as an intervention tool to address aging and various neurological disorders.

References

Abiru, M. (2014). Musical neglect training (MNT). In M. H. Thaut, & V. Hoemberg (Eds.), *Handbook of neurologic music therapy* (pp. 270–298). Oxford: Oxford University Press.

Albert, M. L., Sparks, R. W., & Helm, N. A. (1973). Melodic intonation therapy for aphasia. *Archives of Neurology*, *29*(2), 130–131. Available from https://doi.org/10.1001/archneur.1973.00490260074018.

Altenmüller, E., Marco-Pallare, J., Münte, T. F., & Schneider, S. (2009). Neural reorganization underlies improvement in stroke-induced motor dysfunction by music-supported therapy. *Annals of the New York Academy of Sciences*, *1169*. Available from https://doi.org/10.1111/j.1749-6632.2009.04580.x.

Aschersleben, G., & Prinz, W. (1995). Synchronizing actions with events: The role of sensory information. *Perception & Psychophysics*, *57*(3), 305–317. Available from https://doi.org/10.3758/BF03213056.

Avanzino, L., Pelosin, E., Vicario, C. M., Lagravinese, G., Abbruzzese, G., & Martino, D. (2016). Time processing and motor control in movement disorders. *Frontiers in Human Neuroscience*, *10*. Available from https://doi.org/10.3389/fnhum.2016.00631.

Baird, A., Brancatisano, O., Gelding, R., & Thompson, W. F. (2018). Characterization of music and photograph evoked autobiographical memories in people with Alzheimer's disease. *Journal of Alzheimer's Disease*, *66*(2), 693–706. Available from https://doi.org/10.3233/JAD-180627.

Baldassarre, A., Ramsey, L., Hacker, C. L., Callejas, A., Astafiev, S. V., Metcalf, N. V., ... Corbetta, M. (2014). Large-scale changes in network interactions as a physiological signature of spatial neglect. *Brain*, *137*(Pt 12), 3267–3283. Available from https://doi.org/10.1093/brain/awu297.

Baldassarre, A., Ramsey, L., Rengachary, J., Zinn, K., Siegel, J. S., Metcalf, N. V., ... Shulman, G. L. (2016). Dissociated functional connectivity profiles for motor and attention deficits in acute right-hemisphere stroke. *Brain*, *139*(7), 2024–2038. Available from https://doi.org/10.1093/brain/aww107.

Barrett, A. M., Boukrina, O., & Saleh, S. (2019). Ventral attention and motor network connectivity is relevant to functional impairment in spatial neglect after right brain stroke. *Brain and Cognition*, *129*, 16–24. Available from https://doi.org/10.1016/j.bandc.2018.11.013.

Beaty, R. E. (2015). The neuroscience of musical improvisation. *Neuroscience and Biobehavioral Reviews*, *51*, 108–117. Available from https://doi.org/10.1016/j.neubiorev.2015.01.004.

Belfi, A. M., Karlan, B., & Tranel, D. (2016). Music evokes vivid autobiographical memories. *Memory*, *24*(7), 1–11. Available from https://doi.org/10.1080/09658211.2015.1061012.

Belin, P., Van Eeckhout, P., Zilbovicius, M., Remy, P., François, C., Guillaume, S., . . . Samson, Y. (1996). Recovery from nonfluent aphasia after melodic intonation therapy: A PET study. *Neurology*, *47*(6), 1504−1511. Available from https://doi.org/10.1212/WNL.47.6.1504.

Bernardi, N. F., Cioffi, M. C., Ronchi, R., Maravita, A., Bricolo, E., Zigiotto, L., . . . Vallar, G. (2017). Improving left spatial neglect through music scale playing. *Journal of Neuropsychology*, *11*(1), 135−158. Available from https://doi.org/10.1111/jnp.12078.

Bitan, T., Simic, T., Saverino, C., Jones, C., Glazer, J., Collela, B., . . . Rochon, E. (2018). Changes in resting-state connectivity following melody-based therapy in a patient with aphasia. *Neural Plasticity*. Available from https://doi.org/10.1155/2018/6214095.

Boasen, J., Takeshita, Y., Kuriki, S., & Yokosawa, K. (2018). Spectral-spatial differentiation of brain activity during mental imagery of improvisational music. *Frontiers in Human Neuroscience*, *24*. Available from https://doi.org/10.3389/fnhum.2018.00156.

Bodak, R., Malhotra, P., Bernardi, N. F., Cocchini, G., & Stewart, L. (2014). Reducing chronic visuo-spatial neglect following right hemisphere stroke through instrument playing. *Frontiers in Human Neuroscience*, *8*. Available from https://doi.org/10.3389/fnhum.2014.00413.

Bostan, A. C., Dum, R. P., & Strick, P. L. (2010). The basal ganglia communicate with the cerebellum. *Proceedings of the National Academy of Sciences of the United States of America*, *107*(18), 8452−8456. Available from https://doi.org/10.1073/pnas.1000496107.

Braun Janzen, T., Haase, M., & Thaut, M. H. (2019). Rhythmic priming across effector systems: A randomized controlled trial with Parkinson's disease patients. *Human Movement Science*, *64*, 355−365. Available from https://doi.org/10.1016/j.humov.2019.03.001.

Braunlich, K., Seger, C. A., Jentink, K. G., Buard, I., Kluger, B. M., & Thaut, M. H. (2018). Rhythmic auditory cues shape neural network recruitment in Parkinson's disease during repetitive motor behavior. *European Journal of Neuroscience*, *49*(6), 849−858. Available from https://doi.org/10.1111/ejn.14227.

Breier, J. I., Randle, S., Maher, L. M., & Papanicolaou, A. C. (2010). Changes in maps of language activity activation following melodic intonation therapy using magnetoencephalography: Two case studies. *Journal of Clinical and Experimental Neuropsychology*, *32*(3), 309−314. Available from https://doi.org/10.1080/13803390903029293.

Buard, I., Dewispelaere, W. B., Thaut, M., & Kluger, B. M. (2019). Preliminary neurophysiological evidence of altered cortical activity and connectivity with neurologic music therapy in Parkinson's disease. *Frontiers in Neuroscience*, *13*. Available from https://doi.org/10.3389/fnins.2019.00105.

Bukowska, A. A., Krężałek, P., Mirek, E., Bujas, P., & Marchewka, A. (2016). Neurologic Music Therapy training for mobility and stability rehabilitation with Parkinson's disease − A pilot study. *Frontiers in Human Neuroscience*, *9*. Available from https://doi.org/10.3389/fnhum.2015.00710.

Calabrò, R. S., Naro, A., Filoni, S., Pullia, M., Billeri, L., Tomasello, P., . . . Bramanti, P. (2019). Walking to your right music: A randomized controlled trial on the novel use of treadmill plus music in Parkinson's disease. *Jounral of NeuroEngineering and Rehabilitation*, *16*(1), 68. Available from https://doi.org/10.1186/s12984-019-0533-9.

Callan, D. E., Tsytsarev, V., Hanakawa, T., Callan, A. M., Katsuhara, M., Fukuyama, H., & Turner, R. (2006). Song and speech: Brain regions involved with perception and covert production. *NeuroImage*, *31*(3), 1327−1342. Available from https://doi.org/10.1016/j.neuroimage.2006.01.036.

Cha, Y., Kim, Y., Hwang, S., & Chung, Y. (2014). Intensive gait training with rhythmic auditory stimulaton in individuals with chronic hemiparetic stoke: A pilot randomized controlled study. *NeuroRehabilitation*, *35*(4), 681−688. Available from https://doi.org/10.3233/NRE-141182.

Chen, J. L., Penhune, V. B., & Zatorre, R. J. (2008). Listening to musical rhythms recruits motor regions of the brain. *Cerebral Cortex*, *18*(12), 2844–2854. Available from https://doi.org/10.1093/cercor/bhn042.

Chen, M. C., Tsai, P. L., Huang, Y. T., & Lin, K. C. (2013). Pleasant music improves visual attention in patients with unilateral neglect after stroke. *Brain Injury*, *27*(1), 75–82. Available from https://doi.org/10.3109/02699052.2012.722255.

Comstock, D. C., Hove, M. J., & Balasubramaniam, R. (2018). Sensorimotor synchronization with auditory and visual modalities: Behavioral and neural differences. *Frontiers in Computational Neuroscience*, *12*. Available from https://doi.org/10.3389/fncom.2018.00053.

Corbetta, M., & Shulman, G. L. (2011). Spatial neglect and attention networks. *Annual Review of Neuroscience*, *34*, 569–599. Available from https://doi.org/10.1146/annurev-neuro-061010-113731.

Costa, A., Monaco, M., Zabberoni, S., Peppe, A., Perri, R., Fadda, L., ... Carlesimo, G. A. (2014). Free and cued recall memory in Parkinson's disease associated with amnestic mild cognitive impairment. *PLoS One*, *9*(1). Available from https://doi.org/10.1371/journal.pone.0086233.

Coull, J. T., & Nobre, A. C. (2008). Dissociating explicit timing from temporal expectation with fMRI. *Current Opinion in Neurobiology*, *18*(2), 137–144. Available from https://doi.org/10.1016/j.conb.2008.07.011.

Crasta, J. E., Thaut, M. H., Anderson, C. W., Davies, P. L., & Gavin, W. J. (2018). Auditory priming improves neural synchronization in auditory-motor entrainment. *Neuropsychologia*, *117*, 102–112. Available from https://doi.org/10.1016/j.neuropsychologia.2018.05.017.

Cuddy, L. L., Sikka, R., & Vanstone, A. (2015). Preservation of musical memory and engagement in healthy aging and Alzheimer's disease. *Annals of the New York Academy of Sciences*, *1337*, 223–231. Available from https://doi.org/10.1111/nyas.12617.

de Bruin, N., Doan, J. B., Tumbull, G., Suchowersky, O., Bonfield, S., Hu, B., & Brown, L. A. (2010). Walking with music is a safe and viable tool for gait training in Parkinson's disease: The effect of a 13-week feasibility study on single and dual task walking. *Parkinson's Disease*, *2010*. Available from https://doi.org/10.4061/2010/483530.

de Manzano, Ö., & Ullén, F. (2012). Goal-independent mechanisms for free response generation: Creative and pseudo-random performance share neural substrates. *NeuroImage*, *59*(1), 772–780. Available from https://doi.org/10.1016/j.neuroimage.2011.07.016.

De Swart, B. J. M., Willemse, S. C., Maassen, B. A. M., & Horstink, M. W. I. M. (2003). Improvement of voicing in patients with Parkinson's disease by speech therapy. *Neurology*, *60*(3), 498–500. Available from https://doi.org/10.1212/01.WNL.0000044480.95458.56.

del Olmo, M. F., Arias, P., Furio, M. C., Pozo, M. A., & Cudeiro, J. (2006). Evaluation of the effect of training using auditory stimulation on rhythmic movement in Parkinsonian patients-a combined motor and [18F]-FDG PET study. *Parkinsonism and Related Disorders*, *12*(3), 155–164. Available from https://doi.org/10.1016/j.parkreldis.2005.11.002.

Dreisbach, G. (2006). How positive affect modulates cognitive control: The costs and benefits of reduced maintenance capability. *Brain and Cognition*, *60*(1), 11–19.

El Haj, M., Postal, V., & Allain, P. (2012). Music enhances autobiographical memory in mild Alzheimer's disease. *Educational Gerontology*, *38*(1), 30–41. Available from https://doi.org/10.1080/03601277.2010.515897.

Elston, J., Honan, W., Powell, R., Gormley, J., & Stein, K. (2010). Do metronomes improve the quality of life in people with Parkinson's disease? A pragmtic, single-blind, randomized cross-over trail. *Clinical Rehabilitation*, *24*(6), 523–532. Available from https://doi.org/10.1177/0269215509360646.

Emre, M., Aarsland, D., Brown, R., Burn, D. J., Duyckaerts, C., Mizuno, Y., . . . Dubois, B. (2007). Clinical diagnostic criteria for dementia associated with Parkinson's disease. *Movement Disorders, 22*(12), 1689−16707. Available from https://doi.org/10.1002/mds.21507.

Eustache, F., Giffard, B., Rauchs, G., Chételat, G., Piolino, P., & Desgranges, B. (2006). La maladie d'Alzheimer et la mémoire humaine. *Revue Neurologique, 162*(10), 929−939. Available from https://doi.org/10.1016/s0035-3787(06)75102-5.

Foster, N. A., & Valentine, E. R. (2001). The effect of auditory stimulation on autobiographical recall in dementia. *Experimental Aging Research, 27*(3), 215−228. Available from https://doi.org/10.1080/036107301300208664.

Fox, M. D., Corbetta, M., Snyder, A. Z., Vincent, J. L., & Raichle, M. E. (2006). Spontaneous neuronal activity distinguishes human dorsal and ventral attention systems. *Proceedings of the National Academy of Sciences of the United States of America, 103*(26), 10046−10051. Available from https://doi.org/10.1073/pnas.0604187103.

Freitas, C., Manzato, E., Burini, A., Taylor, M. J., Lerch, J. P., & Anagnostou, E. (2018). Neural correlates of familiarity in music listening: A systematic review and a neuroimaging meta-analysis. *Frontiers in Neuroscience, 12*. Available from https://doi.org/10.3389/fnins.2018.00686.

Fujioka, T., Dawson, D. R., Wright, R., Honjo, K., Chen, J. L., Chen, J. J., . . . Ross, B. (2018). The effects of music-supported therapy on motor, cognitive, and psychosocial functions in chronic stroke. *Annals of the New York Academy of Sciences.* Available from https://doi.org/10.1111/nyas.13706.

Fujioka, T., Trainor, L. J., Large, E. W., & Ross, B. (2009). Beta and gamma rhythms in human auditory cortex during musical beat processing. *Annals of the New York Academy of Sciences.* Available from https://doi.org/10.1111/j.1749-6632.2009.04779.x.

Fujioka, T., Trainor, L. J., Large, E. W., & Ross, B. (2012). Internalized timing of isochronous sounds is represented in neuromagnetic beta oscillations. *Journal of Neuroscience, 32*(5), 1791−1802. Available from https://doi.org/10.1523/JNEUROSCI.4107-11.2012.

Gardiner, J. C., & Thaut, M. H. (2014). Musical executive function training (MEFT). In M. H. Thaut, & V. Hoemberg (Eds.), *Handbook of neurologic music therapy* (pp. 279−293). Oxford: Oxford University Press.

Gentilucci, M., & Dalla Volta, R. (2008). Spoken language and arm gestures are controlled by the same motor control system. *Quarterly Journal of Experimental Psychology, 61*(6), 944−957. Available from https://doi.org/10.1080/17470210701625683.

Ghai, S. (2018). Effects of real-time (sonification) and rhythmic auditory stimuli on recovering arm function post stroke: A systematic review and meta-analysis. *Frontiers in Neurology, 9*. Available from https://doi.org/10.3389/fneur.2018.00488.

Ghai, S., & Ghai, I. (2019). Effects of (music-based) rhythmic auditory cueing training on gait and posture post-stroke: A systematic review & dose-response meta-analysis. *Scientific Reports, 9*(1). Available from https://doi.org/10.1038/s41598-019-38723-3.

Ghai, S., Ghai, I., Schmitz, G., & Effenberg, A. O. (2017). Effect of rhythmic auditory cueing on agin gait: A systematic review and meta-analysis. *Aging and Disease, 9*(5), 901−923. Available from https://doi.org/10.14336/AD.2017.1031.

Ghai, S., Ghai, I., Schmitz, G., & Effenberg, A. O. (2018). Effect of rhythmic auditory cueing on parkinsonian gait: A systematic review and meta-analysis. *Scientific Reports, 8*(1), 1−19. Available from https://doi.org/10.1038/s41598-017-16232-5.

Grahn, J. A., & Brett, M. (2007). Rhythm and beat perception in motor areas of the brain. *Journal of Cognitive Neuroscience, 19*(5), 893−906. Available from https://doi.org/10.1162/jocn.2007.19.5.893.

Grahn, J. A., & Rowe, J. B. (2013). Finding and feeling the musical beat: Striatal dissociations between detection and prediction of regularity. *Cerebral Cortex, 23*(4), 913−921. Available from https://doi.org/10.1093/cercor/bhs083.

Grau-Sánchez, J., Amengual, J. L., Rojo, N., Veciana de Las Heras, M., Montero, J., Rubio, F., ... Rodríguez-Fornells, A. (2013). Plasticity in the sensorimotor cortex induced by music-supported therapy in stroke patients: A TMS study. *Frontiers in Human Neuroscience, 494*. Available from https://doi.org/10.3389/fnhum.2013.00494.

Grau-Sánchez, J., Duarte, E., Ramos-Escobar, N., Sierpowska, J., Rueda, N., Redón, S., ... Rodríguez-Fornells, A. (2018). Music-supported therapy in the rehabilitation of subacute stroke patient: A randomized controlled trial. *Annals of the New York Academy of Sciences*. Available from https://doi.org/10.1111/nyas.13590.

Hackett, T. A. (2015). Anatomic organization of the auditory cortex. In M. J. Aminoff, F. Boller, & D. F. Swaab (Eds.), *Handbook of clinical neurology* (pp. 27−53). Available from https://doi.org/10.1016/B978-0-444-62630-1.00002-0.

Han, E. Y., Yun, J. Y., Chong, H. J., & Choi, K.-G. (2018). Individual therapeutic singing program for vocal quality and depression in Parkinson's disease. *Journal of Movement Disorders, 11*(3), 121−128. Available from https://doi.org/10.14802/jmd.17078.

Harro, C. C., Shoemaker, M. J., Frey, O., Gamble, A. C., Harring, K. B., Karl, K. L., ... VanHaisma, R. J. (2014). The effects of speed-dependent treadmill training and rhythmic auditory-cued overground walking on balane function, fall incidence, and quality of life in individuals with idiopathic Parkinson's disease: A randomized controlled trial. *Neurorehabilitation, 34*(3), 541−556.

Hébert, S., Racette, A., Gagnon, L., & Peretz, I. (2003). Revisiting the dissociation between singing and speaking in expressive aphasia. *Brain, 126*(Pt 8), 1838−1850. Available from https://doi.org/10.1093/brain/awg186.

Heilman, K. M., Watson, R. T., & Valenstein, E. (1984). Neglect and related disorders. In K. M. Heilman, & E. Valenstein (Eds.), *Clinical Neuropsychology* (pp. 279−336). Oxford: Oxford University Press.

Hommel, M., Peres, B., Pollak, P., Memin, B., Besson, G., Gaio, J. M., & Perret, J. (1990). Effects of passive tactile and auditory stimuli on left visual neglect. *Archives of Neurology, 47*(5), 573−576. Available from https://doi.org/10.1001/archneur.1990.00530050097018.

Hoshi, E., Tremblay, L., Féger, J., Carras, P. L., & Strick, P. L. (2005). The cerebellum communicates with the basal ganglia. *Nature Neuroscience, 8*(11), 1491−1493. Available from https://doi.org/10.1038/nn1544.

Irish, M., Cunningham, C. J., Walsh, J. B., Coakley, D., Lawlor, B. A., Robertson, I. H., & Coen, R. F. (2006). Investigating the enhancing effect of music on autobiographical memory in mild Alzheimer's disease. *Dementia and Geriatric Cognitive Disorders, 22*(1), 108−120. Available from https://doi.org/10.1159/000093487.

Jacobsen, J. H., Stelzer, J., Fritz, T. H., Chételat, G., La Joie, R., & Turner, R. (2015). Why musical memory can be preserved in advanced Alzheimer's disease. *Brain, 138*(Pt 8), 2438−2450. Available from https://doi.org/10.1093/brain/awv135.

Jacome, D. E. (1984). Aphasia with elation, hypermusia, musicophilia and compulsive whistling. *Journal of Neurology Neurosurgery and Psychiatry, 47*(3), 308−310. Available from https://doi.org/10.1136/jnnp.47.3.308.

Jamali, S., & Ross, B. (2013). Somatotopic finger mapping using MEG: Toward an optimal stimulation paradigm. *Clinical Neurophysicology, 124*(8), 1659−1670. Available from https://doi.org/10.1016/j.clinph.2013.01.027.

Janata, P. (2009). The neural architecture of music-evoked autobiographical memories. *Cerebral Cortex, 19*(11), 2579−2594. Available from https://doi.org/10.1093/cercor/bhp008.

Jankovic, J. (2008). Parkinson's disease: Clinical features and diagnosis. *Journal of Neurology, Neurosurgery, and Psychiatry, 79*(4), 368−376. Available from https://doi.org/10.1136/jnnp.2007.131045.

Jeffries, K. J., Fritz, J. B., & Braun, A. R. (2003). Words in melody: An H(2)15O PET study of brain activation during singing and speaking. *NeuroReport, 14*(5), 749−754. Available from https://doi.org/10.1097/00001756-200304150-00018.

Jeong, S., & Kim, M. T. (2007). Effects of theory-driven music and movement program for stroke survivors in a community setting. *Applied Nursing Research, 20*(3), 125−131.

Kang, K., & Thaut, M. H. (2019). Musical neglect training for chronic persistent unilateral visual neglect post-stroke. *Frontiers in Neurology, 10.* Available from https://doi.org/10.3389/fneur.2019.00474.

Kenyon, G. P., & Thaut, M. H. (2000). A measure of kinematic limb instability modulation by rhythmic auditory stimulation. *Journal of Biomechanics, 33*(10), 1319−1323. Available from https://doi.org/10.1016/S0021-9290(00)00077-4.

Kessels, R. P. C., Hobbel, D., & Postma, A. (2007). Aging, context memory and binding: A comparison of "what, where and when" in young and older adults. *International Journal of Neuroscience, 117*(6), 795−810. Available from https://doi.org/10.1080/00207450600910218.

Kortte, K. B., Horner, M. D., & Windham, W. K. (2002). The trail making test, Part B: Cognitive flexibility or ability to maintain set? *Applied Neuropsychology, 9*(2), 106−109. Available from https://doi.org/10.1207/S15324826AN0902_5.

Koshimori, Y., Strafella, A. P., Valli, M., Sharma, V., Cho, S., Houle, S., & Thaut, M. H. (2019). Motor synchronization to rhythmic auditory stimulation (RAS) attenuates dopaminergic responses in ventral striatum in young healthy adults: [11C]-(+)-PHNO PET study. *Frontiers in Neuroscience, 13.* Available from https://doi.org/10.3389/fnins.2019.00106.

Koshimori, Y., & Thaut, M. H. (2018). Future perspectives on neural mechanisms underlying rhythm and music based neurorehabilitation in Parkinson's disease. *Ageing Research Reviews, 47*, 133−139. Available from https://doi.org/10.1016/j.arr.2018.07.001.

Large, E. W., Fink, P., & Kelso, J. A. S. (2002). Tracking simple and complex sequences. *Psychological Research, 66*(1), 3−17. Available from https://doi.org/10.1007/s004260100069.

Lee, S., Lee, K., & Song, C. (2018). Gait training with bilateral rhythmic auditory stimulation in stroke patients: A randomized controlled tria. *Brain Sciences, 8.* Available from https://doi.org/10.3390/brainsci8090164.

Leggieri, M., Thaut, M. H., Fornazzari, L., Schweizer, T. A., Barfett, J., Munoz, D. G., & Fischer, C. E. (2019). Music intervention approaches for Alzheimer's disease: A review of the literature. *Frontiers in Neuroscience, 13.* Available from https://doi.org/10.3389/fnins.2019.00132.

Lekeu, F., Marczewski, P., Van Der Linden, M., Collette, F., Degueldre, C., Del Fiore, G., ... Salmon, E. (2002). Effects of incidental and intentional feature binding on recognition: A behavioural and PET activation study. *Neuropsychologia, 40*(2), 131−144. Available from https://doi.org/10.1016/S0028-3932(01)00088-4.

Li, K., & Malhotra, P. A. (2015). Spatial neglect. *Practical Neurology, 15*(5), 333−339. Available from https://doi.org/10.1136/practneurol-2015-001115.

Limb, C. J., & Braun, A. R. (2008). Neural substrates of spontaneous musical performance: An fMRI study of jazz improvisation. *PLoS One, 3*(2). Available from https://doi.org/10.1371/journal.pone.0001679.

Liu, S., Chow, H. M., Xu, Y., Erkkinen, M. G., Swett, K. E., Eagle, M. W., ... Braun, A. R. (2012). Neural correlates of lyrical improvisation: An fMRI study of freestyle rap. *Scientific Reports*, 2. Available from https://doi.org/10.1038/srep00834.

Loui, P. (2018). Rapid and flexible creativity in musical improvisation: Review and a model. *Annals of the New York Academy of Sciences*. Available from https://doi.org/10.1111/nyas.13628.

Mainka, S., & Mallien, G. (2014). Rhythmic speech cueing (RSC). In M. H. Thaut, & V. Hoemberg (Eds.), *Handbook of neurologic music therapy* (pp. 150−160). Oxford: Oxford University Press.

Mainka, S., Wissel, J., Völler, H., & Evers, S. (2018). The use of rhythmic auditory stimulation to optimize treadmill training for stroke patients: A randomized controlled trial. *Frontiers in Neurology*, 9. Available from https://doi.org/10.3389/fneur.2018.00755.

McIntosh, G. C., Brown, S. H., Rice, R. R., & Thaut, M. H. (1997). Rhythmic auditory-motor facilitation of gait patterns in patients with Parkinson's disease. *Journal of Neurology Neurosurgery and Psychiatry*, 62(1), 22−26. Available from https://doi.org/10.1136/jnnp.62.1.22.

Mehrholz, J., Thomas, S., & Elsner, B. (2017). Treadmill training and body weight support for walking after stroke. *Cochrane Database of Systematic Reviews*. Available from https://doi.org/10.1002/14651858.CD002840.pub4.

Merrett, D. L., Peretz, I., & Wilson, S. J. (2014). Neurobiological, cognitive, and emotional mechanisms in melodic intonation therapy. *Frontiers in Human Neuroscience*, 8. Available from https://doi.org/10.3389/fnhum.2014.00401.

Mertel, K. (2014). Therapeutical instrumental music performance (TIMP). In M. H. Thaut, & V. Hoemberg (Eds.), *Handbook of neurologic music therapy* (pp. 116−139). Oxford: Oxford University Press.

Milardi, D., Arrigo, A., Anastasi, G., Cacciola, A., Marino, S., Mormina, E., ... Quartarone, A. (2016). Extensive direct subcortical cerebellum-basal ganglia connections in human brain as revealed by constrained spherical deconvolution tractography. *Frontiers in Neuroanatomy*, 10. Available from https://doi.org/10.3389/fnana.2016.00029.

Molinari, M., Leggio, M. G., Filippini, V., Gioia, M. C., Cerasa, A., & Thaut, M. H. (2005). Sensorimotor transduction of time information is preserved in subjects with cerebellar damage. *Brain Research Bulletin*, 67(6), 448−458. Available from https://doi.org/10.1016/j.brainresbull.2005.07.014.

Moussard, A., Bigand, E., Belleville, S., & Peretz, I. (2014). Learning sung lyrics aids retention in normal ageing and Alzheimer's disease. *Neuropsychological Rehabilitation*, 24(6), 894−917. Available from https://doi.org/10.1080/09602011.2014.917982.

Murgia, M., Pili, R., Corona, F., Sors, F., Agostini, T. A., Bernardis, P., ... Pau, M. (2018). The use of footstep sounds as rhythmic auditory stimulation for gait rehabilitation in Parkinson's disease: A randomized controlled trial. *Frontiers in Neurology*, 9. Available from https://doi.org/10.3389/fneur.2018.00348.

Nasreddine, Z. S., Phillips, N. A., Bédirian, V., Charbonneau, S., Whitehead, V., Collin, I., ... Chertkow, H. (2005). The montreal cognitive assessment, MoCA: A brief screening tool for mild cognitive impairment. *Journal of the American Geriatrics Society*, 53(4), 695−699.

Nieuwboer, A., Baker, K., Willems, A. M., Jones, D., Spildooren, J., Lim, L., ... Rochester, L. (2009). The short-term effects of different cueing modalities on turn speed in people with Parkinson's disease. *Neurorehablitation and Neural Repair*, 23(8), 831−836. Available from https://doi.org/10.1177/1545968309337136.

Nieuwboer, A., Kwakkel, G., Rochester, L., Jones, D., van Wegen, E., Willems, A. M., . . . Lim, I. (2007). Cueing training in the home improves gait-related mobility in Parkinson's disease: The RESCUE trial. *Journal of Neurology, Neurosurgery & Psychiatry, 78*(2), 134–140. Available from https://doi.org/10.1136/jnnp.200X.097923.

Nombela, C., Hughes, L. E., Owen, A. M., & Grahn, J. A. (2013). Into the groove: Can rhythm influence Parkinson's disease? *Neuroscience and Biobehavioral Reviews, 37*(10 Pt 2), 2564–2570. Available from https://doi.org/10.1016/j.neubiorev.2013.08.003.

Nozaradan, S. (2014). Exploring how musical rhythm entrains brain activity with electroencephalogram frequency-tagging. *Philosophical Transactions of the Royal Society B: Biological Sciences.* Available from https://doi.org/10.1098/rstb.2013.0393.

Nozaradan, S., Peretz, I., Missal, M., & Mouraux, A. (2011). Tagging the neuronal entrainment to beat and meter. *Journal of Neuroscience, 31*(28), 10234–10240. Available from https://doi.org/10.1523/JNEUROSCI.0411-11.2011.

Nozaradan, S., Peretz, I., & Mouraux, A. (2012a). Selective neuronal entrainment to the beat and meter embedded in a musical rhythm. *Journal of Neuroscience, 32*(49), 17572–17581. Available from https://doi.org/10.1523/jneurosci.3203-12.2012.

Nozaradan, S., Peretz, I., & Mouraux, A. (2012b). Steady-state evoked potentials as an index of multisensory temporal binding. *NeuroImage, 60*(1), 21–28. Available from https://doi.org/10.1016/j.neuroimage.2011.11.065.

O'Donnell, M. J., Denis, X., Liu, L., Zhang, H., Chin, S. L., Rao-Melacini, P., . . . Yusuf, S. (2010). Risk factors for ischaemic and intracerebral haemorrhagic stroke in 22 countries (the INTERSTROKE study): A case-control study. *The Lancet, 376*(9735), 112–123. Available from https://doi.org/10.1016/S0140-6736(10)60834-3.

Özdemir, E., Norton, A., & Schlaug, G. (2006). Shared and distinct neural correlates of singing and speaking. *NeuroImage, 33*(2), 628–635. Available from https://doi.org/10.1016/j.neuroimage.2006.07.013.

Palisson, J., Roussel-Baclet, C., Maillet, D., Belin, C., Ankri, J., & Narme, P. (2015). Music enhances verbal episodic memory in Alzheimers disease. *Journal of Clinical and Experimental Neuropsychology, 37*(5), 503–517. Available from https://doi.org/10.1080/13803395.2015.1026802.

Paltsev, E. I., & E-lner, A. M. (1967). Change in the functional state of the segmental apparatus of the spinal cord under the influence of acoustic stimuli and its role in bringing about an arbitray movement. *Biofizika, 12*(6), 1064–1070.

Patel, A. (2008). *Music, language, and the brain* (1st ed.). Oxford: Oxford University Press.

Patel, A. D., & Iversen, J. R. (2014). The evolutionary neuroscience of musical beat perception: The action simulation for auditory prediction (ASAP) hypothesis. *Frontiers in Systems Neuroscience, 8.* Available from https://doi.org/10.3389/fnsys.2014.00057.

Pelzer, E. A., Hintzen, A., Goldau, M., von Cramon, D. Y., Timmermann, L., & Tittgemeyer, M. (2013). Cerebellar networks with basal ganglia: Feasibility for tracking cerebello-pallidal and subthalamo-cerebellar projections in the human brain. *European Journal of Neuroscience, 38*(8), 3106–3114. Available from https://doi.org/10.1111/ejn.12314.

Pereira, C. S., Teixeira, J., Figueiredo, P., Xavier, J., Castro, S. L., & Brattico, E. (2011). Music and emotions in the brain: Familiarity matters. *PLoS One, 6*(11). Available from https://doi.org/10.1371/journal.pone.0027241.

Peretz, I., Belleville, S., & Fontaine, S. (1997). Dissociations between music and language functions after cerebral resection: A new case of amusia without aphasia. *Canadian Journal Experimental Psychology, 51*(4), 354–368.

Peterson, D. A., & Thaut, M. H. (2007). Music increases frontal EEG coherence during verbal learning. *Neuroscience Letters, 412*(3), 217−221. Available from https://doi.org/10.1016/j.neulet.2006.10.057.

Petter, E. A., Lusk, N. A., Hesslow, G., & Meck, W. H. (2016). Interactive roles of the cerebellum and striatum in sub-second and supra-second timing: Support for an initiation, continuation, adjustment, and termination (ICAT) model of temporal processing. *Neuroscience and Biobehavioral Reviews, 71*, 739−755. Available from https://doi.org/10.1016/j.neubiorev.2016.10.015.

Pinho, A. L., de Manzano, Ö., Fransson, P., Eriksson, H., & Ullén, F. (2014). Connecting to create: Expertise in musical improvisation is associated with increased functional connectivity between premotor and prefrontal areas. *Journal of Neuroscience, 34*(18), 6156−6163. Available from https://doi.org/10.1523/JNEUROSCI.4769-13.2014.

Pinho, A. L., Ullén, F., Castelo-Branco, M., Fransson, P., & de Manzano, Ö. (2016). Addressing a paradox: Dual strategies for creative performance in introspective and extrospective networks. *Cereb Cortex, 26*(7), 3052−3063. Available from https://doi.org/10.1093/cercor/bhv130.

Piolino, P., Coste, C., Martinelli, P., Macé, A. L., Quinette, P., Guillery-Girard, B., & Belleville, S. (2010). Reduced specificity of autobiographical memory and aging: Do the executive and feature binding functions of working memory have a role? *Neuropsychologia, 48*(2), 429−440. Available from https://doi.org/10.1016/j.neuropsychologia.2009.09.035.

Plailly, J., Tillmann, B., & Royet, J. P. (2007). The feeling of familiarity of music and odors: The same neural signature? *Cerebral Cortex, 17*(11), 2650−2658. Available from https://doi.org/10.1093/cercor/bhl173.

Prassas, S., Thaut, M., McIntosh, G., & Rice, R. (1997). Effect of auditory rhythmic cuing on gait kinematic parameters of stroke patients. *Gait and Posture.* Available from https://doi.org/10.1016/S0966-6362(97)00010-6.

Preston, A. R., & Eichenbaum, H. (2013). Interplay of hippocampus and prefrontal cortex in memory. *Current Biology, 23*(17), R764−R773. Available from https://doi.org/10.1016/j.cub.2013.05.041.

Rajendran, V. G., & Schnupp, J. W. H. (2019). Frequency tagging cannot measure neural tracking of beat or meter. *Proceedings of the National Academy of Sciences of the United States of America, 116*(8), 2779−2780. Available from https://doi.org/10.1073/pnas.1820020116.

Ramig, L. O., Bonitati, C. M., Lemke, J. H., & Horii, Y. (1994). Voice treatment for patients with Parkinson's disease: Development of an approach and preliminary efficacy data. *Journal of Medical Speech-Language Pathology, 2*(3), 191−209.

Rao, S. M., Harrington, D. L., Haaland, K. Y., Bobholz, J. A., Cox, R. W., & Binder, J. R. (1997). Distributed neural systems underlying the timing of movements. *Journal of Neuroscience, 17*(14), 5528−5535.

Repp, B. H. (2005). Sensorimotor synchronization: A review of the tapping literature. *Psychonomic Bulletin and Review, 12*(6), 969−992. Available from https://doi.org/10.3758/BF03206433.

Ripollés, P., Rojo, N., Grau-Sánchez, J., Amengual, J. L., Càmara, E., Marco-Pallarés, J., ... Rodríguez-Fornells, A. (2016). Music supported therapy promotes motor plasticity in individuals with chronic stroke. *Brain Imaging and Behavior, 10*(4), 1289−1307.

Rochester, L., Baker, K., Nieuwboer, A., & Burn, D. (2011). *Movement Disorders, 26*(3), 430−435. Available from https://doi.org/10.1002/mds.23450.

Rossignol, S., & Jones, G. M. (1976). Audio-spinal influence in man studied by the H-reflex and its possible role on rhythmic movements synchronized to sound. *Electroencephalography and Clinical Neurophysiology, 41*(1), 83–92. Available from https://doi.org/10.1016/0013-4694(76)90217-0.

Rowe, G., Hirsh, J. B., & Anderson, A. K. (2006). Positive affect increases the breadth of attentional selection. *Proceedings of the National Academy of Sciences of the United States of America, 104*(1), 383–388. Available from https://doi.org/10.1073/pnas.0605198104.

Salimpoor, V. N., Benovoy, M., Larcher, K., Dagher, A., & Zatorre, R. J. (2011). Anatomically distinct dopamine release during anticipation and experience of peak emotion to music. *Nature Neuroscience, 14*(2), 257–262. Available from https://doi.org/10.1038/nn.272.

Särkämö, T., Ripollés, P., Vepsäläinen, H., Autti, T., Silvennoinen, H. M., Salli, E., ... Rodríguez-Fornells, A. (2014). Structural changes induced by daily music listening in the recovering brain after middle cerebral artery stroke: A voxel-based morphometry study. *Frontiers in Human Neuroscience, 8*. Available from https://doi.org/10.3389/fnhum.2014.00245.

Särkämö, T., Tervaniemi, M., Laitinen, S., Forsblom, A., Soinila, S., Mikkonen, M., ... Hietanen, M. (2008). Music listening enhances cognitive recovery and mood after middle cerebral artery stroke. *Brain, 131*(Pt 3), 866–876. Available from https://doi.org/10.1093/brain/awn013.

Särkämö, T., Tervaniemi, M., Laitinen, S., Numminen, A., Kurki, M., Johnson, J. K., & Rantanen, P. (2014). Cognitive, emotional, and social benefits of regular musical activities in early dementia: Randomized controlled study. *Gerontologist, 54*(4), 634–650. Available from https://doi.org/10.1093/geront/gnt100.

Scahill, R. I., Schott, J. M., Stevens, J. M., Rossor, M. N., & Fox, N. C. (2002). Mapping the evolution of regional atrophy in Alzheimer's disease: Unbiased analysis of fluid-registered serial MRI. *Proceedings of the National Academy of Sciences of the United States of America, 99*(7), 4703–4707. Available from https://doi.org/10.1073/pnas.052587399.

Schauer, M., & Mauritz, K. (2003). Musical motor feedback (MMF) in walking hemiparetic stroke patients: Randomized trials of gait improvement. *Clinical Rehabilitation, 17*(7), 713–722.

Scheltens, P., Blennow, K., Breteler, M., de Strooper, B., Frisoni, G., Salloway, S., & Van der Flier, W. (2016). Alzheimer's disease. *Lancet, 388*, 505–517.

Schlaug, G. (2016). Melodic intonation therapy. In G. Hickok, & S. L. Small (Eds.), *Neurobiology of language* (pp. 1015–1023). Cambridge, MA: Academic Press. Available from https://doi.org/10.1016/B978-0-12-407794-2.00081-X.

Schlaug, G., Forgeard, M., Zhu, L., Norton, A., Norton, A., & Winner, E. (2009). Training-induced neuroplasticity in young children. *Annals of the New York Academy of Sciences.* Available from https://doi.org/10.1111/j.1749-6632.2009.04842.x.

Schlaug, G., Marchina, S., & Norton, A. (2008). From singing to speaking: Why singing may lead to recovery of expressive language function in patients with Broca's aphasia. *Music Perception, 25*(4), 315–323. Available from https://doi.org/10.1525/MP.2008.25.4.315.

Schneider, S., Müünte, T., Rodriguez-Fornells, A., Sailer, M., & Altenmüller, E. (2010). Music-supported training is more efficient than functional motor training for recovery of fine motor skills in stroke patients. *Music Perception, 27*(4), 271–280. Available from https://doi.org/10.1525/mp.2010.27.4.271.

Schneider, E., Schönle, P. W., Altenmüller, E., & Müünte, T. F. (2007). Using musical instruments to improve motor skills recovery following a stroke. *Journal of Neurology, 254*(10), 1339–1349.

Shelton, J., & Kumar, G. P. (2010). Comparison between auditory and visual simple reaction times. *Neuroscience & Medicine, 1*, 30–32. Available from https://doi.org/10.4236/nm.2010.11004.

Sihvonen, A. J., Särkämö, T., Leo, V., Tervaniemi, M., Altenmüller, E., & Soinila, S. (2017). Music-based interventions in neurological rehabilitation. *The Lancet Neurology*, *16*(8), 648–660. Available from https://doi.org/10.1016/S1474-4422(17)30168-0.

Simmons-Stern, N. R., Budson, A. E., & Ally, B. A. (2010). Music as a memory enhancer in patients with Alzheimer's disease. *Neuropsychologia*, *48*(10), 3164–3167. Available from https://doi.org/10.1016/j.neuropsychologia.2010.04.033.

Simmons-Stern, N. R., Deason, R. G., Brandler, B. J., Frustace, B. S., O'Connor, M. K., Ally, B. A., & Budson, A. E. (2012). Music-based memory enhancement in Alzheimer's Disease: Promise and limitations. *Neuropsychologia*, *50*(14), 3295–32303. Available from https://doi.org/10.1016/j.neuropsychologia.2012.09.019.

Soto, D., Funes, M. J., Guzman-Garcia, A., Warbrick, T., Rotshtein, P., & Humphreys, G. W. (2009). Pleasant music overcomes the loss of awareness in patients with visual neglect. *Proceedings of the National Academy of Sciences of the United States of America*, *106*(14), 6011–6016. Available from https://doi.org/10.1073/pnas.0811681106.

Sparks, R., Helm, N., & Albert, M. (1974). Aphasia rehabilitation resulting from melodic intonation therapy. *Cortex*, *10*(4), 303–316. Available from https://doi.org/10.1016/S0010-9452(74)80024-9.

Sparks, R. W., & Holland, A. L. (1976). Method: Melodic intonation therapy for aphasia. *The Journal of Speech and Hearing Disorders*, *41*(3), 287–297.

Squire, L. R. (1992). Memory and the hippocampus: A synthesis from findings with rats, monkeys, and humans. *Psychological Review*, *99*(2), 195–231. Available from https://doi.org/10.1037/0033-295X.99.2.195.

Stahl, B., Kotz, S. A., Henseler, I., Turner, R., & Geyer, S. (2011). Rhythm in disguise: Why singing may not hold the key to recovery from aphasia. *Brain*, *134*(Pt 10), 3083–3093. Available from https://doi.org/10.1093/brain/awr240.

Stephan, K. M., Thaut, M. H., Wunderlich, G., Schicks, W., Tian, B., Tellmann, L., ... Hömberg, V. (2002). Conscious and subconscious sensorimotor synchronization—Prefrontal cortex and the influence of awareness. *NeuroImage*, *15*(2), 345–352. Available from https://doi.org/10.1006/nimg.2001.0929.

Stewart, L., Walsh, V., Frith, U., & Rothwell, J. (2010). Transcranial magnetic stimulation produces speech arrest but not song arrest. *Annals of the New York Academy of Sciences*, *930*, 433–435. Available from https://doi.org/10.1111/j.1749-6632.2001.tb05762.x.

Street, A. J., Magee, W. L., Bateman, A., Parker, M., Odell-Miller, H., & Fachner, J. (2018). Home-based neurologic music therapy for arm hemiparesis following stroke: Results from a pilot, feasibility randomized controlled trial. *Clinical Rehabilitation*, *32*(1), 18–28. Available from https://doi.org/10.1177/0269215517717060.

Tecchio, F., Salustri, C., Thaut, M. H., Pasqualetti, P., & Rossini, P. M. (2000). Conscious and preconscious adaptation to rhythmic auditory stimuli: A magnetoencephalographic study of human brain responses. *Experimental Brain Research*, *135*(2), 222–230. Available from https://doi.org/10.1007/s002210000507.

Teghil, A., Boccia, M., D'Antonio, F., Di Vita, A., de Lena, C., & Guariglia, C. (2019). Neural substrates of internally-based and externally-cued timing: An activation likelihood estimation (ALE) meta-analysis of fMRI studies. *Neuroscience and Biobehavioral Reviews*, *96*, 197–209. Available from https://doi.org/10.1016/j.neubiorev.2018.10.003.

Thaut, C. (2014a). Patterned sensory enhancement (PSE). In M. H. Thaut, & V. Hoemberg (Eds.), *Handbook of neurologic music therapy* (pp. 106–115). Oxford: Oxford University Press.

Thaut, C. P. (2014b). Vocal intonation therapy (VIT). In M. H. Thaut, & V. Hoemberg (Eds.), *Handbook of neurologic music therapy* (pp. 179–184). Oxford: Oxford University Press.

Thaut, M. H. (2005). *Rhythm, music, and the brain: Scientific foundtaions and clinical applications* (1st ed.). New York: Routledge.

Thaut, M. H. (2015). The discovery of human auditory-motor entrainment and its role in the development of neurologic music therapy. In E. Altenmüller, S. Finger, & F. Boller (Eds.), Progress in Brain Research. Available from https://doi.org/10.1016/bs.pbr.2014.11.030.

Thaut, M. H., & Gardiner, J. C. (2014). Musical attention control training. In M. H. Thaut, & V. Hoemberg (Eds.), *Handbook of neurologic music therapy* (pp. 270–298). Oxford: Oxford University Press.

Thaut, M. H., Gardiner, J. C., Holmberg, D., Horwitz, J., Kent, L., Andrews, G., ... McIntosh, G. R. (2009). Neurologic music therapy improves executive function and emotional adjustment in traumatic brain injury rehabilitation. *Annals of the New York Academy of Sciences, 1169*, 406–416. Available from https://doi.org/10.1111/j.1749-6632.2009.04585.x.

Thaut, M. H., & Kenyon, G. P. (2003). Rapid motor adaptations to subliminal frequency shifts during syncopated rhythmic sensorimotor synchronization. *Human Movement Science, 22* (3), 321–338. Available from https://doi.org/10.1016/S0167-9457(03)00048-4.

Thaut, M. H., Kenyon, G. P., Hurt, C. P., McIntosh, G. C., & Hoemberg, V. (2002). Kinematic optimization of spatiotemporal patterns in paretic arm training with stroke patients. *Neuropsychologia, 40*(7), 1073–1081. Available from https://doi.org/10.1016/S0028-3932 (01)00141-5.

Thaut, M. H., Kenyon, G. P., Schauer, M. L., & McIntosh, G. C. (1999). The connection between rhythmicity and brain function. *IEEE Engineering in Medicine and Biology Magazine, 18*(2), 101–108. Available from https://doi.org/10.1109/51.752991.

Thaut, M. H., Leins, A. K., Rice, R. R., Argstatter, H., Kenyon, G. P., McIntosh, G. C., ... Fetter, M. (2007). Rhythmic auditory stimulation improves gait more than NDT/Bobath training in near-ambulatory patients early poststroke: A single-blind, randomized trial. *Neurorehabilitation and Neural Repair, 21*(5), 455–459. Available from https://doi.org/ 10.1177/1545968307300523.

Thaut, M. H., & McIntosh, G. C. (2014). Neurologic Music Therapy in stroke rehabilitation. *Current Physical Medicine and Rehabilitation Reports, 2*(2), 106–113. Available from https://doi.org/10.1007/s40141-014-0049-y.

Thaut, M. H., McIntosh, G. C., Prassas, S. G., & Rice, R. R. (1992). Effect of rhythmic auditory cuing on temporal stride parameters and EMG patterns in normal gait. *Neurorehabilitation and Neural Repair, 6*, 185–190. Available from https://doi.org/10.1177/136140969200600403.

Thaut, M. H., McIntosh, G. C., Prassas, S. G., Rice, R. R., Thaut, M. H., McIntosh, G. C., ... Rice, R. R. (1993). Effect of rhythmic auditory cuing on temporal stride parameters and EMG. Patterns in hemiparetic gait of stroke patients. *Neurorehabilitation and Neural Repair, 7*, 9–16. Available from https://doi.org/10.1177/136140969300700103.

Thaut, M. H., McIntosh, G. C., & Rice, R. R. (1997). Rhythmic facilitation of gait training in hemiparetic stroke rehabilitation. *Journal of the Neurological Sciences, 151*(2), 207–212. Available from https://doi.org/10.1016/S0022-510X(97)00146-9.

Thaut, M. H., McIntosh, K. W., McIntosh, G. C., & Hoemberg, V. (2001). Auditory rhythmicity enhances movement and speech motor control in patients with Parkinson's disease. *Functional Neurology, 16*(2), 163–172.

Thaut, M. H., Miller, R. A., & Schauer, L. M. (1998). Multiple synchronization strategies in rhythmic sensorimotor tasks: Phase vs period correction. *Biological Cybernetics, 79*(3), 241–250. Available from https://doi.org/10.1007/s004220050474.

Thaut, M. H., Peterson, D. A., & McIntosh, G. C. (2005). Temporal entrainment of cognitive functions: Musical mnemonics induce brain plasticity and oscillatory synchrony in neural networks underlying memory. *Annals of the New York Academy of Sciences, 1060,* 243−254. Available from https://doi.org/10.1196/annals.1360.017.

Thaut, M. H., Peterson, D. A., McIntosh, G. C., & Hoemberg, V. (2014). Music mnemonics aid verbal memory and induce learning-related brain plasticity in multiple sclerosis. *Frontiers in Human Neuroscience.* Available from https://doi.org/10.3389/fnhum.2014.00395.

Thaut, M. H., Rathbun, J. A., & Miller, R. A. (1997). Music versus metronome timekeeper in a rhythmic motor task. *International Journal of Arts Medicine, 5*(1), 4−12.

Thaut, M. H., Rice, R. R., Braun Janzen, T., Hurt-Thaut, C. P., & McIntosh, G. C. (2019). Rhythmic auditory stimulation for reduction of falls in Parkinson's disease: A randomized controlled study. *Clinical Rehabilitation, 33*(1), 34−43. Available from https://doi.org/10.1177/0269215518788615.

Thaut, M. H., Schweizer, T. A., Leggieri, M., Churchill, N. W., Fornazzari, L., Vuong, V., & Fischer, C. E. (2018). Neural basis for preservation of musical memory and effects on functional intra network connectivity in early AD and MCI. In *Program no. 741.12 2018 Neuroscience Meeting Planner.* San Diego, CA: Society for Neuroscience, 2018. Online.

Thaut, M. H., Thaut, C. P., & McIntosh, K. (2014). Melodic Intonation Therapy (MIT). In M. H. Thaut, & V. Hoemberg (Eds.), *Handbook of neurologic music therapy* (pp. 140−145). Oxford: Oxford University Press.

Thaut, M. H., Tian, B., & Azimi-Sadjadi, M. R. (1998). Rhythmic finger tapping to cosine-wave modulated metronome sequences: Evidence of subliminal entrainment. *Human Movement Science, 17*(6), 839−863. Available from https://doi.org/10.1016/S0167-9457(98)00031-1.

Thaut, M., Schleiffers, S., & Davis, W. (1991). Analysis of EMG activity in biceps and triceps muscle in an upper extremity gross motor task under the influence of auditory rhythm. *Journal of Music Therapy, 28*(2), 64−88. Available from https://doi.org/10.1093/jmt/28.2.64.

Trombetti, A., Hars, M., Herrmann, F. R., Kressig, R. W., Ferrari, S., & Rizzoli, R. (2011). Effect of music-based multitask training on gait, balance, and fall risk in elderly people: A randomized controlled trial. *Archives of Internal Medicine, 171*(6), 525−533. Available from https://doi.org/10.1001/archinternmed.2010.446.

Tromp, D., Dufour, A., Lithfous, S., Pebayle, T., & Després, O. (2015). Episodic memory in normal aging and Alzheimer disease: Insights from imaging and behavioral studies. *Ageing Research Reviews, 24*(Pt B), 232−262. Available from https://doi.org/10.1016/j.arr.2015.08.006.

Tsai, P. L., Chen, M. C., Huang, Y. T., & Lin, K. C. (2013). Effects of listening to pleasant music on chronic unilateral neglect: A single-subject study. *NeuroRehabilitation, 32*(1), 33−42. Available from https://doi.org/10.3233/NRE-130821.

Tsai, P. L., Chen, M. C., Huang, Y. T., Lin, K. C., Chen, K. L., & Hsu, Y. W. (2013). Listening to classical music ameliorates unilateral neglect after stroke. *American Journal of Occupational Therapy, 67*(3), 328−335. Available from https://doi.org/10.5014/ajot.2013.006312.

Tulving, E. (1972). Episodic and semantic memory. In E. Tulving, & W. Donaldson (Eds.), *Organization of memory* (pp. 381−402). New York: Academic Press.

Van Der Meulen, I., Van De Sandt-Koenderman, M. W. M. E., Heijenbrok, M. H., Visch-Brink, E., & Ribbers, G. M. (2016). Melodic intonation therapy in chronic aphasia: Evidence from a pilot randomized controlled trial. *Frontiers in Human Neuroscience, 10.* Available from https://doi.org/10.3389/fnhum.2016.00533.

Van Der Meulen, I., Van De Sandt-Koenderman, W. M. E., Heijenbrok-Kal, M. H., Visch-Brink, E. G., & Ribbers, G. M. (2014). The efficacy and timing of melodic intonation therapy in subacute aphasia. *Neurorehabilitation and Neural Repair, 28*(6), 536−544. Available from https://doi.org/10.1177/1545968313517753.

Yamadori, A., Osumi, Y., Masuhara, S., & Okubo, M. (1977). Preservation of singing in Broca's aphasia. *Journal of Neurology Neurosurgery and Psychiatry*, *40*(3), 221−224. Available from https://doi.org/10.1136/jnnp.40.3.221.

Zatorre, R. J., Chen, J. L., & Penhune, V. B. (2007). When the brain plays music: Auditory−motor interactions in music perception and production. *Nature Reviews Neuroscience*, *8*(7), 547−558. Available from https://doi.org/10.1038/nrn2152.

Chapter 15

The use of rhythm in rehabilitation for patients with movement disorders

Simone Dalla Bella[1,2,3]

[1]*International Laboratory for Brain, Music, and Sound Research (BRAMS), Montreal, QC, Canada,* [2]*Department of Psychology, University of Montreal, Montreal, QC, Canada,* [3]*Centre for Research on Brain, Language and Music (CRBLM), Montreal, QC, Canada*

Introduction

Humans, across groups and cultures, and from childhood to older age, engage in music activities, and are moved by music. We experience music very often in our everyday environment, by passive or active listening. Some of us deliberately engage in music activities such as playing an instrument, singing, and dancing. These activities involving music are typically multisensory and, owing to their complexity, recruit various neuronal networks mediating sensory, motor, cognitive, and emotional responses. These functions are not devoted to music per se. Some of them are general functions spanning across domains and which can be modified via musical training or activities, as a privileged vehicle for inducing brain plastic changes (Dalla Bella, 2016; Herholz & Zatorre, 2012; Sihvonen et al., 2017). The possibility that music can change the brain is particularly appealing in the context of devising targeted music-based interventions, for rehabilitation in various neurological diseases, such as stroke, dementia, and Parkinson's disease (PD) (Särkämö, 2018; Sihvonen et al., 2017). Indeed, music has a very high potential as a tool for rehabilitation. Music is capable of engaging parallel brain circuitries underpinning reward, sensory and motor processes, arousal, and affective regulation. In addition, music activities are particularly enjoyable, thus making adherence to treatment more likely, and enhancing well-being throughout the life span. Current advances in our understanding of the brain structure and functioning underlying music can add to this endeavor, by fostering theory-driven interventions to be tested in clinical settings (translational approach; Dalla Bella, 2018; Sihvonen et al., 2017). In this chapter I will focus in

Music and the Aging Brain. DOI: https://doi.org/10.1016/B978-0-12-817422-7.00015-8

particular on interventions driven by the rhythmic properties of music, and by their tendency to recruit the motor system. A model of the success of these interventions is PD, to which I will devote particular attention.

Moving to musical beat: a widespread and pleasurable activity

A widespread response to music, deliberate and spontaneous, is to move to its beat. Listening to music with a very salient beat structure (e.g., a march or a waltz) often compels us to move. Human proclivity to move to music and to experience this activity as very pleasurable is linked to what is called musical "groove." This is associated to properties of musical structure such as rhythmic complexity, syncopation, and harmonic complexity (Matthews, Witek, Heggli, Penhune, & Vuust, 2019; Vuust & Witek, 2014; Witek, Clarke, Wallentin, Kringelbach, & Vuust, 2014), as well as individual differences in listeners' attitudes (Senn, Kilchenmann, Bechtold, & Hoesl, 2018). An increasing body of evidence from experimental psychology and cognitive neuroscience indicates that the rhythm conveyed by an auditory stimulus and movement are tightly linked. Music, owing to its temporal regularity and predictability, is ideally suited to engage our body. When we tap our feet or sway our body along with our preferred song, while synchronizing our steps to the beats delivered by our MP3 player during jogging, dancing, or while performing synchronized sports (e.g., swimming), we entrain to the regular pulse of music.

Matching movements to a beat is possible because the temporal dynamics of rhythmic sound (e.g., its periodicity) drives our attention (Large & Jones, 1999), and thereby allows predicting when an upcoming event is going to occur (e.g., the next musical beat). Allocation of attention to the temporal dynamics of a rhythmic stimulus is described by the dynamic attending theory (DAT) (Jones & Boltz, 1989; Large & Jones, 1999). According to DAT, attending is a dynamic process, which can be successfully modeled by internal neurocognitive self-sustained oscillations (Fujioka, Trainor, Large, & Ross, 2012; Nozaradan, Peretz, Missal, & Mouraux, 2011). Internal oscillations, which have been associated to attentional pulses, synchronize to the most prominent aspects of the sound signal (e.g., tones in an isochronous sequences, beats in music). Attention is dynamically shifted to the most salient events in the sound, through a process called "entrainment," thus generating temporal expectations. The mechanisms leading to couple movement to the perceived beat play a critical role in understanding how rhythm can be harnessed to stimulate or reactivate the motor system in patients with motor disorders. These mechanisms are reviewed below.

Moving to musical beat: cognitive and neuronal underpinnings

The majority in the general healthy population are well equipped to move to the beat of music. Apart from some exceptions, namely individuals who poorly synchronize to the beat (Palmer, Lidji, & Peretz, 2014; Sowiński & Dalla Bella, 2013), this ability is very common and relatively independent from musical training (Repp, 2010; Sowiński & Dalla Bella, 2013). The proclivity to move spontaneously to the beat is visible very early during development (within the first 2 years of life; Zentner & Eerola, 2010), while precise audiomotor synchronization appears a bit later, particularly in a social setting (Kirschner & Tomasello, 2009). Motor synchronization to the beat involves both the perception of the main periodicity underlying a temporal pattern, simple or complex, and the motor processes needed to couple motor events to the beat. Beat perception can be tested with tasks such as the Beat Alignment Test (BAT) in which a listener has to detect whether tones are aligned or not with the musical beat (Iversen & Patel, 2008). Motor synchronization to the beat is often assessed by asking participants to tap their finger in synchrony with a pacing stimulus, like a metronome or music (finger tapping paradigm; Repp, 2005; Repp & Su, 2013). More recently, more complex batteries of tests have been devised to assess a full array of rhythmic abilities, perceptual and sensorimotor. Examples are the Battery for the Assessment of Auditory Sensorimotor and Timing Abilities (BAASTA, Dalla Bella, Farrugia, et al., 2017), developed in our lab, and the Harvard BAT (Fujii & Schlaug, 2013). The advantage of these batteries over single tests is their ability to characterize profiles of rhythmic abilities and their sensitivity to individual differences in various populations (for BAASTA, see Bégel et al., 2017, submitted; Benoit et al., 2014; Cochen De Cock et al., 2018; Dalla Bella, Benoit, et al., 2017; Dalla Bella, Dotov, Bardy, & Cochen de Cock, 2018; Dalla Bella, Farrugia, et al., 2017; Falk, Müller, & Dalla Bella, 2015; Puyjarinet, Bégel, Lopez, Dellacherie, & Dalla Bella, 2017). As will be shown below, detecting individual profiles of rhythmic abilities in patient populations may play a pivotal role in devising personalized rhythm-based interventions.

The ability to move to the beat requires the coordinated action of various neuronal networks (Damm et al., 2020). Perceiving the beat of an auditory sequence engages auditory regions of the brain (the superior temporal gyrus; Chen, Penhune, & Zatorre, 2008a; Schwartze & Kotz, 2013; Thaut, 2003). In addition, classical motor regions including the basal ganglia, premotor cortex, presupplementary motor area, and the cerebellum light up during beat perception, notwithstanding the lack of an overt motor response (Chen, Penhune, & Zatorre, 2008b; Coull, Cheng, & Meck, 2011; Grahn & Brett, 2007; Grahn & Rowe, 2009; Paquette, Fujii, Li, & Schlaug, 2017). The coupling of a motor response to the beat is afforded by sensorimotor integration regions (dorsal premotor cortex; Chen, Zatorre, & Penhune, 2006; Coull et al., 2011; Zatorre, Chen, & Penhune, 2007). Malfunctioning of these networks is associated with rhythmic deficits found in neurodegenerative disorders such as PD (Benoit et al., 2014; Grahn & Brett, 2009; Jones & Jahanshahi, 2014; Pastor, Artieda, Jahanshahi, & Obeso, 1992; Spencer & Ivry, 2005), as well as in neurodevelopmental disorders including attention-deficit hyperactivity disorder (Noreika, Falter, & Rubia, 2013; Puyjarinet et al., 2017), developmental coordination disorder (Trainor, Chang, Cairney, & Yao-Chuen, 2018), stuttering (Falk et al., 2015), autism spectrum disorder (Allman, Pelphrey, & Meck, 2012), and speech and language impairments (Bégel et al., submitted; Corriveau & Goswami, 2009; Corriveau, Pasquini, & Goswami, 2007; Goswami, 2011; Huss, Verney, Fosker, Mead, & Goswami, 2011).

In a nutshell, current knowledge of the behavioral and brain mechanisms underpinning rhythmic abilities reveals that rhythmic musical stimuli can engage motor areas in the brain. Interestingly, temporal predictions driven by rhythmic auditory stimuli and their oscillatory neuronal counterpart are reinforced by overt motor production, which in turn improves perception (Morillon & Baillet, 2017; Morillon, Schroeder, & Wyart, 2014). Hence, moving to the beat of a rhythmic stimulus provides ideal conditions to enhance temporal prediction and attending, while improving both perceptual and motor performance at the expected times. This has particular relevance for the aforementioned patient populations showing impaired temporal prediction and rhythmic processes. Moving to an auditory beat can be exploited to pave the way to effective and individualized rhythm-based interventions. Indeed, identifying the components of the rhythm system spared by brain lesion or congenital anomalies may guide individualized rehabilitation strategies. In this chapter I will show how this approach can be used successfully for predicting the success of a music-based rhythm intervention in PD.

Rhythm, a successful tool for motor rehabilitation

The presentation of rhythmic stimuli has shown beneficial effects on motor behavior in patients with movement disorders (e.g., Ghai, Ghai, Schmitz, & Effenberg, 2018; Spaulding et al., 2013), but also in older healthy adults (Ghai, Ghai, & Effenberg, 2018). The vast majority of studies focused on gait disorders, given their functional relevance for patient populations, their deleterious impact on quality of life, and the associated economic burden. Dysfunctional gait, namely a slow, broad-based, shuffling, and cautious walking pattern ("senile gait disorder"; Salzman, 2010) is not uncommon in older adults. It is observed in about one-third of adults above 70 years of age among community-residing older adults (Verghese et al., 2006), a proportion increasing with age (Downton & Andrews, 1991). Particular attention is paid to gait speed, as it is a hallmark of health and functional status (Cesari, 2011), it declines with age and is a strong predictor of disability, healthcare utilization, nursing home admission, and mortality (Blain, Carriere, & Sourial, 2010; Cesari et al., 2005; Ostir, Kuo, Berges, Markides, & Ottenbacher, 2007; Shumway-Cook, Guralnik, & Phillips, 2007; Studenski, Perera, & Patel, 2011). Reduced gait speed in older adults is also treated as a warning sign of cognitive decline and a good predictor of its onset (Aggarwal, Wilson, & Beck, 2006; Buracchio, Dodge, Howieson,

Wasserman, & Kaye, 2010; Inzitari, Newman, & Yaffe, 2007). Importantly, gait dysfunctions are a major cause of falls in older adults. Among community-dwelling older adults over 64 years of age, approximately 28%−35% of people experience falls (Blake et al., 1988).

Gait disorders are exacerbated by neurodegenerative disorders and are a hallmark of PD (Grabli et al., 2012). PD is the second most common neurodegenerative disorder (after Alzheimer's disease), and the most common serious movement disorder (Hirtz et al., 2007). Worldwide, about 4 million people suffer from PD, with more than 1.2 million just in Europe (Andlin-Sobocki, Jönsson, Wittchen, & Olesen, 2005). These numbers will tend to increase as a result of the aging population. For example, the prevalence in Europe is estimated at 160 PD patients per 100,000 among people aged 65 and older; this number is forecasted to double by 2030 (de Rijk et al., 1997; Dorsey et al., 2007).

PD results from the progressive loss of neurons in the substantia nigra, disrupting dopaminergic projections to the basal ganglia (caudate nucleus and putamen) and leading to a deregulation of basal ganglia−thalamocortical (BGTC) circuitries. Three cardinal symptoms characterize PD, namely resting tremor, limb rigidity, and bradykinesia (or akinesia) (Jankovic, 2008; Kalia & Lang, 2015; Samii, Nutt, & Ransom, 2004). The first symptom to appear is resting tremor, an involuntary low-frequency repetitive movement caused by contracting muscles. Tremor usually occurs unilaterally, worsens over time, and sometimes extends bilaterally. Rigidity refers to abnormal muscle stiffness or lack of flexibility in the limbs or other body parts, preventing muscles from stretching and relaxing; it similarly affects agonist and antagonist muscles. Bradykinesia indicates a general slowness of voluntary movement (akinesia, when voluntary movement is practically absent). It is one of the most disabling deficits in PD, has deleterious effects on fine motor control, and is visible in tasks such as writing or finger tapping. Postural instability and gait disorders, albeit they are not treated as cardinal symptoms per se, are also important motor signs in PD, gaining importance as the disease progresses (Bloem, 1992; Grabli et al., 2012; Koller & Montgomery, 1997). At the initial stages of the disease, gait dysfunctions can be detected in conditions of dual-task, for example, when patients walk while performing a concurrent task (e.g., speech or simple arithmetic calculation) tapping into limited attentional resources and executive functions (see Al-Yahya et al., 2011; Kelly, Eusterbrock, & Shumway-Cook, 2012). Parkinsonian gait is characterized by small steps (i.e., reduced stride length), unchanged or slightly increased cadence (steps/min) compensating for the reduced stride length, reduced gait velocity, together with festination and freezing (i.e., difficulty in gait initiation or stopping when turning or approaching an object) (Giladi, 2001; Grabli et al., 2012; Morris, Huxham, McGinley, Dodd, & Iansek, 2001; Morris, Iansek, Matyas, & Summers, 1994).

Gait and balance disorders are major therapeutic challenges in PD as they negatively impact the activities of daily living, and represent a growing economic burden for the healthcare system (Grabli et al., 2012). Gait deteriorates over time, impairing mobility, limiting independence, and reducing quality of life (Elbaz et al., 2002). The increased likelihood of falls (Morris et al., 2001; Samii et al., 2004) is a major reason for morbidity and disability in PD (Contreras & Grandas, 2012), leading to fractures and head injuries that may be fatal (de Lau, Verbaan, van Rooden, Marinus, & van Hilten, 2014). From 38% to 87% of PD patients experience falls (Contreras & Grandas, 2012). Falls are a quite common outcome of motor disorders such as PD. An interesting meta-analysis has reported that the recurrent falling rate for PD patients was 57% among those patients who had reported previous falls (Pickering et al., 2007). Recurrent falls are highly disabling. Falling often leads to severe consequences, including head injuries, fractures (hip in particular), and, in some instances, death (Wenning et al., 1999). Falls are also typically associated to the fear of new falls (Adkin, Frank, & Jog, 2003), which result in loss of independence, reduced mobility, increased osteoporosis, reduced social activity, and depression (Bloem, Hausdorff, Visser, & Giladi, 2004). Falls in PD also increase institutionalization rates. Overall the direct economic burden of falls in PD has been estimated to be twice as big as for of nonfallers (Spottke et al., 2005). Unfortunately, gait and balance disorders respond quite poorly to long-term dopamine-replacement therapy (Grabli et al., 2012; Sethi, 2008). This situation motivates the search for complementary nonpharmacological interventions to improve gait in PD (Tomlinson et al., 2012).

Beneficial effects of music and rhythm in Parkinson's disease

There are several options for alleviating motor symptoms in PD, including pharmacotherapy, surgery, neuromodulation, and nonpharmacological treatments (e.g., physical therapy). A common treatment is to prescribe patients a dopamine-replacement therapy (with levodopa and dopamine agonists), to compensate for the decay of the basal-ganglia dopaminergic track (for a review, Connolly & Lang, 2014). Other methods, some of them invasive, aim at reducing the deregulation of BGTC circuitries via the removal of deep-brain structures (e.g., pallidotomy or thalamotomy; see Lozano, Tam, & Lozano, 2018, for a critical review), surgery combined with deep-brain stimulation (e.g., of the subthalamic nucleus; Benabid, Pollak, Louveau, Henry, & de Rougemont, 1987; Kalia, Sankar, & Lozano, 2013), and, more recently, neuromodulation using transcranial magnetic stimulation or transcranial direct current stimulation (Benninger & Hallett, 2015).

Complementary to pharmacotherapy and the other aforementioned interventions, nonpharmacological treatments are considered as a way to improve quality of life and reduce or control the motor symptoms of PD (Rubinstein,

Giladi, & Hausdorff, 2002). These methods are based on physical and exercise therapies (Kwakkel, de Goede, & van Wegen, 2007), and span from sitting and standing, body resistance training, articulation for posture and balance, to endurance and strengthening exercises for improving general physical conditions. Physical therapy in general has shown some beneficial effects in improving patients' physical functioning, quality of life, leg strength, balance, and gait (Goodwin, Richards, Taylor, Taylor, & Campbell, 2008). Here I will focus on the methods making use of external rhythmic cues, with a particular attention to musical stimulation.

Music is perfectly suited to convey rhythmic stimulation. Moving to a musical beat is not only activating neuronal structures underlying rhythm and motor control, some of which are impaired in PD (see below), but also, being a highly participatory and motivating activity, is known to engage the reward system (Salimpoor, Zald, Zatorre, Dagher, & McIntosh, 2015). Thus therapies using music and rhythm as tools for motor rehabilitation in PD can have positive effects on patients' exercise capacity and motivation, fostering social participation, increase adherence, and ultimately enhance quality of life on top of improving motor symptoms (Pacchetti et al., 2000; Pohl, Dizdar, & Hallert, 2013; Ziv & Lidor, 2011). Along this line, there is growing evidence of positive effects of dance-based interventions, such as tango, on motor symptoms, quality of life, and social participation in PD (Duncan & Earhart, 2012; Earhart, 2009; Foster, Golden, Duncan, & Earhart, 2013; Hackney & Earhart, 2009; for beneficial effects of music and dance in healthy older adults, see Chapter 11: Toward music-based auditory rehabilitation for older adults).

Positive effects of presenting rhythmic cues (rhythmic auditory cueing— RAC) on gait in patients with PD have been reported since 1942 (Von Wilzenben, 1942). PD is a prototypical example showing promising effects of RAC on gait kinematics (Ghai et al., 2018; Kwakkel et al., 2007). The intervention is relatively simple and consists of instructing the patient to walk together with a regular stimulation in the form of a repeated sound (a metronome; e.g., Elston, Honan, Powell, Gormley, & Stein, 2010; Enzensberger, Oberlander, & Stecker, 1997; Howe, Lovgreen, Cody, Ashton, & Oldham, 2003) or a piece of music with a salient beat, sometimes with an embedded metronome (e.g., Benoit et al., 2014; McIntosh, Brown, Rice, & Thaut, 1997; Thaut, Rice, Braun Janzen, Hurt-Thaut, & McIntosh, 1996). The stimulation rate is typically individualized relative to patients' preferred cadence (number of steps/min). Patients typically benefit from auditory cues presented at rates ranging from 80% to 125% of their preferred cadence (Bryant, Rintala, Lai, & Protas, 2009), which usually hovers around 100 steps/min (Nieuwboer et al., 2007). When a rhythmic stimulus is presented, PD patients typically walk faster, increase their step length (McIntosh et al., 1997), and reduce the frequency of freezing episodes (Arias & Cudeiro, 2010). This effect of RAC is immediate but usually disappears once the stimulation is stopped. Interestingly, longer term positive effects on walking in everyday life even in the absence of stimulation are found following RAC-based interventions (Lim et al., 2005). In these protocols patients are submitted to programs in which they are asked to walk with RAC a few times a week for several weeks; gait is tested in the absence of rhythmic stimuli before and after the rehabilitation program. After the intervention, PD patients show faster walking speed (Rochester, Burn, Woods, Godwin, & Nieuwboer, 2009), and a significant reduction of freezing phenomena (Nieuwboer, 2008). Comparable motor benefits can be achieved when rehabilitation via RAC is carried out in a home environment with a stimulating device (e.g., see the RESCUE project—Rehabilitation in Parkinson's Disease: Strategies for Cueing) (Nieuwboer et al., 2007). A critical question is to what extent these beneficial effects of RAC persist over time, considering the inevitable decline linked to neurodegeneration. To date, evidence is not conclusive in this respect. In some cases performance deterioration is observed within 12 weeks after the therapy (Nieuwboer et al., 2001); yet, others report rather negligible decline in gait performance, if at all, after 4−6 weeks (Benoit et al., 2014; Marchese, Diverio, Zucchi, Lentino, & Abbruzzese, 2000).

Which are the mechanisms and brain circuitries supporting the beneficial effects of RAC on walking in PD? A possibility, which has been put forward recently, is that the effect of RAC is mediated by a general purpose system responsible for beat perception and motor synchronization to a beat (Dalla Bella, Benoit, Farrugia, Schwartze, & Kotz, 2015; Dalla Bella, 2018; Nombela, Hughes, Owen, & Grahn, 2013; see also Damm et al., 2020). This is the same system affording tracking the beat of simple and complex rhythmic sequences, and coupling of movement to the beat across various behaviors, such as finger tapping, walking, and speaking (Puyjarinet et al., 2019). This idea builds on processes underlying temporal prediction and timing, identified in the context of auditory processing at different levels of stimulus complexity such as speech and tones (Kotz & Schwartze, 2010; Schwartze & Kotz, 2013; Schwartze, Rothermich, Schmidt-Kassow, & Kotz, 2011). The model, illustrated in Fig. 15.1, involves two parallel networks. The BGTC network (in violet) supports the attention-dependent evaluation of temporal intervals, and self-generation of movements. The network is involved in action initiation and in overt estimate of stimulus duration. The cerebellum−thalamocortical (CTC) network (in cyan) supports the preattentive encoding of the temporal structure of event sequences, and matching movements to external cues (Coull et al., 2011; Kotz & Schwartze, 2011). Functional BGTC and CTC networks are essential for extracting the beat structure of a predictable auditory sequence, developing temporal expectations of the upcoming events (i.e., the following beats), and aligning movements to the beat.

As a result of the progressive loss of neurons in the substantia nigra (Factor & Weiner, 2008) the BGTC is deregulated in PD. This is associated with deficits in the perception and production of temporal intervals

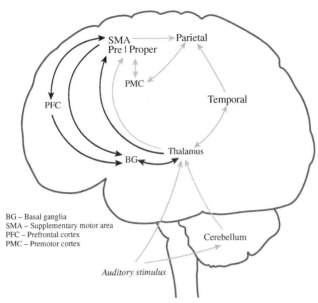

FIGURE 15.1 Networks underlying rhythmic auditory cueing in Parkinson's disease. *From Dalla Bella, S., Benoit, C. E., Farrugia, N., Schwartze, M., & Kotz, S. A. (2015). Effects of musically cued gait training in Parkinson's disease: Beyond a motor benefit.* Annals of the New York Academy of Sciences, 1337, 77–85.

(Allman & Meck, 2011), as well as in beat perception (Benoit et al., 2014; Grahn & Brett, 2009). Yet, the CTC network is spared by the disease, thus allowing for unimpaired coding of prominent discrete events in the temporal structure (e.g., musical beats). This representation of temporal structure paves the way to dynamic attending (i.e., providing attractors for attentional oscillations), generating an expectancy scheme via entrainment (Kotz & Schwartze, 2011) and providing a temporal scaffolding for synchronized action.

Within this framework, two possibilities can be envisioned to explain the effects of RAC. One is that the malfunctioning of the BGTC network in PD is compensated by the recruitment of the CTC network, affected later during the progression of the disease (Dalla Bella et al., 2015; Nombela et al., 2013). In keeping with this hypothesis, enhanced cerebellar activity after gait training with RAC was found in one study (del Olmo, Arias, Furio, Pozo, & Cudeiro, 2006). Another possibility is that the deregulated BGTC network still affords some degree of beat processing (Dalla Bella, Benoit, et al., 2017; Dalla Bella et al., 2018). Residual beat processing may provide sufficient information for temporal pacing of movement initiation and execution so that some of the patients can benefit from rhythmic cues. To date it is still unclear which of the networks support the beneficial effects of RAC. However, in both cases, it is hypothesized that the response to RAC is mediated by beat perception and synchronization mechanisms. Thus individual differences in these abilities are expected to be good predictors of the response to RAC.

Individual differences in rhythmic abilities predict the success of rhythmic auditory cueing

There is a paucity of research on the link between individual rhythmic skills and the widespread ability to walk to the rhythm of an external stimulus. Gait is often treated as mostly an autonomous spinally controlled process with limited adaptability (Dietz, 2003; Dimitrijevic, Gerasimenko, & Pinter, 1998; Pearson & Gordon, 2000), dominated by body dynamics which imposes a preferential rate of stepping. However, top-down cortical contributions to gait control are seen in situations of dual-task. The dual-task paradigm consists of providing the individual a secondary cognitive task (e.g., counting backward) together with a primary task, such as walking (Al-Yahya et al., 2011; Woollacott & Shumway-Cook, 2002). Walking in a dual-task situation is typically more challenging than walking alone, by requiring more cognitive resources such as selective attention and flexibility. This is particularly important in older adults, which are typically more affected by a dual-task due to a reduced cognitive reserve (Yogev-Seligmann et al., 2010). With regard to rhythmic skills, there is recent evidence in healthy young adults that beat perception affects gait when participants synchronize with rhythmic stimuli. Walking to music with a less-salient beat (low-groove) is detrimental to gait (i.e., reducing cadence and step length) in particular for participants with poor beat perception (Leow, Parrott, & Grahn, 2014; Ready, McGarry, Rinchon, Holmes, & Grahn, 2019).

Until very recently, it was unclear whether individual differences in rhythmic abilities in PD patients can act as predictors of their response to RAC. To test this hypothesis we asked patients with PD and matched controls to walk together with highly familiar march music (Cochen de Cock et al., 2018; Dalla Bella et al., 2018). No explicit instruction to synchronize heel strikes to the beat was given, as this is known to hinder gait kinematics (Leow, Waclawik, & Grahn, 2018). The rate of the rhythmic stimuli was 10% faster relative to each participant's preferred cadence. We measured the alignment between the footfalls and the stimulus beat times, reflecting patients' synchronization ability. Moreover, we assessed beat perception with the BAT (Iversen & Patel, 2008), taken from BAASTA (Dalla Bella, Farrugia, et al., 2017), in which participants detected whether a metronome was aligned or not with the beat of musical excerpts. Patients, like controls, positively responded to RAC, by increasing speed and stride length. Yet, patients varied significantly in their response to the stimulation. Out of 39 patients, 22 increased their walking speed above the smallest clinically significant difference (> 6 cm/s) (Hass et al., 2014). The other 17 did not exhibit a positive response to RAC. With our surprise, cueing was detrimental for six patients, who significantly decreased their gait speed (−18 cm/s, on average, compared to no stimulation) and the length of their strides (−11 cm). These different responses to RAC were linked to patients' rhythmic abilities. Patients with a positive response to RAC were more apt to align the footfalls to the beat (good synchronizers) and had relatively spared beat perception relative to controls (see Fig. 15.2). Moreover, patients with positive response to cueing rated their perceptual abilities and musical training higher than the others (Goldsmiths Musical Sophistication Index; Müllensiefen, Gingras, Musil, & Stewart, 2014). In sum, a good response to RAC is related to spared rhythmic abilities, while impaired synchronization to the beat or poor beat perception make the stimulation either useless or, in the worst of the cases, deleterious. This finding is consistent with the view that general rhythm processes may mediate the gait response to RAC. In addition, it provides guidelines to predict a positive effect of RAC based on the performance in simple rhythmic tasks. Along this line, we showed recently that beat perception, gait velocity at baseline, and cognitive flexibility taken together can predict quite successfully whether a patient will respond positively or not to RAC (Cochen de Cock et al., 2018). Interestingly, the link between individual rhythmic abilities and the effects of RAC is not likely to be confined to the immediate effects of the stimulation. Rhythmic abilities can predict the success of a RAC-based intervention. In a recent study in which PD patients were

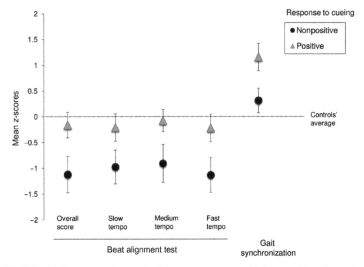

FIGURE 15.2 Performance of patients with positive response (*light-gray triangles*) and nonpositive response to rhythmic auditory cueing (*dark-gray circles*) in beat perception (BAT), and synchronization of footfalls to the beat. Error bars are SE of the mean. *BAT*, Beat Alignment Test. *From Dalla Bella, S., Dotov, D. G., Bardy, B., & Cochen de Cock, V. (2018). Individualization of music-based rhythmic auditory cueing in Parkinson's disease.* Annals of the New York Academy of Sciences, 1423, 308−317.

submitted to a RAC-based intervention (walking with rhythmic music, three times per week, for a month), we found that low synchronization variability and the ability to adapt movement to a stimulation change in a tapping task are good predictors of success for the intervention (Dalla Bella, Benoit, et al., 2017).

In sum, a rhythm-based intervention for gait rehabilitation in PD is well-motivated as it taps into mechanisms either impaired by the disease (BGTC), by partly helping in recovering their functioning, or spared (CTC). Critically, variability in beat perception and synchronization typical of the disease plays an important role in predicting the success of the intervention. An assessment of rhythmic abilities before the intervention may serve to identify the patients who are likely to benefit most from the intervention, and those who may significantly worsen their performance. However, even if for some patients the stimulation brings no effect on their gait, walking with music may still increase a patient's motivation to walk and general mobility. Music is a highly motivating stimulus acting on dopaminergic mechanisms and known for its ability to engage emotions and stimulate the reward system (Blood & Zatorre, 2001; Salimpoor et al., 2015). Thus walking with music, a rewarding activity in itself, may have beneficial effects like increasing mobility and the patient's quality of life.

Harnessing technology for improving rhythm-based rehabilitation

In spite of RAC positive effects on gait in general (Ghai et al., 2018), the possibility of deleterious effects of RAC and in general the variability in patient response mitigate the initial optimism. Patients unable to build on relatively spared rhythmic processing, and generally with reduced cognitive resources, may be confronted with a dual-task situation when asked to walk with music. Walking is particularly affected by dual tasks in older adults (Beauchet, Dubost, Aminian, Gonthier, & Kressig, 2005; Beauchet, Dubost, Gonthier, & Kressig, 2005; Dubost et al., 2006), and even more in PD (Belghali, Chastan, Cignetti, Davenne, & Decker, 2017; Rochester, Galna, Lord, & Burn, 2014).

Variable response to a rhythm-based intervention suggests that treatment individualization is in order to select the appropriate parameters for the intervention. Individualized RAC should (1) capitalize on patients' spared rhythmic abilities, and (2) assist the patient whenever these abilities are impaired (Dalla Bella, 2018; Dalla Bella et al., 2018). This idea has been recently implemented in our lab by harnessing mobile technologies for monitoring motor behavior via dedicated sensors (accelerometers), and for tailoring rhythmic stimulation to patients' performance in real time (Dotov et al., 2019). This technology intervenes to compensate for patients' rhythmic deficits, by assisting them in synchronizing footsteps to the beat. By fostering step-to-beat synchronization via mobile technologies, we expect to increase the effectiveness of music-based interventions, and increase the engagement of spared compensatory mechanisms (i.e., CTC networks). Step-to-beat mapping strategies were adopted in the past to implement bidirectional coupling (WalkMate—Miyake, 2009; Hove, Suzuki, Uchitomi, Orimo, & Miyake, 2012; DJogger—Moens et al., 2014). Another possibility is mutual coordination, in which technology is used to make predictions about the conditions in which spontaneous synchronization of gait is more likely (Dalla Bella, 2018; Dalla Bella et al., 2018; Dotot et al., 2019). The latter solution is particularly desirable as it is expected to foster spontaneous step-to-beat synchronization by mimicking natural interpersonal coordination. We proposed an implementation of this solution by modeling rhythmic (periodic) properties of gait and of the stimulus with a Kuramoto system of coupled phase oscillators. This individualized solution tailors the stimulation to the patient's cadence, thus keeping step-to-beat synchronization, while driving the patient towards an optimal value (i.e., higher cadence). An illustration of this interactive system is provided in Fig. 15.3. We compared gait in the presence of mutually interactive RAC to standard RAC (non-interactive), and to a purely mirroring strategy (i.e., musical rhythm shadowing the patient's gait timing). We found that mutually interactive RAC is the one affording the most improvement in cadence, while fostering the alignment of patients' footfalls to the beat (Dotov et al., 2019). This solution will be implemented in further studies on

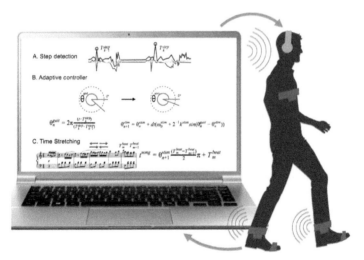

FIGURE 15.3 Interactive rhythmic auditory cueing using mutual synchronization modeled via a Kuramoto system of coupled oscillators. *From Dotov, D. G., Cochen de Cock, V., Geny, C., Ihalainen, P., Moens, B., Leman M., ... Dalla Bella, S. (2019). The role of mutual synchronization and predictability in entraining walking to an auditory beat.* Journal of Experimental Psychology: General, 148(6), 1041−1057.

PD with the goal of further testing its efficacy in a large cohort of patients and to examine the underlying neuronal underpinnings.

Another possibility to implement rhythmic training is to exploit the power of serious games for rehabilitation. A serious game is a game specifically targeted to motor or cognitive rehabilitation, and education purposes. By definition, it is meant to be entertaining, motivating, widely accessible to the public, and cost-efficient (Annetta, 2010; Kato, 2012). Serious games have been extensively used in therapy (for a review, see Rego, Moreira, & Reis, 2010), in stroke (Friedman et al., 2014; Webster & Celik, 2014), PD (Barry, Galna, & Rochester, 2014; Harris, Rantalainen, Muthalib, Johnson, & Teo, 2015; Mendes et al., 2012), and in healthy older adults (Sun & Lee, 2013). Encouraging results in training cognitive functions (working memory, executive functions) were obtained, but with some limitations (Owen et al., 2010). We recently adopted a serious game approach to rhythmic training. Although nowadays there are a few off-the-shelf rhythm-based games, they present limitations, such as reduced temporal precision, and poor selectivity for rhythmic skills, which make them poor candidates for training rhythmic abilities in a clinical setting (Bégel, Di Loreto, Seilles, & Dalla Bella, 2017). For this purpose we devised a new serious game for training rhythm abilities (Rhythm Workers, Bégel, Seilles, & Dalla Bella, 2018), implemented on a tablet device. The game trains rhythmic abilities by asking the player to tap on a tablet device to the beat of musical excerpts of increasing complexity, or to detect whether a metronome is aligned or not to the beat. This protocol was tested recently in a proof-of-concept study, as part of an at-home self-rehabilitation program for training rhythmic abilities in patients with PD (Dauvergne et al., 2018). In this pilot study the serious game showed excellent suitability, as well as an improvement of beat perception in patients. These first results are promising, motivating further research on rhythm-based serious games as a tool for the rehabilitation of rhythmic and motor abilities in patients with PD, and, more generally for patients with rhythm disorders.

Conclusion

In this chapter I reviewed evidence that musical rhythm can act as a powerful tool in rehabilitation for patients with movement disorders. To do so, I adopted a genuinely translational approach building on the widespread and robust relation between musical rhythm and movement (Dalla Bella, 2018). PD was chosen as a model given the peculiar response of patients with the disease to external rhythmic stimuli, and the rich literature on the beneficial effects of rhythm on walking. That gait features can be improved in PD via rhythmic stimulation depending on patients' spared rhythmic abilities is a nice demonstration that rhythm-based interventions can be theory-driven. By capitalizing on current knowledge of normal rhythmic processes, predictions can be made about the success of an intervention knowing patients' individual performance. A standardized assessment of rhythmic abilities thus appears as a critical step to devise individualized RAC programs to limit potential deleterious effects of RAC while maximizing its benefits. Finally, I showed that recent advances in mobile technologies (interactive applications, serious games) can be instrumental to implementing and disseminating rhythm-based music interventions. In particular, assistive rehabilitation strategies implemented via mobile technologies hold particular promise, as they are typically entertaining, motivating, cost-effective, and usable in home-rehabilitation programs. Notably, gait dysfunctions are not uncommon in healthy older adults and deterioration in the neuronal control of movement is also associated with cognitive impairment (in Alzheimer's disease and mild cognitive impairment; Franssen, Souren, & Torossian, 1999; Nadkarni, Mawji, McIlroy, & Black, 2009; Pettersson, Olsson, & Wahlund, 2005; Wittwer, Andrews, & Webster, 2008; Wittwer, Webster, & Menz, 2010). An approach akin to the one adopted for motor rehabilitation in PD can be extended to these populations. Devising individualized rhythm-based musical interventions for older adults, exploiting mobile technologies, may soon become part of the research agenda.

Acknowledgments

The author is funded by a Discovery Grant (RGPIN-2019-05453) from the Natural Sciences and Engineering Research Council of Canada (NSERC), by a John R. Evans Leaders Fund from the Canada Foundation for Innovation (FCI), by starting funds from the Department of Psychology at the University of Montreal.

References

Adkin, A. L., Frank, J. S., & Jog, M. S. (2003). Fear of falling and postural control in Parkinson's disease. *Movement Disorders*, *18*(5), 496−502.

Aggarwal, N. T., Wilson, R. S., Beck, T. L., et al. (2006). Motor dysfunction in mild cognitive impairment and the risk of incident Alzheimer disease. *Archives of Neurology*, *63*(12), 1763−1769.

Al-Yahya, E., Dawes, H., Smith, L., Dennis, A., Howells, K., & Cockburn, J. (2011). Cognitive motor interference while walking: A systematic review and meta-analysis. *Neuroscience and Biobehavioral Reviews*, *35*, 715−728.

Allman, M. J., & Meck, W. H. (2011). Pathophysiological distortions in time perception and timed performance. *Brain*, *135*(3), 656−677.

Allman, M. J., Pelphrey, K. A., & Meck, W. H. (2012). Developmental neuroscience of time and number: Implications for autism and other neurodevelopmental disabilities. *Frontiers in Integrative Neuroscience*, *6*, 7.

Andlin-Sobocki, P., Jönsson, B., Wittchen, H. U., & Olesen, J. (2005). Cost of disorders of the brain in Europe. *European Journal of Neurology*, *12*(Suppl. 1), 1−27.

Annetta, L. A. (2010). The "I's" have it: A framework for serious educational game design. *Review of General Psychology*, *14*(2), 105.

Arias, P., & Cudeiro, J. (2010). Effect of rhythmic auditory stimulation on gait in Parkinsonian patients with and without freezing of gait. *PLoS One*, *5*, e9675.

Barry, G., Galna, B., & Rochester, L. (2014). The role of exergaming in Parkinson's disease rehabilitation: A systematic review of the evidence. *Journal of Neuroengineering and Rehabilitation, 11*(1), 33.

Beauchet, O., Dubost, V., Aminian, K., Gonthier, R., & Kressig, R. W. (2005). Dual-task-related gait changes in the elderly: does the type of cognitive task matter? *Journal of Motor Behavior, 37,* 259–264.

Beauchet, O., Dubost, V., Gonthier, R., & Kressig, R. W. (2005). Dual-task-related gait changes in transitionally frail older adults: The type of the walking-associated cognitive task matters. *Gerontology, 51,* 48–52.

Bégel, V., Benoit, C.-E., Correa, A., Cutanda, D., Kotz, S. A., & Dalla Bella, S. (2017). "Lost in time" but still moving to the beat. *Neuropsychologia, 94,* 129–138.

Bégel, V., Dalla Bella, S., Devignes, Q., Vanderbergue, M., Lemaître, M. P., Dellacherie, D. Rhythm as an independent determinant of developmental dyslexia. Submitted.

Bégel, V., Di Loreto, I., Seilles, A., & Dalla Bella, S. (2017). Music games: Potential application and considerations for rhythmic training. *Frontiers in Human Neuroscience, 11,* 273.

Bégel, V., Seilles, A., & Dalla Bella, S. (2018). *Rhythm Workers*: A music-based serious game for training rhythmic skills. *Music & Science, 1,* 1–16.

Belghali, M., Chastan, N., Cignetti, F., Davenne, D., & Decker, L. M. (2017). Loss of gait control assessed by cognitive-motor dual-tasks: Pros and cons in detecting people at risk of developing Alzheimer's and Parkinson's diseases. *Geroscience, 39,* 305–329.

Benabid, A. L., Pollak, P., Louveau, A., Henry, S., & de Rougemont, J. (1987). Combined (thalamotomy and stimulation) stereotactic surgery of the VIM thalamic nucleus for bilateral Parkinson disease. *Applied Neurophysiology, 50,* 344–346.

Benninger, D. H., & Hallett, M. (2015). Non-invasive brain stimulation for Parkinson's disease: Current concepts and outlook 2015. *NeuroRehabilitation, 35,* 11–24.

Benoit, C.-E., Dalla Bella, S., Farrugia, N., Obrig, H., Mainka, S., & Kotz, S. A. (2014). Musically cued gait-training improves both perceptual and motor timing in Parkinson's disease. *Frontiers in Human Neuroscience, 8,* 494.

Blain, H., Carriere, I., Sourial, N., et al. (2010). Balance and walking speed predict subsequent 8-year mortality independently of current and intermediate events in well-functioning women aged 75 years and older. *The Journal of Nutrition, Health & Aging, 14*(7), 595–600.

Blake, A. J., Morgan, K., Bendall, M. J., Dallosso, H., Ebrahim, S. B., Arie, T. H., et al. (1988). Falls by elderly people at home: Prevalence and associated factors. *Age and Ageing, 17*(6), 365–372.

Bloem, B. R. (1992). Postural instability in Parkinson's disease. *Clinical Neurology and Neurosurgery, 94*(Suppl.), S41–S45.

Bloem, B. R., Hausdorff, J. M., Visser, J. E., & Giladi, N. (2004). Falls and freezing of gait in Parkinson's disease: A review of two interconnected, episodic phenomena. *Movement Disorders, 19,* 871–884.

Blood, A. J., & Zatorre, R. J. (2001). Intensely pleasurable responses to music correlate with activity in brain regions implicated in reward and emotion. *Proceedings of the National Academy of Sciences of the United States of America, 98,* 11818–11823.

Bryant, M. S., Rintala, D. H., Lai, E. C., & Protas, E. J. (2009). An evaluation of self-administration of auditory cueing to improve gait in people with Parkinson's disease. *Clinical Rehabilitation, 23,* 1078–1085.

Buracchio, T., Dodge, H. H., Howieson, D., Wasserman, D., & Kaye, J. (2010). The trajectory of gait speed preceding mild cognitive impairment. *Archives of Neurology, 67*(8), 980–986.

Cesari, M. (2011). Role of gait speed in the assessment of older patients. *The Journal of the American Medical Association, 305*(1), 93—94.

Cesari, M., Kritchevsky, S. B., Penninx, B. W., Nicklas, B. J., Simonsick, E. M., Newman, A. B., et al. (2005). Prognostic value of usual gait speed in well-functioning older people— Results from the Health, Aging and Body Composition Study. *Journal of the American Geriatrics Society, 53*(10), 1675—1680.

Chen, J. L., Penhune, V. B., & Zatorre, R. J. (2008a). Listening to musical rhythms recruits motor regions of the brain. *Cerebral Cortex, 18*(12), 2844—2854.

Chen, J. L., Penhune, V. B., & Zatorre, R. J. (2008b). Moving on time: Brain network for auditory-motor synchronization is modulated by rhythm complexity and musical training. *Journal of Cognitive Neuroscience, 20*(2), 226—239.

Chen, J. L., Zatorre, R. J., & Penhune, V. B. (2006). Interactions between auditory and dorsal premotor cortex during synchronization to musical rhythms. *Neuroimage, 32*(4), 1771—1781.

Cochen De Cock, V., Dotov, D. G., Ihalainen, P., Bégel, V., Galtier, F., Lebrun, C., et al. (2018). Rhythmic abilities and musical training in Parkinson's disease: Do they help? *Parkinson's Disease, 4*(1), 8.

Connolly, B. S., & Lang, E. (2014). Pharmacological treatment of Parkinson disease. A review. *The Journal of the American Medical Association, 311*(16), 1670—1683.

Contreras, A., & Grandas, F. (2012). Risk of falls in Parkinson's disease: A cross-sectional study of 160 patients. *Parkinson's Disease*, 362572.

Coull, J. T., Cheng, R. K., & Meck, W. H. (2011). Neuroanatomical and neurochemical substrates of timing. *Neuropsychopharmacology, 36*(1), 3—25.

Corriveau, K. H., & Goswami, U. (2009). Rhythmic motor entrainment in children with speech and language impairments: Tapping to the beat. *Cortex, 45*(1), 119—130.

Corriveau, K., Pasquini, E., & Goswami, U. (2007). Basic auditory processing skills and specific language impairment: A new look at an old hypothesis. *Journal of Speech, Language, and Hearing Research, 50*(3), 647—666.

Dalla Bella, S. (2016). Music and brain plasticity. In S. Hallam, I. Cross, & M. Thaut (Eds.), *The Oxford handbook of music psychology* (2nd ed., pp. 325—342). Oxford: Oxford University Press.

Dalla Bella, S. (2018). Music and movement: Towards a translational approach. *Neurophysiologie Clinique/Clinical Neurophysiology, 48*(6), 377—386.

Dalla Bella, S., Benoit, C.-E., Farrugia, N., Keller, P. E., Obrig, H., Mainka, S., et al. (2017). Gait improvement via rhythmic stimulation in Parkinson's disease is linked to rhythmic skills. *Scientific Reports, 7*, 42005.

Dalla Bella, S., Benoit, C.-E., Farrugia, N., Schwartze, M., & Kotz, S. A. (2015). Effects of musically cued gait training in Parkinson's disease: Beyond a motor benefit. *Annals of the New York Academy of Sciences, 1337*, 77—85.

Dalla Bella, S., Dotov, D. G., Bardy, B., & Cochen de Cock, V. (2018). Individualization of music-based rhythmic auditory cueing in Parkinson's disease. *Annals of the New York Academy of Sciences, 1423*, 308—317.

Dalla Bella, S., Farrugia, N., Benoit, C.-E., Bégel, V., Verga, L., Harding, E., et al. (2017). BAASTA: Battery for the Assessment of Auditory Sensorimotor and Timing Abilities. *Behavior Research Methods, 49*, 1128—1145.

Damm, L., Varoqui, D., Cochen De Cock, V., Dalla Bella, S., & Bardy, B. (2020). Why do we move to the beat? A multi-scale approach, from physical principles to brain dynamics. *Neuroscience Biobehavioral Reviews, 112*, 553—584.

Dauvergne, C., Bégel, V., Gény, C., Puyjarinet, F., Laffont, I., & Dalla Bella, S. (2018). Home-based training of rhythmic skills with a serious game in Parkinson's disease: Usability and acceptability. *Annals of Physical and Rehabilitation Medicine, 61*(6), 380−385.

de Lau, L. M., Verbaan, D., van Rooden, S. M., Marinus, J., & van Hilten, J. J. (2014). Relation of clinical subtypes in Parkinson's disease with survival. *Movement Disorders, 29,* 150−151.

de Rijk, M. C., Tzourio, C., Breteler, M. M., Dartigues, J. F., Amaducci, L., Lopez-Pousa, S., et al. (1997). Prevalence of parkinsonism and Parkinson's disease in Europe: The EUROPARKINSON Collaborative Study. European Community Concerted Action on the Epidemiology of Parkinson's disease. *Journal of Neurology, Neurosurgery, and Psychiatry, 62*(1), 10−15.

del Olmo, M. F., Arias, P., Furio, M. C., Pozo, M. A., & Cudeiro, J. (2006). Evaluation of the effect of training using auditory stimulation on rhythmic movement in Parkinsonian patients—A combined motor and [18F]-FDG PET study. *Parkinsonism & Related Disorders, 12,* 155−164.

Dietz, V. (2003). Spinal cord pattern generators for locomotion. *Clinical Neurophysiology, 114*(8), 1379−1389.

Dimitrijevic, M. R., Gerasimenko, Y., & Pinter, M. M. (1998). Evidence for a spinal central pattern generator in humans. *Annals of the New York Academy of Sciences, 860*(1), 360−376.

Dorsey, E. R., Constantinescu, R., Thompson, J. P., Biglan, K. M., Holloway, R. G., Kieburtz, K., et al. (2007). Projected number of people with Parkinson disease in the most populous nations, 2005 through 2030. *Neurology, 68*(5), 384−386.

Dotov, D. G., Cochen de Cock, V., Geny, C., Ihalainen, P., Moens, B., Leman, M., ... Dalla Bella, S. (2019). The role of mutual synchronization and predictability in entraining walking to an auditory beat. *Journal of Experimental Psychology: General, 148*(6), 1041−1057.

Downton, J. H., & Andrews, K. (1991). Prevalence, characteristics and factors associated with falls among the elderly living at home. *Aging, 3*(3), 219−228.

Dubost, V., Kressig, R. W., Gonthier, R., Herrmann, F. R., Aminian, K., Najafi, B., et al. (2006). Relationships between dual-task related changes in stride velocity and stride time variability in healthy older adults. *Human Movement Science, 25,* 372−382.

Duncan, R. P., & Earhart, G. M. (2012). Randomized controlled trial of community-based dancing to modify disease progression in Parkinson disease. *Neurorehabilitation and Neural Repair, 26*(2), 132−143.

Earhart, G. M. (2009). Dance as a therapy for individuals with Parkinson disease. *European Journal of Physical and Rehabilitation Medicine, 45*(2), 231−238.

Elbaz, A., Bower, J. H., Maraganore, D. M., McDonnell, S. K., Peterson, B. J., Ahlskog, J. E., ... Rocca, W. A. (2002). Risk tables for parkinsonism and Parkinson's disease. *Journal of Clinical Epidemiology, 55,* 25−31.

Elston, J., Honan, W., Powell, R., Gormley, J., & Stein, K. (2010). Do metronomes improve the quality of life in people with Parkinson's disease? A pragmatic, single-blind, randomized cross-over trial. *Clinical Rehabilitation, 24,* 523−532.

Enzensberger, W., Oberlander, U., & Stecker, K. (1997). Metronome therapy in patients with Parkinson disease. *Der Nervenarzt, 68,* 972−977.

Factor, S. A., & Weiner, W. J. (2008). *Parkinson's disease. Diagnosis and clinical management.* New York: Demos Medical Publishing.

Falk, S., Müller, T., & Dalla Bella, S. (2015). Non-verbal sensorimotor timing deficits in children and adolescents who stutter. *Frontiers in Psychology, 6,* 847.

Foster, E. R., Golden, L., Duncan, R. P., & Earhart, G. M. (2013). Community-based Argentine tango dance program is associated with increased activity participation among individuals with Parkinson's disease. *Archives of Physical Medicine and Rehabilitation, 94*(2), 240−249.

Franssen, E. H., Souren, L. E., Torossian, C. L., et al. (1999). Equilibrium and limb coordination in mild cognitive impairment and mild Alzheimer's disease. *Journal of the American Geriatrics Society, 47*(4), 463−469.

Friedman, N., Chan, V., Reinkensmeyer, A. N., Beroukhim, A., Zambrano, G. J., Bachman, M., et al. (2014). Retraining and assessing hand movement after stroke using the MusicGlove: Comparison with conventional hand therapy and isometric grip training. *Journal of Neuroengineering and Rehabilitation, 11*(1), 76.

Fujii, S., & Schlaug, G. (2013). The Harvard Beat Assessment Test (H-BAT): A battery for assessing beat perception and production and their dissociation. *Frontiers in Human Neuroscience, 7*, 771.

Fujioka, T., Trainor, L. J., Large, E. W., & Ross, B. (2012). Internalized timing of isochronous sounds is represented in neuromagnetic β oscillations. *The Journal of Neuroscience, 32*(5), 1791−1802.

Ghai, S., Ghai, I., & Effenberg, A. O. (2018). Effect of rhythmic auditory cueing on aging gait: A systematic review and meta-analysis. *Aging and Disease, 9*(5), 901−923.

Ghai, S., Ghai, I., Schmitz, G., & Effenberg, A. O. (2018). Effect of rhythmic auditory cueing on parkinsonian gait: A systematic review and meta-analysis. *Scientific Reports, 8*(1), 506.

Giladi, N. (2001). Freezing of gait. Clinical overview. *Advances in Neurology, 87*, 191−197.

Goodwin, V. A., Richards, S. H., Taylor, R. S., Taylor, A. H., & Campbell, J. L. (2008). The effectiveness of exercise interventions for people with Parkinson's disease: A systematic review and meta-analysis. *Movement Disorders, 23*, 631−640.

Goswami, U. (2011). A temporal sampling framework for developmental dyslexia. *Trends in Cognitive Sciences, 15*(1), 3−10.

Grabli, D., Karachi, C., Welter, M. L., Lau, B., Hirsch, E. C., Vidailhet, M., et al. (2012). Normal and pathological gait: What we learn from Parkinson's disease. *Journal of Neurology, Neurosurgery, and Psychiatry, 83*(10), 979−985.

Grahn, J. A., & Brett, M. (2007). Rhythm and beat perception in motor areas of the brain. *Journal of Cognitive Neuroscience, 19*(5), 893−906.

Grahn, J. A., & Brett, M. (2009). Impairment of beat-based rhythm discrimination in Parkinson's disease. *Cortex, 45*(1), 54−61.

Grahn, J. A., & Rowe, J. B. (2009). Feeling the beat: Premotor and striatal interactions in musicians and nonmusicians during beat perception. *The Journal of Neuroscience, 29*(23), 7540−7548.

Hackney, M. E., & Earhart, G. M. (2009). Effects of dance on movement control in Parkinson's disease: A comparison of Argentine tango and American ballroom. *Journal of Rehabilitation Medicine, 41*(6), 475−481.

Harris, D. M., Rantalainen, T., Muthalib, M., Johnson, L., & Teo, W.-P. (2015). Exergaming as a viable therapeutic tool to improve static and dynamic balance among older adults and people with idiopathic Parkinson's Disease: a systematic review and meta-analysis. *Frontiers in Aging Neuroscience, 7*, 167.

Hass, C. J., Bishop, M., Moscovich, M., Stegemöller, E. L., Skinner, J., Malaty, I. A., et al. (2014). Defining the clinically meaningful difference in gait speed in persons with Parkinson disease. *Journal of Neurologic Physical Therapy, 38*, 233−238.

Herholz, S. C., & Zatorre, R. J. (2012). Musical training as a framework for brain plasticity: Behavior, function, and structure. *Neuron, 76*(3), 486−502.

Hirtz, D., Thurman, D. J., Gwinn-Hardy, K., Mohamed, M., Chaudhuri, A. R., & Zalutsky, R. (2007). How common are the "common" neurologic disorders? *Neurology, 68*(5), 326−337.

Hove, M. J., Suzuki, K., Uchitomi, H., Orimo, S., & Miyake, Y. (2012). Interactive rhythmic auditory stimulation reinstates natural 1/f timing in gait of Parkinson's patients. *PLoS One, 7*, e32600.

Howe, T. E., Lovgreen, B., Cody, F. W., Ashton, V. J., & Oldham, J. A. (2003). Auditory cues can modify the gait of persons with early-stage Parkinson's disease: A method for enhancing parkinsonian walking performance? *Clinical Rehabilitation, 17*, 363−367.

Huss, M., Verney, J. P., Fosker, T., Mead, N., & Goswami, U. (2011). Music, rhythm, rise time perception and developmental dyslexia: Perception of musical meter predicts reading and phonology. *Cortex, 47*(6), 674−689.

Inzitari, M., Newman, A. B., Yaffe, K., et al. (2007). Gait speed predicts decline in attention and psychomotor speed in older adults: The health aging and body composition study. *Neuroepidemiology, 29*(3-4), 156−162.

Iversen, J.R., & Patel, A.D. (2008). The Beat Alignment Test (BAT): Surveying beat processing abilities in the general population. In: K. Miyazaki, Y. Hiraga, M. Adachi, Y. Nakajima, & M. Tsuzaki (Eds.), *Proceedings of the 10th International Conference on Music Perception and Cognition* (pp. 465−468).

Jankovic, J. (2008). Parkinson's disease: Clinical features and diagnosis. *Journal of Neurology, Neurosurgery, and Psychiatry, 79*, 368−376.

Jones, C. R., & Jahanshahi, M. (2014). Contributions of the basal ganglia to temporal processing: Evidence from Parkinson's disease. *Timing & Time Perception, 2*(1), 87−127.

Jones, M. R., & Boltz, M. (1989). Dynamic attending and responses to time. *Psychological Review, 96*(3), 459−491.

Kalia, L. V., & Lang, A. E. (2015). Parkinson's disease. *Lancet, 386*, 896−912.

Kalia, S. K., Sankar, T., & Lozano, A. M. (2013). Deep brain stimulation for Parkinson's disease and other movement disorders. *Current Opinion in Neurology, 26*(4), 374−380.

Kato, P. M. (2012). Evaluating efficacy and validating games for health. *Games for Health Journal, 1*(1), 74−76.

Kelly, V. E., Eusterbrock, A. J., & Shumway-Cook, A. (2012). A review of dual-task walking deficits in people with Parkinson's disease: Motor and cognitive contributions, mechanisms, and clinical implications. *Parkinson's Disease, 2012*, 918719.

Kirschner, S., & Tomasello, M. (2009). Joint drumming: Social context facilitates synchronization in preschool children. *Journal of Experimental Child Psychology, 102*(3), 299−314.

Koller, W. C., & Montgomery, E. B. (1997). Issues in the early diagnosis of Parkinson's disease. *Neurology, 49*, S10−S25.

Kotz, S. A., & Schwartze, M. (2010). Cortical speech processing unplugged: A timely subcortico-cortical framework. *Trends in Cognitive Sciences, 14*, 392−399.

Kotz, S. A., & Schwartze, M. (2011). Differential input of the supplementary motor area to a dedicated temporal processing network: Functional and clinical implications. *Frontiers in Integrative Neuroscience, 5*, 86.

Kwakkel, G., de Goede, C. J., & van Wegen, E. E. (2007). Impact of physical therapy for Parkinson's disease: A critical review of the literature. *Parkinsonism & Related Disorders, 13*(Suppl. 3), S478−S487.

Large, E. W., & Jones, M. R. (1999). The dynamics of attending: How people track time-varying events. *Psychological Review, 106*(1), 119−159.

Leow, L.-A., Parrott, T., & Grahn, J. A. (2014). Individual differences in beat perception affect gait responses to low- and high-groove music. *Frontiers in Human Neuroscience, 8,* 811.

Leow, L.-A., Waclawik, K., & Grahn, J. A. (2018). The role of attention and intention in synchronization to music: Effects on gait. *Experimental Brain Research, 236,* 99–115.

Lim, I., van Wegen, E., de Goede, C., Deutekom, M., Nieuwboer, A., Willems, A., et al. (2005). Effects of external rhythmical cueing on gait in patients with Parkinson's disease: A systematic review. *Clinical Rehabilitation, 19*(7), 695–713.

Lozano, C. S., Tam, J., & Lozano, A. M. (2018). The changing landscape of surgery in Parkinson's disease. *Movement Disorders, 33*(1), 36–47.

Marchese, R., Diverio, M., Zucchi, F., Lentino, C., & Abbruzzese, G. (2000). The role of sensory cues in the rehabilitation of parkinsonian patients: A comparison of two physical therapy protocols. *Movement Disorders, 15*(5), 879–883.

Matthews, T. E., Witek, M. A. G., Heggli, O. A., Penhune, V. B., & Vuust, P. (2019). The sensation of groove is affected by the interaction of rhythmic and harmonic complexity. *PLoS One, 14*(1), e0204539.

McIntosh, G. C., Brown, S. H., Rice, R. R., & Thaut, M. H. (1997). Rhythmic auditory-motor facilitation of gait patterns in patients with Parkinson's disease. *Journal of Neurology, Neurosurgery, and Psychiatry, 62,* 22–26.

Mendes, F. A. D., Pompeu, J. E., Lobo, A. M., da Silva, K. G., de Paula Oliveira, T., Zomignani, A. P., et al. (2012). Motor learning, retention and transfer after virtual-reality-based training in Parkinson's disease—Effect of motor and cognitive demands of games: A longitudinal, controlled clinical study. *Physiotherapy, 98*(3), 217–223.

Miyake, Y. (2009). Interpersonal synchronization of body motion and the walk-mate walking support robot. *IEEE Transactions on Robotics, 25,* 638–644.

Moens, B., Muller, C., van Noorden, L., Franěk, M., Celie, B., Boone, J., et al. (2014). Encouraging spontaneous synchronisation with D-Jogger, an adaptive music player that aligns movement and music. *PLoS One, 9,* e114234.

Morillon, B., & Baillet, S. (2017). Motor origin of temporal predictions in auditory attention. *Proceedings of the National Academy of Sciences of the United States of America, 114*(42), E8913–E8921.

Morillon, B., Schroeder, C. E., & Wyart, V. (2014). Motor contributions to the temporal precision of auditory attention. *Nature Communications, 5,* 5255.

Morris, M. E., Huxham, F., McGinley, J., Dodd, K., & Iansek, R. (2001). The biomechanics and motor control of gait in Parkinson disease. *Clinical Biomechanics, 16,* 459–470.

Morris, M. E., Iansek, R., Matyas, T. A., & Summers, J. J. (1994). Ability to modulate walking cadence remains intact in Parkinson's disease. *Journal of Neurology, Neurosurgery, and Psychiatry, 57,* 1532–1534.

Müllensiefen, D., Gingras, B., Musil, J., & Stewart, L. (2014). The musicality of non-musicians: An index for assessing musical sophistication in the general population. *PLoS One, 9,* e89642.

Nadkarni, N. K., Mawji, E., McIlroy, W. E., & Black, S. E. (2009). Spatial and temporal gait parameters in Alzheimer's disease and aging. *Gait & Posture, 30*(4), 452–454.

Nieuwboer, A. (2008). Cueing for freezing of gait in patients with Parkinson's disease: A rehabilitation perspective. *Movement Disorders, 23*(Suppl. 2), S475–S481.

Nieuwboer, A., De Weerdt, W., Dom, R., Truyen, M., Janssens, L., & Kamsma, Y. (2001). The effect of a home physiotherapy program for persons with Parkinson's disease. *Journal of Rehabilitation Medicine, 33*(6), 266–272.

Nieuwboer, A., Kwakkel, G., Rochester, L., Jones, D., van Wegen, E., Willems, A. M., et al. (2007). Cueing training in the home improves gait-related mobility in Parkinson's disease: The RESCUE trial. *Journal of Neurology, Neurosurgery, and Psychiatry*, *78*(2), 134−140.

Nombela, C., Hughes, L. E., Owen, A. M., & Grahn, J. A. (2013). Into the groove: Can rhythm influence Parkinson's disease? *Neuroscience and Biobehavioral Reviews*, *37*, 2564−2570.

Noreika, V., Falter, C. M., & Rubia, K. (2013). Timing deficits in attention-deficit/hyperactivity disorder (ADHD): Evidence from neurocognitive and neuroimaging studies. *Neuropsychologia*, *51*(2), 235−266.

Nozaradan, S., Peretz, I., Missal, M., & Mouraux, A. (2011). Tagging the neuronal entrainment to beat and meter. *The Journal of Neuroscience*, *31*(28), 10234−10240.

Ostir, G. V., Kuo, Y. F., Berges, I. M., Markides, K. S., & Ottenbacher, K. J. (2007). Measures of lower body function and risk of mortality over 7 years of follow-up. *American Journal of Epidemiology*, *166*(5), 599−605.

Owen, A. M., Hampshire, A., Grahn, J. A., Stenton, R., Dajani, S., Burns, A. S., et al. (2010). Putting brain training to the test. *Nature*, *465*(7299), 775−778.

Pacchetti, C., Mancini, F., Aglieri, R., Fundarò, C., Martignoni, E., & Nappi, G. (2000). Active music therapy in Parkinson's disease: An integrative method for motor and emotional rehabilitation. *Psychosomatic Medicine*, *62*(3), 386−393.

Palmer, C., Lidji, P., & Peretz, I. (2014). Losing the beat: Deficits in temporal coordination. *Philosophical Transactions of the Royal Society of London. Series B, Biological Sciences*, *369*(1658), 20130405.

Paquette, S., Fujii, S., Li, H. C., & Schlaug, G. (2017). The cerebellum's contribution to beat interval discrimination. *Neuroimage*, *163*, 177−182.

Pastor, M. A., Artieda, J., Jahanshahi, M., & Obeso, J. A. (1992). Time estimation and reproduction is abnormal in Parkinson's disease. *Brain*, *115*(1), 211−225.

Pearson, K., & Gordon, J. (2000). Locomotion. In E. R. Kandel, J. Schwartz, T. Jessell, S. Siegelbaum, & A. Hudspeth (Eds.), *Principles of neural science* (4th ed., pp. 737−755). New York: McGraw-Hill.

Pettersson, A. F., Olsson, E., & Wahlund, L. O. (2005). Motor function in subjects with mild cognitive impairment and early Alzheimer's disease. *Dementia and Geriatric Cognitive Disorders*, *19*, 299−304.

Pickering, R. M., Grimbergen, Y. A., Rigney, U., Ashburn, A., Mazibrada, G., Wood, B., ... Bloem, B. R. (2007). A meta-analysis of six prospective studies of falling in Parkinson's disease. *Movement Disorders*, *22*(13), 1892−1900.

Pohl, P., Dizdar, N., & Hallert, E. (2013). The ronnie gardiner rhythm and music method—A feasibility study in Parkinson's disease. *Disability and Rehabilitation*, *35*(26), 2197−2204.

Puyjarinet, F., Bégel, V., Gény, C., Driss, V., Cuartero, M. C., Kotz, S. A., et al. (2019). Heightened orofacial, manual, and gait variability in Parkinson's disease results from a general rhythmic impairment. *Parkinson's Disease*, *5*, 19.

Puyjarinet, F., Bégel, V., Lopez, R., Dellacherie, D., & Dalla Bella, S. (2017). Children and adults with attention-deficit/hyperactivity disorders cannot move to the beat. *Scientific Reports*, *7*(1), 11550.

Ready, E. A., McGarry, L. M., Rinchon, C., Holmes, J. D., & Grahn, J. A. (2019). Beat perception ability and instructions to synchronize influence gait when walking to music-based auditory cues. *Gait and Posture*, *68*, 555−561.

Rego, P., Moreira, P., & Reis, L. (2010). Serious games for rehabilitiation: A survey and classification towards a taxonomy. In *Proceedings of the Fifth Iberian Conference on Information Systems and Technologies (CISTI)*, (pp. 349−354).

Repp, B. H. (2005). Sensorimotor synchronization: A review of the tapping literature. *Psychonomic Bulletin & Review*, *12*(6), 969–992.

Repp, B. H. (2010). Sensorimotor synchronization and perception of timing: Effects of music training and task experience. *Human Movement Science*, *29*(2), 200–213.

Repp, B. H., & Su, Y. H. (2013). Sensorimotor synchronization: A review of recent research (2006-2012). *Psychonomic Bulletin & Review*, *20*(3), 403–452.

Rochester, L., Burn, D. J., Woods, G., Godwin, J., & Nieuwboer, A. (2009). Does auditory rhythmical cueing improve gait in people with Parkinson's disease and cognitive impairment? A feasibility study. *Movement Disorders*, *24*, 839–845.

Rochester, L., Galna, B., Lord, S., & Burn, D. (2014). The nature of dual-task interference during gait in incident Parkinson's disease. *Neuroscience*, *265*, 83–94.

Rubinstein, T. C., Giladi, N., & Hausdorff, J. M. (2002). The power of cueing to circumvent dopamine deficits: A review of physical therapy treatment of gait disturbances in Parkinson's disease. *Movement Disorders*, *17*, 1148–1160.

Salimpoor, V. N., Zald, D. H., Zatorre, R. J., Dagher, A., & McIntosh, A. R. (2015). Predictions and the brain: How musical sounds become rewarding. *Trends in Cognitive Sciences*, *19*, 86–91.

Salzman, B. (2010). Gait and balance disorders in older adults. *American Family Physician*, *82* (1), 61–68.

Samii, A., Nutt, J. G., & Ransom, B. R. (2004). Parkinson's disease. *Lancet*, *363*, 1783–1793.

Särkämö, T. (2018). Cognitive, emotional, and neural benefits of musical leisure activities in aging and neurological rehabilitation: A critical review. *Annals of Physical and Rehabilitation Medicine*, *61*(6), 414–418.

Shumway-Cook, A., Guralnik, J. M., Phillips, C. L., et al. (2007). Age-associated declines in complex walking task performance: The Walking InCHIANTI toolkit. *Journal of the American Geriatrics Society*, *55*(1), 58–65.

Schwartze, M., & Kotz, S. A. (2013). A dual-pathway neural architecture for specific temporal prediction. *Neuroscience and Biobehavioral Reviews*, *37*, 2587–2596.

Schwartze, M., Rothermich, K., Schmidt-Kassow, M., & Kotz, S. A. (2011). Temporal regularity effects on pre-attentive and attentive processing of deviance. *Biological Psychology*, *87*(1), 146–151.

Senn, O., Kilchenmann, L., Bechtold, T., & Hoesl, F. (2018). Groove in drum patterns as a function of both rhythmic properties and listeners' attitudes. *PLoS One*, *13*(6), e0199604.

Sethi, K. (2008). Levodopa unresponsive symptoms in Parkinson disease. *Movement Disorders*, *23*(Suppl. 3), S521–S533.

Sihvonen, A. J., Särkämö, T., Leo, V., Tervaniemi, M., Altenmüller, E., & Soinila, S. (2017). Music-based interventions in neurological rehabilitation. *Lancet Neurology*, *16*, 648–660.

Sowiński, J., & Dalla Bella, S. (2013). Poor synchronization to the beat may result from deficient auditory-motor mapping. *Neuropsychologia*, *51*(10), 1952–1963.

Spaulding, S. J., Barber, B., Colby, M., Cormack, B., Mick, T., & Jenkins, M. E. (2013). Cueing and gait improvement among people with Parkinson's disease: A meta-analysis. *Archives of Physical Medicine and Rehabilitation*, *94*(3), 562–570.

Spencer, R. M., & Ivry, R. B. (2005). Comparison of patients with Parkinson's disease or cerebellar lesions in the production of periodic movements involving event-based or emergent timing. *Brain and Cognition*, *58*(1), 84–93.

Spottke, A. E., Reuter, M., Machat, O., Bornschein, B., von Campenhausen, S., Berger, K., ... Dodel, R. (2005). Cost of illness and its predictors for Parkinson's disease in Germany. *Pharmacoeconomics*, *23*(8), 817–836.

Studenski, S., Perera, S., Patel, K., et al. (2011). Gait speed and survival in older adults. *The Journal of the American Medical Association, 305*(1), 50−58.

Sun, T. L., & Lee, C. H. (2013). An impact study of the design of exergaming parameters on body intensity from objective and gameplay-based player experience perspectives, based on balance training exergame. *PLoS One, 8*(7), e69471.

Thaut, M. H. (2003). Neural basis of rhythmic timing networks in the human brain. *Annals of the New York Academy of Sciences, 999*(1), 364−373.

Thaut, M. H., Rice, R. R., Braun Janzen, T., Hurt-Thaut, C. P., & McIntosh, G. C. (1996). Rhythmic auditory stimulation in gait training for Parkinson's disease patients. *Movement Disorders, 11*, 193−200.

Tomlinson, C. L., Patel, S., Meek, C., Herd, C. P., Clarke, C. E., Stowe, R., ... Ives, N. (2012). Physiotherapy intervention in Parkinson's disease: Systematic review and meta-analysis. *British Medical Journal, 345*, e5004.

Trainor, L. J., Chang, A., Cairney, J., & Yao-Chuen, L. (2018). Is auditory perceptual timing a core deficit of developmental coordination disorder? *Annals of the New York Academy of Sciences, 1423*, 30−39.

Verghese, J., LeValley, A., Hall, C. B., Katz, M. J., Ambrose, A. F., & Lipton, R. B. (2006). Epidemiology of gait disorders in community-residing older adults. *Journal of the American Geriatrics Society, 54*(2), 255−261.

Von Wilzenben, H. D. (1942). *Methods in the treatment of post encephalic Parkinson's*. New York: Grune and Stretten.

Vuust, P., & Witek, M. A. (2014). Rhythmic complexity and predictive coding: A novel approach to modeling rhythm and meter perception in music. *Frontiers in Psychology, 5*, 1111.

Webster, D., & Celik, O. (2014). Systematic review of Kinect applications in elderly care and stroke rehabilitation. *Journal of Neuroengineering and Rehabilitation, 11*(1), 108.

Wenning, G. K., Ebersbach, G., Verny, M., Chaudhuri, K. R., Jellinger, K., McKee, A., et al. (1999). Progression of falls in postmortem-confirmed parkinsonian disorders. *Movement Disorders, 14*(6), 947−950.

Witek, M. A., Clarke, E. F., Wallentin, M., Kringelbach, M. L., & Vuust, P. (2014). Syncopation, body-movement and pleasure in groove music. *PLoS One, 9*(4), e94446.

Wittwer, J. E., Andrews, P. T., Webster, K. E., et al. (2008). Timing variability during gait initiation is increased in people with Alzheimer's disease compared to controls. *Dementia and Geriatric Cognitive Disorders, 26*(3), 277−283.

Wittwer, J. E., Webster, K. E., & Menz, H. B. (2010). A longitudinal study of measures of walking in people with Alzheimer's disease. *Gait & Posture, 32*, 113−117.

Woollacott, M., & Shumway-Cook, A. (2002). Attention and the control of posture and gait: A review of an emerging area of research. *Gait & Posture, 16*(1), 1−14.

Yogev-Seligmann, G., Rotem-Galili, Y., Mirelman, A., Dickstein, R., Giladi, N., & Hausdorff, J. M. (2010). How does explicit prioritization alter walking during dual-task performance? Effects of age and sex on gait speed and variability. *Physical Therapy, 90*(2), 177−186.

Zatorre, R. J., Chen, J. L., & Penhune, V. B. (2007). When the brain plays music: Auditory−motor interactions in music perception and production. *Nature Reviews Neuroscience, 8*(7), 547−558.

Zentner, M., & Eerola, T. (2010). Rhythmic engagement with music in infancy. *Proceedings of the National Academy of Sciences of the United States of America, 107*(13), 5768−5773.

Ziv, G., & Lidor, R. (2011). Music, exercise performance, and adherence in clinical populations in the elderly: A review. *Journal of Clinical Sport Psychology, 5*(1), 1−23.

Chapter 16

The impact of music interventions on motor rehabilitation following stroke in elderly

Eckart Altenmüller[1] and Clara E. James[2,3]

[1]*Institute of Music Physiology and Musicians' Medicine (IMMM), University of Music, Drama and Media, Hanover, Germany,* [2]*University of Applied Sciences and Arts Western Switzerland HES-SO, School of Health Sciences, Geneva, Switzerland,* [3]*Faculty of Psychology and Educational Sciences, University of Geneva, Geneva, Switzerland*

Introduction: enriching life with musical activities

It is predicted that by 2050, the global population of older people, in both developed and developing countries, will more than double, reaching nearly 2.1 billion individuals (United Nations Department of Economic & Social Affairs Population Division, 2015). The number of people aged 80 years or over is increasing at an even faster rate, especially in Europe, North America, and the Far East, resulting in a growing number of individuals living for longer with significant disability, reduced quality of life, and multiple chronic conditions (Prince et al., 2014). As a consequence of rapid population aging, there is a rising prevalence of age-related neurological disorders including stroke, Alzheimer's disease and Parkinson's disease (Reitz & Mayeux, 2014; Wirdefeldt, Adami, Cole, Trichopoulos, & Mandel, 2011). To reduce the burden of disease attributable to these disorders, it is important not only to optimize brain development early in life in order to promote lifelong neuronal enrichment and to accumulate what is termed "cognitive reserve," but also to design environments for the elderly, including activities, which promote lifelong brain plasticity, emotional well-being, social connectedness, and autonomy (Altenmüller, Schneider, Marco-Pallares, & Münte, 2009; Altenmüller & Stewart, in press; Kempermann, 2012; Prince et al., 2014).

Music and the Aging Brain. DOI: https://doi.org/10.1016/B978-0-12-817422-7.00016-X
407

It has long been known that physical activity has positive effects on brain health at all stages of the life span. A growing body of literature indicates that it may enhance cognition, offer protection against neurodegenerative disorders, and reduce incidence and severity of psychological conditions such as anxiety and depression (e.g., Craft & Perna, 2004; Tyndall et al., 2018). In terms of mechanisms of action, a direct effect on central nervous system function and morphology may play a significant role: physical activity leads to improved cardiovascular health (Clark, Baker, & Taylor, 2016), including additional brain capillarization, the release of neurotrophic factors, the reduction of stress and inflammatory processes, and therefore may positively influence brain function (Freudenberger et al., 2016; Kennedy, Boylan, Rieck, Foster, & Rodrigue, 2017; Macpherson, Teo, Schneider, & Smith, 2017). Furthermore, physical activity may promote neuroplasticity, the ability of the brain to continually adapt throughout the life span, and neurogenesis, the generation of new neurons, especially in subcortical structures of the hippocampus, a brain region crucial for memory function and regulation of mood states (Ahlskog, Geda, Graff-Radford, & Petersen, 2011; Llorens-Martín, Tejeda, & Trejo, 2010).

Musical activity comprises complex physical activity, and, moreover, adds further dimensions promoting brain plasticity since it is one of the richest human emotional, sensory–motor, and cognitive experiences. Musical activity involves listening, feeling, moving. It requires watching and planning, as well as remembering and anticipating musical events. Finally, all these elements need to be coordinated into a coherent experience or performance. It is frequently accompanied by strong emotions resulting in joy, happiness, and bittersweet sadness or even in overwhelming bodily reactions like tears in the eyes or shivers down the spine, underpinned by a broad spectrum of neurochemical responses (Chanda & Levitin, 2013). Correspondingly, a large number of cortical and subcortical brain regions are involved in music listening and music-making activities (for reviews see Altenmüller & Furuya, 2016; Altenmüller et al., 2009; see also Koelsch, Chapter 1: The musical brain, this volume).

Primary and secondary regions in the cerebral cortex are critical for any conscious perception of sensory information, be it auditory, visual, or somatosensory. Additionally, music also influences and changes activity in multisensory and motor integration regions in frontal, parietal, and temporooccipital brain regions. The frontal lobe is involved in the guidance of attention, in planning and motor preparation, in integrating auditory and motor information, and in specific human skills such as imitation and empathy, based on a frontal-parietal mirror neuron network. Multisensory integration regions in the parietal lobe and temporooccipital areas integrate different sensory inputs from the auditory, visual, and somatosensory system into a combined sensory impression; it is this multisensory brain representation, which constitutes the typical musical experience. Apart from these neocortical areas, a number of other brain structures also play a critical role in musical performance. Basal ganglia are crucial for motor learning, timing, and emotional integration, whereas the cerebellum is important for motor coordination, but it also plays an important role in various cognitive tasks especially when they include demands on timing and working memory (Eriksson, Vogel, Lansner, Bergstrom, & Nyberg, 2015). Apparently, distinct loops exist between cerebellum and neocortex for cognitive (posterior part of the cerebellum) and motor function (anterior part) (Salmi et al., 2009). Typically, basal ganglia and anterior cerebellum are activated in rhythm processing or tapping in synchrony with an external pacemaker such as a metronome (De Pretto & James, 2015). Finally, the emotional network, the limbic system, is crucial for the emotional experience of music and therefore for an individual's motivation to listen to or to engage in any musical activity, underpinned, for example, by dopamine release (for a review see Zatorre, 2015).

Music provokes brain plasticity and strong neurochemical changes

During the past two decades, brain imaging has provided important insight into the capacity of the human brain to adapt to complex demands. As mentioned above, these adaptations are referred to as brain plasticity and do not only include the quality and extent of functional connections of brain networks, but also adaptations of morphological features like fine structures of nervous tissue and even the macroscopic gross structure of brain anatomy (for a classic review see Münte, Altenmüller, & Jäncke, 2002; more recent Altenmüller & Furuya, 2016). Brain plasticity is best observed in complex tasks, including for example temporospatially precise movements with high behavioral relevance. These behaviors are usually accompanied by emotional arousal and motivational activation of the reward system. Although plastic changes are more pronounced when specific activities have started before puberty and when involving intense training—as is the case in professional musicians—brain plasticity can also be observed in healthy elderly novices, undergoing controlled training trials (Altenmüller & Schlaug, 2013; Schneider, Schönle, Altenmüller, & Münte, 2007; Wan & Schlaug, 2010).

To summarize briefly, a comparison of the brain anatomy of skilled musicians with that of nonmusicians shows that prolonged instrumental practice leads to functional and structural adaptations in all brain areas and connections, critical for performing music. Since this chapter focuses on the rehabilitation potential of music making, this section emphasizes the adaptations that have been found to accompany the development of expertise in high-level musicians: prolonged instrumental practice leads to an enlargement of the hand area in the motor cortex (Amunts et al., 1997). Furthermore,

Gaser and Schlaug (2003) demonstrated enhancement of grey matter density in cortical sensory—motor regions, auditory regions, the left dorsolateral prefrontal cortex, and in the cerebellum in professional instrumentalists as compared to nonmusicians and amateurs. These adaptations of brain structures are accompanied by behaviorally relevant improvements of fine finger coordination and two-point discrimination abilities (Ragert, Schmidt, Altenmüller, & Dinse, 2003), enhanced auditory or visual working memory (Oechslin, Van De Ville, Lazeyras, Hauert, & James, 2013; Schneider et al., 2002), and precision of timing (Furuya, Oku, Miyazaki, & Kinoshita, 2015). Interestingly, musicians who start early, before the age of 7, do not display these structural adaptations of the brain at least in the sensory—motor cortices and the callosal fibers, however, they seem to have an "early optimized network," which allows superior performance of motor tasks without enlarged anatomical structures (Steele, Bailey, Zatorre, & Penhune, 2013; Vaquero et al., 2015). In contrast, later starters, after age 7 do show the abovementioned structural adaptations accounting for the effects observed in many morphological brain imaging studies (e.g., Bangert & Schlaug, 2006; Gärtner et al., 2013).

In addition to focusing on structural measures such as grey matter density, several studies have investigated measures that related to structural connectivity between brain regions. Using diffusion tensor imaging (DTI)—a technique which allows for the reconstruction of white-matter tracts and the characterization of their microstructural status using diffusivity measures, such as fractional anisotropy—Bengtsson et al. (2005) and more recently Rueber, Lindenberg, and Schlaug (2015) found structural differences in the corticospinal tract, particularly in the posterior limb of the internal capsule, between musicians and nonmusicians as well as within musicians' groups (keyboard players compared to string players). Halwani, Loui, Rüber, and Schlaug (2011)—also using DTI—reported differences in macrostructure and microstructure of the arcuate fasciculus (AF)—a prominent white-matter tract connecting temporal and frontal brain regions—between singers, instrumentalists, and nonmusicians. Then the right ventral stream altered progressively as a function of musical training and these results could be associated with better musical syntax processing (Oechslin, Gschwind, & James, 2018). Thus structural changes to white matter tracts are not only altered by musical training per se, but by the precise sensorimotor demands of the type of musical training (according to instrument) and—as has been shown in behavioral tests, these morphological adaptations can also be accompanied by faster reaction times and improved coordination (Landry & Champoux, 2017).

The above findings serve to illustrate the potential for musical training to result in structural and functional adaptations across a number of different brain areas and their connections. It is relevant to note that such changes are not only restricted to individuals who have undergone musical training over a period of years but have also been observed through longitudinal studies incorporating relatively short periods of training (e.g., Hyde et al., 2009;

Stewart et al., 2003). Given that active music-based rehabilitation involves multiple components analogous to training and music learning (i.e., iterated practice of movements coupled with auditory feedback and extensive cognitive processing, proprioceptive and visual feedback) it is reasonable to suggest that some of the principles of music-training—induced plasticity can be usefully exploited through the use of music-supported therapy (MST) in neurorehabilitation.

It should be noted that patients who are receiving MST are not only *producing* aspects of music through their movement, they are also *perceiving* the music they produce (in addition to any live or recorded accompaniment that may be part of the protocol). The perception of music can elicit powerful feelings of pleasure, and studies have shown that such experiences (most dramatically seen during musical "shivers" down the spine) strongly activate the dopaminergic mesolimbic system (for a review see Zatorre, 2015). Dopamine release has been shown to have demonstrable effects on the strength of synaptic connections (Wickens, Reynolds, & Hyland, 2003). In a similar vein, music's anxiolytic properties are well-known (see Nilsson, 2008 for a review) and responses to music can produce measurable cardiovascular and endocrine responses, indicated by reduced serum cortisol levels and inhibition of cardiovascular stress reactions (Bradt, Dileo, & Potvin, 2013; Okada, Kurita, & Takase, 2009). In animal models, prolonged stress can have maladaptive effects on neuroplasticity, such as dendritic atrophy, synapse loss, and decreased hippocampal neurogenesis (Radley, Morilak, Viau, & Campeau, 2015), while elevated cortisol levels in patients with acute stroke correlates with increased infarct volume, and increases the risk of depression, poor prognosis, and fatal outcome (Douven et al., 2017). Hence, bearing in mind that that music is perceived as well as produced in music support therapy, it may be that the potential of music to evoke both pleasure and reduce anxiety may confer particular benefits for sensorimotor learning and plasticity, though this remains to be empirically tested.

Besides the abovementioned dopaminergic activation, serotonin, the "feel-good substance," lacking during clinical depressions, is also important for music-induced brain plasticity. It is commonly associated with feelings of satisfaction from expected outcomes, whereas dopamine is associated with the intensity of evoked feelings of pleasure, and the experience of novelty or surprise. In a study of neurochemical responses to pleasant and unpleasant music, serotonin levels were significantly higher when subjects were exposed to music they found pleasing (Evers & Suhr, 2000). In another study with subjects exposed to pleasing music, functional and effective connectivity analyses showed that listening to music strongly modulated activity in a network of mesolimbic structures involved in reward processing including the dopaminergic nucleus accumbens and the ventral tegmental area, as well as the hypothalamus and insula. This network is believed to be involved in regulating autonomic and physiological responses to rewarding and emotional stimuli (Menon & Levitin, 2005). On the other hand, pleasurable musical stimuli are also able to reduce stress and release of stress hormones such as cortisol, which may well be a potent means to facilitate neuroplastic changes following stroke (Hou et al., 2017; Leardi et al., 2007). This underlines the importance of music experiences for human beings, associating their response patterns to those of biologically relevant stimuli.

Taken together, not only brain plasticity, but also these powerful music-induced modulations of neurochemical status (most probably underlying brain plasticity to a significant degree) make music activity a compelling candidate to consider in the search for effective rehabilitation of neuronal dysfunction and loss following stroke. In the following section we will review music interventions in rehabilitation of stroke, starting with MST in upper limb dysfunctions, followed by music-supported gait training and melodic intonation therapy (MIT) to improve recovery from nonfluent aphasia. Finally, we will provide evidence of music-induced brain plasticity together with music's ability to tap into emotion and reward systems in the brain as the main factors to facilitate neurorehabilitation.

Yet, when comparing musicians to nonmusicians, the nature−nurture question cannot be adequately addressed. Gaser and Schlaug (2003) demonstrated gradual enhancement of grey matter density in cortical sensory−motor regions, auditory regions, the left dorsolateral prefrontal cortex, and in the posterior cerebellum when comparing professional instrumentalists to amateurs and nonmusicians, thus investigating three levels of musical expertise. James and colleagues also showed progressive functional and structural brain plasticity of grey and white matter as a function of three distinct levels of musical expertise (nonmusicians, and amateur and professional pianists). The amateur and expert/professional groups were separated based on number of hours practiced over the life span, and also by only selecting professionals that were studying at superior Conservatoires or were already established performers. Meanwhile the authors strictly matched the three groups for age, gender, education level, fluid intelligence, and finally onset age of musical training in the two musician groups, thus supporting the notion of gradual impact of practice intensity on brain plasticity, that moreover could be associated to the behavioral data (James et al., 2014; Oechslin et al., 2013, 2018). In many studies comparing amateurs and experts, the experts started much earlier, which represents a bias. These data highlight that practice drives brain and behavioral plasticity in musicians, and not only predisposition.

Music interventions in rehabilitation of motor skills following stroke

According to the definition proposed by the World Health Organization in 1970, "stroke is rapidly developing clinical signs of focal (or global) disturbance of cerebral function, with symptoms lasting 24 hours or longer, or leading to death, with no apparent cause other than of vascular origin" (Warlow, 1998). Generally, strokes can be classified into two major categories, namely, ischemic stroke and hemorrhagic stroke. Ischemic stroke is caused by interruption of the blood supply to a part of the brain, most often by a blood clot, resulting in sudden loss of function, while hemorrhagic stroke is attributed to rupture of a blood vessel or an abnormal vascular structure. Generally, ischemic strokes account for about 80% of stroke cases while hemorrhagic stroke accounts for 20% (Donkor, 2018).

The public health burden of stroke is enormous: stroke is ranked as the second leading cause of death worldwide with an annual mortality of about 5.5 million people. Not only does the burden of stroke lie in the high mortality but the high morbidity also results in up to 50% of survivors being chronically disabled. According to the current global burden of disease data on stroke, in 2013 there were almost 25.7 million stroke survivors, 6.5 million deaths, 113 million disability-adjusted life years due to stroke, and 10.3 million new strokes (for a recent review on stroke epidemiology see Donkor, 2018). Last but not least the burden of the caregivers of the stroke patients should be mentioned, they are often obliged to reduce their working hours, and thus income, and risk social isolation.

With respect to disability, voluntary movement control is typically impaired after a stroke. Movement control of the body on the contralateral side of the brain lesion proceeds through stages of recovery in which the sensory and motor function are often reestablished abnormally. In the upper extremity, after a period of flaccidity, a common course of recovery includes the development of an uncontrolled flexion synergy, meaning a synchronous activation (cocontraction) of flexors and extensors resulting in the typical posture of stroke patients with flexion of the elbow and the wrist. This is accompanied by a loss of fine motor control and jerky and slow movements. Such a pathological synergy is observed in the hemiparetic limb during efforts to use the arm or hand for functional tasks. Individuals with this uncontrolled flexion synergy have great difficulty isolating joint movements out of synergy. Therefore control of wrist and finger movements is a challenging aspect of upper extremity recovery. Unfortunately, residual dysfunction in the hemiparetic limb is frequently observed for extended periods, plateauing at around 12 months. Moreover, 60% of poststroke individuals are left with residual motor dysfunction, especially of skilled movements of the upper extremities, as a long-term disability after the first year (Cauraugh, Light, Kim, Thigpen, & Behrman, 2000). These chronic motor problems lead to difficulty in the execution of functional movements (e.g., picking up a glass, manipulating objects, etc.), and thus strongly decrease autonomy and everyday life function.

Bearing in mind the above represented effects of short- and long-term music-induced plasticity, it seems adequate to apply musical activities in stroke patients. This approach is now widely established and subsumed under the term of "music-supported therapy in neurorehabilitation." MST is defined as clinical, evidence-based interventions using music to improve motor, sensory, cognitive, and emotional functions following central nervous injury and/or degeneration. The underlying scientific paradigm is music-induced functional brain plasticity, reinforced by motivational factors linked to music listening and music making, as exemplified in the above paragraphs.

Music-supported therapy in upper limb dysfunction in stroke patients

In a recent review, we identified 16 randomized controlled studies that evaluated the efficacy of musical activities in stroke rehabilitation ($n = 664$) (Sihvonen et al., 2017). In most studies, the main outcome measures were standard motor tests (e.g., Fugl-Meyer test, Box and block test, nine-hole pegboard test). Furthermore, mood, cognitive performance, quality of life, and speech abilities were often also assessed in most of these studies. The results of these assessments will be briefly summarized below. In upper extremity paresis, MST aiming at rehabilitation of fine motor hand skills was first systematically investigated by Schneider et al. (2007). The setting included initially eight drum pads digitally set up to produce piano sounds forming a major scale. Patients had to tap with the paretic hands on the drum pads. As the patients progressed from tapping single sounds to well-known simple melodies, such as children's songs or "Ode to Joy," they were transferred to a digital keyboard. Next they had to perform individuated finger movements on the keyboard, again advancing stepwise to include technically more demanding melodies, that is, more complicated sequences of finger flexions and extensions (see Fig. 16.1, illustrating the setting). Thus behavioral shaping, that is, adaptation of task difficulty to the actual state of motor abilities, was achieved. Such gradual progress is an important advantage of natural training regimens like music making, reinforced by the reward and drive to produce a tune as compared to conventional therapies, that principally focus on movement.

Superiority of the music-making group in all behavioral measures of fine motor abilities over conventional physiotherapy was evident after interventions containing five 30-minute sessions per week for 3 weeks (Schneider et al., 2007). This effect was replicated and it was demonstrated that it was specifically caused by musical activity rather than motor training, since patients practicing with mute instruments remained inferior to the music group (Tong et al., 2015).

However, a recent randomized controlled trial found that adding MST to a standard program of rehabilitation did not induce superior outcomes as compared to conventional therapy approaches in the recovery of upper extremity function in stroke patients during the subacute stage

FIGURE 16.1 Setting of the "piano training" in stroke patients with impairments of fine motor function of the upper extremity (Schneider et al., 2007). The affected wrist should be supported when the patient is positioned at the piano in order to reduce spasticity of the hand. In the background, the Zebris-system is shown, which is used to monitor the changes in movement smoothness. The therapist is Dr. Sabine Schneider, who developed the piano training. *With permission of Dr. Schneider.*

(Grau-Sánchez et al., 2018). This discrepancy probably resulted from differences in training intensity between studies. In the abovementioned study of Schneider et al. (2007), patients in both the experimental and the control group (CG) received 13.5 hours of standard rehabilitation for 3 weeks. This standard rehabilitation involved physical and occupational therapy sessions. In addition to that, the experimental group received 15 sessions (30 minutes each) of MST, but no extra sessions were provided to the CG. Similarly, Altenmüller et al. (2009) did not provide additional therapy time to the CG either. In the study of Grau-Sánchez et al. (2018), both groups were enrolled in a standard rehabilitation program that consisted of 40 hours of conventional treatment for 10 extra hours of training with either MST or conventional therapy that included passive mobilization, stretch and progressive resistance exercises, and task-specific training. Therefore the standard rehabilitation program was nearly three times more intense than in previous studies and patients in the CG received extra rehabilitation time, keeping the total hours of training equal. Thus apparently, in subacute stroke patients, when the number of training hours is equal, there are no differences between MST and conventional therapy. However, MST was rated as significantly more pleasant than conventional physiotherapy.

Chronic stroke patients can enhance their upper extremity functionality when treated with MST, even when the treatment is provided years after the stroke (Amengual et al., 2013; Rojo et al., 2012; Villeneuve & Lamontagne, 2013; Villeneuve, Penhune, & Lamontagne, 2014). However, the only randomized controlled trial in the chronic phase, conducted by Fujioka et al. (2018), has shown that MST was not superior to self-administered graded repetitive arm supplementary program (Harris, Eng, Miller, & Dawson, 2009). In this study, both training protocols led chronic stroke patients to slightly reduce their motor impairment and perform functional movements faster.

Only two studies have investigated the progression of motor gains over the course of the training (Grau-Sánchez, Ramos, Duarte, Särkämö, & Rodríguez-Fornells, 2017; Villeneuve & Lamontagne, 2013). Improvements in velocity, key pressure, and note accuracy were achieved rapidly during the first training sessions, which reflects the fast learning pace of motor learning. Rapid improvements occurred in the context of musical task performance, but functional gains and recovery of deficits were more evident at the end of the MST program and were even stronger after a second training period.

Generalization of motor gains to activities of daily living has been explored in two randomized controlled trials in the subacute stage (Grau-Sánchez et al., 2018; Schneider, Münte, Rodriguez-Fornells, Sailer, & Altenmüller, 2010). Patients improved at the performance of functional tasks and activities of daily living after the training and reported a transfer effect to everyday functions. Moreover, adding MST to the standard rehabilitation program promoted the same retention of gains as conventional therapy after 3 months. Interestingly, patients who are more sensitive to experience reward in musical activities seem to show a larger motor improvement when treated with MST (Grau-Sánchez et al., 2018).

In order to apply MST not only to fine motor skills of the fingers, but also to impairments of motor control of the upper arm and the forearm, Scholz et al. (2016) designed a movement sonification—based therapy program. Gross movements of the arm were transformed into discrete sounds, providing a continuous feedback in a melodic way, tuned according to a major scale (i.e., patients could use movements of their paretic arms to "play" this musical instrument, see Fig. 16.2). Here sound perception substituted defective proprioceptive feedback. This sonification therapy significantly reduced joint pain and improved smoothness of movement more than movement therapy without structured sound feedback (Nikmaram et al., 2019).

FIGURE 16.2 Sonification of arm movements. The device contains a movement sensor applied to the forearm and upper arm (Xsense) and allows to transform movements into music coding the vertical axis into pitch, the horizontal axis into timbre and the z-axis into loudness. This way, the paretic arm is enabled to "play" a simple musical instrument, allowing to "move" tunes. *Scholz, D. S., Rohde, S., Nikmaram, N., Bruckner, H. P. P., Großbach, M., Rollnik, J. D., & Altenmuller, E. (2016). Sonification of arm movements in stroke rehabilitation—A novel approach in neurologic music therapy.* Frontiers in Neurology, 7, 106. *<https://doi.org/10.3389/ fneur.2016.00106>, with permission.*

Music-supported therapy in rehabilitation of gait disorders in stroke patients

In paretic patients, range of ankle and shoulder movement are reported to improve after music listening (Yeong & Kim, 2007). In this study mood and quality of life also improved significantly in the music group. Thus MST resulted in significantly improved shoulder and elbow joint function and mood, as compared with controls receiving standard physical therapy (Jun, Roh, & Kim, 2013).

With respect to gait and lower limb malfunction, simple rhythmic cueing with either a metronome or another sound-producing device have both been applied (Cha, Kim, Hwang, & Chung, 2014). Since this is related to musical timing, we subsume this method under MST, although pitches and timbres are not varied and therefore important musical parameters are not included in this form of rehabilitation strategy. Furthermore, it is hypothesized that the mechanisms of action are more related to temporal organization of motor output, and less to emotional and motivational aspects of motor rehabilitation. Thus rhythmic auditory cueing may act mainly on cerebellar and basal ganglia networks involved in timing of movement organization. In a study by Thaut et al. (2007) a 3-week training program for hemiparetic stroke patients resulted in significantly superior increase in gait speed for the music group as compared to conventional physiotherapy. Both stride length and cadence significantly improved. A recent meta-analysis confirmed positive effects of music on gait velocity and stride length (Yoo & Kim, 2016): Analyzing a total of 10 randomized or clinical controlled trials with 356 individuals, large effect sizes were reported concerning walking velocity, cadence, and stride length. Additional subgroup analysis demonstrated that although the type of rhythmic cueing and stage of stroke did not lead to statistically substantial group differences, the effect sizes and heterogeneity values in each subgroup implied possible differences in treatment effect, depending on loudness, timbre, and sound structure of the rhythmic cueing. Briefly summarizing, the results suggest that rhythmic stimulation is more effective with music as compared to a metronome and is more efficient at an early stage of stroke rehabilitation. Furthermore, there is a dose—effect relationship, showing that longer training sessions are more efficient.

Music in the rehabilitation of aphasia: melodic intonation therapy

While the close links between music and movement make motor rehabilitation an obvious avenue for music-supported rehabilitation, recovery of language can also benefit from a music-supported approach. Aphasia is a common and devastating complication of stroke or other brain injuries that results in the loss of ability to produce and/or comprehend language. It has been estimated that between 24% and 52% of acute stroke patients have some form of aphasia if tested within 7 days of their stroke; 12% of survivors still have significant aphasia at 6 months after stroke (Wade, Hewer, David, & Enderby, 1976).

Based on clinical observations that patients with severe nonfluent aphasia can sing lyrics better than they can speak the same words, an intonation-based therapy called MIT was first developed by Albert and colleagues in the 1970s (Albert, Sparks, & Helm, 1973; Sparks & Holland, 1976) and recently further elaborated by Schlaug et al. (Schlaug, Norton, Marchina, Zipse, & Wan, 2010; Wan, Rueber, Hohmann, & Schlaug, 2010). The two unique components of MIT are first the intonation of words and simple phrases using a melodic contour that follows the prosody of speech, and second the rhythmic tapping of the left hand that accompanies the production of each syllable and serves as a catalyst for fluency. Thus MIT emphasizes melody and contour and engages a sensorimotor network of articulation on the unaffected (usually right) hemisphere through rhythmic tapping.

To date, studies using MIT have produced positive outcomes in patients with nonfluent aphasia. These outcomes range from improvements on the Boston diagnostic aphasia examination (Goodglass & Kaplan, 1983), to improvements in articulation and phrase production (increase in syllable production/minute after 40 sessions in the MIT group by 200% vs 120% in the CG; Bonakdarpour, Eftekharzadeh, & Ashayeri, 2000; Wilson, Parsons, & Reutens, 2006) after treatment. The effectiveness of this intervention is further demonstrated in a study that examined transfer of language skills to untrained contexts. Schlaug, Marchina, and Norton (2008) compared the effects of MIT with a control intervention (speech repetition) on picture naming performance and measures of propositional speech. After 40 daily sessions, both therapy techniques resulted in significant improvement of all outcome measures, but the extent of this improvement was far greater for the patient who underwent MIT compared to the one who underwent the control therapy. These positive effects were also confirmed by Raglio et al. (2016) as well as in an enlarged treatment program, including breathing and awareness exercises (Jungblut & Aldridge, 2004).

The therapeutic effect of MIT is also evident in neuroimaging studies that show reorganization of brain functions. MIT resulted in increased activation in a right-hemisphere network involving the premotor, inferior frontal, and temporal lobes (Schlaug, Marchina, & Norton, 2009), as well as increased fiber number and volume of the AF in the right hemisphere (Altenmüller & Schlaug, 2012; Wan, Zheng, Marchina, Norton, & Schlaug, 2014) suggesting an increased audiomotor connectivity of the right hemisphere: these findings demonstrate that intensive therapies such as MIT, when applied over a longer period of time in chronic stroke patients, can induce functional and structural brain changes in a right-hemisphere vocal−motor network, and these changes are related to speech output improvements (Wan et al., 2014).

The mechanisms underlying the recovery-enhancing effects of MIT are not completely clear. Four possible mechanisms by which MIT's therapeutic effect is achieved have been discussed (for details see Altenmüller & Schlaug, 2013): (1) reduction of speed to approximately one syllable/second which may specifically engage right-hemisphere perceptual and perception−action coupling, since the right hemisphere has been shown to integrate sensory information over a larger time window than the left hemisphere (Abrams, Nicol, Zecker, & Kraus, 2008; Poeppel, 2003); (2) syllable lengthening that isolates/emphasizes individual phonemes even as they remain part of the continuously voiced words/phrases; and (3) "chunking" that not only combines prosodic information with meaningful content to facilitate production of longer, more fluent phrases, but has also been shown to lead to more right- than left-hemisphere activation in healthy subjects (Meyer, Alter, Friederici, Lohmann, & von Cramon, 2002; Ozdemir, Norton, & Schlaug, 2006; Zatorre & Belin, 2001). Given that patients with right hemisphere lesions have greater difficulty with global processing tasks (e.g., melody and contour processing) than those with left-hemisphere lesions (Peretz, 1990; Schuppert, Münte, Wieringa, & Altenmüller, 2000) it is possible that the melodic element of MIT does indeed engage the right hemisphere, particularly the right temporal lobe, more than therapies that do not involve tonal information or melodic contour, and again intervention that would integrate information over a larger timescale favoring right over left hemispheric processing (Abrams et al., 2008). The fourth mechanism—left hand-tapping (one tap/syllable, one syllable/second)—is likely to play an important role in engaging a right hemispheric, sensorimotor network capable of providing an impulse for verbal production in much the same way that a metronome has been shown to serve as a "pacemaker" when rhythmic motor activities prime and/or entrain sensorimotor networks (Thaut & Abiru, 2010; Thaut, Kenyon, Schauer, & McIntosh, 1999). In addition, research suggesting that hand movements and articulatory movements may share neural correlates (Meister et al., 2003; Tokimura, Tokimura, Oliviero, Asakura, & Rothwell, 1996) further supports the notion that hand-tapping is critically important for facilitating the coupling of sounds to orofacial and articulatory actions (Lahav, Saltzman, & Schlaug, 2007). Since concurrent speech and hand use occurs in daily life, and gestures are frequently used to emphasize/accompany important and/or elusive concepts in speech, rhythmic hand movements, in synchrony with articulatory movements, may have similarly beneficial effects on speech production and in particular in relearning of speech—motor functions after a stroke.

Effects of music-supported therapy on cognition, mood, and quality of life

Besides effects on motor rehabilitation, subacute patients exhibit better language abilities after MST than those patients treated only with conventional therapy, even when the number of hours of therapies is balanced (Grau-Sánchez et al., 2018). This is probably due to the fact that the processing of relevant features of music, such as rhythm and beat, share several networks with language processing (Brown, Martinez, & Parsons, 2006; Patel, 2011). Moreover, chronic patients improved in processing speed and mental flexibility after the training (Fujioka et al., 2018; Ripollés et al., 2016). These results are in agreement with previous findings on the effects of passive music listening of preferred, individually chosen music on cognitive functions in subacute stroke patients (Särkämö & Soto, 2012; Särkämö et al.,

2008). Here, as the most important mechanisms, effects on mood, reduced depressivity, and reduced stress seem to trigger these improvements (Sihvonen et al., 2017).

Regarding the effects on mood and quality of life, patients treated with MST reported increased quality of life and positive emotions as well as a reduction of negative affect, fatigue, and depressive symptoms (Fujioka et al., 2018; Grau-Sánchez et al., 2018; Ripollés et al., 2016; van Vugt et al., 2016). The results on mood and quality of life are of great significance, because one of the aims of stroke rehabilitation is to improve the patient's quality of life (Albert & Kesselring, 2012). The benefits of MST at the emotional level are in line with previous research on music-based interventions promoting well-being in patients with other conditions (Fredenburg & Silverman, 2014; Ghetti, 2011; Segall, 2018) and healthy population (for a review, see Daykin et al., 2018). Importantly, individuals with stronger musical engagement are the ones that show larger effects on well-being after a music-based intervention (Kreutz, Ott, Teichmann, Osawa, & Vaitl, 2008; Weinberg & Joseph, 2017; Zavoyskiy, Taylor, & Friedman, 2016). Therefore given that MST can promote similar motor improvements as conventional therapy, but that patients' mood and quality of life increases after the training, MST should be favored over conventional approaches.

Effects of music-supported therapy on brain plasticity

With respect to the neurobiological mechanisms underlying the behavioral changes, demonstrated above, experimental studies have reported an increase in the excitability and a cortical motor map reorganization in the affected sensorimotor cortex of subacute and chronic stroke patients after MST (Amengual et al., 2013; Grau-Sánchez et al., 2013). Similarly, in chronic stroke patients, a reduction of the involvement of the unaffected hemisphere during paretic movements after the training occurred, indicating a pattern of hemispheric reorganization within the lesioned hemisphere after the training (Ripollés et al., 2016). However, in these studies, the lack of a CG of patients undergoing a different therapy was a limitation when concluding that these changes are specific to MST since other types of motor therapies can promote similar cortical reorganization and functional changes (Classen et al., 2014; Liepert, Bauder, Miltner, Taub, & Weiller, 2000).

Regarding the neurophysiological basis of behavioral improvement, patients undergoing MST not only regained their motor abilities at a faster rate but also improved in timing, precision, and smoothness of fine motor skills, as well as showing increases in neuronal connectivity between sensory−motor and auditory brain areas assessed by means of electroencephalographic coherence measures (Altenmüller et al., 2009; Schneider et al., 2010). Therefore establishing an audiosensory−motor corepresentation may support the rehabilitation process (see Fig. 16.3).

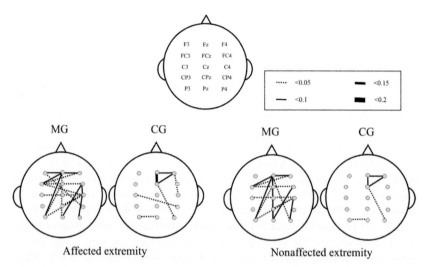

FIGURE 16.3 Topographic task-related EEG coherence maps (indicating the degree of similarity of the microvoltage recorded at two sensors) for the MG compared to the CG during self-paced arm movements for the drum pad condition in the beta band (18−22 Hz). Statistically significant increases in task-related coherence between brain areas involved in motor performance were assessed before and after 3 weeks and 15 sessions of music-supported therapy on sonified drum pads, which allowed the patient to play tunes on a C-major scale. Stroke patients were either trained to tap simple melodies with their paretic arm or underwent conventional physiotherapy. Displayed are the increases in connectivity by means of lines connecting the EEG-sensors, their thickness indicating the strength of their coherence. It is clearly visible that in the MG connectivity was more pronounced and included more brain areas of both hemispheres. *CG*, Control group; *EEG*, electroencephalographic; *MG*, music group. *From Altenmüller, E., & Stewart, L. (in press). Music supported therapy in Neurorehabilitation. In V. Dietz, & N. Ward. Oxford textbook of Neurorehabilitation (2nd ed.). Chapter 31.*

The importance of establishing such an audiosensory−motor corepresentation in rehabilitation is corroborated by findings from a patient who underwent music-supported training 20 months after suffering a stroke. Along with clinical improvement involving both gross and fine motor skills, fMRI follow-up provided evidence for the establishment of an auditory−sensory motor coupling network due to the training procedure (Rojo et al., 2012). In a larger group of 20 chronic stroke patients, changes in motor cortex excitability following a 4-week intervention with the same methods appeared using the transcranial magnetic stimulation technique. These changes were accompanied by marked improvements of fine motor skills (Amengual et al., 2013).

Effects on the rehabilitation of the upper limb after stroke, undoubtedly show that MST is efficient, and seems to be more helpful than functional motor training without auditory feedback, but otherwise offers similar fine motor training. With respect to the underlying mechanisms, a number of open questions still remain. First, the role of motivational factors must be clarified. The patients' informal descriptions of their experience with the MST revealed that the intervention was highly enjoyable and a highlight within their rehabilitation process. Thus as already explored in the first part of this article, motivational and emotional factors may have contributed to the success of the training program. Furthermore, according to a study by Särkämö et al. (2008), music listening activates a widespread bilateral network of brain regions related to attention, semantic processing, memory, motor functions, and emotional processing. Särkämö and colleagues showed that music exposure significantly enhanced cognitive functioning in the domains of verbal memory and focused attention in stroke patients. The music group also experienced less depression as compared to the CGs. These mechanisms may also hold true for the MST we applied.

Another issue relates to auditory feedback mechanisms. It has not yet been clarified whether any auditory feedback (e.g., simple beep tones) would have a similar effect on fine motor rehabilitation or whether explicit musical parameters such as a sophisticated pitch and time structure are prerequisites for the success of the training. This has to be addressed in studies comparing the effects of musical feedback compared to simple acoustic feedback. With respect to the latter, in Parkinson patients, Dalla Bella et al. (Benoit et al., 2014) convincingly demonstrated that musically structured auditory cueing improved walking speed and stride length more than simple metronome cueing. Furthermore, previous musical training led to greater benefits in these patients (De Cock et al., 2018). In contrast, in stroke patients, according to a study by Thaut, Kenyon, Hurt, McIntosh, and Hoemberg (2002), simple rhythmic cueing with a metronome significantly improved the spatiotemporal precision of reaching movements.

Lastly, it is not clear whether timing regularity and predictability is crucial for the beneficial effect of MST using tapping on drum pads or playing on a keyboard. Although it has been argued that the effectiveness of this therapy relies on the fact that the patient's brain receives a time-locked auditory feedback with each movement, new results challenge this viewpoint. In a relatively recent study (van Vugt et al., 2016) 15 patients in early stroke rehabilitation with no previous musical background were studied. They learned to play simple finger exercises and familiar children's songs on the piano. The participants were assigned to one of two groups: in the normal group, the keyboard emitted a tone immediately at keystroke; in the delay group, the tone was delayed by a random time interval between 100 and 600 ms. To assess recovery, standard clinical tests such as the nine-hole pegboard test and index finger tapping speed and regularity were used. Surprisingly, patients in the delay group improved more in the nine-hole pegboard test, whereas patients in the normal group did not. In finger tapping rate and regularity both groups showed similar marked improvements. The normal group showed reduced depression whereas the delay group did not (van Vugt et al., 2016). Thus MST even with a randomly delayed keyboard can improve motor recovery after stroke, possibly because patients in the delayed feedback group implicitly learn to be independent of the auditory feedback and therefore outperform those in the normal condition.

Future research should address the long-term sustainability of improvements and should strive to optimize the length and number of training sessions, according to patients needs and preference. Most probably, a client-tailored treatment algorithm, taking into account severity of impairment, psychological status, motivational drive, and musical background and preferences, will be most efficient. Ideally, if the patient is receptive to MST, making music should become part of the lifestyle of the poststroke patient. This would be an interesting line of future research.

Conclusion

The research of the last two decades summarized in this chapter demonstrates undeniably that music making is a powerful driver of adaptive functional and structural brain plasticity and associated adaptations of motor and cognitive behavior. Consequently, exposure and active musical training can be a strong stimulant for neuroplastic adaptations and behavioral improvements following brain injury after stroke. Making music leads to enhanced coupling of perception and action mediated by sensory, motor, and multi-modal brain regions and affects either in a top-down or bottom-up fashion important relay stations in the brainstem and thalamus. Furthermore, listening to music and making music provokes motions and emotions, increases between-subject communications and interactions, and—mediated via neurotransmitters such as serotonin and dopamine—is experienced as joyous and rewarding through activity changes in amygdala, ventral striatum, and other components of the limbic system. Furthermore, listening to music and making music reduces stress and pain via inhibition of cortisol release, thus laying a fertile ground for the positive effects of music activities and activity-dependent neuroplasticity (Leardi et al., 2007). Making music makes rehabilitation more enjoyable, therefore enhancing motivation to persist exercising and can therefore more effectively remediate impaired neural processes or neural connections by engaging and linking brain regions than classical therapy.

As other interventions, MST and MIT in neurorehabilitation need to be grounded within a neurobiological understanding of how and why particular brain systems are affected. The efficacy of these experimental interventions should be assessed quantitatively and in an unbiased way, also taking into account the influence of the musical history of the patient. We resumed in this chapter the journey of researchers towards a sound neuroscientific basis for music-based interventions. The studies reviewed here, and the first data derived from randomized clinical trials are important steps in establishing neurologically based music therapy that might have the power to enhance brain recovery processes, ameliorate the effects of developmental brain disorders, and neuroplasticity in general, and last but not least increase autonomy and well-being of stroke patients.

Acknowledgments

Eckart Altenmüller and Clara E. James gratefully acknowledge generous support from the German Research Foundation (Al 269) and the Swiss National Science Foundation (100019E-170410). Parts of a joint grant application on music-supported therapy in elderly by EA and CEJ, accepted by these foundations and ongoing at present, are integrated in this book chapter.

Parts of this Review Article are based on previous reviews published together with Aleksi Sihvonen and colleagues in 2017, with Stewart (in press), and with Grau-Sánchez (2019, 2020). We are deeply indebted to the colleagues contributing to these reviews (in alphabetic order): Esther Duarte, Jennifer Grau-Sánchez, Vera Leo, Thomas Münte, Antoni Rodriguez-Fornells, Teppo Särkämö, Aleksi Sihvonen, Seppo Soinila, Lauren Stewart, and Mari Tervaniemi.

References

Abrams, D. A., Nicol, T., Zecker, S., & Kraus, N. (2008). Right-hemisphere auditory cortex is dominant for coding syllable patterns in speech. *The Journal of Neuroscience*, *28*, 3958−3965.

Ahlskog, J. E., Geda, Y. E., Graff-Radford, N. R., & Petersen, R. C. (2011). Physical exercise as a preventive or disease-modifying treatment of dementia and brain aging. *Mayo Clinic Proceedings. Mayo Clinic*, *86*(9), 876−884.

Albert, M. L., Sparks, R. W., & Helm, N. A. (1973). Melodic intonation therapy for aphasia. *Archives of Neurology*, *29*, 130−131.

Albert, S. J., & Kesselring, J. (2012). Neurorehabilitation of stroke. *Journal of Neurology*, *259* (5), 817−832.

Altenmüller, E., & Furuya, S. (2016). Brain plasticity and the concept of metaplasticity in skilled musicians. *Advances in Experimental Medicine and Biology*, *957*, 197−208.

Altenmüller, E., & Schlaug, G. (2012). Music, brain, and health: Exploring biological foundations of music's health effects. In G. MacDonald, & Kreutz L. Mitchell (Eds.), *Music, health, and wellbeing* (2, pp. 12−24). Oxford: Oxford University Press.

Altenmüller, E., & Schlaug, G. (2013). Neurobiological aspects of neurologic music therapy. *Music and Medicine*, *5*, 210−216.

Altenmüller, E., Schneider, S., Marco-Pallares, P. W., & Münte, T. F. (2009). Neural reorganization underlies improvement in stroke induced motor dysfunction by music-supported therapy. *Annals of the New York Academy of Sciences*, *1169*, 395−405.

Altenmüller, E., & Stewart, L., in press. Music supported therapy in Neurorehabilitation. In V. Dietz, & N. Ward., *Oxford textbook of neurorehabilitation* (2nd ed.) Chapter 31.

Amengual, J. L., Rojo, N., Veciana de las Heras, M., Marco-Pallarés, J., Grau, J., Schneider, S., ... Rodriguez-Fornells, A. (2013). Sensorimotor plasticity after music-supported therapy in chronic stroke patients revealed by transcranial magnetic stimulation. *PLoS One*, *8*, e61883. Available from https://doi.org/10.1371/journal.pone.0061883.

Amunts, K., Schlaug, G., Jäncke, L., Steinmetz, H., Schleicher, A., Dabringhaus, A., & Zilles, K. (1997). Motor cortex and hand motor skills: Structural compliance in the human brain. *Human Brain Mapping*, *5*, 206–215.

Bangert, M., & Schlaug, G. (2006). Specialization of the spezialized in features of external brain morphology. *The European Journal of Neuroscience*, *24*, 1832–1834.

Bengtsson, S. L., Nagy, Z., Skare, S., Forsman, L., Forssberg, H., & Ullen, F. (2005). Extensive piano practicing has regionally specific effects on white matter development. *Nature Neuroscience*, *8*, 1148–1150.

Benoit, C. E., Dalla Bella, S., Farrugia, N., Obrig, H., Mainka, S., & Kotz, S. A. (2014). Musically cued gait-training improves both perceptual and motor timing in Parkinson's disease. *Frontiers in Human Neuroscience*, *8*, 494. Available from https://doi.org/10.3389/fnhum.2014.0049.

Bonakdarpour, B., Eftekharzadeh, A., & Ashayeri, H. (2000). Preliminary report on the effects of melodic intonation therapy in the rehabilitation of Persian aphasic patients. *Iranian Journal of Medical Sciences*, *25*, 156–160.

Bradt, J., Dileo, C., & Potvin, N. (2013). Music for stress and anxiety reduction in coronary heart disease patients. *Cochrane Database of Systematic Reviews*, *12*, CD006577.

Brown, S., Martinez, M. J., & Parsons, L. M. (2006). Music and language side by side in the brain: A PET study of the generation of melodies and sentences. *The European Journal of Neuroscience*, *23*, 2791–2803.

Cauraugh, J., Light, K., Kim, S., Thigpen, M., & Behrman, A. (2000). Chronic motor dysfunction after stroke: Recovering wrist and finger extension by electromyography-triggered neuromuscular stimulation. *Stroke; A Journal of Cerebral Circulation*, *31*(6), 1360–1364.

Cha, Y., Kim, Y., Hwang, S., & Chung, Y. (2014). Intensive gait training with rhythmic auditory stimulation in individuals with chronic hemiparetic stroke: A pilot randomized controlled study. *NeuroRehabilitation*, *35*(4), 681–688. Available from https://doi.org/10.3233/NRE-141182.

Chanda, M. L., & Levitin, D. J. (2013). The neurochemistry of music. *Trends in Cognitive Sciences*, *17*, 179–193.

Clark, I. N., Baker, F. A., & Taylor, N. F. (2016). Older adults' music listening preferences to support physical activity following cardiac rehabilitation. *Journal of Music Therapy*, *53*, 364–397.

Classen, J., Liepert, J., Wise, S. P., Hallett, M., Leonardo, G., Baarbé, J., ... Cohen, L. G. (2014). Rapid plasticity of human cortical movement representation induced by practice. *Journal of Neurophysiology*, *79*, 1117–1123.

Craft, L. L., & Perna, F. M. (2004). The benefits of exercise for the clinically depressed. *Primary Care Companion to the Journal of Clinical Psychiatry*, *6*(3), 104–111.

Daykin, N., Mansfield, L., Meads, C., Julier, G., Tomlinson, A., Payne, A., ... Victor, C. (2018). What works for wellbeing? A systematic review of wellbeing outcomes for music and singing in adults. *Perspectives in Public Health*, *138*(1), 39–46.

De Cock, V. C., Dotov, D., Ihalainen, P., Bégel, V., Galtier, F., Lebrun, C., ... Dalla Bella, S. (2018). Rhythmic abilities and musical training in Parkinson's disease: Do they help? *NPJ Parkinson's Disease*, *4*, 8.

De Pretto, M., & James, C. E. (2015). Principles of parsimony: fMRI correlates of beat-based versus duration-based sensorimotor synchronization. *Psychomusicology: Music, Mind, and Brain*, *25*, 380–391.

Donkor, E. S. (2018). Stroke in the 21st century: A snapshot of the burden, epidemiology, and quality of life. *Stroke Research and Treatment, 2018*, 3238165. Available from https://doi.org/10.1155/2018/3238165.

Douven, E., Köhler, S., Rodriguez, M. M. F., Staals, J., Verhey, F. R., & Aalten, P. (2017). Imaging markers of post-stroke depression and apathy: A systematic review and meta-analysis. *Neuropsychology Review, 27*, 202–219. Available from https://doi.org/10.1007/s11065-017-9356-2.

Eriksson, J., Vogel, E. K., Lansner, A., Bergstrom, F., & Nyberg, L. (2015). Neurocognitive architecture of working memory. *Neuron, 88*, 33–46.

Evers, S., & Suhr, B. (2000). Changes of the neurotransmitter serotonin but not of hormones during short time music perception. *European Archives of Psychiatry and Clinical Neuroscience, 250*, 144–147.

Fredenburg, H. A., & Silverman, M. J. (2014). Effects of music therapy on positive and negative affect and pain with hospitalized patients recovering from a blood and marrow transplant: A randomized effectiveness study. *The Arts in Psychotherapy, 41*(2), 174–180. Available from https://doi.org/10.1016/j.aip.2014.01.007.

Freudenberger, P., Petrovic, K., Sen, A., Toglhofer, A. M., Fixa, A., Hofer, E., ... Schmidt, H. (2016). Fitness and cognition in the elderly: The Austrian Stroke Prevention Study. *Neurology, 86*, 418–424.

Fujioka, T., Dawson, D. R., Wright, R., Honjo, K., Chen, J. L., Chen, J. J., ... Ross, B. (2018). The effects of music-supported therapy on motor, cognitive, and psychosocial functions in chronic stroke. *Annals of the New York Academy of Sciences, 1423*(1), 264–274. Available from https://doi.org/10.1111/nyas.13706.

Furuya, S., Oku, T., Miyazaki, F., & Kinoshita, H. (2015). Secrets of virtuoso: Neuromuscular attributes of motor virtuosity in expert musicians. *Scientific Reports, 5*, 15750. Available from https://doi.org/10.1038/srep15750.

Gärtner, H., Minnerop, M., Pieperhoff, P., Schleicher, A., Zilles, K., Altenmüller, E., & Amunts, K. (2013). Brain morphometry shows effects of long-term musical practice in middle-aged keyboard players. *Frontiers in Psychology, 4*, 636. Available from https://doi.org/10.3389/fpsyg.2013.00636.

Gaser, C., & Schlaug, G. (2003). Brain structures differ between musicians and non-musicians. *Journal of Neuroscience, 23*, 9240–9245.

Ghetti, C. M. (2011). Active music engagement with emotional-approach coping to improve well-being in liver and kidney transplant recipients. *Journal of Music Therapy, 48*(4), 463–485.

Goodglass, H., & Kaplan, E. (1983). *Boston diagnostic aphasia examination* (2nd ed.). Philadelphia, PA: Lea & Febiger.

Grau-Sánchez, J., Amengual, J. L., Rojo, N., Veciana de Las Heras, M., Montero, J., Rubio, F., ... Rodríguez-Fornells, A. (2013). Plasticity in the sensorimotor cortex induced by Music-supported therapy in stroke patients: A TMS study. *Frontiers in Human Neuroscience, 7*, 494. Available from https://doi.org/10.3389/fnhum.2013.00494.

Grau-Sánchez, J., Duarte, E., Ramos-Escobar, N., Sierpowska, J., Rueda, N., Redón, S., & Rodríguez-Fornells, A. (2018). Music-supported therapy in the rehabilitation of subacute stroke patients: A randomized controlled trial. *Annals of the New York Academy of Sciences, 1423*(1), 318–328. Available from https://doi.org/10.1111/nyas.13590.

Grau-Sánchez, J., Ramos, N., Duarte, E., Särkämö, T., & Rodríguez-Fornells, A. (2017). Time course of motor gains induced by music-supported therapy after stroke: An exploratory case study. *Neuropsychology, 31*(6), 624–635.

Grau-Sanchez, J., Münte, T. F., Altenmüller, E., Duarte, E., & Rodriguez-Fornells, A. (2020). Potential benefits of music playing in stroke upper limb motor rehabilitation. *Neuroscience and Biobehavioural Reviews*, in press.

Halwani, G. F., Loui, P., Rüber, T., & Schlaug, G. (2011). Effects of practice and experience on the arcuate fasciculus: Comparing singers, instrumentalists, and non-musicians. *Frontiers in Psychology*, 2. Available from https://doi.org/10.3389/fpsyg.2011.001561.

Harris, J. E., Eng, J. J., Miller, W. C., & Dawson, A. S. (2009). A self-administered graded repetitive arm supplementary program (GRASP) improves arm function during inpatient rehabilitation: A multi-site randomized controlled trial. *Stroke; a Journal of Cerebral Circulation*, *40*(6), 2123–2128.

Hou, Y. C., Lin, Y. J., Lu, K. C., Chiang, H. S., Chang, C. C., & Yang, L. K. (2017). Music therapy-induced changes in salivary cortisol level are predictive of cardiovascular mortality in patients under maintenance hemodialysis. *Therapeutics and Clinical Risk Management*, *13*, 263–272.

Hyde, K. L., Lerch, J., Norton, A., Forgeard, M., Winner, E., Evans, A. C., et al. (2009). Musical training shapes structural brain development. *The Journal of Neuroscience*, *29*, 3019–3025.

James, C. E., Oechslin, M. S., Van De Ville, D., Hauert, C. A., Descloux, C., & Lazeyras, F. (2014). Musical training intensity yields opposite effects on grey matter density in cognitive versus sensorimotor networks. *Brain Structure & Function*, *219*, 353–366.

Jun, E. M., Roh, Y. H., & Kim, M. J. (2013). The effect of music-movement therapy on physical and psychological states of stroke patients. *Journal of Clinical Nursing*, *22*(1–2), 22–23.

Jungblut, M., & Aldridge, D. (2004). The musictherapy intervention SIPARI with chronic aphasics – Research findings. *Neurologie & Rehabilitation*, *10*(2), 69–78.

Kempermann, G. (2012). New neurons for "survival of the fittest.". *Nature Reviews. Neuroscience*, *13*(10), 727–736. Available from https://doi.org/10.1038/nrn3319.

Kennedy, K. M., Boylan, M. A., Rieck, J. R., Foster, C. M., & Rodrigue, K. M. (2017). Dynamic range in BOLD modulation: life span aging trajectories and association with performance. *Neurobiology of Aging*, *60*, 153–163. Available from https://doi.org/10.1016/j.neurobiolaging.2017.08.027.

Kreutz, G., Ott, U., Teichmann, D., Osawa, P., & Vaitl, D. (2008). Using music to induce emotions: Influences of musical preference and absorption. *Psychology of Music*, *36*(1), 101–126. Available from https://doi.org/10.1177/0305735607082623.

Lahav, A., Saltzman, E., & Schlaug, G. (2007). Action representation of sound: Audiomotor recognition network while listening to newly acquired actions. *The Journal of Neuroscience*, *27*, 308–314.

Landry, S. P., & Champoux, F. (2017). Musicians react faster and are better multisensory integrators. *Brain and Cognition*, *111*, 156–162. Available from https://doi.org/10.1016/j.bandc.2016.12.001.

Leardi, S., Pietroletti, R., Angeloni, G., Necozione, S., Ranalletta, G., & Del Gusto, B. (2007). Randomized clinical trial examining the effect of music therapy in stress response to day surgery. *The British Journal of Surgery*, *94*(8), 943–947. Available from https://doi.org/10.1002/bjs.5914.

Liepert, J., Bauder, H., Miltner, W. H. R., Taub, E., & Weiller, C. (2000). Treatment-Induced cortical reorganization after stroke in humans. *Stroke; A Journal of Cerebral Circulation*, *31*(6), 1210–1216. Available from https://doi.org/10.1161/01.STR.31.6.1210.

Llorens-Martín, M., Tejeda, G. S., & Trejo, J. L. (2010). Differential regulation of the variations induced by environmental richness in adult neurogenesis as a function of time: A dual birthdating analysis. *PLoS One 16, 5*(8), e12188. <https://doi.org/10.1371/journal.pone.0012188>.

Macpherson, H., Teo, W. P., Schneider, L. A., & Smith, A. E. (2017). A lifelong approach to physical activity for brain health. *Frontiers in Aging Neuroscience, 23*(9), 147. Available from https://doi.org/10.3389/fnagi.2017.00147.

Meister, I. G., Boroojerdi, B., Foltys, H., Sparing, R., Huber, W., & Topper, R. (2003). Motor cortex hand area and speech: Implications for the development of language. *Neuropsychologia, 41,* 401−406.

Menon, V., & Levitin, D. J. (2005). The rewards of music listening: Response and physiological connectivity of the mesolimbic system. *NeuroImage, 28,* 175−184.

Meyer, M., Alter, K., Friederici, A. D., Lohmann, G., & von Cramon, D. Y. (2002). FMRI reveals brain regions mediating slow prosodic modulations in spoken sentences. *Human Brain Mapping, 17,* 73−88.

Münte, T. F., Altenmüller, E., & Jäncke, L. (2002). The musician's brain as a model of neuroplasticity. *Nature Reviews Neuroscience, 3,* 473−478.

Nikmaram, N., Scholz, D. S., Grossbach, M., Schmidt, S. B., Spogis, J., Belardinelli, P., . . . Altenmüller, E. (2019). Musical sonification of arm movements in stroke rehabilitation yields limited benefits. *Frontiers in Neuroscience, 13,* 1378.

Nilsson, U. (2008). The anxiety-and pain-reducing effects of music interventions: A systematic review. *AORN Journal, 87*(4), 780−807.

Oechslin, M. S., Gschwind, M., & James, C. E. (2018). Tracking training-related plasticity by combining fMRI and DTI: The right hemisphere ventral stream mediates musical syntax processing. *Cerebral Cortex, 28,* 1209−1218.

Oechslin, M. S., Van De Ville, D., Lazeyras, F., Hauert, C. A., & James, C. E. (2013). Degree of musical expertise modulates higher order brain functioning. *Cerebral Cortex, 23,* 2213−2224.

Okada, K., Kurita, A., & Takase, B. (2009). Effects of music therapy on autonomic nervous system activity, incidence of heart failure events, and plasma cytokine and catecholamine levels in elderly patients with cerebrovascular disease and dementia. *International Heart Journal, 50,* 95−110.

Ozdemir, E., Norton, A., & Schlaug, G. (2006). Shared and distinct neural correlates of singing and speaking. *NeuroImage, 33,* 628−635.

Patel, A. D. (2011). Why would musical training benefit the neural encoding of speech? The OPERA hypothesis. *Frontiers in Psychology, 2,* 142. Available from https://doi.org/10.3389/fpsyg.2011.00142.

Peretz, I. (1990). Processing of local and global musical information by unilateral brain-damaged patients. *Brain, 113,* 1185−1205.

Poeppel, D. (2003). The analysis of speech in different temporal integration windows: Cerebral lateralization as "asymmetric sampling in time". *Speech Communication, 41,* 245−255.

Prince, S. A., Reed, J. L., Nerenberg, K. A., Kristiansson, E. A., Hiremath, S., Adamo, K. B., . . . Reid, R. D. (2014). Intrapersonal, social and physical environmental determinants of moderate-to-vigorous physical activity in working-age women: A systematic review protocol. *Systematic Reviews, 4*(3), 132. Available from https://doi.org/10.1186/2046-4053-3-132.

Radley, J., Morilak, D., Viau, V., & Campeau, S. (2015). Chronic stress and brain plasticity: Mechanisms underlying adaptive and maladaptive changes and implications for stress-related CNS disorders. *Neuroscience and Biobehavioral Reviews, 58,* 79−91.

Ragert, P., Schmidt, A., Altenmüller, E., & Dinse, H. R. (2003). Superior tactile performance and learning in professional pianists: Evidence for meta-plasticity in musicians. *The European Journal of Neuroscience, 19*(2), 473−478.

Raglio, A., Oasi, O., Gianotti, M., Rossi, A., Goulene, K., & Stramba-Badiale, M. (2016). Improvement of spontaneous language in stroke patients with chronic aphasia treated with music. *The International Journal of Neuroscience, 126*(3), 235−242. Available from https://doi.org/10.3109/00207454.2015.1010647.

Reitz, C., & Mayeux, R. (2014). Alzheimer disease: Epidemiology, diagnostic criteria, risk factors and biomarkers. *Biochemical Pharmacology, 88*(4), 640−651. Available from https://doi.org/10.1016/j.bcp.2013.12.024.

Ripollés, P., Rojo, N., Grau-Sánchez, J., Amengual, J. L. L., Càmara, E., Marco-Pallarés, J., & Rodríguez-Fornells, A. (2016). Music supported therapy promotes motor plasticity in individuals with chronic stroke. *Brain Imaging and Behavior, 10*(4), 1289−1307. Available from https://doi.org/10.1007/s11682-015-9498-x.

Rojo, N., Amengual, J., Juncadella, M., Rubio, F., Camara, E., Marco-Pallares, J., ... Rodriguez-Fornells, A. (2012). Music-supported therapy induces plasticity in the sensorimotor cortex on chronic stroke: A single-case study using multimodal imaging (fMRI-TMS). *Brain Injury, 25,* 787−793.

Rueber, T., Lindenberg, R., & Schlaug, G. (2015). Differential adaptation of descending motor pathways in musicians. *Cerebral Cortex, 25*(6), 1490−1498. Available from https://doi.org/10.1093/cercor/bht331.

Salmi, J., Pallesen, K. J., Neuvonen, T., Brattico, E., Korvenoja, A., Salonen, O., & Carlson, S. (2009). Cognitive and motor loops of the human cerebro-cerebellar system. *Journal of Cognitive Neuroscience, 22,* 2663−2676.

Särkämö, T., & Soto, D. (2012). Music listening after stroke: Beneficial effects and potential neural mechanisms. *Annals of the New York Academy of Sciences, 1252*(1), 266−281. Available from https://doi.org/10.1111/j.1749-6632.2011.06405.x.

Särkämö, T., Tervaniemi, M., Laitinen, S., Forsblom, A., Soinila, S., & Mikkonen, M. (2008). Music listening enhances cognitive recovery and mood after middle cerebral artery stroke. *Brain, 131,* 866−876.

Schlaug, G., Marchina, S., & Norton, A. (2008). From singing to speaking: Why patients with Broca's aphasia can sing and how that may lead to recovery of expressive language functions. *Music Perception, 25,* 315−323.

Schlaug, G., Marchina, S., & Norton, A. (2009). Evidence for plasticity in white-matter tracts of patients with chronic Broca's aphasia undergoing intense intonation-based speech therapy. *Annals of the New York Academy of Sciences, 1169,* 385−394.

Schlaug, G., Norton, A., Marchina, S., Zipse, L., & Wan, C. Y. (2010). From singing to speaking: Facilitating recovery from nonfluent aphasia. *Future Neurology, 5,* 657−665.

Schneider, P., Scherg, M., Dosch, H. G., Specht, H. J., Gutschalk, A., & Rupp, A. (2002). Morphology of Heschl's gyrus reflects enhanced activation in the auditory cortex of musicians. *Nature Neuroscience, 5*(7), 688−694.

Schneider, S., Münte, T. F., Rodriguez-Fornells, A., Sailer, M., & Altenmüller, E. (2010). Music supported training is more efficient than functional motor training for recovery of fine motor skills in stroke patients. *Music Perception, 27,* 271−280.

Schneider, S., Schönle, P. W., Altenmüller, E., & Münte, T. F. (2007). Using musical instruments to improve motor skill recovery following a stroke. *Journal of Neurology, 254,* 1339−1346.

Scholz, D. S., Rohde, S., Nikmaram, N., Brückner, H.-P. P., Großbach, M., Rollnik, J. D., & Altenmüller, E. (2016). Sonification of arm movements in stroke rehabilitation—A novel approach in neurologic music therapy. *Frontiers in Neurology, 7*, 106. Available from https://doi.org/10.3389/fneur.2016.00106.

Schuppert, M., Münte, T. F., Wieringa, B. M., & Altenmüller, E. (2000). Receptive amusia: Evidence for cross-hemispheric neural networks underlying music processing strategies. *Brain, 123*, 546−559.

Segall, L. E. (2018). Music therapy and wellness. In O. S. Yinger (Ed.), *Music therapy: Research and evidence-based practice* (pp. 111−124). St. Louis, MO: Elsevier.

Sihvonen, A. J., Särkämö, T., Leo, V., Tervaniemi, M., Altenmüller, E., & Soinila, S. (2017). Music-based interventions in neurological rehabilitation. *The Lancet Neurology, 16*(8), 648−660. Available from https://doi.org/10.1016/S1474-4422(17)30168-0.

Sparks, R. W., & Holland, A. L. (1976). Method: melodic intonation therapy for aphasia. *Journal of Speech Heart Disease, 41*, 287−297.

Steele, C. J., Bailey, J. A., Zatorre, R. J., & Penhune, V. B. (2013). Early musical training and white-matter plasticity in the corpus callosum: Evidence for a sensitive period. *The Journal of Neuroscience, 33*, 1282−1290.

Stewart, L., Henson, R., Kampe, K., Walsh, V., Turner, R., & Frith, U. (2003). Brain changes after learning to read and play music. *NeuroImage, 20*, 71−83.

Thaut, M. H., & Abiru, M. (2010). Rhythmic auditory stimulation in rehabilitation of movement disoders: A review of current research. *Music Perception, 27*, 263−269.

Thaut, M. H., Kenyon, G. P., Hurt, C. P., McIntosh, G. C., & Hoemberg, V. V. (2002). Kinematic optimization of spatiotemporal patterns in paretic arm training with stroke patients. *Neuropsychologia, 40*, 1073−1081.

Thaut, M. H., Kenyon, G. P., Schauer, M. L., & McIntosh, G. C. (1999). The connection between rhythmicity and brain function. *IEEE Engineering in Medicine and Biology Magazine: The Quarterly Magazine of the Engineering in Medicine & Biology Society, 18*, 101−108.

Thaut, M. H., Leins, A. K., Rice, R. R., Argstatter, H., Kenyon, G. P., McIntosh, G. C., ... Fetter, M. (2007). Rhythmic auditory stimulation improves gait more than NDT/Bobath training in near-ambulatory patients early poststroke: A single-blind, randomized trial. *Neurorehabilitation and Neural Repair, 21*(5), 455−459.

Tokimura, H., Tokimura, Y., Oliviero., Asakura, T., & Rothwell, J. (1996). Speech-induced changes in corticospinal excitability. *Annals of Neurology, 40*, 628−634.

Tong, Y., Forreider, B., Sun, X., Geng, X., Zhang, W., Du, H., ... Ding, Y. (2015). Music-supported therapy (MST) in improving post-stroke patients' upper-limb motor function: A randomised controlled pilot study. *Neurological Research, 37*(5), 434−440.

Tyndall, A. V., Clark, C. M., Anderson, T. J., Hogan, D. B., Hill, M. D., Longman, R. S., & Poulin, M. J. (2018). Protective effects of exercise on cognition and brain health in older adults. *Exercise and Sport Sciences Reviews, 46*(4), 215−223.

United Nations Department of Economic & Social Affairs Population Division. (2015). Retrieved from <https://www.un.org/en/development/desa/population/index.asp>.

van Vugt, F. T., Kafczyk, T., Kuhn, W., Rollnik, J. D., Tillmann, B., & Altenmüller, E. (2016). The role of auditory feedback in music-supported stroke rehabilitation: A single-blinded randomised controlled intervention. *Restorative Neurology and Neuroscience, 34*(2), 297−311. Available from https://doi.org/10.3233/RNN-150588.

Vaquero, L., Hartmann, K., Ripollés, P., Rojo, N., Sierpowska, J., François, C., ... Altenmüller, E. (2015). Structural neuroplasticity in expert pianists depends on the age of musical training onset. *NeuroImage*, *14*, 106−119.

Villeneuve, M., & Lamontagne, A. (2013). Playing piano can improve upper extremity function after stroke: Case studies. *Stroke Research and Treatment*, *2013*, 159105. Available from https://doi.org/10.1155/2013/159105.

Villeneuve, M., Penhune, V., & Lamontagne, A. (2014). A piano training program to improve manual dexterity and upper extremity function in chronic stroke survivors. *Frontiers in Human Neuroscience*, *8*, 662. Available from https://doi.org/10.3389/fnhum.2014.00662.

Wade, D. T., Hewer, R. L., David, R. M., & Enderby, P. M. (1976). Aphasia after stroke: Natural history and associated deficits. *Journal of Neurology, Neurosurgery, and Psychiatry*, *49*, 11−16.

Wan, C. Y., Rueber, T., Hohmann, A., & Schlaug, G. (2010). The therapeutic effects of singing in neurological disorders. *Music Perception*, *27*, 287−295.

Wan, C. Y., & Schlaug, G. (2010). Music making as a tool for promoting brain plasticity across the life-span. *The Neuroscientist*, *16*, 566−577.

Wan, C. Y., Zheng, X., Marchina, S., Norton, A., & Schlaug, G. (2014). Intensive therapy induces contralateral white matter changes in chronic stroke patients with Broca's aphasia. *Brain and Language*, *136*, 1−7.

Warlow, C. P. (1998). Epidemiology of stroke. *Lancet*, *352*(3), 1−4.

Weinberg, M. K., & Joseph, D. (2017). If you're happy and you know it: Music engagement and subjective wellbeing. *Psychology of Music*, *45*(2), 257−267.

Wickens, J. R., Reynolds, J. N., & Hyland, B. I. (2003). Neural mechanisms of reward-related motor learning. *Current Opinion in Neurobiology*, *13*(6), 685−690.

Wilson, S. J., Parsons, K., & Reutens, D. C. (2006). Preserved singing in aphasia: A case study of the efficacy of the melodic intonation therapy. *Music Perception*, *24*, 23−36.

Wirdefeldt, K., Adami, H. O., Cole, P., Trichopoulos, D., & Mandel, J. (2011). Epidemiology and etiology of Parkinson's disease: A review of the evidence. *European Journal of Epidemiology*, *26*(Suppl. 1), S1−S58. Available from https://doi.org/10.1007/s10654-011-9581-6.

Yeong, S., & Kim, M. T. (2007). Effects of a theory-driven music and movement program for stroke survivors in a community setting. *Applied Nursing Research*, *20*(3), 125−131.

Yoo, G. E., & Kim, S. J. (2016). Rhythmic auditory cueing in motor rehabilitation for stroke-patients: Systematic review and meta-analysis. *Journal of Music Therapy*, *53*(2), 149−177.

Zatorre, R. J., & Belin, P. (2001). Spectral and temporal processing in human auditory cortex. *Cerebral Cortex*, *11*, 946−953.

Zatorre, R. J. (2015). Musical pleasure and reward: Mechanisms and dysfunction. *Ann NY Acad. Sci*, *1337*, 202−211. Available from https://doi.org/10.1111/nyas.12677.

Zavoyskiy, S., Taylor, C. L., & Friedman, R. S. (2016). Affect-incongruency in emotional responses to music. *Psychomusicology: Music, Mind, and Brain*, *26*(3), 247−256. Available from https://doi.org/10.1037/pmu0000156.

Afterword: concluding thoughts and future directions

The chapters of this volume have presented the neuronal architecture of the musical brain as a highly complex hierarchical structure, revealed both in healthy responding to music and in the myriad response patterns following brain damage or disease. Not a lot of other activities involve as many brain areas and cognitive/motor/emotional/social/physiological processes, which makes music a very valuable tool for many purposes. Moreover, because musicality is a natural human ability, it may be studied across age and experience in a wide variety of contexts.

The authors of these chapters have documented far-reaching advances in the study of music and the aging brain. In the past 10−20 years, the literature on the topic has exploded with very strong results from brain imaging, neuropsychological assessment, and intervention designs based on neurobiological understanding of how and why particular brain systems are affected. Overall, those studies highlight positive effects of music on mood, cognition or motor functions, and suggest that music may be a powerful tool providing neuroprotection or rehabilitation in later stages of life. Findings speak to the relevance of clinical interventions and provide a scientific demonstration of their efficacy, ultimately increasing functioning, autonomy, and well-being in all persons, including those at risk and those afflicted.

Many challenges have arisen, and much future work remains to be conducted. In a recent (2019) blog [a reprise of her presidential address (2009) to the Society of Music Perception and Cognition[1]], Andrea Halpern points out that music research studies on older adults are underrepresented compared to the prevalence of older adults in the general population. This state of affairs is, Halpern argues, unfortunate, because music research can inform abiding questions about interactions between genetics and life experiences, and has applications for health (both prevention and therapy) and education. We know that aging is associated with a slowing down of functions involving sensory processes, attention, and memory, but there is also an

---

1. https://musicscience.net/2019/12/04/where-are-the-older-adults-in-music-psychology-research/.

enhancement of functions that invoke lifetime knowledge and experience. Because of the latter, we need to challenge a deficit model of aging that consistently interprets age differences in performance as a reduction, impairment, or problem. One future approach is to see aging and the brain as a dynamic object that adapts to changes and to life experiences. New encounters with music may lead to new values and interpretations, an exciting challenge for music interventions. In turn, music can be processed and interpreted differently as people get older and this age-related difference may not necessarily reflect a deficit.

With regard to intervention studies, we need to be aware of the importance of considering methodological limitations when designing or assessing music-based interventions. For instance, when interpreting pre−post improvement without control conditions or with a passive control condition, researchers should note that when an effect is detected, it might not be attributable to music and might not be necessarily better than other less costly or less complicated interventions. Our authors emphasize the need for high standard research designs, for example, randomized trials with an active control and blind assessments of outcome measures; larger samples; inclusion of measures of effect size; and homogeneity of participants' profiles wherever possible. Where randomized control trials are impossible, and only an "imperfect" design is feasible, interpretation of results should be approached with caution. As well, future research needs to attend to the specific mechanisms in action (the "active ingredient") in order to design more targeted and powerful interventions.

Moving to directions for music therapy, it is important to identify the goal of therapy in order to use music in the most efficient and targeted way (e.g., using the rhythmical aspect of music for gait or motor rehabilitation; using the evocative power of old famous songs for reminiscence therapy; using the arousing aspect of energetic music to fight apathy in Alzheimer's disease; etc.). Future research on music intervention and training models with the aging population should be grounded on what we know about aging and the brain. Therapy should be personalized based on the brain or cognitive function profiles of a patient, and should take into account individual preferences (see, in this regard, Chapter 7 in Baird, Garrido, & Tamplin, 2020). Future work could also extend to end-of life issues (looking at the effect of music on families or care workers, for example).

Music is easy to use in clinical/community settings because it is now readily accessible to everyone regardless of their background, age, and pathologies. It is very popular in the widest part of the population, affordable, easy to adjust to all sorts of needs or situation constraints, and so forth. Bridges should be strengthened between research and the community or clinical settings to bring new knowledge and practices to the service of today's citizens, and between research and politics or policy makers to use our data to better shape our institutions and laws. The future is bright and poised for new explorations.

Lola L. Cuddy, Sylvie Belleville and Aline Moussard

Reference

Baird, A., Garrido, S., & Tamplin, J. (2020). *Music and dementia: From cognition to therapy.* Oxford: OUP.

Index